The Scarecrow Author Bibliographies

1. John Steinbeck (Tetsumaro Hayashi). 1973.
2. Joseph Conrad (Theodore G. Ehrsam). 1969.
3. Arthur Miller (Tetsumaro Hayashi). 2d ed. 1976.
4. Katherine Anne Porter (Waldrip & Bauer). 1969.
5. Philip Freneau (Philip M. Marsh). 1970.
6. Robert Greene (Tetsumaro Hayashi). 1971.
7. Benjamin Disraeli (R. W. Stewart). 1972.
8. John Berryman (Richard W. Kelly). 1972.
9. William Dean Howells (Vito J. Brenni). 1973.
10. Jean Anouilh (Kathleen W. Kelly). 1973.
11. E. M. Forster (Alfred Borrello). 1973.
12. The Marquis de Sade (E. Pierre Chanover). 1973.
13. Alain Robbe-Grillet (Dale W. Frazier). 1973.
14. Northrop Frye (Robert D. Denham). 1974.
15. Federico Garcia Lorca (Laurenti & Siracusa). 1974.
16. Ben Jonson (Brock & Welsh). 1974.
17. Four French Dramatists: Eugène Brieux, François de Curel, Emile Fabre, Paul Hervieu (Edmund F. Santa Vicca). 1974.
18. Ralph Waldo Ellison (Jacqueline Covo). 1974.
19. Philip Roth (Bernard F. Rodgers, Jr.). 1974.
20. Norman Mailer (Laura Adams). 1974.
21. Sir John Betjeman (Margaret Stapleton). 1974.
22. Elie Wiesel (Molly Abramowitz). 1974.
23. Paul Laurence Dunbar (Eugene W. Metcalf, Jr.). 1975.
24. Henry James (Beatrice Ricks). 1975.
25. Robert Frost (Lentricchia & Lentricchia). 1976.
26. Sherwood Anderson (Douglas G. Rogers). 1976.
27. Iris Murdoch and Muriel Spark (Tominaga & Schneider-meyer). 1976.
28. John Ruskin (Kirk H. Beetz). 1976.
29. Georges Simenon (Trudee Young). 1976.
30. George Gordon, Lord Byron (Oscar José Santucho). 1976.
31. John Barth (Richard Vine). 1977.
32. John Hawkes (Carol A. Hryciw). 1977.
33. William Everson (Bartlett & Campo). 1977.
34. May Sarton (Lenora Blouin). 1978.
35. Wilkie Collins (Kirk H. Beetz). 1978.
36. Sylvia Plath (Lane & Stevens). 1978.
37. E. B. White (A. J. Anderson). 1978.
38. Henry Miller (Lawrence J. Shifreen). 1979.
39. Ralph Waldo Emerson (Jeanetta Boswell). 1979.
40. James Dickey (Jim Elledge). 1979.
41. Henry Fielding (H. George Hahn). 1979.
42. Paul Goodman (Tom Nicely). 1979.
43. Christopher Marlowe (Kenneth Friedenreich). 1979.
44. Leo Tolstoy (Egan & Egan). 1979.
45. T. S. Eliot (Beatrice Ricks). 1980.
46. Allen Ginsberg (Michelle P. Kraus). 1980.
47. Anthony Burgess (Jeutonne P. Brewer). 1980.
48. Tennessee Williams (Drewey Wayne Gunn). 1980.
49. William Faulkner (Beatrice Ricks). 1981.
50. Lillian Hellman (Mary Marguerite Riordan). 1980.
51. Walt Whitman (Jeanetta Boswell). 1980.
52. Jack Kerouac (Robert J. Milewski). 1981.
53. Herman Melville (Jeanetta Boswell). 1981.
54. Horatio Alger, Jr. (Scharnhorst & Bales). 1981.
55. Graham Greene (A.F. Cassis). 1981.
56. Henry David Thoreau (Boswell & Crouch). 1981.

GRAHAM GREENE:
an annotated bibliography of criticism

by

A. F. CASSIS

Scarecrow Author Bibliographies, No. 55

The Scarecrow Press, Inc
Metuchen, N.J., & London
1981

Library of Congress Cataloging in Publication Data

Cassis, A. F.
Graham Greene: an annotated bibliography of criticism.

(Scarecrow author bibliographies; no. 55)
Includes indexes.
1. Greene, Graham, 1904- --Bibliography.
I. Title. II. Series.
Z8368.987.C37 [PR6013.R44] 016.823'912 81-770
ISBN 0-8108-1418-8 AACR2

Manufactured in the United States of America

To Hilda and the girls

CONTENTS

PREFACE

There seems to be little doubt in both academic and popular circles that Graham Greene is perhaps the leading man of letters on the English literary scene today. Scholars and academics may dispute his stature as a novelist, or whether he can be called a twentieth-century Dickens; but they cannot ignore his contribution to, or impact on, the English novel in the wake of the Joyce/Woolf/Richardson experiment with the "stream of consciousness." Nor can one completely ignore his achievements in the sister arts of drama, the short story, and criticism.

Greene has been writing for over half a century and there seems to be no sign that his prolificacy is diminishing in any way as he moves towards his 77th birthday. Ways of Escape and Dr. Fischer of Geneva or The Bomb Party (both published in 1980) and the curtain-raiser Yes & No and For Whom The Bell Chimes (performed at Haymarket Studio Theatre, Leicester, in March 1980) indicate that the "grand old man" of English literature is as creatively engaged as he was in his forties and fifties.

Criticism, as a handmaid of literature, began to notice Greene's art in the forties. Taking the lead from the French, English critics began to evaluate aspects of his art and two years after the appearance of two French book-length studies of Greene's art and thought, the first English book-length study, as well as the first German one, was published. Since then, the volume of criticism--not all of it by any means first rate--has grown untrammelled and undeterred by Scrutiny's determination to exclude Greene from its pages. Recognition of Greene's art by academic circles followed the lead taken by the popular press in the early fifties, and his works became the subject of many dissertations at German and North American universities.

It became apparent to me that with this ever-increasing volume of criticism in weeklies, general interest periodicals, and scholarly journals, some annotated bibliography of criticism was needed to facilitate the task of the serious student and reader. Criticism in the popular "Catholic" press has been excluded from this volume. The items included are not confined to English and some attempt, perhaps unsuccessful, has been made to ensure comprehensiveness by consulting a wide range of basic bibliographies of English literature ranging from Abstracts of English Studies to the Year's Work in English Studies.

This bibliography is chronologically arranged, and apart from two items on Babbling April, begins in 1929 with The Man Within. The critical items listed do not include works on Greene's books for children, but are restricted to his novels, plays, short stories, critical essays, his autobiography, and his biography of Lord Rochester. The cut-off date is 1979 but I am fully conscious that the items listed for that year are far from "comprehensive" or adequate.

The items for each year, whenever possible, have been subdivided into four or five categories which may be identified under B A R D S: B for books, including chapters in or sections of; A for articles, including selected review articles and letters to the editor; R for reviews of books and performances of plays; D for dissertations; and S for "miscellaneous." Each category is alphabetically arranged with this exception: anonymous articles or reviews in journals or periodicals are given at the end of the category and arranged alphabetically according to the title of the journal. The numbering of each item is meant to indicate category, year and number within the category; e.g., A597 indicates an article, written in 1959, and listed as number 7 in the category.

Some attempt has been made to give, in the case of books, both English and American publishers. In the case of articles, the titles of articles and periodicals, the date (without the year, for that is subsumed in the numbering of the item), and page numbers are given. Generally speaking, the volume number is also given except in those cases where I had to rely on inter-library loan photocopies and had not checked the original. The list of abbreviations for journals is based on the MLA Directory of Periodicals for 1978-79, which has also been supplemented by my own list. Fewer than a dozen items were unavailable for examination and these have been noted as such. Dissertations are Ph. D. works unless otherwise stated and the university to which the dissertation was presented is also given. Wherever possible, reference to Dissertation Abstracts is made and publication information given when pertinent. The annotations indicate the content and attempt to give the central thesis or purpose of the article or book and the works considered in the study, as well as the level of the criticism. This has entailed some evaluation. However, I have tried to keep my biases and opinions to a minimum. For the convenience of the student and scholar, two indexes are appended: one for the critics included and the other containing references to some 55 selected topics and themes, as well as studies of individual works.

Any bibliography of criticism is built on the works of earlier bibliographers and this volume is no exception. It is difficult to tell whether this volume would have achieved its present form without the earlier checklists of W. Birmingham, M. Beebe, P. Hargreaves, N. Brennan, J. Vann, and especially R. A. Wobbe, whose excellent book Graham Greene: A Bibliography and Guide to Research crossed my desk in May. I am particularly indebted to him for the list of M. A. dissertations at U. S. universities.

When speaking of indebtedness, it is difficult for me to mention all those who have helped me in this work. I am particularly grateful to Dr. B. F. Tyson for his support and suggestions; to Dr. G. Hesse for help in translation; to my colleagues in the Departments of Modern Languages and History; to the University Library, especially the Inter-Library Loan Service; to the Library at Trinity College, University of Dublin; and to the Newspaper Section of the British Library at Colindale, London. I am also indebted to the University of Lethbridge for sabbatical leave in 1979-80 which helped me to complete this study which I had begun six years ago.

I wish to thank Miss B. Ramtej for her part in typing the

manuscript; my daughters, Irene and Jehan, for their help in typing and proofreading; and my family for its patience and tolerance.

A. F. Cassis

The University of Lethbridge,
Lethbridge, Alberta

ABBREVIATIONS FOR PERIODICALS

ABR	American Benedictine Review (Atchison, KS)
Abside	Abside: Revista de Cultura Mejicana (San Luis Potosi, Mexico)
Accent	Accent: A Quarterly of New Literature (Urbana, IL)
Adam	Adam International Review (London)
AFMUB	Annali della Facoltà di Magistero dell' Università di Bari
Aidai	Aidai Kulturos Zurnalos
AL	American Libraries (Chicago)
AM	American Mercury (New York)
America	America: A Catholic Review of the Week (New York)
Annotator	Annotator
AnRS	Annual Reports of Studies (Kyoto, Japan)
AntigR	Antigonish Review (N. S.)
APL	Annales Politiques et Littéraires (Paris)
Apostle	Apostle (Detroit)
Approach	Approach (Osaka, Japan)
AR	Antioch Review (Yellow Springs, OH)
Arbor	Arbor Ciencia, Pensamiento y Cultura (Madrid)
ArielE	Ariel: A Review of English Literature (Calgary, Alta.)
ArQ	Arizona Quarterly (Tucson, AZ)
Arts	Arts (Sydney, Australia)
ASch	American Scholar (Washington, DC)
AtA	The Atlantic Advocate
Atlantic	The Atlantic Monthly
Atlantida	Atlantida (Madrid)
AU	L'Action Universitaire (Montréal)
AUBB	Annales de L'Union Belgo-Britannique
AUCP	Acta Universitatis Carolinae-Philologica (Prague)
Ave Maria	Ave Maria (Notre Dame, IN)
AWPR	Atlas World Press Review (Stanley Foundation, New York)
BA	Books Abroad
B&B	Books and Bookmen (London)
BasT	The Basilian Teacher (Toronto)
BB	Bulletin of Bibliography (Westwood, MA)
BBM	British Book of the Month
BBN	British Book News (London)
BC	Books in Canada

Begegnung	Begegnung (Cologne)
Bell	Bell
Best Sellers	Best Sellers
BFL	Bulletin de la Faculté des Lettres de Strasbourg
Blackfriars	Blackfriars (Oxford, England)
BMCN	Book-of-the-Month Club News (New York)
BN	Biography News
Booklist	Booklist
Bookman	Bookman (London)
Bookman	Bookman (N. Y.)
Bookmark	Bookmark
BookW	Book Week
Bookworld	Bookworld
BosT	Boston Transcript
Brit	Britain Today
Brotéria	Brotéria: Revista de Sciencias Naturaes (Lisbon)
BT	Books on Trial (Chicago)
BTod	Books Today
CA	Catholic Action (Fargo, ND)
Caliban	Caliban (Toulouse, France)
CalR	Calcutta Review
C&L	Christianity and Literature (Grand Rapids, MI)
CC	Canadian Commentator (Toronto)
CE	College English (Middletown, CT)
CF	Canadian Forum (Toronto)
CG	Catholic Gazette (London)
CH	Catholic Herald (London)
Chimera	Chimera (Seton Hall Univ., NJ)
ChrC	The Christian Century (Chicago)
ChristW	Christ und Welt (Dusseldorf, W. Germany)
ChrS	Christian Scholar (New York)
ChrSM	Christian Science Monitor
Cithara	Cithara: Essays in the Judeo-Christian Tradition (St. Bonaventure, NY)
CivC	Civilta Cattolica (Rome)
CL	Comparative Literature (Eugene, OR)
CLM	Central Literary Magazine (Birmingham)
CLS	Comparative Literature Studies (Urbana, IL)
CLW	Catholic Library World
ColQ	Colorado Quarterly (Boulder, CO)
Commentary	Commentary (New York)
Commentator	Commentator (Yeshiva Univ., NY)
Commonweal	Commonweal (New York)
ConL	Contemporary Literature (Madison, WI)
ContempR	Contemporary Review (London)
COS	Cleveland Open Shelf
CP	Cahiers Protestants
CQ	Carolina Quarterly (Chapel Hill, NC)
CR	Clergy Review (London)
Cresset	Cresset (Valparaiso, IN)
Critic	Critic: A Catholic Review of Books and the Arts (Chicago)
Criticism	Criticism: A Quarterly for Literature and the Arts (Detroit, MI)

Critique	Critique: Revue Générale des Publications Françaises et Etrangères (Paris)
CritQ	Critical Quarterly (Manchester)
Crosscurrents	Crosscurrents (West Nyack, NY)
CSBW	Chicago Sun Book Week
CST	Chicago Sunday Tribune
CT	Christianity Today
CTr	Catholic Transcript
CultC	Culture Catholique
Culture	Culture: Revue trimestrielle, sciences religieuses et sciences profanes au Canada (Montréal)
CW	Catholic World
Daedalus	Daedalus: Journal of the American Academy of Arts and Sciences (Cambridge, MA)
DaiE	Daily Express (London)
DaiM	Daily Mail (London)
DaiMir	Daily Mirror (London)
DaiN	Daily News (New York)
DaiT	Daily Telegraph (London)
DC	Drama Critique: A Critical Review of Theatre Arts and Literature (Lancaster, NY)
DeutR	Deutsche Rundschau
Dieu Vivant	Dieu Vivant
DM	The Dublin Magazine (formerly The Dubliner)
Dominicana	Dominicana
DR	Dalhousie Review (Halifax, Nova Scotia)
DSPACR	Dun Scotus Philosophical Association Convention Report
Du	Du; Europaeische Kunstzeitschrift (Zurich)
DubR	Dublin Review
DWB	Dietsche Warande en Belfort: Tijfschrift voor Letterkunde, Kunst en Geestesleven (Leuven, Belgium)
EA	Etudes Anglaises: Grande-Bretagne, Etats-Unis (Paris)
E&S	Essays and Studies by Members of the English Association
Echo	Echo: Revue Internationale
Econ	The Economist
EIC	Essays in Criticism: A Quarterly Journal of Literary Criticism (Oxford)
EigoS	Eigo Seinen (Tokyo)
EJ	The English Journal (E. Lansing, MI)
ELLS	English Literature and Language (Tokyo)
ELN	English Language Notes (Boulder, CO)
ELWIU	Essays in Literature (Macomb, IL)
Empreintes	Empreintes
Encounter	Encounter (London)
English	English (Aylesbury, Bucks. England)
Envoy	Envoy: A review of Literature and Art (Dublin)
ES	English Studies: A Journal of English Language and Literature (Gent, Belgium)
Esprit	Esprit (Paris)

Esquire	Esquire (New York)
ETJ	Educational Theatre Journal (Toledo, OH)
Etudes	Etudes (Paris)
European	European (London)
EvS	Evening Standard (London)
EW	Evangelische Welt (Bethel)
Expl	Explicator (Washington, DC)
Extension	Extension (Chicago)
Extracta	Extracta. Resumeer af Special espgaver fra det Filosofiske Fakultet ved Kobenhaus Universitet
FH	Frankfurter Hefte: Zeitschrift für Kultur und Politik (Frankfurt, W. Germany)
Fiddlehead	Fiddlehead (Fredericton, New Brunswick)
FigL	Figaro Littéraire (Paris)
FilmH	Film Heritage
FiR	Films in Review (New York)
FJS	Fu Jen Studies: Literature and Linguistics (Taipeh, Taiwan, Rep. of China)
FMod	Filología Moderna (Madrid)
ForumC	Forum (Canada)
ForumH	Forum (Houston)
ForumZ	Forum (Zaghreb)
FQ	Florida Quarterly (Gainesville, FL)
FR	Fortnightly Review (London)
FrA	France-Asie/Asia (Tokyo)
FrI	France Illustré
FS	French Studies: A Quarterly Review (Cambridge, England)
GaR	The Georgia Review (Athens, GA)
GdiM	Giornalo di Metafisica (Genova, Italy)
GdL	La Gazette des Lettres
GduL	Guilde du Livre (Lausanne, Switzerland)
GH	Good Housekeeping (New York)
Globe	Globe and Mail (Toronto)
Grail	Grail
Guardian	Guardian (Manchester)
GuardianW	Guardian Weekly (Manchester)
HA	Harvard Advocate
H&PR	Homilectic and Pastoral Review (New York)
Harper's Magazine	Harper's Magazine (New York)
HB	Horn Book (Boston)
Hibernia	Hibernia (Dublin)
HM	Hommes et Mondes (Paris)
Hochland	Hochland (Munich)
Holiday	Holiday (Philadelphia)
Horizon	Horizon (New York)
HudR	The Hudson Review (New York)
Humanist	Humanist (London)
HumB	Humanitas: Rivista di Cultura (Brescia, Italy)
HWM	Herald Weekend Magazine
ICS	L'Italia che Scrive: Rassegna per Colore che Leggono (Rome)

IER	Irish Ecclesiastical Record (Maynooth, Ireland)
IEY	Iowa English Bulletin Yearbook (Iowa City, IA)
IJES	Indian Journal of English Studies
IL	Innostrannaja Literatura (Moscow)
ILN	Illustrated London News
IM	Irish Monthly (Dublin)
Indice	Indice (Madrid)
Insula	Insula: Revista Bibliográfica de Ciencias y Letras (Madrid)
IP	Irish Press (Dublin)
IT	The Irish Times (Dublin)
JA	Jahrbuch für Amerikastudien
JAU	Journal of the Annamalai University
JCH	Journal of Contemporary History
JKUR	Jammu and Kashmir University Review
JML	Journal of Modern Literature (Philadelphia)
JO'L	John O'London's
JSH	Journal of Southern History
Káñina	Káñina Revista des Artes y Letras de la Universidad Costa Rica (San José)
Kirkus	Kirkus Reviews (New York)
Kliatt	Kliatt Adult Paperback Book Guide (Newton, MA)
KN	Kwartalnik Neofilologiczny (Warsaw, Poland)
KoK	Kirke og Kultur (Oslo, Norway)
KR	Kenyon Review
KresR	Krestanska Revue (Prague)
Kuban	Kuban (Krasnodar)
KulturaP	Kultura (Maison-Lafitte, France)
KulturaW	Kultura (Warsaw)
Kulturleven	Kulturleven
La Croix	La Croix (Paris)
L&L	Life and Letters (London)
L&P	Literature and Psychology (Teaneck, NJ)
Lang&S	Language and Style: An International Journal (Flushing, NY)
LanM	Les Langues Modernes (Lavausseau, France)
LdProv	Lettore di Provincia (Ravenna, Italy)
Letture	Letture: Libro e Spettacolo/Mensile di Studi e Rassegne (Milan, Italy)
LFQ	Literature/Film Quarterly (Salisbury, MD)
LHY	Literary Half-Yearly (Mysore, India)
Life	Life (Chicago)
Listener	Listener (London)
LitR	Literary Review: An International Journal of Contemporary Writing (Madison, NJ)
Living Age	Living Age
LivL	Livres et Lectures: Revue Bibliographique (Paris)
LJ	Library Journal (New York)
LM	London Magazine
LNL	Linguistics in Literature (San Antonio, TX)
Look	Look
LR	Library Review (Glasgow, Scotland)
LU	London Universe

Luc	Luceafărul (Bucharest, Romania)
LWU	Literatur in Wissenschaft und Unterricht (Kiel, W. Germany)
Maclean's	Maclean's Canada's Weekly Magazine (Toronto)
Mapocho	Mapocho (Santiago, Chile)
Marcha	Marcha (Montevideo, Uruguay)
Marginalia	Marginalia
MBL	Modern British Literature (Butler, PA)
MCR	Melbourne Critical Review
MD	Modern Drama (Toronto)
Meanjin	Meanjin (Victoria, Australia)
MerF	Mercure de France
Merkur	Merkur: Deutsche Zeitschrift für Europäisches Denken (Munich)
MFS	Modern Fiction Studies (West Lafayette, IN)
MLQ	Modern Language Quarterly (Seattle, WA)
Month	Month (London)
MQ	Midwest Quarterly: A Journal of Contemporary Thought (Pittsburg, KS)
MR	Massachusetts Review: A Quarterly of Literature, the Arts and Public Affairs (Amherst, MA)
NA	Neves Abendland (Augsburg)
NAd	The New Adelphi (London)
N&Q	Notes and Queries (Oxford)
Nation	Nation (New York)
NationL	Nation & Athenaeum (London)
NC	Nineteenth Century and After (London)
NCh	News Chronicle (London)
NCR	National Catholic Reporter (Los Angeles, CA)
ND	Negro Digest
NDH	Neue Deutsche Hefte (Berlin, W. Germany)
Newsletter	Newsletter: Catholic Book Club
Newsweek	Newsweek
NH	Die Neue Heimat (Berlin)
NL	Nouvelles Littéraires (Paris)
NLauR	New Laurel Review (Chalmette, LA)
NLea	The New Leader (New York)
NObs	National Observer (Salisbury, Rhodesia)
Norseman	Norseman: A Review of Current Events (London)
Nos Cours	Nos Cours (Montréal)
Novena Notes	Novena Notes
NovM	Novyj Mir (Moscow, USSR)
NR	National Review (London)
NRep	The New Republic (Washington)
NRev	New Review (London)
NS	Die Neueren Sprachen (Frankfurt, W. Germany)
NSoc	New Society (London)
NSta	New Statesman (London)
NW	New World (Chicago)
NY	New Yorker
NYEP	New York Evening Post
NYHT	New York Herald Tribune
NYJ	New York Journal

NYP	New York Post
NYRB	New York Review of Books
NYTBR	New York Times Book Review
NYWT	New York World Telegram
NZZ	Neue Zurcher Zeitung
OB	Ord och Bild (Stockholm)
Observer	Observer (London)
OC	Orbis Catholicus
Odù	Odù (Ile-Ife, Nigeria)
ORom	Osservatore Romano (Rome)
Outlook	Outlook
PAPA	Publications of the Arkansas Philological Association (State Univ., AK)
PBSA	Papers of the Bibliographical Society of America
Periscoop	Periscoop (Antwerp, Belgium)
Perm	Permskii Universitet, Perm'
Person	The Personalist: An International Review of Philosophy (Los Angeles, CA)
Perspectiv	Perspectiv: det danske Magasin
Phoenix	Phoenix (Charleston, SC)
PicP	Picture Post
PLL	Papers on Language and Literature (Edwardsville, IL)
PNW	Penguin New Writing
PP	Philologica Pragensia (Prague)
PR	Partisan Review (Boston, MA)
PRev	Paris Review
Progressive	Progressive (Madison, WI)
PrS	Prairie Schooner (Lincoln, NE)
PsyT	Psychology Today
PURBA	Panjab University Research Bulletin Arts. (Chandigarh, India)
PuW	Poesie und Wissenschaft (Heidelberg, W. Germany)
PW	Publishers Weekly
QQ	Queen's Quarterly (Kingston, Ont.)
Raduga	Raduga (Kiev)
Ramparts	Ramparts (Menlo Park, CA)
RDM	Revue des Deux Mondes
Realities	Realities (Washington, SE)
REL	Review of English Literature (Leeds)
Renascence	Renascence: Essays on Value in Literature (Milwaukee, WI)
RG	Revue Generale (Brussels)
RiL	Religion in Life (Nashville, TN)
RLC	Revue de Littérature Comparée (Tours-Cedex, France)
RLM	La Revue des Lettres Modernes (Paris)
RLMeC	Rivista di Litteratura Moderne e Comparata (Firenze)
RLV	Revue des Langues Vivantes (Liège, Belgium)
RLz	Radjans'ke Literaturoznavstvo: Naukovo-Teoretyčnyj Žurnal (Kiev)
RMS	Renaissance & Modern Studies (Univ. of Nottingham)

RN	Revue Nouvelle (Brussels)
RoLit	România Literarǎ: Sǎptǎminal de Literaturǎ si Artǎ Editat de Uniunea Scriitorilor din Republica Socialistǎ România (Bucharest)
RolS	Rolling Stone (New York)
RP	Revue de Paris
RPF	Revue de la Pensée Française
RRel	Review for Religious (St. Louis, MO)
RUCR	Revista de la Universidad de Costa Rica
RUL	Revue de L'Université Laval
RUO	Revue de L'Université d'Ottawa/Univ. of Ottawa Quarterly
RUSEng	Rajasthan Univ. Studies in English (Jaipur, India)
RyF	Razón y Fe: Revista Hispanoamericana de Cultura (Madrid)
Samtiden	Samtiden: Tidsskrift for Politikk, Literatur og Samfunnssporsmal (Oslo)
S&S	Sight and Sound: The International Film Quarterly (London)
SAP	Studia Anglica Posnaniensia: An International Review of English Studies (Poznań, Poland)
SAQ	South Atlantic Quarterly (Durham, NC)
SatEP	Saturday Evening Post (Philadelphia)
SatN	Saturday Night
SatR	Saturday Review (New York)
SB	Studies in Bibliography: Papers of the Bibliographical Society of the Univ. of Virginia (Charlottesville)
SCB	South Central Bulletin (Houston, TX)
SchLJ	School Library Journal (New York)
Scriblerian	Scriblerian: A Newsletter devoted to Pope, Swift, and their Circle. (Philadelphia)
Scrutiny	Scrutiny (London)
Seele	Seele (Regensburg)
Serif	Serif (Kent State Univ. Library Quarterly)
SFC	San Francisco Chronicle
SHR	Southern Humanities Review (Auburn, AL)
Sign	Sign (Union City, NJ)
SLJ	Southern Literary Journal (Chapel Hill, NC)
SLURJ	St. Louis Univ. Research Journal
SJM	St. Joseph Magazine (Oregon)
SNNTS	Studies in the Novel (Denton, TX)
Soir	Soir (Brussels)
SoR	Southern Review (Baton Rouge, LA)
SovL	Soviet Literature (Moscow)
Spectator	Spectator (London)
SpR	Springfield Republican
SR	Sewanee Review (Sewanee, TN)
SSF	Studies in Short Fiction (Newberry, SC)
STC	Studies in the Twentieth Century
Steaua	Steaua (Bucharest)
StM	The Student Movement
Streven	Streven (Amsterdam)

Studies	Studies: An Irish Quarterly Review (Dublin)
Studium	Studium (Rome)
Style	Style (Fayetteville, AK)
SUB	Studia Universitatis Babes-Bolyai
SunT	Sunday Times (London)
SunTel	Sunday Telegraph (London)
Sur	Sur
SWR	Southwest Review (Dallas, TX)
Symposium	Symposium (Syracuse, NY)
Synthese	Synthese: An International Journal for Epistemology, Methodology and Philosophy of Science (Helsinki, Finland)
SZ	Stimmen der Zeit (Munich)
Tablet	Tablet (London)
TamR	Tamarack Review (Toronto)
T&T	Time & Tide: Indian Journal of International Films (New Delhi, India)
TArts	Theatre Arts
Tashkend	Tashkend. Gosudarstvenni Pedagogicheskii Institut. Uchenye Zapiski.
TCL	Twentieth Century Literature: A Scholarly and Critical Journal (Hempstead, NY)
TCLon	Twentieth Century (London)
TCMel	Twentieth Century (Melbourne)
TCS	Twentieth Century Studies (Univ. of Kent)
Theology	Theology (London)
Thought	Thought: A Review of Culture and Idea (Bronx, NY)
Time	Time (New York)
Times	Times (London)
TLS	Times Literary Supplement
TM	Temps Modernes (Paris)
Today	Today (Tunbridge Wells, Kent)
Tomorrow	Tomorrow (New York)
TP	Temps Présent (Paris)
TPr	Tempo Presente (Rome)
TQ	Texas Quarterly (Austin, TX)
TR	La Table Ronde (Paris)
Transition	Transition: The Literary Magazine for a World of Change (Hillsboro, OR)
Trivium	Trivium (Dyfed, Wales)
TRom	Tribuna României (Bucharest)
TSLL	Texas Studies in Literature and Language (Austin, TX)
TSU	Trudy Samarkandskogo Universiteta
UES	Unisa English Studies: Journal of the Department of English (Pretoria, S. Africa)
UKCR	University of Kansas City Review
Unitas	Unitas: A Quarterly for the Arts and Sciences (Manila, Philippines)
Univ	Universitas: Zeitschrift für Wissenschaft, Kunst und Literatur. (Tübingen, W. Germany)
UPR	University of Portland Review
UTQ	University of Toronto Quarterly: A Canadian Journal of the Humanities

UZKGPI	Učenye Zapiski Kujbyševskogo Gosudarstvennogo Pedagogičeskigo Instituta im. V. V. Kujbyševa (USSR)
VeP	Vita e Pensiero: Rassegna Italiana di Cultura (Milan)
VI	Vie Intellectuelle (Paris)
ViR	Viata Româneascǎ (Bucharest)
VLit	Voprosy Literatury (Moscow)
VMU	Vestnik Moskovskogo Universiteta. (Moscow)
VN	Victorian Newsletter (Flushing, NY)
VolR	The Volusia Review
VQ	Visvabharati Quarterly (Santiniketan, West Bengal, India)
VQR	Virginia Quarterly Review
VV	Village Voice (New York)
WBR	Weekly Book Review
WCR	West Coast Review (Burnaby, B. C.)
WesR	Western Review (New Mexico)
WHR	Western Humanities Review (Salt Lake City, UT)
WisR	Wiseman Review
WLT	World Literature Today: A Literary Quarterly of the Univ. of Oklahoma (Norman, OK)
WRev	World Review (Queensland, Australia)
WSCL	Wisconsin Studies in Contemporary Literature
WSJ	Wall Street Journal
WW	Wort und Wahrheit
WZUR	Wissenschaftliche Zeitschrift der Wilhelm-Pieck-Universität Rostock. Gesellschafts-und Sprachwissenschaftliche Reiche (Rostock, E. Germany)
YR	The Yale Review: A National Quarterly (New Haven, CT)
ZAA	Zeitschrift für Anglistik und Amerikanistik (Leipzig)
ZeitB	Die Zeit im Buch (Vienna)
ZRL	Zagadnienia Rodzajów Literackich (Lódź, Poland)
Zvezda	Zvezda (Leningrad, USSR)

THE BIBLIOGRAPHY

1925

R251 Unsigned. "Poetry: Babbling April." TLS, 1218 (21 May), p. 355. Critical of the volume for being little organized, "full of inconsequences and irrelevancies ... and occasionally of spontaneous expletives...."

1926

R261 Snow, Royall. "Oxford: Thick Smoke and Thin Fire." Poetry (Chicago), XXVIII (May), pp. 112-14. Babbling April is the second of two volumes reviewed. Compliments Greene for being "thoughtful without parade" and for possessing a "literary conscience" without which the poetry would have been "thoroughly flat" as it is without "thrill and fire" and it presents "nothing new."

1929

R291 Allen, Paul. "The Man Within." Bookman (N. Y.), LXX (29 Dec.), p. 449. Appreciative of the "warm and glowing" style, the sense of values given and the "feeling for words" which make the reader follow the story with "sympathy and understanding." Commends Greene for a "satisfying" first novel which is described as a "psychological" novel written with "feeling and much skill." Associates the "inevitability" of the novel with Conrad's Lord Jim.

R292 Baird, Enid. "The Continuing Present." NYHT, (20 Oct.), p. 23. Recognizes the "direct, unpretentious beauty" of the narrative and the "concreteness and strict economy of dramatic production" which characterize The Man Within. Though the outward physical conflict is exciting in itself, it serves as a background for Andrew's inner conflict and never obscures it. The characters walk, think and talk like "real individuals." Describes the novel as "complete and beautiful," as an "accomplishment not merely the promise of future accomplishment," that indicates a literary ability both "cultivated and disciplined."

R293 Brebner, Bartlet. "Promise Almost Fulfilled." SatR, VI (19 Oct.), p. 287. This "exciting tale written in distinct and dignified prose" is an "assured and competent piece of work" that indicates a literary integrity free from "mannerism or trickery." Speculates that The Man Within may be a "forerunner of better fare" that may reach beyond "honesty and subtlety and competence of craftsmanship to outstanding artistic achievement."

R294 Codman, Florence. "Two Literary Generations." Nation, CXXIX:3355 (23 Oct.), pp. 468-69. A "surprisingly adroit" first novel that leaves the reviewer worried whether Greene had "burned himself out in one trial." The "extraordinary lyric phantasm," nearer to drama than fiction, is expressed in language of "rare purity, fluency and richness, in a manner that is strikingly original, forceful and graceful."

R295 Mais, S. P. B. "An Excellent First Novel." DaiT, (21 June), p. 16. Warm praise for Greene who has the "twofold gift of being able to tell an exciting story and to reveal human character." The Man Within is "impregnated with beauty, subtle in construction" and has great dramatic tension. As a first novel it is a "perfect accomplishment" and has all the "makings of a good play."

R296 N., R. W. "The Man Within." SpR, (3 Nov.), p. 7e. Dissents from the general chorus of praise for the novel to point out its "consanguinity" with the stream of consciousness type, and its "long-drawn-out-ness" or "slowness that comes near to tedium," for Greene's work "traces back to intellectual analysis more than imagination." Compares Greene's narrative, artistry and appeal to R. L. Stevenson's.

R297 Robbins, Frances Lamont. "The Man Within." Outlook, CLIII (Dec.), p. 670. A brief review of the novel among others. Considers the novel as perhaps the "most original and possibly strongest new talent of the year" in English fiction. "In the purity, fluency and discipline of his style, in the originality of his conception and in his sure sense of fictional values," Greene's remarkable study of the inward conflict of a dual nature has set a high standard for future work.

R298 Sackville-West, V. "New Novels." Listener, II:27 (17 July), p. 97. A "heavily-charged and brooding" novel that bears "some resemblance" to Conrad's novels, especially in the "muffled, muted atmosphere" and the significance attendant upon apparently insignificant events. Also notices Greene's "real sense of language" and his interest in the complexities of human nature rather than the details of the historical setting.

R299 Thomas, Gilbert. "First Novels: The Man Within." Spectator, CXLII (22 June), p. 982. The last of five novels reviewed. Commends Greene for an "exceptionally fresh and readable story" that moves with "certainty and ease" in a "narrow compass," and for its "picturesque but historically convincing setting."

R2910 Unsigned. "Novel Notes." Bookman (London), LXXVI (July), pp. 228-29. In The Man Within, Greene chose a theme that tested his ability in the extreme but has succeeded in his "wholly psychological" treatment of it in revealing the "battle of a man ... with contrary and nobler elements that are restive within him." Though his dialogue may lack "ease and naturalness," Greene's "economy of expression" and sincerity lend the novel a "quiet force." Its ending achieves an "effect of high drama."

R2911 ________. "The Man Within." BosT, (13 Nov.), p. 5. This is a "thoroughly unusual" first novel, a romance that has both "beauty and strangeness" and in which one vivid scene follows another. "Greene shows himself an artist of discernment and power" in the way he handles the story.

R2912 ________. "The Man Within." Guardian, (28 June), p. 528. A short review noting the "careful and complex dissection of motives" and the descriptive passages of "great power and beauty."

R2913 ________. "Novels in Brief: The Man Within." NationL, XLV (3 Aug.), p. 602. Notices Greene's talent as a writer in this "psychological adventure story, somewhere between Stevenson and Conrad." Maintains that though the characters may be credible separately, "it is difficult to believe in their connection with one another." Describes the dialogue as "perhaps, too modern."

R2914 ________. "'The Man Within' and Other Recent Works of Fiction." NYTBR, (27 Oct.), p. 6. This is a first novel of "excellent promise" that argues for a future worth close watching. Recognizes the merging of the psychological and the dramatic in it as well as Greene's individual world: "circumscribed, elemental, undetailed." Finds the ending lacking something "genuine and inevitable" in spite of its psychological consistency. Notices some resemblance to Lord Jim.

R2915 ________. "History and Romance." Times, (21 June), p. 19. The Man Within is a "notable" first novel whose "psychological analysis of motives" or "dramatized subconscious" is written with "distinction and subtlety" and whose setting is described with "the full beauty of Mr. Greene's sensitive style."

R2916 ________. "New Novels: The Man Within." TLS, 1429 (20 June), p. 492. Remarks favorably on Greene's interest in the spiritual adventures of the "man within" and "delicate, translucent psychologizing" with which he "enhaloes" his characters and the "deftness" with which he wields the "psychological scalpel" generally. Also notices the "plain, breathtaking excitement" which Greene is capable of arousing.

1930

R301 Mais, S. P. B. "Second Novels by Three Men of Promise." DaiT, (10 Oct.), p. 6. Though both exciting and romantic, The Name of Action does not compare with The Man Within in "clarity and plausibility." It is "powerful and uneven," and despite its "polished and beautiful" style, its characters are sometimes inscrutable and at times, verge on absurdity.

R302 "Proteus." "New Novels." NSta, XXXVI (8 Nov.), p. 148. Finds The Name of Action "an oddly unsatisfying book" which is closer to a fantasy than to a novel, even though the style is "sensitive and fine, and some of his descriptions could hardly be bettered."

R303 Tomlinson, Kathleen C. "New Novels." NationL, XLVIII (15 Nov.), pp. 241-42. The Name of Action, the second of five novels reviewed, is a "notable" book; the writing is "sculptural in character," delightful and enriched by similes.

R304 Unsigned. "New Novels." SatR, CL (8 Nov.), p. 598. The Name of Action is one of six novels reviewed. Critical of Greene's handling: the plot "strains the probabilities" and the motives of the characters seem "trumped-up." Declares it "a bogus book" in spite of its sensitive style and readability.

R305 ________. "Critic's Commentary: Being Some Notes from a Reviewer's Note Book." T&T, XI (8 Nov.), p. 1408. Brief note expressing disappointment at Greene's second novel for it asks too much of credulity. Advises Greene to leave melodrama alone.

R306 ________. "The Name of Action." Times, (7 Oct.), p. 8. Qualified praise for Greene's individual treatment of the stirring drama whose actions move with a "fine effect of inevitability," and for the "distinction and individuality" of his literary style.

R307 ________. "New Novels: The Name of Action." TLS, 1497 (9 Oct.), p. 804. Though "admirably written," the book leaves one with the impression that we are living in the author's "peculiar, highly wrought" imaginative world rather than any recognizable era. However, though not familiar, this world is credible and the book suffers no decline from "the tensity and vividness" of the opening description of Oliver Chant within whose consciousness the story takes place.

1931

R311 Bullett, Gerald. "New Novels." NSta, II (14 Nov.), pp. 613-14. Rumour at Nightfall is the fourth of seven novels reviewed. Maintains that though Greene has "abundant talent," he is so "resolutely and laboriously romantic" that he strains the credulity of his readers especially that the emotions of his characters are "largely theatrical."

R312 Fadiman, William J. "The Name of Action." Bookman (N.Y.), LXXIII (April), pp. 195-96. Greene's second novel is a second-rate fashionable melodrama, a "facile and competent piece of writing" which, despite its "supple prose and unconventional ending" remains nevertheless, a "colorful treatment of a cinema theme" and does not justify any "salvo of cheers."

R313 Footner, Hulbert. "A Romantic Tale." SatR, VII (14 March), p. 664. Despite Greene's excellent talent for writing and his "fresh and charming spirit," The Name of Action remains "unsatisfactory"; its leading characters behave in an inexplicable manner and psychoanalysis "stalks" the romance. It is only in its secondary scenes that the story becomes "simple, first-rate and positively thrilling."

R314 Gould, Gerald. "New Novels: Some Imperfect Sympathies." Observer, (13 Dec.), p. 5. A short review of Rumour at Nightfall noticing the oddity of the atmosphere and the quite "magnificently unconvincing" ending as well as Greene's style, especially his "slow, careful sensuous prose in which the oddities of his characters prevail by their own coherence."

R315 Robbins, Frances Lamont. "The Name of Action." Outlook, CLVII (March), p. 374. Commends the novel to readers who demand "story and style," because both psychology and melodrama are "subordinated to and embodied in a spirited narrative, sensitive characterizations and fine descriptions." Notices Greene's interest in style and his use of simile.

R316 Sykes, Gerald. "Too Many Thrillers." NYHT, (15 Feb.), p. 18. The Name of Action is like the "fantasy of a schoolboy who has read--or seen--too many thrillers"; it cannot be justifiably described as romantic and its characters are "inexpressibly unreal."

R317 Walton, Edith H. "An Unusual Tale by Graham Greene." NYTBR, (8 March), p. 7. Accepts The Name of Action as a "very fine book" with a "pleasantly fantastic plot" that receives "brilliant and unexpected" treatment from Greene. As for the characters, they are real, "alive and suffer." Notices a "cruel kernel of truth" in the story of Chant and Anne-Marie and lavishes praise on Greene for his good writing and good prose.

R318 Unsigned. "The Name of Action." Booklist, XXVII:9 (May), pp. 407-08. Brief note narrating the story and describing the people as "unreal" and the psychoanalysis as "unconvincing."

R319 ________. "The Name of Action." BosT, (25 Feb.), p. 3. Critical of the novel because of its lack of "power and clarity," its "unreal" characters and the "leavey" movement of the story. Maintains that Greene has replaced the "romantic note" of his first novel with a "dissonance which rarely resolves satisfactorily."

R3110 ________. "The Name of Action." Forum, LXXXV (May), p. 16. A brief note commending Greene for his successful blend of "sensational adventure with subtle psychological drama," as well as his ability to write "beautifully."

R3111 ________. "The Name of Action." NRep, LXVI (18 March), p. 135. A brief note describing the "exceptional and heartening achievement" of a novel, "uncommonly well written." Praises Greene for investing the "slight" story with a "beautiful lucidity and objectivity."

R3112 ________. "New Novels." Spectator, CXLVII (26 Dec.), p. 892. A brief trenchant note on Rumour at Nightfall which describes Greene as an author who has "something to say but whose turgidity prevents" him from saying it.

R3113 ________. "New Novels: Rumour at Nightfall." TLS, 1557 (3 Dec.), p. 978. Greene attempts the valuable but extremely difficult task of "filtering" circumstances of everyday life through the tortuous and sensitive minds of individual characters. This is vividly done so long as the characters remain spectators; but when they plunge into the action, the author's "double vision" becomes "extremely difficult and almost unwieldy." Notices Greene's elaborate evocation of Spain's remote and exotic atmosphere.

1932

R321 Armstrong, Anne. "New Novels." SatR, CLIV (24 Dec.), p. 673. Commends Greene in Stamboul Train for building up characters--"all very real people"--by "glimpses." Describes the novel as "modern" and "episodic."

R322 Cantwell, Robert. "Graham Greene Captures Glamour of Spanish Drama." NYEP, (30 Jan.), p. 9. Maintains that Greene's talents for vivid pictorial detail and his ability to convey excitement cannot make up for the "complete separation" of romance--often interchangeable with violent melodrama--and psychological analysis in Rumour at Nightfall.

R323 Gould, Gerald. "New Novels: Romance and Humour." Observer, (11 Dec.), p. 6. Stamboul Train is one of four novels reviewed. Maintains that in this novel Greene has replaced the "affectations and absurdities" of his first novel with quiet study of character and construction. It is "original and well written" and, in spite of being somewhat "jerky in method" and occasionally coarse, he predicts the novel will have wide success.

R324 Linklater, Eric. "New Novels." Listener, VIII:205 (14 Dec.), p. 874. Remarks on the advantages derived from Greene's use of the "circumscribed stage" in Stamboul Train, the "swift and compelling" pace of his narrative, his masterly character delineation and his "engaging qualities" of cynicism, sympathy and irony. Also comments briefly on the "comedy of impartial criticism" in the denouement.

R325 Strong, L. A. G. "The Book of the Month: Stamboul Train." Spectator, CXLIX (9 Dec.), p. 842. Pays warm tribute to Greene for his ability to combine interest in external action and in the processes of the mind. Moreover, he has the knack of "surprising his readers into belief" even though his characters appear to be conventional on the surface. Characterization and the speed with which Greene conveys some psychological essential of his characters are two of the novel's most marked features.

R326 Unsigned. "Rumour at Nightfall." Forum, LXXXVII (April), p. 11. A short review describing the novel as a "brilliant example of the psychological novel" reminiscent of Conrad's work.

R327 ______. "Notes on Fiction." Nation, CXXXIV:3489 (18 May), p. 578. A short review describing Rumour at Nightfall as a "passion play in terms of psychological romance" whose "subtlety of style" makes up, in part, "what it lacks in wisdom." Rather critical of Greene's dependence on "strangeness to achieve the effect of beauty."

R328 ______. "Rumour at Nightfall." NRep, LXX (27 April), p. 308. A short review noting Greene's ability "to cover places and objects with atmosphere laid on heavily, like paint," and to maintain suspense in a novel whose principal characters are overwhelmed by "mental questionings and probings." Notices an affinity with Conrad.

R329 ______. "The New Books." SatR, VIII (13 Feb.), p. 527. Notices the "overtones of a typically Conradian stamp" in Rumour at Nightfall. Maintains that so long as he is telling a story, Greene is "sure" in his treatment and "enthralling" but becomes "confused" when he probes into motives or offers interpretations.

R3210 ______. "New Novel." Times, (16 Dec.), p. 8. Remarks on the change from the remote states of mind described in earlier novels to the "brisk and ingenious sketch" of characters in Stamboul Train.

R3211 ______. "New Novels: Stamboul Train." TLS, 1611 (15 Dec.), p. 960. Maintains that Greene's choice of setting determined the method by which the characters were drawn; instead of fine analysis, there is a clever, brisk, ingenious reporting of character but which nonetheless makes them slightly "theatrical." Notices how the atmosphere changes when Greene attempts to give the state and mind of a person in a moment of crisis at the frontier station.

1933

R331 Conrad, George. "Further Recent Fiction." NYHT, (12 March), p. 10. Describes the novel as an "ingenious and colorful narrative" which uses the "intensely dramatic" vehicle of a continental train for "sudden love and swift tragedy." Remarks on the "momentum of style," its compactness, the "gleam of irony" that tinctures the record of events and his "adroit" craftsmanship.

R332 Redman, Ben Ray. "Chance Acquaintances." SatR, IX (18 March), p. 489. As a story to "excite and entertain," Stamboul Train is "very good" current fiction: the interactions of these strangely assorted characters, "vigorously realized," composes Greene's multiple story which tightens into a well-knit whole.

R333 Unsigned. "Orient Express." BosT, (18 March), p. 2. Notes Greene's revelation of character by "glimpses," and finds that the characters are "distasteful" but plausible. As for the story, it moves easily but is neither "gripping nor convincing."

R334 _______. "Fiction." NRep, LXXIV (22 March), p. 168. Brief note commenting on the English Book Society's choice of Stamboul Train.

R335 _______. "Train Passengers." NYTBR, (12 March), p. 21. Remarks on the skillful presentation of the "thoroughly heterogeneous group" on the train by means of "brief glimpses" of the action although it smacks of the cinema technique. Finds in the "tidiness" and the "neatness" of the ending an indication of a "bitter kind of pity for humanity, mingled with a hopeless acceptance of the miserable destiny of human beings."

1934

R341 B[ettinger], B[eatrice] E. "It's a Battlefield." NRep, LXXX (12 Sept.), pp. 139-40. A short review that finds the book "disheartening" though "absorbing," and not "wholly" convincing in spite of its literary economy.

R342 Gould, Gerald. "New Novels: Tragedy and Comedy." Observer, (4 Feb.), p. 6. It's a Battlefield is one of five novels reviewed. Notices the wide canvas, the quick movement, the numerous complications, the admirable construction, and especially the "bitterly tragically ironical" ending.

R343 Muir, Edwin. "New Novels." Listener, XI:267 (21 Feb.), p. 340. Considers It's a Battlefield to be "a graphic picture of the injustice, heartlessness and confusion of society" inspired by a moral passion that is admirably expressed; but as a novel, it is less successful because the characters remain "functions of a social order" whose wickedness Greene is trying to expose, so that by the end, it is difficult to decide whether Greene is condemning society or human nature.

R344 Paterson, Isabel. "'Cells', in the Prison and Out." NYHT, (1 April), p. 7. Finds It's a Battlefield a "grim" story that "skillfully and concisely" presents with "casual deftness" a terrible vision of the postwar world where devotion to duty, affiliation to political parties, even sex, are regarded as "subterfuges of despair"; and even though Greene takes no side in the hopeless issue or tediously emphasizes his thesis, "the pleasure of reading almost balances the discomfort of the after thoughts."

R345 Pritchett, V. S. "A Modern Mind." Spectator, CLII:5511 (9 Feb.), p. 206. Reviews It's a Battlefield favorably and finds great merit in this "genuinely modern novel" which is "adventurous ... without being bizarre ... intelligent without sacrificing sympathy," has something to say without being "pretentious" and whose characters are "carefully but not redundantly drawn." Notices Greene's "ingenious use of cinema technique" in spite of the dangers of the method. Compliments Greene for being more than a visual artist and for his "integrity as a writer, his humanity, his subtle moral sense and his patient, supple and startling intuition of human character."

R346 ________. "The Cinema Method, Successfully." ChrSM, (21 March), p. 11. Reiterates essentially the same views on It's a Battlefield as being "uncommonly intelligent and moving" which he expressed in his review for The Spectator (see R345), but elaborates a little on Greene's "technical innovation" and his use of the cinema method. Believes that Greene has initiated a movement which may "wean" the English novel from its "present competent dullness."

R347 Unsigned. "A Modern Battlefield." L&L, (April), pp. 125-27. Finds It's a Battlefield "moving, bitter, tragic, humorous and beautiful," and a great advance on anything Greene had written so far. Notes the lack of relief in it, the crowding of the reader's consciousness with the moving life of London and the predominance of the thoughts of characters, often "author-conceived rather than author-described."

R348 ________. "London Kaleidoscope." NYTBR, (8 April), p. 7. Considers It's a Battlefield a "distinctive story, engrossing, alive and decidedly well worth reading" which utilizes the cinema technique of shooting a swift-moving "impartial camera lens over the London scene"--a "kaleidoscopic style" that is dramatic and forceful.

R349 ________. "New Novels: It's a Battlefield." Times, (6 Feb.), p. 19. Maintains that the novel is primarily an "indictment of the institutions of the day," and that there is no "intelligible principle" governing people; hence, the futility of human endeavor. Critical of Greene for having nothing to offer in exchange.

R3410 "New Novels: It's a Battlefield." TLS, 1671 (8 Feb.), p. 90. Surmises that the conflict in the novel is being "waged for the overthrow of the existing order," and is critical that Greene has no plans, is "nowhere constructive" and is concerned with men at odds with one another and at cross-purposes, and that he is not "equal to expressing the emotions without distorting the human medium"; his people are visualized "imperfectly" and he has invested the outcome with the "maximum of futility."

1935

R351 Benet, William Rose. "Young English Drifter." SatR, XII (7 Sept.), p. 7. Finds England Made Me "difficult" to review and Greene chiefly interested in "defeat and futility." Maintains that Greene has lost "his sense of direction" and that the novel, in spite of Greene's ability to write, has succeeded only in giving "flashes of unusual characterisation."

R352 Carter, Cora. "England Made Me." NYHT, (22 Sept.), p. 15. Finds the story "forceful and suggestive," the characters absorbing and, in the "austere and subdued intensity" of the novel generally, a "sense of unrest and boding that is almost a nightmare" as Greene explores the problem of futility and waste with "understanding, pity and power."

R353 Hutchinson, Percy. "Graham Greene's Novel of a Ne'er-Do-Well." NYTBR, (8 Sept.), p. 6. Maintains that though he has given us a cynical but "skillfully fabricated" story full of suspense of business skulduggery in England Made Me, Greene had aimed at more than sheer melodrama, but did not fully achieve his aspirations to be a novelist of "psychological discernment."

R354 M., D. L. "The Making of an Englishman." BosT, (19 Oct.), p. 2. Maintains that though every aspect of the story is modern, England Made Me gains force only in those chapters where Greene abandons the stream of consciousness for direct action, and that despite its subtleties, the story is "strongly melodramatic."

R355 Muir, Edwin. "New Novels." Listener, XIV:339 (10 July), p. 88. Though England Made Me is a much better book than his last, its "political thesis is not quite watertight" and the characters, with the exception of Tony Farrant, have a "reality at one remove," having been created by the "intellect" rather than the imagination. The writing is sometimes "brilliant"; details are "unusually vivid" and sensations of sight or movement often reproduced.

R356 Plomer, William. "Mr. Greene's New Novel." Spectator,

(28 June), p. 1116. Praises England Made Me warmly because it is "hard to find fault" with, and it shows "invention, imagination, atmosphere, freshness of eye, adroit character-drawing, and a very personal gift for metaphor and simile." Maintains that it is not so much in his ruthless questioning or blame of surrounding conditions but in his "poetical ability to show the individual in action" in this "excellent and original" novel that Greene shows himself as a mature novelist.

R357 _______. "Fiction." Spectator, 5604 (22 Nov.), p. 42. The Basement Room and Other Stories is briefly noticed. Greene's potential as a writer is mentioned, especially his ability to catch in a few pages "more of the truth as it flies than some novelists catch in a lifetime."

R358 Quennell, Peter. "New Novels." NSta, IX (29 June), p. 964. England Made Me is one of five novels reviewed. Describes it as a "competent" novel that bears "all the marks of a popular success" written with a "fluent and hard-wearing, if not particularly original style." Remarks on Greene's "knack of concise description" but criticizes his "indirect and elusive method" and his habit of sandwiching "scraps of dialogue ... between passages of staccato interior monologue" which seem to exasperate rather than reveal.

R359 Unsigned. "The Novels." SatR, CLIX (27 July), p. 952. Brief notes on the week's list of books. England Made Me is in some ways rather irritating, but there can be no denying the power and "caustic irony of its delineation of character."

R3510 _______. "New Novels: 'The Old School Tie'." Times, (25 June), p. 9. Maintains that the brisk and exciting England Made Me, "not wanting in subtlety," describes the "old school tie" mentality at its worst with telling irony in the character of Anthony. Though Greene may have packed into the novel more than it could conveniently hold, he is credited with having brought "a searching candour of thought and also a taste for formal experiment" to the novel.

R3511 _______. "New Novels: England Made Me." TLS, 1744 (4 July), p. 430. Maintains that Greene's criticism of the "old school tie" is implicit throughout the novel and gives an "astringent and somewhat bitter flavour" to the story which, in spite of "inconsistencies," is told with "notable skill" and power, a fine taste for excitement and an "ironical sensibility."

R3512 _______. "The Basement Room." TLS, 1764 (23 Nov.), p. 767. One of five books by the Cresset Press briefly reviewed. Greene is described as "deft and entertaining" but his intimations of deeper emotions "fail to enforce themselves."

1936

R361 B., L. "On Foot in Africa." Guardian, (19 May), p. 7. Praises Greene for his "serious" quest which took him to Africa, and impressed by the value, the "penetration, the richness, the integrity" of Journey Without Maps as a "moving record" which is subtly arranged and delivered.

R362 C., H. "Travels: Journey Without Maps." SatR, XV (28 Nov.), pp. 26-27. Appreciative of Greene's effort to "weld all the fragments of his experience into some kind of totality" through his jungle trek, but critical of his having "forgotten the African" or the "phenomena of people" in this part of Africa.

R363 Cuppy, Will. "Mystery and Adventure." NYHT, (21 June), p. 14. Recommends A Gun for Sale as a "superior" thriller full of "running excitement, assisted by [a] ... nervous style and constantly changing scene."

R364 Day Lewis, C. "New Fiction." DaiT, (17 July), p. 9. Maintains that reality keeps breaking through the "tough melodramatic crust" of A Gun for Sale, even though it is termed an entertainment. The novel is described as an "early Buchan" but "much more sensitive."

R365 F[erguson], O[tis]. "This Gun for Hire." NRep, LXXXVII (29 July), p. 362. Considers the novel not so much "a bad book as an unfortunate book" which tries to go many "high and devious ways, yet seems to have no workable means of propulsion." Finds Greene's probings a little too "hackneyed," and the novel "forced and somehow discouraging."

R366 Fleming, Peter. "Long Live Liberia." Spectator, CLVI (15 May), p. 890. Considers Journey Without Maps a "brilliant" book but "essentially subjective," and the journey described with "imaginative sincerity." Notes Greene's ability to convey atmosphere and the essential difference between his account and Hemingway's. Slightly critical of Greene for telling us absolutely nothing about his cousin, his travelling companion. (See B381 for her account of the journey).

R367 Gould, Gerald. "New Novels: Cloister, Studio and Stage." Observer, (19 July), p. 6. Regards A Gun for Sale as a "taut and sinister" story where the excitement is maintained at such a pitch that "one never lets plausibility raise its head." The tempo is fast and sustained; "everything is terrifying, complicated, gruesome: the tour de force comes off."

R368 Hearn, L. Cabot. "Two Psychological Thrillers." SatR, XIV (27 June), p. 6. A favorable review of A Gun for Sale that notes not only Greene's talent to create characters that have breadth and vitality and an exciting story told with masterly economy of words, but also Greene's exploration of the criminal mind and "his understanding of sinners."

R369 Hubbard, Margaret Carson. "Africa, Cure for Neuroses." NYHT, (29 Nov.), p. 6. Interprets Journey Without Maps as Greene's attempt to explain "the festers of his own civilization in terms of the primitive," and of evil. Notes that though Greene's answers may be "too blurred," he is at least close to the answer.

R3610 Lehmann, Rosamond. "New Novels." NSta, XII (1 Aug.), pp. 163-64. A Gun for Sale is the third of four novels reviewed. Notices some similarity between the novel and a "long elaborate dream-experience," and especially Greene's capacity for "building up and sustaining a Dark Tower atmosphere." Finds Raven, as a serious criminological study, the "biggest worry" in spite of Greene's "flowing, sensitive and dramatic" style, and his "pointed" dialogue.

R3611 Marsh, Fred T. "Tough Britons." NYTBR, (21 June), p. 17. Finds A Gun for Sale a "readable and more than usually intelligent thriller" with a well contrived and "swift-moving" tale with flashes of "first-rate wit."

R3612 Morton, C. W., Jr. "Rogue's Gallery." BosT, (27 June), p. 2. A brief review of A Gun for Sale recommending the novel as one that will provide severe competition for any "shocker of the past twelve months."

R3613 Muir, Edwin. "New Novels." Listener, XVI:395 (5 Aug), p. 278. Finds A Gun for Sale "a quickly moving and exciting" story with a nightmare atmosphere thrown out at a "white heat of imagination." It drops occasionally into melodrama and verges on sentimentality, especially in conversations between Raven and the girl.

R3614 Pierhal, Armand. "Liberia, Republique Negre: Quand les Noirs se gouvernent eux-mêmes." APL, CVIII (25 Dec.), pp. 627-29. Uses Greene's Journey Without Maps for "spicy" details about Liberia and the life of the whites there.

R3615 Plomer, William. "Fiction." Spectator, CLVII (17 July), pp. 110-11. A Gun for Sale is the second of five books reviewed. Remarks on Greene's technical indebtedness to the cinema in the novel which, even while providing "a topical satire on the seediness and callousness of social and political life," beats both scenario-writers and writers of adventure stories at their own game.

R3616 Q[uennell], P[eter]. "Liberia and Arabia." NSta, NS XI:275 (30 May), pp. 866 & 868. "He writes with admirable vividness when he writes simply; but his philosophic and literary digressions are inclined to pall." Notices a "marked resemblance" between Journey Without Maps and E. Waugh's account of his experiences in British Guiana.

R3617 S., I. "Books in Brief: Journey Without Maps." NRep, LXXXIX (2 Dec.), p. 153. Finds Greene's monologue about himself rather "boring" in spite of his "politeness and grace" and his "sophisticated, graceful and indirect" style, because nearly everything that would be interesting to a reader is "only obliquely referred to." Notices Greene's trip as a "spiritual direction-finder."

R3618 Unsigned. "Journey Without Maps." COS, (Dec.), p. 22. Brief notice of publication.

R3619 ______. "The Listener's Book Chronicle." Listener, XV:387 (10 June), p. 1127. Considers Journey Without Maps a subjective account which does not explain the motives of the journey and whose interest is largely autobiographical. It is written in an impressionist style "full of abrupt transitions and lists of things observed," and the journey is "eminently readable" and often amusing in a grim way.

R3620 ______. "Miscellaneous Brief Reviews: Across Liberia." NYTBR, (8 Nov.), p. 14. Considers Journey Without Maps a "very unusual" but "vivid and absorbing" travel book which describes in its "gravely stylized yet lucid pages" two explorations: the spiritual, a kind of "ultimate psychoanalysis of civilization" and the concrete or physical adventure which makes interesting reading by itself too.

R3621 ______. "In Liberia: An Explorer Explores His Own Mind." Times, (22 May), p. 19. Notes two simultaneous explorations in Journey Without Maps: the physical and the psychoanalytical. Finds the book suggestive, and Greene's command over style and description appealing. Contains essentially the same views as those in the TLS review below.

R3622 ______. "New Novels." Times, (7 July), p. 11. Notes

that "several themes [are] closely and ingeniously interwoven" in A Gun for Sale, that interest is kept alive and that there is much "flaying of the minor characters."

R3623 ______. "A Psycho-Analyst in Liberia." TLS, 1790 (23 May), p. 439. Examines the two minds of Greene found on the journey: the mind concerned with the objective--sightseeing and the routine of the march--and the "psychoanalytical prospector" trying to locate the "real Mr. Greene in his spiritual home." Questions how far this "raiding subconscious mind" has distorted the account of Liberia that is given in Journey Without Maps.

R3624 ______. "Gunman in Revolt." TLS, 1797 (11 July), p. 579. Maintains that Greene has done his "devoir" in A Gun for Sale, for not only does he supply himself with a "double hunt" in the thriller, but his "literary craftsmanship" is also reinforced by an assurance that carries off even improbable situations. He nas also made the gunman himself more important than the "automatic." Also notices the "final touch of Conradian blackness" when Raven discovers that Anne has disclosed his secret.

1938

B381 Greene, Barbara. Land Benighted. London: Geoffrey Bles. An interesting version of Journey Without Maps by Greene's cousin and companion on the trip. Makes occasional references to her cousin's character, especially his "sharp and clear and cruel brain," the seeming vagueness and unpracticality that hid an "astonishing efficiency" and care for "every little detail," his sense of humor, detachment, obstinacy in argument, and absorption in The Anatomy of Melancholy which he nowhere mentions in Journey Without Maps.

R381 Davenport, Basil. "Religious Melodrama." SatR, XVIII (25 June), pp. 6-7. Finds the psychology of Brighton Rock not altogether convincing, unlike the "triangular conflict" between the devoted Catholicism of Rose, the inverted Catholicism of Pinkie and the "sturdy roast-beef Protestantism" of Ida.

R382 J., K. "Notes for the Novel Reader: Fiction of the Month." ILN, (27 Aug.), p. 384. Brief note on Brighton Rock as a novel whose people are "entirely convincing--horridly convincing" but who either "have no soul, or they have no heart."

R383 Kronenberger, Louis. "Three Works of Fiction." NY, XIV (25 June), p. 56. A short but cursory review of Brighton

Rock that misses the importance of the novel and focusses on the story.

R384 Marriott, Charles. "New Novels." Guardian, (26 July), p. 7. Rates Brighton Rock very highly for it traces spiritual conflicts and finds "beauty in squalor without blinking," but criticizes it for lacking anchorage for the reader in understood motives.

R385 Marsh, Fred T. "Brighton Rock." NYHT, (26 June), pp. 11 & 14. Summarizes, for the most part, the story which he thinks the sort of tale one reads for relaxation, but which combines features of the mystery, everyday realism and the psychological novel.

R386 Muir, Edwin. "New Novels." Listener, XX:497 (21 July), p. 153. Regards Brighton Rock as Greene's best novel to date for it gives a "sincere comment on our life which deserves serious attention"; its presentation of theme is "brilliant" and its "little too clipped" dialogue is moving. Ida is the novel's most "original" character, in spite of Greene's "hatred" for her, but Pinkie is made "dreadful and pitiable" by the intensity of Greene's imagination even though he is not a "palpable" character.

R387 Plomer, William. "Pinkie and Rose." Spectator, CLX:5741 (15 July), p. 116. Appreciative of Greene's description of Brighton, with "verve and a clever accumulation of telling detail"--the work of a "quick and sensitive observer" with a "selective eye and intuitive understanding" that is not merely interested in the description of squalor. Perceives the religious dimension in this "psychological thriller" and the forces which Pinkie, Rose and Ida represent in spite of having grown "unaccustomed to theology in fiction." Slightly critical of the "symptoms" of Catholic "Mariolatry."

R388 Poore, Charles. "Books of the Times." NYT, (24 June), p. 17. Finds Brighton Rock "eerie, gory and baroque" in the Poe manner, but an "uncommonly skillful psychological thriller" which relies on melodrama and a sparkling style to give an anatomy of evil and to qualify it as an entertainment.

R389 S., J. "A Brighton Guttersnipe." Times, (26 Aug.), p. 15. Notes that Brighton Rock may be "shocking" and interesting, "horrifying and exciting," but it is also a "good deal deeper than an adventure story."

R3810 Shawe-Taylor, Desmond. "New Novels." NSta, XVI (23 July), p. 158. Maintains that Ida is the "triumph" of Brighton Rock--"one of the most fully imagined characters in recent English fiction." Appreciative of Greene's use of words, the creation of "pictures of startling force" and especially of sinking a "shaft into these twilight regions of belief and conscience," but is critical of what he calls his "literary romanticism."

R3811 Southron, Jane Spence. "The Career of a Gangster Studied by Graham Greene." NYTBR, (26 June), p. 6. Focusses on Brighton Rock as a fictional presentation--"superlatively entertaining," in a "terse and vigorous" prose that breaks out "unexpectedly into imagery that is both original and illuminating"--of the criminal mentality of the thirties and as an "uncompromising indictment" of some aspects of modern civilization.

R3812 "Torquemada." "Greene and Pinkie." Observer, (24 July), p. 6. Notices Greene's acute observation, from the outside, of the "insides" of his characters, the "keyhole reporting" of his narrative and the effective tricks of his prose, but is critical of his inability to select in descriptions.

R3813 Unsigned. "Brighton Rock." NRep, XCV (6 July), p. 260. Brief notice of the novel.

R3814 ________. "An English Killer." SpR, (17 July), p. 7e. Notes that as an "entertainment," Brighton Rock may be "interesting" but not "amusing" because Pinkie is a "most unpleasant character," in spite of Greene's gift for "striking characterization" and "fast-paced narrative."

R3815 ________. "Ascetic Killer." Time, XXXI (27 June), p. 49. A cursory review of Brighton Rock summarizing the story for the most part and describing it as a melodramatic "psychological gangster novel."

R3816 ________. "Novels of the Week: Brighton Rock." TLS, 1902 (16 July), p. 477. Maintains that Greene is only partly successful in exploring Pinkie's twisted moral sense and that he does not give "coherent imaginative expression" to Pinkie as a victim of heredity, environment and Roman Catholicism, or the sense of Mortal sin. However, the novel has an "undeniable dramatic quality" in spite of the recital of trivialities and occasional coarseness.

1939

A391 Bentley, Phyllis. "Is the British Novel Dead?" SatR, XIX (28 Jan.), pp. 3-4, 14-15. Includes Greene among the generation of novelists rising into literary prominence in the thirties, whose achievements she cites to reject J.

Strachey's statement on the "general decay of English imaginative letters." In her brief assessment of Greene's achievements on p. 4, she recognizes "quality" in his works, "tension" in his "never overwritten" prose, "intensity of characterization" to distinguish Stamboul Train from the ruck of such novels, and his investigation of "moral" and psychological problems in A Gun for Sale and Brighton Rock.

R391 B[enet], W[illiam] R[ose]. "The Confidential Agent." SatR, XX (21 Oct.), pp. 19-20. A short review noting Greene's "mastery of the sinister" and his management of suspense in writing this "superior thriller."

R392 B[urnham], P[hilip]. "The Confidential Agent." Commonweal, XXXI (15 Dec.), p. 191. A short review noting the "cerebral" melodrama and Greene's exposition of immorality or "the deadly lack of morality" without "niceness or qualms."

R393 Cuppy, Will. "Mystery and Adventure: The Confidential Agent." NYHT, (1 Oct.), p. 20. Maintains that "D's" adventures may be "hugely impressive, on the somber and serious side," but as a central character, he is a "far cry from the lucid heroes" of international intrigue.

R394 Duffield, Christopher. "Whither Mexico?" Listener, (16 March), p. iv (Spring Book Supplement). Maintains that Greene's account of Mexico in The Lawless Roads is necessarily subjective; not only can he not select from his experiences, but also his account of the journey through Tabasco and Chiapas has a "nightmare quality" about it.

R395 Gibson, Wilfrid. "Four New Novels." Guardian, (6 Oct.), p. 3. Describes The Confidential Agent as an absorbing grim yarn whose sinister atmosphere is skillfully conveyed in the telling phrase, "fresh in invention and exceptionally well written," so that the required suspension of disbelief is induced without effort.

R396 Gruening, Ernest. "On Disliking Mexico." SatR, XX (17 June), p. 13. Finds Greene's "forthrightness and superb writing" and "supremely realistic and often valid descriptions" in The Lawless Roads salutary as a corrective for too much adulation of Mexico. However, his honest and capable craftsmanship exposes a "fundamental paradox," for though Greene deplores the hate he finds in Mexico, "yet he reciprocates it."

R397 Hewitt, Robert A. "Another Mexico." America, LXI (5 Aug.), p. 406. A brief review that notes Greene's minute observation of detail and his "beautiful" writing even though he is describing things that disgusted him.

R398 James, Earle K. "Trouble Below the Rio Grande." Living Age, CCCLVII (Oct.), p. 197. The Lawless Roads is briefly reviewed as one of four books on Mexico that sees the country as offering a challenge to long-standing spiritual values.

R399 "M." "Impressions of Mexico." Guardian, (24 March), p. 7. Considers The Lawless Roads a subjective book written with "sharp jabbing economy" where the writer's mood of repulsion oppresses the reader and leaves an effect of "fatigue rather than pleasure and understanding."

R3910 M., J. "Mexican Travellers." Month, CLXXIV:902 (Aug.), pp. 146-54. A review article on Mexico as described in the accounts by E. Waugh in Robbery Under Law: The Mexican Object Lesson and Greene's The Lawless Roads.

R3911 McS., J. "Another Mexico." CW, CL (Oct.), p. 121. Finds the book "much less serious, yet ... not less interesting" than E. Waugh's Mexico. Recommends it for its "many delectable passages" and as an "acceptable substitute" for a visit to the country.

R3912 Magner, James A. "Another Mexico." Commonweal, XXX (30 June), p. 263. Notes Greene's loathing for the country and the subjective nature of his "authentic and odorous picture of the decay and confusion" in his vivid, spontaneous prose and revealing episodes, "without benefit of Victorian delicacy."

R3913 Mair, John. "New Novels." NSta, XVIII (23 Sept.), p. 432. The Confidential Agent is the second of five novels reviewed. Describes Greene as the most "individual of English novelists," an "intellectuals' novelist" who resembles Dickens in his capacity to create living but improbable types. Though by no means "flawless," this "highbrow thriller" is more than an imaginative adventure story for Greene is as concerned with the conflicts inside "D" as with the actual material of his exploits.

R3914 Martin, Kingsley. "The Lawless Roads." NSta, NS XVII:422 (25 March), pp. 466 & 468. Considers it a "singularly beautiful travel book" written by "an artist" who never seemed to get in touch with the Indian population but seemed interested mainly in the impact which anti-clericalism and the attack on faith had on the people.

R3915 Mathew, Gervase, OP. "The Lawless Roads." Blackfriars, XX:231 (June), pp. 471-72. Maintains that its "unique distinction" is that it can be reviewed as a travel book or as a "treatise De Ecclesia." As a travel book, its white is "always convincingly piebald," and the black "too black." As a study in Catholicism, it is "complete"; no book has come so close to its essential spirit or described it so fully as a "living Church."

R3916 Mishnun, Virginia. "The Mexican Enigma." Nation, CXLIX (2 Sept.), pp. 250-51. Critical of Greene's "almost pathological hatred" of Mexico which leads to his "highly emotional indictment" of it without being "encumbered with reason or a sense of reality." Finds it pitiful that so brilliantly written a book as The Lawless Roads, "stunning because of the economy and impact of its concrete imagery," should be so full of hate and prejudice.

R3917 Muir, Edwin. "New Novels." Listener, XXII:559 (28 Sept.), p. 638. Maintains that the speed of action of The Confidential Agent in describing a nightmare which is "real through and through" is much faster than that of the ordinary thriller. Inclined to read the novel--ostensibly a thriller relying on melodrama--as an example of Greene's "imaginative criticism of society."

R3918 Nicolson, Harold. "A Novelist in Mexico." DaiT, (10 March), p. 7. A short review of The Lawless Roads noticing Greene's rejection of Mexico and the joylessness of this "work of art."

R3919 S., J. "A Hunt in England." Times, (22 Sept.), p. 3. Finds the action of The Confidential Agent to be exciting, well sustained and probable, and based on an understanding of character.

R3920 Swinnerton, Frank. "New Novels: For Dark Evenings." Observer, (17 Sept.), p. 5. Notices briefly that Greene has written without "much conviction" in The Confidential Agent, in spite of being "very fluent."

R3921 Verschoyle, Derek. "Scenario: The Confidential Agent." Spectator, CLXIII (22 Sept.), pp. 418 & 420. Critical of Greene's growing obsession with violence at the expense of the "moral and aesthetic perspective." This lack of a "sense of proportion" makes him write a "straightforward thriller of slight literary pretension" about a "shadowy and unconvincing" character, with Hollywood in mind. The result is a book that seems "sometimes paltry, sometimes tedious, and sometimes absurd."

R3922 "Viator." "Mexican Journey." Tablet, NS CXLI (18 March), pp. 354-55. Makes the association between Greene's account of Mexico in The Lawless Roads and Lawrence's in The Plumed Serpent in spite of their opposing viewpoints. Behind the decay of Mexico which he describes, Greene "sees the mystery of our living with a strong emphasis on the force of evil and sin, and ... gives, with something like genius, the impressions of a deeper and further combat between Darkness and Light, sin and forgiveness."

R3923 Waugh, Evelyn. "The Waste Land." Spectator, CLXII (10 March), pp. 413-14. Expresses admiration for The Lawless Roads but exposes Greene's tendency to become "savage" at times. Though Greene, as "Augustinian Christian," makes no attempt to give the historical background of the Mexican tragedy, his "cinematographic shots" of conditions are revealing especially in that they are not linked by any political thesis.

R3924 Woods, Katherine. "The Confidential Agent and Other New Fiction." NYTBR, (1 Oct.), p. 20. Praises the work enthusiastically as an "even better novel" than Brighton Rock and which is at once a thrilling, flawlessly constructed adventure, a "magnificent tour-de-force among tales of international intrigue" with overtones of a "stranger and more inclusive questioning, a more intimate disturbance of the spirit, in the echoing fantasia of an imaginative nightmare."

R3925 Ybarra, T. R. "A Lugubrious Traveller's View of Mexico." NYTBR, (11 June), p. 10. Maintains that Greene's distaste for Mexico in The Lawless Roads and his extraordinary graphic descriptions of it have produced a travel book "unique in character and flavor."

R3926 Unsigned. "The Confidential Agent." Booklist, XXXVI (15 Nov.), p. 111. Lists novel under "International Intrigue."

R3927 ______. "The Confidential Agent." NY, XV (30 Sept.), p. 64. Briefly noticed.

R3928 ______. "The Church in Mexico." Times, (7 March), p. 19. Questions the objective of Greene's visit to Mexico in The Lawless Roads, especially that he had no previous acquaintance with it and no knowledge of the language.

R3929 ______. "Ruined Churches of Mexico." TLS, 1936 (11 March), p. 146. The review of The Lawless Roads is more concerned with the state of Christianity and Churches in Mexico than in Greene's account, even though it points out one or two "unnecessary mistakes" in the book.

R3930 ______. "The Trial of an Agent." TLS, 1964 (23 Sept.), p. 553. Maintains that the best in The Confidential Agent lies on the "plane of artificial mystery." Critical of Greene's "drastic and often brutal criticism" of the English way of life for the satire is inclined to be "trivial" and a "little pretentious." Notices Greene's "curious means" for achieving effect and contriving an atmosphere of "deepening mental and nervous tension by a habit of blunt and almost wooden statement."

1940

B401 Lehmann, John. New Writing in Europe. London: Allen Lane; Harmondsworth, Middlessex & New York: Penguin Books. Pages 134-36 give a contemporary assessment of Greene in 1940 as an "extremely readable" but minor novelist "influenced" by American models, and who has "pursued speed in dialogue, simplicity of prose structure and colloquialism in diction." Condemns Greene for preferring "theory and propaganda to living creation" in Brighton Rock, but recognizes the "passion and sincerity informing" The Power and the Glory.

A401 Calder-Marshall, Arthur. "The Works of Graham Greene." Horizon, I:5 (May), pp. 367-75. Rpt. in Little Reviews Anthology. London: Allen and Unwin, 1943, pp. 197-204. Recognizes the limitations resulting from Greene's tendency to reduce everything to a "uniform ... version." In his discussion of "Greeneland" and its people, he is critical of Greene's overwhelming concern with the "philosophical theme" of good and evil and the repetition of the formula of the hunted man in both novels and entertainments.

A402 Sylvester, Harry. "Graham Greene." Commonweal, XXXIII (25 Oct.), pp. 11-13. An appraisal of Greene as a young novelist endowed with a "spiritual and intellectual maturity," whose style deserved to be ranked "with Joyce and the best of Hemingway." Focusses on good and evil in Brighton Rock and pity in The Power and the Glory.

R401 Arrowsmith, Jean. "Soul in Torment: Seeking a Niche." BosT, (20 April), p. 2. Maintains that The Power and the Glory reveals a "developing command of language, characterization and mood" as Greene analyses the conflicting loyalties and desires of the Whiskey Priest by utilizing his usual pattern of mystery and adventure.

R402 Bates, Ralph. "Via Crucis." NRep, CII (22 April), p. 549. In spite of its being a "thoroughly honest book" with "topographically exact" imagery, an effective sequence of events, an exciting pace and sudden pauses "felicitous and nuggeted with poetry," The Power and the Glory makes no claim on one's thought because Greene does not seem to know his Catholic faith. With this "underlying defect," the ending becomes incredible for Greene carries over "his pietism into his revolutionary" which results in mere "commentative virtuosity."

R403 Benet, William Rose. "Earthly and Heavenly Quarry." SatR, XXI (30 March), p. 5. Focusses on the Whiskey Priest and Greene's understanding of "the inner stress of responsibility in the priest's soul" which makes him in the end win the reader's sympathy in The Power and the Glory.

Recognizes Greene as "one of the finest craftsmen of story-telling in our time," and one who can create atmosphere and detail convincingly.

R404 Bishop, George W. "New Fiction." DaiT, (9 March), p. 11. Briefly notices The Power and the Glory as an "entirely engrossing" novel whose excitement is all the more intense because it is based on character.

R405 Hartley, L. P. "Records of Defeat." Observer, (17 March), p. 6. Considers The Power and the Glory a "painful and impressive" novel whose "terrible" story is marked and scarred by circumstances of squalor and poverty. Notices the repetition of the pursuit pattern, the "rhythm" of Greene's prose and the visual effects produced, but objects to the "continuity and crescendo of suffering" in the novel.

R406 Herring, Hubert. "Mexico and South America." YR, XXIX (Winter), p. 397. Notices briefly The Lawless Roads as one of five books on Mexico. Though one may tire from Greene's "dyspeptic descriptions" of facilities, the book is "well written, incisive, critical."

R407 Marriott, Charles. "Novels of France and Mexico." Guardian, (5 March), p. 3. Explains the meaning of "the power and the glory" as a title of the novel which, despite its "harrowing tale," leaves the reader "exultant rather than depressed" and marks out Greene as an "imaginative critic of life."

R408 Marsh, Fred T. "The Story of a Haunted Soul." NYTBR, (17 March), p. 6. Describes The Power and the Glory as being "almost Dostoevskan" in its unusual and unconventional study of a haunted soul. As a "graceful writer of the casual," Greene in this "first-rate piece of story telling," gives the effect of easy entertainment.

R409 Maxwell, Joseph R. N. "Provocative of Thought, Offense, Even Disgust." America, (6 April), p. 722. Recognizes Greene's ability to tell an interesting story and create plausible characters in The Power and the Glory, as well as his "modernly real" handling of it, but questions the effect of the novel--as indicated in the title of the review--and doubts whether it will be entirely accepted by many readers.

R4010 Muir, Edwin. "New Novels." Listener, XXIII:582 (7 March), p. 490. A rather short review which describes The Power and the Glory as one of Greene's "most uneven stories" but which shows "powers of a new kind" in depicting the priest's "inward change." Finds the priest's flight not so convincing and the increasing conflict between

Church and State moving because of Greene's "intense effort to be just to both sides."

R4011 O'Brien, Kate. "Fiction: The Power and the Glory." Spectator, CLXIV (15 March), p. 390. The second of three novels reviewed. Welcomes the novel for its preoccupation with man as a conscious sinner--a distinction that lifts it clean from the ruck of contemporary fiction. Finds Greene's study of the humble and contrite heart could not have been done with a "more delicate understanding, with more unmerciful mercy."

R4012 Poore, Charles. "Books of the Times." NYT, (26 Jan.), p. 15. Notes briefly the implausibility of The Confidential Agent, in spite of the "creeping horror" of the tale that holds the reader spellbound.

R4013 Redman, Ben Ray. "Parable of a Nameless Priest." NYHT, (31 March), p. 3. Warm praise for The Power and the Glory as a "drama of character, conscience and circumstance," and for Greene's profound and subtle understanding of the values involved and his ability to communicate these values by means of a well organized narrative that also reveals a fascinating psychological study, and interests readers with questions of morality and faith.

R4014 Skillin, Edward, Jr. "The Labyrinthine Ways." Commonweal, XXXI (22 March), p. 478. A short review that notes Greene's "strong drama of sin and salvation that only a Catholic can completely understand," and his "economy of phrase," his art of suspense and "gift of understanding."

R4015 Vann, Gerald, OP. "The Power and the Glory." Blackfriars, XXI:242 (May), pp. 339-40. A Catholic viewpoint emphasizing the importance of the novel in showing that consciousness of sin can be valuable for salvation insofar as it leads one to the discovery of the love of God; hence, the evaluation of the novel as the "most moving novel ... most illuminating, that one has read for a long time." Notices Greene's ability to create atmosphere and scene.

R4016 West, Anthony. "New Novels." NSta, XIX (16 March), pp. 371-72. The Power and the Glory is the first of five novels reviewed. Argues that it is a mistake to dismiss Greene simply as a "writer of thrillers of the psychological variety" for the novel is a "fierce statement" on the power of religion and its importance to the individual and to society, a "parable" told with "great skill and power."

R4017 Unsigned. "The Labyrinthine Ways." CW, CLI (May), pp. 253-54. Briefly notices the novel and its "rather teazing style, bizarre, jerky, impressionistic" that exaggerates characters "out of all proportion," and predicts it will attract much criticism, from both Protestant and Catholic reviewers.

R4018 ________. "Briefly Noted: Fiction." NY, XVI (16 March), p. 106. Describes The Power and the Glory as a "first-class narrative of a man hunt" with "excellent characterization, [and] admirable local color."

R4019 ________. "Fallen Man." Tablet, NS CXLIII (16 March), pp. 257-58. Maintains that in The Power and the Glory, Greene, the "novelist of guilt," is concerned with the loss of human innocence and the estranged condition of mankind. Greene uses the framework of the flight from men and the fear of the law to depict an "attempted flight from God" and the distance which separates man from God, as well as the appalling predicament of man unable to be saved by his own efforts. Points out that the "main truth" of the novel is a "powerful and graphic statement of religious truth."

R4020 ________. "The Labyrinthine Ways." Time, XXXV (8 April), p. 88. Brief notice of the novel.

R4021 ________. "New Novels: A Priest in Hiding." Times, (8 March), p. 4. The Power and the Glory is the first of four novels reviewed. Remarks on how the story, though exciting, "cannot approach for interest the human being Mr. Greene has put at the center of it," and though deliberately avoiding emotion, "it starts in the reader an irresistible emotion of pity and love."

R4022 ________. "Novels of the Week: Eternal Pursuit." TLS, 1988 (9 March), p. 121. Maintains that Catholic salvationist doctrines are but lightly concealed beneath the thriller devices of The Power and the Glory so that when the religious experience is translated in terms of pursuit, one experiences a "sequence of dramatic or melodramatic shocks." Though the portrait of the priest is expertly done and deliberately left unheroic, the novel is "unsatisfying" in the division between sin, lust and violence on the one hand, and "doctrinal salvation" on the other; it remains not so much an illusion of life as an "illustration of doctrine."

1941

A411 Brady, Charles A. "A Melodramatic Cousin in R. L. S." America, LXIV (25 Jan.), pp. 439-40. Though orotund and ornate in style, this piece draws the general reader's attention to the "fierce vitality" which surcharges Greene's interest in good and evil, and the soul of man with "spiritual significance, and ... spiritual intensity."

A412 Connolly, Francis X. "Catholic Fiction: 4. Two Reactions." America, LXV (13 Sept.), pp. 634-35. A general analysis of literate readers' reactions to Catholic fiction which includes Greene, among others, in the "Be Honest School" whose works shock the "world into the meaning of sin and the need for salvation," and the "Be Prudent School" whose imagination is "accountable to the higher truths of philosophy." Rather disenchanted with the former for rarely allowing the reader "a thrill of joy without making [him] eat dirt."

1942

A421 Kevin, Neil. "Fiction Priests." IER, LX (Oct.), pp. 253-57. More concerned with the public image of the Catholic priesthood created by Father Chisholm in A. J. Cronin's The Keys of the Kingdom than by its literary worth. In a brief comparison to the Whiskey Priest of The Power and the Glory at the end, he concedes that the latter is the "real priest" that Father Chisholm is not.

S421 Hartung, Philip. "Violence in Graham Greene: Labor in Black and White." Commonweal, XXXVI (29 May), pp. 136-37. A review of Paramount's 1942 film version of A Gun for Sale starring Alan Ladd and Veronica Lake.

1943

B431 Calder-Marshall, Arthur. "Graham Greene." Little Reviews Anthology. Ed. Denys Val Baker. London: George Allen & Unwin, pp. 197-205. Rpt. from Horizon, I:5 (May 1940), 367-75. See A401.

B432 Church, Richard. "Graham Greene." British Authors: A Twentieth-Century Gallery with 58 Portraits. The British Council Series. London: Longmans, Green and Co., pp. 137-39. New ed. ... with 53 Portraits. London, New York: Longmans, Green, 1948. A "miniature word-portrait" that attempts to state Greene's outstanding qualities and how they are demonstrated in his novels up to and including The Power and the Glory.

B433 Nicholson, Norman. "Graham Greene." Man and Literature. London: S. C. M. Press, pp. 182-85. A general assessment of Greene as a novelist within the framework of an inquiry into the nature and purpose of Man which underlie much of the writing of the 20th century. Notes Greene's ability to make the novel exist on the three planes of "plot ... characterization and psychology ... and metaphysics," the "moral framework" in which his characters live, his "serviceable prose" as well as a "certain monotony and limitation of view" in the novels.

A431 Allen, Walter. "The Novels of Graham Greene." PNW, XVIII (July-Sept.), pp. 148-60. Rpt. in Writers of Today. Ed. Denys Val Baker. London: Sidgwick & Jackson, 1946, pp. 15-28. Discusses Greene's awareness of evil and his vision of human life as the "point of intersection of heaven and hell," and as the qualities that constitute his uniqueness among contemporary novelists. The Man Within, It's a Battlefield, A Gun for Sale, England Made Me, The Confidential Agent, Brighton Rock and The Power and the Glory.

A432 Murphy, J. Stanley. "Not on All Fours." America, LXVIII (27 Feb.), pp. 577-78. A brief reconsideration of The Power and the Glory occasioned by its choice for the Hawthorden Prize of 1940 as "definitely adult reading, but truly Catholic none the less" in its penetrating study of God's Grace.

A433 Zabel, Morton Dauwen. "Graham Greene." Nation, CLVII (3 July), pp. 18-20. Rpt. in Forms of Modern Fiction. Ed. William van O'Connor. Minneapolis: Univ. of Minnesota Press, 1948, pp. 287-93, and in Critiques and Essays of Modern Fiction, 1920-1951. Ed. John W. Aldridge. New York: Ronald Press, 1952, pp. 518-25. Rev. and rpt. as "Graham Greene: The Best and the Worst." In his Craft and Character: Texts, Method, and Vocation in Modern Fiction. London: Gollancz, 1957, pp. 276-96. Rpt. in Graham Greene: A Collection of Critical Essays. Twentieth Century Views. Ed. Samuel Hynes. Englewood Cliffs, N.J.: Prentice-Hall, 1973, pp. 30-49. A perceptive review article on The Ministry of Fear. Considers the pitfalls Greene has not escaped, his archetypal plot, and Grace and its necessary enemy, Evil. But it is in Greene's use of the thriller as an instrument "for probing the temper and tragedy of his age," since his lonely hunted heroes provide, in their "passion for identity ... the nexus of values in a world that has reverted to anarchy," that he grants Greene the company of men like Kafka, Auden and Mauriac.

R431 B., E. M. "The Ministry of Fear." SpR, (13 June), p. 7e. Argues that to characterize it as an "entertainment" is an "understatement" because it is an "absorbing and fascinating study of crime and criminals." It is also "an extraordinary book, unique in conception and brilliant in execution."

R432 Chapel, America. "Fine Writing and Thrills in Unusual Espionage Story." CSBW, (6 June), p. 4. Maintains that in The Ministry of Fear Greene has established his "literary niche" by his ability to create an exciting story and "to impale on paper" depths of beauty or horror. Finds that Greene has allowed this novel to have a "little more popular appeal than usual."

R433 Cowley, Malcolm. "Graham Greene." NRep, CVIII (24 May), p. 706. Maintains that though his "entertainments" follow the "same fairly pattern," Greene shows in The Ministry of Fear an "amazing gift" for inventing new incidents and placing them against "new backgrounds."

R434 Du Bois, William. "Graham Greene's Dark Magic." NYT, (23 May), p. 3. Lavishes praise on The Ministry of Fear as "top-hole entertainment," or a "hypnotic moonstone of a novel." Notes Greene's ability to "distill drama from a twisted soul" and considers the novel "more than a mere thriller" by illustrating the "schizophrenia that is corroding the world today" through Arthur Rowe.

R435 Este, Rice. "The Ministry of Fear." LJ, LXVIII (1 May), p. 363. Pre-publication notice of the novel.

R436 Fadiman, Clifton. "The Ministry of Fear." NY, XIX (22 May), p. 72. A short notice describing the novel as Greene's "most surrealist" thriller that has little or no connection with realistic politics.

R437 Gibson, Wilfrid. "Books of the Day: New Novels." Guardian, (21 May), p. 3. Brief notice of The Ministry of Fear as an entertaining "yarn."

R438 Hale, Lionel. "New Novels." Observer, (30 May), p. 3. A short review of The Ministry of Fear noting the "calculatedly nonsensical" story which goes through "twilit corridors of horror" but which also grips the reader's attention.

R439 Muir, Edwin. "New Novels." Listener, XXIX:754 (17 June), p. 730. Though not one of his best books or entertainments, The Ministry of Fear, "formally" a secret service thriller, bears the marks of Greene's preoccupation with the drama of salvation where the struggle between good and evil can be gleaned and the "individual drama becomes ... universal." Questions Greene's intent in making the hero forget and then remember.

R4310 O'Brien, Kate. "Fiction." Spectator, CLXX (28 May), p. 508. The Ministry of Fear is the first of three novels reviewed. Finds that Arthur Rowe's "wild, improbable gangster whirl" fits oddly with Greene's "nervous, brilliant probing, off and on, at character and motive," and wholly removed from his earlier preoccupations.

R4311 Prescott, Orville. "Books of the Times." NYT, (24 May), p. 13. In spite of Greene's craftsmanship, The Ministry of Fear remains "a super de luxe spy story." Finds Greene one of the most "overpraised" writers of the day; for even though he is capable of dressing up crime "in a cloak of neuroses," and skillful in the matter of sinister suggestion, he destroys the "suspense and emotional impact ... by a vague illusiveness, a clutter of irrelevant material and unmotivated actions, and an unsatisfactory, disappointing denouement"--The Ministry of Fear, for example, simply "peters out sadly."

R4312 Rothman, N. L. "Greene Atmosphere." SatR, XXVI (26 June), p. 11. Finds the mystery and intrigue of The Ministry of Fear approximating to the atmosphere of suspense that Hitchcock weaves into a film, and the alternation between "cerebral sparring and the explosion of violence" to be one of the greatest pleasures of the novel.

R4313 Soskin, William. "Psychological Horror Story." WBR, (30 May), p. 4. Praises The Ministry of Fear enthusiastically as an "imaginative feat, a study in suspense and a brilliant crescendo of terror," and Greene for his ability to "glamorize the thriller intellectually."

R4314 Toynbee, Philip. "New Novels." NSta, XXV (26 June), p. 422. Though The Ministry of Fear is "typical" Greene and vindicates its claim to entertain--it is at once "an outstanding entertainment and a reputable novel"--it does not make any claim to mark any "progression" in Greene as a novelist.

R4315 Wright, Cuthbert. "The Ministry of Fear." Commonweal, XXXVIII (4 June), pp. 175-76. Praises Greene for arousing the "kindred" emotions of pity and fear and thereby making the novel superior to the run-of-the-mill terror story.

R4316 Unsigned. "The Ministry of Fear." Atlantic, CLXXII (July), p. 127. A brief review commenting on what the novel will lose when it is adapted into a film.

R4317 ________. "The Ministry of Fear." Booklist, XXXIX (15 July), p. 464. Briefly noticed.

R4318 ________. "The Ministry of Fear." CW, CLVII (July), p. 448. This "unorthodox and entertaining mixture of a mystery, spy story and a psychological adventure" rises above the average suspense story by the characterization of the hero and Greene's unusual narrative art.

R4319 ______. "The Ministry of Fear." Time, XLI (14 July), p. 104. Briefly noticed as a "master thriller and a remarkable portrait of a twisted character."

R4320 ______. "Novels of the Week: Film in the Cake." TLS, 2156 (29 May), p. 257. Maintains that The Ministry of Fear, a tensely "atmospheric" thriller, is more "far-fetched than usual ... though the author's characteristic flavour of obscure, complex and undertoned psychological motivation is as pronounced as ever." As for the story, it is exciting with a "sharply teasing psychological suspense" but is also highly artificial in theme.

1944

A441 Benet, William Rose. "The Phoenix Nest." SatR, XXVII (12 Feb.), pp. 36-37. An excerpt from Earle Walbridge's letter to the editor commenting briefly on Greene's essay on Beatrix Potter's work. Greene's essay was first published in London Mercury, (Jan. 1933), pp. 241-55, and later included in Collected Essays, pp. 232-40.

A442 Brady, Charles A. "Contemporary Catholic Authors: Graham Greene, Novelist of Good and Evil." CLW, XVI (Dec.), pp. 67-74, 89. Attempts, in separate sections, a general consideration of Greene's life and literary achievements. Emphasizes in the latter two sources of "confusion" for American Catholic readers: Greene's preoccupation with the "theological absolutes of good and evil" and the use of the "roman policier" as a medium. The brief survey of the works through A Ministry of Fear that follows omits any reference to The Man Within.

A443 McCarthy, Mary. "Graham Greene and the Intelligentsia." PR, XI (Spring), pp. 228-30. A controversial evaluation of Greene, critical of the "sensational incongruity between matter and form" presented in Greene's "modern high-brow" novels written "under the formal discipline of Edgar Wallace and E. P. Oppenheim." Accuses Greene of being "pious and insincere" and an "ersatz serious novelist" whose novels arouse a "sense of embarrassment" as the central emotion. Contains interesting remarks on Greene's rhetoric.

1945

B451 Catholic Profiles: Series 1. Intro. Michael de la Bedoyère. London: Paternoster Publications, pp. 155-57. Besides noticing the distinction between "Novel" and "Entertainment," the two-and-half page profile with photograph, fails to elicit any of Greene's "personal particulars." For this, Greene refers the writer to his work: "Anything which is of any interest" he says, "is obviously there."

A451 Hays, H. R. "A Defense of the Thriller." PR, XII (Winter), pp. 135-37. Rejects, in his defense of the literature of crime with which he is mainly concerned, M. McCarthy's charge that Greene's "serious qualities are ersatz," (see A443) but accuses Greene, perhaps unjustly, of not fusing the story with the "incidental implications which he draws from it" in his "entertainments."

A452 Speaight, Robert. "Littérature anglaise. Ecrivains Catholiques." TP, p. 3. A short article for the general reader that regards G. Greene, E. Waugh and Kathleen Raine as artists rather than apologists for Catholic ideas. Brief mention of The Power and the Glory and The Ministry of Fear.

1946

B461 Allen, Walter. "Graham Greene." Writers of To-day. Ed. Denys Val Baker. London: Sidgwick & Jackson, pp. 15-28. Rpt. from PNW, XVIII (July-Sept. 1943), pp. 148-60. See A431.

B462 Reed, Henry. The Novel Since 1939. London: Longmans Green & Co. The British Council Series. Pages 15-18 discuss and place Greene, a "serious practitioner" of the novel, in a literary perspective by examining his re-introduction of the sense of evil in the English novel, his unprecedented approach to the art of the novel and his utilization of the conventional thriller. Brighton Rock and The Power and the Glory.

B463 Rillo, Lila E. The Power and the Glory: A Novel by Graham Greene. Foreword Patrick Orphen Dudgeon. English Pamphlet No. 12. Buenos Aires: The Argentine Association of English Culture. A general consideration of the novel that touches upon several significant features: viz, character, children, vice and virtue, climate, atmosphere and style.

A461 Delpech, Jeanine. "Graham Greene à Paris." NL, (19 Dec.), pp. 1-2. An account of an interview with Greene in which he explains his choice of the "roman policier," and discusses freely the filming of several of his books and the reading of poetry among other things. The interviewer associates Greene with Bernanos rather than with Kafka, and emphasizes his "cinematic technique" as his major contribution to the English novel.

A462 G[ardiner], H[arold] C. "Taste and Worth." America, LXXV (20 April), p. 53. Rejects, on the occasion of the re-issue of The Power and the Glory in the U.S., E. Wilson's statement in NY (see A468) that the Whiskey Priest is a victim who does not arouse any "spiritual passion" worthy of a saint, and maintains that the priesthood is the main character or protagonist of the novel.

A463 Gardner, Helen. "François Mauriac: A Woman of the Pharisees." PNW, XXXI, pp. 93-104. This study of La Pharisiènne makes a brief comparison of the role of faith in Mauriac, E. Waugh and Greene on pp. 101-02. Makes a few perceptive observations on Greene's "inverted snobbery," his contempt for "works" and sympathy for "Luther's 'Pecca fortiter,'" his "nightmare" world and the "neo-Calvinism" that underlies his attitude to his character.

A464 Jarrett-Kerr, Martin, C.R. "Recent Roman Catholic Fiction." StM, XLVIII (March-April), pp. 95-98. A review of four novels by A. J. Cronin, B. Marshall, G. Greene and G. Bernanos questioning their "design" upon the reader. Even though admitting that Greene has "a much finer mind, a keener sense of literary values," and is less deliberately an apologetic than Cronin or Marshall, he maintains that Greene constructs an "apologetic up n the foundations of Original Sin, and therefore exacerbates Original Sin to do it" in The Power and the Glory. Considers Greene's portrayal of the unrelieved nature of gloom in the novel as a "put-up job," and though he recognizes "intellectual analysis, even perception," he finds no "open sympathy."

A465 M[agny], C[laude]-E[dmonde]. "Graham Greene." Poésie, XLVI:32 (May), pp. 32-37. Rpt. as "De Benito Cereno au Rocher de Brighton." GduL, XVI (July 1951), pp. 150-53, and in Littérature et Critique. Paris: Payot, 1971, pp. 101-06. Remarks on the completeness of the stories generally, economy of means and the two levels on which the narrative unfolds: the concrete and the "metaphysical." In her discussion of the fundamental theme underlying the novels--the substitution of the notion of an inexorable Fatality for "traditional psychological motivation"--she associates Greene with the existentialism of Sartre and Camus which, in turn, opens new territory for later critics. Focusses on Brighton Rock.

A466 Miller, J. D. B[ruce]. "Graham Greene." Meanjin, V (Spring), pp. 193-97. Highlights for the general reader of the novels the main features of Greene's writings. Also examines briefly the "sense of inevitability" in the novels and the "predestined tragic end" of the protagonists, and assesses The Power and the Glory as a "descent into pure propaganda," leaving Brighton Rock as "his finest achievement."

A467 Wilson, Edmund. "Books: Theodore Dreiser's Quakers and Graham Greene's Priest." NY, (23 March), pp. 84, 88-89. Finds The Power and the Glory, now reissued in the U. S. under its English title, "rather disappointing" in spite of Greene's success in "creating a squalid and painful world," for though the "canvas is pretty well painted ... the picture is somehow dead"; the story does not have the suspense of the thriller nor does it stir one with "the spiritual passion that ought to be conveyed by the life of a saint."

1947

B471 Calder-Marshall, Arthur. "Graham Greene." Living Writers: Being Critical Studies Broadcast in the B. B. C. Third Programme. Ed. Gilbert Phelps. London: Sylvan Press, pp. 39-47. A series of talks by writers on their contemporaries broadcast between October and December 1946. Points out Greene's salient features as a post-depression writer. Notices his interest in the theme of the individual as a victim of society, his reliance on contemporary newspapers for ideas and the topical life of the thirties, his conviction of evil and the "comment metaphors" that build up atmosphere in his prose. A fairly good introduction to the novels of the thirties.

B472 Chaigne, Louis, ed. La littérature catholique à l'étranger: Anthologie. Vol. I. Paris: Editions Alsatia. A brief survey of European Catholic writers outside France. Pages 170-73 give a short bio-bibliographical note on Greene up to 1938, followed by an excerpt, in French, from The Man Within. Though of little value to a student, these pages indicate the early French recognition of Greene and the popularity his novels enjoy in France.

B473 Mallinson, Vernon. "Graham Greene." Tendances nouvelles dans la littérature anglaise contemporaine: Le roman, la poésie, le théâtre. Trans. M. C. H. Collection Savoir No. 11. Brussels: Les Editions Lumières, pp. 14-20. Considers Greene as the most "significant" male writer of his generation, who having been influenced by Dostoyevsky, utilizes the thriller to convey his philosophical beliefs, especially the return to human values. Also notices the cinematic element in Greene's novels. Brighton Rock and The Power and the Glory.

A471 Beary, Thomas John. "Religion and the Modern Novel." CW, CLXVI (Dec.), pp. 203-11. Chooses, with 1940 in mind as a watershed, four novels by G. Greene, A. Huxley, E. Waugh and H. Sylvester to treat "some aspect of man's relation with God and with revealed religion." Concentrates on The Power and the Glory as a dramatic "penetrating study of the problem of evil" that relies on the techniques of "introspection, indirection and contrast," but denies "universal significance" to what is warmly described as a "major work of fiction" and a "remarkable book."

A472 Delteil, Francois. "Graham Greene ou de la fatalité à la grace." La Croix, (28, 29 Sept.), p. 3. A brief article that notices a decline in Greene's preoccupation with Fatalism and the rise of Grace as a central concern. Focusses on the four novels translated into French: Stamboul Train, A Gun for Sale, Brighton Rock and The Power and the Glory.

A473 Duche, Jean. "Je n'écrirai plus de romans policiers', nous dit Graham Greene." FigL, (20 Dec.), p. 6. An interview with Greene in Paris before the publication of The Heart of the Matter in which he comments on his belief in fatality, declares his intention not to write more detective novels, is non-committal in his reply when described as a Jansenist, and parries the charge that he is implicated in a world as absurd as Sartre's or Camus's.

A474 "O'Donnell, Donat" [Conor Cruise O'Brien]. "An Epic of the '30's: Graham Greene." Bell, XIII, pp. 7-16. A condemnation of Greene's use of the thriller, his stylistic tricks, his "museum of seedy imagery" and the so-called "neo-Manichean heresy" manifest in the novels. Regards Greene's rejection of "organised society" for the "barbaric world" as characteristic of the 'thirties. Questions W. Allen's claim that Greene is the leading novelist of this generation and admits, perhaps reluctantly, that Greene "imposes his world upon our imagination," even though no single work of his is "quite satisfactory."

A475 ________. "Le Monde de Graham Greene." Echo, (Aug.), pp. 698-93. A translation of "An Epic of the '30's: Graham Greene," with very few minor deletions.

A476 ________. "Graham Greene." Chimera, V, pp. 18-30. An enlarged but slightly toned down version of "An Epic of the '30's: Graham Greene" that expands on the notion that the thriller "in its structure, allows little scope for creative ability," and examines Greene's "system of religious emotions"--the dual nature of man, emotional belief in evil and in hell, identification of "flesh and the devil"--which underlies It's a Battlefield, Brighton Rock and The Power and the Glory.

A477 Pierhal, Armand. "Graham Greene ou le mystère en pleine lumière." GdL, 34 (9 April), pp. 1, 3. A summary of the themes that surface regularly in the novels:

concern for outcasts and human derelicts, Original Sin, and the child-woman. Also mentions his chief qualities as a novelist: creation of atmosphere, style, dialogue and the ability to build a plot. Brief references to England Made Me, Brighton Rock and The Power and the Glory.

A478 Rostenne, Paul. "Introduction à Graham Greene: Romancier catholique." RN, VI (15 Sept.), pp. 193-204. An interesting and perceptive interpretation of the tragic world of A Gun for Sale and Brighton Rock, especially the psychology of their "personnages demoniques," in terms of a Catholic understanding of Original Sin. Also emphasizes the "redemptive" role of a woman and attributes the "realité" and power of the novels to the harmonious alliance of the metaphysician and the novelist in Greene.

A479 Wall, Barbara. "London Letter." America, LXXVII (9 Aug.), pp. 521-22. A few remarks to the general Catholic reader on Greene's "controversial" preoccupation with society's outcast and especially sin. Brief references to The Power and the Glory and Nineteen Stories--the latter lacking the "layer of supernatural Grace," and therefore "so much poorer."

R471 Blanzat, J. "Rocher de Brighton." FigL, 62 (28 June), p. 4. A short review of the French translation by Marcelle Sibon. Paris: Laffont, 1947.

R472 Hale, Lionel. "Dona Dollar." Observer, (13 July), p. 3. Nineteen Stories is briefly mentioned with two other books in one paragraph.

R473 Mauer, Otto. "Dein ist das Reich und die Macht und die Herrlichkeit." ZeitB, I:5/6, pp. 1-3. A review of the German translation of The Power and the Glory as a realistic novel, even on the linguistic level, and as sufficiently Christian to destroy pharisaism and intellectual arrogance.

R474 Newby, P. H. "New Short Stories." Listener, XXXVIII:969 (21 Aug.), p. 316. Nineteen Stories, "by-products" of a novelist's career, are "not very good" with the exception of one or two like "The Basement Room," in which Greene contrives that "angle of perspective which ... saves his narrative of frustration, seediness and despair from being itself frustrated, seedy and despairing."

R475 Unsigned. "Fiction: The Tragic Failure." TLS, 2373 (26 July), p. 377. Selects "The Basement Room," "I Spy," and "The Innocent" from Nineteen Stories--three distinguished stories in the volume--as anticipations of what Greene can achieve in the form, if he cares to. Finds a common theme to be the "maladjusted individual's attempt to escape from the prison of his own unconscious fears and guilt," and that "no unhappier or more pitiful set of humans could be assembled in a volume of stories."

1948

B481 Gable, Sr. Mariella. "New Boundaries." This Is Catholic Fiction. New York: Sheed & Ward, pp. 33-38. Also rpt. as "The Heart of the Matter." Today, (Oct. 1948), pp. 20-21. A review article on The Heart of the Matter written from a Catholic viewpoint and examining in what way the novel is a "challenge to theologians." Maintains that by concentrating on man's relationship to God and analyzing "the peculiar nexus between the moral and the spiritual order," Greene has "expanded the boundaries" of the English novel. Notes that the one artistic flaw in the novel lies in the inability of the reader to "quite believe the urgency of Scobie's problem."

B482 Hoehn, Matthew, ed. "Graham Greene, 1904-" Catholic Authors: Contemporary Biographical Sketches, 1930-1947. Newark, N.J.: St. Mary's Abbey, pp. 289-90. Includes a brief biographical sketch, and a list of his works until 1947.

B483 Woodcock, George. "Graham Greene." The Writer and Politics. London: The Porcupine Press, pp. 125-53. Contends that though Greene may be a "Catholic propagandist," his portrayal of the spiritual struggle of good and evil shows his concern with the actual violence of human life. The struggle is a moral conflict, even more than the conflict of a soul and is "centered in the relationships of men"; this is why his novels show a developed social consciousness and constitute "one of the most comprehensive surveys of modern social violence ... in European fiction," and reflect Greene's sense of social values. The Lawless Roads, It's a Battlefield, The Confidential Agent, The Ministry of Fear, Brighton Rock and The Power and the Glory.

B484 Zabel, Morton Dauwen. "Graham Greene." Forms of Modern Fiction. Ed. William van O'Connor. Minneapolis: Univ. of Minnesota Press, pp. 287-93. Rpt. from Nation, CLVII (3 July 1943), pp. 18-20. See A433.

A481 Baker, Denys Val. "My Favourite Forgotten Book." Tomorrow, VII (July), pp. 63-64. A timely recall amid the controversy over The Heart of the Matter to the neglected and often underrated Journey Without Maps. Considers the double purpose of the journey as the desire to explore the "mysterious region of unknown Africa," and the "dark and mysterious regions of the mind," and speculates on Greene's "less conscious reason" as the desire to recapture "the vivid experiences of terror and fear ... in his childhood."

A482 Brownrigg, Ronald. Letter. Tablet, CXCII:5642 (10 July), p. 26. Letter to the Editor arguing rather humorously against the publication of The Heart of the Matter because of its effect on "the immature, untrained or atrophied thought-processes of the general reader."

A483 Butler, B. C., OSB. Letter. Tablet, CXCI:5640 (26 June), p. 402. Letter to the Editor disagreeing with E. Waugh's review (see A4825) of the drama of the last few moments of Scobie's life, and suggesting, in response to P. Hughes' letter to the Editor (see A4812) that the exclusion of sin from the purview of the novelist reduces him to "the Sunday-School story-writer."

A484 Cartmell, Joseph. "Canon Joseph Cartmell Writes." Tablet, CXCI:5637 (5 June), p. 354. Rpt. in Commonweal, XLVIII (16 July), pp. 325-26, and in Graham Greene: A Collection of Critical Essays. Ed. Samuel Hynes. Englewood Cliffs, N.J.: Prentice-Hall, 1973, pp. 103-05. Brief comments, from a Catholic theological viewpoint, on Scobie's sin, as "a sort of" appendix to Evelyn Waugh's review. See A4825.

A485 Curtis, Jean-Louis. "Impressions de Londres." TR, 1, pp. 155-58. Notices briefly on p. 158 the contrast between English and French reactions to Brighton Rock.

A486 De Hegedus, Adam. "Graham Greene: The Man and His Work." WRev, XV (Aug.), pp. 57-61. Rpt. as "Graham Greene and the Modern Novel." Tomorrow, VIII (Oct.), pp. 54-56. Contrary to M. McCarthy and like M. D. Zabel, he acknowledges Greene as the leading novelist of his generation not only for his style and technique but also for closing the "gap between the so-called 'average' and so-called 'serious' reader" by using the thriller and returning "miracle" into the world of the serious novel.

A487 Delteil, Francois. "Romanciers catholiques anglais: II. Graham Greene." LivL, 17, pp. 433-35. This brief survey of Greene's life and works attributes Greene's success, especially after the publication of The Heart of the Matter, to his mastery of technique, suggestive style and the breadth of the problems he probes. Contains a "Note bibliographique" of the works translated into French, and some seventeen critical essays and reviews in English and French.

A488 Downing, Francis. Letter. Commonweal, XLVIII (6 Aug.), pp. 399-400. Rejects E. Waugh's statements on The Heart of the Matter that "only Catholics can understand the nature of the problem," or that Scobie willed his "own damnation for the love of God." Maintains instead that Scobie's weakness "stems from pity and desire for peace" and that what is important is "less the manner of his sinning than his sense of guilt: his feeling that his personal responsibility cannot be shifted from himself to God."

A489 Duche, Jean. "Du Rocher de Sisyphe au Rocher de Brighton." TR, 2, pp. 306-09. Follows closely C.-E. Magny's view that an inexorable fatality against which human actions are of no avail--a substitute for Camus's Sisyphus Rock--underlies Greene's Jansenist beliefs in Brighton Rock.

A4810 Engle, Claire Elaine. "Einige englische Romanciers von heute." Du, VIII (Jan.), p. 28. A brief examination of the new spiritualism and intellectual tendencies in the novels of H. Green and G. Greene. The Power and the Glory.

A4811 Eustace, C. J. "Dilemma of the Catholic Novelist." Culture, IX (Dec.), pp. 384-98. A Catholic viewpoint on the problems faced by the Catholic novelist and his dilemma in rendering to others "the intensely personal inner vision he possesses ... of the universe, and life." In a brief reference to Greene on p. 388, he contends that the "controlling passion" of Greene's novels is his "obsession over the problem of love ... in relation to the operation of Divine Grace."

A4812 Hughes, Philip. Letter. Tablet, CXCI:5639 (19 June), p. 386. Letter to the Editor indicative of the controversy raging over The Heart of the Matter, deploring Greene's "Shelleyism" which "resolves religion into a feeling" and which offers for contemplation the "bad man who is simultaneously holy."

A4813 Igoe, W. J. Letter. Tablet, CXCII:5643 (17 July), p. 41. Recognizes The Heart of the Matter as a "magnificent work of art" and the Catholic novelist as a "force to be considered" in England.

A4814 Jans, Adrien. "Graham Greene, entre le péché et l'amour." Empreintes, IV (Feb.-April), pp. 46-49. Praises Greene for his characterization and his "dazzling ability" to inculcate his adventure stories with values. Focusses on the French translation of The Power and the Glory.

A4815 Laurens, A. "Comment j'ai introduit Graham Greene en

France." FrA, III (April), pp. 455-59. Impressions and reminiscences of his discovery of Greene as a novelist. Reaffirms his views of Greene as a Christian existentialist and a novelist whose many affinities with the French make him popular in France as one of the "fils spirituels de Proust, dans la grande ligne Janséniste, pascalienne et mauriacienne."

A4816 Leggett, Frances. Letter. Commonweal, XLVIII (20 Aug.), pp. 452-53. Rejects E. Waugh's "conventional disposing of the problems" raised by The Heart of the Matter.

A4816a Lord, Daniel A. SJ. "Along the Way: Tragedy and Graham Greene." NW, (1 Oct.), p. 4. Editorial commending Greene for attempting "fictional tragedy" in The Heart of the Matter and for showing Scobie suffering and destroying himself as a consequence of his sin and weakness.

A4817 McLaughlin, Richard. "Graham Greene: Saint or Cynic?" America, LXXIX (24 July), pp. 370-71. Impressions of Greene after an evening spent with him in New York. Emphasizes his "contradictory traits which make up the whole of the thinking man" and his attitude to Roman Catholicism.

A4818 Martindale, C. C., SJ. Letter. Tablet, CXCI:5640 (26 June), p. 402. Defends Greene against the charge of "neo-Shelleyism" by P. Hughes (see A4812), and acknowledges Greene's "insight into and pity for human nature" whereby he makes us "look into the sinner's eyes with, precisely, the eyes of Christ."

A4819 Mauer, Otto. "Graham Greene: Problematische Katholizitat." ZeitB, II:11-12, pp. 1-4. A review article on the German translation of Brighton Rock (Vienna: Zsolnay, 1948) and The Lawless Roads (Vienna: Herder, 1948). Considers Greene's Catholicism to be problematic in its unorthodoxy, and maintains that with Dostoyevsky, he suffers from the problem of theodicy because his characters achieve salvation often through sin.

A4820 Mauriac, François. "La Puissance et la gloire." FigL, (30 Oct.), pp. 1, 3. Rpt. as "Graham Greene." Renascence, I (Spring 1949), pp. 25-27, and in his Mes Grands Hommes. Monaco: Editions du Rocher, 1949. Trans. Elsie Pell. Men I Hold Great. New York: Philosophical Library, 1951, pp. 124-28. Published in U.K. as Great Men. London: Rockliff, 1952, pp. 117-22. Also in his Oeuvres Completes. VIII. Paris: Fayard, 1950, pp. 429-32. Rpt. in Graham Greene: A Collection of Critical Essays. Ed. Samuel Hynes. Englewood Cliffs, N.J.: Prentice-Hall, 1973, pp. 75-78. A warm appreciation of, and tribute to, Greene as an English Catholic novelist for his incursions into "le royaume de la nature et de la Grace" in The Power and the Glory, and his "utilization of sin by Grace" in the drama of the Whiskey Priest.

A4821 Montesi, Gotthard. "Tragodie der Nachstenliebe." WW, III (Aug.), pp. 610-15. Focusses on The Heart of the Matter as representative of the new realism among Catholic writers and as an uncompromising book whose theological outlook, where even Faith is regarded as a burden, may perhaps alienate the average reader. Greene does not interpret for the reader the paradoxes in the novel but he awakens in him awe for God's judgment--and mercy--and the knowledge too, that man must not judge.

A4822 O'Faolain, Sean. "The Novels of Graham Greene: The Heart of the Matter." BriT, 148 (Aug.), pp. 32-36. Though primarily a review of The Heart of the Matter pointing out its muddled thought and weak characters as its basic weaknesses--"the religious theme breaks its back"--this review article also places Greene within the "English literary tradition" of Bunyan and Donne, and considers the added dimension given his work through the use of realism as technique, "not (as) an end in itself."

A4823 Reynolds, H. A. "Forever Greene." CG, XXIX:10 (Oct.), pp. 178-80. An assessment of the merits and shortcomings of the Catholic novel using The Heart of the Matter as a starting-point.

A4824 Simons, Katherine. "Graham Greene." BMCN, (June), pp. 6-7. A profile of the novelist giving some "bare facts" of his life in an attempt to provide clues to his personality. Contains a rare reference to Mrs. Greene and the house on Beaumont Street, Oxford.

A4825 Waugh, Evelyn. "Felix Culpa?" Tablet, CXCI:5637 (5 June), pp. 352-54. Rpt. Commonweal, XLVIII (6 July), pp. 322-25. A review article on The Heart of the Matter that discusses Greene's "grim style," his "charmless characters," and his "sound exciting plot." Maintains that Scobie is the "complement of Pinkie," and questions whether one can suppose that his love of God "sanctifies his sins." Contends that to will one's own damnation for the love of God is either "a very loose poetical expression or a mad blasphemy," and that to illustrate the "Nouveau Theologie" in human terms necessitates that the literary critic "resign his judgment to the theologian."

A4826 ________. Letter. Tablet, CXCII (17 July), p. 41. Admits the error in his review of supposing that Greene had imputed "sanctity" to his hero, but rejects Mr. Brownrigg's suggestion (see A482) that the novel should not have been published at all.

R481 Brighouse, Harold. "New Novels." Guardian, (28 May), p. 3. A short review of The Heart of the Matter noticing the absence of violence in "word and deed" and Greene's expert handling of character and familiarity with the local scene.

R482 Burger, Nash K. "Books of the Times." NYT, (12 July), p. 17. Notes that though a "constant, well-sustained suspense" underlies the "brisk and exciting" narrative, The Heart of the Matter is concerned with those "inner struggles and compulsions" of Scobie and with posing "age-old questions as man's relation to God." Finds the novel rich in meaning, symbolism and suspense.

R483 Calkins, Hugh, OSM. "Lights and Shadows." Novena Notes, (17 Sept.), pp. 6 & 14. A liberal Catholic viewpoint on The Heart of the Matter that finds the novel "truly great" in its presentation of "an intriguing problem in completely Catholic terms" and in delineating the terrific impact of theology on human souls.

R484 Connolly, Francis X. "The Heart of the Matter." Newsletter, XL:1 (Mid-Summer), pp. 1-2. Maintains that in this "well-plotted story in which atmosphere, character and event are brilliantly organized to form a perfect tragic pattern," Greene scrutinizes with power and intensity Scobie's "tragic flaw of sentimental pity"--the noble and fatal weakness of a character who may well symbolize the typical modern man. Questions whether themes like Grace and Divine Mercy can be interpreted in a "fictitious form which lacks the assistance of an authoritative tragic chorus."

R485 Deacon, William Arthur. "This Policeman's Lot Was Not a Happy One." Globe, (17 July), p. 12. A rather uninformed review that keeps pointing out the "ludicrous contrast" between The Heart of the Matter and Frank Yerby's The Golden Hawk. Considers the novel to have failed to achieve "the dignity of tragedy because the motivation of Scobie is obscure or not acceptable."

R486 Du Bois, William. "A Searching Novel of Man's Unpaid Debt to Man." NYTBR, (11 July), p. 5. Maintains that in The Heart of the Matter, a "crystal-clear allegory" and an "engrossing" novel, Greene explores with "clinical depth" and compassion the "basic malaise" of a man who sees "few bridges between love and reality" and who is a victim of his own "acute kindness."

R487 Evans, Illtud, OP. "The Heart of the Matter." Blackfriars, XXIX (July), pp. 344-45. A searching review, from a Catholic viewpoint, that interprets the heart of the matter to be "the unassailable truth of the supernatural." Praises the novel for its "power ... pity and integrity" in its study of conscience and the fact of sin.

R488 Flint, R. W. "Recent Fiction." HudR, I (1948/49), pp. 590-96. The Heart of the Matter is the third of five novels reviewed. Though "impeccable" as a "tight, absorbing, pathetic narrative" with vivid conversation, the novel is "three kinds of novel joined, spliced or fastened together"--high-class Maugham Holywood, religious drama and modern love--whose symbolism fails to sustain and whose "relentless hammering of atmospheric effects" merely provides a shallow emotional coloring. Finds comparison with Mauriac or Dostoyevsky "a desperate expedient to make one's point."

R489 Gardiner, Harold C., SJ. "Heart of the Matter: Greene's Greatest?" America, LXXIX (17 July), pp. 350-51. Maintains that this "complex, deeply felt and deeply moving book," delineating the "terrific impact of theology on human souls," could only have been written by a Catholic. Raises the question of whether Scobie is damned, but commends Greene for not passing judgment even though he gives the impression, "almost inescapable," that Scobie is a saint--a fact which is considered perhaps the greatest weakness of the book. Believes The Power and the Glory to be Greene's greatest.

R4810 Hale, Lionel. "Mr. Greene." Observer, (30 May), p. 3. A short but warmly appreciative review of Greene's achievement and "economical realism" in The Heart of the Matter, and the restrained use of his "gift of scene and phrase on the colonial scene" in his treatment of the novel's central theme, the love of God.

R4811 Hardwick, Elizabeth. "Loveless Love." PR, XV, pp. 937-39. Focusses on Scobie's pity, "his loveless love," and asserts that Greene pushes "personal heresy to the limits with a greediness that is convincing neither as fiction nor as religion." Complains of the "snobbishness" of serious Catholic writers in their treatment of the conventionally pious--Greene is "positively churlish" in this respect--but finds the novel "interesting and serious for its plain, grim understanding of the moral pain or exaggerated sentiment."

R4812 Hormel, Olive Dean. "A Grave Study in Ambiguities." ChrSM, (2 Sept.), p. 11. Argues that The Heart of the Matter should be more accurately described as man's relationship to his Church rather than to his God as Sr. M. Gable maintains. (See B481). Regards the novel as a "parable" because its people are "consistently two-dimensional" and, as they move in Greene's "twilight world," leave the reader with "unresolved" ambiguities.

R4813 Jackson, Joseph Henry. "Graham Greene Writes About Inner Conflict." SFC, (18 July), p. 18. Examines Scobie's inner conflict and Greene's tender and understanding handling of it. Considers the novel to be "genuinely fine," one of the best novels to come out of England in recent years, and as an example of modern fiction at its top level.

R4814 John, K. "Notes for the Novel-Reader: Fiction of the Week." ILN, (26 June), p. 722. Maintains that Greene preaches "a gospel of joylessness" through his "grimly remarkable" description of the "devitalizing" African scene and its "moral squalor" in The Heart of the Matter. Finds it "hard to reverence the central figure" who is guilty "not so much of despair as of a deep-rooted, joyless pride."

R4815 Jones, Ernest. "Some Recent Novels." Nation, CLXVII (21 Aug.), p. 212. The Heart of the Matter is the last of five novels reviewed. Merely endorses G. Orwell's view which disqualifies Greene from the rank of a major novelist.

R4816 Kennedy, John S. "Books As Christmas Gifts for Adults." CW, CLXVII (Dec.), p. 211. An annotated list which recommends The Heart of the Matter--the first novel listed--to "careful discerning readers only" who will find it "masterly and sound both psychologically and theologically."

R4817 Lalou, René. "Le Livre de la semaine: La Puissance et la gloire." NL, (9 Dec.), p. 3. Notes, in this review of the French translation of The Power and the Glory, the episodic nature of the story and the thriller pattern that Greene gives his "spiritual tragedies." Also notices the controversy aroused by John Ford's film adaptation, The Fugitive, which played in France under the title "Dieu est mort."

R4818 Lehane, J. C., CM. "The Heart of the Matter Is a Superior Example of the Craftsmanship of Fiction." NW, (23 July), p. 15. Includes among the "artistic achievements of this satisfying story" Greene's description of Scobie's internal conflict and his "honest portrayal of white men in a tropical climate," as well as the "superior quality" of plot and characterization.

R4819 Lewis, Elaine Lambert. "The Heart of the Matter." LJ, LXXIII (15 April), p. 651. Briefly noticed as an interesting study but disappointing as a novel.

R4820 McSorley, Joseph. "New Books." CW, CLXVII (Sept.), pp. 564-65. Though he acknowledges that Greene merely presents a problem through an individual, "unclassifiable and unpredictable," and that one cannot emphatically forecast what will take place between man and his Maker, he is rather critical of Scobie's "pitiful absurdity" which invites "moral disaster by divorcing mind from will and substituting means for ends."

R4821 M., J. "Littérature et Beaux-Arts." Critique, (June), pp. 566-68. A lengthy review of Brighton Rock that recognizes the extreme economy of a well-made novel that makes "agréable lecture," and whose incidents converge to one end like a classical play. Examines its four principal characters as representative of four forces in conflict: Pinkie of evil, Rose of charity, Ida of human justice and Brighton of destiny or fatalism. Cautions against any forced analogy between Sartre and Greene.

R4822 Mayberry, George. "The Man Who Loved God." NRep, CXIX (12 July), pp. 21-22. Maintains that though Greene is an interesting and talented writer whose novel "possesses an inner depth and an unmistakable basic philosophy," The Heart of the Matter lacks "the quality of felt life" that makes for greatness, and that Greene's recurring absorption with the "bad Catholic" and his treatment of him leaves the impression of "slickness."

R4823 Monroe, Elizabeth. "On Reading: The Heart of the Matter." BT, VII (Sept.), p. 89. A short review noting Greene's abandonment of the exploration of horror for the study of disillusionment, of character and the probing of conscience.

R4824 Orwell, George. "Books: The Sanctified Sinner." NY, XXIV (17 July), pp. 66, 69-71. Rpt. in The Collected Essays, Journalism and Letters of George Orwell. Vol. IV. In Front of Your Nose: 1945-1950. Eds. Sonia Orwell and Ian Angus. London: Secker & Warburg; New York: Harcourt, 1968, pp. 439-43, and in Graham Greene: A Collection of Critical Essays. Ed. Samuel Hynes. Englewood Cliffs, N.J.: Prentice-Hall, 1973, pp. 105-10. Argues that The Heart of the Matter is not Greene's best and gives "the impression of having been mechanically constructed ... with no attempt at psychological probability." Finds the plot "ridiculous," with motives inadequately explaining actions as a result of "foisting theological preoccupations upon simple people." Finds other improbabilities in the novel in Greene's handling of a love affair and in making everyone "too highbrow." Also rejects the "sort of snobbishness" in Greene's "explicitly Catholic standpoint," because the general attempt "to clothe theological speculations in flesh and blood" will produce "psychological absurdities."

R4825 Painter, George D. "New Novels." Listener, XXXIX:1011

(10 June), p. 946. Maintains that The Heart of the Matter is Greene's "first total victory" where he achieves the "theological triumph" of making the most authoritative statement in the modern novel on the real presence of God. Suggests that the "thriller-form" is a "symbol of the urgency" of Greene's theme which, when fused with the minor successes of local color and an "almost Shakespearean" conversation, becomes an artistic triumph.

R4826 Prescott, Orville. "Outstanding Novels." YR, XXXVIII (Autumn), p. 191. Though not completely convincing--not entirely successful in its major theme--The Heart of the Matter is "provocative and continuously interesting," for it arouses doubt rather than pity or admiration.

R4827 Robinson, Henry Morton. "A God-Smitten Man." SatR, XXXI (10 July), pp. 8-9. Finds Greene's understanding of the supernatural--the "spiritual dimensions" of The Heart of the Matter--refreshing, and when coupled with his "narrative tempo, subtlety of perception" and mastery of style, makes the novel move forward "with the stalking terror of a Sophoclean tragedy." Slightly critical of Greene's "too exotic and melodramatic" binders for the powerful and original material of the novel.

R4828 Sackville-West, Edward. "The Problem of Despair." NSta, XXXV:902 (19 June), p. 504. A sympathetic and perceptive review of The Heart of the Matter. Considers the novel "a triumph of the novelist's art" and "brilliantly professional," where every scene is "planted as carefully as in a play" and where every detail is "a failing to which only the good are liable." Critical of Greene's final chapter.

R4829 Sandoe, James. "America discovers Graham Greene." CSBW, (13 July). Though he concedes that the choice of The Heart of the Matter by the Book-of-the-Month-Club is a major achievement when compared to earlier choices, he does not think the novel equal in power or in resolution to earlier works because Greene manipulates incidents as wilfully as Hardy.

R4830 Smith, R. D. "Fiction: The Heart of the Matter." Spectator, CLXXX (4 June), pp. 686-87. The first of three novels reviewed. Finds the exercise in "the virtues of eternal damnation" more perfectly carried out than the earlier attempts because details given are essential to the author's conception. Focusses on the delineation of character.

R4831 Sugrue, Thomas. "Story of Man's Deepest Spiritual Conflict." NYHTBR, (11 July), p. 1. Finds the tragedy of Scobie, an "average, undistinguished man," powerful and deep-striking as Greene probes the "theological error" of the division of his loyalties between two incompatibles. Greene's "superb craftsmanship" and the memorable gallery of characters he creates make the drama convincing and moving.

R4832 Wall, Barbara. "London Letter." America, LXXIX (28 Aug.), pp. 470-71. Disapproves of E. Waugh's review of The Heart of the Matter (see A4825) and maintains that Greene is "portraying a character, not making a case," and comments on the controversy aroused by the novel in Catholic newspapers.

R4833 Unsigned. "The Heart of the Matter." Booklist, XLIV (15 July), p. 382. Brief note summarizing the story.

R4834 _______. "Some New Novels." DaiT, (28 May), p. 3. The Heart of the Matter is briefly noticed as a "magnificent conception, poignant and convincing."

R4835 _______. "The Heart of the Matter." Kirkus, XVI:4 (15 Feb.), p. 90. Pre-publication announcement of the novel as one of "considerable seriousness and stature" for an "adult and appreciative" audience.

R4836 _______. "Nineteen Stories." Kirkus, XVI (15 Dec.), p. 645. Advance notice of the forthcoming publication in the U.S. of the collection in February 1949. Remarks briefly on the "memorable" and "compelling" stories in the collection.

R4837 _______. "Bishop Attacks Greene's New Novel." LU, (3 Sept.), p. 3. A quotation from Bishop Brown's letter to the Southwark Record condemning the tendency to lessen "the guilt of sins and sex" which The Heart of the Matter is alleged to encourage as well as its "painful want of reticence" when dealing with adultery. This is followed by a news item about Greene recuperating from an operation in a New York hospital.

R4838 _______. "Greene and Catholicism." Newsweek, XXXII (12 July), pp. 84-86. Finds The Heart of the Matter a "most literately readable" religious novel for it probes deeply Scobie's tormented self in a "masterful" way. It is also a tragic "love story" of the heroism of the human soul and is "singularly moving"; the "moral" does not detract from Greene's abilities as a storyteller.

R4839 _______. "What Price Pity?" Time, LII (9 Aug.), pp. 46-47. Recognizes in the West African setting of The Heart of the Matter the "same cruel, sordid, vulturous hell" of Greene's earlier works. Surmises that Green tried to write a "true tragedy and succeeded in writing a suggestive melodrama, with tragic overtones and ironic implications." Maintains that the reader can easily miss the irony because of Greene's sympathy for Scobie.

1949

B491 Allen, Walter. "Eight Novels Discussed. 1. The Power and the Glory. Graham Greene." Reading a Novel. London: Phoenix House; Denver: Alan Swallow, pp. 37-42. Rev. ed. 1956. Discusses, in a simplified manner for the reader willing to read discriminately and critically, the fundamental elements that distinguish The Power and the Glory: title, epigraph, the anti-romantic trend in setting and character, transcendence of the local and contemporary relevance. Attributes its "terrific power" on the reader to style and technique.

B492 Engel, Claire-Elaine. "Graham Greene." Esquisses anglaises: Charles Morgan, Graham Greene, T. S. Eliot. Paris: Editions "Je sers," pp. 57-98. Outlines Greene's belief in evil which haunts the novels and his emphasis on the sense of sin, and his vision of man, lonely and alone, struggling but trapped, incapable of escaping his destiny--a kind of "predestination," because Greene's Catholicism "est teinté pour le moins de jansénisme." Shows how Brighton Rock, The Power and the Glory and The Heart of the Matter reflect this point of view, and notices the French tendency to compare Greene and Mauriac but she finds "les rapports ... fragiles." Discusses Greene's characterization of the "heroes," the women and children, as well as the atmosphere and ambience of the novels. Concludes that Greene's strange talent, "fait de froideur et de passion contenue, atteste une qualité d'esprit et d'âme qui marquent une époque."

B493 Madaule, Jacques. Graham Greene. Paris: Editions du Temps présent. Focusses on four major themes in the novels up to The Heart of the Matter--England, the hunted man, pity and the role of woman--in an attempt to map out Greene's spiritual world. Regards the Christianity depicted in the novels as both tragic and realistic, disturbing rather than edifying and comforting as it describes the soul's confrontation with the essential realities of good and evil, and reminds us of the precariousness of the human condition. Also includes a chapter on the art of the novels.

B494 Mauriac, François. "Graham Greene." Mes Grands Hommes. Monaco: Editions du Rocher. Rpt. from FigL, (30 Oct. 1948), pp. 1, 3. See A4810.

B495 Rostenne, Paul. Graham Greene: témoin des temps tragiques. Paris: Julliard. Includes a Prefatory Letter by Graham Greene. The study regards the works of Greene from the perspective of his age, and as a response to its problems. It discusses briefly the state of the novel, especially the Catholic novel, Greene's use of the "thriller" and his "sensibilité ... vive au surnaturel." The central part of the study focusses on Greene's outlook on sin, despair, the supernatural implications of anarchy, the impact of the world, of woman, and the liberty found in a true vocation. England Made Me, Journey Without Maps, The Lawless Roads, A Gun for Sale, Brighton Rock, The Power and the Glory and The Heart of the Matter.

A491 Aguirre de Carcer, Nuno. "La novela en la Inglaterra actual: II. Graham Greene." Arbor, XIV (Sept.-Oct.), pp. 99-113. Second article of a series on the contemporary English novel. Surveys Greene's life and works, and the world of his novels, and discusses Greene's basic moral assumptions, including his notion of Grace.

A492 Allen, W. Gore. "Evelyn Waugh and Graham Greene." IM, LXXVII (Jan.), pp. 16-22. A talk for the average educated Catholic reader broadcast from Radio Eireann in November 1948. Brings out the differences between the two writers rather than their similarities, and focusses on Greene's concern with Divine Grace, free will and evil, and his ability to see "life in the raw." Brighton Rock and The Heart of the Matter.

A493 _______. "The World of Graham Greene." IER, LXXI:4 (Jan.) pp. 42-49. Contends, in this basically sound article, that Greene's rejection of a world destroyed by war, his caricature of inter-war society and attitude to women, love, marriage and the "permanent laws of human life," are part of a "theological reaction" to a system of thought shaped by the 1930's. The Heart of the Matter.

A494 _______. "Another View of Graham Greene." CW, CLXIX (April), pp. 69-70. An excerpt from "The World of Graham Greene" focussing on the novelist's "veils of negation and sterility."

A495 Auden, W. H. "The Heresy of Our Time." Renascence, I (Spring), 23-24. Rpt. as "A Note on Graham Greene." The Wind and the Rain, VI (Summer 1949), pp. 53-54. Rpt. in Renascence, XXV:4 (Summer 1973), 181-82, and in Graham Greene: A Collection of Critical Essays. Ed. Samuel Hynes. Englewood Cliffs, N.J.: Prentice-Hall, 1973, pp. 93-95. Praises Greene for relating the thriller to the literary form of the allegory in The Ministry of Fear, and for exposing the "vice of pity," that "corrupt form of love and compassion" which constitutes a "great and typical heresy of our time."

A496 Barr, Donald. "Graham Greene's World." NYTBR, (13 Feb.), pp. 3, 28-29. A review article on Nineteen Stories that considers the chronological arrangement of the stories with their "solid virtues" and "quietness and lucid ease," as a "reflection" of Greene's development as a novelist. Notes that the entertainments have rarely been noticed as "rehearsals" for the novels and suggests two reasons why Greene's world, this "criss-cross of tired intrigues, of flickering eternal motives," fascinates the reader: it is a darker world and its crimes seem more wicked--effects achieved by the "rich concentration of poetry" in his style and his interest in the psychology of his characters.

A497 Barrat, R. "Graham Greene's Bekehrung." NA, IV:11, pp. 338-39. Account of an interview that concentrates on the topic of Greene's conversion to Catholicism. The interviewer requests reasons for the conversion, and elicits Greene's expectation for the immediate future and his views on whether Catholics should be simply concerned with their own salvation. The interviewer is disturbed and rather shocked by Greene's reactionary views.

A498 Bayley, John. "Two Catholic Novelists." NR, CXXXII (Feb.), pp. 232-35. Considers The Loved One and The Heart of the Matter by E. Waugh and G. Greene as "moral fantasies" whose characters are "frankly manipulated" by writers who use "their Catholicism as a weapon and a probe" and who should "not be taken too seriously."

A499 Boyle, Alexander. "Graham Greene." IM, LXXVII (Nov.), pp. 519-25. A general assessment, for the interested reader, of Greene as a "modern" novelist whose serious view of life and concern with "the grave moral problems that beset the individual soul," have "skilfully blended" Catholicism and Art in The Heart of the Matter. Hesitates to place Greene among the great novelists because his characters lacked "roundness" and "depth" until The Power and the Glory.

A4910 Connolly, Francis X. "Inside Modern Man: The Spiritual Adventures of Graham Greene." Renascence, I (Spring), 16-23. A perceptive article that examines "predominant and recurring patterns of thought and feeling" in an attempt to explain Greene's artistic intention, his method and the quality of his achievement. After considering Greene's reliance on observation and the construction of his books on the "level of visualized action," Connolly focusses on Greene's paradoxical preoccupation with grace and sin, especially the latter which amounts to an "obsession with evil." Identifies the "hub of the question" as Greene's inability as a novelist to present adequately, on the spiritual level, what he aspires to with much "conceptual clarity." Brighton Rock, The Power and the Glory, The Heart of the Matter and "The Hint of an Explanation."

A4911 Elsen, Claude. "Graham Greene ou la geste de l'homme traqué." TR, 14 (Feb.), pp. 297-301. Argues that Greene's hunted man, though an outcast, differs from the traditional gangster or villain in that he finds himself in the position of a pursued outcast without any logical reason but merely by virtue of the Absurd or fatalism--"le nom 'sacré' de l'Absurde." Brief references to Brighton Rock, The Confidential Agent, Stamboul Train and The Power and the Glory.

A4912 Erba, Luciano. "Incontro con Graham Greene." VeP, XXXII (Sept.), pp. 507-09. Concentrates on Greene's delineation of characters and the moral vision they express. Makes a brief analogy between the art of Conrad and that of Greene, and credits the latter with "prima concessione"--a "first" in literature--for making the protagonist of A Gun for Sale at once hero, hunted man, and culprit.

A4913 Fadiman, Clifton. "The Decline of Attention." SatR, XXXII (6 Aug.), pp. 20-24. Includes a photograph of Greene who, with writers I. Compton-Burnett and Elizabeth Bowen "are not ashamed, nay, are proud, to make stiff demands on the attention of the reader."

A4914 Gardiner, Harold C. "Graham Greene, Catholic Shocker." Renascence, I (Spring), pp. 12-15. Assumes that Brighton Rock, The Power and the Glory and The Heart of the Matter have a "shocking" effect, especially on the Catholic reader, and attributes this effect to Greene's eschatologism and "idealistic realism" which, with his uncompromising attitude to sin, reveal the whole truth about it: its sordidness as well as its relation to the supernatural.

A4915 Grubbs, Henry A. "Albert Camus and Graham Greene." MLQ, X (March), pp. 33-42. Describes several interesting analogies in character, the "leitmotif" of hopelessness, theme and the "keynote" of pity in The Ministry of Fear and Camus's L'Etranger, but wisely refrains from speaking of imitation, influence or sources.

A4916 Hahn, Karl J. "Graham Greene." Hochland, XLI (July), pp. 455-65. A critical appreciation of The Power and the Glory occasioned by its translation into German.

A4917 Herling, Gustav. "Two Sanctities: Greene and Camus." Adam, 201 (Dec.), pp. 10-19. Considers The Power and the Glory and The Heart of the Matter to be "fundamentally Jansenistic novels" in which the "unescapable destiny of sin and damnation" is pitted against human intentions and results in a despair from which escape is only possible through "death, into sanctity--to God." The dismissal of the Catholic notion of sanctity as a "theological abstraction" betrays the critic's preference for the "secular" sanctity or "active fatalism" of Camus which, though rising from the same "pessimistic and tragic philosophy of life" as Greene's, also points to despair but leaves room for hope, for a desperate struggle against the blind automatism of fate to relieve human suffering.

A4918 Hillig, Franz, SJ. "Die Kraft und die Herrlichkeit: zu dem Priesterroman von Graham Greene." SZ, CXLIII (Feb.), pp. 354-66. An appreciation of The Power and the Glory that heaps praise on Greene not so much for his "sparsamer und gedrangter Realismus" as for his ability to focus attention on the real plight of the Church in Mexico through the fortunes of the Whiskey Priest.

A4919 Ihlenfeld, Kurt. "Kann ein Sunder ein Heiliger sein?" EW, III, pp. 636-37. Focusses on the Whiskey Priest and reacts to the German translation of The Power and the Glory with the question: Can a sinner be a saint?

A4920 Jarrett-Kerr, Martin, CR. "The Novel and the Supernatural." StM, LI:3 (March), pp. 11-14. This is the first of two articles in which he describes four ways of presenting the supernatural in fiction. Uses The Heart of the Matter to illustrate "the way of privilege," the way that tends to be more Catholic than Protestant, and which consists of "contrasting the simplicity, uncomplicatedness, but also thinness of life in those who have not the supernatural, with the awful responsibility and terror, the joy and the damnation of those who have it and can't escape it." Inclined to overstate Greene's "Calvinism" in predestinating his characters, especially "when his characters are right outside him."

A4921 Jouve, Raymond. "La Damnation de Scobie." Etudes, CCLXIII:7 (Nov.), pp. 164-77. Surveys briefly the controversy aroused by the novel in England and the U.S., and gives an interesting analysis of the part played by pity in Scobie's sin, and his choice to remain "l'énnemi de Dieu, et son propre énnemi, que de peiner son entourage" which amounts to a lack of belief in the efficacy of Grace. Is not concerned with proving Scobie's salvation and, like Fr. C. Martindale, credits Greene for bringing the sinner to the point "ou Dieu les juge," where the problem of sin is no longer a human problem but remains a "mystère dont Dieu seul retient le secrêt."

A4922 Kennedy, John S. "Nonpareil Novelist." Sign, XXVII:7 (Feb.), pp. 57-58. Rpt. as "Graham Greene." Hibernia, (May), pp. 17-18. Uncritical tribute of praise to Greene as the "greatest of living novelists writing in English" to whom recognition has come "indirectly" in three ways: the movies, the Book-of-the-Month Club, and controversy. Brief reference to The Power and the Glory and The Heart of the Matter.

A4923 Las Vergnas, Raymond. "A Propos de Graham Greene." HM, IX (May), pp. 147-51. Surveys contemporary English fiction and the renewed French interest in it. Also notices the enthusiasm in France for the French translation of The Power and the Glory--"l'un des romans importants ... traitant de problèmes cruciaux ... avec force"--which may be exercising undue influence in determining the French outlook on contemporary English fiction.

A4924 Lemaitre, Henri. "Un Romancier chrétien de l'absurde: Graham Greene." CultC, 4 (Sept.), pp. 106-16. A perceptive article praising Greene for having re-introduced into the English novel "la signification mystique" of psychological analysis and restored metaphysical values to the mechanical necessity of novelistic incidents. Argues that the significant form of the absurd--the "diptyque symbolique" or underlying dialectic that characterizes the structure--is not so much the classic antithesis of good and evil as the union of paradoxical situations at once contradictory and complementary, and that the novels are essentially tragic and have a strong affinity with Greek tragedy. Brighton Rock, The Power and the Glory, The Heart of the Matter and "The Hint of an Explanation."

A4925 Link, Joseph J. "Der Schnapspriester." Seele, XXV, pp. 271-74. Mainly interested in the Whiskey Priest insofar as his experiences reveal the sacerdotal functions of a priest and their value to a people, rather than his worth as a literary figure.

A4926 Marshall, Bruce. "The Responsibilities of the Catholic Novelist." Commonweal, L (27 May), pp. 169-71. Brief reference to Greene and Waugh as "important Catholic novelists" who never fail "to get both the meaning and the accidents of the world right"; i.e., interested in any subject or experience so long as they write about it "under the aspect of eternity."

A4927 Mason, H. A. "A Note on Contemporary 'Philosophical' Literary Criticism in France." Scrutiny, XVI (March), 54-60. Takes to task C. E. M. (Claude-Edmonde Magny) on pp. 54-56 for evaluating Greene's oeuvre on the basic assumption that it is an "attempt to express a truth which can be fully grasped only by a long series of analytic arguments," and attributes its popularity in France to the familiarity of French critics with its philosophical patterns and ideas.

A4928 Mauriac, François. "La Puissance et la gloire." Renascence, I (Spring), pp. 25-27. Rpt. from FigL, (30 Oct. 1948), pp. 1, 3. See A4820.

A4929 O'Connor, John T. "Catholic Writing Today." CA, XXXI (Feb.), pp. 8-9. This review of Catholic writing in the U.S. contains one brief reference to Greene and The Heart of the Matter.

A4930 Parc, Robert du. "Saint ou Maudit? Le Prêtre dans La Puissance et la gloire de Graham Greene." Etudes, CCLX:14 (March), pp. 366-81. Addresses himself to the "psychological and spiritual" question of whether the Whiskey Priest is a "robot mené par la fatalité ou un homme libre." Rejects the simplistic explanation that he is a "desesperé, conscient de marcher écrasé par le destin," and argues, rather convincingly, that he is neither saintly nor damned but "a very poor man, seized by Christ, and made by his situation into an authentic martyr."

A4931 Pfleger, Karl. "Religiose Wirklichkeit...." WW, IV (June), pp. 473-78. This article on religious reality in contemporary novels considers Greene as a novelist whose works are essentially creative and go beyond mere propaganda because they deal with the absolutes of religious reality, rather than the time-bound ideals of religious actuality. The Power and the Glory.

A4932 Pryce-Jones, Alan. "La Crise de la littérature anglaise contemporaine." AUBB, (Dec.), pp. 8-23. This survey of the state of English literature at mid-century considers briefly on pp. 15-16 Greene's position among English novelists as that of a young writer most worthy of consideration. The Power and the Glory.

A4933 Schmidthues, K. G. "Graham Greene." NH, IV, pp. 429-33. A literary portrait that describes the ideas behind Greene's novels and points out the similarities between these ideas and Newman's. Brighton Rock, The Power and the Glory and The Heart of the Matter.

A4934 Young, Vernon. "Hollywood: Lost Moments." Accent, IX, pp. 120-28. Pages 124-26 note instances of the maltreatment of Greene's novels when adapted to the screen owing to the reluctance of the "holywood conscience" to confront the controlling principle of a work--except perhaps in The Confidential Agent--despite the fact that Greene's novels provide "almost perfect conditions" for movie transcription.

A4935 Unsigned. "Catholic Novels and Reprobates." CW, CLXVIII (March), pp. 417-21. A survey of the state of Catholic literature from a narrow but Catholic viewpoint. Singles out The Heart of the Matter as a "masterpiece but not the great Catholic novel" because Greene has failed to present his theme "with sufficient clarity to enable the ordinary educated Catholic to grasp it."

A4936 ______. "Profile--Graham Greene." Observer, (27 Nov.), p. 2. An unbiased descriptive account for the general reader of Greene's wide appeal as a writer which notices his exploration of spiritual decay, his conception of the role of the Church, and his fascination by the "cruelty, wickedness, and self-destructive capacity of man."

A4937 ______. "West African Rock." TLS, 2417 (29 March), p. 302. A review article on The Heart of the Matter which discusses some of the developments that have taken place in Greene's work to date to relate the novel to the rest of the works. Brings out the salient characteristics of the writing and shows that much of Greene's effective and disturbing atmosphere is generated by "the alternation of action and reflection in unexpected contact." Points out that in Brighton Rock, The Power and the Glory and The Heart of the Matter Greene approximates more with the French school of Mauriac and Bernanos than with the English Tradition, with the distinction that in Greene's works the individual character assumes a major rather than a minor role.

R491 Burnham, David. "Books: 19 Stories." Commonweal, XLIX (11 March), pp. 546-47. Though several stories exhibit Greene as not quite sure of himself, some of the stories are "hauntingly perfect," and several of them memorable for having children as protagonists. Notes that at times Greene's "stylistic elements become virtuosity, the compression, the vivid original metaphors, the photogenic intensification of reality, too far outrun the meaning: manner becomes mannerism."

R492 Cournos, John. "God, Existentialism and the Novel." ASch, XVIII (Winter), 116-27. A review article on seven contemporary novels that share a concern with fundamental issues, responsibility and the total absence of romance and propaganda. Finds The Heart of the Matter "Dostoevskian" in theme with all the "Dostoevskian play of nuance on the duality of the human psyche" and "close" to being a masterpiece.

R493 Farrelly, John. "Becoming Modesty." NRep, CXX (21 Feb.), pp. 25-26. Finds that Nineteen Stories emphasizes certain "weaknesses" in Greene's writing. Critical of the acclaim Greene has received for he regards him as a "skilled professional entertainer who manipulates a fashionable 'sense of sin' for its thrill effects," a morbidly romantic writer, whose "melodramatics are the expression of a tough sentimental sensibility," and whose prose is "studded with shock-words."

R494 H., R. F. "19 Short Stories by Graham Greene." SpR, (6 March), p. 9B. A short review that describes the collection as "miscellaneous" ranging from short impressionistic sketches to pure burlesque, but which adds to the reader's understanding of Greene the novelist.

R495 Hughes, Riley. "The New Novel." Thought, XXIV (March), pp. 14-17. An "editorial" that discusses the return to the concept of value in the modern novel which is far from "dead" through a brief review of E. Waugh's The Loved One and Greene's The Heart of the Matter. Describes the latter as a "kind of moral detective story" where the "crime" is patent, but the "motive" is fathomless.

R496 Jackson, Joseph Henry. "A Bookman's Notebook: From Graham Greene." SFC, (11 March), p. 20. Maintains that the short stories will stand on "their own feet" and, in their concern for good and evil, they help one to understand Greene the artist and his way of looking at life. Finds the variety in Nineteen Stories appealing and interesting.

R497 Lalou, René. "Le Livre de la semaine: Le Fond du problème." NL, (24 Nov.), p. 3. Notes that in The Heart of the Matter, as moving and as significant as The Power and the Glory, Greene avoids the thriller pattern he had frequently used.

R498 Match, Richard. "Nineteen Stories." NYHTBR, (13 Feb.), p. 4. Argues that the diffidence Greene expresses in his introduction is "unwarranted," for the stories, "all kinds and all lengths," are interesting, "sound in workmanship" and show Greene as a "talented" user of the English language.

R499 Prescott, Orville. "Books of the Times." NYT, (16 Feb.), p. 23. Finds the short stories, with the exception of "The Basement Room," "A Drive in the Country," "A Chance for Mr. Lever" and "When Greek Meets Greek," to be "slight, bleak, drab and dismal ... disappointing and strangely flat" oozing with "vulgarity," and failing either through "grotesque exaggeration," or the unexpected use of a supernaturalism "out of key with the prevailing realism, and through sheer triviality."

R4910 Redmond, Ben Ray. "Handout for Posterity." SatR, XXXII

(16 April), p. 23. Rather critical of Greene's inclusion of his "narrative miscarriages and slightest tales" appearing "fully dressed between (the) covers" of Nineteen Stories. However, his best stories, "The Basement Room," "The End of the Party," and "I Spy" are notably successful. Also examines Greene's attitude in the stories.

R4911 Sandrock, Mary. "19 Stories." CW, CLXIX (May), p. 157. A short review claiming that in spite of all the "listed debits" of these stories--some are "seemingly crude first drafts"--Greene's "vivid awareness of the basic verities" and his "bared-to-the-bone" prose can keep the reader interested.

R4912 Young, Vernon. "Hell on Earth: Six Versions." HudR, II (Summer), pp. 311-17. Nineteen Stories is the first of six works reviewed. Finds the stories "remarkable for their occasional escapes from the constriction of naturalism" and "less remarkable when facetious ... or ... luridly cinematic." Critical of Greene's "depressing" exploitation of the usefulness of the "negative simile" but concedes that he is a "master story-teller" who compensates for his "piety and pity with an unfaltering visualization of the English city scene." Singles out "The Basement Room" and "The End of the Party" as two stories that can best stand "without qualification."

R4913 Unsigned. "Graham Greene: Nineteen Stories." Booklist, XLV (15 March), p. 242. Brief notice of the volume.

R4914 _______. "Nineteen Stories." NY, XXIV (19 Feb.), pp. 81-82. Briefly notes that if the stories are about fear they are effective and credible, and that one of Greene's great assets is his detachment as storyteller.

R4915 _______. "Black Squares and White." Time, LIII (21 Feb.), p. 60. Maintains that Greene is not at ease with the form of the short story and that what gives the stories literary value is "the clarity with which they confront the author's religious faith with the paradoxes and atrocities of reality." Selects "The Basement Room," "The End of the Party," "Brother," "A Chance for Mr. Lever" and "The Hint of an Explanation" as being worthwhile reading.

D491 Strasill, Edmond. Die Kunst der Personenbeschreibung in Romanen Galsworthy, Maughams und Graham Greenes. Univ. of Graz.

1950

B501 Bernoville, Gaéton. "Quelques Refléxions sur l'état present de la littérature catholique." Le Catholicisme dans l'oeuvre de Francois Mauriac. Robert J. North. Paris: Editions du Conquistador, pp. ix-xlvi. Pages xxii-xxviii of the Introduction disapprove of the current tendency in criticism to discuss and evaluate a novel by the soundness of its theological views and cites the controversy raging over The Heart of the Matter as a case in point.

B502 Guitton, M. Jean. "Y a-t-il encore une nature humaine?" L'Humanisme et la grâce. Foreword Henri Bedarida. Paris: Editions de Flore, pp. 125-42. Brief reference to Greene's concept of Grace in The Heart of the Matter as being in line with much of modern religious thought--"le pharisaisme du publicain"--that regards Grace as "une grâce de visite soundaine et improbable" which often requires preparation "non par l'exercise du bien mais par l'experience du mal, non par la vertu, mais par l'humilité née du désépoir, mais par la fétidité du péché, comme s'il fallait que nous fussions fumier pour que pousse en nous la rose céleste." Article written from a philosophical standpoint.

B503 Heilman, Robert B., ed. Modern Short Stories: A Critical Anthology. New York: Harcourt, Brace & Co. Includes "The Basement Room" followed by a two-page commentary (pp. 264-66) emphasizing Greene's use of the subject of infidelity and the child's point of view.

B504 Jonsson, Thorsten Georg. "Ett Portratt av Scobie." Tva Essayer om Graham Greene. Stockholm: Norstedts, pp. 3-8. In Swedish. The five-page account of Scobie's character points out some of the changes he underwent, and examines briefly the dream sequences.

B505 Lindegreen, Erik. "Graham Greene." Tva Essayer om Graham Greene. Stockholm: Norstedts, pp. 11-16. In Swedish. The short "essay" attempts some evaluation of Greene's literary achievement, his awareness of popular literature, narrative art and the impact of Catholicism on his vision and writing.

B506 Mauriac, François. "Graham Greene." Oeuvres Completes, VIII. Paris: Fayard, pp. 429-32. See A4820.

A501 Alloway, Lawrence. "Symbolism in The Third Man." WRev, NS 13 (March), pp. 57-60. An analysis of the mythological background of the film that sees a biblical allusion to the walk to Emmaus in the title, and associates Lime and Holly to the practices of tree-worship and ritual death.

A502 Barzel, Werner, SJ. "Sunder aus Liebe? Zu Graham Greene Das Herz aller Dinge." SZ, CXLVI (April), pp. 24-28. A discussion of Scobie's "sin" in The Heart of the Matter.

A503 Beirnaert, Louis. "Die menschliche Armseligheit und die Gnade: Zu Graham Greenes Gestalten." Univ, V (Nov.), pp. 1395-97. An abridged version of a paper delivered at the meeting of the Semaine des Intellectuels Catholiques in Paris, 1950. Contends that man's relationship with God does not depend on psychic structures or psychical aptitudes in us, even though traditionally, the notion prevailed that sanctity was already performed in nature. Brief reference to the Whiskey Priest.

A504 _______. "Does Sanctification Depend on Psychic Structure?" Crosscurrents, 2 (Winter), pp. 39-43. A translation by Joseph L. Caulfield of a paper delivered at the meeting of the Semaine des Intellectuels Catholiques in Paris, 1950. See A503. Includes additional reference to A Gun for Sale.

A505 Bowen, Elizabeth. "The Writer's Peculiar World." NYTBR, (24 Sept.), pp. 3, 40. Rpt. in Highlights of Modern Literature: A Permanent Collection of Memorable Essays from 'The New York Times Book Review.' Ed. Francis Brown. New York: The American Library, 1954, pp. 32-36. Discusses Greene's statement in Why Do I Write? that "disloyalty" is as "much the writer's virtue as loyalty is the soldier's," and concludes that it is not so much a "privilege" as a "test and a tax."

A506 Braybrooke, Neville. "Catholics and the Novel." Blackfriars, (Feb.), pp. 54-64. Rpt. with minor changes in Renascence, V (Autumn 1952), pp. 22-32. Maintains, even while tracing the emergence of the novel, especially the "Catholic" novel, and pointing out the decline of critical standards, that the Catholic novelist has an "added power" over his fellow contemporaries. Illustrates from Brighton Rock. Also admits that Greene in 1938 came close to being a Catholic propagandist but moved away from sheer propaganda with The Power and the Glory and The Heart of the Matter.

A507 _______. "Graham Greene." Envoy, III (Sept.), pp. 10-23. A critical survey recognizing the centrality of the theme of pursuit--physical and spiritual--in the novels. Rightly dismisses Greene from the list of "Papist" propagandists in spite of the strong religious views expressed in The Power and the Glory and The Heart of the Matter, but detects "religious partisanship" and "an element of priggishness" in the juxtaposition of characters who are, more or less, archetypes of good and evil, and right and wrong in Brighton Rock.

A508 _______. "Graham Greene, A Pioneer Novelist." CE, XII:1 (Oct.), pp. 1-9, 415-23. A reprint of "Graham Greene," (see A507), with additional footnotes and the omission of the second last paragraph.

A509 ________. "Péguy: The Radiance of His Art." Commonweal, LIII (10 Nov.), pp. 114-15. Interesting to note the critic's association of the two writers whose acceptance of Catholicism "has at least placed their work in a scale of eternal values, and to this extent has deepened their perception of life," and whose stress on the "importance of the heart," unfashionable among contemporary writers, probes the underlying motives of human action.

A5010 Brion, Marcel. "Les Romans de Graham Greene." RDM, 6 (15 March), pp. 367-75. A general article that regards the hunt or the chase as the central theme of the novels, whether it be man pursuing man, or God and/or sin pursuing man, thus giving the thriller a new dimension as a vehicle for "les rapports" between man and God. Rightly maintains that though the characters may find salvation, sometimes ostensibly through sin--Greene an apologist for the great sinner?--they remain nonetheless free agents who seek violence as an antidote to their anxiety.

A5011 Chaput-Rolland, Solange. "Propos sur un roman de Graham Greene." AU, XVI (Jan.), pp. 73-75. A review article on The Power and the Glory that recommends that the novel be viewed from the standpoint of faith and not evaluated merely from a strictly literary viewpoint only.

A5012 Chavardes, Maurice. "Graham Greene ou la nudité de Dieu." VI, 7 (July), pp. 113-17. Contends that Greene's choice of sinners for central characters suggests a vision of a god essentially tragic "depouillé ... broyé ... humilié," the suffering figure on the Cross but who is also a God of Love; hence, the absence of despair in the novels in spite of the "verité ténébreuse" they depict.

A5013 Fouchet, Max-Pol. "Graham Greene." RP, LVII:307 (July), pp. 59-68. Suggests that part of Greene's popularity is due to his description of a world "qui s'accord au notre"--a loveless universe characterized by the absence of Christ and the prevalence of sin, a veritable "kingdom of Satan" that necessitates a violence analogous to the Elizabethans' for its expression. Written from a Catholic viewpoint and emphasizing Greene's universe with little or no literary evaluation. The Confidential Agent, A Gun for Sale, Brighton Rock and The Heart of the Matter.

A5014 Howes, Jane. "Out of the Pit." CW, CLXXI (April), pp. 36-40. Even though she raises the controversial issue of Scobie's fate, the writer seems to be more concerned with the moral consequences of The Heart of the Matter, and her understanding and experience of Grace and God's mercy in her own conversion than the actual novel which, in her opinion, "has failed, because its readers have failed" to understand God's Grace through it.

A5015 Jouve, Père and Marcel Moré. "Propos de table avec Graham Greene." Dieu Vivant, 16, pp. 127-37. Transcript of a luncheon conversation on 20 December 1949 in which Greene briefly explains his preoccupation with sin, debt to Newman, favorite authors, the plight of humanity, interest in the depths into which the "hunted" man can fall, his choice of the "thriller" and his method of creating character. Also refers to Scobie's first error and his pity though, at times, the interviewers seem to be more interested in expressing opinion than in prodding Greene to talk.

A5016 Kemp, Robert. "Nobis peccatoribus." NL, (20 April). A short general appraisal of Greene for interested French readers. Highlights the various themes of the novels translated into French--England Made Me, Brighton Rock, The Lawless Roads, The Power and the Glory and The Heart of the Matter--and gives "quelques vues" of their main characters.

A5017 Marion, Denis. "Graham Greene." TR, (Feb.), pp. 173-79. A simple and lucid assessment of Greene that attributes his success as a novelist, not to his style and technique, but to his vision of life as a veritable hell on earth where man is confined to "une solitude affreuse et désésperée." Brighton Rock, England Made Me, The Power and the Glory and The Heart of the Matter.

A5018 Marshall, Bruce. "Graham Greene and Evelyn Waugh." Commonweal, LI (3 March), pp. 551-53. Regards Greene as the chronicler of the "grimness of grimness without Grace," and commends both for their knowledge of what goes on in "the hearts of human beings." However, a statement like "Graham Greene and Evelyn Waugh make me want to be holy" indicates some undue concern for the "message" of the novels and unease, from a strictly Catholic viewpoint, with Greene's portrayal of "the ugliness of a world which no longer even knows what it has fallen from."

A5019 Moré, Marcel. "A Propos de Newman." Dieu Vivant, 15, pp. 65-81. A review article of French writings on Newman with brief references to Greene's novels and his interest in theology. Also questions whether "la structure religieuse de Newman ne serait-elle pas de même nature que celle des protagonistes de Graham Greene."

A5020 ________. "Les deux holocaustes de Scobie." Dieu Vivant, 16, pp. 77-105. Rpt. in trans. as "The Two Holocausts of Scobie." Crosscurrents, 2 (1951), pp. 44-63, and in Cross Currents of Psychiatry and Catholic Morality. Ed. William Birmingham and Joseph E. Cunneen. Pref. Francis J. Braceland. New York: Pantheon Books, 1964, pp. 274-99. A detailed and literate study, from a Catholic viewpoint, of the phases of progression in the soul of Scobie as he offers himself as a "holocaust for his brothers." Adopts the view that Scobie, to all appearances damned and "crushed by the fatality of sin," is lifted by the "mysterious stream of the Communion of the Saints" to "respond freely to the call" of God. Maintains that Scobie's act of love at the moment of death is but a "marvelous flower secretly budding on the thorny bush of his sacrifice."

A5021 ________, and Père Jouve. "Propos de table avec Graham Greene." Dieu Vivant, 16, pp. 127-37. See A5015.

A5022 Osterman, Robert. "Interview with Graham Greene." CW, CLXX (Feb.), pp. 356-61. Personal impressions of an evening spent with Greene. Of some interest is Greene's statement on the novelist's material and moral theology.

A5023 Pierhal, Armand. "Romancier ou théologien?" NL, (16 March), p. 1. Reviews French criticism of Greene's "oeuvre" which, he believes, "n'est pas déprimante, mais tonique," in spite of its Christian pessimism.

A5024 Pritchett, V. S. "Books in General." NSta, XXXIX (25 March), p. 344. Reviews a new edition of Oliver Twist. London: Hamish Hamilton, 1950, with a Preface by Graham Greene. Focusses on Greene's statement in the Preface that "the world of Dickens is a world without God."

A5025 Rodriguez-Monegal, Emir. "'El Reves de la Trama' o la Mascara del Realismo." Sur, 183 (Jan.), pp. 57-60. This account of The Heart of the Matter emphasizes Greene's variation on the hunter-victim pattern of earlier novels by focussing on Scobie as a man "corralled by his own self."

A5026 Rousseaux, André. "Le Problème de Graham Greene." FigL, (4 Feb.), p. 2. Regards The Heart of the Matter as the most complete expression of Greene's thought which, he thinks, perceives an incompatibility between the life of man and God because man's charity functions "in reverse," and with such vigor "qu'elle organise parfaitement la damnation." Also gives a brief but interesting account of the polarity in thought between Péguy and Greene.

A5027 Roy, Jean-H. "L'oeuvre de Graham Greene ou un Christianisme de la damnation." TM, V (Feb.), pp. 1513-19. Refutes Paul Rostenne's view of woman's "mission métaphysique" and her "vocation redemptrice" in Greene's novels, and contends that Greene's principal character is man who carries within him the "curse" of his Christianity; hence, the "orientation systematique de la religion vers la damnation" in Brighton Rock and subsequent novels. Interprets the absence of external signs of happiness and joy in religion in the novels as the "misère de l'homme avec Dieu, qui appelle en sourdine: grandeur de l'homme sans Dieu."

A5028 Vann, Gerald, OP. "The Sinner Who Looks Like a Saint." Blackfriars, XXXI, pp. 541-46. An explanation, from a Catholic viewpoint, of Péguy's words "le pécheur est au coeur même de la chrétienté." Though it makes only passing reference to Greene, this article speaks indirectly to Scobie's actions and to the controversial issue of his damnation or salvation.

A5029 Viatte, Auguste. "Graham Greene, Romancier de la grâce." RUL, IV:8 (April), 753-58. Describes Greene as a "romancier à idées: non romancier à thèse" in the tradition of Claudel, Mauriac and Bernanos in his exploration of the divine and sacramental sources of Grace in The Power and the Glory and The Heart of the Matter. Although the "tableaux exacts" of these two novels are seized upon as distinct features, there is no reference made to Greene's art and technique.

A5030 Weightman, J. G. "Soft Centres." NC, (Nov.), pp. 331-38. A review that disqualifies five novels by E. Waugh, A. Huxley, S. Maugham and C. P. Snow from the category of "serious literature" because of their "central softness, resulting from a lack of fundamental integrity and coherence" in the treatment of saintliness when contrasted with Greene's in The Power and the Glory.

A5031 Unsigned. "Die menschliche Armseligkeit und die Heiligkeit." OC, 9 (Sept.), pp. 564-68. An analysis of two documents on Greene: the first by a young prisoner and printed for the reader and the second by a Jesuit priest, Louis Beirnaert. The two documents present opposing views and the article questions which is more profound and closer to a Christian understanding of the novels.

R501 Cournos, John. "The Third Man." Commonweal, LII:7 (26 May), p. 182. A short review of the script in book form. Finds it "disappointing" because a screen play makes demands that are different to those made by legitimate fiction.

R502 Dinnage, Paul. "Two Entertainments." Spectator, 6371 (4 Aug.), p. 158. Admits the difficulty of evaluating The Third Man as a literary work because it is well-nigh impossible to dispell the noises and visual images the film has left. But the atmosphere, the irony of situation and the setting are perfectly suited to the "tragi-comic obstacle-chase" plot with its "curt and antiseptic prose."

R503 Doyle, E. D. "The Third Man." SFC, (23 July), p. 20. A short review indicating a preference for the screen version.

R504 Igoe, W. J. "Graham Greene's Bad Men." CH, (17 Nov.), p. 6. A substantial review of The Third Man comparing Harry Lime to Pinkie to show that Greene, as an artist, had the vision of a "poetic theologian who is a man of his times," especially when he exposes the "deeper evil, the masked despair, sublimated into cynicism ... that is the rot in the Christian and unshriven West."

R505 Lambert, Gavin. "Story Into Film." NSta, XL:1019 (16 Sept.), pp. 280 & 282. The Third Man is "more illuminating of Mr. Reed than Mr. Greene." The writing is "no more than a seviceable fabric to hold together strands of a fairly ordinary melodrama" and the characters lack depth. On the other hand, The Fallen Idol acquires the extra dimension by introducing "a Catholic formula" into the fiction. Comments briefly on the differences between the film version and the original story.

R506 Sandoe, James. "The Third Man Appears in Two Forms." CSBW, (7 April), p. 6. A short review describing the "slight but effective" novel as "less thriller than tale of detection."

R507 W., B. "Recent Fiction." IT, (15 July), p. 6. Compares the printed version of The Third Man with the film. Though the story is a "sketch-plan," it is full of "shrewd observation and dry wit," creates a notable climate of despair, has great "subtlety" and a "responsive sense of values."

R508 Unsigned. "The Third Man and The Fallen Idol." Blackfriars, XXXI:366 (Sept.), p. 455. Brief note on the publication of the book after its widespread popularity on the screen.

R509 ________. "The Third Man." Booklist, XLVI (1 June), p. 304. Book merely mentioned under the category of "Mystery and Detective Stories."

R5010 ________. "The Third Man." Bookmark, IX:8 (May), p. 186. Brief notice of the "suspenseful thriller" and reference to the condensed version that had appeared in The American Magazine.

R5011 ________. "The Third Man." Kirkus, (1 April), pp. 218-19. Short note on the forthcoming publication in book form pointing out Greene's mastery of the medium.

R5012 ________. "The Third Man." NY, XXVI (8 April), p. 119. Briefly noted.

R5013 _______. "Mystery and Adventure: The Third Man." NYHTBR, (21 May), p. 19. The last of four books reviewed. The book form lacks the "visual quality" of the screen version, as well as the "introspective quality" of the novels. In other words, it is "neither fish nor fowl."

R5014 _______. "The Third Man and The Fallen Idol." TLS, 2531 (4 Aug.), p. 481. Shows how the "creative mind goes to work on film" but notes, that though The Third Man is written to be seen, the "cinematic" element is "austerely" avoided and the camera "notably absent." Regrets, however, the sacrifice of the "subtlety of atmosphere and characterisation" that gave value to "The Basement Room" in converting it into film.

D501 Cardinale, Vincent G. Graham Greene's Conception of Evil. M.A., Boston College.

D502 Lohf, Kenneth. Novelist of a Degenerate World. M.A., Columbia Univ.

1951

B511 Allott, Kenneth, and Miriam Farris. The Art of Graham Greene. London: Hamish Hamilton; New York: Russell and Russell, 1963. As the first English book-length study of Greene, the volume attempts an evaluation of the novels and entertainments after making inquiries of Greene. The evaluation is clinical in its account of each work, up to and including The Heart of the Matter, and is distinguished by the writers' earnest belief in the importance of Greene as a novelist whose works demand the "poetic" attention of the reader if they are to be fully appreciated. The detailed analysis of plots tends, at times, to read as plot summaries but the accounts of Greene's use of imagery and the development of his skill and technique are revealing and penetrating. On the whole, the volume plays down the importance of Greene's Catholicism.

The study is divided into five chapters. The first, an Introduction, urges that the themes, obsessions or ruling ideas in Greene are related to a "key obsession or ground of obsessions defined as a 'terror of life.'" Ch. 2 isolates the first three works, partly because Greene has described them as Juvenilia and partly owing to the sameness that underlies all three: in theme, in lack of complication in the plots, in setting, in the romantic sensibility and in the influence of Stevenson and Conrad. Ch. 3 identifies the growing influence of Conrad and James, but shows that the "terror of life" is not projected through a central character but is spread out to create a picture of a fallen world in Stamboul Train, It's a Battlefield and England Made Me. Ch. 4 attempts to establish the connection between Greene's fiction and discusses the early symbols of evil, violence, melodrama, the speed of narrative and style in A Gun for Sale, Brighton Rock and The Confidential Agent. Ch. 5 discusses the "affliction" of pity--"an essentially adult virtue and vice"--which forms the essential paradox underlying The Power and the Glory, The Ministry of Fear and The Heart of the Matter, as well as the adoption of a single character as a vehicle for the "terror of life."

B512 Collins, A[rthur] S[ymons]. "Graham Greene and Elizabeth Bowen." English Literature of the Twentieth Century. London: Univ. Tutorial Press. 4th ed. with a Postscript on the Nineteen-Fifties by Frank Whitehead. London: Univ. Tutorial Press, 1960, pp. 247-62. A survey of Greene's achievement as a novelist from The Man Within to The Heart of the Matter, excluding the "entertainments." Considers Greene to have first shown his "full possibilities" in England Made Me, emphasizes his "detachment as a narrator" presenting life in terms of the faith of the Catholic Church, in terms of heaven and hell, "in the main objectively through the minds of his characters, yet with some restrained personal commentary" in Brighton Rock, The Power and the Glory and The Heart of the Matter. Postscript refers briefly to Greene on p. 371.

B513 Dellevaux, Abbé Raymond. Graham Greene et 'Le Fond du problème'. Brussels: Editions La Lecture au Foyer. Lecture delivered at Brussels to the Cercle Academique St. Capistran, 15 Nov. 1951. A detailed analysis of The Heart of the Matter that brings out the doctrinal bases on which the novel rests. Faults Greene for having traced "une image incomplète de la Redemption."

B514 Mauriac, François. "Graham Greene." Men I Hold Great. New York: Philosophical Library, pp. 124-28. See A4818.

B515 Newby, P[ercy] H. The Novel, 1945-1950. The British Council Series. London: Longmans, Green. Rpt. The Folcroft Press, 1970. The 41-page booklet surveys the impact of World War II on the novel. Pages 33-34 attempt to place Greene in a literary perspective and suggest that his first class storytelling, his reaction to the subtle and complex writing of V. Woolf and J. Joyce which coincided with the swinging of the pendulum away from the sophisticated and literary, have enabled Greene to "please the ordinary reader as well as the intellectual."

B516 O'Malley, Frank. "The Renascence of the Novelist and the Poet." The Catholic Renascence. Ed. Norman Thomas Weyand, SJ. Chicago: Loyola Univ. Press, pp. 25-88. Surveys in the second part of the essay, "The Catholic

Novelist: The Tangled Web," pp. 45-63, the insights of L. Bloy, G. Bernanos, F. Mauriac, G. Greene and S. Undset into the condition of man, evil, sin and suffering. Pages 56-58 consider briefly Greene's preoccupation with the relationship man can establish with God, human frustration and evil. Brief references to Brighton Rock, The Power and the Glory and The Heart of the Matter.

B517 Rischik, Josef. Graham Greene und sein Werk. Schweizer Anglistiche Arbeiten. Bern: Verlag A. Francke Ag. An analytical study of Greene's works up to and including The Third Man. Emphasizes the literary aspects of Greene's works and considers his relation to the times. Plays down the religious dimension which both P. Rostenne and J. Madaule had dealt with. Ch. 1 discusses the writer and his times--youth and conversion--and compares Greene's thrillers with the classic "kriminal-romans." Ch. 2 gives a chronological sketch of Greene's works. Notes that England Made Me marks the high point of his first period and points out that the "seediness" of the novels of that period coincides with Europe's economic and intellectual crisis, whereas the theme of good and evil is only fully developed in The Power and the Glory. Ch. 3 discusses Greene's concern and sympathy with those individuals who are either morally or physically weak, or both, but who stand against a stronger collectivity; hence, the loneliness and isolation which are the hallmarks of his heroes. Ch. 4 focusses on social awareness and relationships in the novels and propounds the view that Greene is emotionally committed to revolution but intellectually committed to tradition. Also notes his higher valuation of loyalty based on individual ties rather than to state or party, as well as his attitude to Jews. Ch. 5 examines the influence of his experience as journalist on his style, and notes that the concept of passing time seems especially difficult in Greene. Ch. 6, "The Literary Background and Outlook," examines "influences" on Greene: Conrad, James, Ford, American and Russian writers, and makes a sketchy comparison with his contemporaries.

A511 Allen, Walter. "English Fiction: 1941-1950." BBN, (May), pp. 323-39. A general review that makes brief mention of The Ministry of Fear and The Heart of the Matter among some ninety novels.

A512 A[rnold], G. L. "Adam's Tree." TCLon, CLIV (Oct.), pp. 337-42. Rpt. in Collected Essays. New York: Viking, 1973, pp. 477-82. An informative discussion of The End of the Affair that recognizes its "serio-comic writing" and its power to provoke serious reflection from the duel of opposing principles personified by Sarah and Maurice, and their respective accounts of their love affair. Interprets Sarah's "horror" of the Cross and Maurice's simultaneous acceptance of God's existence and rejection of His law at the end as an indication that the burden of the Cross has become too heavy.

A513 Bedoyère, Michael de la. "From My Window in Fleet Street." CW, CXXIV (Oct.), pp. 56-61. A discussion of Greene's preoccupation with, and treatment of, the many "layers" of motivation, i.e., what makes men behave as they do, as well as his imaginative construction of, from a Catholic viewpoint, and insight into, the mystery of God's relationship with the sinner in The Power and the Glory, Brighton Rock, The Heart of the Matter and The End of the Affair. The "regret" voiced over Greene's "insistent realism" betrays an overriding concern for the Catholicity of Greene's views as a novelist rather than for his art.

A514 Beirnaert, Louis. "'La Fin d'une liaison' par Graham Greene." Etudes, CCLXXII:14 (March), 369-78. A study of Sarah's conversion from a purely doctrinal Catholic viewpoint. Maintains that the conversion is incomplete for it fails "à s'inscrire jusque dans le psychisme" of Sarah and to transform her sufficiently to renew her heart. Points out that Greene's psychological and theological error lay in making Sarah's belief not only an act beyond nature but also contrary to it; hence, the conflict between flesh and spirit, the "situation sans issue," where a solution is only possible through death.

A515 Bertram, Anthony. "The Stirrup and the Ground: Graham Greene's Optimism." Tablet, (26 May), pp. 417-18. Contends, on the occasion of the publication of The Art of Graham Greene (see B511), that Greene is a "creative novelist" who raises "contentious theological and moral issues," and who goes in a "rare direction" by exploring "the lowest depths without pessimism" through characters that are "symbols of man, of the cracked bell," but whose redeeming features are often a summons or call for prayer.

A516 Bertrand, Théophile. "La Culture par la lecture: XV -Deux 'gloires' symptomatiques." Nos Cours, XXII:15 (20 Jan.), pp. 3-4. A non-literary brief "analysis" of the work of Mauriac and Greene deploring, from a narrow Catholic viewpoint, the weakness of their theological views which have turned the "Catholic novel" into a "hybridation de valeurs catholiques et tendances funéstes." Condemns The Power and the Glory for the "self evident flagrant errors" of the Whiskey Priest's theological views and the illusions he believes, and for Greene's "leftist" but deforming social vision and his exploitation of the mystery of God's mercy.

A517 Braybrooke, Neville. "Graham Greene as Critic." Commonweal, LIV (6 July), pp. 512-14. Also in NAd, XXVIII (4th Quarter 1951), pp. 425-30, and in IM, LXXXI (Oct. 1953), pp. 383-88. This assessment of Greene as a critic maintains that his literary criticism is a "defense of the characters of his own creation," throws light on his craftsmanship, and is distinguished by courage and a "Websterian quality" of "slickness and cruelty."

A518 Burns, Wayne. "The Novelist as Revolutionary." ArQ, VII, pp. 13-27. Mostly concerned with the divergent claims of fictional art and ideology. Maintains on pp. 21-22 that Greene realizes his artistic potential only insofar as he has been disloyal to the Church.

A519 Caillet, Gerard. "Un roman n'est pas une histoire." FrI, 7 (17 March), p. 291. On Greene's refusal to sanction the French adaptation of The Power and the Glory for the Athénée. Also points out that the novel is not only a story but also a vision whose adaptation risks "d'être victime du préjugé cinématographique."

A5110 Capel, Roger. "Letter from England." BT, X (5 June), p. 27. Includes a few brief remarks on the importance of The Lost Childhood and Other Essays in revealing Greene's mind.

A5111 Cayrol, Jean. "Autour de l'oeuvre de Graham Greene." RPF, X (April), pp. 69-72. An examination of Brighton Rock as Greene's masterpiece, especially its treatment of evil in a universe reminiscent of the Old Testament, and particularly the Psalms, where God is "absent but not forgotten." Remarks on the similarity between E. A. Poe's William Wilson and Greene's Pinkie even though the former is a sinner by choice and the latter by necessity.

A5112 Crubellier, Maurice. "Graham Greene: La Tragédie de la pitié." VI, 12 (Dec.), pp. 57-78. A detailed study of pity and the pattern it takes in the novels from a Catholic viewpoint. Traces, after summarily defining pity in the novels as "charity without hope," the degeneration of charity into pity in Scobie and his paler forerunner, Rowe, examines Ida's "bloodless" and "moribund" pity born of social norms, and shows that the return of pity to charity begins with Rose, is forcefully affirmed by the Whiskey Priest, and culminates with Sarah whose awakening to "true love" and Grace is inverse to Scobie's despair and death.

A5113 Downing, Francis. "The Art of Fiction." Commonweal, LV (28 Dec.), pp. 297-98. A discussion of Henry James's revival that contains several references to Greene and to The End of the Affair as an "astonishingly effective and profoundly moving and persuasive novel."

A5114 Engelborghs, Maurits. "Kroniek der engelse letteren: Hoogtepunten in het werk van Graham Greene." DWB, (June), pp. 564-66. Highlights the different values and truths, especially the "mystery of love," that underlie Brighton Rock, The Power and the Glory and The Heart of the Matter.

A5115 Escarpit, Robert. "L'arrière-plan Mexicain dans Lawrence et Greene." LanM, XLV, pp. 44-64. A useful outline for undergraduates, in point form, comparing the two writers' experiences in Mexico, attitudes of distrust in the face of the exotic, reactions to external nature, choice of characters and religion. Concludes that Mexico is not just a mere canvas but a necessary background without which the dramas of The Plumed Serpent and The Power and the Glory would lose their significance.

A5116 Gardiner, Harold C. "Second Thoughts on Greene's Latest." America, (15 Dec.), pp. 312-13. Revises his early verdict on The End of the Affair (see R5111) as a "controversial" novel whose language is a "stumbling block even ... to a mature reader," and whose novelistic problem of telling a "profound spiritual truth ... in terms of stark realism" remains unsolved. Maintains that the "weakness" of the book lies in the introduction of "miracles." Discusses reviews of the novel by R. Hughes, M. Turnell and A. West. See R5113 and A5133.

A5117 Hartsdale, Mary Evangeline. Letter. CW, CLXXIV (Dec.), iv. Repudiates the "tortuous vindication of adultery" in The End of the Affair in a letter to the Editor.

A5118 Horst, Karl August. "Argernis der Schoptung, zur Theologie Graham Greene." Merkur, V (Feb.), pp. 184-87. Examines the controversy over Greene's theological views aroused by an epilogue to the German translation of The Heart of the Matter.

A5119 Jameson, Storm. "British Literature: Survey and Critique." SatR, XXXIV (13 Oct.), pp. 24-26, 47. An interesting and perceptive survey that "places" Greene among his contemporaries. Describes Greene as an "established" novelist, attentive to "form," a "first-class teller of stories" whose men and women "examine their hearts in the course of living lives often of violent action," but concedes that Greene's "ironic sense of man's littleness" holds him back from greatness. Brief reference to form in The Heart of the Matter.

A5120 Lohf, Kenneth A. "Graham Greene and the Problem of

Evil." CW, CLXXIII (June), pp. 196-99. An examination, for the general reader, of the notion that though Greene is preoccupied with evil--evil is the "very basis of human nature," pervasive, engendering a "near-hatred of life" in the characters and is the underlying theme of the novels--he is also concerned in his novels with "salvation from evil and the divine grace which makes that possible."

A5121 Magny, Claude-Edmonde. "De Benito Cereno au Rocher de Brighton." GduL, XVI (July), pp. 150-53. Rpt. from Poésie, XLVI:32 (May 1946), pp. 32-37, with one or two minor word changes. See A465.

A5122 Meath, Gerard, OP. "Catholic Writing." Blackfriars, XXXII:381 (Dec.), pp. 602-09. Discusses E. Waugh's statement that the business of the novelist is "to portray man against a background of eternal values," and contends that there is no conflict between poetic and moral truth. Brief references to Greene and The Heart of the Matter which is described as a "decline" from The Power and the Glory.

A5123 Moré, Marcel. "The Two Holocausts of Scobie." Cross-currents, II, pp. 44-63. Trans. Erwin W. Geissman. Rpt. from Dieu Vivant, 16 (1950), pp. 77-105. See A5020.

A5124 Pritchett, V. S. "A Literary Letter from London." NYTBR, (4 Nov.), pp. 55-57. Discusses in the first part of the "letter" the kind of critic the imaginative writer is. Describes Greene as an "introvert" critic who writes about literature from his point of view "not with any deference to the body of literature," and whose criticism may be of value, not so much for "interpreting" the subject but for revealing himself.

A5125 Remords, G. "Graham Greene: Notes Biographiques et Bibliographiques." BFL, XXIX (May-June), pp. 393-99. Includes a biographical note, brief annotations to the works which are chronologically arranged and a short checklist of criticism in English. Notes the absence of a book-length critical work in English, in spite of the warm praise lavished on Greene by critics and writers. Also lists French translations of the works.

A5126 Sackville-West, Edward. "The Electric Hare: Some Aspects of Graham Greene." Month, VI (Sept.), pp. 141-47. A review article on Greene's The Lost Childhood and Other Essays and The Art of Graham Greene (see B511). Discusses Greene as a critic, his belief in the centrality of Original Sin in human life and his elusiveness--he is "the electric hare whom racing dogs are not meant to catch."

A5127 Sheppard, Lancelot. "Graham Greene." BT, (Nov.), pp. 100-02, 134. General comments on Greene's ability to make a "moral and even a theological issue real to people," his "obsession" with the absurdity and uselessness of evil rather than its malignity, the tenuousness of his plots, and the credibility of his characters and the world of his novels. Covers large areas of Greene but without much depth.

A5128 Silva Delgado, Adolfo. "La Carrera Literaria de Graham Greene." Marcha, XIII (23 Nov.), pp. 14-15, 71. A general review of Greene's literary career: novel writing, travels and other activities as film critic.

A5129 Traversi, Derek. "Graham Greene: I. The Earlier Novels." TCLon, CXLIX:889 (March), pp. 231-40. Rpt. Graham Greene: A Collection of Critical Essays. Ed. Samuel Hynes. Englewood Cliffs, N.J.: Prentice-Hall, 1973, pp. 17-30. Examines Greene's preoccupations through a study of his characters' resentment against life--their hatred of normal human activities and frustrations connected with childhood experience--which they are inclined to substitute for positive religious values. Underlying this detailed study of England Made Me and Brighton Rock is the view that the religious values Greene imposes on his characters are merely a "projection of accidental and eccentric personal qualities"; hence, the conclusion that the "theological framework" of Brighton Rock is "founded upon ambiguity and is ... in the last analysis, unreal."

A5130 ________. "Graham Greene: II. The Later Novels." TCLon, CXLIX:890 (April), pp. 318-28. A sequel to the previous article examining the literary consequences of Greene's Catholicism, i.e., the "problem of the relationship in a work of art between subjective experience and objective belief," in The Power and the Glory and The Heart of the Matter. Regards the first novel as a "partial success," and the second as a "sentimental exploitation of religious motives." Though the conclusions reached may be controversial, the two articles are valuable in that they address themselves to the novelistic aspects of Greene's use of Catholicism.

A5131 Turnell, Martin. "The Religious Novel." Commonweal, LV (26 Oct.), pp. 55-57. A literary evaluation of the effect of the religious element on the sensibility of four Catholic writers: F. Mauriac, G. Bernanos, E. Waugh, and G. Greene, and the need for a "balance" between believer and novelist. Critical of Greene's use of "muddled theology" in his desire to create an "entirely spurious frisson" in The Heart of the Matter, and especially the "discrepancy between the private feelings that he releases and the crudity of his symbols." Considers The Power and the Glory as "most successful" because Greene has found in the Whiskey Priest a perfect "objective-correlative."

A5132 Voorhees, Richard J. "The World of Graham Greene." SAQL (July), 389-98. An introduction, for the undergraduate, to "Greeneland" and its inhabitants in A Gun for Sale, Brighton Rock, The Ministry of Fear and The Heart of the Matter. Maintains that though the "sense of universal evil" has become a "corollary of self-consciousness" in his characters, Greene is no Dostoevsky because of the total absence of "gaiety" and "wholesome love" in his world. Contends that Scobie fails to make plausible the paradox that the sinner is at the heart of Christianity, and that the introduction of ecclesiastical imagery in incongruous situations is ludicrous.

A5133 West, Anthony. "Saint's Progress." NY, XXVII (10 Nov.), pp. 141-42, 144. Rpt. as "Graham Greene." Principles and Persuasions: The Literary Essays of Anthony West. New York: Harcourt Brace, 1957, pp. 195-200; London: Eyre & Spottiswoode, 1958, pp. 174-78. A review article on The End of the Affair which describes the novel as a "faultless display of craftsmanship and a wonderfully assured statement of ideas," and shows Greene's "complete control of content and technique." Argues that his three earlier Catholic novels may have been redolent with unorthodox Catholicism and may have revealed his remarkable creative power in inventing situations where the Church may condemn and sinners are left with a certain knowledge of damnation, but in The End of the Affair the emphasis is placed on the redemption and the earlier negative aspects are discarded for the "reality of mystical experience." Maintains that those who cannot subscribe to Greene's views in the novel will find in it "rich aesthetic satisfaction."

A5134 White, Antonia. "Two Catholic Authors: A Comparison." Apostle, (Sept.), pp. 15-16. Besides pointing out that both Greene and Waugh are converts to Catholicism and that they belong to the inter-war generation, the comparison, given from a Catholic viewpoint, stresses their differences in politics, in their attitudes to the Church and to Catholicism, and in their careers as writers.

A5135 Unsigned. "A Bibliography of Graham Greene." Marginalia, II (April), pp. 16-19. A descriptive bibliography of Greene's works published in book form including children's books and literary criticism from The Man Within (1929) to The Lost Childhood and Other Essays (1951). Includes English and American publishers and titles.

A5136 _______. "Shocker." Time, LVIII (29 Oct.), pp. 62-67. A review of well known facts about Greene's life and work on the occasion of the publication of The End of the Affair in the U.S.

R511 Alpert, Ursula K. "The End of the Affair." SpR, (11 Nov), p. 30A. Brief note remarking on Greene's concern with all that may enter into the end of an affair between a man and a woman "rather than the physical aspects of love."

R512 B., P. "Sheep and Goats." Guardian, (20 April), p. 4. A short review of The Lost Childhood expressing the belief that though the essays are "not always good-tempered"-- Greene's "prosecution" of Samuel Butler is "most unfair"-- they are "consistently spirited and provocative."

R513 Bertram, Anthony. "The Personal Vision." Tablet, CXCVII (7 April), pp. 270-71. Commends The Lost Childhood and Other Essays not only because Greene is a good critic but also for the "intensity and the integrity" of his vision which can so shape a "miscellaneous collection of papers that ... it can turn our minds to Dante."

R514 _______. "Books of the Week: Another Part of the Wood." Tablet, CXCVIII (8 Sept.), p. 156. A perceptive review of The End of the Affair that notes Greene's abandonment of the familiar settings and properties that had hitherto served him well in giving "colour and tension to his spiritual pattern," and questions whether this spiritual pattern if left alone as in this novel, can "wholly succeed as work of art or do we suspect too much contrivance for a prearranged spiritual end?" Wonders whether Greene can give the form of the novel the "scale and elasticity which Dante needed" to accommodate the Main Protagonist.

R515 Betjeman, John. "New Fiction: Mr. Graham Greene." DaiT, (7 Sept.), p. 6. Maintains that the "shockingness" of The End of the Affair is "of the spirit" and that Greene is compelling the reader to consider man's most intimate thoughts in this his "finest book" even while not describing in any detail the activities of his three chief characters.

R516 Bogan, Louise. "Good Beyond Evil." NRep, CXXV (10 Dec.), pp. 29-30. Unlike his earlier works that combine the patterns of the novel of suspense with the religious drama of salvation and redemption, The End of the Affair "undertakes to explain sainthood." The first part of the novel is done with "consummate skill" but the second part is marred by pulling his "supernatural events down to the rather childish level of the relic and the message from the grave." Notes, however, Greene's success in adding "moral dimensions" to the English novel.

R517 Carter, Rev. G. Emmett. "Greene's Latest Novel is Written for Sinners." Ensign, III:51 (13 Oct.), p. 14. Describes The End of the Affair as "terrible" in the sense that it touches one deeply for it deals with needs, aspirations and fears that are common to man. Grace is central to this love story as it "moves inexorably to the end" and describes the throb of human hearts and the progress from "imagined hate to realized love."

R518 E[vans], I[lltud], OP. "The Lost Childhood and Other Essays." Blackfriars, XXXII:374 (May), pp. 244-45. A short review that considers the "critical notices" as a "valuable postscript" to Greene's preoccupation as a novelist.

R519 ________. "The End of the Affair." Blackfriars, XXXII:379 (Oct.), pp. 497-99. Voices concern with the moral issue, especially where Greene's perceptions are "disturbingly exact," and wonders whether Greene in the novel is not invading a territory which belongs to God only.

R5110 Fremantle, Anne. "In Pursuit of Peace." SatR, XXXIV (27 Oct.), pp. 11-12. The End of the Affair is Greene's most "brilliantly written" novel that combines many twentieth century techniques to present his two major themes: the hunted man and the peace he is pursuing. It recalls in its "minute neatness, its exquisitely tidy, fugal counterpoint," Stendhal rather than Melville or Dostoevsky. Maintains that Greene emphasizes the "strangeness of woman's unique position" in this and other novels.

R5111 Gardiner, Harold C., SJ. "Mr. Greene Does It Again." America, LXXXVI (27 Oct.), pp. 100-01. Rpt. in his In All Conscience: Reflections on Books and Culture. New York: Hanover House, 1959, pp. 96-99. Finds The End of the Affair objectionable because the terms in which the truth is couched are unacceptable "on grounds of propriety"--the language is a "stumbling block" even to a mature reader. Maintains that a "different narrative device" could have averted the problem in this controversial novel. See A5116.

R5112 Holland, Rev. J. P. "Not Quite the End." CG, (Oct.), pp. 190-91. Strikes a different note from other enthusiastic reviews of The End of the Affair by emphasizing the "improbable" and unconvincing in the character of Sarah, her diary, the reflections of Bendrix and the "brilliant caricatures" of minor characters, and refuses to recommend the novel to Catholic readers.

R5113 Hughes, Riley. "The End of the Affair." Best Sellers, (15 Nov.), pp. 154-55. Maintains that the novel "cannot be recommended because of Greene's presentation of the pursuit of innocence--described in "cognitive terms"--under the guise of evil with all the "promptings and urgings of orexis." Cautions against Greene's "dangerous romanticism" that finds adulthood and corruption synonymous and explains the two senses of "affair" in the title.

R5114 John, K. "Notes for the Novel-Reader: Fiction of the Week." ILN, (10 Nov.), p. 774. Though The End of the Affair is "serious," it has left the reviewer "cold ... not adverse, not protesting, merely untouched," even though it is a love story. The novel is not dull--"good writing and professional arrangement" make it interesting--but the "people have no substance" and merely work together like any two "leading roles of a morality play."

R5115 McLaughlin, Richard. "I've Been Reading...." TArts, XXXV (Dec.), pp. 34-35, 86. The End of the Affair is the first of four books reviewed. Maintains that "love-hate" is the driving emotion of the novel whose pages burn with "anguish and remorseless candor" of the conflict between the spirit and the flesh. Overlooks the theological aspects.

R5116 Mayberry, George. "Mr. Greene's Intense Art." NYT, (28 Oct.), p. 5. Maintains that Greene, in his "moving first-person account of the warped liaison" between Sarah and Bendrix is attracted by both melodrama and irony and, in his warfare with a faith that alternately attracts and repels him, reveals himself as a philosophical novelist in "the tradition, if not stature, of Dostoevsky and Gide."

R5117 Muir, Edwin. "Love and Hate." Observer, (2 Sept.), p. 7. Maintains that Greene's skill and economy in The End of the Affair have reached a point which he will not surpass, and that he is concerned with the relation between love and hate. Considers Bendrix the "most remarkable figure in Mr. Greene's world."

R5118 ________. "Illumination." Observer, (1 April), p. 7. Though "exceptionally miscellaneous," The Lost Childhood and Other Essays has a unity which is derived from Greene's point of view. The essays and reviews are interesting enough to make one want literary criticism in this vein--and length--for Greene uses the image to do the work of both exposition and criticism at once.

R5119 Nowell-Smith, Simon. "Mr. Greene as Essayist." Spectator, CLXXXV (30 March), p. 420. The essays reveal Greene's "three fold gifts of human understanding, critical assurance and economy of words." Also discusses his treatment of Henry James who is often used as a yardstick but regrets the republication of his earlier strictures on a reviewed author.

R5120 O'Brien, E. D. "Books of the Day: The Lost Childhood." ILN, (21 April), p. 630. Finds the collection a "most interesting introduction to a most interesting character." Though the collection is at once "exasperating and charming" he is critical of the "lack of editing" especially that the essays had been written over a period of twenty years.

R5121 Parsons, Luke. "Graham Greene." FR, CLXXVI (Oct.), pp. 704-05. Argues that The Lost Childhood and Other Essays are "occasional, fragmentary, with a tenuous autobiographical thread connecting them," and agrees with earlier reviews that they help the reader gain a deeper understanding of Greene rather than a fresh appraisal of the writers he selects. Also examines briefly Greene's "limitations," especially the "esoteric, purely Catholic way" he presents moral problems.

R5122 Pitt, Don. "A New Greene Novel on Love vs. Hate." SFC, (21 Oct.), pp. 8 & 14. Like his other three "Catholic" novels, The End of the Affair reveals his "special powers of conciseness, poignancy and narrative strength," so that by the end of the novel, Greene's "oblique assault" on distrust and hate leave one with the sense that they can be "partly resolved--short that is of truly learning to love."

R5123 Prescott, Orville. "Books of the Times." NYT, (26 Oct.), p. 21. Maintains that despite Greene's "flair for words and atmosphere" and the prevailing climate of melancholy irony, The End of the Affair fails because its "central situation is not convincing" and it is "not very interesting," for our interest is not in the characters themselves but what happens to them; the minor characters, however, are interesting. Also finds that three conversions in a novel strain credibility.

R5124 Quennell, Peter. "The Complete Mr. Greene." DaiM, (1 Sept.), p. 2. As one of the most "original" European novelists, Greene has a distinctive quality which can be at times "disconcerting." The End of the Affair focusses on the conflict of passion versus Faith and though "grim" at times--it leaves out of account the gentler human impulses "and the milder more durable forms of human happiness" and the sense of sin works "overtime"--it captures the reader's attention in spite of his occasional resentment. "Dialogue and description are beautifully balanced" and the reality of the situation invades the reader's mind. (The novel is The Daily Mail Book of the Month for September.)

R5125 Rolo, Charles J. "Reader's Choice." Atlantic, CLXXXVIII (Nov.), pp. 88-89. Finds the first half of The End of the Affair--the tale of adultery and obsessive jealousy--almost "flawless" except for Sarah whose "personality is blurred." But the second half which shows a religious awakening "through a pane of rigorous skepticism" is "blatantly stage-managed" so that Greene can put across his theological message.

R5126 Russell, John. "The Enlisted Man." Listener, XLV:1156 (26 April), pp. 673 & 675. Argues that Greene's collection of reviews, prefaces, reportages and fragments of autobiography is "inevitably partial," a creator's criticism whose methods are as "obsessional" as his novels, and that he concentrates on areas of interest which bear upon his work. "He is a prisoner of his allegiances...."

R5127 ________. "New Novels." Listener, XLVI:1176 (13 Sept.), p. 433. Fails to see much merit in a novel written "against life, rather than about it." Though The End of the Affair is constructed with Greene's "habitual skill," it strikes the profane reader, "like most novels by members of the Roman Catholic commando, ... as unreal, insensitive, and too openly schematic to give any impression of the immediacy and unexpectedness of ordinary corrupt human existence."

R5128 Scott, J. D. "Polished Answer." NSta, XLII (8 Sept.), p. 258. Pays a "passing but profound tribute" to Greene's "immense skill, compelling writing, weight of thought and feeling which no contemporary disposes with the same ease." Finds The End of the Affair to have two serious faults: the transitions from the narrative of Bendrix to Sarah's diary to Bendrix are "not well-managed" and Greene's expert showmanship of moral sordidness "suddenly goes bad in the sketch of Mr. Parkis's relationship with his son." As for Greene's status as novelist, his "certainty, rigidity, and narrowness" at once his strength and weakness as a novelist, exclude him from the major figures with whom he invites comparison.

R5129 Shrapnel, Norman. "New Novels." Guardian, (7 Sept.), p. 4. The End of the Affair is a "wonderfully written" novel that substitutes a few miracles for melodrama and does away with violence. Regards the novel as Greene's "most moving" and "most audacious" novel.

R5130 Smith, Janet Adam. "The Cutting Edge." NSta, XLI:1049 (14 April), pp. 428 & 430. As a critic, Greene stalks the man with an obsession, and traces the obsession backwards to the circumstances that caused it and forwards to the works it shapes. His sense of evil "provides the cutting edge and gives unity to pieces written for various occasions," and when it "comes into play," it produces his best criticism in The Lost Childhood and Other Essays. Nevertheless, he is not a "Catholic critic," nor is he a "great critic" for he lacks the "necessary balance and diversity of interest."

R5131 Strong, L. A. G. "Fiction: The End of the Affair." Spectator, (7 Sept.), p. 310. The first of three novels reviewed. Pays tribute to Greene for "facing the full range of human experience" in a novel whose characters are "strongly drawn," the writing "clear and relaxed, the construction superb." Notes Greene's detachment which is made possible by telling the story from the viewpoint of Bendrix.

R5132 Sugrue, Thomas. "A Star-Crossed Love Story." NYHTBR, (28 Oct.), p. 8. Notes the "surface" change of place in The End of the Affair and maintains, after a lengthy summary, that the basic problem Greene was getting at was the "question of spiritual union." Also remarks that Greene's handling of his material "slips a little" when the story spreads into a mystical interpretation of Sarah.

R5133 Sullivan, Richard. "A Woman's Spiritual Move from Adultery to Sanctity." CST, (28 Pct.), p. 4. The End of the Affair, "completely religious in conception," is highly charged with the power of "implication," and its characters are viewed as possessing eternal as well as temporal destinies. Finds the "miracle story" at the end to be its weakest point.

R5134 Trease, Geoffrey. "When Greene Was Young." JO'L, (30 March), p. 179. Finds Greene's comments on juvenile literature in The Lost Childhood and the autobiographical clues interesting, his book reviews varied and his writing excellent, even though his verdicts may be often challenged.

R5135 Valentini, Guiseppe. "Graham Greene: narratore e soggettista." Letture, V, pp. 179-82. In Italian. A review of The Third Man and The Fallen Idol. Trans. Gabriele Baldini. Milan: Bompiani, 1951. Finds The Third Man "spectacular" in the field of classical drama and the two "racconti" on the whole as providing justification for Greene's continued success and views.

R5136 Vallette, Jacque. "Lettre Anglo-saxonnes: La Jeunesse de Graham Greene." MerF, 1058 (Oct.), pp. 326-27. Focusses on "The Lost Childhood" and "The Revolver in the Cupboard" because they help one to understand why Greene's universe is full of insignificance and his faith is tied down to despair.

R5137 W., B. "Recent Novels." IT, (8 Sept.), p. 6. Considers The End of the Affair as a "gloomily reflective novel" where the drama of desperate and "unromantically miserable" characters is described on the psychological and spiritual levels. Though the secondary characters are admirably represented, the novel remains "moderately distinguished" in spite of its being "smoothly and subtly written" and of its attempt to sum up Greene's "interpretation of destiny's plans for her unhappy serfs."

R5138 Walbridge, Earle F. "The End of the Affair." LJ, LXXVI (1 Sept.), p. 1333. Briefly but unfavorably noted as a "fearfully depressing triangle novel."

R5139 Watson, John L. "Clarity of the Abstruse." SatN, LXVII (8 Dec.), p. 73. Maintains that Greene's notion of accepting God not being a "peaceful surrender but a humiliating defeat" may be "abstruse," but his writing is meticulously precise and crystal clear. For all its seriousness of theme, The End of the Affair reads like a "first-class thriller."

R5140 Waugh, Evelyn. "The Heart's Own Reasons." Commonweal, LIV (17 Aug.), pp. 458-59. Rpt. as "The Point of Departure." Month, VI (Sept.), pp. 174-76. Asserts that though only Greene could have written this novel--"his unique personality is apparent on every page"--The End of the Affair differs from earlier works in "method and material," in the use of a narrator and the substitution of the contemporary domestic romantic drama for the thriller. Admires Greene's "defiant assertion" of the supernatural but faults him for being "too emphatically sectarian" and overlooking the impact of the loss of the diary on Sarah.

R5141 Unsigned. "The End of the Affair." Booklist, XLVIII (15 Nov.), p. 101. Briefly noted.

R5142 ________. "The End of the Affair." Kirkus, XIX (1 Sept.), p. 492. Pre-publication notice of the novel as a drama of human love that "cauterizes despair with faith" and continues the "implications" of The Heart of the Matter.

R5143 ________. "The Lost Childhood and Other Essays." Kirkus, XIX (1 Dec.), pp. 694-95. Pre-publication notice describing the collection as a "commentary of personal perception and original insight and subtle stimulus on the passing literary scene," or an "appreciative ... market."

R5144 ________. "Dark Lantern." TLS, 2566 (6 April), p. 208. Maintains that Greene's view of people is that of the "romantic, darkly engaged ... l'aperçu vif et créateur flashing and turning like a dark lantern illustrating with unpredictable brilliance the areas picked out"; but this selectiveness of vision tends to give Greene's judgments "an oblique slant" in The Lost Childhood and Other Essays. However, he preserves his balance when he is in sympathy with his subject which he describes by means of the "blinkered lantern gleams" rather than in detail. His essays are full of wit "imaginatively stimulating, original and excellently written."

R5145 _______. "Painful Sanctity." TLS, 2588 (7 Sept.), p. 561. Concentrates on the religious argument of The End of the Affair which he finds "uninspired and rather humourless," and whose characters are "stock" figures.

D511 Neumann, Sr. Sadie Hedwig. Graham Greene, Master in the Fictional Study of Evil. M.A. Univ. of Ottawa.

D512 Schoebel, Evamaria. Die Bedeutung der Zeit in zwei religioesen Romanen Graham Greene, The Power and the Glory, Elizabeth Langgaesser, Das Unaesloeschliche Siegal. Bonn Univ.

1952

B521 Casnati, Francesco. "Il potere e la gloria." Favole degli uomini d'oggi. Milan: Vita e Pensiero, pp. 194-99. Discusses the martyrdom of the Whiskey Priest and the way in which it pays tribute to the Catholic clergy, in spite of the priest's sin and weakness. Notes in a "postilla" the difference between Greene's unheroic priest and the idealized portrait of the "buoni pastori."

B522 Knaap Peuser, Angelica. "Le Novela de Graham Greene." El Espiritu y la Carne en las Grandes Creaciones Literarias. Buenos Aires: Ediciones Peuser, pp. 161-70. This study concentrates on Brighton Rock, The Power and the Glory and The Heart of the Matter as novels that present a "poco común" argument on the transcendental problems of Grace, Divine Mercy and sin as they portray simultaneously the two planes of existence: the visible and the invisible. Notices the centrality of Péguy's thought in Greene's world and finds interesting the ideas and feelings Greene insinuates rather than those which he voices.

B523 Mauriac, François. "Graham Greene." Great Men. London: Rockliffe, pp. 117-22. See A4818.

B524 "O'Donnel, Donat" [Conor Cruise O'Brien]. "Graham Greene: The Anatomy of Pity." Maria Cross: Imaginative Patterns in a Group of Catholic Writers. New York: Oxford Univ. Press, pp. 63-94; London: Chatto & Windus, 1953. Rpt. under his real name. London: Burns and Oates, 1963, pp. 57-83. An exploration into the meaning of pity in The Heart of the Matter. Contends that both the story and the nature of "pity" in the novel "are obfuscated by the insistence on identifying, for an ambitious paradox, this ruinous 'pity' with the love of God," when, in reality, Scobie's pity is merely a "deep sympathy with childhood, inimical to maturity," and his so called sense of responsibility is "essentially unreliable and irresponsible" for it is not a reasoned acceptance of duties and liability "but the outward form of an emotional craving." Moreover, Scobie's personality is "rigidly unreal, fixed in a plaster of paradox," and the novel as a whole is "marred by sentimentality and moral juggling."

B525 Prescott, Orville. "Comrades of the Coterie: Henry Green, Compton-Burnett, Bowen, Graham Greene." In My Opinion: An Inquiry into the Contemporary Novel. Indianapolis: Bobbs-Merrill, pp. 92-109. Asserts that though Greene is not a "deliberate coterie recruit ... he has at least an associate membership," and maintains that whether he is writing murder and espionage thrillers as The Ministry of Fear or concerned with religious and theological themes like The Heart of the Matter, Greene is "savagely sarcastic" and sometimes "morosely misanthropic" as he explores "sinister" psychological depths caused by fear and guilt.

B526 Zabel, Morton Dauwen. "Graham Greene." Critiques and Essays of Modern Fiction, 1920-1951. Ed. John W. Aldridge. New York: Ronald Press, pp. 518-25. Rpt. from The Nation, CLVII (3 July 1943), pp. 18-20. See A433.

A521 Adams, J. Donald. "Speaking of Books." NYT, (9 March), p. 2. A commentary on, and an illustration of, Greene's statement from "The Lost Childhood" that every writer is a "victim: a man given over to an obsession."

A522 Aldridge, John W. "Manners and Values." PR, XIX (May), 347-48. Though mainly a discussion of social manners as a public manifestation of a value system in the contemporary American novel, the article refers briefly to the notion that guilt in the Greene protagonist is seen "not in terms of society but in terms of (one's) own soul."

A523 Birmingham, William. "Graham Greene Criticism: A Bibliographical study." Thought, XXVII (Spring), 72-100. Surveys the relation between Greene and his critics in some forty selected works. Points out critical tendencies in general appraisals as well as themes of special interest.

A524 Boyle, Alexander. "The Symbolism of Graham Greene." IM, LXXX (March), pp. 98-102. Regards Brighton Rock, The Power and the Glory, The Heart of the Matter and The End of the Affair as dealing "symbolically" with the study of love that progresses from the "negative" in Pinkie to the love of God for the "potentially saint-like soul" of Sarah--a "saintliness that Mr. Greene can understand." Describes the obvious and uses "symbol" and "symbolism" rather loosely and indiscriminately.

A525 Boyle, Raymond M. "Man of Controversy." Grail, XXXV (July), pp. 1-7. A profile of the man and his works on the occasion of the 1952 Catholic Literary Award of the Gallery of Living Authors for The End of the Affair.

A526 Braybrooke, Neville. "Catholics and the Novel." Renascence, V (Autumn), pp. 22-32. Rpt. with minor changes from Blackfriars, (Feb. 1950), pp. 54-64. See A506.

A527 ________. "Graham Greene and the Double Man: An Approach to The End of the Affair." DubR, CCXXVI:455 (1st Quarter), pp. 61-73. Rpt. in TCMel, XXIII (1969), pp. 293-304. In Graham Greene. Ed. Harry J. Cargas. St. Louis, Mo.: B. Herder Book, 1969, pp. 114-30. In QQ, LXXVII (Spring 1970), pp. 29-39. In Arbor, CCCIII (1971), pp. 57-68. A study of Bendrix' dual conception of reality, "of seeing himself as both the subject and the object of his experience," and of himself as both pursuer and pursued. Maintains that in his pursuit of Sarah, Bendrix looks into himself and recognizes, momentarily, his true image in accordance with Greene's canon that pursuit becomes the means of salvation.

A528 Castelli, Alberta. "Scrittori Inglesi Contemporanei de Fronte, al Christianesimo, (Huxley & Greene) II." Humanitas, VII (March), pp. 307-16. Pages 311-16 examine the thriller pattern in Brighton Rock, The Power and the Glory and The Heart of the Matter, and Greene's preoccupation with good and evil, damnation and salvation. This is the second of two articles discussing twentieth-century English writers confronted with Christian issues.

A529 Davis, Robert Gorham. "At the Heart of the Story is Man." NYTBR, (28 Dec.), p. 1. Rpt. in Highlights of Modern Literature: A Permanent Collection of Memorable Essays from 'The New York Times Book Review.' Ed. Francis Brown. New York: The New American Library, pp. 57-62. Compares and contrasts The End of the Affair with Hemingway's The Sun Also Rises in his discussion of the "stable order of values" of writers, especially novelists. Notes that "nothing in the history of the novel gives reason for pessimism about its future, so long as the freedom and responsibility and dignity of the individual remain primary concerns in our society, and so long as writers know that they themselves have power to create values."

A5210 Dinkins, Paul. "Graham Greene: The Incomplete Version." CW, CLXXVI (Nov.), pp. 96-102. Attributes the "critical uneasiness" in the secular press to unpreparedness in coping with Greene's outspoken conviction of reality, i.e., his Catholicism, and to the inability of the religious press to accept "moral impropriety," and the absence of traditional piety. Also comments on Greene's "tragic vision" and attacks him for the absence of "Christian joy" in his writing. Brighton Rock, The Power and the Glory and The End of the Affair.

A5211 Downing, Francis. "Graham Greene and the Case for Disloyalty." Commonweal, LV (14 March), pp. 564-66. Thoughts on Greene's "brief and angered visit" to the U.S. following the initial refusal for entry. Finds à propos Greene's belief in the virtue of "disloyalty," especially his conception of the novelist's duty as a "piece of grit in the state machinery," but condemns Greene's sweeping observation that Los Angeles is under "a reign of terror." References to The Lost Childhood and Why Do I Write?

A5212 Duesberg, Jacques. "Chronique des Lettres anglo-saxonnes: un épigone du 'Misérabilisme': Graham Greene." Synthèse, 69 (Feb.), pp. 348-53. Surveys the pessimism and bewilderment that impregnates Greene's universe in both entertainments and novels where humanity "s'y convulse en proie à l'égarement et à la peur," and where characters, whether victims or sinners, are hunted and doomed to misery. Maintains that in this Greene is merely following the contemporary tradition. Also reviews, in the third section, The End of the Affair which, though a "cruel book and a product of an accomplished art," remains nevertheless, a "minor masterpiece" that has failed to enthuse critics.

A5213 Herzog, Bert. "Bemerkungen zur katholischen Literatur der Gegenwart." SZ, CLI (March), pp. 420-26. General remarks on contemporary Catholic literature in French, German and English. Makes passing reference to Greene's use of the thriller and his mystique of sin.

A5214 ________. "Welt unter geschlossenem Himmel: zu den Buchern von Graham Greene." SZ, CLI (Oct.), pp. 20-25. A personal view of Greene's universe. Rather disenchanted by the sameness of the characters or "cases" in Greene's loveless world in his survey of the works, especially the atmosphere of "practical nihilism" that leaves the reader uncomfortable, and even irritated.

A5215 Immaculate, Sr. Joseph. "The Catholic Novelist as Apostle." CLW, XXIII (May), pp. 247-51. Maintains that novelists like Bloy, Mauriac, Bernanos and Greene have widened the scope of Catholic literature by divesting it from the dogmatic, the pietistic or the apologetic. Brief account of the "paradox" in Greene's novels created by the belief in Grace and charity and his fascination by the "spiritual wasteland of contemporary society."

A5216 Jerrold, Douglas. "Graham Greene, Pleasure-Hater." PicP, LIV (15 March), pp. 51-53. Rpt. Harper's CCV (Aug.), pp. 50-52. A first hand view of Greene as a practical and successful businessman, by choice a "life-hater," and of Greene the novelist with his "recipe for farce inverted," the creator of a "living world of inescapable reality in which everything is true except ... the action of the central figure."

A5217 Kerrigan, William J. "Opposed Modalities: Pitfalls for Catholic Writers." Renascence, V (Autumn), pp. 15-21. Though it makes no reference to Greene, this article is useful for its discussion of four pitfalls which Catholic writers encounter. These are 1) The Catholic view of the supernatural is non-experimental and can play no legitimate part in literature; 2) Failure to distinguish between religion and magic; 3) Inadequacy in the conception of these truths as facts of human existence; and 4) Failure to recognize "the tension between truth and its dramatic embodiment."

A5218 Klein, Luce A. "La première pièce de Graham Greene sera jouée à Paris." Arts, 338 (5 Dec.), p. 3. Argues that in his first play to be produced in Paris by Jean Mercure in 1953, Greene has adapted himself to the conventional form of the play with its unity of place and division into acts. Notes that the rich complexity of the Greenean universe and themes of the novels are expressed in the play but from a more visible Catholic, albeit unorthodox, realistic viewpoint.

A5219 Lees, F. N. "Graham Greene: A Comment." Scrutiny, XIX (Oct.), pp. 31-42. Takes exception to the general acclaim and eulogy with which the "theology-conscious" novels have been received, and in a searching study underlies and illustrates "the crude analysis, the obtrusive and deforming emotionalism, and the defective presentational technique" of The Power and the Glory, The Heart of the Matter and The End of the Affair.

A5220 O'Grady, Emmet. "Graham Greene, écrivain éschatologique." RUO, XXII (April), pp. 156-70. A general introduction for the undergraduate and general reader, from a Catholic perspective, to Greene as a novelist who draws the attention of a pagan world to the existence of death, the last Judgment, heaven and hell; i.e., the spiritual dimension of his novels. Also discusses briefly the influence of the cinema on him, stylistic similarities with Hemingway, and his literary debt to English Catholic writers.

A5221 Phillips, William. "The Pursuit of Good and Evil." AM, LXXIV (May), pp. 102-06. Though meant as a review of

The Lost Childhood and Other Essays, the article examines briefly the "pattern" of the novels--the "drama of pursuit in the moral underworld," crime and punishment and the "tension between good and evil within the characters themselves."

A5222 "A Poor Clare." Letter. America, LXXXVI (19 Jan.), p. 432. An interesting letter from a cloistered nun that finds the "images of evil" in The End of the Affair "not nearly so forceful as Sarah's dogged perseverance in her immense sacrifice."

A5223 Prescott, Orville. "Books of The Times." NYT, (30 July), p. 21. A short review article on the Viking publication in an omnibus volume of A Gun for Sale, The Confidential Agent and The Ministry of Fear--novels of "international intrigue" whose "plots are reinforced by a realistic political background." The preference evinced for these thrillers over the "novels about the psychology of adultery and religion" which, he believes, are "ambiguous and unconvincing in their motivation," is perhaps questionable.

A5224 Roland, Albert. "A Rebirth of Values in Contemporary Fiction." WHR, VI (Winter), pp. 59-69. Examines the different directions that fiction has taken in the forties to find a firm ethical foundation for human behavior. Part 2 of the article discusses briefly one of these directions--the reaffirmation of Catholic spiritual values--in Brighton Rock and The Heart of the Matter among other novels.

A5225 Schmid, Dr. Margarete. "Drei Bucher von Graham Greene." ZeitB, VI:12, pp. 1-2. A review article on England Made Me, The Ministry of Fear and Essais Catholiques--all three recently translated into German, the latter as Vom Paradox des Christentums. Concentrates on the problem of loyalty which the Catholic writer faces.

A5226 Simons, J. W. "Salvation in the Novels." Commonweal, LVI (25 April), pp. 74-76. A Catholic perspective on Greene's obsession with evil, prompted by The Lost Childhood and Other Essays, develops into a brief discussion on Grace and the novel, and Greene's preference for "border cases, the fate seekers, the extremes," rather than the "spiritual 'middle classes.'"

A5227 Valentini, Guiseppe. "Rinascita della casuistica." Letture, VII, pp. 135-37. In Italian. Comments on the debate raging over the "delicate" but "unresolved" theological and dogmatic question central to The Heart of the Matter. Trans. Nella Zoja. Milan: Montadori ("Medusa"), 1952.

A5228 Wansborough, John. "Graham Greene: The Detective in the Wasteland." HA, CXXXVI (Dec.), pp. 11-13, 29-31.

An unbiased discussion of Greene as the "detective in the Wasteland of human relationships, in search of God." Having accepted the Catholic Church as the "cynosure" of the novels and that Greene's message is not "the apology of the convert," the article discusses The Power and the Glory, The Heart of the Matter and The End of the Affair as different patterns of spiritual isolation each of which leads to a knowledge of good and evil that "transcends the limits of the purely human, the purely social consequences of sin."

R521 Bonnerot, L. "The Lost Childhood and Other Essays." EA, 2, pp. 170-71. Argues that the essays are bound together by "un fils uniformement sombre," that Greene's obsession as a creative writer can be contained in the words "violence, cruelty, despair, evil." Greene's idiosyncrasies are too powerful to allow for the objective free play of his critical sense, but they are useful in providing an insight into his real self. Includes a review of The Art of Graham Greene. See B511.

R522 Fowlie, Wallace. "The Quest of a Writer Obsessed." NYTBR, (17 Feb.), pp. 1 & 31. Maintains that Greene's literary essays, though personal in tone, are primarily concerned with what constitutes a writer's "obsession," and attempt to illuminate his entire work by an analysis of the obsession. Greene's opening essays, especially the ones on Henry James, are "most developed" and reveal him as a "penetrating critic." Also compares him to Mauriac and examines briefly the debate he carries on in his novels.

R523 Gardiner, Harold C. "Top-flight Literary Criticism: The Lost Childhood." America, LXXXVI (22 March), p. 675. Apart from shedding light on his "philosophy" of literature, the essays, with their "pungency of phrase, ... insight and .. promise of lasting value," are a critic's delight; they startle one into reflection.

R524 Howe, Irving. "The Taint of Manichee." NRep, CXXVI (17 March), pp. 19-20. As a critic, Greene "writes extremely well, with clarity, color and bite, and with a range of reference that might be envied by a professional critic"; but his unending concern with evil as an eternal component of human nature indicates a personal set of beliefs, so that he speaks of himself when he declares Dickens to be marred by the "eternal and alluring taint of Manichee."

R525 Hughes, Riley. "New Novels: The End of the Affair." CW, CLXXIV (Jan.), p. 312. Explains the "twofold" affair in the title and asserts that Greene, "the least Thomistic" of Catholic novelists may successfully portray the fury of the flesh but is "weak and notional" in portraying the spirit.

R526 Levin, Harry. "Essays on Several Occasions." YR, NS XLI (Summer), 615-18. The Lost Childhood and Other Essays is the second of three volumes reviewed. Remarks briefly on Greene's advocacy of his "tractarian commitments" in his critical essays and his condemnation of those who do not share his "religious sense."

R527 Munn, L. S. "The Lost Childhood." SpR, (22 June), p. 10D. Maintains that Greene's intimate literary essays are as much an autobiography as an appreciation of the writers he has selected for appraisal.

R528 "O'Donnell, Donat" [Conor Cruise O'Brien]. "Graham Greene's The Lost Childhood." A. D., III (Winter), pp. 43-47. Maintains that Greene's weakness as a critic is due to his being a "profoundly introspective" writer who, "occasionally and almost by accident" becomes a sound critic when he deals with a writer whose experiences and preoccupations are similar to his own.

R529 Paulding, Gouverneur. "Criticism with a Restoring Sense of Values." NYHTBR, (17 Feb.), p. 5. Appreciative of Greene's restoration of the "religious sense" to the service of criticism. The essays make excellent reading, are witty and sharp, and their opinions "would be interesting even if he had written nothing else."

R5210 Prescott, Orville. "Books of the Times." NYT, (18 Feb.), p. 17. Though he is "extravagantly overpraised" as a writer, Greene is "penetrating" in his remarks in The Lost Childhood and Other Essays, writes provocatively and stimulatingly about the process of literary creation and can also "lash out in malicious ridicule." The "brief forays into criticism" make for good reading: the subject matter is varied and Greene's technical skill is impressive even though his passion for theology leads him at times into "wild exaggeration."

R5211 Sullivan, Richard. "From Essays to Spoofing by Greene." CST, (17 Feb.), p. 4. A short review that finds the collection of essays an extremely satisfying reading experience and the "source book" of a "first rate" critical mind capable of great range and insight, and which both confirms and illuminates Greene the novelist.

R5212 Webster, Harvey Curtis. "Reflections on Men & Letters." SatR, XXXV (16 Feb.), p. 28. A review of The Lost Childhood and Other Essays that finds the collection partial, perceptive and unusually candid, the best of them about writers "whom life has wounded early." Greene's "ingenious partiality sometimes compels strong disagreement" but he supplies "the basis for his own discounting" and never "pretends to objectivity."

R5213 Willis, Katherine Tappert. "New Books Appraised: The Lost Childhood and Other Essays." LJ, LXXVII (15 Jan.), p. 141. The brief "appraisal" notes that Greene's criticism or book reviews are "more balanced when he has complete sympathy with his subject."

R5214 Unsigned. "The Lost Childhood and Other Essays." Atlantic, CLXXXIX (March), p. 85. A brief review noting Greene's tendency towards self revelation whether the subject is specialized or not.

R5215 ________. "The Lost Childhood and Other Essays." Booklist, XLVIII (1 Feb.), p. 182. Brief notice of publication.

R5216 ________. "The Lost Childhood and Other Essays." NY, XXVII (26 Jan.), p. 99. A brief review noting Greene's concern for moral values which give an interesting slant to his articles. Also points out that Greene beats the space limit of an article "by seizing at once on the essential points."

D521 Boswell, William Caldwell. The Individual in the Novels of Graham Greene. M.A. McGill Univ.

D522 Eigner, Franz. Der Symbolcharacter der Landschaftsbildes in der Werken Graham Greene. Univ. of Vienna.

D523 Kreuzer, Wilhelm. Die Auswirking der weltanschaulicher Grundhaltung auf Characktereichnung und Stoffgestaltung in Greenes Werken. Univ. of Graz.

S521 Unsigned. "End of the Affair: Graham Greene denied Visa." NRep, CXXVI (11 Feb.), p. 7. A short note questioning the grounds on which the U.S. State Department denied an entry visa to Greene.

S522 ________. "Graham Greene 'Cleared' to Enter United States." PW, CLXI (16 Feb.), p. 922. A short note on his disqualification to visit the U.S. and subsequent clearance by the State Department and the Department of Justice.

S523 ________. "Visa to Visit U.S. Rejected by Graham Greene." PW, CLXII (6 Dec.), p. 2243. A further item for information in the saga of Greene's 1952 visit to the U.S.

1953

B531 "Alberes, R.-M." [René Marill]. "Graham Greene et la résponsabilité." Les Hommes traqués. Paris: La Nouvelle Edition, pp. 157-87. An informative but asserting article proposing that the "thriller" pattern lends itself to Greene's vision of hunted man, trapped in a lawless universe and divided in his loyalty to systems over which he has no control. In the face of such fatalism, Greene proposes responsibility--a deliberate assumption of it as if man were master of his destiny. This responsibility contributes man's "seule noblesse," his only weapon to defy the absurdity of his existence, and his only means of salvation, for only then can he hope in the fruits of his "coup d'audace," a hope which takes the form of Divine Grace in Greene's works. Like other French critics, he notices the similarity between Greene and Camus in the "raidissement de l'homme contre la fatalité."

B532 De Pange, Victor. Graham Greene. Pref. François Mauriac. Paris: Editions Universitaires. Rev. and enl. 1958. Includes a biographical account of Greene's life until 1958 which had been read by Greene, and a translation of a fragment of a journal by Greene entitled "The Great Bombardment of Wednesday, 16 April 1941." Discusses Greene's work up to 1958 as a "témoignages de nos temps d'angoisse," and the slow evolution of his thought central to which is the conflict between evil and grace. Quotes extensively from French translations of the novels and devotes Ch. 6 to the "thriller" and cinematic techniques of Greene's novels. Tends to regard Greene's conversion more in the line of the Jansenist doctrine of predestination than of orthodox Catholicism.

B533 Fournier, R. P. Gaston, SJ. Le Tourment de Dieu chez les amants de Graham Greene. Toulouse: Imprimerie Parisiènne. Focusses on Sarah and Maurice as two lovers that give the most authentic expression of the "Tourment de Dieu: cette reponse a Dieu douloureuse, tragique, de l'être humain tiraillé entre deux inconciliables amours."

B534 ________. Scobie, ou l'homme victime de sa pitié: 'Le Fond du Problème' de Graham Greene. Toulouse: Imprimerie Parisiènne. A study of Scobie as a victim of his own pity for his wife, his mistress, and even his God, and as a human being torn between two irreconcilable loves whose drama presents the occasion for the "tourment de Dieu": i. e., the total response to the "impérieux appel du Dieu qui est Amour."

B535 Gardiner, Harold C., SJ. Norms for the Novel. New York: The America Press. Rev. ed. New York: Hanover House, 1960. Formulates in Part One, five principles for the moral valuation of novels and extends them in Part Two to include the literary. Reprints in the Introduction, two articles on The End of the Affair from America. The work contains passing and scattered references to four novels: Brighton Rock, The Power and the Glory, The Heart of the Matter and The End of the

Affair. Exonerates Greene of unworthy motives in the depiction of priest characters and the frank and unsparing realism of passages which may be regarded in puritan Catholic circles as "objectionable." Commends Greene for his expression of the consciousness of sin and his ability to make clear, in the "objectionable passages" that some supreme values are at stake.

B536 Kettle, Arnold. "Graham Greene: The Heart of the Matter." An Introduction to the English Novel. Vol. 2. Henry James to the Present Day. London & New York: Hutchinson Univ. Library, pp. 153-59. Contends that The Heart of the Matter is a "moral fable" that illustrates the abstract concept of the "innate sinfulness of man and his need of divine mercy." Attributes the "failure" of the novel to its "perverted sentimentality," and especially to the "pretentiousness" of Greene's pattern as he tries to put human life into a "strait-jacket," or a "narrow mould."

B537 Longaker, Mark, and Edwin C. Bolles. "Graham Greene." Contemporary English Literature. New York: Appleton-Century-Crofts, pp. 374-76. A short note that touches on Greene's ability to transcend the "topicality" of the thirties and forties and escape the "provincialism" of many English novelists. Includes a list of the works to 1949 but, curiously enough, includes England Made Me under "Miscellaneous" with the travel books and British Dramatists.

B538 Nott, Kathleen. "Augustinian Novelists." The Emperor's Clothes. London: Heinemann, pp. 299-311; Bloomington: Indiana Univ. Press, 1954. Discusses the spread of the conception that nature is originally and essentially bad, and its effect on the novel and contemporary criticism of it. Contends that Greene writes powerfully and movingly in The Power and the Glory because he is writing about a real psychological situation in the reaction between the Whiskey Priest's education and his concrete surroundings, unlike the "factitious, even ad hoc" psychological situation of The Heart of the Matter and The End of the Affair.

B539 Rousseaux, André. "Les damnés de Graham Greene." Littérature du vingtième siècle. Vol IV. Paris: Editions Albin Michel, pp. 104-23. Examines Greene's obsession with damnation and his reliance on Grace alone for salvation which reveals itself in his work in the choice of a hero "traqué par le malheur et le mal," who walks towards his damnation with a conviction that it is inevitable--with the exception of the Whiskey Priest, "un damné a rebours." Stamboul Train, The Power and the Glory and The Heart of the Matter.

B5310 Tynan, Kenneth. Graham Greene and a Photograph." Persona Grata. London: Allan Wingate, pp. 53-56. Includes a slightly abridged version of "An Inner View of Graham Greene." See A5325.

A531 Barra, Giovanni. "La conversione di Graham Greene." VeP, XXXVI (June), pp. 310-15. An account of Greene's conversion to Catholicism which claims that his narrative genius was only sparked after his real or inner conversion on the 1938 trip to Mexico.

A532 Becher, Hubert. "Priestegestalten in der Romanliteratur der Gegenwart." SZ, CLIII, pp. 345-55. A brief examination of the priest as hero in The Power and the Glory and other novels by some twenty-five English, American, German, French and Italian twentieth-century novelists.

A533 Braybrooke, Neville. "Graham Greene as Critic." IM, LXXXI (Oct.), pp. 383-88. Rpt. from Commonweal, LIV (6 July 1951), pp. 512-14. See A517.

A534 Brissaud, André. "C'est un champ de bataille/ c'est un homme traqué/ c'est l'univers de Graham Greene." Arts, 434 (22-28 Oct.), p. 5. A brief survey of Greene's works followed by an interesting account of It's a Battlefield as a "psychological novel of exceptional quality" that touches upon the major themes that underlie the later works.

A535 Broger, Niels Chr. "Gudsforholdet: Graham Greenes menneskeskildring." KoK, LVIII, pp. 275-83. In Norwegian. A study of Greene's portrayal of people and their relationship to God. Maintains that Greene portrays an individual relationship which is never generalized and therefore cannot be judged by others or by the Church.

A536 C., G. "Dialogue avec Pierre Bost sur La Puissance et la gloire." FrI, 378 (10 Jan.), p. 65. A short interview with Pierre Bost on his collaboration with Pierre Quet and Pierre Darbon in the French adaptation of The Power and the Glory for the screen.

A537 Cronin, Vincent. "Graham Greene's First Play." CW, CLXXVII (Sept.), pp. 406-10. Echoes the general sense of disappointment that greeted The Living Room whose "intrinsic weakness" lay not in preaching the indissolubility of marriage, but in the "long-drawn arguments" for and against that theme, "unenlivened by wit, undramatized by sufficient action."

A538 Dhoeve, Andries. "Zij misten de Nobelprijs: Graham Greene." Periscoop, (1 Jan.), pp. 1, 9. Highlights of Greene's career and novels for the general reader occasioned by his failure to obtain nomination for the Nobel Prize for literature.

A539 Doyle, Brian. "Morals and Novels." Ave Maria, LXXVII (25 April), pp. 532-33. A discussion of the Catholic position and the general laws and precepts on reading with brief reference to Greene and Mauriac as writers who take the "Catholic message" to non-Catholics.

A5310 Findlater, Richard. "Graham Greene as Dramatist." TCLon, CLVI (June), pp. 471-73. Takes exception to T. C. Worsley's review of The Living Room as a "complete and baffling failure, in language, situation, and characterization," and regards the play as a "theatrical melodrama" that has "intensity and conviction," but whose essential weakness lies in the "inadequacy of the protagonist of Catholic values, and the intangibility of the unpredictable mercy of God."

A5311 Fowler, Alistair. "Novelist of Damnation." Theology, LVI (July), pp. 259-64. Attempts to correct the prevailing notion that Greene contrasts the "Catholic sense of sin with mere Protestant moralism" or that he makes a "dualistic simplification" into good and evil. Argues that in Greene's novels the love of God comes not merely in the midst of sin and suffering but "by means of" sin, that good and evil are "ambivalent and confused," and that the Roman Catholic Church is at its "most demanding, most inflexible"; hence, the tragedy of renunciation of human love in novels like The Heart of the Matter and The End of the Affair.

A5312 Golden, Janet. "Graham Greene and the Sense of Sin." SJM, LIV:6 (June), pp. 8-9, 26. Discusses from a Catholic viewpoint, Greene's emphasis on sin and the sense of sin in England Made Me, Brighton Rock, The Power and the Glory, The Heart of the Matter and The End of the Affair, as well as the difficulties this emphasis creates for Catholic readers. Attributes the "chill" of England Made Me to the absence of a sense of sin in it because the characters have no "true sense of God."

A5313 Gordon, Caroline. "Some Readings and Misreadings." SR, LXI (Summer), 384-407. The "reading" of novels by James, Joyce, Greene, Faulkner, Bernanos, Mauriac and Waugh is based on the assumption that the novelist's imagination often operates "within the pattern of Christian symbolism rather than the pattern of contemporary thought," that novels are based on the "primal plot: the Christian scheme of Redemption." Pages 393-96 regard The Heart of the Matter, like Joyce's The Portrait of the Artist as a Young Man as describing a "soul choosing damnation." Considers the latter superior to the former because

Greene seems to be "in some doubt himself as to the outcome" of the action; hence, the "inconclusive ending" which is also an "anti-climax."

A5314 Gregor, Ian. "The New Romanticism: A Comment on The Living Room." Blackfriars, XXXIV:402 (Sept.), pp. 403-06. Argues rather persuasively that the play lacks "artistic inevitability" owing to the "theological sanctions" so insistently evoked but which "do not belong to the texture of the narrative," and to Rose's immaturity which prevents Greene from exploring "the real complexities that might reasonably be expected to accompany the situation in which she finds herself."

A5315 Hoggart, Richard. "The Force of Caricature: Aspects of the Art of Graham Greene, with Particular Reference to The Power and the Glory." EIC, III (Oct.), 447-62. Rpt. in his Speaking to Each Other: Essays. Vol. II. About Literature. London: Chatto & Windus, 1970, pp. 40-56. Also in Graham Greene: A Collection of Critical Essays. Ed. Samuel Hynes. Englewood Cliffs, N.J.: Prentice-Hall, 1973, pp. 79-93. An appreciative textual examination of setting, style and character to determine the technical basis of the popularity of The Power and the Glory, viz., "simplicity of the overall pattern," "striking visual quality of the scenes," and to determine the connection between Greene's "way of writing and his outlook on experience."

A5316 Koster, Wilhelm. "Dennoch nicht." FH, VIII (April), pp. 314-15. Brief comments on the "failure" of The Living Room occasioned by the Swedish performance in October, 1952.

A5317 "Leabhar." Letter. IM, LXXXI, p. 291. Supports J. D. Sheridan's position (see A5321) and goes a step further to question whether any kind of immorality is permissible at all.

A5318 Monroe, N. Elizabeth. "The New Man in Fiction." Renascence, VI (Autumn), 9-17. Presents three formulas in the search for greatness and the meaning of existence in modern fiction: the communist, the existentialist and the Christian, all of whom invite man to share in the redemption of the world through action. Focusses on the Christian formula in The Power and the Glory, Brighton Rock, The Heart of the Matter and The End of the Affair. Maintains in this cursory account of the novels that by showing the image of God under man's warped nature, Greene is making a "radical departure from the usual method of conceiving greatness of character."

A5319 Neame, A. J. "Black and Blue: A Study in the Catholic

Novel." European, 2 (April), pp. 26-36. Discusses--and disapproves of--the manner in which Greene, among others, conveys Catholicism as an "intelligible and coherent Weltanschauung," for his novels are too "confined" in scope, and private miseries or idiosyncrasies are "inappropriate to the times," especially to non-Catholics, for whom the problems of Greene's "test cases" in moral theology "seem as irrelevant as the premises on which they are based...."

A5320 Peters, W. "The Concern of Graham Greene." Month, X (Nov.), pp. 281-90. A sympathetic but perceptive look into Greene's "obsession" with evil and his sympathy for the sinner. Maintains that the religious sense is an integrating element of his novels and argues that Greene has restored not only "man's due proportions" as a being "worthy to be fought over by Satan and God," but also the mystery of Satan and the mystery of God's love. The Power and the Glory, The Heart of the Matter and The End of the Affair.

A5321 Sheridan, John D. "Graham Greene and the Irish." IM, LXXXI, pp. 211-16. Discusses the problem of morality and art in his attempt to justify the rejection of The End of the Affair by Irish Catholics even while cognizant that American Catholics had chosen the novel as the most distinguished Catholic novel of the year. Argues that morality has a "local flavour" and that the Irish find the "incidentals" of the novel objectionable.

A5322 Shuttleworth, Martin and Simon Raven. "The Art of Fiction. III: Graham Greene." PRev, I (Autumn), pp. 25-41. Rpt. in Graham Greene: A Collection of Critical Essays. Ed. Samuel Hynes. Englewood Cliffs, N.J.: Prentice-Hall, 1973, pp. 154-68. An informative interview in which Greene though not revealing "unknown things" about himself, makes interesting comments on The Living Room, suicide in his works, his use of melodrama and the "fixation"--in his case, "the religious sense"--that gives to a "shelf of novels the unity of a system."

A5323 Sordet, Etienne. "Signification de Graham Greene." CP, XXXVIII, pp. 239-50. Explores the spiritual significance of the individual dramas of Greene's protagonists in The End of the Affair, The Heart of the Matter and The Power and the Glory. Also discusses irony in The End of the Affair, suicide in The Heart of the Matter, and is rather critical of Greene's easeful acceptance of Grace as covering up "la déchéance morale" of man. Perhaps the most disturbing note in the essay is the identification of Scobie's reflections with Greene's.

A5324 Spender, Stephen. "Movements and Influences in English

Literature, 1927-1952." BA, XXVII (Winter), pp. 5-32. An evaluation of its evolution and present situation that notes the emergence of a steady movement away from "individual sensibility as the centre of creative experience in writing, to a periphery of society, or some source of spiritual authority." Refers briefly on p. 31 to The End of the Affair in connection with the latter and to Greene's "almost" successful attempt in the novel to equate the sense of sin with the knowledge of virtue.

A5325 Tynan, Kenneth. "An Inner View of Graham Greene." Harper's, LXXXVI (Feb.), pp. 128-29, 209-10, 214-15. Rpt. in abridged form in Persona Grata. London: Wingate, 1953, pp. 53-56. Surveys Greene's life and focusses on his preoccupation with sin as a "pleasure giver," as a "pain inflictor," and as an "unholy paradox" that "holds within it the seeds of virtue." Credits Greene with dignifying contemporary fiction by combining sensuality and saintliness through an "awareness of sin unparalleled since Hopkins' time." The "inner view" of Greene--an account of striking oddities, perhaps noticed first hand--contributes little to an understanding of the works and increases the mystery surrounding the novelist.

A5326 Unsigned. "Portrait." BA, XXVII:1, p. 31. Brief reference to The End of the Affair as a novel where Greene "almost succeeds in equating the sense of sin with the knowledge of virtue."

A5327 ________. "Biographical Note." PW, CLXIII (3 Jan.), p. 30. Also gives pre-publication notice of England Made Me, published by Viking in 1953 under the title The Shipwrecked.

A5328 ________. "Portrait Gallery: The Angry Man Within." SunT, (12 April), p. 5. An unbiased and reasonable portrait of Greene for the general reader. Includes a photograph.

R531 Brinnin, John Malcolm. "Greene Aground." NRep, CXXVIII (16 Feb.), p. 20. Argues that the reappearance of England Made Me is only of "academic interest in the juvenilia of a fine writer," for the theme of alienation with which the novel is concerned is "without substance, inexpertly maneuvered into something between the comic and the psychopathic." Moreover, the unreality of the characters tends to make many situations "slick."

R532 Brown, Ivor. "Greene Fields." Observer, (19 April), p. 11. An appreciative review of The Living Room and the production. Maintains that the play has every ingredient of "current popularity," is stimulating and has "serious debate, intelligently and infectiously conducted."

R533 Cassidy, T. E. "The Early World of a Major Writer." Commonweal, LVII (6 March), p. 560. Finds England Made Me a "finely executed" novel with a "firmness of style and meaning" characteristic of a "socially conscious" Greene as he explores the deeper reality of man's struggle with himself. The intricate workings of character are sometimes brought out in the Stockholm setting which houses the "pointless and rootless humans, adrift and apart," of Greene's world.

R534 Clurman, Harold. "The Living Room." Nation, CLXXVII (15 Aug.), pp. 138-39. A review of the London production which notices how the play commands the audience's attention but is critical of its "poor fabric," its "schematically sketched" characters, the "foreshortened" situations to accommodate the awkward dramatic structure and the lack of spiritual candor on Greene's part.

R535 Dempsey, David. "Repeat Performances." NYTBR, (11 Jan.), p. 24. On the reissue of England Made Me under the title The Shipwrecked. Describes the "surrealist" quality of Greene's style in the novel as a "composite of nervous, vivid images out of the characters' subconscious, by which the normal syntax of thought is replaced with a kind of emotional shorthand." Notices Minty as one of the "most acutely observed minor characters." Critical of Greene for not allowing the characters to "develop."

R536 Fremantle, Anne. "The Hunted Men of Graham Greene." SatR, XXXVI (10 Jan.), pp. 15-16. On the American publication of England Made Me by Viking under the title The Shipwrecked. Considers the novel a "psychologically simple" story, "theologically bold" in its assumption that it is the "utterly abased who can save." Anthony is described as a "capsule of all future Greene heroes," a definite "anti-hero."

R537 Guerrero Zamora, Juan. "Graham Greene y su cuarto de estar contra la muerte." Indice, VIII (30 Sept.), p. 24. Though The Living Room may be regarded by some as a "Catholic triumph," it is based on Greene's earlier obsessions and is, at bottom, a "new focus on a constant preoccupation."

R538 Hamilton, Ian. "Theatre: The Living Room." Spectator, 6513 (24 April), p. 512. Maintains that Greene mixes "sexuality and religiosity with a tincture of morality" and creates a human condition which is extremely repellant in a sordid setting. Objects to his "remorseless, obsessive drive into the dark," and questions whether the suicide has been demonstrated to be "dramatically inevitable" rather than the morality behind it.

R539 Hill, Ronald. "The Living Room: Prisoner of This World." Tablet, (25 April), p. 354. Examines the play to determine the dissatisfaction that prevails at the end despite the "effective ending" of this "extremely moving drama." Interprets the living room as the "prison of this world" wherein each character, trapped by his or her peculiar circumstances, is not merely "'real' or 'true' in a naturalistic sense" but whose existence is complicated by his or her awareness of spiritual realities.

R5310 Hughes, Riley. "The Shipwrecked." CW, CLXXVI (March), pp. 470-71. A short note on the reissue of England Made Me in the U. S. Considers the novel as one of Greene's more "serious" works.

R5311 Jackson, Joseph Henry. "An Early Graham Greene." SFC, (15 Jan.), p. 15. On the reissue in the U. S. of England Made Me under the title The Shipwrecked. Maintains that the interrelationships of Anthony, Kate and Krogh make up a dramatic story, but it is in their "innate 'lostness'" that Greene makes their "deviousness" an intellectual and spiritual matter.

R5312 Lambert, J. W. "Wages of Sin." SunT, (19 April), p. 9. A review of The Living Room and its production. Describes the play as an exceedingly good first play, a set of moving "variations on the theme of human inadequacy." Its setting is "brilliantly fantasticated" and the "dubious expediency" of Rose's death is almost forgotten as a result of the fine performance.

R5313 Rolo, Charles J. "Reader's Choice: England Made Them." Atlantic, CXCI (Feb.), pp. 81-82. Maintains that though the new title of the reissue of England Made Me may be "apposite," the novel compares favorably with later works for sheer literary effectiveness and atmosphere, especially in its treatment of "drabness--with passion and wry humor."

R5314 Sullivan, Richard. "Reissue of Early Greene Novel Brilliant But Thin." CST, (11 Jan.), p. 5. On the reissue of England Made Me in the U. S. under the title The Shipwrecked. Considers the novel "pretty thin stuff" when measured against his later novels, in spite of its "sharp and clear" writing, its strong narrative drive and the "brilliant technical facility."

R5315 Trewin, J. C. "A Sense of Sin." ILN, CCXXII (2 May), p. 704. A review of The Living Room and its performance at Wyndham's Theatre, London. Finds the piece "disturbing, far from endearing" and though not "first rank" perhaps, it cannot be shaken off; it remains as "one of the most provocative dramas of its time." Also finds this "moral play" sagging at its close.

R5316 Villard, Leonie. "The Living Room." EA, VIII, p. 83. The review highlights the inevitable differences in appreciation between an English audience and a French one in spite of the spiritual reality of which both audiences are aware.

R5317 Unsigned. "The Shipwrecked." Bookmark, XII (Feb.), p. 103. Brief notice on the reissue of England Made Me in the U.S.

R5318 ________. "Letter from London: The Living Room." NY, XXIX (18 July), p. 69. Includes a brief note on the "sell out success" of the London performance.

R5319 ________. "London Bridge." SatR, XXXVI (1 Aug.), p. 24. Includes, in this general review of plays running in London, a brief account of The Living Room as a "domestic tragedy," and remarks on its many similarities with T. S. Eliot's The Cocktail Party.

R5320 ________. "Early Graham Greene." Time, LXI (19 Jan.), pp. 67-68. On the reissue of England Made Me in the U.S. under the title The Shipwrecked. Regards the novel as "swift but erratic in pace, and streaked with a social consciousness," and written in the "vibrato style" characteristic of Greene.

R5321 ________. "Wyndham's Theatre: The Living Room." Times, (17 April), p. 2. A review of the play and its performance. Notes that each character in the play has a sense of sin and refuses to believe "in the universal unreason of things for the sake of the comfort such belief" may bring.

R5322 ________. "The Living Room in a Cellar." Times, (30 April), p. 4. Notice of the addition of the play in German to the repertory of "Contra Kreis," a stock company which gives its performances in a cellar, after its original production of the play had been unfavorably reviewed in Frankfurt.

R5323 ________. "The Living Room." TLS, 2684 (10 July), p. 450. Brief notice of the publication of the text of the play currently running at Wyndham's Theatre, London.

D531 Galen, Ruth E. Graham Greene: A Study of Absolute and Relative Concepts of Morality. M.A. Univ. of New Mexico.

D532 Hagspiel, Robert. Die symbolik in den Werken Graham Greenes. Univ. of Innsbruck.

D533 Sauer, Josef. Die Darstellung des katholischen Menschen bei Archibald Joseph Cronin und Graham Greene. Univ. of Erlangen.

D534 Stahl, Morma M. The Novels of Graham Greene: A Discussion of the Themes of Love and Pity and the Novelist's Technique. M.A. Univ. of Columbia.

D535 Zerman, Malvyn B. The Writer as Technician: A Study of the Literary Methods of Graham Greene. M.A. Univ. of Columbia.

S531 Unsigned. "The Heart of the Matter: Mr. Greene's Novel Filmed." Times, (26 Oct.), p. 11. On the filming of the novel by More O'Ferral with Trevor Howard as Scobie.

S532 ________. "British Film Banned in Malaya." Times, (30 Dec.), p. 4. Brief news item announcing the banning of The Heart of the Matter on the grounds that a deputy commissioner of police is portrayed in an "unfavourable manner" as one of the censors put it.

1954

B541 Bowen, Elizabeth. "The Writer's Peculiar World." Highlights of Modern Literature: A Permanent Collection of Memorable Essays from 'The New York Times Book Review.' Ed. Francis Brown. New York: The American Library, pp. 32-36. See A505.

B542 Chaigne, Louis. "Graham Greene." Vies et oeuvres d'écrivains. III. Montreal & Paris: Fides. Rev. ed. 1966, pp. 175-214. Gives a brief biographical account of Greene and examines his vision of life, noting his interest in the primitive, in the lonely, insecure, overburdened heart, in spiritual matters, and especially in the reality of sin. Also discusses his use of the thriller, the "realistic" in his descriptions and his cinematic technique, and surveys the French translations of his works separately up to The Fallen Idol. The rev. ed. of 1966 merely notes the translation into French of The End of the Affair and later novels up to and including The Comedians.

B543 Davis, Robert Gorham. "At the Heart of the Story is Man." Highlights of Modern Literature: A Permanent Collection of Memorable Essays from 'The New York Times Book Review.' Ed. Francis Brown. New York: The New American Library, pp. 57-62. Rpt. from NYTBR, (28 Dec. 1952), p. 1. See A529.

B544 Jarrett-Kerr, Martin. Studies in Literature and Belief. London: Rockliff Publishing House; New York: Harper Bros. Considers in Ch. 7, pp. 164-66, Greene's reaction to the "erosion of the imaginative soil" in the 20th century as "the way of self-defence," following the line of much contemporary theological apologetics that "constructs its agreement on the foundations of Original Sin." Accuses Greene of a "slight tilt towards sentimentality" in The Power and the Glory, of being frequently guilty of "author's intrusion" in Brighton Rock, The Heart of the Matter and The End of the Affair, and of being rarely interested in more than one character in a novel. This underestimation of Greene's achievement is condensed from two earlier articles. See A464 & A4920.

B545 Mesnet, Marie-Beatrice. Graham Greene and the Heart of the Matter. London: Cresset Press. Rpt. Westport, Conn.: Greenwood Press, 1972. A study of the characters in Brighton Rock, The Power and the Glory and The Heart of the Matter--novels openly concerned with the issue of Salvation and Damnation. Attempts to define the situation of the characters in the world and in time, the principles according to which they act and, in particular, the conditions that seem to determine them so as to raise the problem of determinism versus free will. Part One examines the overwhelming misery of the world that surrounds the existence of his characters and analyzes the structure of their environment and the chain of events leading to their doom. Part Two attempts an analysis of the minds and hearts of the characters in order to focus on the "great tragedy of freedom." Also shows that their "terror of life" stems from opposing an "interior inertia to the real demand made upon them" so that they break down from sheer impotence under an unbearable burden. Part Three argues that "God is, or exists as a living person," and is the principal actor, the "third man" in the three novels, so that the "fatality of evil" and the power of grace are forever at war in man's dual nature.

B546 Moeller, Charles. "Graham Greene ou le martyre de l'esperance." Littérature du xxe siècle et Christianisme. Vol. I. Silence de Dieu. S. A. Tournai (Belgium): Casterman, Rev. ed. 1967, pp. 283-327. Attributes the "apparent impotence" of God in the novels to Greene's obsession with sin, "le véritable visage du mal." Discusses this obsession with sin and evil which can manifest itself in childhood, "incarnate" itself in Anglo-Saxon civilization, and is upheld by "les partisans de l'ordre," the cynics, the "humiliated children," and the rebels against society, and argues that at the very heart of the sin of despair, in the confrontation with damnation, lies the call of God and perhaps, salvation. This call manifests itself in the role played by woman, and the words and actions of our fellow-men, even in the ambiguity or paradox surrounding pity. Discusses Scobie's drama, the motif of pity, his guilt and whether he is "saved." The last section of the essay discusses The Power and the Glory as a manifestation of "la force surnaturelle du paradoxe chrétien."

B547 Sturzl, Erwin. Von Satan zu Gott: religiose probleme bei Graham Greene. Vienna: Graphische Lehr und Versuchs-anstalt.

A541 Blanchet, André. "Un nouveau 'type' de Prêtre dans le roman contemporain." Etudes, CLXXX (March), 303-10. Rpt. with minor changes in his Le Prêtre dans le roman d'aujourd'hui. Bruges: Desclée De Brouwer, 1955, pp. 59-77. This is the second of two articles which discusses the emergence of a new image of the priest in contemporary novels, a priest who is a "witness of God" rather than just a minister of the Church, and whose archetype is l'abbé Donissan in Bernanos' Sous le soleil de Satan. Discusses briefly the Whiskey Priest in the light of this new concept with passing reference to Brighton Rock and The Heart of the Matter.

A542 Brady, Charles A. "A Brief Survey of Catholic Fiction." BT, XII (Jan.-Feb.), pp. 159-60, 190-91. Assumes, in this survey that covers England, France and the U. S. A. in the twentieth century, that the Catholic novel par excellence is the "novel with a metaphysic," an "Augustinian metaphysic of sin and Grace" in the case of Greene whose four Catholic novels make a "contemporary Divine Comedy" of "four Limbos ... but no Paradise."

A543 Doyle, Louis F., SJ. Letter. America, XCI (18 Sept.), p. 604. Letter to the Editor occasioned by Greene's open letter to the Archbishop of Paris over Colette's burial. (FigL, 14 Aug., p. 1). Doubts the "soundness" of Greene's knowledge of the Catholic religion as revealed in his novels, and deplores Greene's "taste for moral questions" because it is "much greater than his talent." A classic example of the outlook that evaluates Greene's works as Catholic "tracts."

A544 Fytton, Francis. "Graham Greene: Catholicism and Controversy." CW, CLXXX (Dec.), 172-75. A general account that deals with too many topics to do justice to any one. Claims that Greene has not become a "first class writer," and will not become one without a "good failure," for the success he has had so far has been "relatively easy."

A545 Grunt, Olav Paus. "Grunntrekk i Graham Greenes Fortellerkunst." Samtiden, LXIII, pp. 341-49. In Norwegian. A discussion of Greene's narrative technique and style. Notes Greene's fascination by the seedy side of society, the structure of his novels around the problems of sin and grace, and the "redemptive" role of woman in the novels. Analyzes Brighton Rock as a "parable" of good, evil and the world.

A546 Hayman, Ronald. "Le Roman anglais d'après-guerre, III." RLM, III (April), pp. 81-96. Rpt. in La Littérature anglaise d'après-guerre. Paris: Lettres Modernes, 1955, pp. 81-112. Pages 24-29 of this lengthy article on the post World War II novels of West, Koestler, Greene, Waugh and Wilson focus on Greene, the "most popular of contemporary serious novelists," and discuss his shortcomings, especially his inability to make "differenciations morales (sauf pour les plus sommaire)" and his reticence to commit himself in The Heart of the Matter. Mention is also made of his strengths, especially his ability to describe atmosphere in a few words, and of the cinematic quality of his novels in general.

A547 Hynes, Sam. "Religion in the West End." Commonweal, LIX (12 Feb.), pp. 475-78. Maintains that religion ties together two dissimilar plays: T. S. Eliot's The Confidential Clerk and Greene's The Living Room. The latter is an intensely Catholic play where "religion does not obtrude, for it is the substance of the play and not simply an intermittent 'level of meaning.'" Its treatment of love and fear "persuades the general secular audience of its own reality." Favors The Living Room as a vividly realized "problem play."

A548 Igoe, W. J. "London Letter." America, XCII (23 Oct.), pp. 99-101. Surveys the English Catholic literary scene following the death of Hilaire Belloc. Includes Greene as one of the three famous Catholic novelists, but urges him to write a novel on a subject "other than the one that preoccupies sad little boys," especially now that his "range of subjects has narrowed to the point of sterility."

A549 Johnston, J. L. "Graham Greene--The Unhappy Man." CLM, XXXVIII (July), pp. 43-49. Maintains that Greene's "feelings for living evil--and to a lesser extent living good," constitutes his "raison d'être" as a novelist, and that his Catholic background, far from inducing "claustrophobia" serves to deepen the tragedy of his characters who seem to step out from "our own shabby world of reality." Focusses on The Power and the Glory and The Heart of the Matter.

A5410 Madaule, Jacques. "El misterio del amor en la obra de Greene." Sur, 226 (Jan.-Feb.), pp. 48-65. Notes that until The End of the Affair, human love occupied a rather modest place in the works of Greene and that the mutual recognition of love--a sign of "el amor verdadero"--abounds in The End of the Affair and The Living Room. Examines the mystery of Divine Love and Grace, with special reference to The Living Room.

A5411 Mauduit, Jean. "Chronique du Théâtre: 'Le Living Room' de Graham Greene." Etudes, 283 (Nov.), pp. 365-71. A review article on the French production condemning Greene for confusing the simple Christian spectator, and for moving "with impunity" from the medium of the novel "ou la pensée de l'auteur s'impose par lente imprégnation," to the "elementary violence of dramatic art" wherein the complex paradoxes of his Christianity are necessarily oversimplified.

A5412 Nicholl, Donald. "La Littérature catholique en Angleterre depuis la guerre." VI, XXV (June), pp. 58-73. Surveys English post World War II writings from the novel to the physical sciences. Notices briefly Greene's inability to portray the transforming power of Grace in the lives of his characters.

A5413 Nicholson, Jenny. "Graham Greene--A Third Man of Real Life." PicP, LXIV (14 Aug.), pp. 18-19. A "candid portrait" of Greene emphasizing his elusiveness, sociability, boredom and his enjoyment of the "fine freshener" of opium and practical joking.

A5414 Peters, W. A. M., SJ. "Graham Greene's Obsessie." Streven, VII:4 (Jan.), pp. 347-53. Maintains that the writer is a victim of his own obsession and convictions, and shows how Greene is primarily concerned with the evil that stalks his characters. See A5320.

A5415 Scott, Nathan A. "Graham Greene: Christian Tragedian." VolR, I:1 (Spring), pp. 29-42. Rev. and rpt. in Graham Greene: Some Critical Considerations. Ed. Robert O. Evans. Lexington: Univ. of Kentucky Press, 1963, pp. 25-49. Rpt. in his Craters of the Spirit: Studies in the Modern Novel. Washington, D.C.: Corpus Books, 1968; London & Sidney: Sheed and Ward, 1969, pp. 201-33. Argues that Greene's searching moral purpose behind the violence, melodrama and the "forlorn world of dereliction" he so often portrays leads to a world of dimensions, not truly to be understood except "sub specie aeternitatis" which, in the later novels, becomes studies of "purgation and sanctity." Maintains that "Christian tragedy" is possible, for the "'imitation of Christ' becomes a tragic spectacle in so far as it becomes, ironically, the occasion for the hero's betrayal into sin" as Scobie, Greene's "exempleum of the Christian hero in a tragic situation," or as Sarah, by her choice of the "dark night" seems to suggest.

A5416 Sewell, Elizabeth. "Graham Greene." DubR, CVIII:463 (1st Quarter), pp. 12-21. Co-published as "The Imagination of Graham Greene." Thought, XXIX (March 1954), pp. 51-60; also in WW, IX (April 1954), pp. 281-88. Contends that Greene is writing not as a Catholic but as a "late neo-Romantic" in the tradition of the literature of decadence with its ambivalence for attraction and repulsion. Includes a rather disparaging detailed analysis of the "ubiquity" of Greene's preoccupation with the body in The Power and the Glory, Brighton Rock, The Heart of the Matter and The End of the Affair.

A5417 Sherry, Gerald E. Letter. America, XCI (25 Sept.), p. 632. Responds to Rev. Louis F. Doyle's letter (see A543) and draws attention to Greene's admission of wrong reported in the English press but not in the U. S.

A5418 Stopp, Frederick J. "Der katholische Roman im heutigen England: Graham Greene und Evelyn Waugh." SZ, CLIII (March), pp. 428-43. Concentrates on Greene's vision of life and its expression in his works, with special emphasis on The End of the Affair.

A5419 Unsigned. "This Is Graham Greene." Newsweek, XLIV (29 Nov.), pp. 92-93. An introduction to the novelist and his works for the general reader, occasioned by the opening of The Living Room on Broadway. Points out the central theme that runs through the four major novels--"the despair of man confronted by evil" and the consequent spiritual torment. See also R5424.

R541 Atkinson, Brooks. "The Theatre: Graham Greene's The Living Room." NYT, (18 Nov.), p. 41. A review of the play and the performance at Henry Miller's. Finds the play a "passionate exposition of the obvious," a "prolix, meandering exegesis that protests too much" without adding much to the "old-fashioned triangle" except a Roman Catholic viewpoint. Also finds something "adolescent" or "boyish" about Greene for taking full note of sin before rejecting it, and is of the opinion that Greene can "certainly make religion sound difficult." Lists the Cast.

R542 ________. "The Living Room: Graham Greene's Drama About Faith, with Barbara Bel Geddes Starred." NYTBR, (28 Nov.), p. 1. Another review of the play critical of Greene's "ferocity" as he "tortures" and "annihilates" his characters. In spite of its "pithy and searching dialogue," the argument between the priest and the psychologist is a case in point, the play is a disappointment both as "horror play" and religious drama; the horror is overplayed beyond credible limits and the play is "destitute of love for human kind."

R543 Barbour, Thomas. "Playwrights or Play-Writers." HudR, VII (Autumn), 470-73. Regards The Living Room as the product of a play-writer not of a playwright. The play presents a "a primarily religious apprehension of the problems of the stage, rather than a fundamentally theatrical apprehension of a problem of religion." It is also "talky"; its crucial conversation and encounter between Fr. Browne and Rose is like that of "two punch-drunk pugilists," deprived at the outset of the dynamism that would make it theatrically effective. Moreover, the affair between Rose and Michael, stripped of its metaphysical overtones, hardly warrants the fate Greene had planned for them.

R544 Bentley, Eric. "Theatre." NRep, CXXXI (13 Dec.), p. 22. Rpt. as "A Real Writer." What is Theatre? New York: Horizon Press, 1956; London: Dennis Dobson, 1957, pp. 25-29. Rev. ed. incorporating The Dramatic Event and Other Reviews, 1944-1967. London: Methuen, 1969, pp. 200-03. An "autopsy" on The Living Room. Finds the play "disappointing" in spite of the pleasure aroused by Greene's language and the portrayal of religion on stage as a substantial part of people's lives because the characters are left "unfinished," the "macabre melodrama" is "incongruous" and Greene is "surprisingly gauche" in his presentation of the intellectual debate. Critical of the direction of the play and the miscasting of the main role.

R545 Brown, John Mason. "Parish Greene." SatR, XXXVII (18 Dec.), pp. 24-25. Maintains that Greene's customary "curdled attitude toward mortals and ... uncertainty in the midst of the certainties promised by faith" is illustrated in The Living Room with "far less dramatic effect" than in his novels. The play does not fulfil the "initial promises of interest" in spite of its "admirable cast"; its action bogs down in talk, and the strong points of conflict are stated in terms either "weak or smudged," and the atmosphere "befoggs" rather than clarifies the conflict, so that Greene's "house of death" seems "more ludicrous than fearsome."

R546 Chapman, John. "The Living Room Lacks Power to Make It an Absorbing Tragedy." DaiN, (18 Nov.). A review of the play and performance. Describes it as a "miniature tragedy" that makes a "frequently dull and generally dispiriting evening."

R547 Clurman, Harold. "Theatre." Nation, CLXXIX (4 Dec.), pp. 496-97. Speaks of the New York production of The

Living Room in "more indulgent terms" than the first night critics. Finds the performance of the "morality play" entirely "creditable," its advocacy of a faith "beyond logic" acceptable, and the play "generally absorbing" in spite of its lack of "creative spontaneity, a sense of direct experience, the eloquence of original emotion."

R548 Coleman, Robert. "The Living Room Opens at the Henry Miller." DaiMir, (18 Nov.). A review of the play and its performance. Considers it a "morbid melodrama about people who fear death and find no pleasure in living," taxing, and infrequently rewarding because the conflict between "materialistic psychology and religion is ... muddled and gives a somewhat empty though pretentious ring." Though it has materials which make "thoughtful, provocative and highly moving drama," the play which "probably reads better than it acts," seems merely depressing and "stained-glassy."

R549 Freedley, George. "The Living Room." LJ, LXXIX (Aug.), p. 1407. Brief notice of publication and forthcoming Broadway production.

R5410 Genet, Janet Flanner. "Letter from Paris." NY, XXX (23 Oct.), pp. 156 & 159. A review of the French production and reception of The Living Room. It is a "decided hit" and the French find it interesting intellectually--it is a "discussible play"--and especially because it questions the mortal sin of adultery and analyzes Catholic doctrine.

R5411 Gibbs, Wolcott. "Mr. Greene's Tragedy." NY, XXX (27 Nov.), p. 86. Reviews the New York performance and remarks that The Living Room remains a "distinguished play, filled with beautiful writing, practically unendurable suffering, and a kind of understanding that ... can at least promise salvation."

R5412 Hawkins, William. "The Living Room Furnished by Britain." NYWT, (18 Nov.), p. 30. A review of the play and performance. Though it has its highly dramatic passages, the play "wallows around in devious, agonizing realms" so that its "line of thought" ends up being "both pompous and beyond pursuit" in spite of its believable characters and situations and good dialogue.

R5413 Hayes, Richard. "The Stage: The Living Room." Commonweal, LXI (24 Dec.), pp. 333-34. Reviews the "compound" of "public apathy, critical boorishness, an indifferent production" and the "singular excesses" of the play that led to its discontinuation at the Henry Miller after twenty performances.

R5414 Kennedy, Rev. John S. "A Play Sure to be Debated." CTr, (4 Nov.), p. 4. Reviews The Living Room and its performance in a pre-Broadway engagement at New Haven's Shubert Theatre. Examines the reasons militating against popularity: it deals with sin and hell and discusses theology, it offends the "sentimental canons" by a stark and uncompromising look at romance, and it will arouse the ire of Catholics too, all of which makes it "not entertainment in the conventional sense."

R5415 Kerr, Walter F. "The Living Room." NYHT, (18 Nov.), p. 1. A review of the play and performance. Finds the play "grim" and "emotionally barren" because Greene, with a "granite detachment," twists the knot between "the forces of religion and the demands of passion" with an "uncompromising candor" that dramatizes the failure of the individual rather than his redemption.

R5416 McClain, John. "Problem Play Stirs Debate." NYJ, (18 Nov.), p. 22. Finds The Living Room "verbose, redundant" and the "simple and age-old problem" posed baffling, even though absorbing and provocative.

R5417 Madden, Joan. "With Crooked Lines: Greene's Living Room." America, XC (6 March), pp. 600-02. A warm and enthusiastic personal reaction to the play. Disagrees with Vincent Cronin's assessment of the theme (see A537) and considers the play not only as belonging to the "thematic tradition" of the Catholic novels but also as an "illumination" of these "enigmatic narratives."

R5418 Stanley, John. "Life in The Living Room." Commonweal, LXI (31 Dec.), pp. 354-55. Rpt. in Commonweal, LXXI (30 Oct. 1959), pp. 123-24. Descriptive notes on the "flop" for the lay Catholic reader. Makes no reference to the play as a literary work but approves Greene's attempt to talk about God in "an acceptable vocabulary and accent" in a world that is "even repelled by the notion of God."

R5419 Watts, Richard, Jr. "Graham Greene's Horror Drama." NYP, (18 Nov.). A review of The Living Room and performance. Describes it as a "religious horror play" which makes both religion and sex seem equally "ugly and unappetizing." Concentrates on the spiritual torment of this "brilliant and absorbing drama" which is overwhelmed by a "curiously unhealthy air of desperation and despair."

R5420 Zamora, Rafael Vazquez. "El cuarto de vivir y los cuartos de morir." Insula, 98 (Feb.), p. 12. Trans. Cecilia R. Sheehan. Rejects The Living Room as a theatrical work because of its pasteboard characters devoid of human worth and who react to circumstances in inconceivable ways.

R5421 Unsigned. "The Living Room." Booklist, L (15 June), p. 396. Brief notice of its publication by Viking.

R5422 _______. "No Living Rooms." Commonweal, LXI (10 Dec.), p. 278. Deplores the "baffled reception" of The Living Room by New York critics which seems to indicate that they are "de-equipped to handle theater that encompasses" suffering, guilt, sin and evil, and which seems to reflect, consequently, a culture "secularized ... somehow de-intellectualized ... stripped of even passing acquaintance with the fundamental concerns which had made it great."

R5423 _______. "The Living Room." Commonweal, LIX (12 Feb.), pp. 477-78. Pays warm tribute to this "vividly realized problem play," intensely Catholic, "about Catholic people and in Catholic terms" and in which Catholicism, though dramatized in a highly realistic form, does not obtrude for it is the substance of the play.

R5424 _______. "Too Much Spiritual Furniture?" Newsweek, XLIV (29 Nov.), p. 92. This Newsweek "box" describes The Living Room as a "cubicle of doom" and a "glum iteration of dogmatic platitudes that have the spiritual subtlety of an early Tibetan prayer wheel." See also A5421.

R5425 _______. "Taut Drama." NYHTBR, (13 June), p. 3. Brief mention of the publication of the text of The Living Room.

R5426 _______. "The Living Room." NYTCR, pp. 251-54. Includes reviews of the play and performances by Brooks Atkinson (NYT), John Chapman (DaiN), Robert Clurman (DaiMir), William Hawkins (NYWT), Walter F. Kerr (NYHT), John McClain (NYJ), and Richard Watts, Jr. (NYP). See individual entries.

R5427 _______. "The Theatre: New Plays in Manhattan." Time, LXIV (29 Nov.), p. 50. A review of The Living Room and its performance. Finds the "grim drama" impressive in the first half but declines to the point of being a "distinguished failure" as a result of Greene's compulsion "to prolong the agony without knowing how to dramatize it."

R5428 _______. "No Living Room for Sin?" Time, LXIV (20 Dec.), p. 55. Quotes extensively from Commonweal's complaint about New York critics. See R5422.

R5429 _______. "The Living Room in New York." Times, (20 Nov.), p. 8. Brief news items on the first performance of the play in New York.

D541 De Vitis, Angelo A. The Religious Theme in the Novels of Rex Warner, Evelyn Waugh and Graham Greene. Univ. of Wisconsin.

D542 Elson, John T. The Concept of Order in the Novels and Entertainments of Graham Greene. M.A. Columbia Univ.

D543 Petitpas, Harold M. Tension in Graham Greene. M.A. Univ. of Ottawa.

D544 Wassum, Hans Dieter. Das Bild des Menschen im Romanwerk Graham Greene. Univ. of Mainz.

S541 Walsh, Moira. "The Heart of the Matter." America, XCII (4 Dec.), pp. 284-85. A brief review of the film version.

S542 Unsigned. "Colette's Burial." Commonweal, LX (17 Sept.), p. 573. An account, from a clerical perspective, of the controversy aroused by the denial of the Archbishop of Paris of a Catholic burial to Colette, a distinguished French writer. Criticizes Greene's open letter to FigL questioning the Archbishop's decision for making the Church appear "uncharitable," as a lay intervention in a matter that belongs to "the teaching authority of the Church."

S543 ________. "Letter from Paris." NY, (21 Aug.), pp. 70, 73-76. An account of Colette's funeral. Refers to Greene's open letter in FigL to the Archbishop of Paris, and quotes part of it.

S544 ________. "British Novelist Barred by U.S. at Puerto Rico." NYT, (1 Sept.), p. 9. Brief news item on Greene's detention overnight by American authorities in San Juan.

1955

B551 Blanchet, André, SJ. "Un nouveau 'type' de prêtre." Le Prêtre dans le roman d'aujord'hui. Bruges: Desclée De Brouwer, pp. 59-77. A reprint of the second of two articles in Etudes, CLXXX (March 1954), pp. 303-10. See A541.

B552 Wyndham, Francis. Graham Greene. Writers and Their Work Series, 67. Published for The British Council and The National Book League. London: Longmans, Green. Rev. ed. 1968. The revised 32-page booklet of 1968 is a valuable survey of Greene's writings through May We Borrow Your Husband? for the general reader and undergraduate. This survey highlights the recurrent themes of fear, pity, violence, pursuit and the endless restless quality of man's search for salvation and of God's love for man in the novels, entertainments and plays. Also notices Greene's technical ability, originality and versatility, and regards The Heart of the Matter as Greene's best because of its "tautness, economy and evenness of style."

A551 Battcock, Marjorie. "The Novels of Graham Greene." Norseman, XIII (Jan.-Feb.), pp. 45-52. An informative study of the novels illustrating Greene's ability to create "a quickly-moving plot, suspense, terror ... and documentary precision," to evoke the eerie and the gruesome, and to write in a style which is consistently "beautiful" and tersely dramatic. Although she perceptively ascribes Greene's popularity to his understanding and lucid interpretation of the times, the more detailed examination of Brighton Rock, The Power and the Glory, The Heart of the Matter and The End of the Affair with which the article concludes contains several controversial assertions.

A552 Catinella, J. R. Letter. SatR, XXXVIII (29 Jan.), p. 23. Disagrees with J. M. Brown's assessment of The Living Room, especially with the compassion Brown thinks that Greene lacks. See R545.

A553 Codey, Regina. "Notes on Graham Greene's Dramatic Technique." Approach, XVII, pp. 23-27. Maintains that though The Living Room is informed by a "moral consciousness" that makes the conflict more profound "than an argument between Roman Catholicism and psychology," it is neither "great" nor "convincing," and that Greene's dramatic technique--"the objectivity that makes characters have independent life," sharp selection, swift moving scenes, symbols and economic stage directions--is more discernible in a novel like The Power and the Glory.

A554 Cosman, Max. "An Early Chapter in Graham Greene." ArQ, XI (Summer), 143-47. Illustrates Greene's indebtedness in the areas of diction, portrayal of evil and the failure that follows success to Marjorie Bowen's The Viper of Milan, an indebtedness which Greene had acknowledged and described in his essay "The Lost Childhood." Claims that the connection is not so much in "direct copy ... as in a complex of consanguinity and preview." Of interest is his notice of Greene's "penchant" for key words.

A555 De Vitis, A. A. "Notes on The Power and the Glory." Annotator, 5 (May), pp. 7-10. These "notes" perhaps most suited for undergraduate needs, describe the growth of the novel from Greene's "first-hand acquaintance" with Mexico, examine the "consistent allegory" of this "novel of character," and assert that its Catholicism far from making the novel a "political tract," intensifies "the conflict and dignifies the action."

A556 Gregor, Ian. "The Green Baize Door." Blackfriars, XXXVI: 426 (Sept.), pp. 327-33. A searching literary appreciation of the nature of Greene's novels and the sense in which they can be described as "poetic." Examines the variations of the episodic use of the symbol of the "green baize door" (see The Lawless Roads, pp. 3-4) as a means to convey a vision of life.

A557 Lewis, Theophilus. "Theatre: Post Mortem Report." America, XCII (8 Jan.), pp. 386-87. Attributes the "premature demise" of The Living Room in New York to the failure of "neutral" reviews and the failure of the public to recognize the nature and consequences of sin--"an almost forbidden word" in the contemporary New York Theatre.

A558 McGowan, F. A. "Symbolism in Brighton Rock." Renascence, VIII (Autumn), pp. 25-35. A discussion of the selection and use of symbols in Brighton Rock that disputes Ian Gregor's statement on the narrative pattern of the novel as being "incapable of carrying the deeper meanings of the tale." See A5314.

A559 Maguire, Mother C. E. "Grace and the Play." America, XCIII (30 July), pp. 433-35. Reflections on the problem of making Grace psychologically acceptable on the stage and the inevitable, erroneous, "grim impression" created on non-Catholics by the attempt to portray the agony of a soul trying to adjust to Catholic values, in a world which had watered down these values and even repudiated them. Focusses on The Living Room and Brooks Atkinson's review of the play. See R541.

R551 Betjeman, John. "An 'Entertainment' by Graham Greene Set in Monte Carlo." DaiT, (4 Feb.), p. 8. Emphasizes the "moral" in Loser Takes All but admits that the book is "amazingly and refreshingly readable," full of suspense and "disturbingly accurate" in its observations on the relationship of men and women.

R552 Champness, H. M. "A New Novel." Spectator, (9 Dec.), p. 820. Maintains that Greene in his "very fine" novel The Quiet American, examines the implications of Pyle's "sinister and lethal" innocence as it intrudes on the situation of "colonial twilight" which is faithfully reflected in the life and personality of Fowler. Notes that the desolate background is "brilliantly covered" and that the lack of explicit emphasis on Catholicism is "of a piece with the despair ... in the scene presented."

R553 Cranston, Maurice. "New Novels." Listener, LIV:1399 (22 Dec.), p. 1097. The Quiet American has one cardinal fault: there is no "tension" at the center between the conflicting Fowler and Pyle. Pyle's character is vastly inferior to Fowler's so that morality, intellect and feeling come down heavily on Fowler's side and there is no balance between them. The merits of the novel are conspicuous, especially its effective "terse, bleak style," Fowler's character, the gripping account of the war and the implicit religious views.

R554 Davenport, John. "New Novels." Observer, (30 Jan.), p. 9. A short review of Loser Takes All describing Greene's "unfortunate excursion into the Pink Fairy Book" as "puzzlingly banal" and hoping that he would return to his "sin-sodden minor-public-school men."

R555 Edelman, Maurice. "Greene Mansions." BBM, (March), p. 15. Though Greene calls it a "frivolity," Loser Takes All is a "serene" story with few rumbles of self-doubt and anxiety, and whose "exquisitely simple and unreal plot" makes it suitable as a fairy story for adults. Also includes a review of Twenty-One Stories which notes Greene's "great and complex power," the world of the short stories and their people whom he describes with a "loathing that is so close to love."

R556 G., R. "Recent Fiction." IT, (17 Dec.), p. 6. By ordinary standards, The Quiet American is "an excellent novel" even though it lacks the "inner compulsion" or "the driving tension" which distinguished Greene's earlier works. Wonders whether Greene is suggesting that a Third Force can never play a part in "the final battle between the Kremlin and the Vatican." Also notices a "sloughing-off of imagery" in the novel.

R557 Hodgart, Patricia. "New Novels." Guardian, (1 Feb.), p. 4. Briefly notices Greene's "unexpected" appearance as a "funny man" in Loser Takes All which is described as an "ephemeral" entertainment.

R558 John, K. "Notes for the Novel-Reader: Loser Takes All." ILN, (9 April), p. 668. A short review that emphasizes the "frivolous" or slight aspect of the book. "The small plot is a perfect soufflé; but the gay, cosy chat struck me as rather below par."

R559 Keelan, B. C. L. "Light and Shady." Tablet, CCV (12 Feb.), p. 160. Loser Takes All is a "brisk little story" that has some "ingenious twists and lives up to the author's classification as an entertainment. Even though it has an air of "glossy conventionality" about it, it should make a successful film.

R5510 Metcalf, John. "Loser Takes All." Spectator, 6606 (4 Feb.), p. 138. Critical of the "long short story" or "moral fairy tale" which "might well have been written for Woman's Own, and the shallowness of the characters in spite of their "coy, clipped dialogue."

R5511 "O'Donnell, Donat" [Conor Cruise O'Brien]. "Mr. Greene's Battlefield." NSta, L (10 Dec.), p. 804. A perceptive review of The Quiet American, one of Greene's "best" and "exciting" novels in which he retains his old subject--the themes of guilt and innocence, loyalty and treachery are all here--but he changes his "method." His "dry and casual prose" and narrative manner indicate the "re-emergence of the reporter and the quiescence of the leader-writer" for whom, in Fowler's words, "God exists." Notes briefly the "cumbrous and confusing" themes of "anti-Americanism, defensive discomfort about colonies and apathetic anti-Communism."

R5512 Quennell, Peter. "Ever-Greene." DaiM, (1 Dec.), p. 6. As The Daily Mail Book of the Month for December, The Quiet American is praised for being a "continuously exciting and well written" novel with a convincing portrait of Fowler, whereas Pyle "remains a collection of attributes." Focusses on Greene as an "extraordinarily gifted storyteller."

R5513 Raymond, John. "New Novels." NSta, XLIX:1248 (5 Feb.), pp. 189-90. The short but favorable review of Loser Takes All finds the entertainment to be "smoothly written" and the usual preoccupation "with brimstone and the worm ... absent." It is a "deft, perfectly executed performance," very much like a film.

R5514 Ridley, M. R. "When Idealism is Ill-Informed." DaiT, (9 Dec.), p. 8. As a novelist "incapable of doing poor work," Greene describes in The Quiet American the "ruinous damage that can be caused when (one is) ill-balanced and ill-informed." His characters and setting are "vivid," and there is much of his best writing in this novel, especially the "quietly deliberate brutality" of his descriptions and the telling phrase.

R5515 Servotte, Herman. "Winst of verlies? Bij de jongste roman van Graham Greene." DWB, VI, pp. 367-70. Finds Loser Takes All an unimportant entertainment whose sole positive aspect is an indication that Greene is in need of renewed inspiration.

R5516 Shrapnel, Norman. "New Fiction." Guardian, (6 Dec.), p. 4. In this "superb" novel, Greene comes down from the spiritual heights of earlier novels to deal with the theme of "innocence abroad in a corrupt world." Notes the "satisfying pattern" The Quiet American makes, Greene's grasp of a "compelling idea ... (his) light yet grave handling of words ... (and) quiet, deadly accuracy of phrase."

R5517 Syke, Christopher. "Culpable Innocence." Tablet, CCVI (3 Dec.), pp. 550-51. Notes the departure of The Quiet American in subject from its predecessors--its major theme is political--even though it has "considerable affinities" with The Heart of the Matter. Considers it Greene's "best" novel in spite of the melodramatic tone in the denouement and the sometimes "tedious over-vivid style of reportage."

R5518 Toynbee, Philip. "The Heart of the Matter." Observer, (4 Dec.), p. 11. Contends that The Quiet American, like the two preceding novels, suffers from a serious and destructive moral flaw that rives the psychological argument: Pyle is a "monstrous and impossible combination of two opposing forms of moral error," of naivete and of experience, of ignorance and heartlessness. On all the other levels, the novel is "magnificent" and flawless.

R5519 W., B. "Recent Novels." IT, (12 Feb.), p. 6. Considers Loser Takes All a "thin little story" which, though "readable," tends to leave one "unsatisfied--as though one had just half-seen through an expert conjuring trick."

R5520 Unsigned. "The Living Room." TArts, XXXIX (Feb.), p. 12. Gives a synopsis of the play and the cast.

R5521 ________. "Fiction: Rewards of Love." Times, (2 Feb.), p. 10. Finds the distinction between novel and entertainment reasonable but inadequate to cover the "vein of popular magazine fiction" in which Loser Takes All is written. Suspects Greene of modelling himself on S. Maugham.

R5522 ________. "Good Intentions." Times, (8 Dec.), p. 13. Though the tragedy of "good intentions gone wrong" is not unfamiliar in tragedy, the setting and the circumstances of The Quiet American, portrayed with Greene's customary "verve and skill," are strange. Regards, in retrospect, the "moral ambiguity" on which the narration hinges as somehow contrived.

R5523 ________. "Loser Takes All." TLS, 2768 (18 Feb.), p. 101. Though its technique may be as neat as ever, Loser Takes All has neither the texture nor the characterization of earlier "entertainments" and is, in both substance and length, little more than a short story.

R5524 ________. "A Battlefield." TLS, 2806 (9 Dec.), p. 737. In The Quiet American, Greene raises a moral rather than a religious issue and, as a master of suspense, he builds up the situation to explode the moral problem which is at the heart of the matter. The conflict is not between East and West but between shades of Western opinion as represented by the contrast between his two central characters. The novel has a powerful and lasting effect and forces one to think out the implications of the issues raised. Wonders whether the change from the religious to the moral shows "a change of heart" in Greene whose tone, in this novel, is "less austere and more human" than in earlier novels.

D551 Lamble, M. D. A Critical Study of the Later Novels of Graham Greene. M.A. Univ. of Liverpool.

D552 Priems, C. W. L. The Moral Problem in the Works of Graham Greene. M.A. National Univ. of Ireland.

D553 Siecke, Gerda. Das Romanwerk Graham Greenes in seinem Verhaltnis zu den Romanen van Georges Bernanos and Francois Mauriac. Friedrich-Alexander Univ. of Erlangen.

S551 Bouscaren, Anthony T. "France and Graham Greene versus America and Diem." CW, CLXXXI (Sept.), pp. 414-17. Deplores Greene's attack on U.S. policy supporting Diem in South Vietnam, and his sympathetic view of the Vietminh and Ho Chi Minh.

S552 "Diem's Critics: Graham Greene and Father O'Connor's Reply." America, XCIII (28 May), p. 225. A brief rejection of Greene's attack on Vietnam's Diem which had been reprinted in NRep, (9 May 1955), pp. 9-11.

S553 "Men Who Fascinate Women." Look, XIX (6 Sept.), p. 43. A brief portrait that promotes the rather popular belief in Greene's boredom and ennui.

1956

B561 Bentley, Eric. "A Real Writer." What is Theatre? A Query in Chronicle Form. New York: Horizon Press, pp. 25-29. London: Dennis Dobson, 1957. Rev. ed. incorporating The Dramatic Event and Other Reviews 1944-1967. London: Methuen, 1969. See R544.

B562 Clarke, D[avid] Waldo. "Graham Greene." Writers of Today. Essential English Library Series. London & New York: Longmans, Green and Co., pp. 59-68. Surveys briefly Greene's works up to, and including The Living Room. Emphasizes Greene's achievement in widening and deepening the scope of the novel by depicting "the full horror of human evil and of man's inhumanity to God, of man's inadequacy and awful sense of despair." Notices Greene's ability to "arouse the reader's pity without any direct appeal to his sympathies," his "sensitive imagery" and the "economy and effectiveness of his writing."

B563 Fetter, J[ohan] C[arel] A[ntonie]. De Priesterroman in een Gesaeculariseerde Wereld. Utrecht: Erven J. Bijleveld. Pages 27-30 examine Greene's portrayal of the priest, especially in The Power and the Glory, to determine whether it conforms with the traditional Catholic viewpoint.

B564 Miller, Alexander. "Man at the End of His Tether. Great Britain: Graham Greene." The Renewal of Man: A Twentieth Century Essay on Justification by Faith. London: Gollancz, pp. 28-34. In their emphasis on the need for a virtue beyond human capacity, Greene's four "Catholic" novels constitute a "prolegomenon," a sustained essay, the "most powerful in modern literature," on the Christian doctrine of the Grace of God.

B565 O'Faolain, Sean. "Graham Greene: I Suffer; Therefore, I Am." The Vanishing Hero: Studies in Novelists of the Twenties. London: Eyre and Spottiswoode, pp. 73-97; Boston: Little, Brown, pp. 45-73. A revised version of a 1953 Seminar in Criticism at Princeton Univ. Argues that Greene's attempt to express the moral destiny of man in terms of this world has the effect of "disintegrating his characters, of liquifying them, possibly of dehumanizing them" even while enlarging the imaginative and visionary content of the work. Examines Greene's "instinctive or emotional" attraction to evil, the sense in which it is regarded as Jansenist, and analyzes four cardinal characteristics of the novels: the obsessive theme of betrayal, the denial of free will, the belittlement of human nature (it is O'Faolain's contention that the "conceptual hero" of the classical novel has been replaced in contemporary fiction by the "anti-hero" or the "tortured martyr"), and the "mystical escape from nature." Stamboul Train, The Power and the Glory, The Heart of the Matter and The Living Room.

B566 Scott-James, R[olfe] A[rnold]. "Novelists--Recent and Contemporary." Fifty Years of English Literature 1900-1950. London & New York: Longmans, Green. Rpt. with a Postscript, 1950-1955. pp. 163-88. Pages 176-79 assess Greene's achievement. Considers Greene as a writer "worth taking very seriously" and as a man with "taste as well as conviction" and whose preoccupation with the painful does not preclude pleasure or wit. Examines briefly The Power and the Glory which, he thinks, will rank "among the major novels of the century."

A561 Allen, Walter. "Awareness of Evil: Graham Greene."

Nation, CLXXXII (21 April), pp. 344-46. A review article on *The Quiet American.* Describes the novel as the "unflawed expression" of Greene's talent, especially of his awareness of the two worlds of heaven and hell, and the "possibilities of betrayal between them." Also notices Greene's "sense of pity" which gives "his later work its resonance," and his "concern" with narrative techniques.

A562 Bowen, Elizabeth. "Story, Theme, and Situation." *Listener*, LVI (25 Oct.), pp. 651-52. The first of three talks on the novelist's craft. Quotes the opening of *Brighton Rock* to illustrate one of the three "essentials" of a story--the good start that sets scene and atmosphere with "tautness" and "quickness."

A563 Cooney, T. E. "Author as Traveller." *SatR*, XXXIX (10 March), p. 12. A brief and elementary account of Greene's travels which have provided the "exotic" backgrounds for his "morality adventure tales."

A564 Daiches, David. "The Possibilities of Heroism." *ASch*, XXV (Winter), pp. 94-106. A scholarly discussion of the stature of the hero in the light of the problems posed by new psychological knowledge, and whether the hero can achieve "moral stature" in modern fiction. Includes a rather controversial statement on Greene's use of religion and his determination to show "the essential incompatibility between human decency and theological virtue."

A565 Davenport, John. "The Dickens of the Modern World: An Assessment of Graham Greene." *B&B*, (Feb.), p. 7. Greene is the Dickens of today for he shares with the earlier novelist the same "feeling for the grotesque, the same understanding of childhood ... the same deep compassion." Though he may not compose on the same scale as Dickens, what Greene "loses in mass," he gains in depth for he is also a "Catholic moralist" who, with great psychological insight, power of dramatic structure, "brilliant economy and sharpness" of dialogue and a "tragic sense of life," brings to the novel a new "sense of sin."

A566 Elistratova, Anna. "Graham Greene and His New Novel." *SovL*, VIII, pp. 149-55. Surveys briefly the "characteristic" works that led to *The Quiet American* from a marxist viewpoint, conveniently omitting *The Power and the Glory*. Capitalizes on the portrayal of Pyle and his destruction, and puts undue emphasis on the novel as a tract against "social injustice," "military aggression" and the "encroachment of a people's freedom."

A567 Ellis, William D., Jr. "The Grand Theme of Graham Greene." *SWR*, XLI (Summer), 239-50. An appreciative discussion of Greene's personal vision of "the appalling mysteries of love moving through a ravaged world" which he has "artistically transmuted" into his writings. The Lost Childhood, Journey Without Maps, The Lawless Roads, The Man Within and Brighton Rock.

A568 Freedman, Ralph. "Novel of Contention: The Quiet American." WesR, XXI (Autumn), pp. 76-81. A perceptive discussion that steers away from surface discussions of the "time-bound and parochial," i.e., American politics and mores, to the deeper issue which gives the novel its "universal scope"--Greene's indictment of la condition humaine and his embodiment of "the principal failure of human involvement and choice in the twentieth century," all of which points to the "existentialist lens" through which the novel is seen. Also considers symbology and irony in the novel.

A569 Hicks, Granville. "In a Novel It's the Life, Not the Politics, that Counts." NYTBR, (12 Aug.), p. 5. Disapproves of R. G. Davis's denouncement of the anti-American bias in The Quiet American (see R569) and maintains that what matters more in a political novel is the "independent life," the qualities that keep a book alive, rather than the transitory character of political issues raised.

A5610 North, Roy. "Graham Greene." VQ, (Spring), pp. 376-99. A lengthy but rather cursory survey of themes and topics with a brief consideration of style. Maintains that the decay of civilization, the sense of evil, and the desire for self assertion are the main themes of Greene's pre-war novels, and that later novels deal fundamentally with moral problems.

A5611 Parinaud, André. "La leçon de vengeance de Graham Greene." Arts, 565 (25 April), pp. 1, 6. An account of an interview which sustains the notion of Greene's customary gentleness, "impassibility and polite resistance," and in which Greene looks back on certain similar but painful experiences at school and college.

A5612 Pick, John. "London Letter." Renascence, IX, pp. 12-14. A running commentary on the writings of Catholic writers in England in 1956. Makes a few desultory remarks on Greene's achievement, the dramatization of The Power and the Glory at the Phoenix Theatre, and the impact of The Quiet American.

A5613 Scott, Nathan A., Jr. "Catholic Novelist's Dilemma." ChrC, LXXIII:31 (1 Aug.), pp. 901-02. A review article on The Quiet American which, though sensitive to the anti-Americanism of "gross nonsense" splashed across the book, considers the novel not only as the "parable of modern politics" with contending parties, but also as a statement on the "politics of salvation" and the fundamental human situation, in keeping with the religious position advanced in earlier novels.

A5614 Silveira, Gerald E. "Greene's 'The Basement Room.'" Explicator, XV:3 (Dec.), item 13. Interprets Philip's story and the test he endured when seven as an "explicit" Catholic statement on the damnation of self which inevitably follows "the rejection of responsibility and the embracing of an egotistic life."

A5615 Trilling, Diana. "America and The Quiet American." Commentary, XXII (July), pp. 66-71. A charged reply to Mr. Rahv's review of the novel. (See R5620.) Condemns Greene's assault upon America, complains of Mr. Rahv's "tolerance" of Greene and comes close to identifying Fowler's "neutralist position" with Greene and pro-communism. Mr. Rahv's reply rejects Mrs. Trilling's reading of the novel as a political tract and maintains that Fowler, the "mouthpiece of anti-American sentiments," is not "literally" Greene.

A5616 Winship, George P., Jr. "Mission to Novelists." ChrC, LXXIII (18 Jan.), pp. 75-76. Calls for the expression of Christian values in religious novels, and gives in three paragraphs, a Protestant perspective on Greene's novels. Emphasizes Greene's advantage over his Protestant confrères in his use of "sacramental acts" and concrete actions as an "objective correlative."

A5617 Woodcock, George. "Mexico and the English Novelists." WesR, XXI (Autumn), pp. 21-32. A sound article that probes into the role of the Mexican myth in the writings of Lawrence, Huxley and Greene. Argues that the "curiously exaggerated" description of Mexico in their novels is an "imposition over the true map" of each author's personal hopes and fears, a projection of a state of mind he dreads most. Section 4, pp. 29-32, shows how the journey remains a constant symbol in Greene's treatment of good and evil, "giving progression to the central theme," and maintains that his journey into Mexico gave him a renewed apprehension of the abundance of Divine Grace.

A5618 Unsigned. "To Get Rave Reviews, Write an Anti-U.S.A. Novel." Editorial. SatEP, CCXXIX (6 Oct.), p. 10. Expresses shock at the fact that The Quiet American "won top place in a poll of leading newspaper reviewers," and contempt for Greene, "an opium smoker." A typical interpretation of the novel as a piece of anti-American invective or a political tract that lends itself to communist propaganda.

R561 Arnold, G. L. "The Quiet American." TCLon, CLIX:94

(Jan.), pp. 90-92. Rpt. in Collected Essays. New York: Viking, 1973, pp. 490-92. Focusses on Greene's indebtedness to the contemporary "hard-boiled school of American fiction," especially Raymond Chandler, in his creation of the "Yankee-baiting" Fowler.

R562 Barr, Donald. "The Quiet American." SatR, XXXIX (10 March), pp. 12-13. Predicts the "indignation" that Greene's "best work since 1940" and the Saturday Review's Book of the Week will arouse in the U.S. Points out the confrontation under the dash and intrigue of the tale as "Innocence and Experience in love; America and Europe in politics." Also comments on Greene's treatment of adultery, suffering and the construction of the novel.

R563 Braybrooke, Neville. "An End to Anguish?" Commonweal, LXIII (20 Jan.), pp. 406-07. Notes the change in the "pattern" of Greene's writing with the latest "entertainment," Loser Takes All, which carries with it some "interesting social implications." The "obsessions" still recur but they seem "less tortured than before."

R564 Brennan, Neil. "Coney Island Rock." Accent, XVI (Spring), pp. 140-42. A perceptive review of The Quiet American partly as an evaluation of two types of Americans--Granger and Pyle--against a "backdrop" of international politics in Saigon, and partly as innocence confronting the reality of political involvement or as a "political moral" on the introduction of a Third Force which, he cautions, will probably lead to misinterpretation. Notes the descent of Fowler and Pyle from earlier Greenean figures, and criticizes Greene's "heavy-handed manipulation of symbols" and especially his manipulation of Pyle, but points out that the "novel's poetic values, brilliant characterization and intellectual honesty" make it a masterly literary creation.

R565 Clancy, William. "The Moral Burden of Mr. Greene's Parable." Commonweal, LXIII (16 March), p. 622. Argues that in The Quiet American Greene has written a parable of Americans abroad and, like all moralistic tales--Greene is "primarily, and inveterately, a moralist"--the novel has the typical flaws: Pyle is a "caricature," a mere foil to Fowler, and the novel represents the vices and virtues of a morality play. But it fails to "come to terms with its own burden"; both Fowler and Pyle are not "at home" at the lofty level of "innocence, suffering and death" nor do they illuminate the darkness Greene sees around.

R566 Clurman, Robert. "In and Out of Books: The Quiet Englishman." NYTBR, (26 Aug.), p. 8. Maintains that The

Quiet American is "religious as well as political" and that a great deal of the controversy--and hostility--raging over the question whether Fowler and Pyle represent "antagonistic political and national points of view" stems from ignorance of the novelist's technique when he uses the first person point of view.

R567 Corke, Hilary. "Matters of Opinion." Encounter, VI (Jan.), pp. 88-89. Maintains that the theme of The Quiet American is Henry James' "innocent American at large, crossed with Mr. Greene's old one of the white man in the dark man's land," and that this "eminently readable" and "promising" novel, with its brilliant though not penetrating character study of Pyle, falls into a "no-man's-land between thriller and psychological novel." Contends that in his earlier fiction, Greene's commitment to certain opinions directed the action, unlike The Quiet American.

R568 D., R. "Tender Spot." SatN, LXXI (12 May), p. 18. A brief review of The Quiet American noting Greene's "galling" criticism of Americans and the bitter comments of American critics.

R569 Davis, Robert Gorham. "In Our Times No Man Is a Neutral." NYTBR, (11 March), pp. 1 & 32. Considers The Quiet American as a "political novel or parable," which employs its "custom-made characters" as representatives of their nations or political factions, and uses the war in Indo-China to produce a specific ideological and political effect, especially when one reads it against the background of Greene's earlier articles to The Times about the war. Angered by Greene's "crude and trite" caricatures of American types, as well as the absence of "real debate" in the novel--Fowler invariably triumphs in his "debates" with the Americans.

R5610 Gardiner, Harold C. "Nature and Grace." America, XCIV (10 March), p. 639. Describes The Quiet American as a "musty-smelling" novel, "disappointing" in its choice of a theme not commensurate with Greene's talent, and whose tone is "needlessly and depressingly unwholesome." Doubts Greene's "competence to comment" on Indo-China and asserts that Greene's "salvation as a writer would seem to depend largely on his sticking to themes with a definite religious element."

R5611 Ghent, Dorothy Van. "New Books in Review." YR, (Summer), pp. 629-30. Maintains that The Quiet American is an "angry" novel hastily written to "an existentialist formula of the guilt of 'engagement'" and that Greene's "dishonesty" in exploiting "his English ... readers' notions of the undried-behind-the-ears Americans ... is of a piece with his dishonesty in the technique of his narrative"--the "gimmick" of Fowler's gratuitous withholding of essential plot information.

R5612 Hackett, Francis. "The Quiet Englishman." NRep, CXXXV (30 April), pp. 27-28. Asserts that The Quiet American can be taken as a "straight story, or as a polemic, or as a symbolic testament." The polemic, however, lacks guidance, and the study of two characters--two "infantilities"--at cross-purposes needs some counter-balancing to reduce the acrimony.

R5613 Hobson, Laura Z. "Innocent Abroad." GH, CXVII (March), p. 13. Focusses on the story element of The Quiet American which she finds one of the "saddest and most touching," and least "dreary or seedy."

R5614 Hogan, William. "Graham Greene Turns to War in Indo-China." SFC, (9 March), p. 17. Finds The Quiet American "tense" and a skillfully wrought complex network of ideas, intrigue and first rate war reporting. Though "anti-American," and generally critical of U. S. intervention in Indo-China, the novel remains the season's "most interesting" and "avidly" read book.

R5615 Hughes, Riley. "The Quiet American." CW, CLXXXIII (April), pp. 68-69. Regards the "marvelously compact, authoritative" novel as a return to the earlier "entertainments," and a "continuation in style, mood, and method" of Greene's religious novels--though an atheist, Fowler "interprets everything in terms of belief." It is also a political novel which is "fun, brisk sharp fun, to read."

R5616 John, K. "The Novel of the Week: The Quiet American." ILN, (14 Jan.), p. 70. Calls it a "problem" novel because of the conflicting views it raises but agrees with the general view that whatever Greene, the "unrivalled storyteller," does, he does "beautifully," whether it is the background of the war in Indo-China, the horror scenes or the creation of character. Describes Pyle as a "factitious" character even though he is "brilliant."

R5617 Lehmann, John. "The Blundering, Ineffectual American." NRep, CXXXIV (12 March), pp. 26-27. Regards The Quiet American as a "most icily anti-American" novel that has not weaned itself from the religious theme of earlier works. The keynote of the book is a "bitter disgusted irony," its construction "masterly in its cunning," its war scenes "brilliant reporting" with each episode picking out a detail "to pin-point the horror and misery"; but it is also flawed by "excessive caricaturing" of American characters in particular, and the "almost unvaryingly tight-lipped curtness of dialogue and comment."

R5618 Liebling, A. J. "A Talkative Something-or-Other." NY, XXXII (7 April), pp. 136-42. A rather humorous and lengthy "review" wherein Fowler is transformed into a wishful thinking American and Pyle into a French conception of an Englishman. Though the review ridicules Greene's anti-Americanism, it inadvertently indicates the concern aroused by Greene's criticism.

R5619 Prescott, Orville. "Books of the Times." NYT, (9 March), p. 21. Notes that though it "isn't a good novel," the story of The Quiet American is "dramatic and interesting" and the "flamboyant local color" well done. Attributes its "bitter anti-American bias," which he finds exasperating and preoccupying, to "several subordinate characters painted in vitriol" and Fowler's "rancorous and stupid" generalizations.

R5620 Rahv, Philip. "Wicked American Innocence." Commentary, XXI (May), pp. 488-90. Agrees with G. L. Arnold's view (see R561) because The Quiet American, "a thriller with political implications," satisfies the patent "irresistible formula" widely used in fiction. The central part of the review discredits the "political content" of the novel and Greene's "clever" but "pettish and fretful" attack on the U. S., and questions whether Greene is "sufficiently political-minded" to deal with the issues. Expresses the view, prejudiced perhaps, that Greene is "generally overestimated," an exceptional writer "more apt to entertain than to disturb," and whose "imaginative faculty is more manipulative than creative."

R5621 Rolo, Charles J. "Reader's Choice: The Quiet American." Atlantic, CXCVII (March), pp. 82-83. Notices the mystery and suspense generated by the narrative manner, the absence of religion and the theme of American "innocence" versus European "experience."

R5622 Roswald, Robert. "Graham Greene op nieuwe paden." Periscoop, (1 Feb.), p. 7. Impressed by the location of the action in The Quiet American on the human plane rather than the supernatural, now that the main character is not a believer.

R5623 Stead, Ronald. "The Disquieting Graham Greene." ChrSM, (22 March), p. 11. Finds The Quiet American a "provocative" novel that is a "brilliantly composed political parable" indicting the U. S., and the two main characters "fatuous." Admits the tendency to identify the "odious narrator" with Greene.

R5624 Sullivan, Richard. "Intricately Plotted Love and Murder in Saigon." CST, (11 March), pp. 1-2. Considers The Quiet American "agonized and tormented," a "political allegory" that relies on "melodramatic event" and "garishly caricatured types" to project a "dim and distorted" view of current continental complexities.

R5625 Ullman, James Ramsey. "A Skillful Tale of Adventure in Saigon and a Burlesque of Yankee Innocence." NYHTBR, (11 March), p. 3. Maintains that The Quiet American reads like a "burlesque" its principal characters are "fantastic," especially Pyle, and the views propounded are "astonishing."

R5626 Walbridge, Earle F. "The Quiet American." LJ, LXXXI (1 March), p. 634. Brief notice of publication recommending the novel to "Public Libraries and College browsing rooms."

R5627 Wilson, Angus. "Tragedy in Indo-China." B&B, (Jan.), p. 14. In The Quiet American Greene has "successfully married his great gifts as a novelist to his intense, almost unbearable sense of pity." Though the "moral issue" has not changed, the book is free from "direct theology" so that Greene has scope to develop his "ironic humour" which, coupled with his excellent storytelling, his "beautifully realised" characters and his "funny" and "neat" dialogue, makes an "exciting, distinguished book."

R5628 Wood, F. T. "Current Literature, 1955." ES, XXXVIII (Aug.), p. 186. Finds The Quiet American "disappointing." In spite of the well created atmosphere and local color and the absence of religious dogma, the "central character and the basis of the plot are alike unconvincing."

R5629 Unsigned. "The Quiet American." Booklist, LII (15 March), p. 292. Briefly noted.

R5630 ________. "The Quiet American." Bookmark, XV (May), pp. 190-91. Briefly noted.

R5631 ________. "Theatre Notes." English, XI (Summer), p. 57. A short note on Peter Brooke's production of the dramatization of The Power and the Glory and the lack of dramatic tension in it, especially when the action remains static after the suspense of the first scene.

R5632 ________. "The Quiet American." Kirkus, XXIV (1 Jan.), p. 13. A short review describing the novel as a "morality ... of impulsive idealism ... up against the moral inertia of the rest of the world," a rather disquieting examination that substitutes political conscience for the spiritual concern of earlier novels.

R5633 ________. "This Man's Caricature of the American Abroad." Newsweek, (2 Jan.), pp. 58-59. Describes The Quiet

American as a "political" novel whose theme is "political innocence." Predicts the "barrage of indignation" which Americans will raise against Greene for his caricature of the American abroad. Finds the novel, in the last resort, "not convincing" because Pyle is "too much of a cardboard lampoon."

R5634 _______. "L'Americain tranquille." NL, (8 March), p. 7. Brief notice of publication and of Greene's forthcoming visit.

R5635 _______. "Greene Hell of Indo-China." Time, LXVII (12 March), p. 88. Like his other novels, The Quiet American translates Greene's "journalist's impressions into one of his novelistic moral conundrums"; but the manner in which Fowler and Pyle are brought into "moral contest is a masterpiece of Greene narrative technique." Finds that Greene's extreme anti-Americanism mars what could have been "first-rate fiction."

D561 Patten, Karl Walson, Jr. The Relationship Between Form and Religious Ideas in the Fiction of Graham Greene. Univ. of Boston.

D562 Sheehan, Thomas M. The Catholic Treatment of Sin and Redemption in the Novels of Graham Greene. Univ. of Ottawa.

S561 Unsigned. "Greene's Disservice to the Church." America, XCIV (11 Feb.), p. 518. Brief comment describing Greene's criticism of the Vatican (SunT, 15 Jan. 1956) for not recognizing Polish acquisition of the Western Territories as "both mischievous and in bad taste."

S562 _______. "When Green Is Red." Newsweek, XLVIII (1 Oct.), pp. 94, 96. Brief comment, rather petulant, on the Russian acclaim of The Quiet American and the interpretation of its characters into "cut-and-dried political symbols" and marxist stereotypes.

1957

B571 Atkins, John (Alfred). Graham Greene. London: Calder; New York: Roy Publishers. Rev. ed. London: Calder and Bayars, 1966. The rev. ed. includes an additional chapter (21) dealing with books published after 1957. The study attempts to assess the development of Greene as a writer utilizing the critical-biographical approach. However, the year-by-year account and novel by novel discussion tend to focus upon and analyze the moral and religious preoccupations behind the works with which the critic seems to have little sympathy. Also tends to associate characters from the novels with Greene himself in his attempt to assess the personality of Greene through the writings. Assessment of works is rather diffuse at times and based on subjective observations. The study has no index and no bibliography; its footnotes are minimal--explicatory notes rather than informative of sources.

B572 Kerr, Walter. "Playwrights: -5." Pieces at Eight. New York: Simon and Schuster. London: Max Reinhardt, 1958. pp. 141-49. Though he does not deny the insights of "the religious intelligence" into the world of playmaking, he attributes the failure of The Living Room which he describes as "arid and unmoving," to Greene's inability to recognize the limitations of the playwright: as a dramatist he can only show "the impasse, the ache, the unintelligibility" but cannot carry us over into "that supernatural understanding that will make everything tolerable, everything just." Greene looks at his people "from a supernatural point of view that is not dramatized." On the other hand, The Potting Shed "permits the supernatural to enter the room and to contend with the natural"; but Greene again attempts what is "almost impossible for the theater to do: to explain, complete, and resolve the fleshly terror ... of his characters, in terms of a Divine pattern ... essentially invisible, essentially incapable of translation into the concrete world...."

B573 Lodge, David. About Catholic Authors. "Tell Me Father" Series. London: St. Paul Publications; Dublin: Browne & Nolan. Notes briefly on pp. 15-16 that The Power and the Glory is Greene's "most powerful novel to date" and its concern for the priesthood to be most Catholic.

B574 Matthews, Ronald de Couves. Mon Ami Graham Greene. Trans. from the English by Maurice Beerblock. Bruges: Desclée de Brouwer. An account of "conversations" with Greene on topics ranging from experiences at school to the writing of The Potting Shed. Makes good reading as "a sort of" biography of Greene but is now partly superseded by the more compact A Sort of Life and the Introductions to the Collected Edition. The "conversations" about the novels, given in the chronological order of the novels, provide some interesting details about their origins and composition.

B575 West, Anthony. "Graham Greene." Principles and Persuasions: The Literary Essays of Anthony West. New York: Harcourt Brace, pp. 195-200; London: Eyre and Spottiswoode, 1958, pp. 174-78; Kraus Reprint, 1970. Rpt. from NY, XXVII (10 Nov. 1951), pp. 141-42, 144. See A5133.

B576 Zabel, Morton Dauwen. "Graham Greene: The Best and the Worst." Craft and Character: Texts, Method, and Vocation in Modern Fiction. London: Gollancz, pp. 276-96. An enlarged and revised version of "Graham Greene." Nation, CLVII (3 July 1943), pp. 18-20. See A433.

A571 Becher, Hubert. "Der Stille Amerikaner." SZ, CLX (April), pp. 68-72. A review article on The Quiet American from a Catholic doctrinal viewpoint. Discusses suspense, structure, language, characterization and the open end where Greene, as a conscious artist, withholds answers from the reader.

A572 Beebe, Maurice. "Criticism of Graham Greene: A Selected Checklist with an Index to Studies of Separate Works." MFS, III (Autumn), pp. 281-88. This is the first extended checklist of Greene criticism. Part I lists some 85 books and articles on Greene and his writings in English, French, Swedish and German, excluding unpublished dissertations and journalistic reviews. Part II is a selection of significant discussions of individual works from this body of criticism as well as other sources.

A573 Beltzikoff, Boris. "Kaj Munk Och Graham Greene: En Studie i Kristen Kriminologi." OB, LXVI, pp. 249-58, 331-36. In Swedish. A study of the two writers. The section on Greene underlines Greene's rejection of "civilization," and concentrates on Brighton Rock to illustrate his interest in "djavuls-teologi," or evil and damnation.

A574 Cassidy, John. "America and Innocence: Henry James and Graham Greene." Blackfriars, XXXVIII:447 (June), pp. 261-67. In view of the common recognition of evil by the two writers, the article makes interesting comparison between the two writers' treatment of the American abroad as a "valid correlative" for innocence "loosed among the tangles of an older and more complex world" in Daisy Miller and The Quiet American.

A575 Cockshut, A. O. J. "Sentimentally in Fiction." TCLon, CLXI (April), pp. 354-61. Defines sentimentality as an "evasion of a clash between desires and principles" and describes variations of it in the works of six novelists. Argues on pp. 359-61 that Greene's "tough" sentimentality, so common today, springs from a "determination not to be impressed by what would be very shocking, surprising and alarming to most people," and is also rooted in his "equivocal attitude to sin"--his fascination for it even while asserting that goodness is more varied and interesting.

A576 Cottrell, Beckman W. "Second Time Charm: The Theatre of Graham Greene." MFS, III (Autumn), pp. 249-55. A pioneering and appreciative essay on Greene as an important religious playwright in the contemporary theatre. Attributes the success of The Living Room to the asking of "embarrassingly fundamental perhaps unanswerable questions," and The Potting Shed to "an almost complete identity of message and form," and because the "search pattern," a common feature of his works, reaches a "kind of apotheosis" in it.

A577 De Vitis, Angelo Antony. "Allegory in Brighton Rock." MFS, III (Autumn), pp. 216-24. Provides a lucid and useful insight into Brighton Rock, Greene's first novel with an explicit religious theme. Argues that to understand the novel, Brighton Rock should not be read as a mere "thriller" but as a medieval allegory whose "chief polarities of good and evil are established by Rose and Pinkie; the middle ground ... by Ida Arnold."

A578 Evans, Robert O. "Existentialism in Graham Greene's The Quiet American." MFS, III (Autumn), pp. 241-48. An analysis, amply illustrated, of the similarity between Greene and Sartre in "aesthetic existentialism," the doctrine of individual freedom of choice, treatment of sexual matters, existentialist anguish, the concept of nothingness, amorality and political philosophy. Maintains that this existential concern "goes a long way towards explaining the anti-Americanism of the novel." As one of the early, perhaps trend setting "existential" readings in English, the article is useful and illuminating although the statement that Greene's movement in the "direction of existentialism has largely escaped his critics" is not wholly accurate. See A465, A4815, and A568.

A579 Fecher, Charles A. "Literary Freedom and the Catholic Novelist." CW, CLXXXIV (Feb.), pp. 340-44. Though it contains two allusions to Greene, this article may be useful in a study of Greene for it depicts the potential the Catholic Faith can have for the Catholic novelist.

A5710 Haber, Herbert R. "The Two Worlds of Graham Greene." MFS, III (Autumn), pp. 256-68. A detailed analysis of the effects of the supernatural in the context of a "grubby, grotesque, and violently inimical" reality in Brighton Rock and The Power and the Glory to prove that both damnation and sainthood are "mirrored counterparts," two sides of the same coin, and that the Whiskey Priest, as a "complex of external demoralization and inner sanctity," reverses Pinkie's "superficial puritanism and deeper malignancy."

A5711 Hargreaves, Phylis. "Graham Greene: A Selected Bibliography." BB, XXII (Jan.-April), pp. 45-48. Rpt. with additions in MFS, III (Autumn 1957), pp. 269-80. An accurate listing of Greene's novels and entertainments, short stories, plays, poetry, children's books, non-fiction books, essays and articles. Also gives date and title of different British and American publications.

A5712 Hewes, Henry. "Resurrection Will Out." SatR, (16 Feb.), pp. 26-27. A review article on The Potting Shed that also gives a brief account of an interview ten days before opening night. Maintains that the play is a "clever manifesto thrown in the teeth of an unbelieving age," a play whose "dramatic construction is less effective than ... (its) dialogue or ... (its) presentation of a vital subject," but which remains "somewhat unsatisfactory."

A5713 Jefferson, Mary Evelyn. "The Heart of the Matter: The Responsible Man." CQ, IX (Summer), pp. 23-31. Rpt. in Graham Greene. Ed. Harry J. Cargas. St. Louis, Mo.: B. Herder Book Co., 1969, pp. 88-101. A rather pedestrian analysis of Scobie in the light of Kierkegaard's "ethical man" and the "teleological suspension of the ethical." This is followed by an examination of the problem of responsibility--Scobie's excessive sense of it--and the attendant guilt against which he struggles desperately.

A5714 Kenny, Herbert A. "Graham Greene." CW, CLXXXV (Aug.), pp. 326-29. Though appreciative of Greene's talent as a "connoisseur of conflict" which he portrays in terms of the soul's salvation or eternal dmanation--its sharpest terms--he challenges Greene, perhaps unjustly, to write a novel on the salvation of a "bien pensant, the self-righteous," the lukewarm.

A5715 Lewis, R. W. B. "The 'Trilogy' of Graham Greene." MFS, III (Autumn), pp. 195-215. Rpt., with minor changes, as a section of Ch. VI in The Picaresque Saint: Representative Figures in Contemporary Fiction. New York: Lippincott, 1959; London: Victor Gollancz, 1960, pp. 239-64, in Graham Greene. Ed. Harry J. Cargas. St. Louis, Mo.: B. Herder Book, 1969, pp. 45-75, and in Graham Greene: A Collection of Critical Essays. Ed. Samuel Hynes. Englewood Cliffs, N.J.: Prentice-Hall, 1973, pp. 49-75. A searching and scholarly article discussing Greene's obsessive subject, "the mystery of the human condition," in Brighton Rock, The Power and the Glory and The Heart of the Matter, "his most strenuous, his most satisfying, and artistically, his most assured" novels, each of which has its "correlative entertainment." Concludes that Greene's awareness of the mystery of the human condition in the "trilogy" reverses the movement from "ignorance to knowledge, ... discord to harmony, darkness ... to light" in The Divine Comedy; it constitutes a movement into darkness, to a "helpless awareness of impenetrable mystery, ... from the deceptive light to the queerly nourishing obscurity."

A5716 ________. "The Fiction of Graham Greene: Between the Horror and the Glory." KR, XIX (Winter), pp. 56-75. After making a few snide remarks on The Quiet American--it has an "air of spurious slickness," "an intricate plot with very little action," it "does not engage us on any serious level,"--the article discusses Greene's attempt to supersede "the 'dull, devitalized novel' of 'pure form'" by nurturing the "religious sense," condemned as Greene's "calamitous involvement with the supernatural," by bringing to life "the best and the worst" in seedy human beings in the seediest settings, and accepting the reality of evil. Contrasts Greene's and Camus' reactions to the knowledge of absurdity, injustice and wretchedness in the human situation. (These views are incorporated in Ch. VI, "Graham Greene: The Religious Affair" of The Picaresque Saint. See B597.)

A5717 McCarthy, Mary. "Theatre Chronicle: Sheep in Wolves' Clothing." PR, XXIV:2 (Spring), pp. 270-74. Rpt. in her Sights and Spectacles, 1937-1958. London: Heinemann, 1959, pp. 177-83. A charged disapproval of Greene's "peculiar, sensational Catholicism," and the "unholy alliance between religion and psychiatry" that makes The Potting Shed a "fashionable success." Condemns the "monotonously bootleg character" of religion in his works, "in the aggregate ... tiresome," and Greene for reducing religion to a "form of obscenity," as the "new pornography" for non-believers.

A5718 McCormick, John O. "The Rough and Lurid Vision: Henry James, Graham Greene and the International Theme." JA, II, pp. 158-67. A detailed analysis of the two writers' treatment of the American abroad, the notion of power and its effects upon human beings, the sexual theme and the idea of "innocence," and argues that Greene in The Quiet American has reversed the Jamesian situation of "American innocence" confronted with "dissolute Europeans." See also A574.

A5719 McDougal, Stuart Y. "Visual Tropes: An Analysis of The Fallen Idol." Style, IX, pp. 502-13. A study of the techniques used in the film adaptation of "The Basement Room" to create a range of visual equivalents for the figurative language of the story.

A5720 McLaughlin, John J. "The Potting Shed and the Potter's Wheel." America, XCVII (4 May), pp. 168-70. Attempts to clear Greene of the charge of heresy, and rejects any condemnation of the play on the basis of its dogmatic content as a "singular disservice to Mr. Greene and his potential audience." Exposes the play's "easy compatibility with Catholic dogma and ascetics," and that the pact with God is merely God taking faith in the only way he can "'take' it: to purify it"; hence, the title of the article where the potting shed is really the potter's wheel "used to reshape an intelligent, sensitive and unselfish soul."

A5721 McNamara, Eugene. "Prospects of the Catholic Novel." America, XCVII (17 Aug.), pp. 505-06, 508. Examines, for the average Catholic reader, Greene's problem of fusing "his faith onto the steely framework of the realist's technic," and his method which "contributes to the murky atmosphere ... the essential ambiguity" of his attitude.

A5721a Monden, L., SJ. "'De Tuinschuur.' Drama van ongeloof?" Streven, (Dec.), pp. 272-77. Discusses the value of skepticism in The Potting Shed and questions whether the drama reveals the mystery of belief or is merely a senseless blasphemous fantasy. Concludes that the "polemic undertones" of the earlier Greene have disappeared as he is disarmed by the "magnitude of the mystery" into a silent acceptance of Catholicism.

A5722 Mondrone, Domenico, SJ. "Uno Sguardo su Graham Greene da l'Ultima Stanza." CivC, II (May), pp. 279-93. Voices his "gravi doverosi" reservations over an Italian telecast of The Living Room on the public Milan T. V. because the play, by dramatizing the basic but disturbing Greenean questions arouses fear over a possible discrepancy between what the audience takes away and what the author has said.

A5723 Neis, Edgar. "Zum Sprachstil Graham Greenes." NS, (April), pp. 166-73. An analysis of Greene's stylistic devices in The Power and the Glory which is also a "structural masterpiece." Illustrates Greene's "grandiose Wortsymbolik" and allusions, his use of the vulture as leitmotif and the contrast between appearance and reality, and his use of paradoxical situations as well as parallel ones.

A5724 Patten, Karl. "The Structure of The Power and the Glory." MFS, III (Autumn), 225-34. Rpt. in Graham Greene. Ed. Harry J. Cargas. St. Louis, Mo.: B. Herder Book, 1969, pp. 101-14. A sensitive and perceptive discussion of The Power and the Glory as a "bistructured" novel fusing Edwin Muir's classic distinction between the temporal and the spatial, "the long, melodramatic pursuit and the slowly-developed, carefully-related radiant wheel" pattern where the priest is at the centre--the hub of the wheel--and the quality and meaning of the other characters--the spokes of the wheel--and their relation to him.

A5725 Rewak, William J., SJ. "The Potting Shed: Maturation of Graham Greene's Vision." CW, CLXXXVI (Dec.), pp. 210-13. Reviews Greene's questioning into the problems of sin, evil and suffering in his recent works to show that the maturation of his insight into the tragic in The Potting

Shed is "completed by, and suffused with, a vision of joy."

A5726 Robertson, Roderick. "Toward a Definition of Religious Drama." ETJ, IX (May), pp. 99-105. A summary view of The Living Room to arrive at a definition of religious drama as that which deals with one or more of the following: "man's state of being unrelated to God," "the process through which man goes in order to achieve his relationship with God" and the "religious hero." Tends to agree with the view that the psychological ideas put forward in the play are "naive and dated, the religious arguments bland and hollow."

A5727 Ryan, Thomas C. "A Talk with Evelyn Waugh." Sign, XXXVI (Aug.), pp. 41-43. Perhaps the most sensational statement in the talk is made when Waugh voices his dislike for the term "intellectual" and says, "And certainly no one could be less of an intellectual than Graham Greene." Disagrees with Greene's view expressed in the words that he is a "writer who happens to be a Catholic, not a Catholic writer."

A5728 Schmidthues, K. "Graham Greenes Katholizismus: Die religiose Erfahrung der Welt in seinem Romanen." WW, XII (Jan.), pp. 39-51. A Catholic viewpoint on the religious experience in the world of the novels. Applies Greene's criterion of the "religious sense" to the novels and exposes the distorted but rather puritanical theological outlook behind the novels whose Catholicism is based more on intellect than feeling. However, most of Greene's works he admits, provide "not more than a hint of an explanation."

A5729 Servotte, Herman. "Levensinzicht en Levensaanvoelen in het werk van Graham Greene." Kultuurleven, XXIV (Jan.), pp. 28-40. Rpt. with a few stylistic changes, as "Levensinzicht en Levensaanvoelen in de 'Katholieke' Romans van Graham Greene." Literatur als Levenkunst. Essays over hedendaagse engelse Literatur. Antwerpen: De Nederlandsche Bockhandel, 1966, pp. 36-51. A study of the structure and constituent elements of the two worlds of the novels from The Man Within to The End of the Affair: the world of his heroes and the world of reality.

A5730 Shaw, Russell. Letter. America, XCVII (8 June), p. 293. Questions the validity of McLaughlin's interpretation (see A5720) and suggests that the "flaw" in the play is the "over-extension of the insight of the writer into areas where it cannot possibly hope to operate successfully."

A5731 Spier, Ursula. "Melodrama in Graham Greene's The End of the Affair." MFS, III (Autumn), pp. 235-40. Maintains, in a simple and descriptive analysis, that in spite of Greene's assertion to the Allotts who were then engaged on The Art of Graham Greene that he is excluding melodrama from The End of the Affair, Greene did not succeed in avoiding melodrama but has succeeded in a more subtle use of it, especially in its characteristic elements of pursuit, both physical and spiritual, his "marginal comments," and the "true confession" quality of his interjection of God, and, on the whole, its incidents.

A5732 Sundaram, P. S. "The Problem of Evil in Modern English Fiction." JAU, XXI, pp. 83-138. A course of three lectures delivered at the Annamalai University, India. Pages 111-18 of the second lecture give a cursory account of evil in the form of "crime and violence" and as a "very human problem" in The Man Within, Brighton Rock, The Power and the Glory and The Heart of the Matter.

A5733 Tallon, Hugh J. Letter. America, XCVII (8 June), p. 293. Questions, on the basis of McLaughlin's article (see A5720) why writers do not tell us about "priests and nuns of our ordinary experience."

A5734 Toynbee, Philip. "Literature and Life--2: Graham Greene on 'The Job of the Writer.'" Observer, (15 Sept.), p. 3. An interview focussing on the relationship between the writer and the social problems of his time. Greene makes several revealing comments on specific works, e.g., The Power and the Glory is an "attempt to understand a permanent religious situation," the priesthood, or that the Catholic element in Brighton Rock "was really an after thought." He also makes general comments on his works, e.g., a writer's job is "to engage people's sympathy for characters who are outside the official range of sympathy."

A5735 Zigerell, James. Letter. America, XCVII (8 June), p. 293. Regrets McLaughlin's contention that to condemn The Potting Shed for its dogmatic content is a disservice to Greene and his audience, (see A5720), and wonders whether it is not possible "to work out the meaning of the play within the framework of the play itself."

R571 Atkinson, Brooks. "Theatre: Greene's The Potting Shed." NYT, (30 Jan.), p. 32. A review of the play and its opening performance at the Bijou Theatre. The play has original characters and provocative ideas, is "underwritten," full of "seeds that flourish and yield a bountiful harvest in the last half of the play."

R572 ________. "The Potting Shed." NYTBR, (10 Feb.), p. 1. Maintains that Greene comes to grips with his theme in the second half of the play which is original and stimulating; but the first half is "pedestrian playwriting," disappointing because it lacks personality, is "toneless" in dialogue and "colorless" in character.

R573 Brown, Ivor. "Set in America." Listener, LVIII (8 Aug.), pp. 215-16. On Stuart Burge's American drama production of The Power and the Glory which, though "rich and rewarding" with rapid and effective scene changes, occasionally lacked the "requisite squalor." Moreover, the Whiskey Priest's eagerness to make us love him led him on a "sentimental journey."

R574 Chapman, John. "The Potting Shed: A Mystical and Intellectually Provocative Play." DaiN, (30 Jan.). A review of the play and its performance. Though the play and the event in the potting shed may be "odd," the characters are interesting and the play, a "spiritual and intellectual detective story," is stimulating.

R575 Clurman, Harold. "Theatre." Nation, CLXXXIV (16 Feb.), pp. 146-47. Rpt. as "Graham Greene." Lies Like Truth. New York: Macmillan, 1958, pp. 176-78. Argues that The Potting Shed is "inauthentic," "propagandist," and "bogus." Accuses Greene of a "certain hypocrisy ... or, ... moral diplomacy," in that "the cards are tricked." The notion that the "raising of the dead through prayer and self-sacrifice or ... through faith as a possible basis for belief in God (is) ... essentially irreligious."

R576 Coleman, Robert. "The Potting Shed is a Study of Faith." DaiMir, (30 Jan.). A review of the play and its performance. After a "stodgy start," the play improves as it progresses and finally makes "an auspicious and idealistic bow." Maintains that as a playwright, Greene is "stiff, prone to substitute argument for emotion."

R577 D'Arcy, M. C., SJ. "The Potting Shed: Mr. Graham Greene's Play in New York." Tablet, (25 May), p. 490. Questions whether Fr. Callifer had a right to stake his own faith even for another's salvation. Maintains that though Greene makes the part played by Providence "decisive but mysterious" and is quite successful in leaving the audience in suspense as to the motives and justifications of the main actions, he shows at the end that "faith overcomes death," and that the priest's loss of faith is more apparent than real.

R578 Donnelly, Tom. "A Detective Story for Grown-Ups." NYWT, (30 Jan.), p. 18. A review of The Potting Shed and its performance. This "absorbing" and "psychological detective story" has "bite ... drive ... wit" and living characters but "tends to go off the rails" when Greene rather "abruptly abandons the priest, in a dramatic sense."

R579 Driver, Tom F. "The Player's the Thing." ChrC, LXXIV (27 Feb.), pp. 262 & 267. Reviews The Potting Shed and the cast. Contends that Greene's belief that miracles occur--and in response to people's prayers too--"makes good theatre, but poor theology," and finds the "total scheme" of the play "absurd" for it has no "argument," and the "experience of doubt" which should be central to any contemporary religious play, is confined to Fr. Callifer. This is followed by an interview with Dame Sybil Thorndike.

R5710 Engelborghs, Maurits. "Graham Greene: The Potting Shed." DWB, IV, pp. 306-10. A negative reaction to the play, especially to the preponderance of the religious elements, which prompts the judgment that Greene's talent does not lie in the field of drama.

R5711 Hayes, Richard. "The Stage: A Novelist's Theater." Commonweal, LXV (15 March), pp. 613-14. A review of The Potting Shed and the production at the Bijou. Though he praises Greene for rendering the "supernatural in terms of the natural," and tempering "grace with the gravity that is human," he maintains that Greene's forays into the theatre are "serious divertissements, interludes ... of a professional novelist's career," because his imagination though "dramatic" is not "theatrical."

R5712 Kerr, Walter. "Theater: The Potting Shed." NYHT, (30 Jan.). A review of the play and its performance. Though the issues that intrigue him are "in themselves dramatically undemonstrable," Greene has managed, with "clarity and candor," to overcome the technical awkwardness of the play and turn it into a "strangely compelling one."

R5713 Lardner, John. "A Strong Greene, A Weak James." NY, XXXII (9 Feb.), pp. 66, 68, 70-72. A review of The Potting Shed and the performance at the Bijou. Recommends the play as a tense and exciting entertainment "in a very good, wide sense of the word," but finds the third act in which the conflicts are resolved "too quickly and easily" downright sentimental and weak.

R5714 Lewis, Theophilus. "Theatre: The Potting Shed." America, XCVI (23 Feb.), pp. 594-95. A short review of the play avoiding comment on its theological aspects but noting Greene's ability to make "the friction of ideas as exciting as a brawl on Pier A." Refers briefly to the cast.

R5715 McLain, John. "A Fine Play for 2 Acts--But 3d Lags." NYJ, (30 Jan.), p. 20. A review of The Potting Shed and its performance. Though "always enlightening, and frequently exciting," the play is regrettably "one act too long"; the third act is repetitious and uneventful. The first two acts, however, bring all that is "skilled and captivating" in Greene's writing "into sharp being."

R5716 Millstein, Gilbert. "Books of the Times." NYT, (3 Sept.), p. 25. Notes briefly the "unvarying characteristics" of Greene's works to show that Loser Takes All is an uninteresting "pale carbon" of earlier works that lacks the tension Greene competently generates, and is a "finger exercise for the author."

R5717 Watts, Richard, Jr. "Graham Greene's Absorbing Drama." NYP, (30 Jan.), p. 64. A review of The Potting Shed and its performance. Finds Greene's "dark and tortured probings into the doubts and torments of religious faith" terribly candid, remarkably moving and set down in "brilliantly effective theatrical terms." The "absorbing and fascinating drama" puts to rest any doubts as to whether Greene's talents are "adaptable" to the purposes of the stage.

R5718 Winterich, John T. "Let the Chips Fall." SatR, XL (5 Oct.), pp. 17-18. A short review of Loser Takes All following its serialization in Harper's. Finds the story told with "deftness, gaiety and wit."

R5719 Wyatt, Euphemia Van Rensselaer. "Theater: The Potting Shed." CW, CLXXXV (April), p. 66. A brief review of the performance at the Bijou Theatre and a sketch of the action noting that the child, the deus ex machina, is the "weakest link."

R5720 Unsigned. "The Potting Shed." Booklist, LIII (15 May), p. 473. Brief notice of publication noting that the characters, "though well realized, are subordinate to the philosophic theme."

R5721 ________. "The Potting Shed." Bookmark, XVI (June), p. 211. A brief descriptive note on the publication of the play.

R5722 ________. "The Potting Shed." LJ, LXXXII (July), p. 1792. Brief notice of publication recommending the play to "appropriate libraries."

R5723 ________. "Mr. Greene Promises No More Miracles." Life, (1 April), p. 68. A brief note on The Potting Shed reiterating the title and Greene's statement that he is "bored with the subject" of miracles.

R5724 ________. "Theater: Greene with a Fine Edge." Newsweek, XLIX (11 Feb.), p. 67. A review of The Potting Shed and the production. Finds the play "very much alive" on the stage, a "psychological detective story" in addition to its religious theme.

R5725 _______. "The Potting Shed." NYTCR, pp. 372-75. Includes reviews of the play and performance by Brooks Atkinson (NYT), John Chapman (DaiN), Robert Coleman (DaiMir), Tom Donnelly (NYWT), Walter Kerr (NYHT), John McClain (NYJ) and Richard Watts, Jr. (NYP) on 30 January 1957. See individual entries.

R5726 _______. "Uncertain Miracle." Reporter, XVI (7 March), p. 41. A short uncritical review of the play including brief reference to the Cast.

R5727 _______. "The Potting Shed." TArts, XLI (April), p. 15. A review of the play and performance which also lists the Cast at the Bijou Theatre. Finds the play "literate and absorbing," of some religious substance, whose "ingenious" plot and psychological suspense make it respectable as "playwriting, per se."

R5728 _______. "The Power and the Glory." TArts, XLI (May), p. 24. A brief review of the English performance of the dramatization of the novel at the Phoenix Theatre.

R5729 _______. "New Plays in Manhattan: The Potting Shed." Time, LXIX (11 Feb.), p. 56. A review of the play and production. The play is "more trenchant than artistically rounded," a gripping "what-done-it" whose disclosures constitute the very heart and soul of the play. It is "less dour" than The Living Room because it is concerned with faith rather than sin.

R5730 _______. "B. B. C. Television: The Power and the Glory." Times, (2 Aug.), p. 10. A review of S. Burge's production of the dramatization telecast on the B. B. C.

R5731 _______. "The Lunts Here." Times, (7 Nov.), p. 3. Includes a note on the forthcoming presentation of The Potting Shed in London.

D571 Pépin, Sr. Luciènne. The Function of Imagery in Graham Greene's Fiction. M.A. Rivier College.

S571 Hartnung, Philip. "Short Cut to Hell." Commonweal, LXVII (15 Nov.), p. 176. Review of the remake of the film version of This Gun for Hire.

1958

B581 Astaldi, Maria Luisa. "L'americano tranquillo." Nuove Letture inglesi. Firenze: Sansoni, pp. 417-25. A review article on what appears to be, at first sight, a novel "del genere hard boiled" and which reflects, from a partisan viewpoint, a belief in English superiority, but which also recognizes those American qualities of candor and trust which, at the turn of the century, were contrasted with the cunning and duplicity of the old world.

B582 Clurman, Harold. "Graham Greene." Lies Like Truth. New York: Macmillan, pp. 176-78. Rpt. from Nation, CLXXXIV (16 Feb. 1957), pp. 146-47. See R575.

A581 Bazin, A. "Pour un cinéma impur." RLM, V:63-38 (Eté), pp. 68-73. The whole issue, pp. 1-196 is called "Cinéma et roman: éléments d'appréciation." This section questions whether the art of Dos Passos, Caldwell, Hemingway or Malraux "procéde de la technique cinetematographique" and contains two brief references to Greene's art and adaptations of Brighton Rock and The Power and the Glory.

A582 Braybrooke, Neville. "The Priest in an Age of Psychology: An Enquiry for Novelists." Renascence, XI, pp. 10-13. Brief reference to Greene as an "analyst of the soul" in The End of the Affair.

A583 Camilucci, Marcello. "Saggi cattolici di Graham Greene." Studium, LIV (Dec.), pp. 823-30. A review article on the publication in Italian of Essais Catholiques. Intro. P. David M. Turoldo. Milan: Mondadori, 1958. Welcomes the volume for throwing light on the "religious problem" which is "alle origini" of his novels which have been discussed often for their ambiguity or contradictory views. Greene the essayist unites with Greene the novelist to confirm, in the face of contemporary despair, that "il Dio crocifisso e anche il Dio risorto."

A584 Cosman, Max. "Disquieted Graham Greene." ColQ, VI (Winter), pp. 319-25. An interesting assessment of Greene's seriousness which "shows with disquiet," his independence of view in "the realm of thought" rather than of dogma, his "compulsiveness" and "ambivalence," and his awareness of the "actuality" of Satan in the world. Verges on speculation when he attributes to Greene a "bitterness" towards sex or the view that contact between the sexes is "inevitable but essentially corruptible," and his "disquiet" to something "terribly personal--the hesitancy, perhaps the inability, of a certain person he knows ... to take the leap to sainthood."

A585 De Vitis, A. A. "The Church and Major Scobie." Renascence, X (Spring), pp. 115-20. A new and fresh reading of The Heart of the Matter as a tragedy complete with Fatality (Catholicism), Necessity (imagery, setting and Yusuf), a dramatic construction of plot leading to the inevitability of the catastrophe, individual struggle where the protagonist at once hero, traitor and scapegoat, knows his antagonist (God) and is pitted against Him, and the restoration of balance and order at the end through Fr. Rank. Attempts to strike a balance between the minimization of the theological by the Allotts in The Art of Graham Greene and the theological controversy that raged after the publication of the novel.

A586 Duffy, Joseph M., Jr. "The Lost World of Graham Greene." Thought, XXXIII (Summer), pp. 229-47. A thoughtful discussion of the "precarious and ambiguous course of innocence in a fallen world," its loss and Greene's bereavement and nostalgia for it. Contends that Greene reveals himself as a "fallen-away Wordsworthian," a romantic whose illusions have become grotesque. Shows in a detailed analysis of The Ministry of Fear that Rowe achieves full identity when he discovers his guilt, i.e., matures by completing his journey away from innocence. Concludes with a sweeping judgment, not backed by evidence, that Greene's work, "observed in full perspective ... appears thin, superficial and monotonous. He has never created a fully dimensioned world but only the worn surface of a world."

A587 Folk, Barbara Nauer. "Fiction: A Problem for the Catholic Writer." CW, CLXXXVIII (Nov.), pp. 105-09. Brief reference to Greene and The End of the Affair in discussing the degree in which Catholicity should appear in works of fiction.

A588 H., T. "The Potting Shed: Figmentum Fidei." DubR, 475 (Spring), pp. 71-73. Discusses, from a theological viewpoint after abdicating judgment on the merits of the play, the concept of divine faith, the analogy between the servitude of Father Callifer and the "Dark Night of the Soul," and whether God is "conditioned" by prayer or sacrifice. Asserts that the play is "theologically false" and though it relies on Catholic terminology and a Catholic character, it "is not Catholic."

A589 Hollis, Carroll C. "Nathanael West and 'Lovely Crowd.'" Thought, XXXIII (Autumn), pp. 398-416. Refers briefly on pp. 400-01 to Greene's concern with, and use of, the paradoxical truth of reality that can be grasped only in terms of violence.

A5810 Kerr, Walter. "Cheers for the Uninhibited U.S. Theatre." Life, (22 Dec.), pp. 82-88. Brief incidental reference on p. 88 recording "impatience" with Greene's division of his work into "entertainments" and "novels."

A5811 McMahon, J. "Graham Greene and The Quiet American." JKUR, I (Nov.), pp. 64-73. Unavailable for examination.

A5812 Mesnet, Marie-Beatrice. "Le 'Potting Shed' de Graham Greene." Etudes, CCXCVI (Sept.), pp. 238-47. A detailed analysis discussing, from a Catholic and sometimes theological viewpoint, the conflict between rational skepticism and the miraculous. Appreciative of Greene's daring confrontation with the issue of miracles, for William Callifer's sacrifice is the culmination of similar prayers in earlier works: the Whiskey Priest for Brigida, Scobie for the child, and Sarah over Bendrix.

A5813 Pritchett, V. S. "The World of Graham Greene." NSta, LV:1399 (4 Jan.), pp. 17-18. Examines Greene's "jansenist" sense of evil and his introduction into English fiction of a religion of pain and suffering in the light of J. Atkins' book on Graham Greene. In spite of his emphasis on loneliness, the ugliness of life and its transience, Greene provides a welcome relief from the optimism of contemporary success cults.

A5814 Seward, Barbara. "Graham Greene: A Hint of an Explanation." WesR, XXII:2 (Winter), pp. 83-95. A searching analysis of the sense of guilt central to the characters and their awareness of innocence, sin, evil, suffering and atonement. Concludes, however, that this sense of guilt stems from Greene's "consuming" sense of guilt and "his worthlessness" which, projected "outward to include the whole race through the doctrine of man's fall" present "a conception of life that is strongly infused with private horror."

A5815 Stanford, Derek. "The Potting Shed." ContempR, 1110 (June), pp. 301-03. Rejects rationalist critics' emphasis on the miraculous as the "king-post" of the play and their lack of detachment and inability to "suspend disbelief," and maintains that the central theme is "one of renewal through sacrifice."

A5816 Wassmer, Thomas A., SJ. "Graham Greene: Literary Artist and Philosopher-Theologian." H & PR, LVIII (March), pp. 583-89. Rpt. with minor changes, as "The Sinners of Graham Greene." In DR, XXXIX (Autumn 1959), pp. 326-32, as "The Problem and the Mystery of Sin in the Works of Graham Greene." ChrS, XLIII (Winter 1960), pp. 309-15, and also as "Graham Greene: A Look at His Sinners." Critic, XVIII (Dec. 1959-Jan. 1960), pp. 16-17, 72-74. A perceptive and clear analysis, from a theological viewpoint, of Greene's treatment of the problem and mystery of sin as a "psychologico-moral" experience, asserting the compatibility "between theological faith and rational disbelief (in the sense of dissatisfaction with rational arguments.)" The End of the Affair, The Potting Shed and "A Visit to Morin."

A5817 Wyatt, Euphemia Van Rensselaer. "God in a Garden." DC, I (Feb.), pp. 45-48. A discussion of the central theme of The Potting Shed--the "existence of God"--and the miraculous in the play from a Catholic viewpoint. Regards the play as a "springboard for discussion" that brings God to the world "less wittily than The Cocktail Party but with forthright drama."

R581 Allen, Walter. "New Novels." NSta, LVI (11 Oct.), pp. 499-500. Our Man in Havana is the first of four novels reviewed. Maintains that the distinction between novel and entertainment is made clear with this novel. Notices how the "fairy-story" is played out in a world made "vividly actual, at any rate for the most part" by the "concreteness of its detail" and the "beautifully rendered atmosphere of corrupt and seedy luxury."

R582 Bishop, George W. "Gielgud's Three Parts in Six Months." DaiT, (20 Jan.), p. 11. Gielgud speaks about his role in The Potting Shed and notices Greene's new third act--"a considerable improvement on the old one."

R583 Brahms, Caryl. "Friend or Foe?" P&P, V:6 (March), p. 11. A review of The Potting Shed and the performance. Rather disappointed by the "bloodless mildew" of the grim play which, on the surface, is a "religious whodunit." Also describes it as a "muddled tract" that creates an effect of "listlessness," in spite of the skill of its actors and actresses.

R584 Cain, Alex Matheson. "A Modern Lazarus." Tablet, CCXI (15 Feb.), pp. 152-53. Reviews the English performance of The Potting Shed at the Globe Theatre and argues that the play is no mere "rehash" of the many elements to which one has become accustomed to in Greene's works; the so-called "significance" of the plot is not something "artificially added," but springs from the situation itself in which the characters find themselves.

R585 Cain, James M. "Out of a Need for Money." NYTBR, (26 Oct.), p. 5. Though Wormold's machinations to make money may be a "distinguished narrative idea," Our Man in Havana "misses needlessly where it might have rung the bell" and its characters "lack bone, flesh and blood and only occasionally seem lifelike."

R586 Carlington, W. A. "Do You Believe in Miracles?" DaiT, (24 Feb.), p. 11. Questions whether the critics' "illogical and uncritical" attitude to The Potting Shed is due to their skepticism or disbelief in miracles, or to Greene's serious tone which upset them. Admires the acting and the writing of this "striking but uneven play," and criticizes Greene for overstressing his argument "beyond the limit of stage plausibility."

R587 Davenport, John. "Greene the Entertainer." Observer, (5 Oct.), p. 21. Maintains that the "entertainments" have the same moral value as the rest of his works. As a "thriller and a satire that is also a farcical morality play," Our Man in Havana makes one's head spin; one believes in the story on all its levels and its characterization is masterly: one recognizes the inhabitants of that "tragi-comic Greeneland."

R588 Derrick, Michael. "Simple Spyman." Tablet, CCXII (18 Oct.), p. 336. Finds the first part of Our Man in Havana very entertaining by being "more farce than satire," but the story, half way through, ceases to be a joke and becomes "sinister, a moral tale of retribution" which, after violent deaths, ends up as a love-story with a happy ending.

R589 DuBois, William. "Books of the Times." NYT, (28 Oct.), p. 33. Regards Our Man in Havana as a "crashing failure--if not a crashing bore" because Greene's approach wavers between "outright spoof" and "serious comment"; satire, of a sort, loses under the "deadweight of Wormold's melancholia."

R5810 Finn, James. "Greeneland." Commonweal, LXIX (5 Dec.), pp. 267-68. Notes that Our Man in Havana is not written in the tradition of earlier thrillers, even though it contains all the elements; its virtues cannot overcome its "deeper flaws"--the "systematizing of real insight, the simplistic duality of forces," and the lack of "focus" in the novel. Also notes the "comic slant" of Greene's angle of vision and includes a brief note on J. Atkins' Graham Greene.

R5811 Fleming, Ian. "Trouble in Havana." SunT, (5 Oct.), p. 18. Considers Our Man in Havana "brilliant and utterly compulsive reading and in the highest class" of what Greene calls "entertainments." The "almost Wodehausian" treatment of the Secret Service constitutes perhaps the only weakness of a book which delights by the "sheer intelligence of the writing."

R5812 Hobson, Harold. "Annus Mirabilis." SunT, (9 Feb.), p. 23. Considers Greene as "God's advocate" in The Potting Shed putting His case forward. Also comments on Sir John Gielgud's "masterly" performance as James Callifer.

R5813 Hope-Wallace, Philip. "Mr. Greene's Lazarus Theme." Guardian, (6 Feb.), p. 5. Describes The Potting Shed as a "most interesting moral drama," a "little weak technically" and failing to put the weight of the play behind the pivotal uncle-nephew encounter. Criticizes Greene for having loaded the dice against non-Christians and for preaching at Doubting Thomases.

R5814 Hughes, Riley. "Our Man in Havana." CW, CLXXXVIII (Dec.), p. 248. Describes the novel as an "ironic romp" in which Greene, in a relaxed way, follows the "implications of his light-hearted tale" with occasional "satiric touches."

R5815 Inglis, Brian. "Dungeons of the Mind." Spectator, CC (14 Feb.), p. 203. A review of The Potting Shed and its production at The Globe. Though much of the review goes to a discussion of the real choice Greene is suggesting between "Freud's Way and God's Way," the review maintains that, on the intellectual level, the play is "trite"--a fact which is not of much consequence because The Potting Shed is "less a play of ideas than a conflict of feelings." Critical of the casting.

R5816 John, K. "The Novel of the Week: Our Man in Havana." ILN, (8 Nov.), p. 820. Does not find the novel "entertaining enough"; one does not get much joy out of the farce "for all its skill and brilliance in detail," because the "nightmare" lies on the other side. Objects to the rather "immoral" ending and the lack of regard for "public concern and effort."

R5817 Kermode, Frank. "Havana Rock." Spectator, CCI (10 Oct.), p. 496. Finds it difficult to regard Our Man in Havana as a comedy for Greene's "drollery so closely resembles his despair" and the "posture of his farce is so like that of his tragedy; terror and pity break in" in spite of the "pure absurdity" of his deftly built plot.

R5818 Kilpatrick, C. E. "Our Man in Havana." LJ, (Nov.), p. 3256. Brief notice of publication describing the novel as "a mere imitation" of earlier entertainments.

R5819 Lambert, J. W. "Plays in Performance." Drama, 49 (Summer), pp. 18-19. A brief review of The Potting Shed and its performance. Describes the play as a "disappointment ... determined to avoid drama at all costs: and succeeded."

R5820 Lister, Richard. "Mr. Greene Laughs at Espionage." EvS, (7 Oct.), p. 12. "However unreal the story (of Our Man in Havana) the hot, sleazy, sexy tourist centre of Havana is as real as could be; the dialogue crackles; and the people ... have that air of sad actuality which Mr. Greene injects into all his characters."

R5821 Maddocks, Melvin. "Cuba, Israel and New Mexico in Novels." ChrSM, (4 Dec.), p. 17. Regards Our Man in Havana as a "semi-parody" of the thriller genre whose moods fluctuate between a "gaiety that is a bit too resolute and a violence that is a little too cynical."

R5822 Malcolm, Donald. "Off Broadway: The Power If Not the Glory." NY, (20 Dec.), pp. 68-70. Reviews the dramatization of The Power and the Glory and its production. Argues, rather persuasively, that the dramatization of any novel is, at best, an "unsettling experience," for any gains achieved cannot be offset by the losses in atmosphere and especially character; hence, the "coolness" with which he views the "impeccable" presentation at the Phoenix Theatre.

R5823 Martindale, C. C. "The Potting Shed Exorcised." Month, XIX, pp. 237-39. Surmises, from a Catholic viewpoint, that W. Callifer's offering though heroic, is still imperfect and so, had partial effect on the boy. God does not retract the gift of faith he had given because of a mere mistake; ... the priest "felt as if he had lost his faith." Expresses amazement at the imperceptiveness of the Press about the personality of Anne.

R5824 Offord, Lenore Glen. "The Gary Road." SFC, (14 Dec.), p. 30. A brief review of Our Man in Havana noting the return to earlier "entertainments with a wry twist of laughter added to the melodrama."

R5825 Rees, Goronwy. "New Novels: Graham Greene and Others." Listener, LX (30 Oct.), p. 702. As the "most accomplished" of living novelists, Greene has given us a plot in Our Man in Havana which has the "basic simplicity of good farce"; the story is narrated humorously with the "ease and assurance" of a master and his characters are nourished by an acute sense of time and place. Though the powers of evil are not entirely absent, they are played out by figures of fun.

R5826 Rolo, Charles. "Thrillers: Our Man in Havana." Atlantic, CCII (Nov.), pp. 175-76. In spite of its "wry comedy" which he finds "often very funny," he reads into the novel "Greene's doctrine that human goals are irremediable, sordid and pointless; that man is saved by grace alone."

R5827 S., V. B. "Rough Island Story." IT, (18 Oct.), p. 8. Our Man in Havana shows Greene's "masterly descriptive powers" as well as his narrative ability. As a "comic artist," Greene refuses to let the fundamentally lighthearted narrative become bogged down in special pleading.

R5828 S., W. G. "Our Man in Havana." B&B, (Nov.), p. 39. A short review describing the "entertainment" as "mainly farcical, largely in early Evelyn Waugh style," that has "touches of satire at international affairs, catholicism, and bureaucracy, rounded off with a neat ironic ending."

R5829 Sandoe, James. "Mystery and Suspense." NYHTBR, (26

Oct.), p. 17. Includes a brief review of Our Man in Havana as an entertainment, a joke which is, as a whole, "hard-labored and much more foolish than sardonic."

R5830 Shebs, Robert L. "Greene's First Thriller in 17 Years." CST, (26 Oct.), p. 8. Notes a few differences between Greene's latest entertainment, Our Man in Havana, and his earlier ones.

R5831 Shrapnel, Norman. "A Farce with Overtones." Guardian, (14 Oct.), p. 4. Voices a few "misgivings" about the material of Our Man in Havana: not its spiritual overtones but the tone in relation to the content, because the grave skills and insights made to bear upon what is "sheerly frivolous" arouses "nagging thoughts" that remain unsolved.

R5832 Strikski, O. "Their Man in Habarovsk." Spectator, CCI (14 Nov.), p. 650. Humorous, in the form of a letter by a Russian agent--presumably to the KGB--submitting the following "conclusions": the novel appears at first sight to be a "mere fantasy" but its significance lies in "the general impression" produced, its "ostensible purpose is to amuse; its real aim ... to present ... the British Secret Service as a set of incompetent bunglers."

R5833 Trewin, J. C. "Miracle Play." ILN, CCXXXII (22 Feb.), p. 314. Reviews the performance of The Potting Shed at The Globe. Brief comment on Greene's challenge to "modish nihilism and disbelief," and his "too conscious" manipulation of the "elaborate plotting," but credits Greene with his "sincerity of thought and emotion and his ability to make the audience "feel deeply for his characters."

R5834 Tynan, Kenneth. "Whiskey Galore." Observer, (9 Feb.), p. 13. Rpt. in Curtains. London: Longmans, Green; New York: Atheneum, 1961, pp. 207-09. This is the review in which K. Tynan speculates on "Dog" as "God" spelled backwards. Rejects the principle of "supernatural intervention" for human problems--he is most critical of Greene for it--because such a move has "shot us back overnight to the dark ages."

R5835 W., D. "Talking at Random: Not to be Missed." Tablet, CCXI (15 Feb.), p. 161. A short note advising people to see The Potting Shed for it is "extraordinarily well cast, and interesting from the first moment to the last." Moreover, Greene is very skilled at conveying "a sense of the unseen world, and the reality of Grace."

R5836 Worsley, T. C. "The Art and Entertainment: The English Theatre-at-its-Best." NSta, LV (15 Feb.), p. 196. A review of The Potting Shed and the English production. Mainly concerned with the production though he does criticize Greene, in a way, for not succeeding in making James Callifer's discovery "as dramatic a turning-point, or even as important an event, as we feel it should have been." However, the "beautifully taut, evocative dialogue and ... cunning construction" make the quest "unfailingly interesting."

R5837 Yaffe, James. "Of Spies and Lies." SatR, XLI (15 Nov.), p. 19. Though more "broadly comic" than its predecessors and "farcical" in the manner of E. Waugh, Our Man in Havana remains "flat and disappointing" not only because of its "deficiencies" but also for its "simple minded" political philosophy.

R5838 Unsigned. "Our Man in Havana." Booklist, LV (1 Nov.), p. 126. A short review of this "moderately funny" novel that satirizes the British Secret Service.

R5839 ________. "Greene in Havana." B&B, (Oct.), p. 9. Includes a note on Our Man in Havana in the Autumn preview of new fiction.

R5840 ________. "Theatre Notes: The Potting Shed." English, XII (Summer), p. 58. Notes that this "provocative" play uses a "long-ago" incident shrouded in mystery and guilt to maintain steadily a "quality of tension with the suspense of a kind of spiritual thriller."

R5841 ________. "Our Man in Havana." Kirkus, XXVI (1 Sept.), p. 674. Pre-publication notice of the "entertainment" as a "genial form of nonsense" that offers a "questionable diversion."

R5842 ________. "London Letter: The Grin in Graham Greene." Guardian, (11 Oct.), p. 4. Brief remarks on "damnation and degradation" in the Greene world and of his being "hypnotically readable," occasioned by the publication of Our Man in Havana.

R5843 ________. "The Power and the Glory." Nation, CLXXXVII (27 Dec.), p. 502. Reviews the dramatization which "fails to touch" him because all that finally emerges from it is a "man-hunt" where the hunter and the hunted do not arouse interest.

R5844 ________. "The Way to Doomsday." Newsweek, LII (22 Dec.), p. 46. A review of the dramatization and performance of The Power and the Glory, "an absorbing theater piece," directed by Stuart Vaughan.

R5845 ________. "Our Man in Havana." NY, XXXIV (8 Nov.),

p. 197. Briefly noted as a "cold, thin, generally fascinating story" with an "ironic, fantastic" end.

R5846 _______. "The Quiet Englishman." Time, LXXII (27 Oct.), p. 100. Finds in Our Man in Havana Greene's formula of "suspense plus sin" to be entertaining with a "heavily ironic" ending. Includes a portrait of Greene.

R5847 _______. "The Arts: Globe Theatre: The Potting Shed." Times, (6 Feb.), p. 12. Reviews the play and the performance. Also lists the Cast. Admits that though the "ambiguous nature of the revelation" to which Greene leads up to with "deft strokes of characterization" comes in for "somewhat desultory discussion," the play, as a piece of theatre, has "some fine moments," especially in the powerful scene in Father Callifer's room.

R5848 _______. "New Fiction." Times, (9 Oct.), p. 13. The first of five novels reviewed, Our Man in Havana is described as a "joke inclined to lose itself in sadness and fantasy" that gives an "ironic side-glance" at Secret Service heroes, and moves in a "No-Man's Land between realism and fantasy."

R5849 _______. "The Potting Shed." TLS, (21 Feb.), p. 107. Listed under "Books received" and mentioned as a play running at the Globe Theatre.

R5850 _______. "Mr. Greene Entertains." TLS, 2954 (10 Oct.), p. 573. Points out that there is no "discernible difference" between the subject matter of Our Man in Havana and that of his more austere novels. The novel, though "enjoyable" is not satisfying because its weakness lies in the "impossible conjunction of comedy and farce," and its characters generally drawn from stage and screen rather than from life. What it wants in the sense of form, the novel makes up by being fully entertaining, with every scene masterly "in its placing, its indication of character, its flow of dialogue" and especially in its ability to convey a "well-founded and articulate comic sense."

D581 McLeod, Sr. Madelene S. An Indexed Synthesis of the Critical Thought of Graham Greene and Patrick Braybrooke. M.A. Siena Heights College.

D582 Murchland, Bernard G. The Religious Mission of Woman in the Novels of Graham Greene. M.A. Univ. of Ottawa.

D583 Weales, Gerald Clifford. Religion in Modern English Drama. Columbia Univ. Published. Philadelphia: Univ. of Pennsylvania Press, 1961. See B615.

1959

B591 Davies, [Daniel] Horton. "The Confessional and the Altar." A Mirror of the Ministry in Modern Novels. New York: Oxford Univ. Press; Books for Libraries, 1970, pp. 100-10. Ch. IV, Sec. 3 of a survey of how the Ministry is present in modern English and American literature. Mostly concerned with the portrait of the Whiskey Priest--"the unbaying beagle of the invisible Hunter God" in The Power and the Glory--as a remarkable portrayal of the paradox of Grace, especially in the Priest's consciousness of his unworthiness and his attempt "to evade God and God's pursuit of him." Brief references to Greene's use of symbols and style.

B592 Gardiner, Harold C., SJ. "Why I Liked Some." In All Conscience: Reflections on Books and Culture. New York: Hanover House, pp. 89-123. Includes, on pp. 96-102 of this chapter "Mr. Greene does it again," and "Second thoughts on Greene's latest." Rpt. from America, 27 Oct. 1951, pp. 100-101, and 15 Dec. 1951, pp. 312-13. See R5111 and A5116.

B593 Graef, Hilda. "Existentialist Attitudes and Christian Faith: Graham Greene." Modern Gloom and Christian Hope. Chicago: Henry Regnery Co., pp. 84-97. Examines The Power and the Glory, The Heart of the Matter and The End of the Affair as expressions of the contemporary pessimism of a "hopeless, 'existentialist' world" in which a believer must necessarily "take the Kierkegaardian 'leap'" in order to escape from the despair that is threatening human existence.

B594 Hassan, Ihab H. "The Anti-Hero in Modern British and American Fiction." Proceedings of the Second Congress of the International Comparative Literature Association. Ed. Werner P. Friederich. Chapel Hill: Univ. of North Carolina Press; Johnson Reprint Co., 1970, pp. 309-23. Includes Pinkie, among others, as an anti-hero with whose situation we may identify rather than with his character which is neither "clown" nor "prey" but "saint and devil conjoined," and whose spiritual struggle restores "even in damnation, some of the potency he has lost."

B595 Karl, Frederick R. "Graham Greene's Demonical Heroes." A Reader's Guide to the Contemporary English Novel. New York: Noonday Press; London: Thames and Hudson, 1960, pp. 85-107; rev. and enl. 1972. Contends that Greene attempts to recover the stature of the "hero" for a basically irreligious democratic age, through suffering and pain, and, in keeping with Aristotle's "fall," makes the hero's fall a descent from grace, and his attempt "to embrace faith ... the measure of heroism," thus recasting the Greek hero to suit a Christian framework even while maintaining similar tensions. However, Greene's hero parts company with his Greek counterpart when salvation appears possible for him through God's "almost arbitrary use of grace." The second part of the article examines The Power and the Glory from this perspective.

B596 Kunkel, Francis L. The Labyrinthine Ways of Graham Greene. New York: Sheed & Ward. Originally a Diss. presented to Columbia Univ., 1959, entitled "A Critical Study of Graham Greene." Discusses Greene's themes and ideas, his ethical and theological preoccupations as well as the characters' responses to moral crises. Also attempts to see the works in their setting and to compare Greene with others in his tradition and tendencies. Biographical elements are scattered throughout the book.

The work is divided into five chapters. Ch. 1 discusses Greene's preoccupation with evil by examining his travel books and essays and indicates that Greene is "half-Manichean"--Manichean in his tendency to regard humanity "as fodder" in a battle between heaven and hell, and non-Manichean in his repeated emphasis on "the bottomless plentitude of God's mercy" and the ceaseless flow of His grace. Ch. 2 examines the early novels to show the shift in Greene's preoccupation with man's dual nature, the central theme of The Man Within, to the social and economic problems of It's a Battlefield and England Made Me. Also points out that "points of resemblance" among the characters are more pronounced than the similarities in plot which are saved from repetition by the "tempo" of the story, the complex insight of the author, and the fact that the "trapped man formula" is varied with each novel. Ch. 3 examines each entertainment separately. Taken together, they are distinguished from the novels by Greene's "greater use of melodrama, by a comparative lack of development in the characters, and by a concession to the happy ending"; but, like the novels, they also dramatize sometimes moral problems. Shows affinites with James and Conrad. Ch. 4 discusses the "Catholic" novels: the sense in which they are "Catholic"--their overt inclusion of doctrine, dramatization of theological problems like salvation and damnation, evil and grace--without being "aggressively sectarian ... or piously evangelical." Also examines Greene's presentation of heroines and The Quiet American because it has a "religious theme." Ch. 5 examines Greene's two plays, The Living Room and The Potting Shed as "by-products" of Greene's career as a novelist and focusses on the role played by the priest in the novels generally, and the plays in particular. Maintains that The Potting Shed is "artistically inferior" to The Living Room in spite of being better received by New

York critics. The appendix examines the role of dreams in Greene's fiction.

B597 Lewis, R. W. B. "Graham Greene: The Religious Affair." The Picaresque Saint: Representative Figures in Contemporary Fiction. New York: Lippincott; London: Victor Gollancz Ltd., 1960, pp. 220-74. Incorporates the views expressed in "The Fiction of Graham Greene: Between the Horror and the Glory" (see A5716) and reprints, with minor changes, "The 'Trilogy' of Graham Greene." (See A5715.) After crediting Greene for treating "major preoccupations of our day" with an "unsettling literalness and immediacy," he points out the "emotions of human love" lacking in Greene's works, and examines The End of the Affair as a thorough documentation of the "various relationships, alternatives and paradoxes" that make the world of Greene.

B598 McCarthy, Mary. "Sheep in Wolves' Clothing." Sights and Spectacles, 1937-1958. London: Heinemann, pp. 177-83. Rpt. from PR, XXIV:2 (Spring 1957), 270-74. See A5717.

B599 Mondrone, Domenico. "L'Ultima stanza." Scrittori al turguardo. (Nuova Serie). Torino: Societa Editrice Internazionale, pp. 401-13. A critical essay from a Catholic viewpoint on The Living Room. Focusses on the controversial views propounded and considers the play to be representative of Greene's views. Also discusses the part played by Fr. Browne and the role of the priest and priesthood generally in the Catholic novels.

B5910 Mueller, William R[andolf]. "Theme of Love: Graham Greene's The Heart of the Matter." The Prophetic Voice in Modern Fiction. New York: Association Press. Rpt. New York: Doubleday, Anchor Books, 1966, pp. 135-58. One of six studies of modern novels that consider the relationship between novel and Bible to gain a deeper understanding of theme. Examines Scobie's departure from the tenets of conventional morality and religion, and questions whether Scobie is accurate in his reflection that human love "has robbed him of love for eternity." Concludes that the novel is a "tour de force" whose theme implements Christ's "new commandment" and that Scobie, despite the dimensions of his sin, is perhaps the only character in fiction who actually carries out St. Paul's willingness to be cut away from Christ in Romans 9:3. "For I could wish that I myself were accursed and cut off from Christ for the sake of my brethren, my kinsman by race."

A591 Adam, George. "Graham Greene établit son panthéon des littératures anglaise et francaise." FigL, 680 (2 May), p. 4. An account of an interview in Paris in which Greene expresses views on Our Man in Havana, leading contemporary novelists and poets in England and France, and the "Angry Young Men."

A592 Barlow, G. "L'Art de Graham Greene." Esprit, XXVII (March), pp. 517-25. An account of Greene's indebtedness to, and use of, journalism, the cinema, and the "thriller," and the "signification profonde" he was able to give to the techniques he adopted. Rumour at Nightfall, Stamboul Train, The Power and the Glory and The Quiet American.

A593 Blajot, Jorge, SJ. "La renuncia a la fe de Father William Callifer." RyF, CLX (Dec.), pp. 441-50. Establishes the central themes in The Potting Shed before discussing Greene's "indignidad humana del sacerdote" which he finds theologically difficult to explain, especially that Greene seems to find Divine Mercy most resplendent among the derelicts and the abandoned.

A594 Costello, Donald P. "Graham Greene and the Catholic Press." Renascence, XII (Autumn), pp. 3-28. An informative study of the reaction of the Catholic press to The Heart of the Matter and The End of the Affair, as it appeared in the most "influential" Catholic publications--Commonweal, America, The Catholic World and The Tablet--the "less influential"--Dublin Review, Irish Monthly and Cross Currents--the diocesan weeklies of Chicago and Hartford, Connecticut, and a selection of "lesser known" Catholic publications. The study reveals that the raging controversy that swirled around the two novels had little or nothing to do with literary considerations, that there was no such thing as "a 'Catholic' criticism of Greene, ... nothing approaching unanimity in the attitude of Catholic critics," in spite of the "real enthusiasm for Graham Greene, not untouched by ... pride." Includes a descriptive bibliography of some 80 items representative of the interest of the Catholic press.

A595 Glicksberg, Charles I. "Graham Greene: Catholicism in Fiction." Criticism, I:4 (Fall), pp. 339-53. Rpt. as "Catholicism in Fiction." In his Modern Literature and the Death of the God. The Hague: Martinus Nijhoff, 1966, pp. 122-39. A sensitive and discerning analysis of Greene's endless struggle with sin, his "uncompromising revelation of the power of evil, his psychological interest in the sinful and the suffering, his all-embracing compassion for the torments men endure as they finally face the certain knowledge of doom" to show that the novels, essentially tragedies, rise "above the pull of theological considerations." Maintains that Greene is not writing about Catholicism, but about men and women who happen to be Catholic. Brighton Rock, The Power and the Glory, The Heart of the Matter and The End of the Affair.

A596 Graef, Hilda. "Marriage in Our Catholic Novelists." *CW*, CLXXXIX (June), pp. 185-90. Questions why both Mauriac and Greene depict marriage as an institution "doomed to failure ... as something horrible or boring, or, if physically satisfactory, necessarily sinful." Attributes to Greene, perhaps unjustly, the view that "monogamous marriage seems impossible," and asserts that such an attitude is due to a "jansenist contempt for the physical aspect of marriage and contemporary pagan scorn of the inviolability of its bond."

A597 Hughes, Catherine. "Innocence Revisited." *Renascence*, XII (Autumn), pp. 29-34. Shows that Greene's concern for innocence--often interchanged with childhood--is twofold: a concern for corrupted innocence and an absorption in the moment in childhood that shapes the remainder of life. Of interest to the student and general reader. References to works from *The Lawless Roads* to *Our Man in Havana*.

A598 Hughes, R. E. "*The Quiet American*: The Case Reopened." *Renascence*, XII (Autumn), pp. 41-42, 49. Rpt. in *Graham Greene*. Ed. Harry J. Cargas. St. Louis, Mo.: B. Herder Book, 1969, pp. 130-33. Provides a new insight into Greene's most advanced use to date of dramatic irony wherein Fowler is at once the object of the reader's and the author's criticism, as well as the "obtuse narrator ... who offers his experiences without fully understanding them."

A599 Lanina, T. "Paradoxes of Graham Greene." *IL*, 4 (April), pp. 188-96. Claims that Greene's "moment of crystalisation" when his "private universe" becomes visible to his reader is made possible by external contemporary events, as can be seen from *The Quiet American*.

A5910 Murphy, John P., SJ. "*The Potting Shed*: Dogmatic and Dramatic Effects." *Renascence*, XII (Autumn), pp. 43-49. Refutes an earlier reading of the play (see A5720) and asserts that the absence of balance in Greene's works between compassion for the sinner and condemnation of sin has given rise to "exaggeration and artificiality" in plots whose catastrophes seem to be "forced rather than to flow from the dramatic situation" as can be seen from *The Heart of the Matter*, *The Living Room*, and especially, *The Potting Shed* where "Greene's dramatic statement is theologically and psychologically false."

A5911 Puentevella, Renato, SJ. "Ambiguity in Greene." *Renascence*, XII (Autumn), pp. 35-37. Reviews critics' varied responses to the ambiguity surrounding the "inconclusive exits" of Scobie, Harry Lime, Pinkie and Coral, which ambiguity, he maintains, "rings a truer note [from the believer's viewpoint, presumably] in a reality where no IBM can tabulate God's miracles of Grace."

A5912 Tarnawski, Wit. "Przemiany Graham Greene'a." Kultura, 138 (April), pp. 131-37. In Polish. A review article on Our Man in Havana that discusses the shift in Greene's philosophical stance from his advocacy of man's relationship with God in The Potting Shed to his emphasis on the value of the individual, independent of God and country in the novel. Points out that Greene's belief in the value of man echoes Pasternak's in Doctor Zhivago.

A5913 Tracy, Honor. "Life and Soul of the Party." NRep, CXL (20 April), pp. 15-16. Argues that it is Greene the story-teller with the "original" eye and an "ear no less acute, with a prodigious knack of description, dialogue and narrative" who commands our admiration, and not Greene the philosopher or moralist. For the general reader.

A5914 Wassmer, Thomas A., SJ. "The Sinners of Graham Greene." DR, XXXIX (Autumn), pp. 326-32. Also published as "Graham Greene: A Look at His Sinners." Critic, XVIII (Dec./Jan.), pp. 16-17, 72-74. See A5816.

A5915 ________. "Faith and Belief: A Footnote to Greene's 'Visit to Morin.'" Renascence, XI, pp. 84-88. Rpt. as "Reason and Faith as Seen by Graham Greene." DC, II (Nov.), pp. 126-30, and as "Faith and Reason in Graham Greene." Studies, XLVIII (Summer), pp. 163-67. Affirms, from a theological viewpoint, that there can exist a "valid tension" between "theological faith and rational disbelief (in the sense of dissatisfaction with rational arguments)." Illustrates this point--raised in an earlier article (see A5816)--through an examination of Morin's views in "A Visit to Morin."

A5916 Unsigned. "Whose Man in Havana?" Commonweal, LXX (3 July), p. 342. Reflections on the communist praise accorded to Our Man in Havana by the Moscow press.

A5917 ________. "Religion on the Stage." Commonweal, LXIX (16 Jan.), p. 402. An editorial on the deference shown to "religion" and the "comfortable ignorance of things religious," especially in the theatre. Cites critics' ignorance of the use of bread and wine in the dramatization of The Power and the Glory as a case in point.

A5918 ________. "Graham Greene." P&P, VI:10 (July), p. 5. Greene is presented as the Personality of the Month whose play The Complaisant Lover has just opened at the Globe Theatre. Notes that his previous two plays have proved "less successful on both counts than his novels."

R591 Brien, Alan. "Theatre, London." TArts, XLIII (Dec.), pp. 21-23. Page 22 reviews The Complaisant Lover and the English production. Finds the play to be constructed with "professional cunning, full of effective twists, strong curtain lines and forceful confrontations," and its characters to be puppets of stock farce. Greene seems to be interested in "the idea of people on stage rather than in the people themselves."

R592 ________. "Christmas Cavil." Spectator, CCIII (18 Dec.), pp. 907-08. A general review of the West End Theatres of London and performances. Describes The Complaisant Lover as an "old French farce standing on its head" and Greene's stagecraft as "too consciously expert with ... curtain tableaux, unexpected confrontations, changes of mood and ironic twists."

R593 Buckle, Richard. "Keep Britain Black." P&P, VI:11 (Aug.), p. 13. A review of The Hostage by B. Behan and The Complaisant Lover. Points out the contrast between the two plays and chooses the Behan play for being "all blood and guts" to Greene's which is all "intelligence." Finds The Complaisant Lover to hold "no surprises"; the ending is predictable and the play on the whole "heavy going."

A594 Butcher, Maryvonne. "Greene Pastures," Tablet, CCXIII (4 July), p. 583. Argues that Greene is a "disconcerting writer" who switches the mood of The Complaisant Lover from "sophisticated comedy" in the first half to near-tragic realism in the second. But the play remains his "best"; the construction and action is well manipulated and the dialogue has that "bite and inevitability" characteristic of Greene. Also comments on the casting and performance at the Globe.

R595 Driver, Tom F. "Theatre: The Bread and the Wine." NRep, CXL (12 Jan.), p. 22. A review of the dramatization of The Power and the Glory and the American Phoenix production of the play. Critical of Greene's "baroque" Catholic writing, and his lack of "subtlety and taste" in his excursions into "sacramental theatricality." Finds the acceptance of the sacramentalist view which is basic to the plot detrimental to the eighth scene of the "religious melodrama." Associates Greene with Jacobean dramatists like Ford, Webster and Tourneur.

R596 Engelborghs, Maurits. "De nieuwe Roman van Graham Greene." Kultuurleven, XXIV:2 (Feb.), pp. 119-22. Finds Our Man in Havana a relaxing entertainment that pleasantly surprises its readers by the skill and cleverness of its creator, in spite of the somewhat unsatisfactory characterization.

R597 ________. "The Complaisant Lover: Een Blijspel van Graham Greene." DWB, 8 (Oct.), pp. 497-501. The play is intelligent, easy, well constructed and written with zest and gusto. Regards the absence of the purely Catholic as an asset contributing to its success.

R598 Forster, Peter. "Sin and Tonic." Spectator, CCIII (3 July), p. 7. A review of The Complaisant Lover and performance at the Globe Theatre, London. Appreciative of Greene's "increased sureness of comic touch" as he transforms the "tired trivia" of gulled husband, bored wife and jealous lover into a "sin-and-tonic work of art" with compassionate wit and technical skill. Regards the play as Greene's "most successful" even though the transition to the end is a "little wobbly and abrupt."

R599 Frank, Elizabeth. "Brighter Greene Without a Shadow." NCh, (18 June), p. 3. A review of The Complaisant Lover and its first night performance at the Globe Theatre. Regards the "ubiquitous triangle" of husband, wife and lover and the ménage à trois which follows as constituting Greene's most successful play in which, as a writer of natural dialogue, he is "second only to Tchekov."

R5910 Gassner, John. "Broadway in Review." ETJ, XI (March), pp. 29-39. Includes a brief review of the performance of the dramatization of The Power and the Glory at the Phoenix Theatre on pp. 33-34. Reserved in his praise because the "intrinsic repetitiousness of pattern and turbid character-relations weaken a play that has to be extraordinarily dynamic to compensate for the dramatic inadequacy of the central point."

R5911 Hayes, Richard. "The Stage: Tragedy and the Savaged Pieties." Commonweal, LXIX (2 Jan.), pp. 362-63. Reviews the dramatization of The Power and the Glory and its production at the Phoenix Theatre. Finds the theatre event "of the first magnitude," for it retains the "essential character and trajectory as passion drama" of the original. Calls the elimination of the final prison scene from the play "distinctly a loss." Reviews the performance in some detail.

R5912 Hewes, Henry. "Broadway Postscript: Love and Marriage." SatR, XLII (4 July), p. 25. Includes an unsubstantial review of The Complaisant Lover and its performance in London.

R5913 Hobson, Harold. "The Greatest of These...." SunT, (21 June), p. 21. A review of The Complaisant Lover and its production. Describes the play as "sophisticated and tender," but even though clever and amusing, it is not as good as La Parisiènne by Henri Becque, to which it is compared.

R5914 Jones, Mervyn. "Two Unhappy Families." Observer, (21

June), p. 17. A short review of The Complaisant Lover and its performance. Though Greene "spotlights an intriguing aspect of snobbery," he does not dwell upon it but is mainly concerned with the relationships of the "triangle." Notices the change that occurs in the dentist after the interval.

R5915 Panter-Downes, Mollie. "Letter from London: The Complaisant Lover." NY, XXXV (29 Aug.), pp. 80-82. A general review of plays in London theatres and performances. Includes a brief note on The Complaisant Lover as a "routine French farce," with a Greenean theme of adultery.

R5916 Pritchett, V. S. "The Arts and Entertainment: Take Away Sin." NSta, LVII (27 June), pp. 886 & 888. A perceptive review of The Complaisant Lover and its performance. Contends that without the notion of sin--Greene's "form of artifice"--the play "lacks the edge and penetration of artificial comedy." Makes a distinction between general humor and the comic idea in the play.

R5917 Sch[oonderwoerd], N. "Heeft Graham Greene ons weer Teleurgesteld?" Kultuurleven, XXVI (Nov.), pp. 703-04. The initial reaction is that Greene has indeed disappointed us with his third play which might well have been written by Noel Coward but, on second thoughts, concedes that he has succeeded because The Complaisant Lover is moving and enjoyable.

R5918 Simon, Irene. "Some Recent English Novels." RLV, XXV, pp. 219-30. See pp. 220-21. Concludes that Greene's "main concern is with the farce itself" in Our Man in Havana which turns into comedy when we are allowed to see through Wormold's eyes. Connects its "success" with its "topical interest," and questions Greene's "purpose" in the novel.

R5919 Stanford, Derek. "And His New Play: The Complaisant Lover." Critic, XVIII (Dec.-Jan.), pp. 16-17. Though the play may have the traditional "amorous triangle" reminiscent perhaps of Restoration comedy, it is not only funny but sad and realistic too, for Greene seems to be concerned with "the actuality and not the stage-convention of marriage" in spite of the traditional machinery of farce he uses in the Amsterdam hotel scene.

R5920 Thompson, John. "This Play Brings Greatness to the Theatre." DaiE, (18 June), p. 11. A review of The Complaisant Lover and its first night performance at the Globe Theatre. Welcomes enthusiastically the play for being "the best, most truly theatrical" of the year and for showing the richness of talent in the British theatre.

R5921 Trewin, J. C. "The World of the Theatre: In Retrospect." ILN, (15 Aug.), p. 32. A brief review of The Complaisant Lover at the Globe Theatre. Regards it as a "connoisseur's play" because Greene manages "to modulate without embarrassment from something near farce to a passage of (for a moment) something near tragedy."

R5922 Wilson, Cecil. "Still Tears As Greene Turns to Comedy." DaiM, (18 June), p. 3. A review of The Complaisant Lover and its first night performance at the Globe Theatre. Maintains that the play is Greene's "nearest approach" to stage comedy, for though there are no "religious complications" to sex and sin, it contains "serious sentiment."

R5923 Wyatt, Euphemia Van Rensselaer. "Theater: The Power and the Glory." CW, CLXXXVIII (March), p. 504. Reviews the production of the dramatization at the Phoenix, and expresses concern over the representation of the consecration of Mass on the stage.

R5924 Unsigned. "Theatre: The Power and the Glory." America, C (10 Jan.), p. 438. Review of the dramatization and the performance. Finds in the adaptation a grand drama of "magnificence and power" that probes into the "complexities of human relationships and needs."

R5925 _______. "'Lovers,' by Greene, Begins London Run." NYT, (19 June), p. 28. Short note on the first night reception of The Complaisant Lover by English reviewers.

R5926 _______. "Bare Feet Do Not a Peasant Make." Reporter, XX (8 Jan.), p. 37. A review of the performance of Denis Cannan and Pierre Bost's dramatization of The Power and the Glory. Underlines the miscasting of the American production.

R5927 _______. "The Power and the Glory." TArts, XLIII (Feb.), p. 67. An evaluation of the American production of Denis Cannan and Pierre Bost's dramatization.

R5928 _______. "Theater Abroad: Black Comedy." Time, LXXIII (29 June), pp. 43-44. A short review of The Complaisant Lover occasioned by its opening at the Globe Theatre, London. Describes it as "'black comedy' moving from glossy front-room comedy to boudoir farce to the tender pathology of love."

R5929 _______. "Who Laughs Last." TLS, 2996 (31 July), p. 448. Though Greene may call The Complaisant Lover a "comedy" much of the laughter caused by the play is of a "painful kind" about emotions and feelings too "intimate and naked for comfortable exposure." Notes Greene's assuredness as a dramatist and his mastery of mood changes.

D591 Bedard, Bernard John. The Thriller Pattern in the Major Novels of Graham Greene. Univ. of Michigan. D. A., XX:5 (Nov.), 1779-80.

D592 Consolo, Dominick Peter. The Technique of Graham Greene: A Stylistic Analysis of Five Novels. State Univ. of Iowa. D. A., XX:1 (July), 297.

D593 Crull, Mary E. Down the Labyrinthine Ways: A Study of Graham Greene's Novels. M. A. Colorado State College.

D594 Fitzgerald, Ellen F. Difficulty Squared: Is Graham Greene a Great Catholic Novelist? M. A. Columbia Univ.

D595 Jean-de-la Charité, Sr. Structure and Theme in Graham Greene's The Potting Shed. M. A. Rivier College.

D596 Kunkel, Francis Leo. A Critical Study of Graham Greene. Columbia Univ. D. A., XX:2 (Aug.), 670-71. Published as The Labyrinthine Ways of Graham Greene. New York: Sheed & Ward, 1959. See B596.

1960

B601 Buckler, William E. and Arnold B. Sklare, eds. Stories from Six Authors. New York: McGraw-Hill Book Company. Includes four of Greene's short stories: "The Basement Room," "Across the Bridge," "When Greek Meets Greek" and "The Hint of an Explanation." Pages 60-63 list questions for discussion on each of the stories, gives suggested interpretations and eight subjects for written composition.

B602 Gassner, John. "Religion and Graham Greene's The Potting Shed." Theatre at the Crossroads. New York: Holt, Rinehart & Winston, pp. 155-57. Maintains that the play is satisfactory "only on the level of a mystery story"; but its "detective-story pattern" has detracted from concern with any deeper values of the work, and especially the "explorations of character conflict through which spiritual struggles can be brought to full life." The play remains, regardless of its intent, "part potboiler and part propaganda."

B603 Herbert, James. "Graham Greene." Modern English Novelists. Tokyo: Kenkyusha; The Folcroft Press, Inc., 1970. An interpretative survey indicating salient characteristics of the novels and their world. Dwells separately on the "secular" novels of the thirties with their rather gloomy picture of life culled out from the economic depression and political tension of the times, and the "Catholic" novels where the typical figure changes from the criminal rebelling against society to the typical figure of the sinner "crippled by his human state and rebelling against God's law" in Brighton Rock, The Heart of the Matter and The Power and the Glory. Also notices the transition in The Quiet American where the "predicament is not of the Spirit but only of external causes."

B604 Quennell, Peter. The Sign of the Fish. London: Collins; New York: The Viking Press. Pages 60-63 give the writer's reminiscences of his school days at Berkhamstead. Finds Greene's recollections of school days as provided in The Lawless Roads to be "strangely transmogrified" and suggests that the account may be inaccurate. Provides his personal impressions of Greene at school and notes his exuberance then and "great capacity for cynical humour." "Accuses" Greene of a "touch of artificiality, even of artistic fraud" in his novels.

B605 Rosenberg, Edgar. From Shylock to Svengali: Jewish Stereotypes in English Fiction. Stanford, California: Stanford Univ. Press; London: Peter Owen, 1961. Brief reference on pp. 300-01 to Greene's usage of the "old convention" wherein "the jew operates as a metaphor" but which takes the form of "nauseating figures and allusions" in the novels, e. g., Colleoni in Brighton Rock, Wyatt in Stamboul Train and Sir Marcus in A Gun for Sale. It is interesting to note that Greene desists from using "jewish stereotypes" in later novels.

A601 Gonzales Salas, Carlos. "Tres libros y tres autores discutidos: Graham Greene contra Mejico." Abside, XXIV, pp. 358-61. Critical of Greene's "lightning" trips to Mexico which serve as his only source of information on Mexico and Mexicans about whom he writes rather dogmatically and petulantly, and condemns Greene's inaccurate and unfavorable characterization of the land and its people.

A602 Happel, Nikolaus. "Formbetrachtung an Graham Greene Short Story 'The Hint of an Explanation.'" NS, pp. 81-86. A discussion of the short story as an artistic masterpiece. Also determines its suitability for second language instruction purposes.

A603 Hinchliffe, Arnold P. "Good American." TCLon, CLXVIII (Dec.), pp. 529-39. Examines the image of the good American as portrayed by H. James, G. Skyes, G. Greene and W. J. Lederer and E. Burdick. The discussion of The Quiet American is rather cursory.

A604 Kauffmann, Stanley. "With Graham Greene in Havana." NRep, CXLII (15 Feb.), pp. 22-23. A review of the film version of Our Man in Havana attributing the "disappointment" to the clash of the "two tones"--the dramatic and the funny--and to the lack of purpose, in spite of Greene's "pointed, taut, nicely implicative" dialogue.

A605 Pujalo, Esteban. "The Globe Theatre, Londres." FMod, I, pp. 59-63. A review article on The Complaisant Lover and A Man for All Seasons--two well organized, traditionally structured plays with lively dialogue. Maintains that though A Complaisant Lover is made up of "elementos más corrientes" than his earlier plays, and is comic and humorous, it expresses nevertheless a streak of Greene's pessimistic thought that life is "grey and monotonous" and leads to suffering, that a little happiness and comedy inevitably entail suffering and sacrifice.

A606 Spinucci, Pietro. "L'ultimo dramma di Graham Greene." HumB, XV, pp. 820-25. Attempts an assessment of Greene's place in the contemporary European theatre, especially the English theatre, or even the "catholic" theatre, if one can use that term without confusing between theme and artistic rendition. The Living Room, The Potting Shed and The Complaisant Lover.

A607 Vieira, Manuel. "Notas para um estudo sobre Graham Greene." TPr, 20, pp. 46-52. In Portuguese. The "notas" attempt an analysis, from a theological viewpoint, of Greene's conception of the chaos and disorder in the world and the need to establish order. Brighton Rock, The Power and the Glory and The Living Room.

A608 Wassmer, Thomas A., SJ. "The Problem and Mystery of Sin in the Works of Graham Greene." ChrS, XLIII (Winter), pp. 309-15. Rpt. from H&PR, LVIII (March 1958), pp. 583-89. See A5816.

A609 Unsigned. "The Workaday World That the Novelist Never Enters." TLS, 3054 (9 Sept.). Special Number on 'The British Imagination,' p. vii. Affirms that Greene utilizes the "apparatus" of the crime novel for his serious purposes of conveying truths of Roman Catholicism, and about the forms of society and the nature of man, thereby merging the "crime novel" with the "novel proper." Also examines the fictional achievements of other novelists in the article. Includes a portrait of Greene.

R601 Wood, F. T. "Current Literature: Our Man in Havana." ES, XLI, p. 50. Notes that though Greene may have returned to "entertainments," the book is unlike his earlier work; it is also "more of an extravaganza than a satire."

R602 Unsigned. "A Burnt-Out Case." Kirkus, XXVIII (15 Nov.), pp. 967-68. Pre-publication notice calling attention to the "impossible indifference" of Querry and describing the "finale" of the novel as "regrettably closer to farce than to tragedy."

D601 Currie, John Sheldon. Religion and Romanticism in the Novels of Graham Greene. M.A. Univ. of New Brunswick.

D602 Geen, Stewart Cameron. The "Entertainments" of Graham Greene. M.A. McMaster Univ.

D603 Koban, Charles. Theme, Character and Style in the Work of Graham Greene. M.A. Columbia Univ.

D604 Schu, Hermann. Untersuchungen zur Perspektivtechnik in den Romanen Graham Greenes. Freiburg Univ.

D605 Sheehan, Thomas M. The Catholic Treatment of Sin and Redemption in the Novels of Graham Greene. Univ. of Ottawa.

D606 Slate, Audrey Nelson. Technique and Form in the Novels of Graham Greene. Univ. of Wisconsin. D.A., XXI:3 (Sept.), 629-30.

D607 Walters, Dorothy Jeanne. The Theme of Destructive Innocence in the Modern Novel: Greene, James, Cary, Porter. Univ. of Oklahoma. D.A., XXI:8 (Feb. 1961), 2300-01.

S601 Dworkin, Martin S. "Across the Bridge." CC, 4 (Nov.), p. 15. A brief review of the film based upon Greene's short story.

S602 Taber, Robert. "Castro's Cuba." Nation, XCX (23 Jan.), pp. 63-64. Contains negligible reference to Our Man in Havana in the first two paragraphs of this long article on the Cuban revolution.

1961

B611 Kohn, Lynette. Graham Greene: The Major Novels. Stanford Honors Essays in Humanities, No. 4. Stanford, Cal.: Stanford Junior Univ. The essay is divided into four parts, each of which examines the central theme of a novel: evil and the mystery of love in Brighton Rock, the "deceptive perversity" of pity in fallen man which disguises "fear and egotism" in The Heart of the Matter, the mature treatment of love as it is transformed from "lust to human passion and finally to divine love" in The End of the Affair, and the "integration" of all three themes in a study of the salvation of the Whiskey Priest's soul through the "metaphor of the journey" in The Power and the Glory.

B612 Stewart, Douglas. "Graham Greene--Catholicism." The Ark of God: Studies in Five Modern Novelists. London: The Carey Kingsgate Press Limited, pp. 71-99. This is the third lecture of the W. T. Whitley Lectures for 1960 which are concerned with the "message" novelists have, not simply for the world, but for the church, too. Argues that just as Brighton Rock depicts "the triumph of hell over heaven," The Power and the Glory is the "victory of heaven over hell," and lays bare the essential heart of the church in the Whiskey Priest's "protest" against the "law" of the church, as well as Greene's insistence on salvation by Grace rather than a mere observance of the word. But in The End of the Affair, Greene conceives of "Divine-human encounter" in rather "mechanical terms" so that faith and grace are perceived as impersonal forces. Contends that in The Heart of the Matter, Greene's message is that the church should face the revolution that has occurred within the moral consciousness of man and not rely simply on the rules.

B613 Turnell, Martin. "Problems of Belief: Claudel-Mauriac-Greene." Modern Literature and Christian Faith. London: Darton, Longman and Todd; Westminster, Md.: Newman Press, pp. 49-69. This is the third of the Lauriston Lectures for 1959. Examines the work of the three Catholic writers: Claudel disregarding the "changes of the past 400 years," and Greene and Mauriac pushing "compromise to the point at which it becomes complicity," in attempting a Christian interpretation of the modern world. Attributes rather erroneously and without convincing evidence Mauriac's and Greene's poor view of human nature, their "sad, twisted religion," and the element of violence exhibited in their work to the inferiority of their "religious to their artistic experience." Hints at these two novelists' unawareness of the "complexity of human nature," and describes their outlooks as "theological rather than religious."

B614 Tynan, Kenneth. Curtains. London: Longmans, Green; New York: Atheneum. Includes a review of The Living Room, pp. 47-49, in which he asserts that Greene is "surefooted" all the way up to the climax but he slips and falls there. Implies that Greene is advocating Roman Catholicism. Also includes a review of The Potting Shed, pp. 207-09, rpt. from The Observer, (see R5834) and, in his "Summing Up: 1959," pp. 231-32, he maintains that The Complaisant Lover bears the same relationship to the earlier plays that his "entertainments" bear to his serious novels. Maintains that Greene's mastery of dialogue is "no substitute for mastery of characterization."

B615 Weales, Gerald. "Commercial Drama: A Reprise." Religion in Modern English Drama. Philadelphia: Univ. of Pennsylvania Press, pp. 243-54. Pages 242-47 survey Greene's contribution to the post-war commercial theatre in England. Finds The Living Room could have ended, dramatically speaking, with Rose's prayer; but the scene which is added after her suicide is "like the moral after a medieval play." As for The Potting Shed, it fails "not only in communicating its central miracle" but also "in providing a reason for its plot." The Complaisant Lover is cursorily dismissed: "there is no religious emphasis in the play; in fact, there is not much play." Notices the dramatization of The Power and the Glory.

A611 Browne, E. Martin. "Graham Greene: Theatre's Gain." TArts, XLV (Nov.), pp. 20-24. Considers The Living Room, The Potting Shed and The Complaisant Lover in the order of their appearance to show that the last, though a comedy of urban domesticity providing a "wry kind of fun," is concerned with the same values that are found in the other two serious plays. Also believes that Greene will prove "as assured a master of the stage as of the other mediums."

A612 De Vitis, A. A. "The Entertaining Mr. Greene." Renascence, XIV (Autumn), pp. 8-24. An investigation of the nature of the "entertainments"--their "secular" outlook, secondary preoccupation with religious and ethical problems, predominance of causality, characterization, cinematic element, motif of the chase, themes of pity, betrayal and innocence, religious symbolism, irony, flair for comedy--making a clear distinction between them and the novels, and pointing out, like R. B. W. Lewis (see A5715), how, very often, "the entertainments are preliminary studies for the more elaborate novels that follow them."

A614 Duprey, Richard A. "Morris West, A Witness for Companion." CW, CXCIII (Sept.), pp. 360-66. Makes, in a passing comparison of West and Greene on p. 363, a sweeping generalization that Greene "seems cruelly objective, almost sadistic with his characters," never bestowing on them "the great compassion" of M. West.

A615 Eishiskina, N. "Graham Greene's Novels." VLit, VI (June), pp. 149-69. Analyzes the novels, especially The Quiet American, Our Man in Havana and A Burnt-Out Case, from a Marxist viewpoint, to show that Greene's range of subject matter has extended beyond the notion of sin and the individual to a more concrete and humanistic concern for the fate of man in a capitalist society.

A616 Flood, Ethelbert, OFM. "Christian Language in Modern

Literature." Culture, XII (March), pp. 28-42. Distinguishes three uses of language to gauge how and when literature is Christian: "Christian language merely as symbol; Christian language that betrays Christ; or Christian language through which he walks." Maintains that Greene falls in the second category and shows, through an analysis of The End of the Affair, that he uses language to bring off "a literary experience that is Christian," without throwing at his reader "the full set of Christian terms and symbols."

A617 Hess, M. Whitcomb. "Graham Greene's Travesty on 'The Ring and the Book.'" CW, CXCIV (Oct.), pp. 37-42. Points out the parallelism between the two works--Pompilia/Marie? Guido/Rycker? and Priest/Querry?--and, in a sweeping judgment of A Burnt-Out Case, considers the novel's "... preoccupation with the inner lives of individuals ... subtlety of thought and pregnancy of style ... not enough to save (it) ... for use on the side of angels ... its graphic appeal ... turn(s) the reader away in disgust from the human race it represents," and it is not "realistic in a spiritual sense."

A618 Igoe, W. J. "Living Writers--7. Graham Greene." John O'London's, IV (6 June), 24-25. A sympathetic portrait drawing the attention of the general reader to Greene's personality, convictions and various talents as a novelist.

A619 Joseph, Brother, FSC. "Greene's 'The Hint of an Explanation,'" Explicator, XIX:4 (Jan.), item 21. Maintains that the meaning, structure, in fact, "complete intelligibility and aesthetic integrity" of the "story-within-a-story" can only be understood in relation to the question of how God allows evil to exist in the world.

A6110 Kermode, Frank. "Mr. Greene's Eggs and Crosses." Encounter XVI:4 (April), pp. 69-75. Rpt. in Puzzles and Epiphanies: Essays and Reviews: 1958-1961. London: Routledge & Kegan Paul; New York: Chelmark Press, 1962, pp. 176-88. Also in Graham Greene: A Collection of Critical Essays. Ed. Samuel Hynes. Englewood Cliffs, N.J.: Prentice-Hall, 1973, pp. 126-38. A stimulating review article on A Burnt-Out Case. Contends that the novel, in spite of the "economy and skill" with which its fable is constructed, the "exact" timing of the story, the "tact" with which clinical details are disposed of, its "satisfying Greeneian" idiom and the "evidence of competent arrangements" everywhere, falls "far below one's expectations," because the resultant tension between the "religious interpretation" of Querry's life and his own naturalist explanations of it, is minimal. This is due to Querry's inadequate presentation of his explanation which is the result of Greene's inability to stand clear of his hero who is merely a "poseur," a "thinly disguised" Greene. Proceeds to show how The Power and the Glory and The End of the Affair make use of that tension and how the latter, "beyond question Mr. Greene's masterpiece," succeeds because Greene objectifies his obsession and embodies his "God-hatred in the fiction" more fully and more outspokenly than he does in The Heart of the Matter.

A6111 Lehmann, John. "English Letters in the Doldrums? An Editor's View." TQ, IV:3 (Autumn), 56-63. A survey of English letters since World War II. Maintains that G. Greene, A. Wilson and W. Sanson still remain as the main writers in spite of the present generation of new writers who are mainly interested in the topical and the contemporary.

A6112 Lodge, David. "Use of Key Words in the Novels of Graham Greene: Love, Hate and The End of the Affair." Blackfriars, XLII (Nov.), pp. 468-74. An interesting approach to a "neglected" aspect of Greene's art: probing the "obsessive word" rather than the writer's obsession, to reveal that even "thoughtful meditations on the human situation are anchored to a particular word or group of words," which may epitomize the theme of a novel. Shows how "every possible permutation" of love and hate in The End of the Affair is revealed through a study of these keywords.

A6113 Murphy, John P. "On Graham Greene." WisR, CCXXV (Spring), pp. 85-89. A review article on A Burnt-Out Case accusing Greene of his "contrived disloyalty" as an artist in "registering" the different phases of belief and unbelief as a process of relishing "all the delights of Catholic thinking without ever begetting any issue, Catholic or otherise," and that, as in The Potting Shed, this amounts to "outrageous mischief." Also accuses Greene of lack of taste for what may be called "coarseness, (or) vulgarity" in his "irreligious" book about Catholicism.

A6114 Peters, W., SJ. "A Burnt-Out Case, Een mislukte roman." Streven, (Nov.), 161-66. A review article discussing the various stages of belief and unbelief with special reference to A Burnt-Out Case.

A6115 Rolo, Charles J. "Graham Greene: The Man and the Message." Atlantic, CCVII (May), pp. 60-65. A "literary portrait" of Greene for the general reader. Reviews the major themes of the "dramatized theology" of Greene's novels which admit of no human solution to the problems of evil, his "deeply passionate and searching concern about the human situation," and his "bleak" vision of life where the ravaged landscape portrayed is a "scenic image of the human condition--a view, so to speak, of original sin." Brighton Rock, The Power and the Glory, The Heart of the Matter, The End of the Affair, The Quiet American and A Burnt-Out Case.

A6116 Rudman, Harry W. "Clough and Graham Greene's The Quiet American." VN, 19, pp. 14-15. A brief note contending that the two quotations from Byron and Clough in the Preface, and a second from Clough's Dipsychus in the novel, demonstrate Greene's "employment of poetry conversational in tone, realistic and practical in point of view, moralistic in intent to illuminate the theme."

A6117 Servotte, Herman. "Bedenkingen bij 'A Burnt'Out Case,' Graham Greene's jongste roman." DWB, CVI (June), 371-75. Considers A Burnt-Out Case to be a poor amalgam of the old formulas of his earlier successful novels, a "cocktail" of weariness, religiosity and eroticism mixed with some irony and the attendant paradoxes.

A6118 Smith, A. J. M. "Graham Greene's Theological Thrillers." QQ, LXVIII (Spring), pp. 15-33. Shows, through a searching analysis of Brighton Rock, The Power and the Glory, The Heart of the Matter and The End of the Affair, that Greene's "obsession" is not merely limited to "seediness, frustration, failure and sin" but in reality dramatizes the theology of "salvation through grace," and though the novels may present readers with the "seemingly intractable material" of stock situations in melodrama, Greene, through his skillful use of irony, makes tragedy out of it.

A6119 Stratford, Philip. "Graham Greene: Master of Melodrama." TamR, 19 (Spring), 67-86. Though longwinded at times, the article carefully notes Greene's rejection of "patent" aspects of melodrama--"poetic justice operating in the happy ending," staging a "deus or diabolus ex machina," and conflict in character by "eliminating the white" and emphasizing the black--and attributes his mastery of form to the influence of James and his use of Catholicism as a foundation for his novels. Shows how Greene in Brighton Rock avoided melodrama "by suspending judgment and exercising pity" and how the change from pity to sympathy and love turned The Heart of the Matter into tragedy. Maintains that beginning with The End of the Affair until A Burnt-Out Case the "increasingly comic vein" provides another way of meeting "the melodramatic sense of despair and absurdity."

A6120 ________. "Greene's Hall of Mirrors." KR, XXIII (Summer), pp. 527-31. A review article on A Burnt-Out Case which considers the many ways in which the novel acts as a "trap for critics" and reviews the flaws in some fifteen reviews of the novel and the pitfalls into which they had fallen.

A6121 _______. "The Uncomplacent Dramatist: Some Aspects of Graham Greene's Theatre." WSCL, II:3 (Fall), pp. 5-19. Rpt. in Graham Greene: A Collection of Critical Essays. Ed. Samuel Hynes. Englewood Cliffs, N.J.: Prentice-Hall, 1973, pp. 138-54. Considers the movement away from the "popular, melodramatic macrocosm to the bourgeois domestic microcosm, from a tragic to a comic vision," in the light of Greene's early criticism of drama, especially in British Dramatists, and examines the "narrowing compass of action and tightening of situation" in the novels of the forties and early fifties, and the "latent comic gift" he reveals in the delineation of minor characters. Focusses on The Complaisant Lover as the most revealing example of Greene's dramatic skills and outlook to show that the move towards "sophisticated comedy" entailed some sacrifice of his "original talent."

A6122 Unsigned. "Greenland Aboriginal." NSta, LXI (13 Jan.), pp. 44-45. A portrait of Greene's "complex" personality--perhaps by one who has met him or observed him closely. Highlights the impression of "loneliness and boredom" Greene creates as well as his "angry pity for his fellow sinners."

A6123 _______. "Faith and the Winter: Christian Dimensions in Literature." TLS, 3111 (13 Oct.), pp. 696-97. Surveys Christian dimensions in the literature of Ireland, Spain, Holland, Germany, England and France. Describes Greene as a writer portraying in prose "the waste land of a world without God, where most men are hollow," as a novelist whose "popular success is deserved" and who has been able "to impose his beliefs or obsessions, on a public which does not share them."

R611 Brandstrup, Ole. "Til Helvede med succesen." Perspectiv, VIII:7, pp. 47-50. In Danish. Mainly a summary of A Burnt-Out Case. The last two paragraphs assert that the novel is written "unmistakeably" and with "distressful delight," by "en frafalden katolik" who suffers from the same malady as the main character.

R612 Caute David. "The Birth of A Burnt-Out Case." SunT, (29 Oct.), p. 31. A parody of Greene's ideas and style as they are recorded in the Congo Journal.

R613 Chadwyck-Healey, Charles. "In Search of a Character." Go, (Dec.), p. 6. Finds the Congo Journal readable and interesting not only as a diary showing the evolution of a novel in the author's mind, but also for giving an "uncommon insight into the harsh loneliness of the writer's mind."

R614 Chapin, Victor. "Leprosy in the Soul." NLea, XLIV (6 Feb.), pp. 24-25. Appreciative of Greene's "spiritual comedy" in A Burnt-Out Case and his clear statement of his thesis that life without God is absurd. Though the familiar ingredients are present in this "simplest" and "most profound" of his novels, the flaws of earlier novels are also missing as Greene makes his point and "dramatizes his paradoxes by the juxtaposition of fully realised characters."

R615 Chapman, John. "The Complaisant Lover a Sickly and Stylishly Acted Sex Comedy." DaiN, (2 Nov.). A review of the play and its performance. Finds Greene's skillfully arranged "ménage-à-trois" excellent comedy which is sometimes not funny at all as it probes deeply into the hearts of its characters.

R616 Clurman, Harold. "Theatre: The Complaisant Lover." Nation, CXCIII (25 Nov.), p. 437. A review of the play and the performance at the Ethel Barrymore Theatre, New York. Describes it as a "nice old-fashioned play" whose dialogue is "comfortable, fluent, unobtrusively graceful" but which contains a certain "hypocrisy" that may be "typical of English stage convention," because Greene evades the issues he sets up; and such a "lack of clarity ... robs the play of substance."

R617 Davis, Robert Gorham. "A Man Must Suffer to Be Whole." NYTBR, (19 Feb.), p. 4. Finds A Burnt-Out Case appealing, "wise, gentle and sympathetic" and a "fascinating study of the relationship of suffering ... to wholeness," free from the theological excesses of earlier novels, as well as of their color, richness or "freshness of detail." It is not a novel of "great intensity of feeling" but its "quietness, its retrospective air" and its conversations show a "changed and milder mood in Greene."

R618 Denniston, Robin. "Greene Pastures." T&T, XLII (13 Jan.), p. 64. Considers A Burnt-Out Case to be "pitched deliberately in a minor key" and clearly "no masterpiece." Little or no evidence given for such an assessment.

R619 Derrick, Christopher. "Grammar of Assent." Tablet, CCXV (21 Jan.), p. 58. Describes A Burnt-Out Case as Greene's "best treatise," "splendid" but not "topical in the headline sense," a novel about "lies and self deception," and especially "the circumstances in which one can honestly claim to believe or disbelieve, and the grammar most suitable for such utterances."

R6110 Didion, Joan. "Marks of Identity." NR, X (25 March), pp. 190-91. "... Less a novel, less a piece of working fiction than notes towards it." A Burnt-Out Case lacks the "marks of identity," the "sense of what people remember and how they dissemble and how they give themselves away," because Querry is too "self-conscious" and articulate to give himself away.

R6111 Driver, Tom F. "Drama: Catching Up." ChrC, LXXVIII (20 Dec.), pp. 1532-33. A review of The Complaisant Lover and its performance in New York. Contends that in spite of his "terribly sick" view of God, man and woman, Greene writes well so long as he stays within the conventions of the "French bedroom farce"; but the content of his play, based on the thesis that love and sex are two different things, is not only different but "preposterous" and tends to make the third act "neither funny nor real."

R6112 Engelborghs, Maurits. "Graham Greene: A Burnt-Out Case." Kultuurleven, XXVIII (Oct.), pp. 610-15. Disapproves of the novel for lacking fire and conviction, for being the work of a tired and weary writer, and because it reads like a parody of his earlier works.

R6113 Fadiman, Clifton. "A Burnt-Out Case." ClubN, (Feb.), pp. 2-3. Explains the reasons behind its choice as Book-of-the-Month, especially its "tonic value" in arousing one into a "new awareness of the aridity of certain aspects of modern life."

R6114 Fleming, Peter. "The Quest for Querry." Listener, LXVI (26 Oct.), p. 673. In Search of a Character will always have a certain fascination for it shows Greene's mind "consciously, deliberately at work on his raw material"; but it can also alter the value of the finished work.

R6115 Fuller, Roy. "Stuff for a Story." SunTel, (29 Oct.), p. 6. Questions why Greene's "fascinating Journal" in In Search of a Character is more truthful than the novel it begat, and suggests that Greene's "recklessness about facts" may have prevented him "ever quite fulfilling his great endowments."

R6116 Gamble, R. M. "The Lonely Battle." IT, (14 Jan.), p. 6. A Burnt-Out Case is one of Greene's major contributions which provides good reading because of its "assuredness, [and its] complete inevitability and exactness of character and conversation." Maintains that Greene implies, in his analysis of the intense loneliness of Querry, that Faith and Grace will return once the hero has gone through "the pit of nothingness."

R6117 Gardiner, Harold C. "Seekers, Finders in the Congo." America, CIV (18 Feb.), pp. 671-72. Welcomes Greene's return to his serious treatment of theological themes in A Burnt-Out Case--"probably ... [his] masterpiece" though without the grandeur of The Power and the Glory. Also notes the "functional quality" of Greene's style.

R6118 Gilbert Justin. "'Lover' Squares Triangle Amusingly." NYMir, (2 Nov.). A review of The Complaisant Lover and its performance. Finds this latest and "brightest word on how to build a ménage-à-trois" particularly enjoyable because of its "aplomb while plumbing what would normally seem like a tragedy."

R6119 Gilman, Richard. "The Stage: Mixture Almost as Before." Commonweal, LXXV (24 Nov.), pp. 233-34. Rpt. in Common and Uncommon Masks: Writings on Theatre 1961-1970. New York: Random House, 1971, pp. 249-51. Recognizes Greene in The Complaisant Lover in one of his moods of "romantic despair" smuggling behind the "mask" of sophisticated wit and humor, a "potentially tragic and actually pathetic situation" in the "immutably opposed pairs of truths: supernatural and fleshly love, pity and love, marriage and passion." Such an attempt to combine genres--his seriousness "tips the play toward pathos, if not tragedy"--leads to lack of "vitality and real passion" in the lover, and to an "inordinate amount of time" spent in getting the "mechanics of amorous comedy" underway.

R6120 Gregor, Ian. "Dead Centre." Guardian, (20 Jan.), p. 7. A searching review of A Burnt-Out Case that elicits a "curious sense of frustration" as a result of the "little play" made between the carefully assembled and interesting pieces in the novel because Greene creates around a "fancy"; he depends on the reader to take a different view of Querry than that which the novel projects if he is to become involved in Querry's drama.

R6121 Griffin, Lloyd W. "A Burnt-Out Case." LJ, LXXXVI (15 Jan.), p. 258. A short review that finds the novel "provocative" and concerned with "suffering, sin, faith and spiritual agony."

R6122 Hewes, Henry. "An Adult Look at Adultery." SatR, XLIV (2 Dec.), p. 36. A review of The Complaisant Lover and its production. Finds the play "sophisticated and entertaining" and an expression of Greene's "profound dissatisfaction with a life and times that can turn deep if illicit passion into grotesque farce, and love into complaisance."

R6123 Hicks, Granville. "An Inner Climate of Emptiness." SatR, XLIV (18 Feb.), p. 16. Finds the "peculiar strength" of A Burnt-Out Case in the "ambiguity" of Querry's experience, and maintains that the novel is not an "effective argument" for Catholicism because Greene writes out of his doubts and not his convictions.

R6124 Highet, Gilbert. "Our Man in Purgatory." Horizon, III:5 (May), pp. 116-17. Though appreciative of Greene's treatment of Querry's "spiritual leprosy," this review article is critical of the "political" novels because of Greene's "limited" experience and awareness of the modern world.

R6125 Hogan, William. "Graham Greene's Soul-Searching." SFC, (15 Feb.), p. 39. Favorably impressed by A Burnt-Out Case as a "first-rate" philosophical discourse on a man's search for his own soul, "an intellectual and moral parlor game," in an exotic setting in which Greene mixes "art and entertainment with diabolical wit and enormous grace."

R6126 Hollis, Christopher. "The Quest for Querry." Tablet, CCXV (28 Oct.), pp. 1028 & 1030. Finds the West African Journal in In Search of a Character a "very thin affair," and the Congo Journal in "no kind of way a notebook for the novel" that would stimulate a reader's interest. It is, however, of doubtless value to Greene, and shows how "experience and imagination are fused" to make a novel. Surmises that Greene's reason for publishing the notebook is his irritation at critics' identification of his state of mind with Querry's.

R6127 Holloway, David. "Character Hunting." DaiT, (27 Oct.), p. 19. In Search of a Character is not in any sense a "major work" and the second diary, even though it may have some amusement value, adds little to our understanding of the novelist's craft as the first does in spite of being "jumpy and rough."

R6128 ________. "Lepers and Sinners." DaiT, (20 Jan.), p. 17. Maintains that there is always an element of the dentist's drill in reading Greene. Though A Burnt-Out Case "promises so much"--we get to know the setting and the characters in depth--it remains an "imperfect" book because it is "contrived," so that "the power" is there but not the "full glory of Graham Greene."

R6129 Hughes, Riley. "A Burnt-Out Case." CW, CXCIII (April), p. 47. The novel is "vintage" Greene, austere in its presentation of the varieties of belief and unbelief with the "fulcrum of irony located outside rather than inside the story."

R6130 Hutchens, John K. "A Burnt-Out Case." NYHT, (17 Feb.), p. 17. Maintains that the novel in its action and dramatic dialogues brings out the concept of "redemption by suffering" for the characters with a "humanizing warmth" that was absent in earlier novels.

R6131 Jackson, Katherine Gauss. "Books in Brief: A Burnt-Out Case." Harpers, CCXXII (March), pp. 120-22. As a serious book and a "very good one," it is often "outrageously funny" in showing the similarity between a person afflicted with leprosy and one who "bears the emotional stigma of too much success."

R6132 Jennings, Elizabeth. "New Novels." Listener, LXV (2 Feb.), p. 237. A Burnt-Out Case is the first of two novels reviewed. The "chief strength" of this "brilliant and deeply moving" study of the futility of worldly success and of the failure of a vocation is Greene's "beautiful descriptions of Africa" and the subtle interplay of characters. It is marred, however, by a "forced and artificial sense of irony," the "easy ending, the too neatly tied-up plot" brought about by the "pasteboard figure" of Marie Rycker.

R6133 Johnson, Shinwell. "Greene in the Congo." Guardian, (3 Nov.), p. 9. In Search of a Character records Greene's search for authentic medical details and the evolution of "the faceless protagonist" into Querry. Greene's graphic details are vivid but he has "more trouble portraying a character in embryo."

R6134 Keown, Eric. "New Fiction." Punch, CCXL (25 Jan.), p. 189. A Burnt-Out Case is the first of four novels briefly reviewed. Notes Greene's acute "understanding of the human dilemma," and wonders how the Vatican views his writings.

R6135 Kerr, Walter. "First Night Report: The Complaisant Lover." NYHB, (2 Nov.). A review of the play and the performance. Emphasizes Greene's unconventional mind and treatment of adultery in this "champagne cocktail of a comedy that is superbly dry and most engagingly inventive." See also B6316.

R6136 Klausler, Alfred P. "No Inner Laughter." ChrC, LXXVIII (24 May), p. 65. Recognizes Greene as a "skilled technician" and an "astute satirist" in A Burnt-Out Case, but finds his humor "grisly and sardonic" without the "saving grace of an inner divine laughter," as his ironic gaze contemplates the spiritual emptiness of Querry's soul.

R6137 Kunkel, Francis L. "The Hollow Man." Renascence, XIII (Autumn), 48-49. Concentrates first on Querry in A Burnt-Out Case as one who aspires to "the condition of a Hollow Man," whose prototype is Fowler but who does not enhance the novel dramatically by his refusal to become entangled. However, the novel is "full of character gems, ... thought-provoking epigrammatic observations," dramatic dialogue and excellent functional descriptions.

R6138 Lister, Richard. "The New Graham Greene--I Find It Riveting." EvS, (17 Jan.), p. 10. Remarks on Greene's capacity to ferret out the "seamy side of things" and his masterly skill as a teller of stories in A Burnt-Out Case. "Taut, concise and concentrated, with only a handful of brilliantly realised characters," the novel has the "precision and inevitability of a finely made work of art."

R6139 McCarten, John. "The Complaisant Lover." NY, XXXVII (11 Nov.), pp. 117-18. A short review of the play and its performance in New York. Finds the "snag" in the development of the "farce" to be the emergence of the dentist as a "first-rate sort."

R6140 McClain, John. "Graham Greene Play Has Middling Merit." NYJ, (2 Nov.). A review of The Complaisant Lover and its performance. Has "serious misgivings" about the future of this "slick and largely inconsequential triangle play" that has difficulty in sustaining the "comedic pitch" promised by the early scenes.

R6141 McLaughlin, Richard. "A Burnt-Out Case." SpR, (16 April), p. 5D. A short review noting Greene's "mellower, more sympathetic" view of good and evil in the novel as he writes, like Mauriac, of "self-tortured, sin-conscious" people.

R6142 Maddocks, Melvin. "Greene's New Novel: A Burnt-Out Case." ChrSM, (23 Feb.), p. 7. Finds the theology in the novel "curious," Querry "more existentialist than Catholic," and Greene, as a "powerful romancer of evil," titillated by damnation, his main weakness being the boredom felt after evil's defeat.

R6143 Mallett, Richard. "Notes: In Search of a Character." Punch, CCXLI (15 Nov.), p. 732. Notes that the mixture of direct observation and imaginative use of it gives the two journals "a distinctive and interesting flavour."

R6144 Mannes, Marya. "Just Looking." Reporter, XXV (7 Dec.), p. 62. Brief note on The Complaisant Lover describing it as "beautifully irreverent and often extremely funny."

R6145 May, John L. "Books: A Burnt-Out Case." Extension, LV (May), p. 8. Summarizes the novel and recommends it to adults for being thought provoking.

R6146 Mayhew, Alice Ellen. "An Enclosed System Where Cosmic Forces Battle." Commonweal, LXXIV (31 March), pp. 19-20. As Greene's "best-written" serious novel, "full of dramatic insight and suspense," A Burnt-Out Case, like his earlier novels, shows the "enclosed system" of Greene's world "where cosmic forces battle for domination" of a soul. Its "elaborate symbolism" is brilliantly executed, and the dramatic narrative is unimpeded.

R6147 Mortimer, Raymond. "Gangrene of Success." SunT, (15 Jan.), p. 25. With a humor "profoundly sardonic" and images "dingy and grim," and a language always correct and "often exquisite in its neatness," Greene, with a "Maugham-like mastery of narrative" focusses the reader's attention in A Burnt-Out Case on his central subject: the suffering of the mind and the heart, and so produced a novel "more persuasive, more deeply-felt or more powerful" than he had ever written.

R6148 Nadel, Norman. "'Lover' Opens at Barrymore." NYWT, (2 Nov.). A review of The Complaisant Lover and performance. Maintains that most reaction to this penetrating play will be "personal rather than coldly objective" even though it is a comedy.

R6149 Norrie, Ian. "A Major New Novel from Graham Greene." B&B, (Jan.), p. 21. A "fine" novel with an intensely topical setting that uses the symbolism of a burnt-out case to convey "sparingly ... effectively, the psychological state of Querry." Greene is "technically perfect" and he has "the great writer's tragic sense of life," as well as power in his "beautiful, crisp prose."

R6150 O'Brien, E. D. "A Literary Lounger." ILN, (11 Feb.), p. 246. Does not consider A Burnt-Out Case as good as Brighton Rock or The Power and the Glory because the atmosphere of the Congo is "a trifle steamy" and Querry never finds "a conscious solution; his very death is an irrelevant absurdity."

R6151 "O'Donnell, Donat" [Conor Cruise O'Brien]. "Our Men in Africa." Spectator, 6917 (20 Jan.), p. 80. Concedes that Greene is much cleverer in A Burnt-Out Case in manipulating the "theological hoops" in the progress of Querry, the "ambiguous pilgrim," than he was with Scobie. Skeptical of Greene's theology and of the readers, too, who have made a success of his earlier works.

R6152 O'Donovan, Patrick. "Graham Greene's Leper Colony." NRep, CXLIV (20 Feb.), pp. 21-22. Finds Greene's focus on Querry's "agony of loss" in A Burnt-Out Case a "rare" Anglo-Saxon phenomenon, an "unfashionable" preoccupation that may make the novel "uncomfortable," expecially when it is set in a world as "bitter and as flat and as tedious as old left-out beer."

R6153 Parker, Dorothy. "A Burnt-Out Case." Esquire, LV (June), p. 38. Brief reference to the novel as a "big disappointment" in its overly concern with "heavenly mystique."

R6154 Paulding, Gouverneur. "A Loss of Feeling." Reporter,

XXIV (2 March), p. 48. Finds Greene in A Burnt-Out Case "ruthlessly impolite to the reader" for questioning a believer's faith or its memory and an unbeliever's belief. Gives a lengthy summary of the novel.

R6155 Prescott, Orville. "Books of the Times." NYT, (17 Feb.), p. 25. Contends that in A Burnt-Out Case Greene expresses his earlier conviction that "sexual guilt is the beginning of wisdom and that adultery is one of the better paths toward grace." Does not find Querry "a well-realized character" nor his end "dramatically interesting" or "psychologically convincing." Offsets his tribute to Greene's description of the setting by remarking on his "morose and sour distaste for life and people," and his attempt to deal with themes that do not lend themselves to fiction.

R6156 Pritchett, V. S. "The Congo of the Mind." NSta, LXI (20 Jan.), pp. 102-04. A perceptive review of A Burnt-Out Case that notices the importance of Greene's theme and the many merits of the novel, but finds a basic flaw in the figure of Querry--he "has extent but no size," he is a "generalization," and other characters do not react to him but to his opinions. Attributes this flaw to Greene's conception of A Burnt-Out Case as "a play not a novel"; even its dialogue is "stage dialogue," convenient to the limits of the theatre. Finds Greene's "assimilation of cinema technique" more life giving to the novel than the theatre.

R6157 Pryce-Jones, David. "In Search of Africa." T&T, XLII (9 Nov.), p. 1889. Finds In Search of a Character of "less value" than the earlier travel books for an understanding of Greene, but it provides a deep insight into his private obsession by Africa--as a background, as a source in his quest for material with which to tell "an unknown and shapeless story," and as a world where he finds "the direct juxtapositions of personality and morality that fit the conflict of his mind."

R6158 Pugh, Griffith T. "For Special Attention: A Burnt-Out Case." EJ, L (April), p. 291. A short review noting that this "memorable" novel engages the reader on at least two levels: surface action and philosophical thought, and also poses many difficult questions of faith.

R6159 Richardson, Maurice. "Quest for Querry." NSta, LXII (27 Oct.), p. 616. Finds the Congo Journal in In Search of a Character fascinating but "slightly disquieting" perhaps because "part of its subject is itself subjective"; but as a diarist, Greene is "sharply observant."

R6160 Rolo, Charles. "Reader's Choice: A Burnt-Out Case." Atlantic, CCVII (March), pp. 108 & 110. Describes the novel as Greene's "most bizarre ... most memorable" and "absorbing" as an allegory of the journey that carries man toward a genuine awareness of God."

R6161 Sackville-West, Edward. "Time-Bomb." Month, XXV (March), pp. 175-78. Though objecting to the careful "rigging" or heavy reliance on coincidence in A Burnt-Out Case and to the "implausible" behavior of Marie Rycker, the review is appreciative and praiseful of the union of Greene's "sheer narrative with his spiritual pre-occupations to produce so miraculously accomplished a work of art."

R6162 Smith, Francis J., SJ. "The Anatomy of A Burnt-Out Case." America, CV (9 Sept.), pp. 711-12. Considers the novel "an ambiguous work with subtle pretensions to being the modern equivalent of a morality play," dramatic in structure, "charged heavily with dialogue" but which has not artistically fused the "religious sense" and the "importance of the human act," and a story that is melodramatic and peopled by caricatures.

R6163 Spector, Robert Donald. "Spiritual Quest in a Dark World: A New Graham Greene Novel." NYHTBR, (19 Feb.), p. 33. Finds that A Burnt-Out Case "vastly oversimplifies characters" in showing man's inability to exist in a vacuum through Querry's struggle to identify himself. Notices the similarity between Greene and Conrad in the use of exotic backgrounds, interest in dialogue and commitment as a price for living.

R6164 Sullivan, Richard. "A Man in Whom Sin Must Run Its Course." CST, (19 Feb.), p. 3. A short review of A Burnt-Out Case that notices Greene's depiction of a "joyless creation," the irony at the end, and Querry "never so much a character as a fictional contrivance."

R6165 T., W. "Greene in Africa." IT, (25 Nov.), p. 7. In Search of a Character, valuable in that it reveals Greene himself, brings out "the sense of struggle" in the creative process between "the sensual man and the man of faith." Its companion piece may be entertaining but it is "hardly worth reviewing."

R6166 Taubman, Howard. "Theatre: Comedy About a Triangle." NYT, (2 Nov.), p. 43. A review of The Complaisant Lover and the opening night performance at the Ethel Barrymore Theatre. Greene assembles the "conventional machinery" for a comedy about marriage and adultery which is "shocking without raising its voice," witty and funny, and which is, in the end, "thoroughly thin stuff."

R6167 Toynbee, Philip. "Graham Greene at His Best." Observer,

(15 Jan.), p. 29. A warm appreciation of A Burnt-Out Case as Greene's "most serious" novel since The End of the Affair and his "best" since The Power and the Glory. Maintains that Greene's skill lies in the "gentle and unemphatic commentary which accompanies a story ... beautifully and brilliantly told" with his habitual natural vividness, free from his predilections for religious drama or private feuds.

R6168 ______. "Log-Books of the Creative Process." Observer, (5 Nov.), p. 29. A short review which finds In Search of a Character interesting partly because it shows how Greene worked towards the conception of Querry, but mainly for revealing how much Querry is the recurring hero of the novels, so the temptation to say that Greene is a burnt-out case himself is strong but contradicted, or at least qualified, by the novelist's "curiosity which sustains him against the tides of ennui."

R6169 Walker, Peregrine. "A Burnt-Out Case." Blackfriars, XLII:490 (March), pp. 138-39. A novel of "formidable strength" in which a more "tangled world" than the traditional Greenean territory of sin and grace is explored. Though it makes little or no literary assessment, the review calls for an acceptance of the novel for what it is, and not for what "the apologete might want it to be."

R6170 Wall, Bernard. "A Burnt-Out Case." TCLon, CLXIX (March), pp. 308-09. Rejects the "confusion" and the judgment of Greene's Catholicism by the amount of religion that enters into his novels. Notices the influence of the theatre on Greene.

R6171 Warnke, F. T. "New Books in Review: A Burnt-Out Case." YR, L (June), pp. 631-32. The short review finds the novel "desperately disappointing" and "unconvincing" and the hero a "tedious latter-day Byron," in spite of its "valid material," and the successful establishment of atmosphere.

R6172 Watts, Richard Jr. "Two on the Aisle: Mr. Greene Looks at a Triangle." NYP, (2 Nov.). A review of The Complaisant Lover and its performance. Finds the "drawing-room comedy" intelligent, written with "grace and deftness," and "polished, urbane and moderately entertaining" but lacking in purpose.

R6173 Waugh, Evelyn. "Last Steps in Africa." Spectator, (27 Oct), pp. 594-95. A sensitive review of In Search of a Character that perceives and explains the value of the Congo Journal "not as a literary exercise, but as a study of the motions of a literary imagination, and is of very high value indeed."

R6174 Weyergans, Franz. "La saison des pluies, de Graham Greene." RN, XXXIII:4 (April), pp. 417-20. Disappointed by the novel for it leaves him with the impression of "déjà vu" and a certain dissatisfaction with Greene's "création factice," especially that the characters, with the exception of Querry, the doctor, the Father Superior and possibly Marie, lack depth and substance.

R6175 Wyndham, Francis. "A Burnt-Out Case." LM, VIII (March), pp. 62-63. This "elaborately plotted spiritual melodrama, executed with the economy of a master" and evoking atmosphere and establishing setting effortlessly contains much that is "typically Greene," and is among his "finest" novels, owing to his successful delineation of the character of Querry.

R6176 Unsigned. "A Burnt-Out Case." Booklist, LVII (15 Jan.), p. 293. Pre-publication notice.

R6177 ________. "A Burnt-Out Case." Bookmark, XX (Feb.), p. 100. Brief note describing the novel as "cerebral and provocative" for the thoughtful reader.

R6178 ________. "Mr. Greene Looks into His Diary." EvS, (31 Oct.), p. 16. Brief notice of the publication of In Search of a Character.

R6179 ________. "In Search of a Character: Two African Journals." Kirkus, XXIX (1 Nov.), pp. 994-95. Pre-publication notice announcing the "fragmentary" and "revealing" nature of the journals.

R6180 ________. "Where the Lepers Are." Newsweek, LVII (20 Feb.), p. 94. Describes Greene's technique in A Burnt-Out Case as "almost blatant" virtuosity where high "skill and dazzle" are used at the expense of the "rich, underlying music."

R6181 ________. "Vivisected Triangle." Newsweek, LVIII (13 Nov.), p. 95. A review of The Complaisant Lover and its performance in New York. The "excessively civilized" and "lighthearted approach" to the problem of adultery is "polished, often amusing and, in one scene, ... deeply touching." Finds the people "cardboard" and the characterization generally thin.

R6182 ________. "A Burnt-Out Case." NY, XXXVII (11 March), p. 169. Briefly noted as a "silly, pretentious parable that ... might have passed unnoticed in the pages of a Sunday-school magazine."

R6183 ________. "The Complaisant Lover." NYTCR, pp. 184-87. Includes reviews of the play and performance by John

Chapman (DaiN), Justin Gilbert (NYMir), Walter Kerr (NYHB), John McClain (NYJ), Norman Nadel (NYWT), Howard Taubman (NYT), and Richard Watts, Jr. (NYP) on 2 Nov. 1961. See individual entries.

R6184 ________. "Briefly Noted: A Burnt-Out Case." Progressive, XXV (May), p. 50. Notes Greene's excessive concern for the "dialectic" in this "parable."

R6185 ________. "Love Among the Lepers." Time, LXXVII (17 Feb.), pp. 72-73. A review of A Burnt-Out Case that considers the novel Greene's "greatest." As a "parable," with "certainly the most intensely sustained metaphor in modern fiction," the novel shows the persistence of love among "god's grotesques" and can also be described as "existentialist."

R6186 ________. "A Burnt-Out Case." Time, LXXVIII (29 Dec.), p. 55. Briefly noticed as the second choice in the year's Best Fiction.

R6187 ________. "New Fiction." Times, (19 Jan.), p. 15. A Burnt-Out Case is the first of five books reviewed. As one of Greene's "most memorable" books that is "deeply interesting and eminently worth reading," the novel has one central weakness: Querry's reasons for running away are revealed in a "disappointingly abstract way," because the entire book is a "diagnosis of his spiritual state."

R6188 ________. "Novelist's Notes." Times, (2 Nov.), p. 16. A short review of In Search of a Character remarking on how fashionable Greene has become if his "jottings" are made public. Also takes Greene to task for accusing H. Belloc of a "fundamental falsity."

R6189 ________. "Destination Unknown." TLS, 3073 (20 Jan.), p. 37. A review of A Burnt-Out Case which finds the universal relevance of the first part about emptiness "impressive and cogent," and valuable; but the novel "topples into sentimentality and even improbability" with the story element in spite of Greene's "over-efficient, almost slick story-telling" in the latter part.

R6190 ________. "Novelist's Blueprints." TLS, 3113 (27 Oct.), p. 772. A review of In Search of a Character critical of the publication of Greene's working notes in book form because it "smacks of arrogance," an impression heightened by his "didactic footnotes." Besides, the publication of the Congo Journal is too close in time to A Burnt-Out Case and tends to "blur the remembered pattern of the fiction."

D611 Conroy, Esther A. American Critics on Four Novels of Graham Greene. M.A. Rivier College.

D612 Ginn, Regis C. The Imaginary World Created by Graham Greene. M.A. Univ. of Arizona.

D613 McCarthy, David R. The Priest in Graham Greene: His Use and Failure. M.A. Columbia Univ.

D614 McClendon, Margaret A. God in a Godless World: A Study of Graham Greene 1929-1951. M.A. Univ. of Texas at Austin.

D615 Swift, B. C. François Mauriac and Graham Greene: A Study of Atmosphere in the Novel. M.A. Univ. of Manchester.

1962

B621 Browne, E. Martin. "Contemporary Drama in the Catholic Tradition." Christian Faith and the Contemporary Arts. Ed. Finley Eversole. New York and Nashville: Abingdon Press, pp. 132-41. Maintains that the cosmic and eternal values implicit in God's plan--of which human life and history are a part--dominate the works of writers like P. Claudel, T. S. Eliot and G. Greene. Pages 140-41 give a rather sketchy account of how Greene's presentation of the working of Grace in The Living Room, The Potting Shed and The Power and the Glory belongs to the tradition of the old Persian and Resurrection drama.

B622 Crowley, Rev. C[ornelius] P[atrick], CSB. "The Theological Universe of Graham Greene." The Human Image in Modern British Fiction. Toronto: The Radio League of St. Michael. This is the second of a series of five talks on the Trans-Canada Catholic Hour sponsored by the Radio League of St. Michael, Toronto. Talk is dated 25 Feb. 1962. Argues that though Greene's world is sordid and seedy, a "moral no-man's land which lies outside the normal frontiers of Christianity," where the "human image" is least flattering, his vision of the tension between human weakness and the possibility of finding God and redemption in this "no-man's land of morality" transfigures and gives meaning to man's very absurdity and opens wider the "theological universe of man." A Gun for Sale, The Power and the Glory and The Heart of the Matter.

B623 Gregor, Ian, and Brian Nichols. "Grace and Morality." The Moral and the Glory. London: Faber and Faber, pp. 185-216. Rpt. in part in Graham Greene: A Collection of Critical Essays. Ed. Samuel Hynes. Englewood Cliffs, N.J.: Prentice-Hall, 1973, pp. 110-26. Describes briefly the "Greene-Mauriac 'world'"--its inhabitants, the "deception of appearances" in it, and the devaluation of human action which results from an emphasis on Grace--

to discuss the implications of this world on the writing of fiction and how the "presence of Grace" and the "religious sense" affect traditional moral judgment. Makes a useful distinction in his discussion of The End of the Affair between "theology and theology--in fiction" and contends that Greene may have become involved in a situation that "exceeds the novelist's province" in stating and asserting "supernatural grace in the presence of the natural order" in the novel rather than communicating it in human terms--he admits that there is no "a priori reasons why successful novels should not be written about Grace." In Sarah, however, the "fortuitous, inexplicable" action of Grace can only be understood in "extra-fictional terms"; the "fundamental mysteriousness of sanctity" in the novel is at once theme and manner of expression.

B624 Hardwick, Elizabeth. "Loveless Love: Graham Greene." A View of My Own: Essays in Literature and Society. New York: Farrar, Straus and Cudahy; London: Heinemann, 1964, pp. 93-102. A reprint of a review of The Heart of the Matter (PR, XV (1948), pp. 937-39) and of A Burnt-Out Case, (PR, XXVIII:5-6 (1961), pp. 702-09). See R4811.

B625 Kazin, Alfred. "Graham Greene and the Age of Absurdity." Contemporaries. Boston, Mass.: Little, Brown and Co. London: Secker and Warburg, 1963, pp. 158-61. Maintains that the pervasive anxiety and dread of the Hitler Age reflected in the melodrama of The Confidential Agent and The Ministry of Fear have changed, in these Khrushchev-Dulles times, to the farce and absurdity of Our Man in Havana, even though the hero remains the same "defeated, sad ... clown of love."

B626 Kermode, John Frank. "Mr. Greene's Eggs and Crosses." Puzzles and Epiphanies: Essays and Reviews, 1958-1961. London: Routledge and Kegan Paul; New York: Chelmark Press, pp. 176-88. Rpt. in Graham Greene: A Collection of Critical Essays. Ed. Samuel Hynes. Englewood Cliffs, N.J.: Prentice-Hall, 1973, pp. 126-38. Rpt. from Encounter, XVI:4 (April 1961), 69-75. See A6110.

B627 Levi, Albert William. Literature, Philosophy and the Imagination. Bloomington: Indiana Univ. Press. Pages 266-72 of Ch. VII consider The Heart of the Matter as a perfect illustration of "the causal chain producing the mathematical annihilation of an individual," that Scobie's suicide, though an act of free will in all its painful consciousness" is still following "a premediated plan" where the sense of sin is the "'moral' and 'religious' destiny." An interesting viewpoint that deals with the mechanism of fate in the novel.

B628 Varela Jacome, Benito. "Las novelas de Graham Greene."

Novelistas del Siglo xx. San Sebastian: Agora, pp. 35-41. A brief assessment of Greene as one of the "most vigorous" novelists of our times whose technical dexterity in novels depicting the problem of evil and man's conflict with divine grace make his novels attractive. Refers to The Power and the Glory, The End of the Affair and The Heart of the Matter in his brief discussion of "el pensamiento de Green."

B629 Wilson, Colin. "Evelyn Waugh and Graham Greene." The Strength to Dream: Literature and the Imagination. London: Victor Gollancz; Boston: Houghton & Mifflin, pp. 53-63. Examines the symbols of Greene's world as he seizes upon the most depressive details to characterize a scene, and his stylistic effects and dramatic devices in "The End of the Party" and Brighton Rock, but finds the religious theme in the latter cheapened by melodrama and "pseudo-impressive writing."

A621 Barnes, Robert J. "Two Modes of Fiction: Hemingway and Greene." Renascence, XIV (Summer), 193-98. Distinguishes broadly two world views distinctly different: one from the vantage point of Christian tradition, tending to discount the "concept of time as a limiting factor in man's life" where the "important locus" is the tormented conscience of the individual, and the empiricist's where the "time sense is paramount." Contends that these world views of Greene and Hemingway, "prescribe, to a certain extent, the narrative point of view and type of image which will carry forth that theme."

A622 Bryden, Ronald. "Graham Greene, Alas." Spectator, CCIX: 7005 (28 Sept.), pp. 441-42. Rpt. in The Unfinished Hero and Other Essays. London: Faber and Faber, 1969, pp. 210-15. A review article on the publication in Penguin paperbacks of The Power and the Glory, The Heart of the Matter, The End of the Affair, The Quiet American and Our Man in Havana revealing that the English are reluctant to admit Greene to be the finest English novelist writing because of his concern for the eternal and the world at large--like Conrad--rather than the local, provincial, English contemporary scene.

A623 Castelli, Ferdinando. "Graham Greene, un romanziere che affascina e sconcerta." Letture, XVII, pp. 563-80. Greene utilizes the "thriller" to engage the reader with themes that are relevant to the time and to his future destiny. He may fascinate or disconcert the reader, but he never leaves him indifferent. Examines the "grandi temi dell-esistenza" in the novels of the thirties, and separately, from a Catholic viewpoint, Brighton Rock, The Power and the Glory, The Heart of the Matter, and The End of the Affair, and concludes with an evaluation of The Living Room.

A624 Consolo, Dominick P. "Music as Motif: The Unity of Brighton Rock." Renascence, XV (Fall), pp. 12-20. Rpt. in Graham Greene. Ed. Harry J. Cargas. St. Louis, Mo.: B. Herder Book Co., 1969, pp. 75-88. Asserts, and proves, that Brighton Rock, whether it is regarded as "entertainment" or novel, is a book that has "unity of design ... discovered in the repetition and recurrence of song titles and lyrics that, acting as a motif, fabricate a consistent pattern of meaning." Contends that the associations and reactions of characters to music reveal the different values they have, e.g., Ida and Pinkie, and that music as motif functions as a "stitching agent" to bring the values of opposed realms to bear on the immediate action, "makes the conflict meaningful on the second level," and, on the whole, unifies the novel's design.

A625 Ivasheva, Valentina. "Legende und Wahrheit uber Graham Greene." ZAA, X, pp. 229-58. In German, translated from Russian by Hans Heidrich. A marxist approach that focusses on the development of Greene's realism and his search for humanity as he grows disenchanted with religion because its "inhuman laws contradict man's most precious property: his reason and his activity in creative work." The Heart of the Matter, The End of the Affair and The Quiet American.

A626 Kermode, Frank. "Myth, Reality and Fiction." Listener, LXVIII:1744 (30 Aug.), pp. 311-13. A summary of his symposium "The House of Fiction." Discusses with Greene the relationship between myth and reality. Greene illustrates his views from The Heart of the Matter, The Power and the Glory, The End of the Affair and A Burnt-Out Case.

A627 Martin, Guy. "The Heart of the Graham Greene Matter." Realities, pp. 60-63. Though ostensibly a report of an interview, this article discusses Greene's childhood, his conversion to Catholicism, aspects of his novelistic technique--description of scene, images, commitment to truth, and the tragic element--as well as his "singular" attitude towards Catholicism. Of interest is Greene's admission of the change that has come over his Catholicism since The Power and the Glory--"the emotional element has tended to disappear"--and of the impression of St. Augustine and Kierkegaard on him, especially Teillard de Chardin's The Human Phenomenon, when writing A Burnt-Out Case.

A628 Noxon, James. "Kierkegaard's Stages and A Burnt-Out Case." REL, III:1 (Jan.), 90-101. A critical essay probing the "meaning" of the novel, and proposing that one read it as a dramatic counterpoint of Kierkegaard's existential types: the aesthetic, the ethical and the religious, wherein there exists an "inherent contradiction" in attempting to serve one category from the standpoint of another. Such a reading, endorsed by John Atkins' interpretation that the stresses and flaws in Greene's fiction are "signs of spiritual disorder ... symptomatic of the inevitable conflict between artist and man of faith,"--an interpretation accepted without question--leads him to diagnose a case of "spiritual malaise" because Greene the novelist is "so out of harmony with ... the Catholic apologist."

A629 Orwell, George. "Some Letters of George Orwell." Encounter, XVIII (Jan.), pp. 55-65. Describes Greene briefly in a letter on pp. 64-65 to "Tosco" T. R. Fyvel, literary editor of The Tribune, as a Catholic who "takes sides politically with the Church" but is, in outlook, "a mild left with faint CP leanings."

A6210 Paleivskij, P. "Fantomy: Burzuaznyj mir v romanax Grema Grina." NovM, XXXVIII:6, pp. 229-43. In Russian. "Phantoms: The Bourgeois World in the Novels of Graham Greene." Discusses Greene's ironical interest in the dehumanizing forces of capitalist society and its channelling of man into roles which lack any kind of reality. The Quiet American, Our Man in Havana and A Burnt-Out Case.

A6211 Spaventa Filippi, Lia. "Produzione poliziesca di Graham Greene." ICS, XLV, p. 87. Claims that to classify Greene as a writer of "thrillers" casts no aspersion on his achievement, because Greene, even while describing the violence common to our times, transcends the particular act of violence to express his own inner reality.

A6212 Stratford, Philip. "Unlocking The Potting Shed." KR, XXIV (Winter), 129-43. Cites instances of Greene as a "practical joker" who often throws up a "smoke screen of ambiguity" to hide the secrets of his art and who carefully "disguises his life in fiction, and so ingeniously fictionalizes his life, that no frontal attack of research, however painstaking, will reveal the hidden author." But it is difficult to accept the new but interesting and seemingly plausible "key" suggested--Greene's fascination with his own name and a "predilection for his name colour"--for it is based partly on speculation and partly on impression.

A6213 Tucker, Martin. "The Real Africa: Heart Before Politics." NYHT, (23 Sept.), p. 11. An account of an interview with Greene in his London flat. Focusses on Greene's fascination for what is called black Africa, and his views on the output and viewpoints of black African writers and Englishmen, and the question of miscegenation.

A6214 Tysdahl, Bjorn. "Graham Greene--fluktens og forfolgelsens dikter." KoK, LXVII, 293-98. In Norwegian. A study of the pattern of flight and pursuit which takes place in Greene's novels on the physical or external plane and the spiritual or inner world of the individual.

A6215 Waugh, Evelyn. "Sloth." SunT, 7234 (7 Jan.), p. 21. Examines briefly Querry as the "plainest representation" of sloth--a condition he defines as one in which a "man is fully aware of the proper means of his salvation and refuses to take them because the whole apparatus of salvation fills him with tedium and disgust"--or what St. Thomas calls "sadness in the face of spiritual good." Also describes Greene's intention in his later novels as "obscure."

A6216 Wexler, Alexandra. "Der abgeschuittene Kopf." DeutR, LXXXVIII, pp. 50-55. Examines different aspects of the "sickness of the times" as depicted in novels by D. H. Lawrence, I. Murdoch, S. Delaney, A. Sillitoe and A Burnt-Out Case by G. Greene.

R621 Barrett, William. "Africa and Original Sin." Atlantic, CCIX (Feb.), pp. 117-18. Finds the first journal of In Search of a Character a "fascinating notebook on the laboratory of the imagination." Though he acknowledges that it is a mistake to identify an author with his character, he contends that Greene has secreted in Querry his own undercurrent of despair, and that consequently, Querry's judgment of himself as an architect reflects Greene's on his writing.

R622 ________. "Master Craftsman." Atlantic, CCIX (June), pp. 109-11. Maintains that the conciseness of the short story form in Twenty-One Stories gives a "greater intensity" to Greene's macabre imagination. The stories are not Chekhovian in the evocation of mood, moment or character but revolve around a "definite and very well plotted narrative idea."

R623 Barron, Louis. "In Search of a Character." LJ, LXXXI (15 Jan.), p. 226. A short review noting the interest and the pleasure which Greene's brief diary will have for readers and students.

R624 Black, Susan M. "Play Reviews: The Complaisant Lover." TArts, XLVI (Jan.), pp. 15 & 17. A review of the play and the American production. Finds the play a "variation on the classic theme of ménage à trois."

R625 C., E. "In Search of a Character." BA, XXXVI (Spring), pp. 213-14. Shows how the Congo Journal records technical details, small actions, sensory impressions and above all, the material which Greene used to authenticate the medical background and enabled him to communicate the "theme of the deep, overwhelming sadness of the spirit submerged, overcome, lost in the flesh."

R626 D., K. "Heart of Darkness." SatN, LXXVII (3 Feb.), p. 32. A short review of In Search of a Character noting the "growth of character and ideas for his fiction" in the journals.

R627 Davis, Robert Gorham. "A Novelist in Quest of Himself." NYT, (7 Jan.), pp. 4, 38. Draws the analogy between Conrad's Congo diary and Greene's Congo Journal in In Search of a Character. Shows how the latter makes some "fascinating revelations" about Greene's literary method, and his temperament.

R628 Engelborghs, Maurits. "Dagboek van een romancier." DWB, CVII (May-June), p. 372. Does not find "Convoy to West Africa" useful as a diary in contrast to the "Congo Journal" which is revealing and informative.

R629 Gilman, Richard. "The Stage: The Amber Light District." Commonweal, LXXVII (14 Dec.), pp. 316-17. A review of the revived off-Broadway production of The Living Room. Wonders about the reasons behind its revival, even though the play does live by its "half-evasion and sentimentality and more melodramatic ingenuity," and its "unconvincing" resolutions which are merely "crippling but not fatal."

R6210 Griffin, Hilary. "In Search of a Character." CW, CXCV: 1165 (April), pp. 55-56, 58. Regrets the publication of this "peculiar little volume" which is regarded as a "breach of artistic modesty" on Greene's part, for it brings the reader closer to Greene and arouses in the former a "devilish curiosity" to spy at the novelist at work, a sort of "'Peeping Tomism.'"

R6211 Hicks, Granville. "Gestation of a Brain Child." SatR, XLV (6 Jan.), p. 62. Finds the "process" by which A Burnt-Out Case was brought into being "endlessly interesting and truly important," even though the Congo Journal in In Search of a Character is by itself "slight" and does not throw any "dazzling light" on the novel.

R6212 Hogan, William. "A Novelist's Journal; Other News and Notes." SFC, (5 Jan.), p. 39. The short review considers In Search of a Character a "minor" Greene book at best, a "literary curiosity" which is only "fairly interesting" and of value to practicing writers.

R6213 K., H. T. "In Search of a Character." ForumC, XLII (Oct.), p. 167. Finds the book of "considerable interest for its insights into the nuclei of Greene's ideas," Africa being for Greene a "source of this power," whose seediness he seeks out as much as that of the English underworld.

R6214 McDonnell, Thomas P. "Greene's Search." Commonweal, LXXV (2 March), pp. 601-02. Though In Search of a Character may be a "fascinating" record of Greene's search for "X," it raises the question: to what extent can the novel "continue to depend upon the psychological (if not narcissistic) gropings of authors?"

R6215 McLaughlin, Richard. "Interesting Book by Graham Greene." SpR, (Jan.), p. 4D. A short review of In Search of a Character that finds Greene's impressions of the tropical landscape immensely interesting and the "candid inside-the-craftsman's-brain view" provided of great importance.

R6216 Poore, Charles. "Books of the Times." NYT, (13 Jan.), p. 19. Does not find Greene's revelations in In Search of a Character "awfully exciting" and the penetration of his privacy doomed to disappointment.

R6217 R., S. P. "21 Stories." SpR, (13 May), p. 4D. Briefly noted as a republication of Nineteen Stories with the omission of one of these and the addition of three others.

R6218 Ross, Mary. "The Start of the Matter." NYHT, (4 March), p. 13. A short review of In Search of a Character noting its fascination for readers who want to know more about the creative process.

R6219 Ryan, Stephen P. "21 Stories." CW, CXCV (Sept.), pp. 373-74. Finds the republication of Nineteen Stories, after adding "The Destructors," "Special Duties" and "The Blue Film," an "interesting publication stunt" but also an opportunity to review old acquaintances.

R6220 Sullivan, Richard. "Experience Into Fiction: Hints at the Way of Literary Genesis." CST, (21 Jan.), p. 2. A review of In Search of a Character that describes it as an "honest, illuminating but too brief journal" and an engrossing book that reveals, technically, the conception and gestation of a novel, and autobiographically, how "a writer responds to the stimuli of existence."

R6221 Taubman, Richard. "Theatre: Revival of 'Living Room.'" NYT, (22 Nov.), p. 43. A review of the play and its revival at the Gramercy Arts Theatre. (Off-Broadway). Remarks on Greene's absorption with the dialogue rather than characters whom he regards as "means to an end." Lists members of The Cast.

R6222 Tracy, Honor. "Two Voices Are There." NRep, CXLVI (5 Feb.), pp. 20-21. A review of P. Toynbee's Pantaleau and Greene's In Search of a Character. The publication of the latter baffles him and "passes all comprehension" for it is "indiscreet and unwise to demand to know how the conjuror 'does' it."

R6223 W[ickenden], D[an]. "Twenty-One Stories." NYHT, (22 April), pp. 6-7. Though not exactly a "new" book, the collection is "astonishingly fresh"; it has a wide range and the stories are "brilliantly told, neatly constructed."

R6224 Wood, Frederick T. "Current Literature: A Burnt-Out Case." ES, XLIII:3 (June), pp. 208-09. Notes briefly the novel as a "compelling" work whose characters are convincing though its conclusion is a "little conventional." Greene does not "moralise" but he leaves the reader with a series of questions.

R6225 Unsigned. "In Search of a Character." Booklist, LVIII (1 Jan.), p. 273. Brief notice of publication and its value in giving glimpses of a "writer's development of characters and use of casual or random material and experience."

R6226 ________. "21 Stories." Booklist, LVIII (15 May), p. 646. Brief notice of publication noting the story omitted from Nineteen Stories.

R6227 ________. "The Complaisant Lover." ETJ, XIV (March), p. 67. A short review describing the play as a "well written but inconsequential domestic triangle" which is at best only "very moderately amusing."

R6228 ________. "21 Stories." NY, XXXVIII (5 May), p. 192. Brief notice of publication.

R6229 ________. "Twenty-One Stories." Time, LXXIX (4 May), p. 62. A short review that regards the "present bouquet of Greenery" a tribute to "publishing ingenuity." Remarks briefly on Greene's "unsophisticated" talent that does not despise mystery and plot.

R6230 ________. "In Search of a Character." TCLon, CLXX:1012 (Winter), pp. 190-91. Brief notice of publication noting the importance of "these diary-scraps."

R6231 ________. "In Search of a Character: Two African Journals." VQR, XXXVIII (Spring), pp. xlvi, xlviii. Notes the importance of the Congo Journal for those who like to watch "the artist at work," and in revealing Greene himself, his taste in literature and his thoughts on a wide range of subjects.

D621 Sanders, Marvin C. The Use of Ambiguity and Paradox in the Catholic Novels of Graham Greene. M.A. Univ. of Idaho.

1963

B631 Adler, Jacob H. "Graham Greene's Plays: Technique Versus Value." Graham Greene: Some Critical Considerations. Ed. Robert O. Evans. Lexington: Univ. of Kentucky Press, pp. 219-31. Rpt. Kentucky Paperbacks, 1967. Attempts to examine The Potting Shed, The Living Room and The Complaisant Lover from the point of view of an educated playgoer. Makes an interesting analysis of the "Ibsenian" in character, situation and "complex overall symbol" in The Potting Shed, an "interesting, civilized, literate play ... minor where it behaves as though it is major." Dismisses The Living Room for its "amateurishness and lack of focus and economy" as giving the effect "of an early draft for a novel," and appreciates Greene's increasing dramatic competence in the "bittersweet middle-class comedy-triangle" of The Complaisant Lover.

B632 Allott, Miriam. "The Moral Situation in The Quiet American." Graham Greene: Some Critical Considerations. Ed. Robert O. Evans. Lexington: Univ. Kentucky Press, pp. 188-207. Rpt. Kentucky Paperbacks, 1967. Examines the Jamesian affinities of the novel--an "Anglo-American 'international situation,' ... juxtaposition of representatives from the 'New' and the 'Old' worlds ... motivations of treachery and betrayal ... and the close interdependence of its tragic and its comic elements"--and argues persuasively that one should interpret the novel in terms of a concern with the "nature of effective moral action"--rather than on existential terms as Evans advocated (see A578). Maintains, after a careful analysis of the evidence, that though theological dilemmas are absent in the novel, Fowler establishes a "thematic continuity" with Greene's Catholic novels and characters by his pity for humans, by his willingness to take responsibility for wrong-doing to diminish pain and by his longing for peace.

B633 Atkins, John. "Altogether Amen: A Reconsideration of The Power and the Glory." Graham Greene: Some Critical Considerations. Ed. Robert O. Evans. Lexington: Univ. of Kentucky Press, pp. 181-88. The "reconsideration" examines Greene's presentation of death as a "condition" of the novel: it is "its ambiance, its air, its food and drink, its matrix, its love, its demiurge, even its priest." Finds, twenty years later, the extent and nature of loading and hammering the point objectionable, especially that Greene, as a "propagandist of the Catholic Church ... is not persuasive." Resents Greene's violent assault on the reader's allegiance and especially the "disagreeable sense of defeat, of irremediable human defeat" aroused by the novel.

B634 ________. "The Curse of the Film." Graham Greene: Some Critical Considerations. Ed. Robert O. Evans. Lexington: Univ. of Kentucky Press, pp. 207-19. This is a reprint of Ch. 7 of his book Graham Greene. (See B571). Discusses Greene as a film critic after summarizing his views on the popularity of the art. Maintains that Greene's criticism is that of a creative writer, derived from his faculty of apprehending "significant symbols." Illustrates Greene's attacks--a "combination of ferocity and malice"--on film actresses and Americanism in general, and insinuates that the change in Greene's attitude to beautiful actresses stems from his frustration at their inaccessibility--"Greene was a highly-sexed young man," the writer claims.

B635 Borinski, Ludwig. "Graham Greene and Aldous Huxley." Meister des modernen englischen Romans. Heidelberg: Quelle and Meyer, pp. 221-49. This is chapter IX of the volume. The section on Greene (pp. 221-29) is a brief general survey of prominent themes, especially good and evil, betrayal and the "third dimension" created by religion in England Made Me, Brighton Rock, The Power and the Glory, and The Heart of the Matter. Identifies Greene's debt to Conrad and the "puritanical legacy" in the form of Faith which Greene, like T. S. Eliot has inherited.

B636 Brennan, Neil. "Bibliography." Graham Greene: Some Critical Considerations. Ed. Robert O. Evans. Lexington: Univ. of Kentucky Press, pp. 244-76. This is the most comprehensive bibliography to date and is divided into ten sections. Sect. 1 lists Greene's works. Each work is followed by data of TLS and NYT reviews, critical articles and books or monographs, if any, on the work. Sect. 2 lists books written in part by Greene and Sect. 3 is a general note on his contributions to periodicals. Sect. 4 lists seven doctoral dissertations and twelve books on Greene and Sect. 5 lists four dissertations and sixteen books in part on Greene. Sect. 6 lists one hundred and eleven selected periodical articles and Sect. 7 notes the dramatization of his novels and the films made of his short stories and novels. Sections 8 & 9 list the contents of special numbers on Greene by MFS and Renascence, and Sect. 10 lists the five bibliographies and checklists to date.

B637 Burgess, Anthony. The Novel Today. British Council Series, London: Longmans, Green. Rpt. Folcroft Library Editions, 1971. Ch. 5 places Greene in a literary perspective with P. H. Johnson, W. Golding and others as a novelist whose works probe into the problems of good and evil and the wretchedness of the human condition.

B638 Consolo, Dominick P. "Graham Greene: Style and Stylistics in Five Novels." Graham Greene: Some Critical Considerations. Ed. Robert O. Evans. Lexington: Univ. of Kentucky Press, pp. 61-96. The essay focusses on point of view, character, structure and aspects of language, image and symbol in Brighton Rock, The Power and the Glory, The Heart of the Matter, The End of the Affair and The Quiet American to show that the devices Greene uses are not mere "stylistic tricks" but that his style is "cumulative"; the devices are an integral part contributing to his esthetic pattern and incorporate much of the meaning and the action of those novels. See also D592.

B639 De Vitis, A. A. "The Catholic as Novelist: Graham Greene and François Mauriac." Graham Greene: Some Critical Considerations. Ed. Robert O. Evans. Lexington: Univ. of Kentucky Press, pp. 112-27. Shows that both Greene and Mauriac are similar in that they write within the framework of Catholicism, are aware of the difficulties involved in writing from a Catholic viewpoint, are concerned with the problem of good and evil and with observing life and "creating the experience of it." They differ, however, "in method rather than theme" because Greene writes within the traditional form of the English novel, and though he creates the "life-experiences" in "unchartered theological waters," he establishes the ethical norms of behavior and religious perspective at the end of his novels.

B6310 Evans, Robert O., ed. Graham Greene: Some Critical Considerations. Lexington: Univ. of Kentucky Press. A collection of essays by H. C. Webster, Nathan A. Scott, F. L. Kunkel, D. P. Consolo, D. H. Hesla, A. A. DeVitis, H. E. Haber, R. O. Evans, K. Laitinen, J. Atkins, M. Allott, J. H. Adler, C. D. Scott and a bibliography by N. Brennan. See individual entries.

B6311 ________. "The Satanist Fallacy of Brighton Rock." Graham Greene: Some Critical Considerations. Ed. Robert O. Evans. Lexington: Univ. of Kentucky Press, pp. 151-69. Rejects interpretations of Pinkie as a tragic hero and the novel as a masterpiece of horror, and contends that Brighton Rock was conceived as "serious literature" and excuses Greene's intention to depict the human struggle on the ethical and spiritual plane, not without edification, and that he has succeeded in weaving a "Jamesian pattern into the carpet" for the reader to discover. Examines the various devices by which Greene conveys his serious intention of relating the disparate reality of a modern brutal world to the ideals of Christianity.

B6312 Foster, Joseph R. "Graham Greene." Modern Christian Literature. London: Burns and Oates, pp. 47-55. A brief survey of Greene's major novels through A Burnt-Out Case. Concentrates on exposition rather than literary evaluation, and regards the novels as readings or interpretations of life based on the author's "attitude to life."

B6313 Haber, Herbert R. "The End of the Catholic Cycle: The Writer Versus the Saint." Graham Greene: Some Critical Considerations. Ed. Robert O. Evans. Lexington: Univ. of Kentucky Press, pp. 127-51. Contends that in The End of the Affair Greene demonstrates an unprecedented concern with "certain religious imperatives" which beset the believing novelist, and questions whether Greene had in mind some "extraliterary intent." The discussion of the narrative manner in the novel--this is Greene's first attempt as the first person narrator--entails a critical examination of the values and psychology of the artist himself, including his antagonism to time.

B6314 Hartt, Julian N. The Lost Image of Man. Baton Rouge: Louisiana State Univ. Press. Examines briefly on pp. 116-18 of Ch. VI the "hunger for sanctification" in two "late contenders for sainthood in the ranks of traditional piety"--the whiskey priest in The Power and the Glory and Sarah in The End of the Affair.

B6315 Hesla, David H. "Theological Ambiguity in the 'Catholic Novels.'" Graham Greene: Some Critical Considerations. Ed. Robert O. Evans. Lexington: Univ. of Kentucky Press, pp. 96-112. Contends that the "confusion and contradictoriness" of criticism on Greene's novels may be largely traced to the critics' unawareness of the "deep incoherence" resulting from Greene's "qualification of a Gnostic or neo-Gnostic doctrine of creation by a Catholic and orthodox doctrine of the Incarnation." Examines "affinities" which Greene's Catholic novels have with Gnosticism and shows that suicide in the novels is undertaken either as a "means of escape from an ugly and hopeless world" or as the inevitable consequence of the life of "suffering love ... lived in imitation of Christ," for he considers the death of the whiskey priest and Sarah "suicidal," too.

B6316 Kerr, Walter. "The Complaisant Lover." The Theatre in Spite of Itself. New York: Simon and Schuster, pp. 157-60. The review of the play included in this collection of "first-night reviews, Sunday pieces, and magazine articles" emphasizes Greene's "reserve" and "power of suggestion" which gives rise to the "special delight" of the spectator as he watches the "undercurrent of frolic buried deep within the plausible."

B6317 Killinger, John. The Failure of Theology in Modern Literature. Nashville, Tenn.: Abingdon Press. This "running commentary" on works "related" to the Christian faith makes scattered references to themes in three works by

Greene: the Resurrection in The Potting Shed with James Callifer as the modern-day Lazarus (pp. 183-86), the "imago Dei" in The Power and the Glory (pp. 60-61), the sacramental side of the ministry in both works (pp. 144-45), and the high regard in which the Sacraments, especially the Eucharist, are held by Catholics in The Heart of the Matter.

B6318 Kunkel, Francis L. "The Theme of Sin and Grace in Graham Greene." Graham Greene: Some Critical Considerations. Ed. Robert O. Evans. Lexington: Univ. of Kentucky Press, pp. 49-61. Rpt. with some changes, from The Labyrinthine Ways of Graham Greene. New York: Sheed and Ward, 1959, pp. 132-45. Argues that though the pessimism of Jansenism is "most endemic" in Greene's works which often describe the "wretchedness of man with God," Greene never portrays man so mired in sin to be beyond redemption, nor does he glorify sin. Rejects the "sin mysticism" or "felix culpa" notion attributed to Greene and asserts that Greene instills a reverence for the individual, despite his sin, thereby cultivating a "more profound respect for the mysterious transforming power of grace."

B6319 Laitinen, Kai. "The Heart of the Novel: The Turning Point in The Heart of the Matter." Graham Greene: Some Critical Considerations. Ed. Robert O. Evans. Lexington: Univ. of Kentucky Press, pp. 169-81. The essay is translated from the Finnish by Ants Oras. Maintains that the "watershed," the focal point in the novel--in the sense that it constitutes a vantage point from which "the reader may view the total landscape, examining the series of events both forward and backward"--is in Ch. 1 of Book Two. All the "central threads of the novel intersect" here; it is compact, the stage is narrowed, the dramatis personae are concentrated in one place, and decisive events occur to motivate further incidents. Also notes that the various letters quoted in the novel are like "lenses concentrating the problem pattern of the novel into one point."

B6320 Pongs, Hermann. "Graham Greene." Romanschaffen im Umbruch der Zeit Eine Chronik von 1952 bis 1962. Tubingen: Verlag der Deutschen Hochschullehrerzeitung, pp. 129-31. A short study of Greene's "brutal realism" which maintains that Greene manifests what Schiller feared: that an imitation of nature may become an imitation of "gemeine Natur." Beside the realism of The Power and the Glory and The Heart of the Matter, German Catholic fiction seems almost "sentimental-idealistic."

B6321 Pryce-Jones, David. Graham Greene. Writers and Critics Series. London: Oliver & Boyd. New York: Barnes &

Noble, 1967. Rev. ed. 1973. Traces the development of Greene's art and thought as a writer. The evaluation of his art as a major novelist focusses on discussions of technique and style; the evolution of his thought involves an objective evaluation of his Catholicism and its relation to his work without attempting to justify or exonerate Greene for his views. Ch. 1 considers the "topicality" of Greene and argues that his early novels seen in retrospect, are very much a part of the thirties and an interesting reflection of it; but as he moved away to a position that believes in the inevitability of sin and the necessity for suffering, his "social and emotional involvement has dwindled accordingly." Ch. 2 discusses the novels up to, and including, Brighton Rock. The novels express the themes of betrayal and arbitrary justice, and as Greene becomes "progressively more assured and more professional in construction," he tends towards Catholicism as a "moral criterion against the human anarchy." Ch. 3 focusses on The Power and the Glory as it pleads the "paradoxes of sainthood," and sees in the novel "limitations" imposed by Greene's Catholicism. Ch. 4 examines the "entertainments" including The Complaisant Lover, but is reluctant to "lump the secular novels," A Gun for Sale, The Confidential Agent and The Ministry of Fear under this generic title. Ch. 5 discusses Greene's "ontological exercises" in The Heart of the Matter, The End of the Affair, The Potting Shed and The Living Room, The Quiet American and A Burnt-Out Case as Greene attempts to prove the connections between sin and God's purposes, and the attendant suffering. Ch. 6 corrects any impression that Greene is an apologist by emphasizing his "disloyalty" to any one group, and proceeds to reveal that Greene's religious vision, his subversion of doctrine into an unconventional world picture--including that of his works in the sixties--is a "clamp" that centers the reader's attention on the "imaginative inferno" of his works.

B6322 Scott, Carolyn D. "The Witch at the Corner: Notes on Graham Greene's Mythology." Graham Greene: Some Critical Considerations. Ed. Robert O. Evans. Lexington: Univ. of Kentucky Press, pp. 231-44. Contends that the central symbol of the myth Greene has created is the "heart of Africa, seat of our fall," which is neither good nor evil but is a "haunting, compelling synthesis of both" that can bring order from external or internal chaos; hence, Greene's fascination for the primitive and compelling ritual of the Liberian bush devil whose power simultaneously combines good and evil in initiating the young. Discusses the struggle for power and the initiation of Philip in "The Basement Room," David's baptism of terror in "The Hint of an Explanation," and Pendele in A Burnt-Out Case.

B6323 Scott, Nathan A., Jr. "Graham Greene: Christian Tragedian." Graham Greene: Some Critical Considerations. Ed. Robert O. Evans. Lexington: Univ. of Kentucky Press, pp. 25-49. Rpt. from VolR, I:1 (Spring 1954), pp. 29-42. See A5415.

B6324 Webster, Harvey Curtis. "The World of Graham Greene." Graham Greene: Some Critical Considerations. Ed. Robert O. Evans. Lexington: Univ. of Kentucky Press. Rpt. as "Graham Greene: Stoical Catholic." After the Trauma: Perspective British Novelists Since 1920. Lexington: The Univ. of Kentucky Press, 1970, pp. 97-124. Surveys the novels to show that as an artist, Greene is committed to a faithful representation of his personal vision which he realizes with "nearly progressive fidelity" from The Man Within to The Quiet American. Betrayal, lust without love, and violence without motive figure far more prominently in this world rather than fidelity, true love and kindly gentle action; and though the novels of the thirties may be "savagely pessimistic," they, by exaggeration, suggest truths about men and the moral and social universe in which they live just as later novels show his concern with "man's hope of God and the danger of his too frequent hubristic self-reliance."

A631 Abirached, Robert. "Le Paria, de Graham Greene." Etudes, 11 (Nov.), 241-44. Attributes the audience's "malaise" that stems from lack of conviction in Jean Mercure's adaptation of The Potting Shed at the Théâtre Saint-George primarily to Greene's usage of the miraculous as the deus ex machina in a realistic drama, and, to a lesser degree, the thesis play in the modern theatre.

A632 Arnesen, Aksel. "Graham Greenes ideverden." Samtiden, LXXII:9 (Nov.), 636-44. In Norwegian. Focusses on Greene's works in the fifties, especially The End of the Affair, to show that the love of God, seemingly irresistible and even irrational, leads to faith in His power and goodness in a world corrupted by sin and evil. Also comments on Greene's Catholicism.

A633 Bellow, Saul. "The Writer as Moralist." Atlantic, CCXI (March), pp. 58-62. Argues that the "moral function cannot be divorced from art" for the writer "bears the burdens of priest or teacher." On the other hand, he examines briefly A Burnt-Out Case as an example of the "mutual destruction" that may take place between the "tendency of a novel to oppose the conscious or ideological purposes of the writer," even the "most constructive intentions."

A634 Dooley, D. J. "A Burnt-Out Case Reconsidered." WisR, CCXXXVII (Summer), 168-78. Rpt., with minor changes and the addition of an introductory paragraph, as "The Suspension of Disbelief: Greene's Burnt-Out Case." DR, XLIII (Autumn), pp. 343-52. Refutes, rather persuasively, James Noxon's contention (see A628) that A Burnt-Out Case is symptomatic of Greene's spiritual malaise" and illustrative of the incompatibility of the aesthetic approval of the novelist and the philosophic or religious commitment of the man. Establishes in the process the unreliability of Atkins' controversial book, considers the novel in relation to contemporary existentialists like Sartre and Camus, and contends that the novel, in its dramatization of the process of a "numbed person discovering new capacities in himself," is one aspect of modern man "in search of his soul."

A635 Gainham, Sarah. "Grim Grin." Spectator, CCX:7040 (31 March), p. 694. An account of Greene's three-day visit to East Berlin when he was in Germany as guest of Hamburg's Die Zeit. Expresses outrage at Greene's "double standard of values" when he talks of East and West Germans.

A636 Harmer, Ruth Mulvey. "Greene World of Mexico: The Birth of a Novelist." Renascence, XV (Summer), 171-82, 194. Traces, for the undergraduate and literate reader, the parallelism between Greene's trip in Mexico and the Whiskey Priest's, but shows that there are enough discrepancies between place and detail noted in The Lawless Roads and The Power and the Glory, e.g., presence of children, especially Coral, "to make it apparent that Greene had no blue print before him" while writing the novel. Attributes the "phenomenal" transformation in the novel to Greene's "extraordinary perceptiveness," "his film-like ability to capture impressions indelibly," and his imagination which "realizes fullest expression" in reordering and redefining people as characters.

A637 Kermode, Frank. "The House of Fiction: Interview with Seven English Novelists." PR, XXX (Spring), pp. 61-83. Conversations ... abridged from longer talks ... entirely free and unprepared." Discusses the relationship between reality and fiction or "ethical myth" and plot with Greene on pp. 65-68. Of interest are certain admissions by Greene: his passionate liking for melodrama ... a liking for action that conflicts with his desire to produce "a good novel" with "a central figure who represents some idea of reasonable simplicity," and the "appalling mistake" of introducing "something which had not got a natural explanation" in the last third of The End of the Affair.

A638 Kiely, Robert. "The Craft of Despondency--The Traditional Novelists." Daedalus, XCII, 220-37. Discusses E. Waugh, G. Greene and K. A. Porter, "austere allegorists" profoundly influenced by traditional Christian concerns, whose novels are characterized by "sheer mastery of language, eccentricity of characterization, precision and popularity," in spite of their joylessness or gloom. The discussion on Greene focusses on his view of human nature, the "primitive and predatory" nature of his world in The Heart of the Matter, which, in spite of its "sordid, unlikely, overly-contrived dilemma" affords "a possibility of renewal--not escape ... which gives Greene a moral and psychological vitality" not attained by the other two.

A639 Kunkel, Francis L[eo]. "The Priest as Scapegoat in the Modern Catholic Novel." Ramparts, I:4 (Jan.), pp. 72-78. Examines the "recurrence of the archetype" of the priest as a Christ-like figure in a novel by each of Greene, Mauriac, Stolpe and M. West. Shows in his discussion of The Power and the Glory that the events preceding the execution of the priest "intentionally" imitate the actions that led up to the crucifixion.

A6310 Lejeune, Anthony. "Graham Greene as a Thriller Writer." B & B, (Aug.), pp. 25 & 33. The assessment, occasioned by the Penguin Paperback edition of Stamboul Train, A Gun for Sale, The Confidential Agent and The Ministry of Fear, also notes their "unique, bitter flavour" which lingers as an after-taste in the mind, and discusses the "new dimension" which they have given to the writing of thrillers.

A6311 Leland, Charles W., CSB. "The Whiskey-Priest--Lamb of God?" BasT, VIII, pp. 52-58. An examination of the "theological substructure" of the novel--the "dimensions of sin and the mysterious workings of grace"--to explain for the undergraduate the "true martyrdom" of the Whiskey Priest. Shows that the priest is an "alter Christus" living in this world and following the "sacrificial ideal of the Master."

A6312 Lerner, Lawrence. "Graham Greene." CritQ, V (Autumn), pp. 217-31. A searching, critical article contending that Greene is "not merely a skilful craftsman" but a humanist whose vision of the world as a "place of intrinsic evil" is essentially religious but "without religious joy." Following this view of the world, he divides Greene's characters into four categories: the pious, the sinners, the innocent and the humanists, and discusses each category. Also draws attention to Greene's fondness for irony and cautions critics not to "reconstruct his biographical self from his literary self."

A6313 McCaffrey, Bertrand, OP. "Graham Greene: A Catholic Writer?" Dominicana, XLVIII, pp. 120-27. Discusses, from an unpartisan but Catholic viewpoint, four weighty objections, perhaps obvious, to Greene's writings: the implication that he is not a good Catholic, rejection of theological views embodied in his works, excessive use of sex, and lastly, being too Catholic for the non-Catholic and too non-Catholic for the Catholic. The Power and the Glory, The Heart of the Matter, The End of the Affair and A Burnt-Out Case.

A6314 McDonnell, Laurence V., CSP. "The Priest-Hero in the Modern Novel." CW, CXCVI:1175 (Feb.), pp. 306-11. Contends that the portrayal of the Priest-Hero in a novel by each of Bernanos, Greene, Mauriac, E. O'Connor and M. West indicates a "limited" concept of the sacerdotal function of the priest by concentrating on his human foibles or inadequacies and minimizing the supernatural function of the priest's vocation. A brief analysis of The Power and the Glory purports as much, even while admitting that the Whiskey Priest in "his weakness and his heroism ... bears witness to the power and the glory of God."

A6315 Markovic, Vida E. "Graham Greene in Search of God." TSLL, V (Summer), 271-82. Maintains, in his discussion of the novels, that "Greene, the artist, is hampered by God," that his "work and his personality represent the situation of the man of Western civilization caught in the nets of his own culture and unable to extricate himself from them." Full of sweeping assertions: e.g., Greene's "acceptance of the Roman Catholic faith implied a turning away from the burning social and political problems"; or, Pinkie is "on the side of the Catholic God. On the opposite side is ... Ida." No mention of The End of the Affair. Maintains that Greene shows his characters searching for meaning in a hopeless world but they are only saved through religious faith. Brighton Rock, The Power and the Glory, The Heart of the Matter and A Burnt-Out Case.

A6316 Monteiro-Grillo, J. "Tradicao e crise no romance ingles contemporaneo." Broteria, LXVII, 144-64. Considers the novel, in this survey of English writers from D. H. Lawrence to Colin Wilson, as a useful means of revealing man and the society he lives in, and not just as mere entertainment. Brief assessment of Greene on pp. 160-62.

A6317 Schumann, Hildegard. "Zum Problem des Anti-Helden in Graham Greenes neueren Romanem." WZUR, XII, pp. 71-77. A marxist approach to the concept of the anti-hero in Greene's more recent novels. Focusses on The Quiet American and Our Man in Havana to show that the novels of the fifties mark a profound and ideological transformation from the individual problems and conflicts of earlier novels to social realism and current political problems. Sets the humanistic contents of the two novels against the political and social background of post-war England.

A6318 Sheed, Wilfrid. "Enemies of Catholic Promise." Commonweal, LXXVII (22 Feb.), pp. 560-63. A discussion, from a Catholic viewpoint, of the "unresolved moral problem" of Catholic novelists. Pays tribute to Greene in The Power and the Glory for the "perfection of compromise achieved" between "telling his story right" and "giving the right impression about Catholic doctrine."

A6319 Skonieczny, P., OFM. "The Dimensions of Evil in Graham Greene." DSPACR, XXVII, pp. 145-71. An intelligible account, from a philosopher-theologian's viewpoint, attempting to shed light on Greene by explaining his work in terms of evil. Discusses the notion of evil in the light of Greene's personal life and autobiographical writings, the presentation of evil, especially in "The Hint of an Explanation," Brighton Rock and A Gun for Sale, and the exposition of existential themes which reveal modern man to himself, because Greene, a realist with "thoroughly pessimistic tendencies," is not a Manichean: even while believing evil is "rationally absurd," he also emphasizes, unlike contemporary existentialism, God's part in the universe.

A6320 Voorhees, Richard J. "Recent Greene." SAQ, LXII (Spring), 244-55. Contrasts Greene's development from The Quiet American to A Burnt-Out Case with his earlier "obsessions" with good and evil, innocence and experience, and, on the whole, his seriousness. Shows a change in his point of view manifested by a growing concern with innocence in The Quiet American, by an ability to make jokes, even treat original sin in a "new and bizarre way" in Loser Takes All, by his burlesque of both Catholicism and melodrama and parody of spy stories in Our Man in Havana and in his aversion to success, power and greatness in A Burnt-Out Case. Maintains that his "recent work is even more compelling [than his earlier work] because of the dilemma by which it is plagued: innocence is dynamite, and experience is atom bomb."

A6321 Wichert, Robert A. "The Quality of Graham Greene's Mercy." CE, XXV (Nov.), pp. 99-103. In both Scobie and the Whiskey Priest, Greene, like Péguy, presents a personal morality that seems to challenge God "in the cause of the damned," for though Scobie and the Whiskey Priest die in the presence of "monstrous, heinous sin," they "make it impossible for us to damn them. And, if we can't ... can God?" (See also A4818).

A6322 Wilson, Angus. "Evil in the English Novel: Evil and the Novelist Today." Listener, LXIX:1764 (17 Jan.), pp. 115-17. The last of a series of four talks on the BBC Third Programme. Rpt., with minor revisions, as one article. (KR, XXIX:2 (March 1967), 167-94). Contends that the central tradition of English writing did not have "any clear theological pattern" in which to embody the sense of evil, and that a "continental sense of good and evil transcendent" is imperative if the traditional novel is to break its "provincial, encaging shape." Criticizes Greene, "so exotic (and) un-English" a novelist for "over-schematization" in Brighton Rock which, even while embodying the "transcendent view that accounts for his apprehension of evil," also has the quality of "felt life" in keeping with the tradition of the English novel.

A6323 Unsigned. "Novelist Whitewashes Castro Regime." Editorial. ChrC, LXXX (27 Nov.), pp. 1457-58. Accuses Greene of not knowing the meaning of religious freedom because of his broadcast announcing that there is no evidence of religious persecution in Cuba under the Castro regime.

R631 Allsop, Kenneth. "Greene: The Religious Questioner Who Turns to Fantasy." DaiM, (20 June), p. 10. A brief review of A Sense of Reality remarking on Greene's "unexpected departure into undisguised fantasy," and which describes his prose as an "intense meticulous plaiting of reality and imaginative discovery."

R632 Alter, Robert. "Graham Greene." NYHT, (23 June), p. 5. Regards A Sense of Reality as an "artistic grouping" that reflects Greene's "real mastery" of the art of the short story. Examines each of the four pieces separately and shows that technical accomplishment and literary craftsmanship are common factors in all four.

R633 Barrett, William. "Reader's Choice: A Sense of Reality." Atlantic, CCXII (July), pp. 128-29. Maintains that the stories are only of "middling success," and though they add the new "dimensions of fantasy and myth" to Greene's works, they elaborate the "moral and intellectual themes that haunt" his mind.

R634 Bemis, R. "Books in Brief: A Sense of Reality." NR, XV (24 Sept.), p. 249. Maintains, in this short review, that the stories describe man's "compulsive affair with illusion" and expose the "raw edges of reality in varieties of mental and spiritual isolation," and that Greene carries his theme to a "further border of despair" as he defeats his characters with "irksome assiduousness."

R635 Bradbury, Malcolm. "New Novels." Punch, CCXLIV (26 June), pp. 937-38. A Sense of Reality is the first of four works reviewed. Notes the slight revival of romance--three of the four stories are so classified--and the interest aroused by these "not particularly successful stories." Maintains that Greene does not quite shape the "plentiful Freudian and religious symbolism" of "Under the Garden" because of the "crudity in characterisation and conversation of the man who is intended to be a significant mouthpiece."

R636 Brooke, Jocelyn. "New Fiction." Listener, LXIX (20 June), p. 1049. A Sense of Reality is the first of five books reviewed. Considers the volume "one of the best things" Greene has ever done, especially "Under the Garden" which is regarded as a "small masterpiece."

R637 Copeland, Edith. "In Search of Reality." BA, XXXVII:4 (Autumn), p. 452. A short review that describes briefly each short story separately.

R638 Corke, Hilary. "A Strong Smell of Fish." NRep, CXLIX (31 Aug.), pp. 31-33. A rather lengthy review of A Sense of Reality that examines each of the short stories separately and describes Greene's curious mind as "lavatorial" and "grossly paradoxical."

R639 Fulford, R. "On Graham Greene: Slippers, Pipe and Raw Terror." Maclean's, LXXVII (7 Sept.), pp. 69-70. Remarks on the change from the realistic settings of earlier works to the "several worlds which are (apparently) imaginary," notices the point made by the title and condemns the book as "rather second class" whose style and precision of detail cannot make up for the "incomprehensible private symbolism with which it abounds." Also comments on the affinity between Greene and Buchan in their selection of "adventure in familiar surroundings happening to unadventurous men" when the Penguin paperbacks of The Ministry of Fear, The Confidential Agent, A Gun for Sale and Stamboul Train are introduced.

R6310 Furbank, P. N. "New Novels?" Encounter, XXI (Oct.), pp. 82-83. A Sense of Reality is the first of six volumes reviewed. Questions whether they have much of the "new" in them. Focusses on "Under the Garden" and its "19th century flavour," especially the kind of relationship it presupposes between the imaginary and the real.

R6311 Greacen, Robert. "Short Stories." DaiT, (19 July), p. 19. A short review of A Sense of Reality that gives credit to Greene for attempting something new and for exploring the "shadowy territory of dream, fantasy and myth," but finds that the collection, though interesting and readable, does not add anything to the "topography of Greeneland."

R6312 Gregor, Ian. "A Sense of Reality." Blackfriars, XLIV:520 (Oct.), pp. 439-41. Maintains that in spite of the "self-contained air" of the four stories, the volume remains as a "by-product of his activities as a novelist." Critical of "Under the Garden," especially its "coy whimsicality ...

which, in the end, blunts the sense of reality of the world above and below the garden," and full of praise for "A Discovery in the Woods" for its irony and imagination.

R6313 Griffin, Lloyd W. "A Sense of Reality." LJ, LXXXVIII (1 June), pp. 2274-75. A short review that "mildly" recommends the volume for its rather "pale Greene" because it leaves one dissatisfied even though it approaches reality "through the dark side of dream, fantasy, and legend."

R6314 Grosvenor, Peter. "Graham Greene Tries a Weird New Tack." DaiE, (20 June), p. 14. Maintains that the title A Sense of Reality "belies" the contents of this volume which stems from a truly feverish imagination. Singles out "A Visit to Morin" as the "most interesting" story.

R6315 Grumbach, Doris. "A Sense of Reality." Critic, XXII (Aug.-Sept.), p. 84. Briefly notices the volume as "unimpressive" because not one of the stories is "convincing."

R6316 Herr, Dan. "Greene Breaks Even." CST, (7 July), p. 5. A review of A Sense of Reality that finds in "Under the Garden" and "A Discovery in the Woods" a "new and not particularly successful approach to Greene," but admits that all four stories have vivid dialogue, sharp characterization and are "characteristically readable and superbly written."

R6317 Hicks, Granville. "Strangers in Paradox." SatR, XLVI (22 June), pp. 35-36. This review of A Sense of Reality notes the irony in the title and Greene's love of paradox. Discusses each of the stories separately.

R6318 Hindus, Milton. "Graham Greene Reports from Underground." NYTBR, (14 July), pp. 4, 20. A review of A Sense of Reality which claims that Greene is not "at home in a world of fantasy" nor can he plumb the psychological, intellectual and emotional depths of Kafka's or Tolstoy's parables.

R6319 Igoe, W. J. "A Sense of Reality." Month, NS XXX:3 (Sept.), pp. 180-82. Greene's works "become more and more like an anatomy of belief and disbelief" depicting all the stresses which faith is heir to as one can see from "A Visit to Morin." On the other hand, "Under the Garden" "represents a new departure," and is primarily the story of a man's search for the lost world of his childhood.

R6320 Lodge, David. "The Liberty of Fantasy: Graham Greene's New Departure." Tablet, CCXVII (22 June), pp. 679-80. A Sense of Reality is not one of Greene's best books but it represents "a new departure." Examines "Under the Garden" in some detail emphasizing the "religious meaning" at the "deepest level of the fable." Finds in Morin a "composite caricature" of Mauriac and Greene himself but cannot "see the point" in "Dream of a Strange Land."

R6321 MacInnes, Colin. "Involved and Aloof: A Sense of Reality, by Graham Greene." Spectator, CCX:7043 (21 June), p. 812. Argues that Greene's involvement lies in his presentation of the "fatality hanging over man"--struggle between good and evil, life and death--but his aloofness is further emphasized by his little sense of human beings and the absence of any "hope" for redemption.

R6322 Mayne, Richard. "Where God Makes the Scenery." NSta, LXVI (2 Aug.), p. 144. An unfavorable review of A Sense of Reality suggesting "some doubts" on his general assessment that the novels and entertainments provide "escape" and "actuality," and critical of Greene's "mannerisms," and the "too mechanical presentation of paradox" in spite of his best known verbal habit of the "evocative catalogue." Maintains that Greene's vision is "too facile to be tragic" for where was, or is, "the hope to merit all that disillusion."

R6323 Noyes, Henry Drury. "A Sense of Reality." CW, CXCVIII (Nov.), pp. 126, 128. Finds the range of the volume great and the stories in direct contrast to his earlier work but still retaining the "distorted perspective in belief, sex and the meaning of a seemingly fantastic world." Also finds the "autobiographical implications" of "A Visit to Morin" "delightfully malin."

R6324 O'Brien, E. D. "A Literary Hunger: A Sense of Reality." ILN, (13 July), p. 70. Brief reference to the "parable" element in three "short-long stories" which the critic would not be bothered to discover.

R6325 Prescott, Orville. "Books of the Times." NYT, CXII (21 June), p. 27. Recommends A Sense of Reality to Greene's admirers only. Finds "Under the Garden" perplexing and mysterious, and "A Visit to Morin" cryptic.

R6326 Quinn, John J. "A Sense of Reality." Best Sellers, XXIII (15 July), p. 141. Regards the collection as representative of Greene's "pristine perfection," of his penetrating insight "chiselled in paradox and unforgettably capsulized in neat simile."

R6327 Quinton, Anthony. "Greene the Fantasist." SunTel, (23 June), p. 17. Examines each story in A Sense of Reality separately and admits that though the skill is there, the "sense of reality" claimed by the title is "peculiar" and far removed from the "marvellous perceptiveness about the common world" which his novels give.

R6328 Shrapnel, Norman. "New Maps of Greeneland." Guardian, (21 June), p. 6. The review of A Sense of Reality remarks on the paradox of Greene: his "urge for abstracting himself from actuality and his unequalled gift for presenting it," so that in this collection of myth, dream and hallucination, the "sense of actuality is sharper than normal." Questions why Greene is such a compelling novelist in spite of his belief that man, by himself, cannot come to any good.

R6329 Stratford, Philip. "What Seems Is." KR, XXV:4 (Autumn), pp. 757-60. A searching review of A Sense of Reality that discusses each of the four stories separately, and emphasizes Greene's revolt against surface realism and exploration of the realm of pure fantasy in "A Discovery in the Woods" and "Under the Garden."

R6330 Wain, John. "Graham Greene Takes a Liberty." Observer, (23 June), p. 25. Maintains that Greene's new departure in A Sense of Reality into the "realness" of myth and fantasy does not fare very well. "Under the Garden" gives the impression of a "fantasy uneasily blended with naturalism," and of the other three, only "A Discovery in the Woods" combines "economy and impact."

R6331 Waterman, Jack. "Fantasy from Mr. Greene." EvS, (25 June), p. 10. A short review of A Sense of Reality focussing on "Under the Garden" and expressing disappointment at the "mental mystery tour of which the chart unfortunately remains with the author."

R6332 Wilkie, Brian. "Stories by Greene." Commonweal, LXXVIII (12 July), pp. 432, 434. Points out that the way in which Greene uses myth in A Sense of Reality is original: the myth itself in "Under the Garden" is Greene's "invention, not just its application." Questions whether "A Visit to Morin" is self-parody.

R6333 Zinnes, Harriet. "21 Stories." BA, XXXVII (Spring), p. 206. Notes the republication of older stories which are "a little dreary" to reread, even though the short story encourages Greene's "facile wit or irony, ... the neat paradox and the slick if unusual presentation of man's morbidity."

R6334 Unsigned. "Back to the Source." Newsweek, LXII (24 June), p. 119. A review of A Sense of Reality that singles out "Under the Garden" as a tale of "sheer artistry," a fantasy that packs "more quick, vibrant reality ... than may be found in a score of realistic novels."

R6335 ________. "Our Man in London." Newsweek, LXII (15 July), p. 50. A review of the opera at Sadler's Wells based on Our Man in Havana.

R6336 ________. "A Sense of Reality." NY, XXXIX (10 Aug.), p. 89. Briefly noticed.

R6337 ________. "The Paper Chase." Time, (28 June), p. 67. A review of A Sense of Reality that maintains that Greene's religious writings draw the readers inevitably into speculation about his own "apparently tormented belief." Focusses on "A Visit to Morin" as a fascinating story that seems to carry Greene "a razor's edge closer to despair than A Burnt-Out Case."

R6338 ________. "New Fiction." Times, (20 June). p. 15. A Sense of Reality is the first of five works briefly reviewed. The work "enlarges" Greene's reputation as a creative artist who can use myth, legend and dream effectively.

R6339 ________. "Old Magic." TLS, 3199 (21 June), p. 457. Finds the title, A Sense of Reality, enigmatical for each of the four stories--considered separately in the review--and either "mysterious" or "other-worldly." Wonders whether this "interesting, incomprehensible and probably haunting book" is a writer's "self indulgence in dreams or something thrown off from work in progress."

R6340 ________. "A Sense of Reality." VQR, XXXIX:4 (Autumn), pp. cxxi, cxxiv. A short review pointing out the variety of novelistic talents displayed in the work. Finds "Under the Garden" most "engaging."

D631 Boardman, Gwenn Rosina. Graham Greene: The Aesthetics of Exploration. The Claremont Graduate School. D.A., XXIV:6, 2474. Rev. and published. Gainesville: Univ. of Florida Press, 1971. See B712.

D632 Koithara, James Aggaeus. The Pattern of Border Struggle in Graham Greene. Univ. of Montreal.

D633 Suarez, Ralph P. The Application of Catholic Criteria to the Works of Graham Greene. M.A. C. W. Post College.

1964

B641 Allen, Walter. Tradition and Dream: The English and American Novel from the Twenties to Our Time. London: Phoenix House. Published in the U.S. as The Modern Novel in Britain and the United States. New York: E. P. Dutton. Section 3 of "The Thirties: British," pp. 202-07, is a succinct and masterly account of Greene's achievement as a novelist, within the framework of the development of English and American fiction. Notices the influences of the thirties on Greene's works, his rapport with the temper of the times, the dominant themes of the novels and his jansenistic outlook. Examines Brighton Rock as the "archetypal Greene novel, " and disapproves of The End of the Affair as a novel "overlaid by parable" in contrast to The Power and the Glory which rises "triumphantly clear of the parable. "

B642 Browne, E. Martin. "The Christian Presence in the Theatre. " The Climate of Faith in Modern Literature. Ed. Nathan A. Scott, Jr. New York: The Seabury Press, pp. 128-41. Brief reference on p. 140 to The Living Room, The Potting Shed and The Complaisant Lover as plays that have contributed to "the Christian presence" in the theatre by displaying human lives in which "the fact of Christianity and the author's belief in it" are crucial and determining factors.

B643 De Vitis, A. A. Graham Greene. Twayne's English Authors Series. New York: Twayne Publishers, Inc. Argues that since the religious idea informs Greene's major works, an analysis of his use of religious subject matter and belief rather than a definition of them will be of more value in evaluating his success or failure "in having used artistically and imaginatively the properties of Roman Catholicism. " The analysis of plots, characters and situations, especially of the major novels beginning with Brighton Rock, reveals that Greene's Catholicism is not "one stance, but a variety of stances, " sometimes incompatible with doctrinarian interpretations.

The book is in eight chapters. Ch. 1 discusses the social and economic milieu of the thirties and forties to show Greene's contemporaneity and to establish his position within the mainstream of English fiction. Ch. 2 is a revised version of the first part of "The Catholic as Novelist" (see B639), and establishes Greene's concern with good and evil as a novelist and not as a theologian or philosopher. Ch. 3 is a revised version of "The Entertaining Mr. Greene" (see A612), which discusses Greene's notion of the nature of the thriller and makes a quick examination of each entertainment separately, from Stamboul Train to Our Man in Havana. Ch. 4 examines the early novels, It's a Battlefield and England Made Me, "brilliantly planned and executed, " but nevertheless, tentative efforts that look forward to the more provocative and serious novels. Ch. 5, the longest in the book, discusses Brighton Rock, The Power and the Glory, The Heart of the Matter, The End of the Affair, The Quiet American, and A Burnt-Out Case separately to show that the religious note animates the narrative. Views on the first three novels are basically those expressed in A577, A555, and A585. Ch. 6 examines The Living Room, The Potting Shed, and The Complaisant Lover separately and finds that they add to the theatre a "dimension which might be termed religio-philosophical dilemma." Ch. 7 is a revised version of the second part of "The Catholic as Novelist" (see B639), and emphasizes Mauriac's influence on Greene. Ch. 8 reviews literary opinions and interpretations of Greene's religious outlook. The book is well documented. The "Selected Bibliography" includes a chronological listing of Greene's works with the data of original publication, and a list of seventy four critical works, briefly annotated.

B644 Fraser, George Sutherland. "The 'Serious' 1930s." The Modern Writer and His World. London: D. Verschoyle, 1953. Rev. ed. London: A.Deutsch; New York: F. Praeger, pp. 131-47. Pages 133-38 discuss Greene as the "great master of symbolic melodrama" in an examination of the main innovating figures in the novel. Surveys briefly the novels up to A Burnt-Out Case and focusses on England Made Me as an "underrated" novel of the thirties which displays "Greene's powers and his typical thematic pattern." Also describes Greene's "workmanlike" qualities as a novelist.

B645 Grenzmann, Wilhelm. "Graham Greene." Weldichtung der Gegenwart: Probleme und Gestalten. Frankfurt & Bonn: Athenaum Verlag, pp. 359-80. An analysis of The Power and the Glory, The Heart of the Matter, The End of the Affair, and The Living Room. Maintains that a certain Protestantism characterizes Greene's works because of his focus on two purely "Protestant" elements: the hidden God, and the radical question of conscience. Also includes on pp. 464-65 a brief bibliographical note on Greene's works and lists German translations of the works up to 1952.

B646 Jarrett-Kerr, Martin. "The 491 Pitfalls of the Christian Artist." The Climate of Faith in Modern Literature. Ed. Nathan A. Scott, Jr. New York: Seabury Press, pp. 177-207. Perceives Greene, on pp. 191-97, as a "test case in England of the dangers facing the Christian artist." This cursory review of The Living Room, The Potting Shed and The Complaisant Lover underrates Greene's ability to create character whereas the review of A Burnt-Out Case attempts to document the erroneous conclusion that it is impossible for Greene "to escape from the playpen he has built round himself" in his earlier novels.

B647 Joselyn, Sister M., OSB. "Graham Greene's Novels: The Conscience in the World." Literature and Society: A Selection of Papers Delivered at the Joint Meeting of the Midwest Modern Language Association and the Central Renaissance Conference, 1963. Ed. Bernice Slote. Lincoln: Univ. of Nebraska Press, pp. 153-72. Maintains that Greene gives "the solidity of specification" to his moral vision of the world--a "distinct mutation of the general English moralist"--in Brighton Rock, The Power and the Glory and The Heart of the Matter by creating several "compelling metaphors" of the world as prison, as desert and as battlefield, and, in his realistic manner, creating a roster of prevailing moral types: "saints" or "anti-heroes" like the Whiskey Priest, the "righteous" like Ida, "pseudo-saints" like Scobie and the "damned" like Pinkie.

B648 Martin, Graham. "Novelists of Three Decades: Evelyn Waugh, Graham Greene, C. P. Snow." The Pelican Guide to English Literature. Vol. VII. The Modern Age. London: Cassell, 1961-64; Harmondsworth: Penguin Books, 1972, pp. 394-414. Pages 401-09 discuss why Greene is a "minor" novelist who is "highly topical" and also "popular without being any the less serious." Examines Greene's "pervasive" and "deep-seated" topicality and relates it to his serious themes, but finds it difficult to identify Greene's "social consciousness" owing to the exclusion of any explicit comment in his earlier novels and to the insistence on theology in later ones. Questions how far "the official interpretation" evades or confuses the meaning of the situation in The Heart of the Matter.

B649 Moré, Marcel. "The Two Holocausts of Scobie." Cross Currents of Psychiatry and Catholic Morality. Ed. William Birmingham and Joseph E. Cunneen. Pref. Francis J. Braceland. New York: Pantheon Books, pp. 274-99. See A5020.

B6410 Reed, John R. Old School Ties: The Public Schools in British Literature. Syracuse, N.Y.: Syracuse Univ. Press, pp. 161-93 passim. Includes, in the examination of the novelists' utilization of experiences acquired in the Public School system, Greene's criticism of the system and its products in Brighton Rock, England Made Me, It's a Battlefield, The Heart of the Matter, The End of the Affair, and Our Man in Havana.

B6411 Scott, Nathan, ed. The Climate of Faith in Modern Literature. New York: Seabury Press. Includes two articles by E. Martin Browne and Martin Jarrett-Kerr. See B642 and B646.

B6412 Stratford, Philip. Faith and Fiction: Creative Process in Greene and Mauriac. Notre Dame, Indiana: Univ. of Notre Dame Press. A full-length comparison of the two writers which defines the common traits they share but which also isolates the distinguishing characteristics of each novelist in order to display what is "mutually illuminating" in their theory and practice of the art of the novel. Discusses the "complex interplay" of faith and fiction which provides the tension that gives "singularity and distinction" to their novels. Ch. 1 introduces the comparative method to be used and outlines the main themes to be treated by using Le Baiser au lepreux (A Kiss for the Leper) and A Burnt-Out Case as paradigm novels. Chs. 2-6 survey the works and progress of the two writers chronologically from childhood and adolescence to artistic maturity showing the parallel course the careers of the two writers have taken. (Chs. 4 & 5 are exclusively devoted to Greene). Chs. 7 & 8 discuss the influence of Catholicism on the novelist in "conditioning" his imagination as well as in providing him with themes and material, and by avoiding argument with other critics, tests the novelists' statements on their art against their accomplishment. Ch. 9 investigates the novelists' experiments with drama and Ch. 10 discusses the novelists' views on commitment.

A641 Anisimov, I. "Romany Grekhema Grina." IL, 10 (Oct.), pp. 221-26. In Russian. "The Novels of Graham Greene." Surveys the works briefly and distinguishes three genres: entertainments, novels and travel books. Maintains that though Greene did not take sides in ideological struggles, he was deeply concerned with social and moral problems prior to his interest in the spiritual crises of individuals, as can be evinced from his treatment of the criminality of capitalist society in It's a Battlefield. Regards A Burnt-Out Case as his most profound and mature novel.

A642 Callaghan, Morley. "An Ocean Away." TLS, 3249 (4 June), p. 493. Brief reference to "the dank and dismal Catholicism" in Greene's novels which he finds "interesting." Regards the "hopeless spiritual trap" and the awareness of evil in Greene as the "old English puritanism being fanned into flame again."

A643 Dechet, Ferruccio. "Suggestioni e limiti della tematica de Graham Greene." GdiM, XIX, pp. 75-89. As a convert to Catholicism who has left a profound impression by his existentialist views, Greene is aware of the need to turn "alle fonte dell-essere, all-albro della vita," but has not reached his proposed goal because every "problematica della crisi rinchiusa in uno sterile narcisismo." Describes the encounter of "il grandi tema dell'esistenza" with evil, suffering, and weakness--all of which Greene has made central to Christianity--as characteristic of "la Weltaschauung greeniana." The Power and the Glory, The Heart of the Matter and The Living Room.

A644 Engelborghs, Maurits. "Graham Greene op de terugweg?" DWB, CIX, pp. 55-63. A rev. art. on A Sense of Reality, the republication of The Power and the Glory in the Modern Novel Series and David Pryce-Jones' monograph Graham Greene. (Writers and Critics Series). Edinburgh and London: Oliver and Boyd, 1963. Appreciative of "Under the Garden" but questions whether Greene, perhaps the most widely discussed novelist alive, is losing his talent.

A645 ________. "De opvatting van roman en romanschrifter bij Graham Greene." DWB, CIX, pp. 172-98. A lengthy essay on Greene's views on the novel and novel writing based on Why Do I Write, The Lost Childhood and Other Essays, excerpts from novels and interviews, and reviews.

A646 Fielding, Gabriel. "Graham Greene: The Religious Englishman." Listener, LXXII:1852 (24 Sept.), pp. 465-66. Also in JSH, LXXII (24 Sept.), pp. 185-87. An assessment of Greene's work by probing the state of his moral as well as his literary conscience. Comments on Greene's "evasiveness" and the "misprised sexuality" of, and the recurrent symbols of policeman and priest in, his novels. Considers the inability "to take the long view, to transcend the absurd" to be Greene's "greatest failing" as a novelist.

A647 Grenzmann, Wilhelm. "Das Leiden der Literatur--das Leiden an der Literatur." Begegnung, XIX (July-Aug.), pp. 5-10. Includes brief reference to The Power and the Glory and The End of the Affair as novels which portray essentially, a way of life on the brink of human possibilities. The article explores the theme of suffering in literature.

A648 Hortmann, Wilhelm. "Graham Greene: The Burnt-Out Catholic." TCL, X, pp. 64-76. Stimulating but controversial. Argues that in the "Catholic Trilogy," Brighton Rock, The Power and the Glory and The Heart of the Matter, Greene's doctrine of damnation and the Church's view of Divine Mercy bring him dangerously close to heresy and possible excommunication; but The End of the Affair marks his "capitulation as a Catholic novelist" and he is forced into the role of the "Catholic apologist" who turns from his being an "advocate of human weakness into an advocate of the Church," especially on marriage, which he takes up in The Living Room. Points out that after The End of the Affair Greene becomes an "author of topical semi-documentary novels" that reflect his travels to political trouble spots.

A649 Jacobsen, Josephine. "A Catholic Quartet." ChrS, XLVII (Summer), pp. 139-54. Discusses the "diverse" angles or approaches of M. Spark, G. Greene, J. W. Powers and F. O'Connor to their material after pointing out the qualities they share: they are witty, not passive or "parochial"; they decry the artificial gulf between the worldly and the supernatural; they abhor the mincings of religiosity; they are at no time far from violence. Pages 143-46 consider Greene's characteristics: his pessimism and his "addiction to paradox," and the three states which "haunt" him: innocence, failure and pity. References to "The Innocent," Brighton Rock, The Heart of the Matter and The Quiet American.

A6410 Lerner, Laurence. "Love and Gossip: Or, How Moral Is Literature?" EIC, XIV:2 (April), pp. 126-47. The discussion of this controversial issue involves three speakers, "A," "B" and "C," and moves from Ben Jonson and Shakespeare to Greene's The Quiet American and other works. Pages 135-38 show "B" and "C" taking opposed views: "B" maintaining that Greene comes down in favor of Fowler as he expounds the anti-American sentiment of the novel and its moral, "Beware of the Innocent," and "C" arguing that Greene has thrown enough doubt on Fowler's motives for having Pyle killed, and consequently, on his political wisdom. Greene's objectivity is also discussed.

A6411 Maclaren-Ross, J. "Excursions in Greene Land." LM, IV (Dec.), pp. 56-65. Rpt. in Memoirs of the Forties. London: Alan Ross, 1965, pp. 13-28. An account of an interview with Greene held in 1938. Presents a rare picture of Greene's family life, though one questions the accuracy of the statement that Mr. and Mrs. Greene are "cousins."

A6412 Maxwell, J. C. "'The Dry Salvages': A Possible Echo of Graham Greene." N&Q, XI (Oct.), p. 387. Notes a "fairly close resemblance" between T. S. Eliot's statement in Section V--the "music heard so deeply"--and what Andrew says in Ch. 4 of The Man Within.

A6413 Nemec, Jiri. "Svedecka Sluzba Umeni: K duchovnimy pozadi romanoveho dila Grahama Greena." KresR, 6, pp. 155-62. Unavailable for examination.

A6414 Nolan, Jack Edmond. "Graham Greene's Movies." FiR, XV (Jan.), pp. 23-35. Rpt. in LFQ, II:4 (Fall 1974), pp. 302-09. A chronological account of Greene's involvement with the cinema as film critic and script writer, as well as the adaptation of his many works for the cinema and T.V. Describes Greene's "Weltanschauung" as a "distillation of despair."

A6415 Pitts, Arthur W., Jr. "Greene's 'The Basement Room.'" Expl, XXIII (Oct.), item 17. Rejects Silveira's interpretation (see A5614), and argues that the story portrays "the destruction of a personality, not the damnation of a soul."

A6416 Poole, Roger C. "Graham Greene's Indirection." Blackfriars, XLV:528 (June), pp. 257-68. Rpt. in Graham

Greene. Ed. Harry J. Cargas. St. Louis, Mo.: B. Herder Book, 1969, pp. 29-45. Attempts an explanation of Kierkegaard's "Indirect Communication"--"'to step out in character,' or to reduplicate something believed"--through a study of passages in The Power and the Glory, The Heart of the Matter and The End of the Affair.

A6417 Quinn, Edward. "Argernis an Graham Greene. Die Katholiken und seine 'angewandte Theologie.'" WW, XIX, pp. 611-15. Discusses two problems which readers find irritating in Greene's works: his portrayal of Catholics and his "theology" and its application or manifestation. Shows that the implications of Greene's theology are closely related to the "new theology" of which K. Rahner is the leading exponent, and that Greene's distinction between faith and belief, confusing and incomprehensible at times, is "not altogether wrong" as some pastoral experience and an understanding of the principles of Catholic theology will indicate.

A6418 Rillie, John A. M. "The Sweet Smell of Failure." TCLon, CLXXII (Spring), pp. 85-99. On "the changing status of success" as reflected in selected writers from J. Austen to J. Braine. Pages 89-90 mention Greene and his "fugitives" to whom failure is the "only worthwhile kind of success." Brief reference to A Burnt-Out Case.

A6419 Ruotolo, Lucio P. "Brighton Rock's Absurd Heroine." MLQ, XXV (Dec.), pp. 425-33. Argues that Greene affirms through Rose the central tenet of existentialism that "man is his future." Approaches Rose through the "distorted, triangular relationship" of Pinkie, Ida and Hale who reflect the experience of an age without faith. Shows how Rose's concern for loving is the basis of her willingness to suffer damnation with Pinkie, and that "her life extends absurdly beyond the limitation" of her knowledge that "existence is a sickness unto death and that, moreover, Hell is other people."

A6420 Simon, John K. "Off the Voie Royale: The Failure of Greene's A Burnt-Out Case." Symposium, XVIII, pp. 163-70. Attributes the failure of the novel not so much to Greene's inattention to the "consistent presence of the dark landscape" which, in this case, is used in "suggestive contrast" to the fame which Querry has escaped, as for the absence of an "undiminished" mystery about the hero--the mystery about Querry continues into the middle of the book only--and the absence of a "consistently equivocal point of view precluding any deep and lasting sense of mystery" for Querry.

A6421 Stratford, Philip. "Chalk and Cheese: A Comparative Study of A Kiss for the Leper and A Burnt-Out Case." UTQ,

XXXIII:2 (Jan.), pp. 200-18. An intelligently conceived study examining setting, atmosphere and character in each of the two novels to define the differences in style and tradition. Despite these differences, the underlying "significant" similarities are emphasized, especially the creative problems they confronted, the domination by a strong religious concern and their "compassionate identification with their characters," so that their solutions "often complement one another."

A6422 Wardle, Irving. "Graham Greene." P&P, XII:1 (Oct.), p. 7. A profile that concentrates on his contributions to the theatre. As a dramatist, Greene is no innovator; he sticks to the rules of West End naturalism and is a godsend to theatres who like to "combine an eminent author with a traditional poet."

R641 Bryden, Ronald. "Somebodaddy." NSta, LXVIII:1750 (25 Sept.), p. 462. Carving a Statue is a comedy built "on the largest blasphemy possible" where "every joke is a miniature blasphemy," and built around the theatrical prohibition against depicting God. Though its plot is "underdeveloped, its dialogue too symbol-laden for plausibility ... its best effects ... oblique and extra-dramatic," the play brings into the theatre "a wit and intelligence few playwrights would dare, and the immense generosity of a great moral writer."

R642 Dooley, D[avid] J. "Greeneland Explored." CF, XLIV (Aug.), pp. 115-16. Argues that A Sense of Reality explores familiar areas of Greene's universe and reveals his ridicule of "two kinds of complacency--complacent pharisaism and complacent unbelief." Examines each of the four stories separately and asserts that Greene's investigation of certain areas of human experience is from "an artist's, not an apologist's, point of view."

R643 Hobson, Harold. "On Zeffirelly and Greene." SunT, (20 Sept.), p. 31. A short review of Carving a Statue and its production. Focusses on Greene's vision of God but finds the play cold in spite of Sir Ralph Richardson's performance and the many symbols in it.

R644 Holland, Mary. "The Greene Image of God." Observer, (20 Sept.), p. 27. A review of Carving a Statue at the Haymarket. Critical of Greene's "heavy-handed parable of man's inhumanity to his fellows" and his maxims about God as he tries to stage some attitudes to God and man. Inadequate characterization and a creaking plot that lacks the Greene "master touch with telling a story" are characteristics of the play's confusion.

R645 Holmstrom, John. "Sans Everything." P&P, XII:2 (Nov.),

pp. 40-41. A review of Carving a Statue and the performance. Maintains that the play "shows no sign of a redeeming talent at all"; short as it is, it is "shamelessly padded" with weak jokes, aphorisms and gratuitous comic turns with practically nothing happening. Attributes Greene's failure to a "lack of material and a lack of passion."

R646 Hope-Wallace, Philip. "Carving a Statue." Guardian, (18 Sept.), p. 13. The play does not quite come off even though the big names connected with the performance may ensure "a run of some sort." It is a "laboured parable" that does not take wing; "the main character is still explaining himself to himself and to us within ten minutes of curtain fall."

R647 Rutherford, Malcolm. "God Only Knows." Spectator, 7108 (25 Sept.), p. 402. An unfavorable review most critical of Carving a Statue which he thinks is "shamefully passed off as a play." Finds it hard to believe how the play which can hardly be seen as "an isolated failure" of Greene, ever made it to Haymarket, even if one were to grant the pulling power of Greene and Sir Ralph Richardson.

R648 Trewin, J. C. "Places of Play: Carving a Statue." ILN, (3 Oct.), p. 520. A brief review of "an odd piece" at the Haymarket. "With its anxious analogies, its determined symbolism, the piece wanes ... into clamorous monotony, relieved ... by a scatter of shrewd lines, but never by eloquence," and remains for the most part "pretentious and steadily untheatrical."

R649 Wood, Frederick T. "A Sense of Reality." ES, XLV (June), pp. 262-63. Briefly noted for its stories that are "compact and concise," and which bear the marks of Greene's "unusual style" even though it is difficult to determine "the idea behind them."

R6410 Unsigned. "See-Saw of Pride and Contrition." Times, (18 Sept.), p. 15. A review of Carving a Statue and its performance at the Haymarket. Discovers the premise of the play to be an "extended simile between God and the artist"; but owing to the liberty Greene takes in changing sides, the issues and questions raised by the play become more foggy than illuminating.

D641 Barratt, Harold. Existentialism in Graham Greene's 'The Name of Action,' The 'Heart of the Matter' and 'A Burnt-Out Case': The Theme of Betrayal. M.A. Univ. of Windsor.

D642 Bowes, Sr. Saint Martin of Lima. Graham Greene: Religious Dramatist. M.A. Villanova Univ.

D643 Siferd, Nancy K. Graham Greene's Attitudes Toward Love and Marriage. M. A. Bowling Green State Univ.

D644 Wagner, Nora E. The Foundations of Graham Greene's Thought, with Particular Emphasis on the Concepts of Evil and Redemption as Presented in His Early Work. M. A. George Washington Univ.

S641 Unsigned. "Mr. Graham Greene to Re-word Play." Times, (10 Aug.), p. 6. Brief news item indicating Greene's agreement to alter "four or five words" that may have some "double entendre" in Carving a Statue, after his meeting with the Lord Chamberlain.

1965

B651 Chapman, Raymond. "The Vision of Graham Greene." Forms of Extremity in the Modern Novel. Ed. N. A. Scott, Jr. Richmond, Va.: John Knox Press, pp. 75-94. Approaches Greene, not as a Christian apologist but as a popular Christian writer who startles readers by "extremism," by depicting the inner struggle of individuals to reach perfection in an environment of instability and violence; hence, his anti-heroes characterized by loneliness, isolation and insecurity, depicted against the drab grubby background of a seedy world, and whose actions condemn the "technical" morality of the world, and to whom total "commitment to a Person," to the saving power of Grace is the only certainty in spite of their sin and failures. Notes an affinity between Greene's novels and morality plays.

B652 Goller, Karl Heinz. "Graham Greene: The Power and the Glory." Der moderne englische Roman: Interpretationem. Ed. Horst Oppel. Berlin: Erich Schmidt Verlag, pp. 245-61. An interpretation of the novel that recognizes its originality and uniqueness in the main tradition of the English novel for establishing a relationship with the protagonist rather than a confrontation with the world. Considers the novel as a paradigm of the "absolute loneliness and abandonment" of modern man.

B653 Hortmann, Wilhelm. "Katholische Romanciers: Waugh, Greene." Englische Literatur im 20. Jahrhundert. Bern: A. Francke AG Verlag, pp. 146-50. Surveys, in these pages from Ch. V, Greene's achievement as a novelist and his concern with Catholic themes and issues in Brighton Rock, The Power and the Glory and The Heart of the Matter, as well as The Living Room and The Potting Shed. Regards the Catholic trilogy as the epitome of Greene's novelistic technique wherein one can see his "subordination of material to the artistic conception."

B654 Maclaren-Ross, Julian. "Excursions in Greeneland." Memoirs of the Forties. London: Alan Ross Ltd., pp. 13-28. Rpt. from LM, IV (Dec. 1964), pp. 56-65. (See A6411).

B655 Markovic, Vida E. "Gream Grin." Engleski Roman. xx Veka. Vol. II. Beograd: Nancna Rnjiga, pp. 40-54, 230-32. (See A6315 & A658).

B656 Moeller, Charles. "Literature That Is Not for Everyone." Man and Salvation in Literature. Trans. Charles Underhill Quinn. Notre Dame and London: Univ. of Notre Dame Press, 1970, pp. 97-99. Originally published as L'Homme moderne devant le salut. Paris: Les Editions Ouvrières, 1965. Uses The Heart of the Matter as an example of Christian literature that is not for everyone but which is, nevertheless, "extremely important."

B657 Wells, Arvin R. "Graham Greene." Insight II: Analyses of Modern British Literature. Ed. John V. Hagopian and Martin Dolch. Frankfurt am Main: Hirschgraben-Verlag, pp. 152-69. Critical analyses of The Power and the Glory and "The Basement Room" followed by questions and suggested answers for junior undergraduate class discussion.

A651 Barratt, Harold. "Adultery as Betrayal in Graham Greene." DR, XLV (Autumn), pp. 324-32. Scobie, at heart "an existential situationalist" for whom truth is "functionalized and temporalized" with no transcendent norms, believed that love led inevitably to suffering, failure, pain and frustration owing to a decided lack of communication. He is ruined by adultery, is guilty of self-deception and self-betrayal, all of which leads ultimately to his suicide. An existentialist viewpoint on The Heart of the Matter.

A652 Blehl, Vincent Ferrer, SJ. "Literature and Religious Belief." CLS, II:4, pp. 303-14. Rpt. in Mansions of the Spirit: Essays in Literature and Religion. Ed. George A. Panichas. New York: Hawthorn Books, 1967, pp. 105-18. Discusses the relationship between the cognitive aspects of literature and religious belief and the problem arising from writers who consider Christian belief to possess "only imaginal, not objective, cognitive value." Considers briefly on pp. 308-09 Greene's use of religious symbolism and his use of the Christ figure in The Power and the Glory.

A653 Boardman, Gwenn Rosina. "Greene's 'Under the Garden': Aesthetic Explorations." Renascence, XVII:4 (Summer), 180-90, 194. Contends that the story is a "mythic rendition" of Greene's preoccupations with the mystery of Faith, the difficulties of belief, the "loss of 'mystique' from today's religious life," the loss of innocence and aesthetic discoveries. In this myth, Greene provides a new form of legend and figures: Wilditch comes close to expressing the problems of a writer, or even a believer, and Javitt and Maria dramatizing "both personal fantasy and moral consciousness."

A654 Decap, Roger. "La tradition puritaine dans la littérature anglaise: John Bunyan and Graham Greene." Caliban, NS 1, pp. 129-45. Attributes Greene's "préoccupation primordialle" with the destiny of the individual soul, the total absence of the "phénomène mystique," the systematic confrontation between, and the interweaving of, the positive realities of Good and Evil, and the "individualistic" approach to religion in the novels to the Puritan tradition which Greene had inherited prior to his conversion to Catholicism. Uses Bunyan as the norm of the Puritan tradition, and describes the similarities that exist between the two writers' attitudes to Salvation, Grace and individual tensions, and contrasts these views with orthodox Catholicism.

A656 Marian, Sister, IHM. "Graham Greene's People: Being and Becoming." Renascence, XVIII (Autumn), pp. 16-22. Maintains that Greene's basic approach to the reality of life is essentially existential for the typical Greene hero, "sunk in the morass of a private despair ... guilty of sexual lapses ... enervated, weary" of himself, his fellow men, and of God, struggles against the apparent absurdity of the "scheme of things life has ordained for him"--the "inevitability of the absurd" as Camus put it--and it is in the dawning consciousness of what his being is and "what it means to become" that Greene's existential qualities are exhibited. Brighton Rock, The Power and the Glory and A Burnt-Out Case.

A657 Marie-Celeste, Sister. "Georges Bernanos et Graham Greene: le prêtre dans Journal d'un curé de campagne et La Puissance et la gloire." RLM, V, pp. 127-29, 43-70. Though Greene should not be mistaken for an English Bernanos, both writers show a remarkable similarity in the special interest they evince in the priest as a central character whose experience is a testimony to his sacerdotal apostolate which is characterized by personal, physical, and moral suffering, a "naive" love for souls, the growth of the habit of prayer, a humble acceptance of injury and poverty, and a devotion and fidelity to the priesthood. Also shows how both writers use the thriller "pour en revêtir le tragique chretien."

A658 Markovic, Vida E. "Engelski Roman Pre Drugog Svetskog Rata." Forum, (May), pp. 125-76. In Serbo-Croatian. Pages 128-45 survey Greene's novels of the thirties and discuss Brighton Rock, The Power and the Glory, The Heart of the Matter and A Burnt-Out Case and his vision of life, and reiterate her earlier thesis (see A6315) that, "Greene, the artist, is hampered by God," and though determined to move forward, he is relentlessly pulled back by his past, his culture and is unable to extricate himself from the web of western civilization.

A659 Nichol, Davidson. "Our Critics and Lovers: Three Reassessments." Transition, V:22, pp. 32-37. Not so much a "reassessment" of Greene--he is the second to be "reassessed," the other two being Albert Schweitzer and Joyce Cary--as a discussion of the import of Greene's "affection for the uneducated African and his seeming uneasiness with the educated."

A6510 Sandra, Sister Mary, SSA. "The Priest-Hero in Modern Fiction." Person, XLVI:4 (Autumn), pp. 527-42. Maintains that the priest-hero's problem in E. O'Connor's The Edge of Darkness, J. F. Powers' Morte D'Urban, Bernanos' The Diary of a Country Priest and Greene's The Power and the Glory lies in reconciling and fusing his "dual response" to any situation, as a product of his culture and as a priest. Pages 538-42 examine the constant conflict between priest and man in the Whiskey Priest and his attempt to come to terms with himself and his situation by evaluating his views of himself, his function and the Mexican persecution, i. e., his "present" situation or culture. Only then does he find meaning in his activity and achieve a clear view of life and Christian love.

A6511 Sonnenfeld, Albert. "Twentieth Century Gothic: Reflections on the Catholic Novel." SoR, I:2 (April), pp. 388-405. A consideration of the nature of the novel in England, Germany and France where it is "a reaction to disorder and the threat of imminent chaos" rather than "celebrative" as in Italy or Spain. Several references to Greene and A Burnt-Out Case.

A6512 Taylor, Marion A. and John Clark. "Further Sources for 'The Second Death' by Graham Greene." PLL, 1, pp. 378-80. Remarks on the striking parallelism in language, too close to be "accidental," between the narrator's memory of his friend's second death and the passage from Mark VIII:22-25. Also notes that the point about the "blindness" of the narrator indicates another source, John IX:39-41 besides the acknowledged one from Luke VII:11-15.

A6513 Turnell, Martin. "Graham Greene: The Man Within." Ramparts, (June), pp. 54-64. Questions the validity of Greene's distinction between "entertainments" and "novels," and though admitting the craftsmanship of both categories, is highly critical of Greene for using his books as an "outlet for something in his personal make-up"; hence, the "limitations of the novels and the intrusion into the 'entertainments' of some of the themes of the novels." Argues that the "seediness" Greene describes is but a "substitute for a genuinely searching criticism" of the decaying social system, and that there is no "genuine apprehension of evil" in the novels. Discusses the growth of the religious element and Greene's prose style in the novels to assert that Greene projects into them a personal "highly idiosyncratic religion" (see A5131) that is well-nigh a "deliberate destruction of (moral) perspective in the interests of melodrama." Original and controversial. The Man Within, Brighton Rock, The Power and the Glory, The Heart of the Matter and The End of the Affair.

R651 Schellenberg, Johannes. "Graham Greene: Unser Mann in Havana." Biblio, XIX, pp. 966-69. A review of Lida Winiewicz's German translation of Our Man in Havana now published in paperback. Notices Greene as a "fable" writer and his vivid characterization and unexpected ending. Also includes a short biography.

R652 Unsigned. "The Comedians." Booklist, LXII (15 Dec.), p. 396. Pre-publication notice of the novel.

R653 ______. "The Comedians." Kirkus, XXXIII (15 Nov.), p. 1163. Pre-publication notice describing the book as being "to an extent," a novel but "superlatively" an entertainment.

R654 ______. "Carving a Statue." TLS, 3286 (18 Feb.), p. 133. Briefly noticed under "Books Received." Notes the difference between the play as it emerged in the theatre and what Greene says about it in the introduction.

D651 Flynn, Sr. M. Robert of Citeaux. The Utility of Suffering in the Novels of Graham Greene. M.A. Boston College.

D652 Hoodecheck, Donald J. The Theme of Purgation in Graham Greene's 'The Power and the Glory.' M.A. Mankato State College.

D653 Kambeitz, Clemens Gabriel. The Pessimistic Realism of Graham Greene. M.A. Univ. of Toronto.

D654 Ledeboer, Leroy D. The Despair that Leads to Faith: A Study of the Major Religious Novels of Graham Greene. M.A. Moorhead State College.

D655 McDonald, Marjorie H. Sacred and Profane Love as Depicted in the Writings of Graham Greene. M.A. Saint Mary's Univ.

D656 Quirk, Frank B. Graham Greene and the Human Condition. M.A. Univ. of Massachusetts.

D657 Read, Donald R. Pattern and Meaning in the Novels of Graham Greene. M.A. Trinity College.

D658 Rozsnafszky, Jane S. The Search for Meaning of the Characters of Graham Greene. M.A. Drake Univ.

D659 Stowe, Mary L. The Significance of Interpersonal Relationships in the Novels of Graham Greene. M.A. Washington State Univ. at Pullman.

D6510 Tolbert, Evelyn O. The Greene Priest. M.A. Univ. of Houston.

1966

B661 Electrowicz, Leszek. "Greene'a alegoryczne "dreszczowce." Zwierciadlo w okruchach: Szkice o powiesci amerykanskiej i angielskiej. Warsaw: Panstwowy Instytut Wydawniczy, pp. 289-99. In Polish. A study of the allegorical elements in the novels. Considers Greene's heroes as allegorical figures who make their way to salvation through evil, hatred and sin. References to Brighton Rock, The Power and the Glory, The Quiet American, and A Burnt-Out Case.

B662 Fricker, Robert. "Der englische Roman unserer Zeit." Der moderne englische Roman. Göttingen: Vandenhoeck and Ruprecht, pp. 174-96. Notes the diversity of Greene's works in his discussion of the major novels and their characteristics. Discusses the weaknesses of Brighton Rock as a thriller--a "splendid failure"--especially Pinkie with whom the reader cannot identify, shows that The Power and the Glory, though designed on the detective novel pattern, may be interpreted as an aesthetic, as distinct from theological, proof of God, and maintains that Greene's focus on the soul in The Heart of the Matter is indicative of his artistic development. Though his novels are not in any sense propagandist or aimed at the reader's conversion, they show man following the "centrifugal power of his soul" in an attempt to free himself from the "centripetal power of the Church" without losing God.

B663 Glicksberg, Charles I. "Catholicism in Fiction." Modern Literature and the Death of God. The Hague: Martinus Nijhoff, pp. 122-39. Rpt. from Criticism, 1:4 (Fall 1959), 339-53. [See A595]

B664 Lodge, David. Graham Greene. Columbia Essays on Modern Writers. No. 17. New York and London: Columbia Univ. Press. Rpt. in The Novelist at the Crossroads and Other Essays on Fiction and Criticism. London: Routledge

& Kegan Paul; Ithaca: Cornell Univ. Press, 1971, pp. 87-118, and in Six Contemporary British Novelists. Ed. George Stade. New York: Columbia Univ. Press, 1976, pp. 1-56. The Essay questions academic skepticism with regard to Greene's reputation and achievement as well as sectarian "Catholic" criticism because Greene, a "master technician," has cultivated the virtues and disciplines of prose, and uses Catholicism as a "system of concepts, a source of situations, and a reservoir of symbols" with which he can dramatize intuitions about the nature of human experience. Analyzes the works on a purely literary basis to emphasize the creative, inventive and rhetorical side of Greene's work, from the characteristic themes of betrayal and pursuit in The Man Within and the "obsessions" revealed in the early entertainments where one can best observe the genesis of his mature art, to the increasing power and complexity of later works up to and including The Comedians. Notes that The End of the Affair represents "his art at its most mature."

B665 Roy, Gregor. Greene's 'The Power and the Glory' and Other Works. Monarch Notes and Study Guides. New York: Monarch Press, Inc. Though elementary, the study is more comprehensive than the general run of "notes" and "Study Guides" and should be useful to junior undergraduates and the literate reader. The Introductory chapter gives a brief summary of Greene's life and works, discusses Greene's position in the contemporary novel, his attitude to the heroic ideal and modern values, and ends with a short account of the state of Catholic literature. Ch. 2 discusses plot, analysis of character, thematic materials and their interrelationships in the Catholic trilogy: Brighton Rock, The Power and the Glory and The Heart of the Matter. Ch. 3 gives a cursory examination of Greene's "entertainments" from A Gun for Sale to Our Man in Havana. Ch. 4 points out inconsistencies in criticism of Greene and presents critical opinion on six major themes: sin and grace, freedom, natural and supernatural orders, interpersonal communication, pity and technique. Also includes a three-page bibliography of criticism.

B666 Servotte, Herman. "Levensinzicht en levensaavoelen in de 'katholieke' romans van Graham Greene." Literatuur als Levenkunst. Essays over Kedendaagse Engelse Literatuur. Antwerpen: De Nederlandsche Boekhandel, pp. 36-52. Rpt. with a few stylistic changes from Kultuurleven, XXIV (Jan. 1957), pp. 28-40. See A5729.

B667 Temple, Ruth Z., and Martin Tucker, comps. & eds. "Greene, Graham (1904-)." A Library of Literary Criticism: Modern British Literature. Vol. I. New York: Frederick Ungar, pp. 378-85. Includes fifteen selected excerpts from critical works which describe Greene's qualities as a writer, and which attempt to "define his status, indicate ... something of his life and personality ... and sp3cify other pursuits."

B668 West, Paul. "Graham Greene." The Wine of Absurdity: Essays on Literature and Consolation. University Park & London: The Pennsylvania State Univ. Press, pp. 174-85. Contends that if Greene, unlike Mauriac or Bernanos, scandalizes people by his treatment of religion, it is because he presents "the full spectrum of his obsessive fictional world" instead of routine cases. Moreover, Greene writes "the same novel" most of the time because what interests him is not only the opposition between Infinite Love and human love, and the consequent allegation that our world is absurd, but also the promotion of this awareness in the least doctrinal way, not so much by argument as by "trying to express the inescapable mystery of life in which it is impossible not to participate." Brighton Rock, The Power and the Glory, The End of the Affair and A Burnt-Out Case.

A661 Burgess, Anthony. "Religion and the Arts: 1. The Manicheans." TLS, 3340 (3 March), 153-54. Considers, among other topics, "the legitimate source of fascination" in the process which turns a sinner into a saint, with reference to The End of the Affair, and the "states of sin and sainthood as possible aspects of each other" in The Heart of the Matter.

A662 Davidson, Richard Allan. "Graham Greene and L. P. Hartley: 'The Basement Room' and The Go-Between." N&Q, XIII (March), pp. 101-02. Points out enough "striking" parallels between the two works in plot details and theme--"Greene's story is thematically almost a microcosm of Hartley's novel"--that may warrant a "further comparative study of their canons."

A663 De Vitis, A. A. "Greene's The Comedians: Hollower Men." Renascence, XVIII:3 (Spring), 129-36, 146. Discusses Greene's further pursuit of the nature of innocence and commitment, and the move away from the "highly stylized allegorical presentations" of his early novels. Brown's "tragi-comic compassion" becomes the chief mood of this the "gloomiest" of Greene's novels, "full of comic touches and humour of a macabre and grotesque nature." Maintains that as an anti-hero who has no "real love," Brown is a failure. Inscfar as Catholicism is concerned, he "does not illustrate a religious breakdown; his is a failure of character."

A664 Gilman, Richard. "Up From Hell with Graham Greene." NRep, CLIV (29 Jan.), pp. 25-28. A review article on

The Comedians. Critical of Greene's "pretension" and "inauthenticity" especially when he reflects on society, and his inability to offer a "personal, singular, unaccommodating vision" whose intensity gives "urgency," shape to plot, "self-sufficiency" and purpose to his earlier novels. Owing to the failure of the "obsessional element to operate in any but the most mechanical manner," The Comedians, "something approaching to an artistic failure," suffers from "insuffіcency, perfunctoriness, vulnerability to attack," resulting in "platitude, obviousness and, ... assertion in the place of struggle."

A665 Grazyte, Ilona. "Graham Greene." Aidai, CLXXXVI (1966), 200-05. Unavailable for examination.

A666 Ibanez Langlois, José Miguel. "Catolicismo y protestantismo en la novela de Graham Greene." Atlantida, 22, pp. 381-97. The conflicts in Greene's characters have meaning only in terms of sin and grace and the Catholic Faith. The novels testify to the supernatural reality of Catholicism, to the transcendence of Faith over morality, the affirmation of the personal forces of good and evil, heaven and hell, to the supremacy of the Church, the priesthood and the efficacy of the Sacraments. The novels also show the Protestant streak Greene had inherited: a belief in original sin as an intrinsic corruption of human nature, and belief in grace "como justificacion extrinseca" of man, as well as pessimism with regard to man's freedom in choosing good.

A667 Jones, James Land. "Graham Greene and the Structure of the Moral Imagination." Phoenix 2, pp. 34-56. A paper delivered before the Quarante Club of New Orleans, Spring 1964. Divided into three sections. Section 1 examines the similarities between Greene and Conrad, his "spiritual ancestor in the British novel," and the former's "moral imagination" which did not solidify into theological dogma but applied itself to the problems of moral conflict and the drama of conscience in the contemporary world. Section 2 discusses the constituent elements of this moral imagination--Piety or the "varieties of self-righteousness," Pride, Pity, Peace or the desire to escape from the pain and complexity of life, Passion and Apathy or total spiritual dryness and paralysis of feeling--in Brighton Rock, The Power and the Glory, The Heart of the Matter, The End of the Affair, The Quiet American and A Burnt-Out Case. Section 3 examines Greene's craftsmanship and command of technical resources.

A668 Lambert, J. W. "Graham Greene: The Next Move." SunT, (16 Jan.), pp. 41-42. An account of an evening with Greene occasioned by his new appointment as Companion of Honour and his upcoming move to Paris and Antibes. Greene, in a relaxed and mellow mood, reminisces on his works, political views, work in the theatre, the cinema and his dislike of appearing on T. V.

A669 Laski, Marghanita. "How Well Have They Worn? 7. Brighton Rock." Times, (17 Feb.), p. 15. The increasing regard for Greene as "Catholic novelist rather than novelist pure and simple," and the growing "intellectual fascination with some constituents of the environment" make it difficult to reconstruct the impact of this "seminal" novel when it first appeared. Hindsight alters one's first impression as a "first-class thriller"; the "contemporaneity of the environment" and the Catholicism "beautifully integrated into the argument of the plot though not necessarily more than plot machinery," indicate a novel "admirably invented and constructed, and original beyond possible realization in 1938."

A6610 Lewin, David. "Friendship, Sex ... and a Sense of Doom." DaiM, (22 March), p. 8. A talk with Greene in Nice in which he speaks, facetiously perhaps? of the "dominant forces" in his life as being friendship, sex and politics. Insists that Greeneland is not a world created in fantasy or imagination, but is factual and real.

A6611 Lodge, David. "Graham Greene's Comedians." Commonweal, LXXXIII (25 Feb.), pp. 604-06. A review article on The Comedians. Greene uses the term "comedians" in its "traditional, theatrical sense, denoting the improvisation of roles and the wearing of masks," because the pursuit of happiness in the conditions of Haiti is inevitably attended by "absurd incongruities ... which compel the individual to the adoption of a 'comic' role." Also maintains that over the previous decade, Greene has reflected the changes in the contemporary intellectual climate rather than the "anti-humanist Catholic tradition" of his "catholic" novels.

A6612 McCall, Dan. "Brighton Rock: The Price of Order." ELN, III:4 (June), 290-94. Argues that the novel, besides being a "detective story" is also a "statement in fictional terms of a fundamental contrast" between the opposing consciousness of Pinkie and Ida, and their two ways of ordering experience, rather than the "mutually exclusive" interpretation of R. W. B. Lewis and A. A. De Vitis. (See A5715 & A577). Notices the "Catholic vocabulary" Greene uses in describing Pinkie's emotions.

A6613 Mayhew, Alice. "Upwards from Jansenism." NCR (30 March), p. 9. Rpt. as "The Comedians." Graham Greene. Ed. Harry J. Cargas. St. Louis, Mo.: B. Herder Book, 1969, pp. 134-41. Maintains that The Comedians is "more complicated ... least jansenistic and most optimistic" of his novels, one in which Greene is most socially conscious of a world filled with "farcical, impertinent, confusing strains" and where his tone is "humanist, less dogmatic and more compassionate, less arrogant."

A6614 Pritchett, V. S. "Brown's Hotel: Haiti." NSta, LXXI (28 Jan.), p. 129. Review article on The Comedians. A book with the "usual zest in the sardonic, self-lacerating view," but in which one wishes Greene were "less a contriver and would let the characters show for themselves what their meaning is" even though his mind is "courageous, charitable and compassionate." Greene condemns indifference more harshly than violence, describes "brilliantly" the filthy conditions of the tropics, and is always on "the qui vive for the ironies of impotence and desire ... betrayal ... and treachery." Maintains that Greene "overcrowds with the apparatus of horror" and that his laughter sometimes is at cross purposes with the reader.

A6615 Pryce-Jones, David. "Graham Greene's Human Comedy." Adam, Nos. 301-03, pp. 19-38. Basically a discussion of Greene's "religious sense" which gives "unity" to his work and which, especially in his later novels, no longer depends "on outside intervention ... but on relationships," on his imaginative vision of man's inhumanity to man rather than "Church Latin." This is followed by a lengthy review of The Comedians, a presentation of "the secularist value on human affairs" growing out of The Quiet American.

A6616 Tressin, Deanna. "Toward Understanding." EJ, LV, pp. 1170-74. "A unit in understanding" for twelfth grade students illustrating "problems of adjustment faced by young people" in four short stories by W. Cather, S. Fitzgerald, C. Aiken and Greene. Examines briefly the thrust of "responsibility" on Philip's "isolation" from life in "The Basement Room," and the "selfishness and hardness that take over Philip's heart when fear and confusion vacate it." Also refers briefly to the "religious theme" or Philip's spiritual deterioration, and the use of symbols in the story.

A6617 Wilshere, A. D. "Conflict and Conciliation in Graham Greene." E & S, XIX, pp. 122-37. Shortened version of a paper read at the invitation of the Salisbury Branch of the English Association to the English Teachers' Conference, University College of Rhodesia and Nyasaland, September 1963. Argues that Greene has an "ambivalent attitude to religion which swings from "challenge to affirmation," from conflict with "prescriptive theology" and the inevitable "theological sclerosis" it entails to conciliation with Catholicism because he is unable to treat any other form of religion seriously. It would appear then that "Greene the writer is at loggerheads with Green the Catholic"; i.e., the humane artist believes that Catholicism comes to grips with the reality of evil but he cannot accept the logical conclusions the propositions set before him, thus leading to his sympathy with his sinners. Analyzes the character of Pinkie, the Whiskey Priest and Scobie from this viewpoint.

A6618 Unsigned. "A New Honor and a New Novel." Life, LX (4 Feb.), pp. 43-44. Includes a recent "close up" as well as three other photographs, and interesting snippets from an interview on the occasion of his being named a Companion of Honour by the Queen "for conspicuous service of national importance."

R661 Allen, Walter. "The Comedians." LM, V:12 (March), pp. 73-80. A lengthy searching review that reveals the "Greene world of the extreme situation" without any compensation, whose preoccupations are wholly removed from those of the "Catholic novels." The view of life expressed within the framework of the novel and the need for commitment makes the novel his "most Conradian" and "finest" since The Power and the Glory. Distinguishes between the different kinds of comedians in the novel.

R662 Amis, Kingsley. "Slow Boat to Haiti." Observer, (30 Jan.), p. 27. Critical of the "elaborate double prelude" of the first hundred pages of The Comedians, the "irritating" style of fanciful images and "clumsy word order," and the lack of incidents in general so that the action moves "slowly, circuitiously, along lines that converge, touch, and move apart again." Considers Greene's "straight forward and angry reporting" of what Haiti is like to be the most lively parts of the novel.

R663 Barker, Paul. "The Masks of Graham Greene: The Comedians." NSoc, (27 Jan.), p. 29. Does not think it is a "very good book" for it has "too big an element of pasteboard" and many images of the "theatre and chance bob up again and again." What the book, like most of his novels, lacks is "true involvement, either of the author with his characters, or of the characters with their own fate." Greene has hitherto disguised it by a "kind of generalised pity," by the "technical excitements of the thriller" and by the "agonies of Catholic dialectic"; for Greene is not a "Bloomsbury-sensitive novelist" but a "writer of roles."

R664 Barthelme, Donald. "The Tired Terror of Graham Greene." Holiday, XXXIX (April), pp. 146, 148-49. An extremely unfavorable review of The Comedians. It is not even a good entertainment but a "ghostly self-parody" merely retaining the "manner" and the "trademark" atmosphere of earlier works, poorly written and arguing "exhaustion at the deepest level, at the level of feeling," with a desire to be "complex and bloody at any cost."

R665 Bedford, Sybille. "Tragic Comedians." NYBR, (3 March), pp. 25-27. A lengthy review of The Comedians, a novel whose strength and freshness make it "fine and important" and "very moving." Finds the novel rich in incident and situations, even though the "worst takes place off stage," with a flaw in the "implied limitation" of choices before the "tragic comedians."

R666 Bims, Hamilton. "The Comedians." ND, XV (May), pp. 92-93. Maintains that the setting of the novel transcends "spatial limits" and approaches the "realm of dream" even though the novel, for all its promise of allegory, "bogs down in the shadow of poetics, sociology and Bible morality." Greene operates easily in the realm of myth but balks at the challenge of probing into "the unresolved regions of human personality."

R667 Bowen, John. "The Doomed Are Everywhere." NYTBR, (23 Jan.), pp. 1, 43. Attempts to prove that the idea of failure "informs" The Comedians--a novel written with "liveliness and skill, and with such a will and ability to please and carry us along." Also notes that Greene cannot always be trusted as a "guide to his own work."

R668 Burgess, Anthony. "New Fiction." Listener, LXXV (3 Feb.), p. 181. The Comedians is the first of five novels reviewed. Maintains that Greene "homes" to evil, which in this novel is not approached as a theological proposition but is "Sartrean--self-evident, palpable, unredeemable"--and is in the State and not primarily in the plot.

R669 Byatt, A. S. "Evil as Commonplace." Encounter, XXVI (June), pp. 66, 68-70. A review article on The Comedians. Argues that the casual and factual description of Haiti and its violence make the power of the book. Its comedians are those who are obsessed "with the fortuitous, chaotic aspects of existence," whose sense of aimlessness necessitates a "series of deliberately assumed parts." Though they do not suffer, they soon find out that "comedy and tragedy are not altogether distinguishable." Brown's character, a comedian, comes off convincingly, but the unreality of Martha and Jones "mars the final sequence when Brown ... takes Jones to the hills and death."

R6610 Casey, Florence. "Variations for Voodoo Dreams." ChrSM, (3 Feb.), p. 7. Maintains that Greene is a "critic's bane" for he explores the "same taut problem" but in different situations. In The Comedians, the problem assumes an interrogative shape: "Who is the funniest of them all--the jokester in a deck of human assortment?"

R6611 Cheuse, Allan. "Graham Greene's Bonbon du Bon." Nation,

CCII (21 Feb.), pp. 218-19. As the "most interesting" novel of his career, The Comedians is "more satiric than divine" and closer to tragedy than anything Greene has written; his continuing pessimism has led to the "farcical atmosphere and the despairing comic tone." Attributes the "richness" of the novel to Greene's "political variations" on his old theme that "innocence prevents one from becoming eligible for salvation."

R6612 Crombie, Robert. "The Horror of Life Without Freedom." BTod, III (30 Jan.), p. 1. Maintains that The Comedians is "Greene at his best" as he presents our "icily-angry picture of what life is like when freedom vanishes," and that the label comedian is used for those characters who are not really engaged in the struggle that life offers.

R6613 Davenport, Guy. "A Round of the Same." NR, XVIII (22 March), pp. 278-79. Includes a rather cursory review of The Comedians. Focusses on Greene's ability to tell a tale of suspense and adventure and his eye for the grotesque, especially where evil is concerned.

R6614 Davenport, John. "The Last Albigensian." Spectator, CCXVI:7179 (28 Jan.), pp. 110-11. Recommends, in his review of The Comedians, the abandonment of the term "Greeneland" for Greene's world is the world in which we live, and considers Greene's position as a Catholic novelist. Maintains that the comedians are "men of no real faith" who have opted out and are uncommitted and indifferent to essential things.

R6615 Dienstfrey, Harris. "Personal Salvation." Progressive, XXX (April), pp. 47-48. Argues that in The Comedians the action unfolds with "an easy, almost nonchalant plausibility" which, though controlled by careful design, serves "to undercut and contradict" the necessity for engagement which is the theme of the novel.

R6616 Dolbier, Maurice. "Innocence and Guilt--Graham Greene Returns." NYHT, CXXV (24 Jan.), p. 21. Maintains that though the characters in The Comedians are "exotic," the setting is authentic; the events may be "harsh, sinister, violent" and grim for the characters and the country, but the book is neither grim nor oppressive, and the story, "swiftly and suavely told," repeats the familiar theme of the ruin that innocence can wreak.

R6617 Fleischer, Leonore. "Fiction: The Power and the Glory." PW, CXC (12 Dec.), p. 58. Forecast of The Bantam paperback edition to be published 1 February 1967.

R6618 Fremont-Smith, Eliot. "Books of The Times: Opting Out in Never-Never Land." NYT, (28 Jan.), p. 45. Though by no means Greene's "best" novel, The Comedians is enjoyable as a "good fast tale, full of vivid scenes," a melodrama "shot through with dramatic hints and pauses and incredible coincidence." But its failure stems from an "oppressive sadness" rather than a suppressed passion that informs the novel--"an obligation ... set down upon the surface of the novel, instead of an angry revelation to spur it from beneath."

R6619 Fuller, Edmond. "Reading for Pleasure: Pale Greene." WSJ, XLVI (24 March). p. 18. Maintains that The Comedians neither makes it as an entertainment nor as a great novel; it is marred as a novel by "uncertainty of direction and an alarmingly blind view ... of what would be a viable alternative to Duvalier." Voices rather undue concern for Greene's "unsupported intemperateness" in his attacks against the U. S.

R6620 Gray, Ken. "Book of the Day: Greene's New Novel." IT, (29 Jan.), p. 9. Recognizes the "pure Greenery" of the violent background in The Comedians "full of cross-currents of right and wrong ... against which the scrupulously drawn characters probe their motives and wrestle with their inner selves." But the greatest comedian is Greene, "wryly and ironically manipulating his characters with brilliant skill and subtlety."

R6621 Griffin, Lloyd W. "The Comedians." LJ, XCI (Jan.), p. 276. A short critical review noticing the "savage humor and irony," and a certain "disjointed, meandering structure" in the novel whose strength lies in the portrayal of character and the creation of atmosphere.

R6622 Grosvenor, Peter. "Back from the Dark Places, Greene's Best for Years." DaiE, (27 Jan.), p. 6. The story of The Comedians, a "typical brew of seedy adventure and furtive sex," describes the plight of Greene's comedians in an "ironic sense" because their destinies seem to be controlled by a divine practical joker.

R6623 Halton, Rev. Thomas. "Graham Greene's New Novel." Hibernia, XXX:3 (March), p. 19. Though it notices the characteristic virtues of Greene as a novelist in The Comedians--craftsmanship, swift and taut dialogue, realism etc.--and its characteristic weaknesses too--the episodic nature of the plot, melodrama and the "almost pathological concern with adultery"--the review does not evaluate the novel but relies heavily on summarizing other reviews.

R6624 Hicks, Granville. "Trials of the Uncommitted." SatR, XLIX (29 Jan.), pp. 29-30. A review of The Comedians that considers the "commitment" of each of the comedians and notices the "breadth of sympathy" that Greene shows in the novel.

R6625 Hill, Roland. "Bekenntnisse eines Hotelbesitzers." Hochland, LIX, pp. 90-94. A review of Hilde Spiel's translation of The Comedians. Vienna/Hamburg: Paul Zsolnay Verlag, 1966. Concentrates on Greene's development of farce, irony and the absurd in the novel, discusses his political standpoint and questions, in spite of Greene's indication to the contrary, whether Brown who cannot be counted among the indifferent is really Greene.

R6626 Hodgart, Patricia. "Revelations at the Heart of Darkness." ILN, (5 Feb.), p. 40. Maintains that Greene has the ability to tell an intricate story with the simplicity and apparent effortlessness of a master thus combining the traveller's passion for exotic places and the writer's instinct to describe human behavior in exceptional circumstances. Though the "heroes" may be the resistance fighters in The Comedians, those who fascinate Greene play out "their various roles as if life were a farce and nothing really mattered." Notices Greene's "ironic acceptance" of the relationship and balance between the tragic and the comic in the novel.

R6627 Holloway, David. "Recent Fiction: Mr. Greene's New Purgatory." DaiT, (27 Jan.), p. 21. Notices the remarkably low-key tone of the narration in The Comedians where desperate deeds are revealed by "implication, and often by flashback." Maintains that the black purgatory of the setting tests the characters' motives to the breaking point. These characters are immediately "established" in the first few pages of the novel which he considers the best since The Power and the Glory. Also comments on the irony of the title.

R6628 Igoe, W. J. "The Faith and the Mask." Month, NS XXXV: 4 (April), pp. 246-48. The main characters of The Comedians are "transients," its theme is "vacuity" and its setting "an obscure political and moral vacuum." Each character, often having made a mask for itself, creates its own melodrama remote from the enigmatic reality of a human soul, and is "trapped in the ephemeral."

R6629 Jackson, Katherine Gauss. "The Comedians." Harper's, CCXXXII (Feb.), p. 118. A short review asserting that though Greene "makes much of examining the motivations" of Brown and Jones, the story is dramatic and the background vivid. Recommends it as a book "to enjoy and ponder over."

R6630 Kunkel, Francis L. "Greeneland Improved." Renascence, XVIII (Summer), pp. 219-21. Argues that the characters, plot and themes of The Comedians, though much the same as before, are subject to "fresh direction, deepened insights, a newly discovered artistic restraint and ... a novel point of view." What is new is the "fictionalization of the existentialist notion of the absurd"; in other words, the human anxieties and agonies "conceived in terms of black comedy loom over like a human-divine tussle" now that Greene has surmounted "the antihumanistic catholic literary tradition" of the "Catholic" novels.

R6631 Lauras, Antoine. "Sommes-nous des comediens?" Etudes, CCCXXIV (April), 510-13. Notices the "tableau hallucinant" that gives the double dimension of comedy and death to The Comedians, and distinguishes between two categories of characters: those committed to some form of belief or ideal and the uncommitted who have no option but to play a role in the comedy.

R6632 Levine, Norman. "Mr. Greene, Mellowed." AtA, LVI (Feb.), p. 72. Maintains that with The Comedians Greene has rediscovered his main strength to be in the world we live in. Sees the novel as "almost entirely Jones'"--a mellowed Greenean version of Anthony Farrant--and its freedom from the dramatization of Catholic dogma as a further "mellowing" of "England's finest living novelist."

R6633 Lister, Richard. "Greene's Savage Island." EvS, (1 Feb.), p. 10. The bottomless depth of disillusion and despair that is at the heart of The Comedians--the "very best" of "the master at the height of his power"--is alleviated by the "formal perfection" of Greene's art so that every action has the "rightness of inevitability."

R6634 Lodge, David. "Books for the Week: Black Comedy." Tablet, CCXX (29 Jan.), p. 128. Considers The Comedians a further exploration into the "literary and philosophical discussions of the absurd," a kind of fiction conceived in terms of "comedy and irony in which the possibility of religious faith has all but retreated out of sight in the anarchic confusion of human behaviour." Also notes the "key-word" of the novel and the sense in which "comedian" and "comedy" are used.

R6635 Lynch, William F., SJ. "Our Man in Hell." Critic, XXIV (Feb.), pp. 66-68. A lengthy review of The Comedians as a novel that re-enforces the differences between the comic and the tragic but which admits uncertainty as to the "final direction of Mr. Brown or The Comedians."

R6636 MacGillivray, Arthur, SJ. "The Comedians." Best Sellers, XXV (1 Feb.), p. 417. Examines briefly Greene's use of simile and the flashback technique, and notes his "seriousness of intent" in the novel.

R6637 Massingham, Hugh. "Haiti Rock." SunTel, (30 Jan.), p. 24. The Comedians, a "modern morality" with the "authentic Greene touches," is not as good as Brighton Rock but better than The End of the Affair. Greene makes the evil pervasive and embracing by setting the action in Haiti. Because his characters are uncommitted, they are futile figures, comedians, "faceless, lost humanity." What the book lacks is Greene's compassion and understanding for such characters.

R6638 Murray, James G. "The Comedians." America, CXIV (5 Feb.), pp. 203-04. Maintains that the novel attempts to present the fundamentally theological problem of evil in "non-personal terms," but confusion arises because the ideas are "jumbled up ... irregularly conveyed" and they "merely suggest" rather than convince; hence, the "mish-mash of a book" that suffers not only from "delusions of grandeur" but also from "conflicts of genre and from confusions of approach and intent."

R6639 Natan, Alex. "Neuer Graham Greene: The Comedians." ChristW, XIX:10 (March), p. 27. Critical of Greene's narrator and his focus on evil rather than good, even though he admits that human failure, "eine konstante Grosse," is a key to the reader's understanding because God, too, fails at every battle but wins the war in the end.

R6640 Nettell, Stephanie. "Fiction: Graham Greene." B&B, XI (Feb.), p. 28. As a novel, The Comedians reflects a "gentler, more charitable Greene" with a "warmer tolerance" than usual, in spite of its passionate indictment of police tyranny and diplomatic hypocrisy. Finds the comedy "grey" leaving one with a "puzzled bleakness, not excitement."

R6641 O'Brien, Conor Cruise. "Old Black Magic Has Him in Its Spell." BookW, (6 Feb.), p. 5. Maintains that the strength of The Comedians does not lie in its characterization, nor in "moralizing or in political analysis, but in the skillful and sympathetic working of a great mine of evil experience" that is Haiti.

R6642 Ostermann, Robert. "The Comedians Play Their Parts in Mr. Greene's Forbidding World." NObs, V (31 Jan.), p. 23. Maintains that Greene's vision in The Comedians is "mordant" but basically religious, even theological, and few can doubt the validity of his "chill, forbidding world" because as a "reflective, conscious master" of his art, Greene is a "fantasist" who shows a creation whose parts may seem familiar "but taken together is a new universe."

R6643 Price, R. G. G. "New Novels." Punch, CCL (26 Jan.),

p. 138. The Comedians is the first of four novels briefly reviewed. The novel reveals more the "Ambler side" of Greene rather than the Mauriac side for the theology is "less outré" and the "complex melodrama goes with a swing." Notices also the thickly laid local color.

R6644 Pugh, Marshall. "Assassins in the Greene Hell of Haiti." DaiM, (27 Jan.), p. 12. Notices "signs of wavering confidence ... moments of padding purplish similes" in The Comedians in spite of Greene still being the "master craftsman." Though he distinguishes between Greene and Brown, the reviewer tends to attribute to Greene the narrator's belief that Haiti is not the exception but "a small slice of everyday taken at random."

R6645 Rosenthal, Raymond. "Over the Border to Haiti." NLea, (14 Feb.), pp. 19-20. Finds The Comedians, as a "medieval morality play," entertaining only "in spots," and "frazzles out in the usual, depressing, throw-it-away contemporary sense"; it has neither "enchantment" nor the "adventure" of the "entertainment." Each of its characters is "stock and meaningless without the others, as the cast of any Grade-B movie," and the "spirit of Restoration comedy that hovers about the moments of relative brightness only helps to stress the surrounding dullness and mechanical novelistic proficiency."

R6646 Sale, Roger. "High Mass and Low Requiem." HudR, XIX (Spring), pp. 123-34. Pp. 132-34 review The Comedians and describe it as a "novel-entertainment," one of Greene's "best" books with "crystal prose and a magnificent sense of detail," "mordant, often disagreeable and generally defeated." Pays tribute to Greene's narrative power, especially his ability to "dramatize inaction as a kind of action."

R6647 Weeks, Edward. "Black Rule Gone Mad." Atlantic, CCXVII (March), p. 157. Maintains that The Comedians reveals Greene at his best with superbly drawn characters, style, irony and invention.

R6648 Wilson, Angus. "Topical Greene." Guardian, XCIV (3 Feb.), p. 10. Maintains that the aim of The Comedians is to awaken the affluent society in the insulated provincialism of modern England to the horrors of the "manichaen reality" of western backed reactionary governments. Finds the novel a "compound" of Greene's old stage properties simulating the "varieties of seediness, frustration and decay" to which he is attached.

R6649 Wolfe, Peter. "Greene Thoughts in a Green Shade." PrS, XL (Summer), pp. 178-81. Besides showing an awareness of modern man's political and spiritual state, The Comedians is conceived with a "new reverence and loving charity for suffering humanity." This "new maturity of vision" is managed in this novel with the same artistry and rich imagination of earlier novels which have made Greene one of the "major" writers of this century.

R6650 Unsigned. "The Comedians." Choice, III (March), pp. 32 & 34. A short account of the novel which finds the portrait of Haiti "vivid and convincing."

R6651 ________. "Greene Hell." Newsweek, LXVII (31 Jan.), p. 86. In The Comedians, Greene shifts between "fact and fiction, lacing his story with topical reality" and makes revolution and love dominate the narrative. But the old "thickly fictionalized story" stops short of probing beneath the superficial features of the characters.

R6652 ________. "Guided Tour of Greeneland." Time, LXXXVII (28 Jan.), p. 72. Maintains that in The Comedians Greene takes his characters through predestined paths to nowhere but without the intensity and the passion of the search which marked earlier explorations of the "ambiguous border between good and evil."

R6653 ________. "Mr. Greene in Haiti." Times, (27 Jan.), p. 27. The Comedians is the first of three novels reviewed. Though "less strictly disciplined" than his recent works, The Comedians "takes and makes the best" of both novels and entertainments. Foresees the endless critical argument about the meaning of the novel.

R6654 ________. "Plain Mr. Brown." TLS, 3335 (27 Jan.), p. 57. Finds that Greene in The Comedians has acquired a new humility, gentleness and patience with our sad humanity because his characters seem to accept with perseverance and sad humor their miserable destiny. The novel contains the characteristic faults and virtues in a Greene novel: adultery seems as dreary as ever, characters wooden and caricatured and, on the other hand, excellence of craftsmanship, swift dialogue, "the touch of drollery, the play of great wit and funniness."

R6655 ________. "Notes on Current Books: The Comedians." VQR, XLII (Spring), xlviii. Notes the effect of the "entertainment" on the novel which has many exciting and humorous moments in it but whose central character seems so "convincingly phlegmatic" that he is not worth attention. Faults Greene for leaving the most interesting character--Duvalier--offstage.

D661 Bell, Martha F. Graham Greene and the Idea of Childhood. M.A. North Texas State Univ.

D662 Brooks, Sammy K. Graham Greene and Mexico: A Critical Study of 'The Power and the Glory' and 'Another Mexico.' M.A. Univ. of Austin at Texas.

D663 Cawthon, Daniel D. The Themes of Alienation in the Major Novels of Graham Greene. M.A. Univ. of Tulsa.

D664 Clines, Patrick. The Child and Being: Key to the Novels of George Bernanos and Graham Greene. M.A. Fresno State College.

D665 Davidson, Arnold C. Graham Greene: A Writer of the Cross Rather Than the Resurrection. M.A. Kansas State Teachers College.

D666 Groven, John O. The Influence of Religion on the Works of Graham Greene. M.A. Univ. of Colorado.

D667 Hooper, Walter D. The Péguy Motif in the "Catholic" Novels of Graham Greene. M.A. Univ. of Rhode Island.

D668 Kelleher, James Patrick. The Orthodoxy and Values of Graham Greene. Boston Univ. Graduate School. D.A., XXV, 1825-A.

D669 La Chance, Louis. Types of Fantasy in the Fiction of Graham Greene. M.A. Univ. of Montreal.

D6610 Sorbara, Joseph Dominic. Character in Satire and the Novel: A Study of Evelyn Waugh and Graham Greene. M.A. Univ. of Toronto.

D6611 Sullivan, Virginia M. The Heart of Darkness in Graham Greene: Some Critical Considerations of Greene's Vision of the World as It Relates to His Preoccupation with Death in His Novels and Entertainments, with Particular Emphasis on 'It's a Battlefield.' M.A. Columbia Univ.

1967

B671 Adelman, Irving, and Rita Dworkin. Modern Drama: A Checklist of Critical Literature on 20th Century Plays. Metuchen, N.J.: The Scarecrow Press, Inc. Mentions ten items on Greene as a dramatist, seven on The Complaisant Lover and six on The Potting Shed. Makes no mention of The Living Room.

B672 Blehl, Vincent Ferrer, SJ. "Literature and Religious Belief." Mansions of the Spirit: Essays in Literature and Religion. Ed. George A. Panichas. New York: Hawthorn Books, pp. 105-18. See A652.

B672a Burgess, Anthony. "The Greene and the Red: Politics in the Novels of Graham Greene." Urgent Copy: Literary Studies. London: Faber & Faber. New York: W. W. Norton & Company, 1968, pp. 13-20. Rpt. "The Politics of Graham Greene." The Best of 'Speaking of Books' from 'The New York Times Book Review.' Ed. with Intro. Francis Brown. New York: Holt, Rinehart and Winston, 1969, pp. 284-91. Co-published in JCH, 2 (April 1967), 92-99. See A671.

B673 ________. "Good and Evil." The Novel Now: A Student's Guide to Contemporary Fiction. London: Faber & Faber. Rev. ed. 1971, pp. 61-72. Published in U.S.A. as The Novel Now: A Guide to Contemporary Fiction. New York: W. W. Norton. Pages 61-64 examine Greene's probings into the problem of good and evil and the wretchedness of the human condition in Brighton Rock, its "complement" The Power and the Glory, The Heart of the Matter and The End of the Affair.

B674 Friedman, Maurice Stanley. "Coccioli, Bernanos and Greene." To Deny Our Nothingness: Contemporary Images of Man. New York: Delacorte Press; London: Victor Gollancz, pp. 117-32. Pages 128-32 concentrate on Greene's Whiskey Priest as a "Modern 'Saint'" who takes on himself the "contradictions of contemporary existence" rather than "transcend" them through personal holiness, as one who is not only unconcerned with his own salvation and sainthood but "deliberately takes on damnation for the sake of others," one of whose singular aspects is the paradox that only in corruption does he learn to love.

B675 Ibanez Langlois, José Miguel. El mundo pecador de Graham Greene. Santiago de Chile: Empresa Editora Zig-Zag. This lengthy study in Spanish is primarily concerned with the theological aspect of the novels, especially sin and grace, hope and despair, good and evil, and damnation and salvation from a Catholic viewpoint. Gives lengthy analyses of the central characters in The Power and the Glory, The Heart of the Matter, The End of the Affair and A Burnt-Out Case.

B676 Kaam, Adrian van, and Kathleen Healy. "Querry in Greene's A Burnt-Out Case." The Demon and the Dove: Personality Growth Through Literature. Pittsburgh, Pa.: Duquesne Univ. Press, pp. 259-85. The analysis of Querry's personality is based on the assumption that a close partnership between literature and psychology can unveil the depths of human experience. Makes a detailed psychological analysis of Querry which demonstrates the relationship between loss of belief and his "existential neurosis," and reveals Querry's disease as a "complete ennui of existence" that has led to an "encounter with nothingness" and whose cure was achieved through suffering.

B677 Larrett, William. "Graham Greene." The English Novel from Thomas Hardy to Graham Greene. Frankfurt/Main: Verlag Moritz Diesterweg, pp. 151-65. One of seven essays in the volume each of which focusses on the salient features of one novelist. Attributes Greene's popularity to his undemanding storytelling, straightforward readable style and his ability to reveal character in a few lines or conjure the atmosphere of a scene with a few bold strokes. The "essentially dynamic quality" of his writing embodies successfully his basic themes of violence, persecution, pursuit and Catholic conscience in The Power and the Glory, The Heart of the Matter, The End of the Affair and A Burnt-Out Case. His treatment of the visible and spiritual world, combined with "his epic skill" makes him a "rare" novelist in the English tradition.

B678 Lumley, Frederick. "Britain: Graham Greene." New Trends in 20th Century Drama: A Survey Since Ibsen and Shaw. Oxford Univ. Press, pp. 289-92. Originally published as Trends in 20th Century Drama: A Survey Since Ibsen and Shaw. London: Rockliffe, 1956. Examines the weaknesses of the four plays: the "painstakingly contrived" situations that "never ring true" in The Living Room and The Potting Shed--the latter having "stock protagonists"--the "abrupt change of tempo" from the "hilarity" of the first half to the "serious problems of human relations to be solved" in the second half of The Complaisant Lover, and the "alternance of farce and Soho sordidness" which obscures the simplicity he was attempting in Carving a Statue. Greene thus remains an "outsider" in the theater where his technique "seems to stifle his broader vision ... and the ability to carry us with him."

B679 Paul, Leslie. "The Writer and the Human Condition." Alternatives to Christian Belief: A Critical Survey of the Contemporary Search for Meaning. New York: Doubleday. London: Hoffer & Stoughton, pp. 160-83. Rpt. from KR, XXIX:1 (Jan. 1967), 21-38. See A678.

B6710 Tucker, Martin. Africa in Modern Literature: A Survey of Contemporary Writing in English. New York: Frederick Ungar Publishing Co. Describes Greene, in this survey of literature about Africa written in English, as a novelist writing in the Conradian tradition that regards Africa "as a journey by way of experience to painful maturity." Concludes that religion and journalism frequently cause damage and despair rather than promote understanding between individuals and groups, as Greene's scathing portraits of Catholic missionaries and Parkinson in A Burnt-Out Case among others evince, and that the police officer, more often than not, "creates the bridge on which understanding travels to a more profound level," e.g., Scobie. Refers twice to an interview with Greene in London, April 1962 (pp. 129 & 155). See A6213. Scattered references to Journey Without Maps, The Heart of the Matter, A Burnt-Out Case and In Search of a Character.

B6711 Turnell, Martin. "Graham Greene: A Critical Essay." Contemporary Writers in Christian Perspective. Grand Rapids, Mich.: William B. Eerdmans. Though introductory in character and suitable for readers without specialized training in literature or religion, this essay is essentially an enlarged version of an earlier article (see A5131 & A6513) and argues from the same premises. Discusses the absence of a "compelling apprehension of evil in the Jamesian sense," and the advantages of his topical setting and the pattern of the novels, traces the growth of the religious element, and argues that what is defective with the "quality" of the religion in the novels is reflected in Greene's prose style, in his tendency to operate by overstatement, to introduce a "dash of sensationalism into the commonplace," and the conjunction of religion and sex to heighten emotional appeal. Analyzes The Power and the Glory and The Heart of the Matter separately from this perspective, as well as "The Later Novels" and the plays.

A671 Burgess, Anthony. "Politics in the Novels of Graham Greene." JCH, 2 (April), pp. 92-99. Rpt. as "The Politics of Graham Greene." NYTBR, 10 Sept. 1967, pp. 2, 32, 34; as "The Greene and the Red: Politics in the Novels of Graham Greene." Urgent Copy: Literary Studies. London: Faber & Faber, 1967; New York: W. W. Norton & Company, 1968, pp. 13-20; and in The Best of 'Speaking of Books' from 'The New York Times Book Review.' Ed. with Intro. Francis Brown. New York: Holt, Rinehart & Winston, 1969, pp. 284-91. Just as Greene's Catholicism has an "international character," so are his politics "world politics." Discusses Greene's reputation for anti-Americanism--his rejection of the "unforgivable hypocrisy" masquerading as a crusade for democratic rights and freedom when, in reality, it is a drive for "more feverish material consumption" wherein "matters of spiritual faith seem to have no role"; hence, his preference for a place that "seems to breathe sin" as being paradoxically, "spiritually healthier" than "an aseptic garden city."

A672 Clancy, L. J. "Graham Greene's Battlefield." MCR, 10, pp. 99-108. Attempts an assessment of Greene's achievement as a novelist. Examines each of the so-called "religious" novels and suggests reasons why Greene's achievement has not been greater; e.g., in Brighton Rock, "Greene preempts the reader's responsibility by prejudging the issues"; The Power and the Glory suffers from "his most consistent fault as a novelist: his inability or unwillingness to dissociate himself from the character with whom he is most in sympathy"; The Heart of the

Matter raises doubts as to whether the rendering of Scobie's dilemma is "an honest one"; The End of the Affair "marks an impasse" because the "religious dilemma was impossible of solution." Contends that Greene regards human and religious needs as essentially opposed and that man, perpetually at war with himself, can either "retire" from human feeling or lead a life of cynicism and despair.

A673 Davies, Horton. "Catching the Conscience: Graham Greene's Plays." RiL, XXXVI (Winter), pp. 605-14. A study of The Living Room and The Potting Shed from a Christian viewpoint with special emphasis on themes. The Living Room, in spite of its surface narrative, the fear of life and the fear of death it expresses, the "subtle points about true and false love," and its symbolism, remains "not entirely convincing." On the other hand, the nature of the conflict in The Potting Shed, a "twentieth-century representation of the story of Lazarus," is clear and its paradox "that the religious are open-minded and the rationalists have minds as closed as a jail" is unmistakable.

A674 Hebblethwaite, Peter. "How Catholic Is the Catholic Novel?" TLS, 3413 (27 July), pp. 678-79. "It is horizon--or vocation--which gives a 'Catholic novelist' his identity, and vocation is simply the lived aspect of coherence." Shows how the "sense of difference" often characteristic of Catholic novelists like E. Waugh and M. Spark can lead, in Greene's works, to "in-jokes, in-situation, in-vocabulary" as in Our Man in Havana, or to the challenge to miracle and conversion as in The End of the Affair.

A675 Ivasheva, V. V. "Tri vstrechi s Anglici." VMU 1, pp. 80-87. In Russian. An account of three separate opportunities between 1964 and 1966 to meet with English novelists. Refers, in one paragraph, to a meeting with Greene prior to his departure to his new home in Paris which, she claims, helped her understand his works.

A676 Liventseva, Liliya. "Kamo gryadeshi? Problema gibeli Geroya V. romanakh G. Grina." Kuban, (Sept.), pp. 106-09. In Russian. Examines the conflict of the hero with society in A Burnt-Out Case and The Comedians, which conflict leads the hero to spiritual destruction and ruin.

A677 Orlova, R. "Strana Grina." Moyvi Miz, IV, pp. 259-62. In Russian. A review article on the Russian translation of The Comedians by N. Volzhina in Innostrayana Literatura, 9 & 10, 1967.

A678 Paul, Leslie. "The Writer and the Human Condition." KR, XXIX:1 (Jan.), pp. 21-38. Rev. and rpt. in Alternatives to Christian Belief: A Critical Survey of the Contemporary Search for Meaning. New York: Doubleday, 1967, pp.

160-83. On the judgment of modern writers, especially novelists, on the present age--"sick without seeming to know how to cure itself"--and their documentation of the affliction. One sign of this affliction is the capacity, though innocent oneself, "to bear the evil done by others as though one were personally guilty." Examines Scobie, among others, in the light of this paradox, because in "bearing the burden of another's existence," Scobie's crimes appear to the reader "as the very consequence of integrity."

A679 Seehase, Georg. "Kapitalistische Entfremdung und humanistische Integration: Bemerkungen zum englischen proletarischen Gegenwartsroman." ZAA, XV:3, pp. 383-400. Brief reference to Greene as one novelist, among others, who advocates a "humanistic integration" as distinct from novelists like E. Waugh, W. Golding and L. Durrell who maintain the present "alienation." A marxist viewpoint. References to Greene's works confined to The Quiet American.

A6710 Sever, Alexander. "Un catolic nelinistit: Graham Greene." ViR, XX:4 (April), pp. 148-61. In Romanian. Concentrates on the "Catholic" novels in their exploration of the relationship between conscience and religion to show that they stand out as a "literary monument" to a Catholicism in Europe which is faced with all kinds of dissidences.

A6711 Wilson, Angus. "Evil in the English Novel." KR, XXIX:2 (March), 167-94. See A6322.

R671 Allen, Walter. "Greene Thoughts in a Greene Shade." NYTBR, (30 April), p. 5. Maintains that the "sense of the author at play" dominates May We Borrow Your Husband?--a collection of stories that vary in merit from the "macabre jokes" of "The Overnight Lag" and others to the "chilling parable on the theme of human vanity and mortality" in "Beauty." Finds further evidence in "Cheap in August" of the new phase in Greene's development which combines pity with sympathy or charity.

R672 Burgess, Anthony. "More Comedians." Spectator, CCXVIII: 7243 (21 April), p. 454. Admires the craftsmanship and "ruminate(s) the somehow appalled humour and sweet-sour compassion" of May We Borrow Your Husband?--"autumnal pieces" whose backgrounds stand to close examination, and whose literary allusions "imply rich dimensions behind the small surface plot."

R673 Butcher, Maryvonne. "Chamber Music." Tablet, CCXXI (29 April), p. 469. Finds the stories in the collection May We Borrow Your Husband? of unequal merit; but credits Greene with the ability to capture, with "fiendish accuracy," the different tones of voice in the story that gives its title to the collection, and to write a "most moving" and accomplished story in "Cheap in August."

R674 Casson, Allan. "Greene's Comedians and Amis' Anti-Death League." MR, VIII (Spring), pp. 392-96. Remarks on the "mechanical unreality" of Magiot, the "uncompromising ambiguity" and the "subtle motions in the mind of Brown, the only surviving comedian." Also notices the "anti-American bias" of The Comedians and its "tendentiousness."

R675 Coffey, Warren. "May We Borrow Your Husband?" Commonweal, XXIV (25 Aug.), pp. 527-28. Maintains that in this collection Greene has "written his way back to comic North Temperate Zone" away from the heat and intensity of the "theological thriller." Finds the collection consisting of three stories he calls "skip," four "fell," and the remaining five "shrewd and funny."

R676 Cook, Roderick. "May We Borrow Your Husband?" Harper's, CCXXXIV (May), pp. 119-20. A short review that finds the collection "first-rate entertainment" balanced by funny pieces.

R677 Corke, Hillary. "New Fiction." Listener, LXXVII (27 April), p. 565. May We Borrow Your Husband? is the second of four books reviewed. A "pretty round condemnation" of Greene generally and of the collection in particular which is not even an entertainment for it induces a "feeling of nausea when one shuts the book."

R678 Davenport, Guy. "And a Cool Drink by the Hammock." NR, XIX (25 July), pp. 811-12. May We Borrow Your Husband? is the second book reviewed. Regards the collection as comedy arising from the "claims of nature on convention," and written in as "frolicsome and bemused an attitude as the best English comedy can strike," but above all, with a "wide and very human grin."

R679 Dempsey, Michael. "As Mr. Greene Gets Older." ILN, (22 April), p. 30. In these "Comedies of the Sexual Life" Greene is "flexing his literary muscles, assured of his powers, complete, accurate, expert," and seems to be concerned with the "mechanics of storytelling, with form."

R6710 G[rady], R. F. "May We Borrow Your Husband?" Best Sellers, XXVII (1 May), p. 52. In spite of being subtitled "sexual comedies," there is nothing "blatant" about them. Singles out "Cheap in August" as a memorable story, "rueful, compassionate" and done with "exquisite taste."

R6711 Gardner, John. "An Invective Against Mere Fiction." SoR, III:2 (April), pp. 454-59. Includes on pp. 457-58 a review of The Comedians as a "fine novel, especially for reading on a train," one that makes a "casual pass at art." The truth behind it "rides easy" because it is "comfortable and familiar" and is expressed in a popular form and manner.

R6712 Grosvenor, Peter. "Graham Greene Observing: The Funnier Side of Sex." DaiE, (6 April), p. 12. Though Greene's ironic edge is still "pretty sharp" in comedies of May We Borrow Your Husband? there is a new kind of "mellowness and tolerance" in these stories which are often concerned with loneliness and the striving for friendship.

R6713 Gzowski, Peter. "When a Book Is Bad Today, It's Horrid." Maclean's, LXXX (July), p. 67. Includes a short review of May We Borrow Your Husband? as a collection of stories that are "just plain good writing--sure, calm and wise."

R6714 Hamilton, Alex. "May We Borrow Your Husband?" B & B, XII:10 (July), p. 49. Does not find much merit in this collection which cannot be saved from being a "let down" by its "valetudinarian tone," its "casual snickering worldly wisdom" or mastery of technique.

R6715 Hamilton, Ian. "Recent Fiction: Fallen Among Stylish Louts." DaiT, (6 April), p. 23. A short review of May We Borrow Your Husband? noticing that "seediness in the product of reflection rather than injection," and that the shortest and lightest of these 12 stories "spoil one for cruder hashes."

R6716 Hern, Anthony. "The Honeymoon Couple...." EvS, (11 April), p. 11. A brief but warm review of the collection of short stories May We Borrow Your Husband?--"almost all of them as successful" as the title story--which shows Greene at his best, "magnetic," with spoiled adults.

R6717 Holicky, Bernard H. "May We Borrow Your Husband?" LJ, XCII (1 April), p. 1509. A short review focussing on the title story and which describes the remaining eleven as "humorously and compassionately told ... free from right-wrong dualism."

R6718 Junker, Howard. "Greene's Grotesqueries." Newsweek, LXIX (8 May), p. 107. Considers most of the stories in May We Borrow Your Husband? to be "tiny, tart grotesqueries" and a long way from the splendid passion and the anguish it entailed in his earlier works.

R6719 King, Francis. "Wrenched from Obscurity." SunTel, (9 April), p. 9. Tends to regard the stories in May We Borrow Your Husband? as fragments or summaries of unwritten novels and considers the title one to be the best because of its "psychological complexity lacking in the rest of the book," even though Greene adapts the Jamesian device of the narrator whose powers of perception are heightened by what goes around him. The predictability of Greene's reactions narrows down what would have been a wide range.

R6720 Kunkel, Francis L. "May We Borrow Your Husband?" America, CXVI (20 May), p. 761. Focusses on Greene's anti-Americanism--the "old shade of Greene"--in "Cheap in August," and finds the "new shade" lighter with the sense of fun, especially in those where sex figures prominently; but the "unfamiliar addition" in this "cruel comedy borrowed from Black Humor" lies in the "intrusion of the absurd."

R6721 Ostermann, Robert. "In New Greene Collection, There's Ample Proof of the Master's Touch." NObs, VI (15 May), p. 21. A review of May We Borrow Your Husband? emphasizing Greene's "oblique" approach to his art and noting the "Greene dialog" and imagery in the collection.

R6722 Petersen, Clarence. "The Power and the Glory." BTod, IV (5 Feb.), p. 11. Brief notice of a paperback edition.

R6723 Poore, Charles. "Books of The Times: Gamey Tales Told Out of Season." NYT, (26 April), p. 45. Regards May We Borrow Your Husband? as a collection of "acrid love stories" that show Greene's determination to write even when he hasn't much inspiration.

R6724 Price, R. G. G. "New Fiction." Punch, CCLII (12 April), p. 544. May We Borrow Your Husband? is the first of four books reviewed. Finds the collection more than "just very amusing or agreeably sentimental" for it shows the "genial side" of Greene, how funny he can be, when his attitude is that of "charitable attention and, ultimately, rueful justice."

R6725 Pryce-Jones, David. "Workshop Chips." SunT, (9 April), p. 53. Though they are "small, uneven chips from his workshop," the stories in May We Borrow Your Husband? still convey the care and skill of his art. In these comedies, one is uncertain whether to love or to pity the players.

R6726 Raven, Simon. "No Laughing Matter." Observer, (9 April), p. 26. Argues that though May We Borrow Your Husband? may have "verbal wit in plenty," "exquisite satire," "straight laughs and even occasional slapstick," the final impression it leaves is one "far from comic," because comedy is what happens to people who are ignorant of the issues involved and Greene's people are too well aware of issues. Chooses "Cheap in August" to show the "elegiac," the pitiful on a "friendly, very human level."

R6727 Rück, Heribert. "Graham Greene: Die Stunde der Komödianten." NDH, XIV, pp. 170-73. A review of the German translation of The Comedians. Maintains that Greene belongs to the "alten Garde" of Chesterton, Waugh and Belloc and that he remains a "Diagnostiker" in spite of the changes in literary trends. Attaches great importance to what has not been said in the novel.

R6728 Samstag, Nicholas. "Cupid's Blasé Blush." SatR, L (5 Aug.), p. 36. A review of May We Borrow Your Husband? that considers the stories comedies "only in the literary sense"; Greene "seems intent on taking all the fun out of sexual wrong-doing."

R6729 Scott, Paul. "New Fiction." Times, (6 April), p. 9. May We Borrow Your Husband? is the second of five books reviewed. Notes the absence of the "familiar trappings" but the "supreme skill in presentation, the immediate kindling of the vitalizing spark of reality" is always present.

R6730 Scott-Kilvert, Ian. "English Fiction: 1966." BBN, 322 (June), pp. 409-14. Indicates "the absence of radical innovations" in the novel even while it remains the "most convenient and flexible form" for the expression of ideas and experience. Brief reference to The Comedians as a novel that does not "rank" among Greene's two or three finest novels but which "demonstrated his usual masterly economy of presentation as well as his sharp awareness of the moral climate of the times."

R6731 Sullivan, Richard. "A Faint Disillusionment." BTod, IV (14 May), p. 6. A review of May We Borrow Your Husband? that notes the change "not altogether for the better," in Greene's attitude and cautions the reader that though the stories are called comedies, they do not have the "ribaldry, plain fun or the happy ending" one associates with it but an "irony, detachment and a faint bittersweet disillusionment."

R6732 Trevor, William. "Sex and Sensibility." GuardianW, XCVI (13 April), p. 11. May We Borrow Your Husband? is the first of two books reviewed. Considers the collection to be "as fine as anything Mr. Greene has written"; in his combination of the opposites of "economy" and a "degree of repetition," in the short story, he has shown himself to be as "crafty and versatile as ever." Its "steamy sex" is not shocking in itself.

R6733 Trodd, Kenith. "Voyeur." NSta, LXVII (7 April), p. 476. This review of May We Borrow Your Husband? welcomes Greene's change of taste from "damnation" to the "ironic chagrin" with which he looks at his characters. Focusses on Greene's narrator in the collection, the "literary voyeur with a mock-respectfully Jamesian pose" who produces a rather "piquant and sometimes pleasantly salacious" effect.

R6734 Williamson, Bruce. "Greene Land." IT, (8 April), p. 8. Whether one treats the short stories as a "by-product" of his works or a "warming up exercise" for his next novel, one is left with the impression that Greene can never be "less than compulsively readable" and entertaining in May We Borrow Your Husband?

R6735 Unsigned. "May We Borrow Your Husband?" Booklist, LXIII (1 April), p. 837. Brief pre-publication note pointing out that the stories focus on "the narrow line between absurdity and tragedy in personal relationships."

R6736 ________. "Scraps of Sex from Greene." DaiM, (6 April), p. 8. A short review of May We Borrow Your Husband? noting that the "bizarre fragments of prose and ultra-short stories" are given under a misleading label. Though comic, they still exude the now familiar "sour, knowing sadness" which one associates with Greene.

R6737 ________. "May We Borrow Your Husband?" Kirkus, XXXV (15 Feb.), p. 219. Pre-publication note, unenthusiastic and rather negative.

R6738 ________. "May We Borrow Your Husband?" PW, CXCI (13 Feb.), p. 75. Pre-publication notice calling the volume a "major disappointment" for the stories are too "slight and wispy" to linger in the memory.

R6739 ________. "Autumnal View." Time, LXXXIX (21 April), p. 92. May We Borrow Your Husband? may be "down-to-earth escapist fare" but must not be dismissed too lightly; the "bittersweet poignancy" that underlies the "artful and impeccable" style reveals a "mellow and compassionate, comedic yet concerned" Greene whose "chill and final reminders of mortality add pungency rather than detract from the pleasures" of this collection.

R6740 ________. "Awful When You Think of It." TLS, 3399 (20 April), p. 325. May We Borrow Your Husband? is the first of three works reviewed. Maintains that Greene is emulating James in this collection. The refusal of the middle-aged writer-narrator to judge and interfere--he has taken "a holiday from moral judgment"--gives the collection its "strange gaiety, its lopsided grin," and the subtitle, "comedies of the sexual life" emphasizes how untypical events "tend to have a comic relationship with real life."

D671 Coroneou, Marianthi. Suffering as Part of the Human Condition in the Fiction of Graham Greene, A. Camus and Nikos Kazantzakis. Univ. of Kentucky. D. A. I., XXX:7 (1970), 3454-A.

D672 Currie, John Sheldon. Supernaturalism in Graham Greene: A Comparison of Orthodox Catholicism with the Religious Vision in the Major Novels. Univ. of Alabama. D. A., XXVIII (1968), 3176A-77A.

D673 Lynes, Charles M. The Whiskey Priest, an Atypical Martyr: An Examination of the Whiskey Priest of 'The Power and the Glory' as a Reworking of the Standard Martyr Story. M. A. Fresno State College.

D674 Meyers, Jeffrey. The Hero in British Colonial Fiction. Univ. of California, Berkeley. D. A., XXVIII:7, 2690-A. Published as Fiction and the Colonial Experience. Totowa, N. J.: Rowman & Littlefield, 1973. See B7313.

D675 Mills, Joseph L. Plutchik's Emotive Theory as Applied to Eschatology Elements in Key Works of Graham Greene. M. A. Morehead State Univ.

D676 Omibiyi, A. A. The Treatment of Pain and Death in Five Novels of Graham Greene: 'The Man Within,' 'It's a Battlefield,' 'Brighton Rock,' 'The Power and the Glory,' 'The Heart of the Matter.' M. Phil. Birbeck College, Univ. of London.

D677 Phillips, Kenneth Allan. A Study of the Catholic Attitudes in the Novels of Graham Greene and Evelyn Waugh. M. A. Univ. of New Brunswick.

1968

B681 De Vitis, A. A. "Religious Aspects in the Novels of Graham Greene." The Shapeless God: Essays on Modern Fiction. Ed. Harry J. Mooney, Jr., and Thomas F. Staley. Pittsburgh: Univ. of Pittsburgh Press, pp. 41-67. Contends that Greene's novels from The Man Within onwards indicate "an ever-widening circle of interests and beliefs" away from "dogmatic Roman Catholicism toward a wider-ranging humanism." However, Brighton Rock, The Power and the Glory, The Heart of the Matter and The End of the Affair which are examined at some length, describe a "single pattern, a movement, from definition and qualification of a religious conviction to a thumping avowal of the reality of goodness in the real world." Also maintains that The Quiet American is in reality a "further illustration" of the fascination of power and its destructive potential which had interested Greene in The Heart of the Matter. The section on The Comedians as a black comedy which begins with p. 57 is a revised version of his article in Renascence. See A585.

B682 Fredericksen, Emil. "Graham Greene." Fremmede Digtere i det 20. arhundrede. Bind III. Ed. Sven Moller Kristensen. Kobenhavn: G. E. C. Gads Forlag, pp. 199-215. An evaluative survey of Greene's life and works. Points out the great variety of Greene's works after 1951 and his potential for surprising his readers. Also notes the centrality of failure, the cost of success, pursuit, and good and evil in the novels. Tends to read autobiographical elements in the novels.

B683 Fricker, Robert. "Graham Greene." Christliche Dichter im 20. Jahrhundert: Beitrage zur europaischen Literatur. Ed. Otto Mann. Bern and Munchen: Francke Verlag, pp. 253-66. A survey of the major novels that emphasizes the Christian element in them. Shows how Brighton Rock marks the turning point from the early novels to the religious themes of The Power and the Glory, The Heart of the Matter and The End of the Affair and that though there is an increasing secularization in later novels, the Christian pattern can still be traced. Argues that the characters' self-analysis, their guilt and the "zentrifugale und zentripetale" forces they contend with give rise to Greene's dramatic dialectic which reaches beyond the "confessional" to probe the essence of humanity in our time.

B684 Hall, James [Wilford]. "Efficient Saints and Civilians: Graham Greene." The Lunatic Giant in the Drawing Room: The British and American Novel Since 1930. Bloomington: Indiana Univ. Press, pp. 111-23. Discusses the "old opposites" of "bourgeois effectiveness and saintly heroism" which "coalesce" in Greene as he moves "to symbolize" these newer standards of conduct in Brighton Rock, The Power and the Glory, The Heart of the Matter and The Quiet American by elevating the "puritan drive left after all creating anew of the conscience of the race," and relating it to "twentieth-century self-kicking, self-pity, and humaneness."

B685 Maurois, André. "Grahan Greene." Points of View: From Kipling to Graham Greene. Foreword Walter Allen. New York: Ungar; London: Frederick Muller, 1969, pp. 383-409. This is an enlarged edition of Prophets and Poets. New York: Harper, 1935; London: Cassell, 1936, a translation from the French of Magiciens et logiciens. Paris:

B. Grasset, 1935, with additional chs. 10 & 11 on V. Woolf and G. Greene. Considers Greene as a "sensual" but "metaphysical" novelist who has restored to the English novel the religious sense and to human actions their significance by making the "concept of redemptive love" central to his novels. Finds The Heart of the Matter a "magnificent" novel where the "metaphysical character of the 'problem'" saves the novel from "over-naturalistic realism," and finds the "metaphysical depth of a Catholic novel" in The Power and the Glory. Also notes Greene's technical skill and the "objections" of non-religious readers to the constant recurrence of the religious theme.

B686 Orwell, George. "122. Review. The Heart of the Matter by Graham Greene." The Collected Essays, Journalism and Letters of George Orwell. Vol. IV. In Front of Your Nose: 1945-1950. Ed. Sonia Orwell and Ian Angus. London: Secker and Warburg; New York: Harcourt, pp. 439-43. Rpt. in Graham Greene: A Collection of Critical Essays. Ed. Samuel Hynes. Englewood Cliffs, N. J.: Prentice-Hall, 1973, pp. 105-10. Rpt. from NY, XXIV (17 July 1948), pp. 66, 69-71. See R4823.

B687 Salem, James M. A Guide to Critical Reviews. Part III. British and Continental Drama from Ibsen to Pinter. Metuchen, N. J.: Scarecrow Press. Pages 113-15 list three of Greene's plays in alphabetical order. Entries indicate date of opening, the number of performances in Broadway as well as performances off Broadway, if any. Reviews listed are restricted to American periodicals.

B688 Scott, Nathan A., Jr. "Graham Greene: Christian Tragedian." Craters of the Spirit: Studies in the Modern Novel. Washington, D. C.: Corpus Books; London & Sydney: Sheed and Ward, 1969, pp. 201-33. Rev. & rpt. from VolR, I:1 (Spring 1954), pp. 29-42. (See A5415).

A681 Burstall, Christopher. "Graham Greene Takes the Orient Express." Listener, LXXX (21 Nov.), pp. 672-74, 676-77. A transcript of Greene's conversation which formed the basis of the "omnibus" BBC production of "The Hunted Man." Covers a wider range of topics than has been reported so far in interviews, and shows Greene speaking rather freely about his experiences, his novels and his beliefs.

A682 Duran Justo, Leopoldo. "La última gran novela católica de Graham Greene." FMod, 29-30, pp. 167-78. A lengthy analysis of The Comedians that stresses its "catholic" elements and discusses character, especially Brown, as a vehicle that embodies the central idea of the novel.

A683 Filyushkina, S. "Roman Grema Grina 'Chelovck vnutri.'"

Perm, CLXXXVIII, pp. 3-18. In Russian. A study of The Man Within showing Greene's concern for the inner world and the conflict between good and evil rather than the social aspects of existence.

A684 French, Philip. "Screen Greene." LM, VIII (April), pp. 54-57. Surveys briefly Greene's involvement with the cinema and reviews the film version of The Comedians adapted by Greene and directed by Peter Glenville.

A685 Gallagher, Michael P. "Human Values in Modern Literature." Studies, LVII:226 (Summer), pp. 142-53. Argues that the literature of today runs counter to the conscious progressive and humanist ideals of our time, and that Christian writers, brought up in the "over-all myth ... that life is irretrievably afflicted and bitter," fail to provide a new dimension and display an "excessive distrust and even disdain for what is human." G. Greene is one writer, among others, who expresses this "anti-human tendency" and conveys "a message of human inadequacy." Brief reference to The Heart of the Matter.

A686 Greacen, Robert. "Social Class in Post-War English Fiction." SoR, IV (Winter), pp. 142-51. A survey suggesting that English novelists tend to be wary of taking sides, dislike political parties and prefer to remain artists to reflect society rather than change it. Refers briefly to the "almost classless milieu of delinquency and semi-delinquency" that Greene portrays in Brighton Rock.

A687 Harris, Wendell V. "Molly's 'Yes': The Transvaluation of Sex in Modern Fiction." TSLL, X, 107-18. Traces the "evolution from the insistence that sexual satisfaction is important for happiness to the use of the sexual act as a symbol of fulfillment, and thence to the confusion of this symbolic representation with complete fulfillment of the human personality" in key works by English novelists of the twentieth century. Shows how Greene in The End of the Affair has refused to honor "the usual twentieth century absolute value" of the sexual experience, and has found a "viable alternative" by affirming values beyond those experienced in this life.

A688 King, Bruce. "Graham Greene's Inferno." EA, XXI:1, 35-51. A scholarly article pointing out the parallelism that exists between Dante's Inferno and The Heart of the Matter in both structure and character. Maintains that just as Joyce and Eliot resorted to myth, to some vision of a past order, to set against the disorder of present reality, Greene resorted to imitation, to Dante's Inferno, to "raise the theology of his novel beyond the paradoxical" and give it "a formal structure, a satiric perspective and a destiny lacking in most of his other novels."

A689 Manuel Torres, M. "El socio y Our Man in Havana, novelas paralelas." Mapocho, 17, pp. 61-67. Points out the parallelism between the two novels even though there is little likelihood that Greene has been aware of the Chilean Jenaro Prieto's novel.

A6810 Michener, Richard L. "Apocalyptic Mexico: The Plumed Serpent and The Power and the Glory." UKCR, XXXIV (June), pp. 313-16. Examines the "similar sympathies and criticism" both writers express in their respective novels against a "mechanistic materialism" deadening the soul of modern man and imposed by socialist economics, and the need for a "spiritual influence" to achieve stability and contentment. However, the different bases which both writers conceive for religious conviction lead them to "ultimately antagonistic resolutions."

A6811 Sonnenfeld, Albert. "The Catholic Novelist and the Supernatural." FS, XXII (Oct.), pp. 307-19. Examines Mauriac, Bernanos and Greene to determine the narrative devices resulting from their "adumbration of the supernatural" to give metaphysical dimension to their novels. Shows the devices of "purposeful incompleteness" and the creation of the "double as a substitute for necessarily inadequate fictional psychology" in The Heart of the Matter, and the change in narrative point of view and the reversals of plot resulting from "the answered prayer" as well as the "efficacy of sacrament" in The End of the Affair.

A6812 Sternlight, Sanford. "The Sad Comedies: Graham Greene's Later Novels." FQ, I:4 (Oct.), pp. 65-77. Asserts that Greene's later writing beginning with The End of the Affair through The Quiet American, Our Man in Havana, A Burnt-Out Case and climaxing with The Comedians expounds the "comic nature of existence"; but it is not ultimately "a literature of despair," for not only is there hope in an afterlife but also hope in the possibility of "living in dignity" in this world because the man who accepts and believes in a system regardless of what it is, can never be reduced "to the absurd state and the loss of human dignity," the isolation, into which one who does not believe, can fall. Emphasizes the "godless" or Sartrian aspect of existentialist characters in the novels.

A6813 Waugh, Auberon. "Profile: Graham Greene." DaiMir, (22 May), p. 18. Though the profile, based on an interview, refers to his being "a man of the Left," it emphasizes his "wanderlust," his openness of mind, his dislike for the "brutalising affluence of America," his concern for the human spirit and his compassion.

R681 Lauras, Antoine. "Notes Bibliographiques, II." Etudes, CCCXXIX (Aug.-Sept.), 302. Includes a brief review of the French translation of May We Borrow Your Husband? Finds the collection a "deception" which, in spite of Greene's ability for narration, leaves an "imprêssion de vide," rather disconcerting because the themes of the stories are "bien mincês."

R682 Sullivan, Dan. "The Theater: Graham Greene's Carving a Statue." NYT, (1 May), p. 43. A review of the play and its performance at the Gramercy Arts Theatre, New York. The play has "too many symbols, too much unmotivated theological conversation and, above all, too much explication."

D681 Flake, Elaine M. Graham Greene's Obsession with the Lost Childhood Theme in His Novels, Short Stories and Essays. M.A. Brigham Young Univ.

D882 Gunn, D. W. The American and British Author in Mexico, 1911-41. Univ. of North Carolina. Rev. & published as American and British Writers in Mexico, 1556-1973. Austin: Univ. of Texas Press, 1974. See B741.

D683 Gusdorf, Barbara Neuroth. Concepts of Sainthood in the Novels of Albert Camus and Graham Greene. Michigan State Univ. D.A., XXIX, 1895A-96A.

D684 Longree, Georgia A. The Concepts of Belief and Non-Belief in the Writings of Graham Greene. M.A. Texas Christian Univ.

D685 Mensah, A. N. The Treatment of Private Codes of Conduct and Religious Themes in the Novels of Graham Greene. M.Phil. Univ. of Leeds.

D686 Muller, C. H. The Novels of Graham Greene: A Critical Study, with Particular Reference to the Religious Themes. M.A. Univ. of Wales (Aberyswyth).

D687 Roy, John Francis. A Study of Graham Greene's Recent Works. M.A. Univ. of Saskatchewan.

D688 Sabine, Francisco John. Graham Greene's Heroes: Regeneration Through Experience. M.A. Univ. of British Columbia.

D689 Whidden, Sr. Mary B. The Prophetic Artistry of Graham Greene. M.A. Univ. of New Hampshire.

D6810 Wight, Marjorie. An Analysis of Selected British Novelists Between 1845 and 1966 and Their Critics. Univ. of Southern California. D.A., XXVIII:11, 4651-52A.

1969

B691 Braybrooke, Neville. "Graham Greene and the Double Man: An Approach to The End of the Affair." Graham Greene. The Christian Critics Series. Ed. Harry J. Cargas. St. Louis, Mo.: B. Herder Book Co., pp. 114-30. Rpt. from DubR, CCXXVI:455 (1952), 61-73. See A527.

B692 Bryden, Ronald. "Graham Greene, Alas." The Unfinished Hero and Other Essays. London: Faber & Faber, pp. 210-15. Rpt. from Spectator, CCIX:7005 (28 Sept. 1962), pp. 441-42. See A622.

B693 Burgess, Anthony. "The Politics of Graham Greene." The Best of 'Speaking of Books' from 'The New York Times Book Review.' Ed. with Intro. Francis Brown. New York: Holt, Rinehart and Winston, pp. 284-91. See A671.

B694 Cargas, Harry J., ed. Graham Greene. The Christian Critic Series. St. Louis, Mo.: B. Herder Book Co. A collection of nine essays by C. D. Scott, C. Poole, R. W. B. Lewis, D. P. Consolo, M. E. Jefferson, K. Patten, N. Braybrooke, R. E. Hughes and A. Mayhew, reprinted from periodicals--with the exception of C. D. Scott's which was "done exclusively" for the book. The Editor points out in his one-page Introduction that the articles were selected because they express "mature views," and are "worthwhile pieces" to circulate for they treat "Greene's fiction as fiction" and do not focus on side issues. See individual entries.

B695 Consolo, Dominick P. "Music as Motif: The Unity of Brighton Rock." Graham Greene. The Christian Critics Series. Ed. Harry J. Cargas. St. Louis, Mo.: B. Herder Book Co., pp. 75-88. Rpt. from Renascence, XV (Fall 1962), 12-20. See A624.

B696 Hoskins, Katharine Bail. Today the Struggle: Literature and Politics in England During the Spanish Civil War. Austin and London: Univ. of Texas Press. Pages 36-40 of Ch. 2 describe Greene's attitude to the Spanish War as that of a "social and political radical" Catholic whose sympathies were so divided that he made no direct statement about the War, and, consistent with his Catholicism, believed in the "fallibility of men and the futility of their aspirations toward an ideal society." Examines briefly the "marxist dream" as expressed in The Power and the Glory and Greene's indirect expression of his feelings for the war in The Confidential Agent--not a "political novel."

B697 Hughes, R. E. "The Quiet American: The Case Reopened."

Graham Greene. The Christian Critics Series. Ed. Harry J. Cargas. St. Louis, Mo.: B. Herder Book Co., pp. 130-33. Rpt. from Renascence, XII (Autumn 1959), 41-42, 49. See A598.

B698 Jefferson, Mary Evelyn. "The Heart of the Matter: The Responsible Man." Graham Greene. The Christian Critics Series. Ed. Harry J. Cargas. St. Louis, Mo.: B. Herder Book Co., pp. 88-101. Rpt. from CQ, IX (Summer 1957), 23-31. See A5713.

B699 Lewis, R. W. B. "The 'Trilogy' of Graham Greene." Graham Greene. The Christian Critics Series. Ed. Harry J. Cargas. St. Louis, Mo.: B. Herder Book Co., pp. 45-75. Rpt. from MFS, III (Autumn 1957), 195-215. See A5715.

B6910 Mayhew, Alice. "The Comedians." Graham Greene. The Christian Critics Series. Ed. Harry J. Cargas. St. Louis, Mo.: B. Herder Book Co., pp. 134-41. Rpt. from NCR (30 March 1966), p. 9. See A6613.

B6911 Patten, Karl. "The Structure of The Power and the Glory." Graham Greene. The Christian Critics Series. Ed. Harry J. Cargas. St. Louis, Mo.: B. Herder Book Co., pp. 101-14. Rpt. from MFS, III (Autumn 1957), pp. 225-34. See A5724.

A6912 Poole, Roger C. "Graham Greene's Indirection." Graham Greene. The Christian Critics Series. Ed. Harry J. Cargas. St. Louis, Mo.: B. Herder Book Co., pp. 29-45. Rpt. from Blackfriars, XLV:528 (June 1964), pp. 257-68. See A6416.

B6913 Price, Alan. Brighton Rock. Graham Greene. Notes on English Literature. Oxford: Basil Blackwell. Designed primarily for High School students and undergraduates, the "Notes" provide under "The Comprehensiveness of Brighton Rock" relevant information on Greene's ability to combine the topical and the universal and, through the first section of Part Four of the novel, illustrate Greene's awareness of the social, mental and spiritual forces that permeate Brighton Rock. The section entitled "The Crime-Thriller and Graham Greene" explains what is meant by the crime thriller and why Greene uses it. This is followed by three sections on "Structure and Narrative," "Character and Setting," and "Style, Involvement and Achievement" in the novel. Each of the five sections is followed by a few questions on the text.

B6914 Reinhardt, Kurt F. "Graham Greene: Victory in Failure." The Theological Novel of Modern Europe: An Analysis of Masterpieces by Eight Authors. New York: Frederick

Ungar Publishing Co., pp. 170-203. Examines Greene's realization of the immensity of evil within man and his world in the three "theological" novels whose protagonists are "exceptional individuals in catastrophic limit-situations." Analyzes each novel separately: The Power and the Glory to reveal the theme of the "huge abandonment" which provides the tragic suspense in the priest being hunted by the police and his own consciousness of guilt; the "sophisticated" The Heart of the Matter to expose the "theological, ontological and psychological differences among pity, compassion and love," and The End of the Affair to show the pursuit on the human and super-human levels, as well as the dialectical ambivalence of hate and love.

B6915 Scott, Carolyn D. "The Urban Romance: A Study of Graham Greene's Thrillers." Graham Greene. The Christian Critics Series. Ed. Harry J. Cargas. St. Louis, Mo.: B. Herder Book Co., pp. 1-29. Discusses the difference between Greene's "entertainments" and "novels" by trying to determine the meaning of the former term as Greene uses it, the relationship of the entertainments to the mystery story genre, and in what way Greene's thriller form carries a serious intent.

A691 Allen, Walter. "Recent Trends in the English Novel." English, XVIII:100 (Spring), pp. 2-5. Expresses surprise at the achievement of the novel over the past 25 years in spite of the age being "unpropitious to the novelist's art"--the novel has had to yield ground to newspapers, periodicals, radio and T. V.--and the failure of the post-war novel "to produce a paradigm of man's life in society." Pays tribute to Greene for his success in these circumstances which is due to his "narrative power, the brilliance of his observations, the depth of his pity," and especially his ability to "encompass in his own mind and beliefs so many of the stresses and antagonizing of the contemporary world."

A692 Bergonzi, Bernard. "Greeneland Revisited." NSoc, (20 Nov.), pp. 824-25. A review article on Travels With My Aunt maintaining that the emphasis on "Catholic" topics in his earlier novels represented only one phase of Greene's development and that the present shift to the historical and political simply reveals the same "weary familiarity with corruption" without the "spiritual drama." Regards the last novel as an "embarrassment," a "farce" that "constantly dwindles into facetiousness" with the "self-imitation that ... suggests a failure of real imagination." Suggests that the "abandonment or resolution" of his earlier obsessions, coupled with "tiredness and boredom" may have "sharply diminished (Greene's) raison d'être as a writer."

A693 Braybrooke, Neville. "Graham Greene and the Double Man:

An Approach to The End of the Affair." TCMel, XXIII, pp. 293-304. See A527.

A694 Cameron, J. M. "The Catholic Novelist and European Culture." TCS, 1 (March), pp. 79-94. Examines Catholic thought as it shows itself in the novels of Bernanos, Mauriac, E. Waugh and Greene. Compared to E. Waugh, Greene is a "pre-eminently European writer" whose range of theological problems resembles Bernanos' and Mauriac's, and whose readability is founded upon his command of the cinematic technique. His theological themes belong to his "middle period." Discusses Greene's "vulgarization of text-book theology for dramatic purposes" in Brighton Rock and briefly in The Heart of the Matter.

A695 Cargas, Harry J. "Graham Greene: 100 Articles Through 1965: An Annotated Checklist." CLW, XL:8 (April), pp. 488-90; XL:9 (May-June), pp. 566-69. According to the author, "the basis of selection has been maturity of the critic's view in assessing Greene's writings." The annotations attempt to give the substance or central thesis of the article. Alphabetically arranged--Part I runs from 'A' to 'Min'--and is confined to articles in English in periodicals of the U.K. and U.S.A. Excludes "pietistic" articles in the popular Catholic press.

A696 Celeste, Sister Marie, SC. "Bernanos and Graham Greene on the Role of the Priest in The Diary of a Country Priest and The Power and the Glory." Culture, XXX (Dec.), pp. 287-98. Examines the two authors' interest in, and revelation of, the psychological complexities in the life of the two priests whose apostolates, similarly characterized by physical and moral suffering, lead them to discover solutions to their problems and awaken in the reader "a consciousness of the supernatural."

A697 Desmond, John F. "Graham Greene and the Eternal Dimension." ABR, XX (Sept.), pp. 418-26. Discusses the "religious dimension" wherein the significance of a human action is "valued first of all in itself," against an objective and absolute norm, the "immutable 'now'" from which human actions derive value, and not valued "in relation to the self or something outside it only as it exists within time and circumstance." It is Greene's consciousness of this distinction that separates him radically from modern subjectivist British novelists. Illustrates from "The Basement Room," The Heart of the Matter and The End of the Affair.

A698 Dneprov, V. "Vera i bezverie." Zvezda, 4, pp. 202 & 210; 5, pp. 204-15. In Russian. Part one focusses on the various stages of faith and unbelief in A Burnt-Out Case. Part two examines the breakdown of belief and the destruction of values in the post World War II generation and focusses on The Comedians with the suggestion that the communism of the revolutionary Dr. Magiot may provide a resolution for the contemporary spiritual problems.

A699 Filyushkina, S. A. "Iskusstvo Grina-romanista." VMU, 4, pp. 18-29. In Russian. An analysis of Greene's art as a novelist. Remarks on his fame as a novelist outside England, and pays tribute to his psychological insight, his portrayal of the tragedy of humans in a disordered universe, his unrivalled mastery of the word and his style.

A6910 Grob, Alan. "The Power and the Glory: Graham Greene's Argument from Design." Criticism, XI (Winter), pp. 1-30. Argues that the novel is a "spiritual romance" without any "significant reduction" of the "deeply entrenched ironies of texture and structure" which are generally subversive to patterns of romance. Describes the irony fostered by the presupposition of abandonment by God and by the conduct and fate of the Whiskey Priest, and how Greene offsets the novel's "counter current of random mischance" by the parallel he develops between the life of the priest and that of Christ. Focuses on the "real" as distinct from the figurative sainthood of the priest, and shows how Greene's usage of the dream extends the "purely naturalistic limits" of the novel to discover the message of "providential care," evidence of whose existence lies in the efficacy of the answered prayer--another device Greene uses as a "structural axis" to reveal the hidden presence of God; hence, the "implied salvation" of Brigida, Calver and the lieutenant, which can also be attributed to Greene's belief in universal salvation and the complementary relationship of infinite love. These personal views and conflicts, however, are subdued in The Power and the Glory and "subordinate" to Greene's "massive yet intricate system of design."

A6911 Jones, Grahame C. "Graham Greene and the Legend of Péguy." CL, XXL:2 (Spring), pp. 138-45. Investigates the "rather curious case of literary influence" of Péguy's "actual personality rather than his writings" on the novels of Greene. Maintains that Greene had "forged" for himself a heroic legend of a "Promethean figure" defending the damned against God, and that this manifests itself in his preoccupation with self-damnation in the face of Divine retribution in Brighton Rock, The Ministry of Fear and The Heart of the Matter.

A6912 King, James. "In the Lost Boyhood of Judas: Graham Greene's Early Novels of Hell." DR, XLIX (Summer), pp. 228-36. Though it may lack "the repetitive and overwhelming implications of Brighton Rock," A Gun for Sale is nevertheless a "dress rehearsal" for the later novel.

Examines the "remarkable look-alike" criminals of these two "novels of apprenticeship" and shows how "strikingly modern" the two novels are in their "insistence on the fragmentation and chaos of modern life and their ability to mirror effectively such a vision in the ironic derangement of the sacred."

A6913 Knipp, Thomas R. "Gide and Greene: Africa and the Literary Imagination." Serif, VI (June), pp. 3-14. A comparison of the two writers' works reveals that, as part of the Conradian tradition, they regard Africa as "an objective correlative" which, if explored and discovered would discover self for them. Maintains that Journey Without Maps, the "more artful book," develops into an "imaginative ordering" of a deep and significant experience, and that it is "carefully structured" as a pyramid at whose apex Greene "encounters aspects of the primitive--of the noncerebral" which the West seems to have lost, and in which he finds values and virtues.

A6914 Laquaniti, Guiseppa. "Temi e forme nei romanzi esotici si Graham Greene." Annali Della Facolta Di Magistero Dell Universita Di Bari, VIII, 155-71. Unavailable for examination.

A6915 Perrott, Roy. "Graham Greene: A Brief Encounter." Observer, (16 Nov.), p. 25. An account of a day spent with Greene in Paris on the occasion of the publication of his 19th novel, Travels With My Aunt. Greene makes the, by now, familiar remarks on boredom which, he says, is at the bottom of his "rootlessness." Of interest is his admission that the 1938 trip to Mexico brought about "a big change" for he became "emotionally involved" in Catholicism and, "of course, that changes one's own writing, one's whole life."

A6916 Phillips, Gene D. "Graham Greene: On the Screen. An Interview." CW, CCIX (Aug.), pp. 218-21. Rpt. with minor changes in Month, CCXXIX (June 1970), pp. 362-77; in TCLon, XXV, (Summer 1970), pp. 111-17, and in Graham Greene: A Collection of Critical Essays. Ed. Samuel Hynes. Englewood Cliffs, N.J.: Prentice-Hall, 1973, pp. 168-76. The interview focusses on Greene's interest in the screen, and in a secondary way, in writing fiction. Greene admits that his narrative style was influenced by his going to the cinema, and discusses his script writing and the adaptations of his novels generally for the screen.

A6917 Poole, Roger. "'Those Sad Arguments': Two Novels of Graham Greene." RMS, XIII, 148-60. Discusses The Quiet American and A Burnt-Out Case as two novels illustrating Cartesian or Systematic doubt and Pascalian or wagering doubt respectively. These doubters, whether Pascalian or Cartesian, inhabit a space which seems to them "meaningful or meaningless." Sometimes both forms of doubt are present in one person, i.e., when the Pascalian doubter accepts Cartesian skepticism at the "center of his committed doubt," e.g., Vigot and Dr. Colin.

A6917a Reynolds, Louise T. "Our Spies and Their Spies." New Renaissance, I (Winter), pp. 52-63. Makes brief reference to Greene's introduction to K. Philby's My Silent War and compares on p. 55 Greene's conception of the Secret Service as "a farce and a fantasy, capable of waste and treachery"--based on a reading of Our Man in Havana--to Hemingway's ironic viewpoint.

A6918 Sharrock, Roger. "Graham Greene: The Tragic Comedian." Tablet, CCIII (4 Jan.), p. 8. Expresses some disappointment at a recent BBC arts program interview with Greene, and discusses briefly his professionalism and "romantic feeling for the poetry of modern urban life." Maintains that the Catholicism of the novels and plays constitutes a "phase" in Greene's oeuvre and is not "the true centre"; that center is the "troubled humanism" to which he has returned in the late fifties and sixties, with a "greater compassion and a marvelously developed technique."

A6919 Solov'eva, N. M. "Gumanizm Grekhema Grina." Raduga, IV, pp. 153-61. In Russian. The "humanism" described is really an account of Greene's "concern" for communist ideals in his writings, especially in The Quiet American and Our Man in Havana. Very nearly co-opts Greene into the communist pantheon.

A6920 Thomas, D. P. "Mr. Tench and Secondary Allegory in The Power and the Glory." ELN, VII:2 (Dec.), pp. 129-33. Argues that the allegorical complexity of the novel extends beyond the Christian scheme and that a "secondary allegory" based on the legendary significance of the tench as a fish that is not prey to the pike which it heals, as in Isaac Walton's The Compleat Angler and T. H. White's The Once and Future King, is also plausible.

A6921 Trifu, Sever. "Graham Greene." Tribuna, 40 (Oct.), p. 8. In Romanian. A literary profile that notes Greene's interest in psychological analysis and a moral sense and values.

A6922 White, W. D. "The Power and the Glory. An Apology to the Church." UPR, XXI:I (Sept.), pp. 14-22. Contends that though the novel may be understood at once in both "religious" and "psychological" categories, Greene's focus is on the office of the priest as a "symbol of and a concrete expression of the Church"; for it is the priest who brings forcefully to our consciousness the "objectivity and given reality of the Church as the Body of Christ" and builds up the realization that the Church is lasting. Also discusses the "paradox of Grace" in the novel.

R691 Adalbert, Sr. Mary. "Collected Essays Including The Lost Child(hood)." RRel, XXVIII (Sept.), p. 841. A short review noting Greene's "thorough penetration" of the craftsmanship of James and Conrad, his "deep literary perspicuity" and his "encompassing character sketches."

R692 Adams, Phoebe. "Collected Essays." Atlantic, CCXXIII (June), p. 118. Briefly noted.

R693 Blakeston, Oswell. "Projecting Greene Rays." B&B, XIV:8 (May), pp. 14-15. A review of Collected Essays which considers the collection "... a treasure trove" bound to enrich and to provide "wonderful stimulation" to readers, not so much by Greene's pleasing "colourful snippets" as by the "serious 'new lights'" which Greene brings to bear upon a wide field of authors and topics.

R694 Brennan, Bernard P. "Collected Essays." LJ, XCIV (1 June), p. 2234. A short review noting that the criticism is "apt and perceptive" and that Greene's presence is strongly felt throughout.

R695 Brophy, Brigid. "Collected Essays." NYT, (25 May), p. 7. A perceptive review appreciative of the collection as an "exciting rarity" for it uses Greene's fictive method and "instruments"--"the relentless compassion, slicing out a character's inner life and the beautiful flat pulse of the prose"--on "real characters." Examines Greene's style and shows that Greene does not bring an "analytic intellect" to bear on his subject but a "working intelligence" without a "thought out esthetic" for Catholicism is the only "ready-made" intellectual structure beneath the essays.

R696 Casey, Kevin. "In the Greene Country." IT, (29 March), p. 8. Collected Essays are worth reading for the insight which they provide into Greene's own mind and methods. As a critic, Greene displays a wide knowledge of Restoration literature and a gift for discovering areas of value in little known or forgotten works. Most of the essays are of equal interest.

R697 ________. "Light and Shade." IT, (15 Nov.), p. 8. Travels with My Aunt shows the familiar preoccupations "filtered through a new ironic tolerance and a droll yet compassionate humour." Though the landscape may be recognizable, the change in point of view to a narrator who is an aging uninvolved observer, "amused yet sharply self-mocking," brings about variations of "light and shade," so that instead of the characteristic "paradox," we get a "sad humour," a pointed or pointless irony, but never without the "familiar, superbly-controlled hypnotic skill" to tell an anecdotal story without losing the reader's interest.

R698 D., R. "Catholic Reflections." TCLon, 1039-40, p. 92. Describes Collected Essays as a "catholic selection with Catholic overtones, though none the less liberal in approach," and a fruitful study of the "how and why of authorship."

R699 Dennis, Nigel. "Sign of the Greene Man." SunTel, (9 March), p. 13. This review of Collected Essays argues that Greene's obsessions are the "driving force" behind his storytelling for the "whole world of an author is what his temperament makes of it"; after all, Gagool, the witch in King Solomon's Mines, which Greene finds in every writer is a "matter of personal temperament and private need." Also impressed by the "vast amount" Greene has read and his "extraordinary intelligence."

R6910 ________. "Bank Managers, Take Heart!" SunTel, (16 Nov.), p. 10. Written "deftly and lightly ... nearly always funny," Travels with My Aunt is an "impious" but gay and happy novel that removes the fear that Greene was becoming too Calvinistic, too much preoccupied with sin. Greene seems to have fallen in love with his characters so that his "inbred scepticism" has rotted away.

R6911 Finn, James. "An Obsession with Failure." NRep, CLXI (5 July), pp. 30-31. Considers Collected Essays a "relatively cohesive and satisfying oeuvre" that is interesting for the biographical information it provides, for its "sharp aperçus on life and literature," especially when pressed into the service of a definitive judgment, and for its sympathetic and discriminating analyses of minor figures. Also notes that Greene, like "a good, persuasive critic ... leads us to discuss his work in his own terms."

R6912 Foot, Michael. "Graham Greene: My Debt to a Viper." EvS, (11 March), p. 14. A short review of Collected Essays that attributes Greene's zest for writing and his attitude toward the darker side of human nature to Marjorie Bowen.

R6913 Forbes-Boyd, Eric. "Of Fidel Castro, Henry James, and 'Two Bad Mice.'" ChrSM, LXI (13 June), p. 9. Considers Collected Essays "entertaining reading" in which Greene is more impressive and memorable as a critic than as a delineator of characters which are "engagingly and revealingly presented."

R6914 Forrest, Alan. "Greene Takes a Hippy Turn." DaiM, (21 Nov.), p. 12. With not a "single tortured Catholic" in sight in Travels with My Aunt, Greene takes a look at pot-smoking, illicit sex, in fact all "the sins of permissiveness as benignly as if he were a 22-year-old hippy intellectual doing the scene."

R6915 Furbank, P. N. "A Fine Joke." Times, (22 Nov.), p. v. Travels with My Aunt is "... A genial and Christmassy affair and as hypnotically readable as always," but which remains, nevertheless, an allegory about story telling. Finds Henry Pulling "the tiredest of stock figures" and Aunt Augusta's narratives the center of interest and entertainment.

R6916 Grosvenor, Peter. "Revelations of Grim Grin the Great." DaiE, (6 March), p. 15. A short review describing Collected Essays as an "absorbing" volume which provides a "revealing insight" into the mind of Greene.

R6917 Hern, Anthony. "Auntie Mame--Graham Greene Style...." EvS, (18 Nov.), p. 21. A short review of Travels with My Aunt that calls for the recognition of the successful farce which Greene's novel is. Compares Aunt Augusta to Patrick Dennis's Auntie Mame.

R6918 Hope, Francis. "Soupsweet." NSta, LXXVII (7 March), p. 332. A review of Collected Essays critical of Greene as a literary egoist, of his "bland chattiness," and of the universalizing of his experiences by rhetorical means. Considers Greene "deeply erudite on minor writers" and finds no better description for his "sometimes lazy oeuvre" than "soupsweet."

R6919 Hughes, Catharine. "Obsessed with Sin." Progressive, XXXIII (Sept.), pp. 50-51. Finds Collected Essays to be "continually absorbing" for it reveals the same compassion and absorption with sin and damnation as the novels. Also notes that Greene's criticism is "deeply personal" and reveals as much of the reviewer as the reviewed.

R6920 Hughes, Robert. "Aspects of the Imagination." SunT, (9 March), p. 58. In spite of the considerable range of Collected Essays and the reader's consciousness of the "ticking" of Greene's Catholic conscience the essays read very smoothly with very few of the judgments not wearing well.

R6921 Jordan, John. "Fun and Morals." Hibernia, XXXIII:22 (21 Nov.), p. 16. Maintains that though Travels with My Aunt "bedazzles in its variety of comic invention," it is also one of Greene's most serious novels for in it, and through his creation of Aunt Augusta--"one of the great eccentrics of English literature"--he is protesting against "conformity in living."

R6922 Laski, Marghanita. "The Author Suppresses Himself." Times, (8 March), p. 20. Finds the flaws in presentation in Collected Essays an impediment to appreciation for it is not really a collection but a selection which presupposes suppressions--a fact that may be of interest to future critics perhaps, but is "riling" to present day readers. Also very critical of the "bibliographical messiness" of the volume and the very selection itself which is called a "rag-bag in weight and length as well as subject-matter," all of which indicate "adhoc journalism" rather than serious contributions in literature.

R6923 LeFoe, Dominic. "Travels with My Aunt." ILN, (13 Dec.), p. 28. "An endearing and delightful book ... humorous and witty" whose language is "meticulously measured" and whose characters are "fresh and original." Regards the novel as a "triumphant success" which combines irony and compassion and wit with "the hint of tears."

R6924 Magid, Nora L. "The Tantalizing Two-Way Mirrors of Graham Greene." Commonweal, XC (19 Sept.), pp. 567-68. A review of Collected Essays which, though it does not evaluate the collection, finds the friendships described "varied" and the reviews and appreciations given with the "perceptions of a man who reads as well as he writes" gracefully, with an "understanding of intention and technique." Compares the selection with The Lost Childhood and notes the way Greene surfaces from time to time in everything he writes.

R6925 Maurer, Robert. "Belles-Lettres." SatR, LII (2 Aug.), pp. 26, 31. Collected Essays is the first of four books reviewed. Though the collection is made up of occasional pieces, the pieces hang together and seem to maintain a unified impression by their central core of thought on the "sense of man's fundamental inadequacy." Finds it difficult to pin down reasons for the attraction of the reader to Greene.

R6926 Millar, Gavin. "Smuggler's Arms." Listener, LXXXII (20 Nov.), pp. 708-09. Travels with My Aunt is the first of two books reviewed. Maintains that in the novel the traditional Greene ingredients are pushed to "the point of caricature," and that Greene's "bizarre conception of character" fogs the "lesson of the book."

R6927 Mitchell, Julian. "Grim Grin in the Gloom." NSta, LXXVIII (21 Nov.), p. 733. Maintains that Travels with My Aunt is "a fairy story," a "grotesque and improbable tale" made "resonant with over-and under-tones" by Greene's incomparable skill as storyteller. Points out two "puzzling contradictions" in Pulling's narrative, and maintains that in spite of Greene's self-parody and funny comic passages, the book has "the authentic and mordant gloom" one has come to associate with Greene.

R6928 Muggeridge, Malcolm. "Books." Esquire, LXXII (Aug.), pp. 16-22. A review of Collected Essays that admires Greene's "total dedication to writing" but prefers his essays to the novels because in the former he seems much nearer to the reader than he is, for example, in the person of a Scobie. Besides, Greene's "style, temperament and gifts ... suit the essay form exceptionally well," and he has the "great merit of being professional rather than critical."

R6929 Petersen, Clarence. "May We Borrow Your Husband?" Bookworld, III (27 July), p. 13. Notice of the Bantam edition publication.

R6930 Pettingell, Phoebe. "A Catholic Taste." NLea, LII (7 July), pp. 16-18. A lengthy review of Collected Essays that maintains that though the breadth of Greene's subject matter "defies classification," the collection is valuable for the "insight it gives into Greene the novelist," his views on the novel and his incongruous religious outlook. Finds Greene's criticism a "welcome antidote" to C. S. Lewis and Chesterton and also notes his "considerable wit and humor."

R6931 Price, R. G. G. "Ever Greene." Punch, CCLVII (17 Dec.), p. 1017. Finds Travels with My Aunt enjoyable, amusing and "essentially fun, not fun used to lure readers into moral speculation"; but though his laughter may be "pure and infectious," it brings a "chill in its wake."

R6932 Pritchard, William. "One Man's Evil." Listener, LXXXI (6 March), p. 317. The review of Collected Essays notices the absence of "The Revolver in the Corner Cupboard" which would have provided some relief from the "long parade of English authors." Critical of Greene's emphasis on the religious sense and his "hit-and-run treatment" which passes as criticism in his essays on James and Mauriac. Also finds that Greene's sense of evil seems to "obliterate whatever sense of humour there might have been."

R6933 Pritchett, V. S. "A Polished Dissenter." NYRB, XIII (10 July), pp. 8-9. A searching review of Collected Essays which describes Greene's reviews as an "artist's raids," their opinions having an "artist's necessity" in them. With a "patient almost pedantic eye of the connoisseur of 'brief lives,'" Greene searches for the "seat of unease" in his subject, and is "free of the snobbery that pretends (he) has had no time for the juvenile or second rate."

R6934 Raven, Simon. "Merry-go-round in Greene-land." Observer, (16 Nov.), p. 31. Though the "anecdotes are elegant," and the descriptions "concrete yet evocative, comprehensive yet concise," the development of Travels with My Aunt is "scrappy and its climax definitely scruffy" in spite of the looseness of its traditional picaresque mode.

R6935 Scott, Michael Maxwell. "Recent Fiction." DaiT, (20 Nov.), p. 9. Describes Travels with My Aunt as a "lark, a farcical cosmopolitan jaunt" without any of Greene's earlier compassionate concern for sin and guilt. Maintains that Henry's innocence is "really only a spoof"--in fact the whole entertainment is a spoof where Greene is parodying himself.

R6936 Sharrock, Roger. "The Illuminated Margin." Tablet, CCXXIII (8 March), p. 233. Though Collected Essays may be "marginal" to Greene's major achievement, the "range and good sense" of the criticism in the collection make it delightful. The criticism, "relaxed yet precise," is free from any "academic compulsion to relate the work ... to some hypothetical tradition"; Greene's approach to a work is through "the personal deficiency of the artist" to lay bare the flaw which releases "the personal imaginative process like a coiled spring." Also notes Greene's consistency of outlook in his occasional essays as well as his consistent intellectual gaiety.

R6937 ________. "Books for the Week: Innocent Abroad." Tablet, CCXXIII (22 Nov.), p. 1147. Examines the narrative manner of Travels with My Aunt--"the most entertaining of his books so far" with its "gallery of amoral picaresque rogues"--and suggests that "human complexity and the compassion which this complexity arouses" have displaced metaphysical Evil as his main theme.

R6938 Shrapnel, Norman. "Greene Thoughts in a Greene Shade." Guardian, (20 Nov.), p. 8. Considers Travels with My Aunt as a "hilarious" novel with the unmistakable Greene tone--"laconic, downbeat, mordantly serious however unsolemn." Greene's "superlative skill" and tone enable him to spin any yarn he chooses; what would have been "sheer vulgarity" becomes "bitterly funny" with his handling.

R6939 ________. "Journey Through Greeneland." GuardianW, CI (29 Nov.), p. 18. Travels with My Aunt is the first of three novels reviewed. Reiterates the same views as in R6938.

R6940 Sokolov, Raymond A. "The Short Greene." Newsweek, LXXIII (19 May), pp. 110, 112, 114. A journalistic review that finds Collected Essays "truly odd" because of the "way it brings its intellectual suavity to bear on literature and personalities on whom so penetrating a light has rarely played before."

R6941 Solomon, Petre. "Eseurile lui Graham Greene." RoLit, 19 (May), p. 20. In Romanian. The publication of Collected Essays prompts a survey of Greene's literary obsessions, including his "shady" Catholicism, as well as his professional seriousness as a novelist.

R6942 Thomas, Edward. "Selected Books: Collected Essays." LM, IX (June), pp. 83-87. Notes that Greene's interest in his chosen novelists is in the "moment of extreme strain which ... reveals what a man really is," and that though he never sounds the note of "moral righteousness," he reserves his harshest lines for those who lack imagination to understand the sufferings of others. Also notes the "tremendous consistency of thought" in the Collection and examines his view of life.

R6943 Toynbee, Philip. "The Best of Greene." Observer, (9 March), p. 30. Rpt. as "Greener Than Greene." Critic, XXVIII (Sept.), pp. 78-80. A perceptive review that argues that Greene is a "better essayist than he is a novelist"; the "superb" essays are written by a "drier though no less generous Graham Greene ... freed from the novelist's temptation to transform them into melodrama." Also examines Greene's particular tastes and qualities which emerge and notes that Greene is a "finer poet than even his finest novels would have allowed us to suspect."

R6944 Trevor, William. "Personal Essays." Guardian, (6 March), p. 9. The essays are full of concern for the author's craft, are not "dry" and bring the reader into closer contact with Greene than his travel books or novels do. As a critic, he is modest and sympathetic, and writes "as a person rather than a literary man," always aware of the "human frailty" of the person he writes about.

R6945 ________. "An Enemy of the Ungenerous." GuardianW, C (13 March), p. 15. A review of Collected Essays reiterating the same view as in R6944.

R6946 Waugh, Auberon. "On the Rocks." Spectator, CCXXII:7341 (7 March), pp. 308 & 310. Prefers the novels with their central emotion of charity to Collected Essays, even though the latter may be "superbly deft" and may add to our understanding of his books, especially for his own craving for revolutionary violence which he expresses with a baldness that a few might find disconcerting.

R6947 ________. "Mystery Tour." Spectator, CCXXIII:7378 (22 Nov.), pp. 717-18. Welcomes the comedy that finally creeps out from behind Greene's tragic mask in Travels with My Aunt which is regarded as a "spanking good collection of short stories, portrait-sketches and funny happenings, but whose crowning denouements are" sheer pantomime.

R6948 Weales, Gerald. "There Are Demons at the Bottom of the Garden." KR, XXXI:4, pp. 554-60. As a "fuller, richer, more repetitious statement" than The Lost Childhood, this volume, nevertheless, does not qualify Greene as a "literary critic" because each essay is a "penetration into self," a kind of confession of secrets and truths that "force their way, unwanted, to the ... surface." Though one may read with "more fascination than pleasure" to discover how he shall reduce every topic or author "to a greene thought in a greene shade," one leaves the volume with a "bad taste in the mouth."

R6949 Weinig, Sr. Mary Anthony, SHCJ. "Collected Essays." Best Sellers, XXIX (1 June), p. 84. Finds the total effect of these "ephemera" to include "some tedium and disappointment" in spite of their "penetrating observations," and that the few "acid judgments" seem to stem more from incompatibility of temperament rather than literary fault finding.

R6950 Whitley, John. "A Trip Worth Taking." SunT, (16 Nov.), p. 56. Travels with My Aunt is a "consciously relaxed, stylised book" with a "pervasive sense of detachment" so that the occasional moral lecture does not disturb the "uproarious comic" story.

R6951 Unsigned. "Collected Essays." AR, XXIX (Fall), p. 445. A short review noting that Greene's criticism is always touched with the "Midas force" of his own preoccupations.

R6952 ________. "On the Top Shelf: Travels with My Aunt." GuardianW, CI (20 Dec.), p. 19. One of twenty books mentioned for the year.

R6953 ________. "Collected Essays." Kirkus, XXXVII (15 March), p. 349. A prepublication descriptive note on the collection.

R6954 ________. "Travels with My Aunt." Kirkus, XXXVII (15 Nov.), p. 1222. Prepublication notice of the novel which describes it as a "mixed success."

R6955 ________. "Collected Essays." NY, XLV (14 June), p. 116. Brief notice of the collection as "unmistakably the work of a novelist ... rich in anecdote, in character, and in drama."

R6956 _______. "May We Borrow Your Husband?" Observer, (9 Nov.), p. 31. Publication notice of paperback edition.

R6957 _______. "Travels with My Aunt." Observer, (21 Dec.), p. 17. Briefly noted as John Gielgud's personal choice for "Best of the Year."

R6958 _______. "Collected Essays." PW, CXCV (10 March), p. 66. Prepublication notice of the collection that notes Greene's "erudition, irony" and wide range and how "urbane" and "eminently readable" he is in spite of the "continual listing with the winds of his Catholicism."

R6959 _______. "May We Borrow Your Husband?" PW, CXCV (2 June), p. 138. Notice of Bantam paperback edition.

R6960 _______. "The Third Man." Theology, XXV (Jan.), p. 486. Briefly mentioned.

R6961 _______. "Travels with My Aunt." PW, CXCVI (10 Nov.), p. 43. A prepublication notice remarking on Greene's awareness of the tragic irony of the human condition, the pathos as well as the comedy in our search for love, in spite of the superb comedy of the novel.

R6962 _______. "Studies in Black and Grey." Time, XCIV (22 Aug.), p. 74. A review of Collected Essays which does not consider Greene's compulsive and compassionate visiting of his own moral preoccupations upon the life and art of others as "calculated to enhance his reputation for balanced judgment" as much as it reveals him.

R6963 _______. "The Dark Truster in God and the Thwarted Believer in Man." TLS, 3498 (13 March), pp. 257-58. Compares and contrasts Collected Essays with J. B. Priestley's Essays of Five Decades. Throughout the essays, Greene remains a man "nursing an obsession," more of the novelist reflecting rather than the essayist.

R6964 _______. "Portrait of No Lady." TLS, 3534 (20 Nov.), p. 1329. Travels with My Aunt is described as an entertainment in Greene's "most stylish--and stylized--manner" in which he interweaves two stereotypes of English fiction: the Indomitable Old Lady and the Innocent Abroad. Notes the part played by "curious places" in the shaking of Pulling to life, Greene's "literary playfulness," his melancholy directness and the mildness with which he draws out the entertainment.

D691 Guest, Lawrence A. Christian Tragedy and the Works of Graham Greene: A Redefinition as Applied to 'Brighton Rock,' 'The End of the Affair,' 'A Burnt-Out Case' and 'The Power and the Glory.' M.A. Fresno State College.

D692 Kellogg, Gene. The Catholic Novel in a Period of Convergence. Univ. of Chicago. Published as The Vital Tradition: The Catholic Novel in a Period of Convergence. Chicago: Loyola Univ. Press, 1970. See B701.

D693 Lebensold-Adamson, Judith Emily. Laughter in the Novels of Graham Greene. M.A. Univ. of Montreal.

D694 Love, Frances A. Graham Greene's Use of the Christian Concept of Descent. M.A. Texas Agricultural and Mechanical Univ.

D695 McDonald, Ann Gilbert. A Bibliography of the Periodical Contributions of Graham Greene. George Washington Univ.

D696 Manly, Jane Burt. Graham Greene: The Insanity of Innocence. Univ. of Connecticut. DAI, XXX:7 (1970), 3016A.

D697 Marlowe, Jeanne A. A Comparison of Religious Themes in the Fiction of Graham Greene and Flannery O'Connor. M.A. Bowling Green State Univ.

D698 Rusyn, Br. August S. Ambiguity as a Literary Technique in Selected Novels of Graham Greene. M.A. Univ. of Rhode Island.

D699 Sternberg, Carl Edward. The Quest for Justice in the Fiction of Graham Greene. Univ. of Connecticut. DAI, XXX:7 (1970), 3024A.

D6910 Stine, Norma Contryman. As It Is and As It Ought to Be: Graham Greene on the Cinema. M.A. Univ. of Nebraska.

S691 Lennon, Peter. "French Honour Graham Greene." Guardian, (2 Jan.), p. 9. A short report on his popularity in France on the occasion of his appointment as Chevalier of the Legion of Honour by the French State.

1970

B701 Bati, Laszlo, and Istvan K. Nagy, eds. Az angol irodalom a huszadik szazadbam. 2 vols. Budapest: Gondolat, pp. 31-56. Unavailable for examination.

B702 Bryer, Jackson R., and Nanneska N. Magee. "The Modern Catholic Novel: A Selected Checklist of Criticism." The Vision Obscured: Perceptions of Some Twentieth-Century Catholic Novelists. Ed. Melvin J. Friedman. New York: Fordham Univ. Press, pp. 241-69. Part I is a highly selective list of general studies divided into books and articles. Part II gives a checklist of criticism of eleven individual authors--American, English, French, Italian and German. Pages 255-58 list some fifty selected works on Greene--30 of them are pre-1960--as well as cross-references to items in Part I. Lists all books on Greene with a selection of standard articles generally based on relevance to Greene as a Catholic writer.

B703 Eagleton, Terence. "Reluctant Heroes: The Novels of Graham Greene." Exiles and Emigres: Studies in Modern Literature. London: Chatto and Windus; New York: Schocken Books, pp. 108-37. This is one of the "critical explorations" around the problem raised by the "émigré" theme in 20th-century literature. Discusses the "tensions" that exist in Greene's novels between the characters' conscious commitment to orthodoxy and their active rejection of its limits which often lead to "unresolved ambiguities" as in The Power and the Glory and The End of the Affair, or between the possibility of outstanding virtue and its affirmation "in the context of a radical suspicion of goodness" as in Querry, or between involvement and detachment--the latter only to the degree that it does not "sterilise the humane feelings" in order to criticize the involvement of the committed--as in The Quiet American. Examines briefly Greene's pervasive belief that God is "most concretely present in suffering, guilt and weakness" in the novels and discusses the tensions in Brighton Rock for they seem "least satisfactorily resolved." Maintains at the end that "in feeling and attitude," Greene is closer to Orwell, "and to a specific strain in the English novel, than to the more overtly theological writers with whom he is often compared."

B704 Friedman, Melvin J., ed. The Vision Obscured: Perceptions of Some Twentieth-Century Catholic Novelists. New York: Fordham Univ. Press. Includes A. Sonnenfeld's "Children's Faces: Graham Greene," and J. A. Bryer's and N. N. McGee's "The Modern Catholic Novel: A Selected Checklist of Criticism." pp. 109-28 and pp. 241-69 respectively. See B7011 & B702.

B705 Guseva, E. A., ed. The Basement Room by Graham Greene: Short Stories. Moscow: Vysshaya Shkola. Includes a Russian Foreword, pp. 5-9, to fourteen stories in English.

B706 Hoggart, Richard. "The Force of Caricature: Aspects of the Art of Graham Greene." Speaking to Each Other: Essays. Vol. II. About Literature. London: Chatto and Windus, pp. 40-56. Rpt. from EIC, III (Oct. 1953), 447-62. See A5315.

B707 Kellogg, Gene. "Graham Greene." The Vital Tradition: The Catholic Novel in a Period of Convergence. Chicago: Loyola Univ. Press, pp. 111-36. This is Ch. 8 of a volume--originally a thesis--describing the rise and decline of the Catholic novel in France, England and America. Examines briefly Greene's "origins": James, Conrad and Mauriac, makes a few observations on his technique, especially the "rapidity" of movement that can only be described as cinematographic, before discussing "the theme of universal love" in Stamboul Train, England Made Me, and his handling of Catholic themes and characters in Brighton Rock--"a fearful study in the Catholic's belief in human freedom"--The Power and the Glory where the "focus is on men's hearts rather than their actions" and The Heart of the Matter which recalls the "Aeschylean mode of religious wonder and awe." Maintains that the last three novels are symptomatic of "Catholic thinking that was increasing in depth" but which had to collide "inevitably ... with the pious rigidity inherited from the nineteenth century," because the novels indicate an "accelerated convergence between the Catholic and non-Catholic worlds."

B708 Mazkovic, Vida E. "Major Scobie." The Changing Face: Disintegration of Personality in the Twentieth-Century British Novel, 1900-1950. Pref. Harry T. Moore. Carbondale and Edwardsville: Southern Illinois Univ. Press; London and Amsterdam: Feffer and Simons, Inc., pp. 82-97. Asserts that Scobie is Greene's "maturest statement" on the tragic situation of man which deprives life of both value and joy until death seems "the best way out of an existence devoid of meaning." Claims that Scobie, a "modern saint ... who gives glamour to failure (and) glories in the degradation of man," reveals variations of Greene's "nihilism."

B709 Robson, W. W. "Graham Greene." Modern English Literature. London & New York: Oxford University Press, pp. 138-41. A critical account that considers Greene as the English exponent of "existentialist-psychological" fiction, and the serious use he made of the thriller. Notes Greene's "absurd" conception of faith and his reliance on melodrama or "proleptic eschatology."

B7010 Shakhova, Kira, ed. The Quiet American and Our Man in Havana. Kiev: Dnipro. Ukrainian translations of the two novels followed by an Afterword, pp. 351-62.

B7011 Sonnenfeld, Albert. "Children's Faces: Graham Greene." The Vision Obscured: Perceptions of Some Twentieth Century Catholic Novelists. Ed. Melvin J. Friedman. New York: Fordham Univ. Press, pp. 109-28. Maintains that Greene writes for "the lonely and tormented schoolboy he had been," because the experience of apprenticeship in the work of adults goes back to the traumas of childhood. Shows that two formative traumatic experiences constitute Pinkie's "psychic inheritance and provide the matrices of the novel's imagery." Children's faces also constitute Scobie's failing as he feels an "adult-like pity toward children." He even sees a projection of children's faces when he deals with adults: e.g., Helen, The Captain of the Esperenca, Pemberton, and even Ali.

B7012 Vann, Jerry Don. Graham Greene. A Checklist of Criticism. The Serif Series: Bibliographies and Checklists, No. 14. Kent: Kent State Univ. Press. A compilation of criticism about Greene divided into five sections: Bibliographies, Books about Greene, Chapters about Greene and References to Greene in Books, Articles about Greene, and lastly, Greene's Novels: A Chronological Listing with Reviews. Cut-off date for entries seems to be 1966, with several exceptions. Items are listed alphabetically in the first four sections. A few dissertations are also included in the fourth section. Not annotated. Leaves out criticism on the plays, films, travel books and short stories even though A Sense of Reality is included.

B7013 Wall, Stephen. "Aspects of the Novel 1930-1960." The Twentieth Century: The Sphere History of Literature in the English Language. Vol. VII. Ed. Bernard Bergonzi. London: The Cresset Press, pp. 222-76. Pages 228-33 examine Greene's achievement as a novelist and indicate some of his distinctive qualities: popularity in spite of the "intensely personal, even obsessive" world he creates, the topicality of his themes, cinematic elements and the "doctrinal open-endedness" of his novels. The Quiet American, The Heart of the Matter and The Comedians.

B7014 Webster, Harvey Curtis. "Graham Greene: Stoical Catholic." After the Trauma: Representative British Novelists Since 1920. Lexington: Univ. Press of Kentucky, pp. 97-124. Rpt. from Graham Greene: Some Critical Considerations. Ed. Robert O. Evans. Lexington: Univ. of Kentucky Press, 1963, pp. 1-25. See B6324.

A701 Astier, Colette. "La Tentation du roman policier dans deux romans: Un crime, de Georges Bernanos, Le Rocher de Brighton, de Graham Greene." RLC, XLIV (April-June), pp. 224-43. Shows how the typical characteristics of the thriller are present in Brighton Rock and the first two parts of Un crime, and discusses how Bernanos and Greene charged the thriller pattern with "une valeur métaphorique" to express "une pensée tragique" of a universe "ou le mal seul a sa place."

A702 Biles, Jack I. "An Interview in London with Angus Wilson." SNNTS II:1 (Spring), pp. 76-87. A. Wilson expresses how much he detests the concept of "the saved sinner and the lost good man" which, he thinks, is behind Greene's "really awfully dotty" work. Attributes Greene's widespread readership to his being the first to write about the "anonymous man" and his "ability to build up tension and pursuit." Regards his recent work beginning with the The Quiet American as a "sort of wrong-headed nonsense taking over, that has destroyed this tension and power (of his earlier novels). And he is a very bad playwright."

A703 Braybrooke, N. "Graham Greene--The Double Man: An Approach to His Novel, The End of the Affair." QQ, LXXVII (Spring), pp. 29-39. See A527.

A704 Bryden, Ronald. "Graham Greene Discusses with Ronald Bryden the Collected Edition of His Novels Which was Published Not Long Ago." Listener, LXXXIII:2143 (23 April), pp. 544-45. In the course of the "discussion"--more of an interview, with Greene responding to specific questions--Greene also remarks on the "key books" of his life and the influence of Conrad, and unexpectedly announces that Travels with My Aunt is his "second best book." Also comments on a novel he could not write and on another he could not finish.

A705 Cheney, Lynne. "Joseph Conrad's The Secret Agent and Graham Greene's It's a Battlefield: A Study in Structural Meanings." MFS, XVI (Spring), pp. 117-31. Discusses the importance and the use of structure in fulfilling the "functions of unifying and intensifying" thereby playing an "essential role in communicating meaning," especially with the disappearance of the reliable commentator. Though the structure of It's a Battlefield may have failed "to focus precisely and emphasize clearly"--compensated for by the reliable commentator--the structure nevertheless played a "key role" in communicating Greene's meaning of de-emphasizing the "cause and effect relationship" so that "instead of certainty, there was probability."

A706 Cox, Gerard, H. 111 "Graham Greene's Mystical Rose in Brighton." Renascence, XXIII:1, pp. 21-30. Focusses attention on Rose rather than on Pinkie and Ida as the only character "to confront her own situation and, in existential terms, to constitute herself as an individual" whose vocation is associated with that of the Virgin Mary. Examines three occasions in which she asserts her identity until her final self affirmation in the confessional when she "affirms by assent the infinite personality of God" and accepts her vocation to hope and pray for Pinkie's salvation. Acceptance of her vocation, the suggestiveness of her name and Pinkie's association of Rose with the characteristics of the Virgin indicate that Greene has given Rose "the leading role in his divine comedy."

A707 Cunningham, Laurence. "The Alter Ego of Greene's 'Whiskey

Priest.'" ELN, VIII (Sept.), pp. 50-52. Proposes another source for the Whiskey Priest other than the one Greene mentions in his introduction to The Lawless Roads; viz., the actual fugitive priest Miguel Pro Juarex SJ who bears "striking similarities and contrived differences" to the Whiskey Priest, and to whom Greene alludes without mentioning his name. Suggests a reading of the novel against the background of the heroic and dashing Father Pro with the Whiskey Priest as his "anti-type."

A708 Davidson, Arnold C. "Graham Greene's Spiritual Lepers." IEY, 15 (Fall), pp. 50-55. Maintains that the pattern of uninvolvement in The Quiet American, A Burnt-Out Case and The Comedians indicates that Greene's fictional people are running away from commitment and lapsing into pathetic alienation, detachment, boredom and ennui--a nadir from which they can only escape by being spiritually reborn and "committed" once again.

A709 French, Philip. "The Red and the Greene." NSta, LXXIX: 2039 (10 April), p. 516. A review article on The Collected Edition of Brighton Rock, It's a Battlefield, England Made Me and Our Man in Havana. Regards Greene's introductions as a "piecemeal autobiography from the mid-twenties," and which, though brief, are "beautifully wrought, sly, ironic, simultaneously guarded and revealing, each containing several illuminating anecdotes."

A7010 Houle, Sister Sheila, B.V.M. "The Subjective Theological Version of Graham Greene." Renascence, XXIII:1 (Autumn), pp. 3-13. A largely "negative" presentation of Greene's world-view. Assumes that the theological vision is rooted in his temperament and not a product of experience and though it has not changed essentially, it does not have the "unity of system" Greene deemed important. Examines Greene's interest in Time, his portrayal of children as part of his preoccupation with the nature of man, the themes of betrayal, commitment and the reality and desirability of the spiritual. Contends that the "unity" of his personal theological vision is achieved at the expense of credibility and breadth of vision, and its "weakness" lies in its "monotony," the "sentimentality" with which Greene resolves major problems and conflicts, his misunderstanding of Grace and his vague concept of God. Endorses E. Sewell's view of Greene's literary decadence. (See A5416). The Man Within, The Quiet American and the Short Stories.

A7011 Jones, Grahame C. "Léon Bloy et Graham Greene: l'influence de La Femme pauvre sur The End of the Affair." RLC, XLIV, pp. 540-46. Contends that though the indignation and aversion for Bloy in The Lost Childhood may be genuine, Greene has retained, nevertheless, from his reading of Bloy, certain ideas "qui respondaient aux thèmes majeurs de ses propres écrits et qu'il a developpées et approfondies lui-même"; viz., the idea of the adulterous woman reaching sanctity, and like Bloy's two "modalités éssentielles"--the "unicité" of love--Greene makes little or no distinction between Divine Love and sensual human love. The passion for suffering is somewhat different in Sarah's case because it is endured for the salvation of others.

A7012 Kellogg, Gene. "The Catholic Novel in Convergence." Thought, XLV, pp. 265-96. Defines the term "Catholic novel," describes how the movement began, what it achieved, and why it has ebbed in France, England and America. Section 2 deals with England and pp. 281-83 with Greene whose "great theme ... responsibility" is reversed to become "self destructive" as in Scobie's obsession, or to arouse indignation as in The Quiet American.

A7013 Kellogg, Jean D. "A Burnt-Out Case?" America, CXXII (14 March), pp. 273-74. Develops the theme of "responsibility" treated in the preceding article to cover The Power and the Glory as well, and states that toward mid-century, Greene "painfully revised" this belief.

A7014 Kort, Wesley. "The Obsession of Graham Greene." Thought, XLV, pp. 20-44. An illuminating discussion of Greene's obsession with "a no-man's-land between the Catholic and the secularist world" in his major fictions pointing out the "thematic continuity" achieved by his vision of this tragic separation which may be unacceptable to the Church. Argues that Greene's exploration of the attitude of his characters to the Church, their suffering and their struggle for meaning and identity as they are caught between the irreconcilable opposites of the Church on the one hand and the non-religious attitudes of its opponents on the other, constitute an "aesthetic obsession ... a faithful intuition of the contemporary religious dilemma."

A7015 Kubal, David L. "Graham Greene's Brighton Rock: The Political Theme." Renascence, XXIII:1, pp. 46-54. Maintains that the novel is only "reservedly" theological. It is political in the sense that it dramatizes Greene's belief in the inadequacy of liberalism, especially its insistence upon man's exclusively natural origins and its search to "establish the definition of the individual within the confines of society" to the exclusion of the supernatural and the Divine.

A7016 Levin, Gerald. "The Rhetoric of Greene's The Heart of the Matter." Renascence, XXIII:1, pp. 14-20. Discusses the problem that arises from Greene's "indiscriminate irony." The reader, conscious of the narrator's reliability in his account of the facts, becomes conscious also of the narrator's unwillingness to make a "normative statement without a qualifying and generally indiscriminate irony." This consciousness urges the reader "into a scepticism that is ultimately incompatible with the emotional and intellectual investment" he had made in Scobie's character and fate.

A7017 MacSween, R. J. "Exiled from the Garden: Graham Greene." AntigR, I:2 (Summer), pp. 41-48. Surmises, from what seems to be personal impressions fostered by the reading of several works, that Greene is a "strange personality that seems to be in love with disease, death, sin and God," and is enamored with the "exotic of decay, despair and the uncanny." This dangerous exercise, especially so with Greene who seems to elude his very interviewers, leads to many sweeping and controversial statements; e.g., "Greene lives in a devastated world and its interest lies precisely in its devastation"; "later works (after Brighton Rock) seem almost the product of an unfeeling professionalism"; Querry "is Greene in a stance of his later life."

A7018 Mayne, Richard. "Collected Guilt." Listener, LXXXIII: 2160 (2 April), pp. 455-56. A review article on the first four novels in The Collected Edition: Brighton Rock, It's a Battlefield, England Made Me and Our Man in Havana. Attempts an "indentikit portrait of the Greene man."

A7019 Mesnet, Marie Beatrice. "La Vision politique de Graham Greene." Etudes, CCCXXXIII (Dec.), pp. 686-705. Rpt., in translation, in The Politics of Twentieth-Century Novelists. Ed. George Andrews Panichas. Foreword John W. Aldridge. New York: Hawthorn Books, 1971, pp. 100-24. Discusses Greene's concern for justice and truth which infuses his work and gives the universe he creates "the complex dimensions of reality," so that his novels, drawn from life, have the present with all its violence as a "backdrop" for his "global" observations. His characters, grounded in life, are at once unique individuals and human types. Faith gives them a spiritual dimension lacking in the novel since James. Surveys the works up to A Burnt-Out Case to show Greene's pursuit of justice and truth and what it reveals of the world and our times.

A7020 Newcombe, Jack. "Greene, The Funny Writer, on Comedy." Life, LXVIII (23 Jan.), p. 10. An uninterrupted monologue in which Greene talks to Life's London bureau chief about his new reputation as a "writer of funny books" that Travels with My Aunt had earned him. Comments on the evolution of his novel, comedy and tragedy, and the appropriateness of the names he has chosen in the novel.

A7021 Phillips, Gene D. "Graham Greene Interviewed." Month, CCXXIX (June), pp. 362-67. Rpt. TCLon, XXV (Summer), pp. 111-17. A reprint of an earlier article (See A6916) with the omission of three short paragraphs in the opening page.

A7022 Sternlight, Sanford. "Two Views of the Builder in Graham Greene's A Burnt-Out Case and William Golding's The Spire." CalR, NS 1 (March), pp. 401-04. Notices the parallelism between the characters and fates of the two central characters, Jocelin and Querry, and investigates their motivations and actions in an attempt to determine which is the "more religious act" since both novels end "in affirmation."

A7023 Symons, Julian. "Waiting for the War." SunT, (5 April), p. 32. "Takes stock" briefly of Greene as a "most accomplished novelist who is not a great writer" on the occasion of The Collected Edition of Brighton Rock, It's a Battlefield, England Made Me and Our Man in Havana. Suggests that a more useful label than "seedy" or "catholic" for these "period" novels would be "Low Romance," and remarks on Brighton Rock as the one novel that "wears least well."

A7024 Wolfe, Peter. "Graham Greene and the Art of Entertainment," STC, 6 (Fall), pp. 35-61. Distinguishes three stages in Greene's attitude to the "entertainments": in 1955 Greene describes them as having "just enough character to give interest to the action"; in 1961, he "finds relief" in them "for melodrama as much as farce is an expression of a manic mood"; in 1970, he dissolves the distinction altogether. The entertainments are "surface narratives whose irony and sharpness of detail save them from artificiality." Greene's belief in original sin carries them beyond the "crime-puzzle formula" and his avoidance of documentary data gives them "narrative drive." Essentially melodramatic, full of suspense, pursuit and flat characters, this thriller mode is "well geared to Greene," and brightens "his dark ontology." Also shows the influence of J. Buchan and E. Wallace on Greene.

R701 Algren, Nelson. "No Ashes in the Urn." Critic, XXVIII (Jan.-Feb.), pp. 84-86. This review of Travels with My Aunt maintains that the author's lack of feeling or personal involvement with his character communicates itself to the reader who does not feel concern for them. Seems to suggest that by consciously contriving an entertainment out of literary observations and travel notes, Greene is merely continuing his "war against boredom."

R702 Bell, P. K. "Travels with My Aunt." NLea, LIII (2 Feb.), p. 20. A short review which condemns the novel as a "current laundry list" which Greene "has roguishly but unsuccessfully tried to disguise as a parody" of his novels.

R703 Boston, Richard. "Travels with My Aunt." NYTBR, (25 Jan.), pp. 4-5, 18. Maintains that though this "peculiarly Greenean" comedy can be seen as "deliberate self-parody," it is also concerned with the inevitable approach of death.

R704 Cosgrave, M. S. "Travels with My Aunt." HB, XLVI (April), p. 187. Gives a summary of the plot and describes it as a "hilariously funny novel that spoofs the sacred but is never sacrilegious."

R705 Davenport, Guy. "Britannia in Negligée." NR, XXII (24 March), pp. 314-15. Travels with My Aunt is the second of three novels reviewed. Attributes its "triumphant comedy" to the awkwardness with which Greene's perception of the world and one's moral view fit together.

R706 Donoghue, Denis. "The Uncompleted Dossier." NYRB, XIV (12 March), pp. 25-27. Travels with My Aunt is one of two works reviewed. Maintains that the novel is an enjoyable comedy, sometimes a farce in which Greene, "a happy decadent, turns things into rogues," and whose characters exist "in latitude, not in depth." But in spite of its lightness, it is also Greene's "De Senectute turned upon age and death." Surmises that the novel is a "comic translation" of James' "The Jolly Corner."

R707 Finn, James. "The Living Dead End." NRep, CLXII (14 Feb.), pp. 26-28. An appreciative review of Travels with My Aunt that also praises the nature of Greene's achievement. Notices the similarities between this novel and earlier works and also the changes in style and feeling. Maintains that Greene's view of life in the novel, though more agreeable and relaxed than in earlier works, is still one of amusement and deep melancholy. As for the novel, it is "solid, mature, amusing and disturbing."

R708 Frankel, Haskel. "Travels with My Aunt." SatR, LIII (24 Jan.), p. 38. Describes the novel as an entertaining "soufflé" of "highly civilized fun," episodic to the point where "it wearies in midstream" and, with Greene's gift of evoking a sense of place, almost "a sentimental journey" through scenes of his past triumph.

R709 Fuller, Edmund. "Of Bankers and Byron." WSJ, CLXXV (5 Feb.), p. 10. Travels with My Aunt is the first of two books reviewed. The novel is "funny" and stems from a comic view which arises from Greene's "penetration of human nature." Though Greene does not recommend Aunt Augusta as a model, she is preferable to Henry's "emotional-spiritual constipation."

R7010 Grady, R. F. "Travels with My Aunt." Best Sellers, XXIX (1 Feb.), pp. 413-14. As the February Book-of-the-Month Club choice, the novel is bound to be a best-seller and shows Greene at "his polished and unpredictable best."

R7011 Hill, William. "Fiction: Travels with My Aunt." America, CXXII (2 May), p. 478. Brief annotation narrating outline of story.

R7012 Horrocks, Norman. "Travels with My Aunt." LJ, XCV (1 Jan.), p. 83. A short review describing the novel as "richly comic" in which intrigue is blended with fun "in a most successful jeu d'esprit."

R7013 Ivanescu, Mircea. "Virtutile divertismentului." RoLit, III:3 (July), p. 20. In Romanian. Considers Travels with My Aunt to be a novel that announces a change in Greene's vision. Although ostensibly an entertainment, the novel attempts to show a particular initiation, a shock of the conscience, for the therapeutic purpose of stimulating a more fruitful spiritual life.

R7014 Kunkel, Francis L. "Little Profit But the Name." America, CXXII (14 April), p. 373. Considers Travels with My Aunt "a departure" from Greene's usual fiction for two reasons: it is in part a "self-parody" and, from the point of technique, it is really "a protracted character sketch."

R7015 Lehmann-Haupt, Christopher. "Books of the Times." NYT, (19 Jan.), p. 45. Travels with My Aunt is the second of two books reviewed. Though "unhappily titled," the novel is "the flip side" of all the things Greene used to brood about; in it too, Greene indulges in a "considerable amount of forced whimsey," but his "effortlessly professional prose" makes it all interesting.

R7016 Maddocks, Melvin. "From Sackcloth and Ashes to Cap and Bells." Life, LXVIII (23 Jan.), p. 10. Travels with My Aunt is "a barrel of laughs" in which Greene, with a "barroom monologuist's abandon," writes a "middle-aged parody of all those novels whose lusty Tom Joneses journey their way to an education of the heart." But Greene as a comedian has a way of going "morbid" even when "he is giddiest"; in fact, no one can call him a "devil-may-care or don't-give-a-damn--even in joke."

R7017 Mambrino, J. "Voyage avec ma Tante." Etudes, CCCXXXII (May), 775-76. Rather disturbed by the description of the book as a novel and not as an entertainment. Maintains that Greene's narrative art is wasted by exalting "le rien, le néant de la vie"; the novel is "drôle" and leaves a feeling "d'ennui désespéré."

R7018 Mencken, Nancy. "Travels with My Aunt." LJ, XCV (15 April), p. 1660. Gives a brief account of the plot with a note that "sophisticated young adults will enjoy the wit and satire treated in an understated style."

R7019 Monod, Sylvère. "Travels with My Aunt." EA, XXIII:4, pp. 453-54. Describes it as a "masterpiece of comic narrative," that provides a perfect illustration of how a narrative can entertain and give the reader all that he expects of a novel "au sens plein du terme," as it contrasts the world of Henry Pulling with that of Aunt Augusta.

R7020 Ostermann, Robert. "Greene's 'Travels' is a Milestone in His Long Novelistic Evolution." NOb, IX (2 Feb.), p. 19. A review of Travels with My Aunt as a "small masterpiece" that reveals Greene's "thorough, bitter and intense" jibe and sardonic skepticism for the hopes, values and institutions cherished in the Western world by endorsing their opposites with "bold satiric thrusts."

R7021 Pritchard, William H. "Senses of Reality." HudR, XXIII (Spring), pp. 162-70. Travels with My Aunt is one of some twelve novels reviewed. Maintains that by "relaxing his powers" in the novel, Greene is always highly accomplished, has presented a warmer Greeneland than his earlier novels did--but is less entertaining.

R7022 Rascoe, Judith. "Chaucer Was Here." ChrSM, LXII (12 Feb.), p. 11. Argues that Greene is indebted to Chaucer for the framework of Travels with My Aunt, in its "tales short and tall," and in Aunt Augusta who bears a strong resemblance to the "evergreen" wife of Bath.

R7023 Sheed, Wilfrid. "Racing the Clock with Greene and Pritchett." Atlantic, CCXXV (April), pp. 109-13. Rpt. The Morning After. Selected Essays and Reviews. New York: Farrar, Straus, 1971, pp. 66-75. A review of Travels with My Aunt by Greene and Blind Love & Other Stories by Pritchett. Examines Greene's strategy to outlive his generation or "beat the clock" with comedy. Notes that Greene is also making a study of old age in Aunt Augusta, "half-stage and half-real," as he depicts tolerance and sensuality "à la Française."

R7024 Sissman, L. E. "Evergreen." NY, (28 Feb.), pp. 110, 113-14. Describes Travels with My Aunt as an "enigma," "a pastiche of Graham Greene ... unbuttoned and expansive," to be read "for the fun in it"--the "agreeable jokes, amusing descriptions and witty dialogue." There is something "less than serious ... about the author's attitude towards the book"--it "does not get off the ground"--which raises the question whether it is an "extended piece of self-parody."

R7025 Sokolov, Raymond A. "Greene Goes Waughward." Newsweek, LXXV (26 Jan.), p. 80. Though he praises Greene for the opening of Travels with My Aunt, he cannot accept, and is not amused, by Greene's sudden "Waughward turn," from "the black velvet of the confessional" to the "music-hall motley."

R7026 Stern, Daniel. "The Greene Landscape Revisited." Book World, IV (8 Feb.), p. 3. Does not find Travels with My Aunt representative of Greene "at top form"; it has a "certain heaviness of tone" that betrays Greene's intention of being comic, and as the fun wears thin, one becomes aware of the too elaborate plot that carries "the light luggage."

R7027 Sullivan, Walter. "'Where Have All the Flowers Gone?' Part II: The Novel in the Gnostic Twilight." SR, LXXVIII:4 (Oct.-Dec.), pp. 654-64. One of seven novels reviewed. See pp. 656-57. Though not a "good novel," Travels with My Aunt is "largely inoffensive." The "skill" and "delicacy" with which it is written cannot make up for the "surprise" of the reader at much in it that is "second best."

R7028 Thomas, Edward. "Veteran Propellors." LM, X (April), pp. 100-01. Travels with My Aunt is the first of three novels reviewed. Argues that the novel is "anything but a pot-boiler" and that in spite of the "saucy" West End comedy conventions it adopts, it is the "element of seriousness in it that keeps us going, and the light entertainment that very nearly sinks it beyond recovery."

R7029 Thomson, John. "Travels with My Aunt." Harper's, CCXL (March), p. 108. Perceives the book as a self-parody for the benefit of the reader, and Pulling as a comic or farcical hero redeemed "out of middle class virtues" by an initiation into sin.

R7030 Wimsatt, Margaret. "Travels with My Aunt." Commonweal, XCII (8 May), pp. 200-02. Argues that in spite of the action holding together, the neat plot and the amusement it generates, the novel fails because it is built on an "unequal yoking together in the book of two characters from different sources of literary vision and value."

R7031 Wolfe, Peter. "Travels with My Aunt." STC, 6 (Fall), pp. 119-23. Regards the novel as a "romantic protest against age, infirmity, and death"--which preoccupation "blurs the novel's focus." In addition, Augusta Bertram's character fails to come to life in spite of the "workmanlike and unpretentious" aspects of the novel, Greene's "professional touch" and "relaxed conversational style."

R7032 Unsigned. "Travels with My Aunt." Booklist, LXVI (1 April), p. 109. Briefly noted as an "engaging tour-de-force in which Greene satirizes most of the subjects that he has previously dealt with in an absorbing seriousness."

R7033 _______. "Travels with My Aunt." Choice, VII (Sept.), p. 842. A short review describing the novel as "somewhat slight yet almost always unfailingly entertaining" and "old fashioned."

R7034 _______. "1970: A Selected List from Books of the Year." NYTBR, (6 Dec.), p. 102. Travels with My Aunt is briefly noted.

R7035 _______. "Collected Essays." Observer, (25 Oct.), p. 32. Notice of the paperback publication of the "catholic, erudite collection."

R7036 _______. "Hamlet's Aunt." Time, XCV (19 Jan.), p. 66. A review of Travels with My Aunt which regards the "picaresque tale" as it sprawls over Christendom as a "comic masterpiece" which is also a "neat parable" demonstrating that "the surface of a man's life, however wildly comic it seems, it not really funny unless it is a parodic replay of The Man Within." Maintains that in his masterful self-parody, Greene has given "a sociopsychological striptease" of Aunt Augusta.

R7037 _______. "Collected Essays." VQR, XLVI (Winter), pp. xv, xviii. A short review describing the collection as "one of the wisest and most entertaining" that gives full play to Greene's "range, understanding, honesty and humour" and reveals his prejudices, weaknesses and strengths.

D701 Beckles, W. A. Catholicism in the Fiction of Graham Greene. Univ. of Alberta.

D702 Eberly, Ralph Stevens. Joyce Cary's Theme of Freedom and a Comparison with James Joyce and Graham Greene. Univ. of Michigan. DAI, XXXI:12 (1971), 6601A.

D703 La Chance, Paul Richard. Man and Religion in the Works of William Golding and Graham Greene. Kent State Univ. DAI, XXX:11 (1971), 6062A.

D704 Macoubrie, Margery Cunningham. Modern Religious Drama in the Secular Theatre. Univ. of Minnesota. DAI, XXXI:7 (1971), 3555A.

D705 Spann, Ekkehard. "Problemkinder" in der englischen Erzaehlkunst der gegenwart. Univ. of Tübingen.

D706 Willig, Charles Lloyd. The Short Fiction of Graham Greene. Univ. of Tulsa. DAI, XXXI:6, 2945A.

1971

B711 Aoki, Yuzo. Graham Greene. Guide to Twentieth Century English and American Literature, 24. Tokyo: Kenkyusha. Unavailable for examination.

B712 Boardman, Gwenn R. Graham Greene: The Aesthetics of Exploration. Gainesville: Univ. of Florida Press. Originally a Ph. D. dissertation at the Claremont Graduate School, 1963, now published with an additional Ch. 8. Argues that Greene's explorations were at once aesthetic as well as psychological adventures, and shows that Liberia, Indo-China, Mexico and the Congo each led to a new level of artistic consciousness in Greene. Maintains that the metaphor of the map, central to Greene's works, expresses his artistic quest, and uses the controlling metaphor to explain the pattern traced by the works.

Ch. 1 records Greene's explorations of unmapped Liberia which had become to him a "symbolic representation" of his dissatisfaction with European civilization, as well as his new awareness of "the way men really act," his new kind of hope in human nature and even a "love of life." Ch. 2 shows Greene reconstructing his map of lost childhood where the metaphor of the child's "dissected map" helps us understand his artistic purpose in A Gun for Sale and Brighton Rock. Ch. 3 shows how Greene, after the "theological Limbo" observed in Africa found in Mexico a landscape that "could be simultaneously charted in its familiar, secular aspect and with his personal, religious symbols," as in The Power and the Glory. Ch. 4 reveals Greene as charting the "confusions" of love, pity and hate in The Ministry of Fear, The Heart of the Matter and The End of the Affair which last novel rejects the "adolescent ... confusion" of The Heart of the Matter for the "Mystery of God's love." Ch. 5 discusses Greene's journey to Indo-China which led to the confrontation of today's adult representation of the guilt of Europe with the innocence of the New World. Ch. 6 examines the comical terrain of Loser Takes All, Our Man in Havana and The Complaisant Lover for it became apparent after Indo-China that "under the shadow of the Cross, it is better to be gay." Ch. 7 goes to the Congo where Greene, in search of Querry, pieces together a picture of man and artist in A Burnt-Out Case, and Ch. 8 examines "Under the Garden" as the "finest expression" of Greene's own years of exploring the theory and practice of the craft of fiction. Includes an assessment of Barbara Greene's Land Benighted and a valuable bibliography of Greene's Novels, Short Stories, Poems and Plays, as well as his Travels, Essays and Criticism, and a useful Index.

B713 Camilucci, Marcello. "I Saggi cattolici di G. Greene." Il Viaggiatore curioso: Testimonianze critiche. Milan: Bietti, pp. 315-22. See A583.

B714 Capey, Arthur. "The Post-War English Novel." Literature and Environment: Essays in Reading and Social Studies. Ed. Fred Inglis. Foreword Denys Thompson. London: Chatto & Windus, pp. 15-40. An analysis of selected novels, not necessarily "established classics," but which represent the age and bring into focus contemporary values and attitudes. Pages 19-21 examine briefly Greene's seriousness, the pervading atmosphere of "impersonal disgust" in the novels, and contends that his "artistic imagination has become imprisoned by the material it focusses on" because Greene never seems to supply in his books the "positive values" needed to measure the "degradation" he portrays. These values the reader has to supply from his own knowledge of life and literature.

B715 Fisch, Harold. The Dual Image: The Figure of the Jew in English and American Literature. London: World Jewish Library. Pages 87-89 discuss Greene's portrayal of the Jewish mythic stereotype, the "jew-Devil," in both Colleoni in Brighton Rock and Sir Marcus in A Gun for Sale. Makes no reference to Wyatt in Stamboul Train.

B716 Foster, J. "Gertrud von Le Fort and Graham Greene." Affinities: Essays in German and English Literature. Dedicated to the Memory of Oswald Wolff (1897-1968). London: Oswald Wolff, pp. 321-29. This is the text of Gertrud von le Fort's essay "The Paradox of Christianity (An Essay on Graham Greene)" which originally formed the "preface to a collection of Greene's occasional pieces published in German translation under the title Vom Paradox des Christentums. (Zurich: Verlag der Azche, 1952). The essay maintains that, as a writer, Greene is aware of the difficult conflict that may arise between Christian morality and human life from his probing into the motive of sin, the depth of the abandonment of the sinner, and the hopelessness of the sinner's situation. This "tensional relationship" between literature and moral theology extends beyond the human sphere into the metaphysical, to the very concept of God.

B717 Gilman, R. "Mixture Almost as Before." Common and Uncommon Masks: Writings on Theatre 1961-1970. New York: Random House, pp. 249-51. Rpt. from Commonweal, LXXV (24 Nov. 1961), pp. 233-34. See R6119.

B718 Lodge, David. "Graham Greene." The Novelist at the Crossroads, and Other Essays on Fiction and Criticism. Ithaca: Cornell Univ. Press, pp. 87-118. Rpt. from Columbia Essays on Modern Writers, No. 17. See B664.

B719 Magny, Claude-Edmonde. "Préface au Rocher de Brighton, de Graham Greene." Littérature et critique. Paris: Payot. Rpt. from Poésie, XLVI:32 (May 1946), pp. 32-37. See A465.

B7110 Mesnet, Marie Beatrice. "Graham Greene." Trans. Richard J. Ricard. The Politics of Twentieth-Century Novelists. Ed. George Andrews Panichas. Foreword John W. Aldridge. New York: Hawthorn Books, pp. 100-24. Rpt. from Etudes, CCCXXXIII (Dec. 1970), pp. 686-705. See A7019.

B7111 Sheed, W. "Racing the Clock with Greene and Pritchett." The Morning After: Selected Essays and Reviews. Foreword John Leonard. New York: Farrar, Straus, pp. 66-75. Rpt. from Atlantic, CCXXV (April 1970), pp. 109-13. See R7023.

B7112 Woodward, Anthony. "Graham Greene: The War Against Boredom." Seven Studies in English. For Dorothy Cavers. Ed. Gildas Roberts. Cape Town & London: Purnell & Sons, pp. 64-105. Discusses Catholicism as a primary inspiration in Greene's works and his later fascination by the broader, less doctrinaire but potent ethic of commitment and involvement. Argues that desperation forms "a principal ingredient of the massive theological injection" Greene has given the modern novel, that his seedy "anti-heroes" are endowed with "the dignity of affliction" by his Christian imagination, that Greene is not a "late Romantic, drunk on spiritual extremism" but a powerful writer who has thrown into relief some of the main features of traditional pessimism. Also accounts for Greene's large reading public. Brighton Rock, The Heart of the Matter, The Lawless Roads, The Power and the Glory and The Lost Childhood.

B7113 Yamaguchi, Tetsuo. 'Moetsukita Ningen' in tsuite no Moetsukita Shiron. Tokyo: Seium Shobo, pp. 3-19. In Japanese. "A Burnt-Out Essay on A Burnt-Out Case." This is closer to a book review than an essay and is one of five essays on modern English novelists, and is also the title of the volume.

A711 Allain, Marie-Françoise. "Dossier Graham Greene: Profil de l'écrivain." LanM, LXV, pp. 47-50. Attributes the anguish and anxiety aroused by the characters, events and atmosphere of the novels to Greene's own obsessions.

Also comments on his "clairvoyance ... l'élement caracteristique du génie de Greene" and his ability to communicate his vision without posing as moralist or apologist.

A712 Bitterli, Urs. "Graham Greene und der Kolonialismus." NZZ, VIII, pp. 601-05. Notes how seldom is the relation between Europeans and inhabitants of the third world credible in Greene's novels. Maintains that though the novels reveal a three-fold relationship between Europeans and the colonies--the personal level where representatives from two cultures meet, white colonial society in relation to its environment, and the political/economic relations between colonial powers and developing countries--Greene always returns to the problems arising from personal relationships.

A713 Blondel, Jacques. "The Heart of the Matter: Le cas de Scobie." LanM, LXV, pp. 51-55. Examines the character of Scobie the "just," the ambiguity surrounding him and his "hamartia" to show that his inner life is determined as much by the "éxigences de la morale du devoir comme d'une conscience scrupuleuse" as by the Christian vision that lends a tragic sense to his actions, and that the specific Catholic perspective just adds a metaphysical dimension and theological debate to what is essentially a psychological experience.

A714 ________. "The Heart of the Matter: Roman Catholique." LanM, LXV, pp. 56-60. A sequel to the previous article. Maintains that the dualism between Greene's imaginative vision and the strictly Catholic orthodox vision creates a dialectic that cuts across the novel raising controversial questions about grace, salvation of Scobie and other theological issues.

A715 Braybrooke, Neville. "Graham Greene y el 'hombre desdoblade': un estudio de The End of the Affair." Arbor, CCCIII, pp. 57-68. Trans. Norman Baraclough. See A527.

A716 Coulthard, A. R. "Graham Greene's 'The Hint of an Explanation': A Reinterpretation." SSF, VIII:4 (Fall), pp. 601-05. Suggests a new interpretation of the short story as an "understated satire on a proud complacent priest" who is unconsciously ironical as he thinks that God allowed him to trample down an outcast like Blacker to indicate the call to the priesthood, rather than the generally accepted interpretation of the priest's experience with Blacker at face value.

A717 Davis, Robert Murray. "Contributions to 'Night and Day' by Elizabeth Bowen, Graham Greene, and Anthony Powell." SNNTS, III:4, pp. 401-04. Includes on pp. 402-03 a list of Greene's contributions as film critic in twenty-four of the twenty-six issues of the periodical. Subtitles and the movies reviewed are also given.

A718 Fougner, Ingeborg Prytz. "Sjelens 'obotliga ansamhet,'" KoK, LXXVI, pp. 355-360. In Norwegian. A study of The Heart of the Matter with special emphasis on the theme of loneliness and the inability of people to communicate in the novel.

A719 Gomez, Joseph A. "The Theme of the Double in The Third Man." FilmH, VI:4 (Summer), pp. 7-12, 24. Not so much a study of The Third Man as much as an attempt to exonerate Carol Reed from the criticism that he could never come to grips with the literary themes of Conrad and Greene. Shows Reed's influence in dropping Martins' split-personality and in expanding the double relationship between Martins and Lime, and his ability to transform literary conceptions into visual artistry.

A7110 Hamilton, Alex. "Graham Greene." Guardian, (11 Sept.), p. 8. A "sort of interview" in Greene's residence at Antibes at which the novelist "chats" rather than answers prepared questions about chance encounters, his forthcoming novel The Honorary Consul, the "hell of writing," and the areas of the world "where his re-entry would promote too much adrenalin." Rules out further plays or autobiographies.

A7111 Hawton, Hector and Roger Manvell. "A Sort of Roman." Humanist, LXXXVI, (Oct.), pp. 303-35. A discussion of Greene's works in the light of A Sort of Life. Touches upon Greene's direct association with the experiences of his characters, the subject of pain, his fascination by failure which constitutes part of his preoccupation with "the dangerous edge," and the mysterious relationship of opposites in his novels. Also includes a "portrait study" by Karsh of Ottawa.

A7112 Larsen, Frans O. "Menneskesyn og livstolkning i tre katolske romaner af Graham Greene." Extracta, III, pp. 160-65. In Danish. The essay attempts to find a common denominator in the characterization of people in Brighton Rock, The Power and the Glory and The Heart of the Matter in order to illustrate Greene's view of life. Maintains that if the characters find themselves trapped in situations of conflict, it is only God's grace that can reach out to them in their weakness and sets them free.

A7113 McDonald, James L. "Graham Greene: A Reconsideration." ArQ, XXVII, pp. 197-210. An "unorthodox" approach arguing that the richness and density of the novels do not arise from Greene's preoccupation with theological issues but from his concern with the social and political issues of the times, that his use of Catholicism is "overtly political" and a mere "frame of reference" for probing these concerns. In this context, Brighton Rock becomes a "proletarian novel dealing directly with class struggle in England," The Power and the Glory an "examination of the nature and effects of one result of class struggle--the revolution," and The Heart of the Matter a "war novel focussing on ... the moral and religious complications," resulting from the War. Traces Greene's "political sympathies" from England Made Me through The Ministry of Fear to The Quiet American and The Comedians.

A7114 McInery, Ralph. "The Greene-ing of America." Commonweal, XCV (15 Oct.), pp. 59-61. Taking his lead from A. Burgess (see A671), he reiterates that Greene's anti-Americanism is essentially theological; i.e., Americanism is to Greene a "medieval evil: a progressivism and secularism disguised in the remnants of faith, a confusion of categories."

A7115 Majid, S. H. "The Existential Concern in Graham Greene." IJES, XII, pp. 75-85. Argues that though Greene has moved in the direction of Sartrean existentialism where he views man's freedom "in the context of the modern psychological and scientific determinism," his resulting experience with the sordidness and the absurdity of human existence does not lead to affirmation and optimism but into an "abysmal pessimism" where he is closer to Céline and Kafka than Camus and Sartre. Examines Fowler, Querry and especially Brown--the failures of all three in their attempt to find a principle that would lend meaning to their existence--to illustrate Greene's descent into "abysmal pessimism."

A7116 Milner, Ian. "Values and Irony in Graham Greene." AUCP, XIV, pp. 65-73. Focusses on A Burnt-Out Case to show how Greene uses, as main literary mode, an irony that "suffuses both the dramatic movement of the story and the narrational point of view" to represent Querry's slow search for recovery from his alienation, and to emphasize "the significance of the human act." Also examines The Power and the Glory to show the effects obtained in the expression of religious values by irony. Maintains that the ironical contrast between the priest's human weakness and his sacerdotal duties is abandoned in the final stages of the novel and replaced by the "affirmations of the apologist."

A7117 Munzar, Jiri. "Graham Greene, Essayist." PP, XIV, pp. 30-38. "A mosaic of quotations, brief characteristics and attempts at evaluation." The survey covers The Lost Childhood and Collected Essays, Essai Catholiques, British

Dramatists and Why Do I Write, and attempts to focus on "Greene's conception of reality in general and upon his approach to literature and individual authors."

A7118 Roberts, Cecil. "Graham Greene's Sort of Life." B&B, XVII (Oct.), pp. 28-31. Though ostensibly a review of A Sort of Life, the writer takes Greene to task for his remarks on The Nottingham Journal and on himself as editor and novelist. Accuses Greene of being a "careless and inaccurate writer" who may have been an "acute observer of prostitutes" but is most inaccurate in his observations on Nottingham.

A7119 Sale, Walter. "An Interview in New York with Walter Allen." SNNTS, III:4 (Winter), pp. 405-29. On pp. 416-17, W. Allen discusses his view that comedy is more serious than tragedy and considers Greene as a novelist who has "often comic strains" in his novels but is not a "comic" novelist.

A7120 Scruton, Roger. "Graham Greene." Spectator, (15 May), pp. 667-68. Takes stock of Greene as a novelist on the occasion of the Collected Edition of The Confidential Agent, The Power and the Glory and The Heart of the Matter--novels of unequal merit and "ill-written." Critical of Greene for not being interested in relations between people--he chooses his characters from a "limited and predetermined range" of human attitudes and relies on "spiritual conflicts" to give them life. Greene is also at his best when portraying the "anxiety-ridden introversion" of a hunted man in solitude. Acknowledges Greene's "gift for construction" but takes him severely to task for his inability to bring his taste for "exotic surroundings into any true relation with his theme," and also for his "slight" interest in language. Prefers the "witty and delicate" Travels with My Aunt over The Power and the Glory and The Heart of the Matter.

A7121 Shenker, Israel. "Graham Greene at 66." NYTBR, (12 Sept.), pp. 2 & 26. An interview in which Greene speaks of his coming visit to the U. S. to see his new American publisher, Simon & Schuster. Comments on his attempt to achieve accuracy in A Sort of Life and the, by now, familiar topics of boredom and his method of writing. Also makes interesting remarks on the theology which accommodates evil in his forthcoming novel.

A7122 Sternlight, Sanford. "Prologue to the Sad Comedies: Graham Greene's Major Early Novels." MQ, XII, pp. 427-35. Analyzes Greene's "Christian existentialist" protagonists--Fred Hale, the Whiskey Priest, Scobie--in an attempt to prove that these characters prefigure the "mutilated men" of Greene's later absurd, non-Christian, Godless or Sartrian existentialist characters in the fifties and sixties.

A7123 Tyrrell, Gerrard. Letter. CH, (1 Oct.), p. 5. Responds to W. Igoe's review of A Sort of Life. Makes a distinction between Greene's "creative ability and religious faith." Finds little "Catholic content" in the novels and the autobiography with which the "Catholic literate" may relate without straining his religious beliefs.

A7124 Unsigned. "The Man Within." TLS, 3, 629. (17 Sept.), pp. 1101-02. Rpt. in Graham Greene: A Collection of Critical Essays. Ed. Samuel Hynes. Twentieth Century Views. Englewood Cliffs, N.J.: Prentice-Hall, Inc., 1973, pp. 8-16. A review article on A Sort of Life and the Collected Edition of Brighton Rock, The Confidential Agent, England Made Me, The Heart of the Matter, It's a Battlefield, Our Man in Havana and The Power and the Glory, and an assessment of Greene as a novelist. Considers A Sort of Life as having the "virtue of a good autobiography: it is frank, honest and entertaining." There is, however, another autobiography that emerges from the Introductions to the Collected Edition. This edition is important as a monument to the major English novelist writing in the tradition of the "art-novel," and one who has expressed the "religious sense, and created a fictive world in which human acts are important." Though his art may offer little comfort to the religious since he "celebrates minimal virtues," Greene has nevertheless created a world in which "creative art is a function of the religious mind."

R711 Allen, Trevor. "The Young Graham Greene." ContempR, CCXIX:1269 (Oct.), p. 218. A review of A Sort of Life that notes the "mental turbulence" of the early years and the "typical Greene touches" in the writing. Though some of the details may be "too doting," for the "distinctive recall the book is inimitable."

R712 Alvarez, A. "In the Gloomy Country of Graham Greene's Heart." SatR, LIV (25 Sept.), pp. 33-35, 49. Notes the strength of Greene's terseness, "his liverish, morning-after realism" and morbid taste for the macabre in A Sort of Life, as well as his possession by "the demons of failure and boredom." Also notices the deceptive "ease and limpidity" of his prose and the "adult tone of voice."

R713 B., B. A. "A Sort of Life." PW, CC (12 July), p. 71. Pre-publication notice describing the memoirs as "quietly fascinating, coolly understated and irresistible reading."

R714 Bayley, John. "The Greening of Graham Greene." Listener, LXXXVI (16 Sept.), pp. 375-76. Greene is not exactly the best of memoirists for no one could be "less confessive" than him. Though it describes his world as having been "anonymous, drab, desolatingly predictable," the memoir is admirable in that it is never pretentious, and its interest lies not so much in revealing his early life as in the "analysis of how he came to be a writer, and the suggestion of what sort of writer he became."

R715 Bedient, Calvin. "The Nihilism of Boredom." NRep, CLXV: 14 (2 Oct.), pp. 23-34. Though "less lovable" than his novels and "self-indulgently steeped in defeat and loss," the autobiography cannot fail to please by "its commanding style." However, because the "tone ... is joyless, the precision is crabbed ... the book is like a burrow in which Greene, conscious of an advancing age, returns gratefully to a prepared nest of failure."

R716 Bell, Pearl K. "Writers & Writing: Rejecting Greatness." NLea, LIV (20 Sept.), pp. 16-17. A review of A Sort of Life that finds the "surprisingly flaccid autobiography" disappointing; it is "rarely amusing ... mainly tedious and tired as if patched together to fulfill a rather distasteful obligation," and it is only toward the end that Greene writes with the "personal intensity that distinguishes autobiography from book keeping."

R717 Bergonzi, Bernard. "Antecedents: A Sort of Life." Month, 2nd NS IV:5 (Nov.), p. 158. Like The Prelude, it offers an account of the growth of a "novelist's" mind, and has all the fascinating "narrative interest, and much of the atmosphere" of a Greene novel.

R718 Calder-Marshall, Arthur. "A Failure, Rich and Famous." EvS, (28 Sept.), p. 20. A short review of A Sort of Life describing Greene's method in the autobiography as "abreactive"--reliving his early life with all the emotions he felt at the time.

R719 Clemons, Walter. "A Sort of Life." NYTBR, (12 Sept.), pp. 3, 34. Finds the autobiography "odd, calm, saturnine ... unexpectedly moving" and one of Greene's "best books," and his concluding remarks on success and failure without any "fake modesty." Also notices the interesting "thread of selective obliviousness" that is one of the themes of the memoirs.

R7110 Connolly, Cyril. "Hair-shirt and Happiness." SunT, (19 Sept.), p. 35. Finds A Sort of Life "a rather frustrating book" whose general tone is "rather tepid" as if Greene were not sufficiently concerned to pass on much enthusiasm to his reader, who, like the author, is merely observing the young Greene from the outside, "recording a case-history for which some of the key data are lacking."

R7111 Dennis, Nigel. "Battle with Boredom." SunTel, (19 Sept.), p. 18. "... The most interesting aspect of (A Sort of Life) is not what it recounts but the way Mr. Greene serves it all up." He is so "offhand" about the truths he tells the reader--almost a book with "throw-away lines."

R7112 Enright, D. J. "Edge of Danger." NSoc, (16 Sept.), pp. 524-25. Rpt. as "The Man Within: The Memoirs of Graham Greene." Man Is an Onion: Reviews and Essays. London: Chatto & Windus, 1972, pp. 16-19. A review of A Sort of Life that questions whether the autobiographer imposes on his past his later vision of life, or whether the later vision grows out of early insights and blindnesses incurred. Finds autobiography "not an overtly personal work but rather an account of the growth of a writer" who works with a "light touch ... reflecting briefly and moralising very little."

R7113 Field, J. C. "The Literary Scene: 1968-1970. Travels with My Aunt." RLV, XXXVII:6, p. 766. Finds Greene's attempt to create an anti-hero a pleasant surprise in this "highly amusing" and "brilliantly told" fantasy which maintains a "tenuous relationship with reality."

R7114 Finn, James. "A Sort of Life." Commonweal, XCV (29 Oct.), pp. 113-14. Finds the memoirs arousing a "distinctly mixed" pleasure because they arouse one's expectations and curiosity which are left unsatisfied. They also provide "few real surprises" or additions to the "contours" already discerned from the novels and their "selectivity" and focus on failure make them a "sort of fiction."

R7115 Foote, Timothy. "The Man Without." Time, XCVIII (27 Sept.), p. 64. A journalistic review of A Sort of Life that notes its "considerable shortcomings" as well as its merits--Greene is better at "emotional reticence than at revelation," and at his brief notes and perceptions than at his own literary influences and evolution.

R7116 Fuller, Edmund. "Graham Greene Views Himself Darkly." WSJ, CLXXVIII (4 Oct.), p. 12. A review of A Sort of Life that regards it as "thoroughly interesting as far as it goes" but is also an "oddly grudging book" that infects the reader with Greene's own "curious distaste for himself," and disappointing in that it falls short of a story of his full life.

R7117 Fuller, Roy. "The Success of Failure." LM, XI (Nov.), pp. 143-46. A review of A Sort of Life that finds that its "extreme readability and satisfaction of our curiosity," as well as the "autobiographical tone," contribute to its success. Also discusses briefly its "purely literary aspect."

R7118 Grosvenor, Peter. "A Man Who Took a Gamble on Life." DaiE, (16 Sept.), p. 4. A short review of A Sort of Life describing the autobiography as being "not unlike a Greene--a somewhat gloomy, guiltridden tract about the first half of his life."

R7119 Hill, William B. "A Sort of Life." Best Sellers, XXXI (1 Dec.), p. 399. Finds the autobiography a "penetrating sort of self-analysis" beautifully written but with too much that is hidden from the reader. Speculates that Greene may have been "looking for himself" when he started the work, as the "curious emphases" and equally "curious lacunae" indicate.

R7120 Holloway, David. "Graham Greene, an Unfinished Portrait." DaiT, (16 Sept.), p. 6. Finds A Sort of Life an "incomplete" book that has something "perfunctory" about it "not only in point of time but in its general approach." Greene repeats himself and it is quite possible that he may have been bored by his own life. Still it remains an "amiable book, a gentle book, the work of a remarkable man, determined to show that he is not particularly remarkable."

R7121 Hughes, Catharine. "Growing Up as Greene." America, CXXV (2 Oct.), pp. 230-32. A review of A Sort of Life that finds the "compendium of memories, reactions and impressions" very fascinating and confirms the view that Greene's "work is linked to his spiritual autobiography."

R7122 Kennedy, William. "Let Us All Now be Thankful for Mr. Greene's Deadly Boredom." Look, XXXV (19 Oct.), p. 64. The review calls A Sort of Life a "fragment of autobiography" in which Greene imaginatively restructures his life but dwells on events "only long enough for a cursory development of the condition."

R7123 Klausler, Alfred P. "Somber Joy." ChrC, LXXXVIII (24 Nov.), p. 1395. The review of A Sort of Life emphasizes the importance of Greene's conversion to Catholicism and notices the "controlled irony ... understated tragedy" that made the "memoirs" a "journey of self-discovery for the sensitive reader."

R7124 Las Vergnas, Raymond. "Une curiosité affamée." NL, XVII (Sept.), p. 9. A review of the French translation of A Sort of Life by Georges Belmont and Hortense Chabrier. Considers the book to contain the essential in what constitutes the personality of the author, and to be interpreted as "une confession par association d'idées ou par allusions cryptiques." Also disappointed by the reiteration of familiar notions and ideas.

R7125 Lehmann-Haupt, Christopher. "The Other Side of Boredom."

NYT, (17 Sept.), p. 39. A review of A Sort of Life that admits some disappointment over Greene's decision to leave so much out but which also recognizes the reasons behind such a decision, and notes that the autobiography "written in a deliberately minor key," is the "ground plan, not the architecture, of a writer's life."

R7126 Lewis, Peter. "When an Author Decides to Tell Should He Tell All?" DaiM, (16 Sept.), p. 7. Describes A Sort of Life as a "bleak book" full of "bleak truths" that leaves much untold, especially about Greene's "failures in adult love, or in his pursuit of religious beliefs,"--just a few "beautifully crisp biscuits" when one had anticipated a meal instead.

R7127 Lodge, David. "Compost of the Imagination." Tablet, CCXXV (18 Sept.), pp. 906-07. Argues that the "key word" of A Sort of Life is "failure," and describes it as a "muted, discreet, carefully selective book" that confirms and fills out earlier sketches, does not provide startling new revelations, but whose details are of absorbing interest. Notes that the more we know about Greene's life, the less it explains "the character and peculiar power of his imagination."

R7128 Lopez Ortega, Ramon. "Travels with My Aunt." FMod, XI (June), pp. 329-31. Maintains that Greene's "cosmovision" makes "Greeneland" a realistic rather than a fantastic universe. As for the novel, it is not as comic as it appears because it portrays human existence with all its crudity and, like Our Man in Havana, the "funniness comes from the situation rather than the man." Rather perplexed by the circumstances surrounding Wordsworth's death.

R7129 Mambrino, J. "Une sorte de vie." Etudes, CCCXXXV (Nov.), 625. Irritated by "la vanité absolue de l'écriture" and "l'aveu d'un ennui plus profond encore que le désespoir." Admits, however, that the autobiography helps one to see Greene better even though the details about his schooldays do not differ much from the experiences of many others.

R7130 Meyer, Catherine. "Books in Brief: A Sort of Life." Harper's, CCXLIII (Nov.), p. 144. Finds the autobiography a "somewhat maussade record" of Greene's evolution as a writer which engages the interest of the reader "almost reluctantly."

R7131 Muggeridge, Malcolm. "The Man Within." Observer, (19 Sept.), p. 31. A sympathetic review of A Sort of Life that notes Greene's "extraordinary elusiveness" for the autobiography tells us no more about Greene than do his "invented or imagined characters in his fiction." Also notes his "complete lack of pretentiousness about his success as a writer."

R7132 O'Brien, R. A. "Books: A Sort of Life." Commentator, XV (Oct.), pp. 22-23. The review is mostly a summary of this "fragment of autobiography" which is described as full of "candid, shining perception ... honest, clearly seen and full of horrors."

R7133 O'Riordan, John. "The Greene Years." LR, XXIII:4 (Winter), pp. 162-63. A review of A Sort of Life as one of those "delightful sentimental prose-fantasies" in which Greene relates his childhood reminiscences with an "engaging candour, a Peter Pan honesty...." Notes that neither Greene himself nor his critics have yet laid bare "the inmost nature of the novelist's obsession."

R7134 Ostermann, Robert. "In A Sort of Life, Mr. Greene Joins Himself and His Creations." NObs, X (25 Sept.), p. 21. Maintains that in the autobiography Greene the novelist "lives" as a result of his self-examination, and his fidelity in capturing the movement between the real world and the imaginary one "raises the book to the level of literature."

R7135 Perez-Minik, Domingo. "'Viajes con mi tía,' de Graham Greene." Insula, XXVI:292 (March), p. 10. A review of the Spanish translation of Travels with My Aunt. Maintains that Greene moves into the realm of comedy to the point of satire with great ease and suggests that Aunt Augusta may well be an "allegory" of Great Britain.

R7136 P[rescott], S. P[eter]. "Ice in the Heart." Newsweek, LXXVIII (20 Sept.), p. 94. A journalistic view of A Sort of Life which notes Greene's "famous pessimism" wedded to the "kind of aphorism old men favor in their memoirs--the kind young men dare not use," and regards the book as Greene's best since A Burnt-Out Case.

R7137 Pritchett, V. S. "The Shadow of Unease." NSta, LXXXII:2113 (17 Sept.), pp. 366-67. As a "Greene-addict," he recognizes Greene's two basic difficulties which lead to the "sort of life" he describes: the loss of the novelist's freedom when he turns autobiographer and the dull monotony of success when narrated compared to the struggle against failure. Regrets the abrupt ending and the omission of more details of Greene's criticism.

R7138 Ratcliffe, Michael. "The Dangerous Edge." Times, (16 Sept.), p. 12. Argues that in A Sort of Life Greene shows great artistic control in this rather short autobiography characterized by "deceptive simplicity and steely strength," at once delightful and orderly without being dry.

R7139 Sayre, Nora. "'Success Is Only a Delayed Failure.'" Book World, V (10 Oct.), p. 8. A review of A Sort of Life that emphasizes Greene's almost gleeful "reveling" in failure and the "voluptuous gloom" of the memoirs which remain, however, "as rewarding as his best novels."

R7140 Scott-Kilvert, Ian. "English Fiction, 1969-70." BBN, (June), pp. 425-30. Refers briefly to Travels with My Aunt as a novel breaking new and unexpected ground and written "with the lightest of touches in a mood of pure farce."

R7141 Sheed, Wilfrid. "The Greene-ing of Graham Greene." Life, LXXI (24 Sept.), p. 10. A review of A Sort of Life that considers the autobiography "an artifact, a sort of fiction and one of his finer ones at that." Also notes Greene's "extraordinary courtesy," humor and "surprising, insinuating charm."

R7142 Sissman, L. E. "Graham Greene Begins." NY, XLVII (2 Oct.), pp. 126-27, 129-30. A review of A Sort of Life that finds the memoirs to contain a great deal of description and evocation--Greene "creates an atmosphere for the reader that is totally his and totally involving"--but little of intimate personal history; the memoirs do not probe into his own motivations and reactions and seem to present the view of an "observer" rather than of a "participant."

R7143 Smith, Jennifer Farley. "One Man's Bear Dance." ChrSM, LXIV (18 Nov.), p. 7. Discontented with A Sort of Life because it covers childhood and early adult years only, and considers it "yet another well-told story ... perhaps the most sophisticated 'entertainment'" Greene has written.

R7144 Solomon, Petre. "Autobiografia: lui Graham Greene." RoLit, IV:43 (Oct.), pp. 27-28. A review of A Sort of Life followed by extracts from the work, translated into Romanian by the reviewer.

R7145 Thompson, Richard J. "A Sort of Life." LJ, XCVI (Aug.), p. 2487. A short review that finds the autobiography limited and hopes for a "more affirmative volume on his mature years."

R7146 Thoorens, Leon. "Graham Greene: Une sorte de vie." RG, X, pp. 102-03. A review of the French translation of A Sort of Life. The autobiography may disappoint because it does not say anything on subjects or topics hitherto regarded as important; but in it, Greene, "le grand timide" explodes any false images created by his admirers and narrates with modesty and courageous sincerity, his "pauvre petite vérité humaine."

R7147 Trevor, William. "The Battlefield." Guardian, (16 Sept.), p. 9. Points out that A Sort of Life is no "great canvas of the times," but a very selective and "quiet touching account of yet another journey without maps." As always with Greene, there is much more to it than what is stated.

R7148 ________. "Journey Without Maps." GuardianW, CV (25 Sept.), p. 20. A review of A Sort of Life. See R7147.

R7149 Weeks, Edward. "The Peripatetic Reviewer." Atlantic, CCXXVIII (Oct.), p. 132. This review of A Sort of Life mostly summarizes Greene's early life but notes his "painfully vivid imagination and the love for escapade that he has never lost."

R7150 White, Terence de Vere. "Greene on Salad Days." IT, (18 Sept.), p. 8. Finds A Sort of Life interesting only insofar as it reveals Greene's "marked detachment" and an Edwardian childhood and a Georgian boyhood now as remote as ever. But as an autobiography, it is "disappointing"; novelists use themselves in their work so that when they turn to autobiography the material is simply not there and the result is "dessicated."

R7151 Wilson, Colin. "Graham Greene's Autobiography." Spectator, 7,473 (18 Sept.), pp. 413-14. Though it is "an excellent little book, beautifully written," it confirms earlier suspicions that Greene's pessimism is shallower than it seems, "merely a grown up version of adolescent misery and Swinburnian world-rejection" wherein failure is not inevitable or the result of original sin as much as of "romanticism and lack of self-discipline."

R7152 Unsigned. "A Sort of Life." AL, II (Dec.), p. 1225. Briefly noted as a nomination for the "notable Books Council."

R7153 ________. "A Sort of Life." Booklist, LXVIII (1 Oct.), p. 128. A brief review noting that the autobiographical reminiscences quietly evoke the ambience of his childhood without humor or irony.

R7154 ________. "Graham Greene in Adversity." Bookseller, (4 Sept.), p. 1470. A review of A Sort of Life describing the autobiography as being "incomparably written" and "engaging." Quotes extensively from it.

R7155 ________. "Fifty Notable Books: A Sort of Life." Bookworld, V (5 Dec.), p. 26. Briefly noted.

R7156 ________. "A Sort of Life." Commonweal, XCV (3 Dec.), p. 236. Brief notice.

R7157 _______. "Loom of Youth." Econ, CCXL (18 Sept.), pp. 59-60. A review of A Sort of Life as an autobiography where the camera is focussed on Greene's youth with a "sort of unsurprised sadness" and which displays adequately "the natural imbalance of an adolescent mind."

R7158 _______. "A Sort of Life." Esquire, LXXVI (Dec.), pp. 94 & 278. Describes the autobiography as "immensely accomplished, beautifully written, honest and vivid" and "most moving" when Greene lifts the edge of his reserve and reveals part of the loneliness and pain he had experienced.

R7159 _______. "Graham Greene Reveals How He Lived Like a James Bond." IT, (16 Sept.), p. 5. This is a mere narration of the more sensational incidents in the autobiography: Greene's brief flirtation with espionage and Russian roulette.

R7160 _______. "A Sort of Life." Kirkus, XXXIX (15 July), p. 783. Pre-publication note remarking on the value of the autobiography as it "prefigures, isolates and supplements" material that is used later in the novels.

R7161 _______. "A Sort of Life." NYTBR, (5 Dec.), p. 80. Briefly noted.

R7162 _______. "Travels with My Aunt." PW, CXCIX (4 Jan.), p. 58. Pre-publication notice of the Bantam paperback.

R7163 _______. "Travels with My Aunt." SatR, LIV (27 March), p. 42. Brief notice of Bantam paperback.

R7164 _______. "A Sort of Life." SatR, (27 Nov.), p. 52. Briefly noticed as a suitable gift book.

D711 Gonzales, Ramond Joseph. The Latin American Dictator in the Novel. Univ. of Southern California. DAI, XXXII:10 (April 1972), 5787A-88A.

D712 Hanlon, Robert Michael. Graham Greene's Religious Sense. Univ. of Massachusetts. DAI, XXXII:7 (1972), 4001A.

D713 Ingersoll, Earl George. Imagery in the Novels of Graham Greene. Univ. of Wisconsin. DAI, XXXII:6, 3308A.

D714 O'Grady, Walter Anthony. Political Contexts in the Novels of Graham Greene and Joyce Cary. Univ. of Toronto. DAI, XXXII:12 (1972), 6995A.

D715 Steadman, E. M. 'Lord Jim' and 'The Heart of the Matter.' M. Phil. Univ. of Sussex.

D716 Wobbe, Roland A. Rhetoric in the Novels of Graham Greene. Univ. of Exeter.

1972

B721 Allen, Walter. "Graham Greene." Contemporary Novelists. Ed. James Vinson. Pref. Walter Allen. London: St. James Press; New York: St. Martin's Press. Rpt. 1973, pp. 530-34. Includes a biographical sketch, a bibliography of his writings up to 1972 and a critical essay evaluating Greene's achievement, his status as a "learned" international novelist, his superb storytelling, his choice and use of images to give his action "pace, diversity, contract and immediate impact on the reader," all of which results in "concision, compactness, intensity of focus ... for which Greene has not been given sufficient credit."

B722 Atkinson, F. G. "Floreat Augusta--or, On First Looking into Travels with My Aunt." Gleanings from Greeneland. Ed. J. S. Ryan. Armidale, N. S. W.: Univ. of New England, pp. 81-90. Text of a lecture delivered at Summer School. (See B7210). Rejects the "unviable critical approach" that gives excessive attention to Greene's Catholic novels because of their theology, and contends that Travels with My Aunt is his "most serious and most well-wrought work," the "culmination" of his development, different from previous novels because it is a "thorough-going piece of stylisation." It also expresses in a dramatic way other tendencies in Greene's thought and method; viz., humor and the predominance given to female character.

B723 Croft, J. C. "Graham Greene and Africa (Journey Without Maps and The Heart of the Matter)." Gleanings from Greeneland. Ed. J. S. Ryan, Armidale, N. S. W.: Univ. of New England, pp. 70-80. Text of a lecture delivered at a Summer School. (See B7210). Outlines six motives behind Greene's journey to Africa and speculates that the journey into Liberia contained a "veiled suggestion" of a "life-threat and possibly a suicidal gesture ... a roulette revolver of Greene's adolescence," and suggests that its gains reside mainly in his better understanding of self, as well as a deeper insight into the human heart. The section on The Heart of the Matter regards Freetown as the "quintessence of the seedy, and Scobie ... its seedy Christian," seediness being the twentieth century "equivalent" of nineteenth-century ennui.

B724 Dubu, Jean. La poetique de Graham Greene dans "La Puissance et la Gloire." "Situation" No. 26. Paris: Minard "Lettres Modernes." A Study of The Power and the Glory that discusses Greene's perspective or "optique" and the devices he used to give the novel its "puissance de vie." The work is divided into five chapters. The Preface examines briefly the Biblical sources of the title and Ch. 1 maintains that Greene has borrowed more than the title from the Gospels and discusses the moral and religious significance of the geographical and historical framework of the action as an illustration of the use of prophecy on the end of time, "une projection dans le monde contemporaine de l'évangile de la fin du monde." Ch. 2 discusses the spiritual growth of the whiskey priest, his aspirations for sanctity and the notion of martyrdom. Ch. 3 examines Greene's indebtedness to French novelists, and especially to André Malraux in his delineation of the lieutenant. Ch. 4 is an interesting, fruitful and detailed comparison with Dryden's allegorical The Hind and the Panther, noting Greene's frequent borrowings from the animal kingdom, and Ch. 5 analyzes the stylistic devices Greene uses to achieve his end. The Postscript finds confirmation and support for the findings of the study in A Sort of Life which was published when the work was in press.

B725 Enn, Josef. Graham Greene's Romane: Eine Neuinterpretation ihres religiosen Gehalts. Vienna: Verlag Notring. Originally a Ph. D. dissertation. Devotes a chapter for the analysis of each of Brighton Rock, The Power and the Glory, The Heart of the Matter, The Quiet American, A Burnt-Out Case, The Living Room and The Potting Shed, and the most recent works of the sixties. Attempts to indicate the religious dimension of the works and to trace its development in them. Concerned with the representation of religion in the works, the world or the ambience which made the representation possible, and not with any special system or theology. In this context, he concentrates on the Catholic elements, the conception and ideas that form the bases of the novels rather than "Catholic themes." Also analyzes the stylistic aspects. Includes an extensive and valuable bibliography of primary and secondary sources.

B726 Enright, D. J. "The Man Within: The Memoirs of Graham Greene." Man Is an Onion: Reviews and Essays. London: Chatto and Windus, pp. 16-19. Rpt. from NSoc, (15 Sept. 1971), pp. 524-25. See R7112.

B727 McInherny, Frances C. "It's a Battlefield--A World in Chaos." Gleanings from Greeneland. Ed. J. S. Ryan. Armidale, N. S. W.: Univ. of New England, pp. 20-30. An essay written exclusively for the collection. (See B7210). The discussion of the novel centers on Greene as a revolutionary social thinker, à la Orwell, Isherwood and the early Waugh, as one who is not confined to specifically religious writing but who can indict society, with its highly mechanized ruthless system, for dehumanizing the individual and alienating him.

B728 ________. "Some Thoughts Occasioned on Rereading The Power and the Glory." Gleanings from Greeneland. Ed. J. S. Ryan. Armidale, N. S. W.: Univ. of New England, pp. 31-43. Text of a lecture delivered at a Summer School on Graham Greene. (See B7210). Discusses the novel as a work of art that reflects Greene's major preoccupations, and whose driving force is the religious sense which determines the importance of the human act. Examines the contract between the priest and the lieutenant and the sense of responsibility that each has, as well as the main themes of betrayal, childhood and violence of the "world as battlefield"--themes which manifest themselves in the novel.

B729 Murray, Edward. "Graham Greene and the Silver Screen." The Cinematic Imagination: Writers and the Motion Pictures. New York: Frederick Ungar Publishing, pp. 244-60. A judicious and informative account of Greene's "ambivalent attitude" to the motion picture industry, his mindfulness of the effects that can be achieved in both forms, followed by a brief discussion of the filmic technique in the "entertainments" he wrote while film critic to The Spectator and a more detailed discussion of the cinematic elements in The Heart of the Matter, The End of the Affair and The Quiet American. The comparison of the novels to their film adaptations lead him to conclude, quite rightly, that Greene's "filmic approach remains ancillary" to his novelistic vision; i.e., his "cinematic imagination is 'literarised.'"

B7210 Ryan, J[ohn] S[prott], ed. Gleanings from Greeneland. Armidale, N. S. W.: Univ. of New England. A collection of six essays by J. S. Ryan, F. C. McInherny, J. C. Croft, and F. G. Atkinson, four of which--the first, the third, the fifth and the sixth--are drawn in part or in toto from texts of lectures delivered at a Summer School on Graham Greene at the Univ. of New England, New South Wales, Australia, in January 1972. The second and fourth essays have been written for the collection. See B722, B723, B727, B728, B7211 and B7212.

B7211 ________. "Men of Affairs--The Greenes of Berkhamstead." Gleanings from Greeneland. Ed. J. S. Ryan. Armidale, N. S. W.: Univ. of New England, pp. 1-19. This essay on Greene's family and the author's temper is drawn from two lectures on Graham Greene. (See B7210). Gives an account of each member of the family using "official sources" other than Greene's, and regards Greene's appointment to a "department of the Foreign Office" as the "third seminal event in his adult personal life." Uses Kim Philby's book and another on Philby by Bruce Page, et al., as major sources of Greene's activity during the forties, and attempts to indicate changes in Greene's apparent attitude after the general identification of him with the stance of Catholicism, especially his later social concerns, a synthesis of which can be found, he claims, in The Comedians.

B7212 ________. "Structure, Imagery and Theme in The Power and the Glory." Gleanings from Greeneland. Ed. J. S. Ryan. Armidale, N. S. W.: Univ. of New England, pp. 44-69. Examines the "carefully proportioned" structure, both "stylized and symmetric" in the novel which is viewed as an "allegorical prose account of a man who is ... the bearer of a cosmic truth for all men." Focusses on the "thematic 'threading' of images" in the novel which sometimes "occur in triplets," and the "continual barrages of faunal attackers"; chooses recognition "of oneself, of people and of the need to express concern for one's fellow beings" as one of the major themes, so that deception is put aside and characters escape from "chaos to order." However, the book is not a "great novel" in spite of structure, imagery and theme because the central figures are conceived less as characters than as "vehicles for argument."

B7213 Tracy, H. L. W. "Graham Greene." The Critic as Artist: Essays on Books, 1920-1970; with Some Preliminary Ruminations by H. L. Mencken. Ed. Gilbert A. Harrison. New York: Liveright, pp. 315-20. A reprint of "The Life and Soul of a Party." NRep, CXL (20 April 1959), pp. 15-16. See A5913.

B7214 Wolfe, Peter. Graham Greene: The Entertainer. Pref. by Harry T. Moore. Carbondale and Edwardsville: Southern Illinois Univ. Press; London and Amsterdam: Feffer and Simons, Inc. This is the first book length study devoted to Greene's entertainments. The study attempts a critical assessment of each entertainment in a separate chapter, from Stamboul Train up to and including Our Man in Havana, by discussing, more often than not, style, technique, structure, characterization and design, and underlining general merits and defects. Investigates their role as entertainments and the underlying serious themes. Quotes and refers extensively to other critics. The first chapter that discusses Greene's art as an entertainer is basically a reprint of an article in Studies in the Twentieth Century. See A7024.

B7215 Yamamoto, Yukio. "Graham Greene's Place." Gendai Eikoku Sakkaron: Maugham and Greene. Tokyo: Kirihara Sohten, pp. 165-91. In Japanese. This is ch. 8 of the book and only part of it discusses Greene's place in contemporary English writing. The previous seven chapters deal exclusively with S. Maugham and ch. 10 examines the prevailing tendencies in recent English novels.

B7216 Ziolkowski, Theodore. "The Power and the Glory." Fictional Transfigurations of Jesus. Princeton, N.J.: Princeton Univ. Press, pp. 214-325. An analysis of the New Testament symbolism and motifs in The Power and the Glory--one of twenty modern novels analyzed. Maintains that its New Testament title describes the "enduring qualities in mankind, and specifically in the lapsed whiskey priest" and suggests the "secularization" of the figure of Jesus and the Christian "message," and also serves to alert the reader to the symbolic or allegorical dimension of the novel.

A721 Adamson, Jyd. "Graham Greene as Film Critic." S&S, 41 (Spring), pp. 104-06. Discusses Greene's views on the cinema: his wish that it would give the common people what the great Elizabethan dramatists had--a cinema both poetic and common--his realization of the cinema as a "physical medium" and his aesthetic concern for its realism. Greene's weekly reviews, however, left him little scope "for the formulation of original theory."

A722 Chaudhury, M. K. "Graham Greene's Travels with My Aunt: A Picaresque Novel." PURBA, III:2, pp. 79-85. Contends that the novel responds fully to the requirements of a pure picaresque novel in its action, characters and its lack of moral point of view. Like Tom Jones its basic plot is a quest--Henry Pulling for his mother--in which, under her tutorship, he is transformed "from a toff into a tart." As for Aunt Augusta, she is a "highly polished picaro, a modern Moll Flanders."

A723 Hynes, Joseph. "The 'Facts' at The Heart of the Matter." TSLL, XIII:4 (Winter), pp. 711-26. A new reading that "interaccommodates more of the book's details than any other" after taking to task earlier interpretations by almost every major critic and suspending religious belief or unbelief, even while insisting that "some knowledge" of Catholicism is legitimately required of anyone reading the novel. Contends that the critic's job is to see "what is given rather than to issue restrictions in advance" whether it is with regards to joy and Christianity or Scobie's dilemma, and that the distancing resulting from the omniscient point of view shows that the narrative point of view is not only different from Scobie's views but also often militates against it, thus requiring the reader to "balance attitudes." Examines the mistakes that Scobie commits "unawares" as well as those he commits as a "conscious sinner within definable limits" and argues that these mistakes provide a sound basis for supposing him ultimately saved."

A724 Mookerjee, R. N. "Graham Greene on the Art of Fiction." RUSEng, VI, pp. 91-101. Reconstructs Greene's views on the novel, its function and place in the modern world as well as the relationship he envisages between the artist, his times and society from his non-fictional writings: Journey Without Maps, The Lawless Roads, Why Do I Write, In Search of a Character and Collected Essays..

A725 Muller, Charles H. "Graham Greene and the Justification of God's Ways." UES, X:1 pp. 23-35. A detailed discussion of good and evil in Brighton Rock. Shows a certain degree of parallelism between Milton's Satan and Greene's Pinkie; but whereas the former proves the majesty of God by poetic suggestion, the latter, by emphasizing the positive existence and intensity of evil, implies the limitlessness of its heavenly counterpart, goodness. This dualistic theodocy of defining the Unknown in terms of its opposite is best seen in Pinkie's demoniacal pride and Rose's love which symbolizes the presence of Grace. "It is the incomprehensible mystery of this goodness that counterbalances and, so to speak, cancels out the insoluble problem of evil."

A726 ________. "Graham Greene and the Absurd." UES, X:2, pp. 34-44. Argues that the "radical absurdity of the universe" manifests itself in Fowler, "l'homme absurde who becomes, through existentialist anguish, l'homme revolté," and especially in Brown, "l'homme absurde," perhaps par excellence, whose restless rootlessness and inability to revolt or act is the result of his vision of the meaninglessness of an irrational universe. Contends that by portraying such a universe, Greene has affirmed, without falling back on Catholic theology, that life without Grace or God is bound to remain meaningless, empty and absurd. Points out an interesting parallelism between Chardin's views on man's development in The Phenomenon of Man and Colins' in A Burnt-Out Case.

A727 O'Brien, John. "The Novel of Salvation." Cresset, XXXV:3 (Jan.), pp. 12-15. Argues for the recognition of the "novel of salvation" that has its own theme and structure. One of two ways in which the religious writer can show the salvation of a character without straining credibility lies in the choice of "'active' writers." Refers briefly to the Whiskey Priest's heroic love and Scobie's "extreme compassion" among others.

A728 Podlipskaya, E. I. "O roli obraza-simvola v raskrytii ideinogo soderzhaniya romana Greme Grina 'Komedianty.'" Tashkend, LXXXVI, pp. 168-81. In Russian. Examines the role of the image-symbol in revealing the ideology of The Comedians.

A729 Rossani, Wolfango. "Graham Greene fra gazia e peccato," ORom, (26 April), p. 3. A "spiritual portrait" of Greene as a Catholic writer--not in the orthodox sense--of great talent whose ambivalence between sin and grace in his major novels makes him worthy of being called an Anglo-Saxon Mauriac. Gives a biographical sketch of Greene and surveys briefly his major novels.

A7210 Tsuchiya, Tetsu. "Kindai Utopia no Shumatsu-Graham Greene no Baai," EigoS, CXVIII:3 (1 June), pp. 126-28. In Japanese. A short essay showing that Greene's treatment of Catholicism, loneliness, conflict, and God by utilizing the thriller pattern in The Power and the Glory and The End of the Affair indicates the end of modern Utopia.

R721 Allen, Trevor. "Collected Stories." B&B, XVIII (Dec.), p. 94. The review notes that though the collection may constitute a "novelist-author's own recreational 'escape,'" it reveals Greene's best narrative qualities, and his acute feeling for character and background. Comments briefly on some ten stories separately.

R722 Blocker, Gunter. "Der befreite Graham Greene." Merkur, XXVI, pp. 195-97. A review of A Sort of Life that regards Greene as "liberated" in the autobiography--his "best" book--for he is no longer a comedian wearing the mask of the novelist.

R723 Brudnoy, D. J. C. "Books in Brief: A Sort of Life." NR, XXIV (21 Jan.), p. 55. The review finds the "off-hand manner" of this rather "casual, semi-impressionistic" autobiography pleasing, and though A Sort of Life may give a few valuable insights into boyhood, it is almost "maddeningly vague" about his adult romances and marriage.

R724 Butcher, Maryvonne. "The Incisive Critic." Tablet, CCXXVI (9 Dec.), p. 1180. The reviews included in The Pleasure-Dome make the "most compulsive reading" for the film addict as well as the Greene devotee. His technical knowledge enables him to see below the surface of any movie, he is reluctant to pass moral judgments though one can easily detect where he stands and he "writes like an angel," and can be, at times, "wickedly funny."

R725 Coleman, John. "Before the Flood." NSta, LXXXIV (10 Nov.), pp. 687-88. Finds Greene's film reviews collected in The Pleasure-Dome "at best, examples of pithiness, wit and commonsense." They provide the reader with the opportunity to witness the reaction between novelist and reviewer. As a reviewer, Greene was no "theorist" but had a "vivid, descriptive gift, flexibility and that necessary touch of relevance." Considers the use of "criticism" in the subtitle as too strong for reviews.

R726 Forrest, Alan. "B & B's Look at 1971." B&B, XVII (Feb.), pp. 26-27. Makes brief reference to A Sort of Life for being "nicely grumpy, wonderfully evocative in places.... The work of a real professional."

R727 French, Philip. "Perceptive Film Reviewer." Times, (30 Oct.), p. 9. The Pleasure-Dome is for anyone interested in the movies, in Greene, in the thirties or "in plain good writing." Rather critical of John Russell Taylor's editing, and the omission of Greene's important essay in the fifties, "The Novelist and the Cinema--A Personal Experience." However, the collection ensures for Greene a place among the most perceptive movie reviewers of the time.

R728 Green, Martin. "Greeneland." Month, 2nd NS V:12 (Dec.), pp. 376-77. A review of Collected Stories. Argues that the "modest and intelligent" introduction stresses the "gay unexpectedness" with which these stories got themselves written, yet they seem to evoke primarily "pity and indignation" in the reader: pity by the life experience described and indignation at the assemblage of "trivial anecdotes" passed as literature in which nothing has been "explored," "described" or "created."

R729 Gregor, Ian. "A Sort of Fiction?" Blackfriars, LIII (March), pp. 120-24. A review of A Sort of Life that finds the autobiography "so spectacularly not the kind of book" one expected, and regards it as a "failed fiction" in which the central figure--the novelist, the only figure Greene feels justified in portraying--does not come alive. "Stripped of the fiction to which it gave rise, it seems bleak and inconsequential."

R7210 James, Clive. "Greene on Film." Observer, (5 Nov.), p. 38. Describes The Pleasure-Dome as the "journalism of a master writer" and as a "pressure-packed cornucopia, a bounteous horn of epigrams." Though Greene does not set out to entertain, his criticism is "readability incarnate" and reveals his receptivity to the movies.

R7211 Keils, R. M. "A Sort of Life." DR, LII:1 (Spring), pp. 159, 161, 163. A review that maintains that the memoirs complement earlier nonfictional autobiographical material with their "penetrating definition" of the early but significant and formative years. Criticizes the book for not having an index and for leaving much unsaid about his parents or his own relationships with "loved ones."

R7212 Linehan, Fergus. "Greene on Film." IT, (11 Nov.), p. 10. The Pleasure-Dome is "very well worth reading in its own right," giving a run down on the cinema of the 30s, "perceptive, witty and of course, supremely well written." One cannot ignore the opinions put forward in the collection even though one may dissent from them.

R7213 Lodge, David. "Greeneland Revisited." Tablet, CCXXVI (21 Oct.), pp. 1002-03. A perceptive review of Collected Stories commenting upon and evaluating Greene's achievement as a short story writer. Maintains that the short story has never been his "metier"--it is almost always "peripheral" rather than central to his imaginative interests--and that his best efforts belong to his earlier rather than later period. Finds "Under the Garden" which Greene claims as one of his best productions rather "heavy going"--a quality almost always absent from Greene's writings.

R7214 Lopez Ortega, Ramon. "Graham Greene: A Sort of Life." FMod, XII:45 (June), pp. 340-43. Finds the autobiography informative especially of Greene's frustrations and conflicts during adolescence, but maintains that the "arbitrary" conclusion is not convincing and deserves a sequel.

R7215 McDowell, Frederick P. W. "Time of Plenty: Recent British Novels." ConL, XIII:3 (Summer), pp. 361-94. Includes a review of Travels with My Aunt among some fifty or so other novels. Page 369 describes the novel as "not his best" because it lacks the ethical and metaphysical issues of moment which Greene always analyzes with passion and insight.

R7216 Malcolm, Derek. "Greene Shades." GuardianW, CVII (11 Nov.), p. 24. Maintains that The Pleasure-Dome is a "frightening delight" to read: it gives the man behind the writing and the cinema of the thirties in consistent quality writing that elegantly conveys what it is to be confronted with "the horrifying inanity of human entertainment."

R7217 Miller, Kari. "Father, Son and Holy Ghost." NYRB, XIX (20 July), pp. 12-15. Includes a review of A Sort of Life. Finds the book "pleasant" and "agreeable" for both its "frankness and bluntness," but is rather puzzled by Greene's indifference to so much, and exasperated and bored by it at times, especially "when he reaches for his revolver."

R7218 Phillips, Gene D. "Graham Greene on Film: Collected Film Criticism, 1935-40." America, CXXVII (30 Dec.), pp. 576-77. Maintains that the collection boasts some of "the wittiest and most perceptive film criticism." Quotes from reviews in which Greene is "lethal" and "kind" and also from his notice of Shirley Temple's "Wee Willie Winkie" which is not included in the collection.

R7219 Roud, Richard. "Greene Around the Edges." Book World, VI (31 Dec.), p. 5. Regards the collection of film reviews as "quirky, unreliable" and giving a "selective picture" of the last half of the 30s. Concedes that Greene knows "how to write," can sum up qualities accurately but he remains "an amateur in the worst sense of the word"; his standards remain "all too literary," and he has "something of a tin ear."

R7220 Sayre, Nora. "Graham Greene on Film." NYTBR, (17 Dec.), pp. 3, 16. The review of The Pleasure-Dome quotes from Greene's film criticism to show his conception of the film as a popular medium, and the care with which he judged films. Attempts to show what attracted Greene in the reviews, especially his demand for "reality."

R7221 Wilson, F. A. C. "A Sort of Life." WCR, VI (Jan.), pp. 76-77. The review is mainly concerned with the "redeployment" of the material of Greene's "essentially prosaic account" of his early life in the works, and notes that the "Life" does not say anything of "the cultural pressures underlying the metaphysical stances."

R7222 Wolfe, Peter. "Greene Books." PrS, XLVI (Spring), pp. 83-85. A review of A Sort of Life that also includes a short note on Triple Pursuit! A Graham Greene Omnibus. Finds the autobiography both "self-exploration and self-discovery," and though it may be criticized for evasiveness, there is nothing escapist about Greene's discussions of his lifelong obsessions in the volume which reveals "a good deal, maybe more than some readers can take."

R7223 Unsigned. "Travels with My Aunt." B&B, XVII (March), p. viii. A brief note that also remarks on the confusion created by, and the inadequacy of, the division into novel and entertainment in the case of this novel.

R7224 ________. "Graham Greene on Film: Collected Film Criticism 1935-1940. Ed. by John Russell Taylor." Book World, VI (17 Dec.), p. 15. Brief notice.

R7225 ________. "A Sort of Life." Choice, VIII (Jan.), p. 1452. The brief review does not elicit the value of the autobiography but finds the intensity of Greene's disillusionment "denigrating" because Greene seems to relish reflecting upon it before his audience.

R7226 ________. "A Sort of Life." PW, CCII (20 Nov.), p. 67. Brief notice of Pocket Books edition.

R7227 _______. "A Sort of Life." VQR, XLVIII (Winter), p. viii. A short review noting its extraordinary style. The book is a pleasure to read for the "sheer skill" with which words are put together and its glimpses into Greene's youth.

R7228 _______. "Escape Hatch." TLS, (20 Oct.), p. 1245. Argues that the Collected Stories are not an escape from the novelist's world because the familiar Greene landscape and the familiar occupants are still there, and so is the "force and individuality" of Greene's imagination to be seen in these stories in the "interstices" of his novelist's career.

D721 Christman, Elizabeth A. Hell Lay About Them: Childhood in the Work of Graham Greene. New York Univ. DAI, XXXIII (1973), 6345A.

D722 Enn, Josef. Graham Greenes Romane: Eine Neuinterpretation ihres religiosen Gehaltes. Univ. of Vienna. Published. Vienna: Verlag Notring, 1972. See B725.

D723 Geist, Joseph E. The Critical Reception of Graham Greene in Selected American Catholic Periodicals, 1930-1970. Univ. of Kansas. DAI, XXXIII, 2933A.

D724 Harmer, Ruth M. Mexico, Modern Literature, and the Search for Soul. Univ. of Southern California. DAI, XXXV:1 (July 1974), 452A-53A.

D725 MacDonald, Sara Jane. The Aesthetics of Grace in Flannery O'Connor and Graham Greene. Univ. of Illinois at Urbana-Champaign. DAI, XXXIII (1973), 5734A.

1973

B731 Auden, W. H. "The Heresy of Our Time." Graham Greene: A Collection of Critical Essays. Twentieth Century Views. Ed. Samuel Hynes. Englewood Cliffs, N.J.: Prentice-Hall, pp. 93-95. Rpt. from Renascence, I (Spring 1949), 23-24. See A495.

B732 Bitterli, Urs. Conrad, Malraux, Greene, Weiss: Schriftsteller und Kolonialismus. Zurich: Benziger Verlag. The section on Greene, pp. 109-147, examines Journey Without Maps, The Heart of the Matter and The Quiet American not so much for their literary value, but as "historical" sources that express the times and reveal the stance of Europe on colonialism and the range of problems that colonialists encounter.

B733 Cartmell, Canon Joseph. "A Postscript to Evelyn Waugh."

Graham Greene: A Collection of Critical Essays. Twentieth Century Views. Ed. Samuel Hynes. Englewood Cliffs, N. J.: Prentice-Hall, pp. 103-05. Rpt. from Tablet, CXCI:5637 (5 June 1948), p. 354. See A484.

B734 Charvat, Eva. Die Religiositat und das Thema der Verfolgung in sechs Romanen von Graham Greene. Anglelsachsische Sprache und Literatur 14. Bern: Herbert Lang; Frankfurt: Peter Lang. Originally a Doctoral Dissertation at the University of Bern, 1973. Divided into two parts. Part one gives a general analysis of the novels, and analyzes individual characters in Brighton Rock, The Power and the Glory, The Heart of the Matter, The End of the Affair, A Burnt-Out Case and The Comedians, from the standpoint of their role in the narrative and their relationships with others to determine Greene's intentions and the extent in which they are realized. Regards The Power and the Glory as the focal point of Greene's work. The "Exkurs" that follows examines connections between Greene and his work, from his youth to his conversion, especially in the themes he chooses and the way he works them out. Part two discusses briefly religiosity or piety but analyzes at length the theme of pursuit in the novels, and shows the influence of these two themes on the creation of character and explains the relationship between them. Also includes in a separate chapter, critics' views, favorable or otherwise, on the problem stated.

B735 Gregor, Ian. "The End of the Affair." Graham Greene: A Collection of Critical Essays. Twentieth Century Views. Ed. Samuel Hynes. Englewood Cliffs, N. J.: Prentice-Hall, pp. 110-26. Rpt. from his The Moral and the Story. London: Faber & Faber, 1962, pp. 192-206. See B623.

B736 Hoggart, Richard. "The Force of Caricature: Aspects of the Art of Graham Greene with Particular Reference to The Power and the Glory." Graham Greene: A Collection of Critical Essays. Twentieth Century Views. Ed. Samuel Hynes. Englewood Cliffs, N. J.: Prentice-Hall, pp. 79-93. Rpt. from Speaking to Each Other. London: Chatto & Windus, 1970, pp. 40-56. See B706 & A5315.

B737 Hynes, Samuel L., comp. Graham Greene: A Collection of Critical Essays. Twentieth Century Views. Englewood Cliffs, N. J.: Prentice-Hall. A collection of fourteen well-known essays reprinted from periodicals and books by D. Traversi, M. D. Zabel, R. W. B. Lewis, F. Mauriac, R. Hoggart, W. H. Auden, E. Waugh, Canon J. Cartmell, G. Orwell, I. Gregor, F. Kermode, P. Stratford, M. Shuttleworth and S. Raven, and G. D. Philips. The first essay is unsigned. (See individual entries). The introduction by the editor notes Greene's use of melodrama to furnish the texture of his world and to express truths that are essentially religious. Also notes Greene's interest in film and the convention of the thriller, as well as his scrupulous concern for style. No reasons given to justify the selection.

B738 Kermode, Frank. "Mr. Greene's Eggs and Crosses." Graham Greene: A Collection of Critical Essays. Twentieth Century Views. Ed. Samuel Hynes. Englewood Cliffs, N.J.: Prentice-Hall, pp. 126-38. Rpt. from Puzzles and Epiphanies: Essays and Reviews 1958-1961. London: Routledge & Kegan Paul; New York: Chelmark Press, 1962, pp. 176-88. See B626 & A6110.

B739 Lewis, R. W. B. "The 'Trilogy.'" Graham Greene: A Collection of Critical Essays. Twentieth Century Views. Englewood Cliffs, N.J.: Prentice-Hall, pp. 49-75. Rpt. from The Picaresque Saint: Representative Figures in Contemporary Fiction. New York: J. B. Lippincott, 1959; London: Gollancz, 1960, pp. 239-64. See B597 & A5715.

B7310 Lichtheim, George. Collected Essays. New York: Viking. Includes reprints of "Adams's Tree" pp. 477-82, and "Anglo-American" pp. 490-92 from TCLon, CLIV (Oct. 1951), 337-42 and CLIX (Jan. 1956), 90-92. See A512 & R561.

B7311 "The Man Within." Graham Greene: A Collection of Critical Essays. Twentieth Century Views. Ed. Samuel Hynes. Englewood Cliffs, N.J.: Prentice-Hall, pp. 8-16. Rpt. from TLS, (17 Sept. 1971), pp. 1101-02. See A7124.

B7312 Mauriac, François. "Graham Greene." Graham Greene: A Collection of Critical Essays. Twentieth Century Views. Ed. Samuel Hynes. Englewood Cliffs, N.J.: Prentice-Hall, pp. 75-78. Rpt. from Men I Hold Great. New York: Philosophical Library, 1951, pp. 124-28. See A4820.

A7313 Meyers, Jeffrey. "Graham Greene: The Decline of the Colonial Novel." Fiction and the Colonial Experience. Totowa, N.J.: Rowman and Littlefield, pp. 97-115. Originally a Diss. entitled "The Hero in British Colonial Fiction." Univ. of California, Berkeley, 1967. Greene is the fifth and last novelist discussed who is writing in the tradition of the colonial novel that deals with questions of cultural conflicts and race relations, and that offers a "humanistic approach to the problems of colonialism." Contends that The Heart of the Matter, fortified by the "voluptuousness of Baudelaire and the austerities" of T. S. Eliot, which are "eclectically knitted together," is an "attenuated form" of the colonial novel in the tradition of Kim, Conrad and Forster, and that A Burnt-Out Case, "an imaginative failure," and a weaker version of The Heart of the Matter, demonstrates the unmistakable imitation of Conrad's Victory and also marks the end of the colonial novel.

B7314 Orwell, George. "The Sanctified Sinner." Graham Greene: A Collection of Critical Essays. Twentieth Century Views. Ed. Samuel Hynes. Englewood Cliffs, N.J.: Prentice-Hall, pp. 105-10. Rpt. from The Collected Essays, Journalism and Letters of George Orwell. Ed. Sonia Orwell and Ian Angus. London: Secker & Warburg; New York: Harcourt, 1968, pp. 439-43. See B686 & R4823.

B7315 Palmer, Helen H. and Anne Jane Dyson. "Graham Greene." English Novel Explication: Criticisms to 1972. Hamden, Conn.: Shoe String Press, Inc., pp. 130-36. Indexes some seventy critical items--books, articles and reviews--in alphabetical order under Brighton Rock, A Burnt-Out Case, The Comedians, The Confidential Agent, The End of the Affair, A Gun for Sale, The Heart of the Matter, Our Man in Havana, The Power and the Glory and The Quiet American. Page numbers in the critical items relevant to each of these novels are given. Criticism, with one or two exceptions, covers material published from 1958 to 1972.

B7316 Phillips, Gene D. "Graham Greene: On the Screen." Graham Greene: A Collection of Critical Essays. Twentieth Century Views. Ed. Samuel Hynes. Englewood Cliffs, N.J.: Prentice-Hall, pp. 168-76. Rpt. from CW, CCIX (Aug. 1969), pp. 218-21. See A6916.

B7317 Pownall, David E., ed. "Graham Greene." Articles on Twentieth Century Literature: An Annotated Bibliography 1954 to 1970. Vol. 3. New York: Kraus-Thomson Organization, pp. 1354-71. The annotations are, in the main, pertinent quotations from the text. Annotates forty-four general articles, six on A Burnt-Out Case, five on each of Brighton Rock and The Potting Shed, four on each of The Power and the Glory and The Quiet American, two on each of The Comedians, The End of the Affair, The Heart of the Matter and The Living Room, and one on each of It's a Battlefield and Loser Takes All. Also includes articles on individual short stories: three on "The Basement Room," and one on each of "The Hint of an Explanation," "The Second Death," "Under the Garden" and "A Visit to Morin." The annotation for Ursula Spier's article, "G907," is incorrect.

B7318 Ruotolo, Lucio P. "Rose Wilson." Six Existential Heroes: The Politics of Faith. Cambridge, Mass.: Harvard Univ. Press, pp. 39-53. A more elaborate treatment of Rose as an existentialist heroine than his earlier attempt. (See

A6419). Traces her growth from an inauthentic life to her becoming an "existentialist advocate for a churchless Christianity," with a "passion for life" and a heroic "affirmation of hope" in the face of denial.

B7319 Shuttleworth, Martin and Simon Raven. "The Art of Fiction: Graham Greene." Graham Greene: A Collection of Critical Essays. Twentieth Century Views. Ed. Samuel Hynes. Englewood Cliffs, N.J.: Prentice-Hall, pp. 154-68. Rpt. from PRev, I (Autumn 1953), 25-41. See A5323.

B7320 Stratford, Philip. "The Uncomplacent Dramatist." Graham Greene: A Collection of Critical Essays. Twentieth Century Views. Ed. Samuel Hynes. Englewood Cliffs, N.J.: Prentice-Hall, pp. 138-54. Rpt. from WSCL, II:3 (Fall 1961), 5-9. See A6121.

B7321 Traversi, Derek. "Graham Greene: The Earlier Novels." Graham Greene: A Collection of Critical Essays. Twentieth Century Views. Ed. Samuel Hynes. Englewood Cliffs, N.J.: Prentice-Hall, pp. 17-30. See A5129.

B7322 Waugh, Evelyn. "Felix Culpa?" Graham Greene: A Collection of Critical Essays. Twentieth Century Views. Englewood Cliffs, N.J.: Prentice-Hall, pp. 95-103. Rpt. from Tablet, CXCI:5637 (5 June 1948), pp. 352-54. See A4825.

B7323 Wiley, Paul L., comp. "Graham Greene (1904-)." The British Novel: Conrad to the Present. Northbrook, Ill.: AHM Publishing Corporation, pp. 54-57. A selected checklist that aims at a "balanced rather than exhaustive coverage, with a reasonable selection from earlier as well as more recent scholarship." Lists some sixty-five items--four texts, four bibliographies, thirteen critical and biographical books, and forty-four critical essays in books and periodicals.

B7324 Zabel, Morton Dauwen. "The Best and the Worst." Graham Greene: A Collection of Critical Essays. Twentieth Century Views. Ed. Samuel Hynes. Englewood Cliffs, N.J.: Prentice-Hall, pp. 30-49. Rpt. from Craft and Character: Texts, Method, and Vocation in Modern Fiction. London: Gollancz, 1957, pp. 276-96. See B576 & A433.

A731 Alcantara-Dimalanta, O. "Christian Dimensions in Contemporary Literature." Unitas, XLVI, pp. 213-23. Contends that novelists like Salinger, Golding, Camus and Greene have achieved a "basically humanistic approach ... ultimately touch on God, and become ultimately Christian." Shows how Greene, the most outspoken of the four, uses the "unspectacular heroism" of the contemporary novel in The Power and the Glory to "demean the priesthood in order eventually to elevate it" in his presentation of Christianity "without the didactic sanctimony of religion."

A732 Antip, Felicia. "Greeneland." RoLit, VI:40 (Oct.), p. 30. In Romanian. Surveys different critical opinions on Greene occasioned by the publication of The Honorary Consul.

A733 Auden, W. H. "The Heresy of Our Time." Renascence, XXV:4 (Summer), pp. 181-82. Rpt. from Renascence, I (Spring 1949), 23-24. See A495.

A734 Avvisati, Marilena. "Graham Greene contra se." RLMeC, XXVI, 221-30. Maintains that the "personal mythology" of Travels with My Aunt is not necessarily a rejection of the "dimensione 'sacra,'" even though Greene has refused the title of "Catholic novelist," and examines the ways in which the religious theme is introduced in Travels with My Aunt.

A735 Boyd, John D. "Earth Imagery in Graham Greene's The Potting Shed." MD, XVI:1 (June), 69-80. Discusses Greene's frequent use of earth imagery as a major factor in developing the theme of search and its suspense which are central to the play. Maintains that the various forms of earth imagery have made the world of James' search "emotively real and tangible," and helped to make Father Callifer "somewhat more plausible than he would otherwise be." By creating a "convincing emotive climate" and an "emotive meaning of the action," earth imagery has contributed largely to the acceptance of the rather "perilous" action of the play.

A736 Boyum, Joy Gould. "Graham Greene, Screen Writer." WSJ, (16 Nov.), p. 14. Maintains that the adaptation of England Made Me into film has deprived Anthony, Kate and Krogh of their "distinct individuality" and turned them into mere elements in an outer landscape. This is largely due to the limited means of film in expressing inner psychological states; hence, the "not fully satisfying" adaptation into film of his other works because the camera has not yet figured ways of photographing the landscape of the soul.

A737 Cassis, A. F. "A Note on Point-of-View and Self-Revelation in Graham Greene's Novels." DM, X:3 (Autumn/Winter), pp. 69-73. Illustrates three divergent viewpoints of the "varied hues of Catholicism" from The Power and the Glory, The Heart of the Matter and "A Visit to Morin" in an attempt to show that though a pattern may emerge from the viewpoints adopted in the works, it is not representative of Greene's personal stance towards Catholicism, nor is any one set of ideas, much less a character of his, a "facet" of Greene's mind.

A738 Clemence, Esme. "In Search of Graham Greene." Fiddlehead (Spring), pp. 82-89. A semi-humorous fantasy of an adult undergraduate's experiences and attempt to "research" Greene for a class presentation.

A739 Davis, Robert M. "From Standard to Classic: Graham Greene in Transit." SNNTS, V:4 (Winter), 530-46. A timely review essay on the Collected Edition of eleven novels, J. R. Taylor's The Pleasure Dome, P. Stratford's The Portable Graham Greene, J. Don Vann's Graham Greene: A Checklist of Criticism, S. Hynes' Graham Greene: A Collection of Critical Essays, G. R. Boardman's Graham Greene: The Aesthetics of Exploration and P. Wolfe's Graham Greene: The Entertainer. Dismisses "contemporaneity" as a basic criterion of Greene's art, takes stock of criticism on Greene, evaluates the works mentioned and their contributions towards the creation of Greene as an "institution," and concludes that "first-rate criticism remains to be written."

A7310 Liberman, M. M. "The Uses of Anti-Fiction: Greene's 'Across the Bridge.'" GaR, XXVII, 321-28. Maintains that by deliberately employing the anti-fictional stance--"the tone of despair" the narrator adopts as he exalts his inability to apprehend a reality to imitate--Greene not only tells a story that "'means' but explicitly invokes classical genres for whatever they can mean for his purpose."

A7311 Nichita, Radu. "Masura pentru masura." Luc, XVI:7 (Feb.), p. 9. In Romanian. Quotes from and comments on Greene's speech at the University of Hamburg on the role of the artist and the virtue of disloyalty.

A7312 Nye, Robert. "How to Read Graham Greene Without Kneeling." B&B, XIX (Oct.), pp. 18-21. A review article on A Sort of Life, The Comedians and The Honorary Consul. Describes Greene's personal brand of Catholicism as being closer to Calvin than to Claudel and his work as "the fascinated recoil of a man who sees the beauty in the snake that can kill him." Discusses Greene's "terse, hard and attentive" style, "too obtrusive" at times, and his "passion for human imperfection" which marks his best writing. Also examines serious faults in the "clever architecture" of The Comedians, especially the "limitations of Brown's vision (which) do not marry well with the incisiveness of Greene's style."

A7313 O'Brien, Conor Cruise. "A Funny Sort of God." NYRB, XX (18 Oct.), pp. 56-58. A review article on The Honorary Consul and Collected Stories which focusses on Greene's concept of God in the two works: God, "cruel as well as funny," loving but also a "great kidder" whose "game" with humans is likened to that of "cat and mouse." Contends that "Under the Garden" brings us closest to Greene's "personal God" even though he is not sure whether "parody has got into the allegory or allegory into the parody." Also notes the absence of "overt apologetics" in the series of novels that opened with The Quiet American and which are "crisp and increasingly irreverent in tone," often apparently cynical, preoccupied with the absurd, and especially the cruel absurdities of politics.

A7314 Purcell, James Mark. "Graham Greene and Others: The British Depression Film as an Art Form." AntigR, XV, pp. 75-82. Examines, rather loosely, the professional problems of the film reviewer in the thirties "as they can be inferred from browsing through The Pleasure Dome."

A7315 Shor, Ira Neil. "Greene's Later Humanism: A Burnt-Out Case." LitR, XVI (Summer), pp. 397-411. Examines briefly the "galaxy of social cynicism" in Greene's novels up to The End of the Affair to show that the "positive trend to engage concern with social problems" that began with The Quiet American finds further expression in A Burnt-Out Case which is then fully discussed as representing a "new humanistic approach to reality." Argues that the novel is mainly an account of Querry's "integration into life" after his rejection of, and flight from, humanity. This "salvation in life through life-efforts devoted to a collective good" at the leproserie indicates Greene's later humanistic view that the way out of despair lies through communal action.

A7316 Shpektorova, N. Yu. "Opyt lingvostilisticheskogo analiza individual'-nogo stilya G. Grina, na materiale romana 'Tikhii Amerikanets.'" TSU, 243, pp. 89-97. In Russian. A linguo-stylistic analysis of Greene's style based on a study of The Quiet American.

A7317 Stinson, John J. "Graham Greene's 'The Destructors': Fable for a World Far East of Eden." ABR, XXIV, 510-18. A discussion of the short story as a "parable-like comment on man's inborn depravity and the primacy of evil in the world." Examines the strongly "Augustinian" theological "scaffolding" underlying the narrative.

A7318 Strange, Roderick. "Graham Greene: The Writer." New Blackfriars, LIV:632 (Jan.), pp. 29-35. Admits that there is an autobiographical element in the novels but the part it plays is "considerably less important than is commonly supposed." Contends that Greene's assessment of his works in A Sort of Life when he says "Perhaps a novelist has a greater ability to forget than other men--he has to forget or become sterile. What he forgets is the compost of the imagination" is both accurate and true, and that a reading of the works in the light of what he has written will be more fruitful than a "predominantly autobiographical interpretation."

A7319 Tanazhko, L. G. "Angliiskii antikolonial'nyi roman i poslevoennye romany G. Grina." Perm, CCLXX, 310-26. In Russian. A study of the English anti-colonial novel of Conrad and Forster followed by Greene's post-war novels that touch upon the colonial theme. The Heart of the Matter and The Quiet American.

A7320 Vilangiyil, Sebastian O. "The Demonic Heroes of Graham Greene." SLURJ, IV:2 (June), 201-11. A term paper in the course "Philosophy of Literature." Attempts to show that Greene's demonic heroes--people like Pinkie, the Whiskey Priest and Scobie--turn accepted values and traditional morality upside down by consciously seeking salvation and God through sin and the devil, unlike the pious and self complacent who have a "morbid desire" to keep themselves "uncontaminated," and are obsessed with a "fetish of cleanliness and purity." In their torment and suffering, the sinners come to terms with their individual salvation.

A7321 Walker, Ronald G. "Seriation as Stylistic Norm in Graham Greene's The Heart of the Matter." Lang & S, VI, pp. 161-75. A useful and detailed study of the central stylistic features of the novel, especially seriation as a "mode of utterance which tends to emphasize patterns of correspondence" and to produce a variety of effects, and to what extent Greene, as a writer, has his stylistic "obsessions" under control.

A7322 Willig, Charles L. "Greene's 'The Basement Room.'" Explicator, XXXI:6 (Feb.), item 48. Rejects both A. W. Pitt's and G. E. Silveira's interpretations (See A6415 & A5614) as inadequate explanations of evil in the story and suggests that because of Philip's "carefully dichotomized" world, Mr. Baines is conceived as "recognizable and absolute good," and Mrs. Baines as the "recognizable opposite" of her husband. On the other hand, Emmy, Baines' mistress, introduces the "complexity of adulthood" and an ambiguity that threatens this simple world and she becomes a "symbol of evil" Philip never understands.

A7323 Zimmermann, Peter. "Graham Greene's Auseinandersetzung mit der imperialistischen Vietnamaggression in dem Roman The Quiet American." ZAA, XXI, pp. 34-49. Analyzes Greene's exposition of the "imperialist aggression" on Vietnam. Attributes the origin of Greene's disillusionment with Colonialism to his Journey Without Maps, and examines Greene's portrayal of the crisis of French Colonialism in Vietnam, early American intervention through Pyle's "Third Force," and his attitude to the national liberation movement. Discusses the position of Fowler as narrator--not to be identified with Greene for he is a distinct and separate character--and considers The Quiet American as Greene's contribution to critical realism.

A7324 "Grim Greene." TLS, 3711 (20 April), p. 437. A review article on the Collected Edition of A Gun for Sale, Ministry of Fear and The Quiet American. (Vols. 9, 10 & 11). Notices, from his autobiographical introductions, Greene's two selves: "the public, literary, self-conscious and improbable" Greene and the "old-fashioned popular figure of fiction ... the opium-smoking, brothel-collecting wanderer, stimulated by danger and oppressed by boredom, the last poète maudit."

A7325 "The Cost of Caring." TLS, (14 Sept.), pp. 1055-56. A review article on The Honorary Consul. Maintains that the problem with Greene had always been the adaptation of his great "story telling skill to metaphysical subjects." In The Honorary Consul, Greene "is back at his old stand, as good as he ever was," presenting with his familiar "sour, joyless voice": a new melodrama, "skillful, professional, flawless," with "more than melodramatic meaning," and a topical situation full of "violent action and religious speculation." Also discusses the inevitability of commitment, the social and political relevance of Greene's art and the new note of urgency in Greene's impatience with the Church which makes The Honorary Consul a "serious and moving indictment, at once religious and political." Includes a portrait by Islay Lyons.

R731 Abrahams, William. "The Noble and the Absurd." Atlantic, CCXXXII (Nov.), pp. 114, 116, 118. Considers The Honorary Consul to be one of Greene's "best" novels, vivid and alive, expressing a highly personal view of life and the "incongruities and contradictions" that make life; but he gives the "absurd" in life a "comic, ironic, sympathetic, touching, and finally even noble expression."

R732 Ackroyd, Peter. "Of Gods and Men." Spectator, CCXXXI: 7577 (15 Sept.), pp. 344-45. Finds The Honorary Consul "generally a wearying book" because of a certain "fatality about the narrative, a sense of privation and abandonment which invades the central characters and which generates the tone" of the novel despite its "classical brevity and lucidity."

R733 Bailey, Paul. "Special Notices: The Pleasure-Dome." LM, XIII (June-July), pp. 157-59. Finds the collection "hugely enjoyable" and proves Greene, as a film critic, fit to rank with James Agee and Pauline Kael. Illustrates Greene's proper awareness of the limitations of the cinema and his "disrespect for fame and reputation."

R734 Bazrov, Konstantin. "The Greene Eye." Month, 2nd NS VI: 3 (March), pp. 126-27. Considers The Pleasure-Dome as an example of "criticism at its most perceptive"; it conveys the flavor of the pleasure-dome and the assessments generally stand the test of time.

R735 Bell, Pearl K. "Sinners and Saints." NLea, LVI (15 Oct.), pp. 16-17. Regrets the "mechanical flabbiness of thought, incident, language, and especially religious argument" that "blights" the core of The Honorary Consul, as well as Greene's failing power as a novelist who is now content with "hackneyed questions and easy non-answers."

R736 Breslin, Sean. "Ripe Greene." IP, (22 Sept.), p. 12. Like all "classic romantics," Greene is obsessed by lost causes. But The Honorary Consul moves on a "warmer, more compassionate plane" than his earlier novels, and has a "mellow ripeness that suggests an autumnal acceptance, if not solution, of the issues that have dominated his artistic living." It is also an "object lesson in the novelist's craft," with a narrative "clear, clean, uncluttered with the language at peak function."

R737 Brittain, Victoria. "Recent Fiction: The Honorary Consul." ILN, (Nov.), p. 91. Hails Greene's triumphant return to the serious themes of his earlier books and his ability to create characters that are neither "unbearably tragic, nor pale enough to be shrugged as unimportant misfits." The climax of the book is a "brilliantly sustained piece of suspense"; and though Greene's view of women is as sad as ever, The Honorary Consul remains a "memorable novel, a reminder of a standard most modern fashionable novelists no longer even try for."

R738 Broyard, Anatole. "Books of The Times: A Talked-Out Case." NYT, (6 Sept.), p. 35. Does not find Greene at his best in The Honorary Consul because he has become wordy and has lost the "economy or intensity" of earlier works. Moreover, his characters have "declined from inevitability to plausibility."

R739 Cuffe, Edwin D. "Other Voices, Other Lands: Fiction and Foreign Policy." America, CXXIX:9 (29 Sept.), pp. 219-20. In spite of its "tiresome metaphysical and religious terribilita" and the "bargain-basement process theology" between Father Leon and the doctor, The Honorary Consul remains "an enthralling piece of narrative" written in an easy, unobtrusive and clear style that is characteristic of "this most brilliant of all contemporary storytellers."

R7310 De Foe, R. "The Honorary Consul." HudR, XXVI (Winter), pp. 783-84. Maintains that the characters remain "thin" and "predictable" and that the novel itself gets "bogged down" in the kidnap business and "unlikely discussions of love, God and the Church." However, Greene maintains throughout "a serene, slightly cynical, world weary voice" which is attractive but it fails to bring to life the "static, implausible second section" of the novel.

R7311 Dollard, Peter. "The Honorary Consul." LJ, XCVIII (Aug.), p. 2333. A short review noting Greene's blend of plot, character and ideas in a novel that is "engrossing, timely, thoughtful and finely wrought."

R7312 Donoghue, Denis. "A Visit to Greeneland." Commonweal, XCIX:9 (30 Nov.), pp. 241-42. Argues that The Honorary Consul is "not merely more of the same Greene" but one of his "darkest comedies" where God is more often than not "a black comedian, shrewd, complicated in His ways, incalculable, the joker in the pack." Attributes the "strange tone which the book leaves in the mind" to Dr. Plarr, "Greene's man," and the father "motif" in the novel.

R7313 Elliott, Janice. "Signs of a Silver Lining." SunTel, (16 Sept.), p. 17. Though the territory and the theme in The Honorary Consul are familiar, Greene's taste for the "ironic, absurd failure, as a dramatic device," and his style--that of a "depressed angel"--entice the reader on to meet his central characters, who are "compassionately and fully realised." Notices also the "wry hope" with which the novel ends.

R7314 Enright, D. J. "Opium Fumeries." Listener, LXXXIX (12 April), p. 486. Though meant as a review of The Collected Edition of The Quiet American the article focusses on Greene's writing about opium smoking and his experiences which are mentioned in his Introduction of the novel.

R7315 Foote, Timothy. "Our Man in Gehenna." Time, CII (17 Sept.), p. 66. Notes the "extraordinary suspense and subtlety" of The Honorary Consul, Greene's control over the novel and his sophisticated and powerful dramatization of his message--that those who know their need of God are blessed. Rather critical of the "claptrap scene" at the end.

R7316 Foster, Roy. "Thank God for Greene." IT, (15 Sept.), p. 10. Though it does not break new grounds, The Honorary Consul is "pure Greene" in that it continues to take the reader by surprise and the excitement in the development of the plot is only equalled by the pleasure of reading it. Characteristic of Greene is the "fusion of economical but fluent characterization with a literary style of open perfection and an unparalleled feeling for a plot which develops at once unforeseeably and yet with perfect logic." Sees Charley Fortnum as the focus which gives unity to the novel.

R7317 French, Philip. "On the Frontier." NSta, LXXXVI (14 Sept.), pp. 353-54. Maintains that in The Honorary Consul, Greene deliberately conceals his purpose "beneath layers of irony, paradox and contradiction." Though it does not rank among Greene's best work because it lacks the "political complexity and sheer excitement" of The Quiet American, it is nevertheless, a "highly accomplished novel, ... witty, elegant, suspenseful, if oddly comforting." Its characters are "impressive creations or re-creations"--Plarr is a descendant of Fowler and Brown--and its plot is "carefully oiled."

R7318 Fuller, Edmund. "Personifying the Crucial Issues of Our Time." WSJ, CLXXXII (3 Oct.), p. 16. A review of The Honorary Consul that includes a brief descriptive notice of Collected Stories. Maintains that the "masterly crafted" novel is "vintage Greene" and displays his skills at their best as he resolves several strands of moral dilemmas merging into one another. Also finds the themes of the novel resonating most closely with those of The Power and the Glory.

R7319 Gale, George. "From a View to a Death." Spectator, CCXXX:7558 (5 May), pp. 555-56. A review article on The Collected Edition of The Quiet American. Infers from the new Introduction that there is a "much closer relationship between the novelist and his 'I'" in the novel than is usual, and discusses the novel as "an illuminatingly prophetic work" and as the "best book" on the Americans in Vietnam.

R7320 Gallagher, Michael Paul. "The Honorary Consul." Month, 2nd NS VI:12 (Dec.), p. 427. Bears the unmistakable imprint of a Greene novel with its "obsession of ambivalences," and a mingling of "tension, intelligent dialogue and ideological horizons." However, Greene's proneness for caricature exposes him to the attendant danger of "stridency or shrillness of effect."

R7321 Grosvenor, Peter. "Once Again It's Greene for Go." DaiE, (13 Sept.), p. 13. As the Express Book of the Month, The Honorary Consul is described as "vintage Greene" with a very "effective mixture of moral debate and topicality." Notices also "Greene's uncanny nose for trouble spots in the making."

R7322 Halpern, Henry. "Graham Greene on Film." LJ, XCVIII

(1 Jan.), p. 83. A short review noting Greene's "fine talent for evoking ... the action, mood, and visual beauty of the films he enjoyed."

R7323 Hill, William B. "Fiction: The Honorary Consul." America, CXXIX (17 Nov.), p. 381. Brief notice.

R7324 Holloway, David. "Full of Power and Glory." DaiT, (13 Sept.), p. 9. Though in many ways it is "a despairing book shot through with wry humour," The Honorary Consul is nevertheless second only to The Power and the Glory, despite its low key start. The ending may be "savagely" ironical but its construction is perfect--"never can a flashback have been more effortlessly slipped in--and the writing is calmly exact."

R7325 Hope, Francis. "True to Formula." Observer, (16 Sept.), p. 36. Maintains that The Honorary Consul, "witty, ingenious, persuasive, topical, and humane," is not a bad "self parody" for it is a "perfect replica" of a Greene novel.

R7326 Howard, Elizabeth Jane. "Honorary Characters." Guardian, (13 Sept.), p. 11. "Drab, although not dull ... and sometimes mildly entertaining." Criticizes Greene in The Honorary Consul for being preoccupied with "theological mincemeat" which he sees inherent in any human situation. As for characters, they lack a "third dimension" even though they are not just mere caricatures.

R7327 ________. "Two-Dimensional Greene." GuardianW, CIX (22 Sept.), p. 22. See preceding review.

R7328 Howes, Victor. "Latest from Graham Greene." ChrSM, (3 Oct.), p. 11. "Taut, compressed, topical" and well made, The Honorary Consul remains nevertheless a "tragic-comedy, a cliff-hanger with a religious motif" that dwells in the problematic borderline between popular commercial fiction and senior contemporary literature, between melodrama and morality drama, in keeping with many of Greene's works.

R7329 Hughes, Catharine. "That Greene World." Progressive, XXXVII (Nov.), pp. 53-54. Maintains that The Honorary Consul comes up with "mixed results" to Greene's obsession with "metaphysical meanderings and religious exhumations" which, despite the "moment-by-moment effectiveness" of the novel, "almost submerge the narrative and characters" and lead to loss of tension, and a loss of drama.

R7330 Kennedy, Eugene C. "Books: Critics' Choices for Christmas." Commonweal, XCIX:10 (7 Dec.), pp. 270-71.

Notices briefly the value of The Honorary Consul in making one ask questions about one's belief in, and understanding of, values.

R7331 Lander, Robert E. "Collected Stories." America, CXXIX (22 Dec.), pp. 488-89. The review points out that the collection caters to those who enjoy "the slightly ribald" as well as those who prefer "the theological paradox." The three new stories included show Greene in a "familiar atmosphere: paradox reveals the mundane world not to be as mundane as it seems." Though the form of the short story may not be Greene's forte, he excels in it nonetheless.

R7332 Leonard, Hugh. "Greene at the Cinema." B&B, XVIII (Jan.), p. 53. Doubts whether The Pleasure-Dome would have been published if Greene had not achieved fame as a novelist. Asserts that Greene takes about two years "to hit his critical stride and begins to enjoy himself as a film critic."

R7333 Lewis, Peter. "Graham Greene: All Action (and Anguish) Where the News Is." DaiM, (13 Sept.), p. 29. This "beautifully-formed tragic-comedy whose melancholy music ... reverberates exquisitely on the mind," is perhaps Greene's "most enduring novel." Besides showing Greene's "uncanny sense" of where the news is going to be, The Honorary Consul has those "felicities" which one associates with Greene: prose "monkishly spare and taut" and minor characters "brilliantly and sardonically drawn."

R7334 Lodge, David. "Romantic Realist." Tablet, CCXXVII (15 Sept.), pp. 873-74. Because neither Rivas nor Fortnum are "fully realised characters, The Honorary Consul, brave and memorable, remains flawed." With a "journalist's" instinct and a realistic novelist's insight into the "harsh actualities" he wishes to portray, Greene picks on a topic of great interest but handles it with the "novelist's characteristic irony and displacement of conventional attitudes." However, it is the romantic within him that provides "the energy that drives his literary imagination." This romantic realism makes his personal vision and style distinctive.

R7335 Mambrino, J. "Le Consul honoraire." Etudes, CCCXXXIX (Dec.), 779. Appreciative of Greene's mastery over technique and of his interest and willingness to address himself to topical and pressing questions; viz., social justice, revolution and the role of the Church. Notes Greene's "ironie lucide et décapante" and his compassion for "les visages humilies par leur médiocrité et leur misère."

R7336 Morton, James. "New Books on the Cinema." ContempR,

CCXXII (March), pp. 166-67. The Pleasure-Dome is the first of five books briefly reviewed. Finds the collection "fascinating" to read partly because of Greene's style and partly as an early example of reviews of the sound cinema.

R7337 Ostermann, Robert. "Charley-Plarr or Jesus-Judas? With Greene, Take Your Pick." NObs, XII (6 Oct.), p. 23. Advocates an "experience it, then make of it what you will" approach to The Honorary Consul which marks yet another stage in the "theological debate" that Greene has conducted in his fiction which forms a "seamless whole" with its significance.

R7338 Prescott, Peter S. "Another Word for Living." Newsweek, LXXXII (17 Sept.), p. 96. Considers The Honorary Consul one of Greene's best novels which, though it does not advance "his art or vision by an inch," indicates a perfection of form which few novelists ever attain.

R7339 Price, Reynolds. "The Honorary Consul and Collected Stories." NYTBR, (9 Sept.), pp. 1, 18-19. The review praises Greene for retaining the story element in The Honorary Consul which he regards as a "development" in Greene's skills as a searcher "in the honesty of his methods and the liability of his findings." It is Greene's "lithest" novel resembling the two preceding ones by being "comic" and reaching its "calm" end only after violence and "unfathomable brutality." Includes a brief note on Collected Stories which calls attention to "the winning candor and lean wit" of the Introduction, and Greene's remarks on the role of the unconscious mind in his work.

R7340 Raphael, Frederic. "Bonds Honoured." SunT, (16 Sept.), p. 40. Maintains that in spite of being a veritable "citizen of the world," Greene is a "regional writer" whose Wessex is a "metaphysical parish" with characters bearing a strong family resemblance. Considers the last third of The Honorary Consul as a "philosophical setpiece ... rendered unacademic by approaching death." The novel has "tension without novelty," is expertly contrived but "smacks of calculation" and lacks any "play between the writer and his actual material."

R7341 Ratcliffe, Michael. "The Exemplary Graham Greene Novel." Times, (13 Sept.), p. 10. Though not one of his "most richly invented novels--it is too leisurely for that"--The Honorary Consul is characteristic of Greene's novels; it is "melancholy, ironic and towards the end, horribly exciting," and parts of it are written "within a whisker of self-parody." Notices the "Father" motif in the novel and recognizes Edwardo Plarr as the central character and not Charley Fortnum.

R7342 Roban, Jonathan. "Bad Language: New Novels." Encounter, XLI (Dec.), pp. 76-80. Includes a review of The Honorary Consul on pp. 79-80. Finds the novel to be a "work of religious totalitarianism" where "manner and message are in perfect harmony." Notes Greene's incapacity to be "surprised by sin" even though he writes about sermons and "smells the mortality in the souls" of his characters who are invariably "possessed of a terrible resignation and knowingness."

R7343 Rothberg, Abraham. "Graham Greene: One More River to Cross." SWR, LVIII (Autumn), pp. viii and 351-53. Regards The Honorary Consul as an "updated version" of The Power and the Glory without "the force and conviction" of the earlier novel. Though "interesting" and "well-written," its style is "plain, severe, almost without simile or metaphor, or imagery," and it retains and expresses Greene's "fine observation of the anguish of the human condition."

R7344 Ryan, Frank L. "The Honorary Consul." Best Sellers, XXXIII (15 Oct.), p. 327. The short review focusses on the "narrative point-of-view in the novel, the way in which the narrator and the characters interpret Greene's world and converge on troubles which "spring from eternity and shall not fail."

R7345 ________. "Collected Stories." Best Sellers, XXXIII (15 Nov.), pp. 375-76. The review describes the three divisions in the collection but notes that the stories seem to need the "moral structure" of the novels, and that too often Greene relies on a "wavering silhouette of characterization and action."

R7346 Share, Bernard. "Greene and White." Hibernia, XXXVII:15 (21 Sept.), p. 18. Compares The Honorary Consul with Patrick White's The Eye of the Storm. Praises Greene for his "unfailing mesmerism" in getting an "unpromising" bunch of characters to perform their "insignificant gyrations in a maddeningly significant way," so that the "spiritual struggle" appears compelling to the reader.

R7347 Sheed, Wilfrid. "The Honorary Consul." BMCN, (Fall), pp. 2-3. Finds the plot to be one of his best since the thirties, the people real, "lovingly but ruthlessly observed," and the novel generally a "splendid satire on history as publicity." The old issues of loss of faith, betrayal, etc. are present but are regarded as "tragic but not serious," for the drama has absorbed the comedy to the benefit of both.

R7348 Theroux, Paul. "Graham Greene's The Honorary Consul &

Collected Stories." Book World, VII (30 Sept.), pp. 1-3, 10. Considers The Honorary Consul a "major" work in the context of Greene's work and important for the statement it makes about the paradoxes of political struggle. Notes the "Chaplinesque dimensions" the characters acquire in the novel and Greene's insistence on the comedy. Praises the Collected Stories for its "evenness" and the tremendous range of its stories, some of which deserve comparison "with the best of their kind."

R7349 Waugh, Auberon. "Our Man in Argentina--Dazzling as Ever." EvS, (18 Sept.), p. 261. A warm appreciation of Greene's talents as the novelist who exercises an "enormous, brooding presence" over the English. Not only is The Honorary Consul enjoyable--doubts whether another like it will appear for a long time--but it also weds "the hopeless outrage of a 20-year-old idealist" to the "cynical, faultless precision of an old master."

R7350 W[eaver], R[obert]. The Honorary Consul. TamR, 61 (Nov.), p. 73. As one of his "major fictions," the novel takes us back to the "heart of Greeneland" to which, amid the chaos of ambiguous motives and spiritual decay, Greene brings his own commitment to the writer's craft.

R7351 Wyndham, Francis. "A Pitiable God." Listener, XC (13 Sept.), pp. 350-51. A review of The Honorary Consul that focusses on the rather unorthodox views expressed and the spiritual pessimism which had informed Greene's artistic vision of the world and its moral complexity. Notes the "atmospheric richness" of the novel and its central irony from which "a chain of interlocking ironies is constructed, which complement and sometimes contradict each other."

R7352 Unsigned. "A Sort of Life." Best Sellers, XXXII (1 Feb.), p. 503. Brief notice.

R7353 ______. "The Honorary Consul." Booklist, LXX (15 Nov.), p. 320. Briefly noted for its "philosophic core" and for Greene's projection of the "desperation of man's condition."

R7354 ______. "Collected Stories." Booklist, LXX (1 Dec.), p. 368. Notes briefly the original appearance of the stories.

R7355 ______. "The Honorary Consul." Booklist, LXX (15 Dec.), p. 440. Brief notice of the "engrossing tragicomical novel."

R7356 ______. "The Honorary Consul." Book World, VII (9 Dec.), p. 1. Brief notice.

R7357 ________. "A Sort of Life." CLW, XLIV (Feb.), p. 424. Briefly noted as a "literary autobiography."

R7358 ________. "Graham Greene on Film." Choice, X (April), p. 298. The short review maintains that Greene is "not a very good film critic" and the collection is valuable as a "time-capsule" of a very intelligent viewer's reactions to a body of film than as criticism per se."

R7359 ________. "Greene Hell." Econ, CCXLVIII (15 Sept.), pp. 148-49. Attributes the sense of "déjà vu" in The Honorary Consul to the shadows of Camus and Conrad that flit behind the inhabitants of this "commanding fiction." However, to transport his reader to that nameless city to expound on his "text" of political violence is at once distracting and unnecessary. Moreover, by permitting the "'relevance' of polemicists and doctors to exceed his own, Mr. Greene has failed a duty to the fiction he has served with outstanding faith."

R7360 ________. "Graham Greene on Film." FilmQ, XXVI (Summer), p. 34. Brief descriptive notice of the volume.

R7361 ________. "Collected Stories." Kirkus, XLI (1 July), p. 716. Brief notice of publication.

R7362 ________. "The Honorary Consul." Kirkus, XLI (1 July), pp. 704-05. Pre-publication notice describing the novel as his best since The Heart of the Matter and intensely involving in the conflicts which take place on more than one level.

R7363 ________. "Collected Stories." NRep, CLXIX (3 Nov.), p. 31. A short review that predicts the endurance of the collection "by virtue of the cumulative force of its individual items," some of which are "among the best" in the language.

R7364 ________. "The Honorary Consul." NYTBR, (2 Dec.), p. 76. Untitled notice referring to God as "an ambivalent terrorist" in the Argentine of Greene.

R7365 ________. "Graham Greene on Film." PsyT, VII (June), p. 103. Briefly noticed.

R7366 ________. "The Honorary Consul and Collected Stories." PsyT, VII (Dec.), p. 126. Briefly noticed.

R7367 ________. "The Honorary Consul." PW, CCIV (2 July), p. 78. Brief notice. Remarks on Greene's return to "the devastating no man's land that has always been the locale of his best writing," and how he plumbs with great effectiveness and power the "thin wavering line between good and evil, life and death, responsibility and evasion."

R7368 _______. "Collected Stories." PW, CCIV (16 July), p. 108. Pre-publication notice of the "wonderful collection, well worth the price" which shows Greene's skill off to advantage.

R7369 _______. "A Selection of the Year's Best Books." Time, CII (31 Dec.), p. 46. The Honorary Consul is the fourth novel selected.

R7370 _______. "An Amateur at the Press Show." TLS, 3704 (2 March), p. 228. Maintains that Greene's film reviews in The Pleasure-Dome belong to the tradition of the "gentleman-essayist": they are examples of "fine writing, often brilliant but they do not constitute criticism in any meaningful sense." However, the reviews reflect an "enthusiasm, a responsiveness of his material and a desire to articulate his response," are "unique, reflective, discursive and at times polemical," but lack a "sense that the cinema has a history and forms of artistic organization."

D731 Charvat, Eva. Die Religiosität und das Thema der Verfolgung in sechs Romanen von Graham Greene. Univ. of Bern, 1973. Published. See B734.

D732 Duffy, William R. Graham Greene: Entertainer and Novelist. Univ. of Chicago.

D733 Duran Justo, Leopoldo. El substrato teológico en la obra de Graham Greene. Univ. of Madrid.

D734 Fay, Marguerite Mary. Graham Greene: A Study of Five Major Novels. Purdue Univ. DAI, XXXIV (March 1974), 5965A.

D735 Kaehler, Klaus. Die Sytax des Dialogs im modernen Englisch, Dargestellt an Werken von Harold Pinter und Graham Greene. Univ. of Berlin-Humboldt.

D736 Keegan, Maureen Therese, S. C. M. M. The Man-God Relationship: A Comparative Study of the Fiction of Rabindranath Tagore and Graham Greene. The Catholic Univ. of America. DAI, XXXIV (May 1974), p. 7324A.

D737 Korn, Frederick B. 'Condemned to Consequences': A Study of Tragic Process in Three Works by Joseph Conrad and Graham Greene. Univ. of Illinois at Urbana-Champaign. DAI, XXXIV (March 1974), p. 5977A.

D738 Perez Lapuente, Felix. The Sense of Failure in Graham Greene. M. A. Duesto.

S731 Cowley, Malcolm. "The Greene-ing of the Portables." Book

World (29 April), p. 13. The story of the Viking Portable Library from its origins in 1943 to Philip Stratford's The Portable Graham Greene.

1974

B741 Gunn, Drewey Wayne. "Matters of Church and State, 1938." American and British Writers in Mexico, 1556-1973. Austin: Univ. of Texas Press, pp. 181-92. Reviews, in this 19th chapter of the chronological survey, Greene's disgust with the ugliness and cruelty that was part of Mexico, its government, its people, and his concern with the religious question as revealed in "Across the Bridge," The Lawless Roads and The Power and the Glory. Tends to overstate the importance of Mexico in Greene's career, and especially of The Power and the Glory--an "almost impartial" novel, "nearly flawless in its development" where "abstract thesis, characters, action and setting all fit into a piece."

B742 Harkness, Bruce. "Conrad, Graham Greene, and Film," Joseph Conrad: Theory and World Fiction. Proceedings of the Comp. Lit. Symposium, Vol. VII, 23-25 January 1974. Ed. Wolodymyr T. Zyla & Wendell M. Aycock. Lubbock: Texas Technical Univ., pp. 71-87. Attributes the failure of turning Conrad's novels into film to the disjunction that occurs--"radically harmful to film versions"--when his novels shift focus from the internal and individualistic to the social, whereas Greene's are successful because they stay on one level or plane, regardless of whether it is the internal or the social. Illustrates from Conrad's The Secret Agent and Greene's The Third Man among others.

B743 Kennedy, Alan. "Inconsistencies of Narrative in Graham Greene." The Protean Self: Dramatic Action in Contemporary Fiction. London: Macmillan; New York: Columbia Univ. Press, pp. 231-49. Focusses on the "fictiveness of novel writing"--the metaphors of drama in the novel or the conscious playing of roles--in Our Man in Havana, The Comedians and Travels with My Aunt to show that Greene's inconsistency or ambivalence to the character who indulges in fictions--Greene has a "wholly pragmatic" attitude that justifies his characters when they produce desirable ends, and not when they do not--results from his failure to think thoroughly about "the nature of dramatic fictions, and about the nature of controlled, conscious, ritual action or self-dramatization."

B744 Noguchi, Keisuke, ed. Guream Grin kenkyu. Tokyo: Nansosha. Unavailable for examination.

B745 Phillips, Gene D., SJ. Graham Greene: The Films of His Fiction. Studies in Culture and Communication. New York and London: Teachers College Press, Teachers College, Columbia University. A timely evaluative study of the film adaptations of Greene's fiction. Discusses and evaluates each work adapted to the screen as a fiction first, Greene's talent as a scriptwriter, as well as the differences between the film adaptations and their fictional models. Quotations and references to what seems to have been a lengthy interview with Greene on the subject of his work for the cinema are scattered throughout the book. Ch. 1 discusses Greene's association with the cinema: his film reviews and criticism and his serious interest in the motion picture medium. Ch. 2 focusses on eight of Greene's "entertainments" as adapted by other screenwriters and Ch. 3 examines four of Greene's own film adaptations of his entertainments. Ch. 4 examines five of Greene's novels as adapted by other screenwriters, and Ch. 5 examines Greene's own adaptations of Brighton Rock and The Comedians. This is followed by a select bibliography of primary and secondary sources and an up to date list of film scripts by Greene as well as a list of adaptations of Greene's fiction by other screenwriters and a useful index.

B746 Taylor, John Russell, intro. Masterworks of the British Cinema. London: Lorrimer Publishing Ltd.; New York: Harper & Row; Toronto: Fitzhenry & Whiteside Ltd. Includes the film script of The Third Man, written in close consultation with Carol Reed, the Director, and Greene's description of the characters, as well as a substantial excerpt from Joseph A. Gomez' "The Theme of the Double in The Third Man." Film Heritage, VI:4 (Summer 1971).

A741 Alves, Leonard. "The Relevance of Graham Greene." ELLS, XI, pp. 47-76. Examines The Quiet American, The Power and the Glory, The Comedians and The Honorary Consul to show that Greene's continuing relevance in today's context lies in "his uncanny sense of the Zeitgeist of modern times." Also discusses Greene's novelistic vision of the world and the need he sees for divine compassion in human life.

A742 Bedard, B. J. "Reunion in Havana." LFQ, II:4 (Fall), pp. 352-58. Describes the "gestation" of Our Man in Havana both as a novel and a film, the collaboration of Reed and Greene--this is their third attempt--and the few changes and additions that were made to the novel when translated into film. Also comments on the casting and maintains that "the weaknesses of the film are ultimately the weaknesses of the entertainment."

A743 Broker, Uwe. "Henry James, Graham Greene und das Problem der Form," LWU, VII, pp. 16-33. A stylistic and structural analysis of The Power and the Glory that attempts to determine the extent in which Greene's asceticism is related to James and where he fits into the general pattern.

A744 Brock, D. Hayward and James M. Welsh. "Graham Greene and the Structure of Salvation." Renascence, XXVII:1 (Autumn), pp. 31-39. Analyzes The Power and the Glory, "a literary masterpiece of the twentieth century," to show it anticipated the "general movement toward Ecumenism" and the "social responsibility that Christians and Catholics have since embraced." Contends that the novel, far from being an exercise in Catholic propaganda, criticizes both the Church and revolutionary society and, from a modern Christian humanist viewpoint, justifies the ways of God to modern man by "portraying the ineffability of the omnipresence of grace" in the world of fallen man.

A745 Cassis, A. F. "The Dream as Literary Device in Graham Greene's Novels." L&P, XXIV, pp. 99-108. The survey of dreams in the major novels shows how Greene uses the dream as a literary device mainly for the revelation of character and its development, at times to influence the course of action and to ensure the reader's acceptance of the change, and also, though rarely, as a rather subtle unobtrusive authorial comment.

A746 Castelli, Ferdinando, SJ. "Graham Greene alle presse con gli antichi amori." CivC, CXXV:1, pp. 240-49. A review article on The Honorary Consul. Maintains that as a novelist, Greene aims to "turbare, inquietare, irritare, enthisiasmare. Anything but to leave one indifferent." As a "synthesis" of Greenean motifs, The Honorary Consul recalls The Power and the Glory in its principal characters, setting and theme even though it may not have the theological and psychological force or charge of the earlier novel. Discusses the dilemma of Fr. Rivas and regards the novel as a love story rather than a political one. Notes three levels on which the novel unfolds: in the external action, in the change of perspective and most important of all, in the "genialità" of the narrator.

A747 Cendre, Anne. "Graham Greene: 'Non, Je n'écrirai pas de Memoires ... Ce serait indiscret!.'" Soir, 1-2 (Jan.), p. 7. An account of an interview in which Greene rejects the notion of further memoirs, and "chats" about novelists, novel writing and the countries he has visited.

A748 Chaudhury, M. K. "The Significance of Caricature in Graham Greene's The Comedians." PURBA, V:2, pp. 51-56. Examines the "secret bond and interchangeability" of Brown and Jones and attempts to show through an examination of the incidents of the novel how "Brown's caricature and hatred of Jones get transformed into love and identification."

A749 Davis, Robert M. "More Graham Greene on Film: Uncollected Reviews and Fragments of Reviews." LFQ, II:4 (Fall), pp. 384-85. Includes some 55 items, ten of which had not appeared in Graham Greene on Film (The Pleasure-Dome), three reviews of books about films and forty-two that had been cut. All reviews had appeared in The Spectator between 23 March 1934 and 15 March 1940.

A7410 Drążkiewicz, Joanna. "Understanding Suspense," ZRL, XVII:2, pp. 21-30. Defines suspense as a "literary device" based on arousing a question--asked directly or indirectly, suggested by a statement on characters' reactions--"in the minds of characters, the narrator and the addressee of a work"; i.e., in the literary work not the reader. Illustrates from A Gun for Sale and Brighton Rock among other works by A. C. Doyle and J. Conrad.

A7411 Duran, Leopoldo. "Graham Greene's 'A Visit to Morin.'" CR, NS LIX:10 (Oct.), pp. 643-47. A discussion of Morin's "faith" from a Catholic theological viewpoint which maintains that "the spirit of man is impenetrable to ... human scrutiny" and that the Grace and Love of God cannot be charted by theologians.

A7412 Elliott, David. "Graham Greene's Singular Success in the Perilous Switch from Print to Film." BN, I (June), p. 648. Examines briefly Greene's successful film career, relying mainly on Gene D. Phillips' The Films of His Fiction. Attributes Greene's success to his cinematic writings--"his books are movie naturals"--and to his attempt, as a screen writer, to "help the spirit of the original." Examines "The Fugitive," the 1947 screen version of The Power and the Glory, and "The Third Man."

A7413 Fagin, Steven. "Narrative Design in Travels with My Aunt." LFQ, II:4 (Fall), pp. 379-83. Analyzes the novel and film version in terms of narrative structure and looks at the way each of them tells a story and how the film substitutes for the first person narrative a method which "equates the audience somewhat loosely with the person to whom we are closest in relation" to release the information.

A7414 Gomez, Joseph A. "The Third Man: Capturing the Visual Essence of Literary Conception." LFQ, II:4 (Fall), pp. 332-40. Shows how the film exhibits that all "too rare marriage" between director and scriptwriter in evolving "a unique transformation" to capture the visual essence of literary conception through "aural/visual patterning" rather than excessive dialogue or other literary narrative devices. (Some of the material in this article had appeared earlier. See A719).

A7415 Gossett, Thomas F. "Flannery O'Connor's Opinions of Other Writers: Some Unpublished Comments." SLJ, VI:2 (Spring), pp. 70-82. Includes brief reference to Greene and M. Spark as "the most important English Catholic writers" today.

A7416 Keyser, Les. "England Made Me." LFQ, II:4 (Fall), pp. 364-72. Discusses the script-writers' methods to translate Greene's use of the stream of consciousness "technique" and his shifting perspective on the events of the story by providing a prologue to the main action of the film and switching the setting from Stockholm to the Nazi-plagued Germany of the thirties. England Made Me remains, however, despite its "visual excitement and thematic intensity" an actor's film, "a showcase for professional talents."

A7417 Kolesnykov, V. P. "Sljazamy social'nyx posukiv: Pro evoljuciju pohljadiv Grema Grina," RLz, XVIII:2, pp. 40-50. In Ukrainian. Examines the evolution of Greene's views.

A7418 Lauder, Robert E. "The Catholic Novel and the 'Insider God.'" Commonweal, CI (25 Oct.), pp. 78-81. Contrasts the visions of Greene and Walker Percy to illustrate the "Blondelian Shift" which is currently taking place in the Catholic novel--a shift in emphasis that stresses God's presence in human history, that God is immanent in man's self-making, that the divine mystery of redemption is operative everywhere in human life, that God is not totally extrinsic to man.

A7419 Lenfest, David S. "Brighton Rock/Young Scarface." LFQ, II:4 (Fall), pp. 373-78. Considers the transformation of Brighton Rock into film as a "relatively pure" transition partly because Greene controlled the screenplay. Finds in his examination of the "curious paradigm" of the fundamental structure of the novel/film, a "lack of clear motivation" in both Ida and Pinkie, and suggests that if the novel or film seems unbalanced, it is because "the stylistic experiments are not consistent with the didactic message."

A7420 Literature/Film Quarterly. II:4 (Fall). Special Issue: Graham Greene. Includes articles on adaptations of Greene's novels into film and film reviews by B. J. Bedard, R. M. Davis, S. Fagin, J. A. Gomez, L. Keyser, D. S. Lenfest, R. E. McGugan, R. Mass, J. E. Nolan, J. S. Skerrett, W. F. Van Wert, J. M. Welsh & G. R. Barrett, and A. L. Zambrano. See individual entries.

A7421 McGugan, Ruth E. "The Heart of the Matter." LFQ, II:4 (Fall), pp. 359-63. Argues that the "virtual disappearance of one of the major characters--God--from the 1953 film version as a result of the inability to render on film the third person omniscient accounts of Scobie's conversations with God which reveal the central conflict of the novel, reduces this "modern version of the Faust story to the level of domestic drama."

A7422 Mass, Roslyn. "The Presentation of the Character of Sarah Miles in the Film Version of The End of the Affair." LFQ, II:4 (Fall), pp. 347-51. A consideration of the changes effected in the film in the character of Sarah Miles. Maintains that in both film and novel, she is a "fragmented individual" who performs a series of roles as an "instrument for use by others."

A7423 Muller, Charles H. "Graham Greene: The Melodramatic Character," UES, XII:3, pp. 31-37. Argues, in a review article on the Collected Edition of Brighton Rock, The Heart of the Matter and Collected Stories that melodrama enables Greene to project character dramatically. Brighton Rock is the first novel that successfully adapts plot to "the cliche of melodrama," but it is in The Heart of the Matter that the two are "most successfully adapted for the exploration" of Scobie's character which is shown to be methodically and respectively revealed in relation to his wife, his mistress and his God. Also concentrates on "Under the Garden" as Greene's attempt to find "Pendele" in the realm of a lost childhood.

A7424 Nolan, Jack E. "Graham Greene's Films." LFQ, II:4 (Fall), pp. 302-09. Rpt. from FiR, XV (Jan. 1964), pp. 23-35. See A6414.

A7425 Routh, Michael. "Greene's Parody of Farce and Comedy in The Comedians." Renascence, XXVI:3 (Spring), pp. 139-51. Maintains that it is impossible to classify the novel generically because it is not based on the "decorum" of a single genre but rather on a parody of the two genres of farce and comedy. Shows how Brown's use of farce becomes an "unintentional parody" as he attempts to create a facade of comedy over his interpretation of life and twisted perspective of character whereas his action argues for a darker category.

A7426 Skerrett, Joseph T., Jr. "Graham Greene at the Movies: A Novelist's Experience with Film." LFQ, II:4 (Fall), pp. 293-301. Examines Greene's involvement with the cinema as movie-goer, film reviewer, screenwriter and novelist. Shows how the influence of the film surfaced clearly in A Gun for Sale and how Greene's dissatisfaction with the movies increased as they grew more escapist and derivative so that he never lost a "certain sense of disappointment in the medium and contempt for the industry."

A7427 Stalling, Louise. "It's to Do with Opposite Forces: Graham Greene's 'Destructors.'" SCB, XXXIV, p. 115. Includes the abstract of a 15-minute talk which maintains "that the central motif of the short story is the circular staircase in the Wren House." "Both the structure of the story and the character of the protagonist are sustained, like the staircase, by 'opposite forces.' The result is a circular development which produces Greene's ambiguous statement about the survival of humane values in an inhumane world."

A7428 Trifu, Sever. "Graham Greene, Contemporanul Nostru." SUB, XIX:1, pp. 59-66; also as "Un contemporan neliniştit: Graham Greene." Steaua, XXV:10, pp. 52-54. In Romanian. Examines briefly the evolution of the English novel in the 20th century to determine Greene's place in contemporary literature. Discusses Greene's literary achievement which presents the reader with the ferment and changes in the spiritual, social and political contemporary life.

A7429 Van Wert, William F. "Narrative Structure in The Third Man." LFQ, II:4 (Fall), pp. 341-46. Shows how the "entertainment" rises to the level of structure of The Power and the Glory when adapted into film and becomes "self-serious and self-serving ... a masterpiece of reduction and refinement." Also examines the "intricately patterned counterpoint arrangement between the image track and the sound track" to show the film's "denotative" narrative structure.

A7430 Welsh, James M. and Gerald R. Barrett. "Graham Greene's Ministry of Fear: The Transformation of an Entertainment." LFQ, II:4 (Fall), pp. 310-23. The first section of the essay attributes Fritz Lang's unsuccessful adaptation of The Ministry of Fear to the assumption that the mass of filmgoers will find the introspection and interior development of the central character to be boring and to the resulting emphasis on action and plot. Section 2 discusses Lang's role in the film's transformational failures and the satisfaction a viewer might gain from the film.

A7431 Zambrano, Ana Laura. "Greene's Visions of Childhood: 'The Basement Room' and The Fallen Idol." LFQ, II:4 (Fall), pp. 324-31. Shows how the film version even while reinterpreting the story, expands characters and scenes which Greene had only hinted at in "The Basement Room" as a result of the collaboration of Greene and Carol Reed.

R741 Adams, Phoebe. "Short Reviews: Lord Rochester's Monkey." Atlantic, CCXXXIV (Oct.), p. 118. Notes briefly the "sensible, low-keyed biography" written forty years ago.

R742 Bogart, Gary. "Elderly Books for Youngerly Readers." WLB, XLVIII (Jan.), p. 381. Includes The Portable Graham Greene. Ed. Philip Stratford. New York: Viking, 1973, and The Honorary Consul for their "relevance to youthful interests, readability ... and general moral/ethical thrust."

R743 Broyard, Anatole. "An Ixion's Wheel of Wit." NYT, (10 Sept.), p. 39. Surveys significant characteristics and details in Rochester's life as depicted by Greene in his "fascinating" but "frustrating" biography.

R744 Bryant, Dorothy M. "The Colonel's Men Killed Plarr." Nation, CCXVIII (27 April), pp. 535-36. Considers The Honorary Consul, like all good fiction, an "illumination of the meaning" behind current political kidnapping, and on whom the responsibility falls for such acts. Notes the reader's sympathy for Dr. Plarr, the circumstances of whose death, though hidden, cannot be destroyed.

R745 Clemons, Walter. "Lord Rochester's Monkey." NYTBR, (15 Sept.), pp. 3, 24-25. This is Greene's "best early work" in which he responds by intuition, to the discord in Rochester's character, and yields insights that "academic caution might prohibit." However, forty years work on Rochester's writings have left Greene in a "number of unprotected positions," but his claim for Rochester as a character that can be "dramatized" is justified.

R746 _______. "Lord Rochester's Monkey." Newsweek, LXXXIV (30 Dec.), p. 63. Brief notice.

R747 Cox, C. B. "Rochester's Roistering." SunTel, (15 Sept.), p. 12. Though "entertaining and lively" and reading like a "popular historical romance," the biography is rather "thin in its treatment of psychology, and thin in its literary criticism"--it does not take into account the scholarship of the past forty years.

R748 Dodsworth, Martin. "Rake's Progress." Guardian, (12 Sept.), p. 14. Rpt. in GuardianW, CXI (21 Sept.), p. 22. Describes the biography as an "original and convincing interpretation of a complex life" whose historical research has been conscientiously done and which is as readable as any of his novels. However, one can take exception to the statement that the life of this Restoration libertine and poet "would seem to fit Mr. Greene's tastes admirably."

R749 Freedman, Richard. "Lord Rochester: Spoiled Idealist or

Plain Rake?" NObs, XIII (5 Oct.), p. 27. Finds the biography a "fascinating" introduction to Rochester, a "prototype" of Greene's own "doomed heroes," even though it does not take full account of recent scholarship.

R7410 Grosvenor, Peter. "The Devil Who Roistered at the Side of King Charles." DaiE, (12 Sept.), p. 17. Gives the story of the typescript and a brief summary, and describes the volume as a "classic" study of good and evil.

R7411 Hastings, Selina. "Unhappy Libertine." DaiT, (19 Sept.), p. 11. Greene's "dispassionate," "discreet" and objective treatment of the Earl of Rochester's life has produced a "somewhat pedestrian effect" because the account is "scrupulously unsensational"; in spite of his "sympathetic understanding of the Earl's dissipated genius," Greene gives a "just and dutiful report in honest black and white rather than the scarlet and gold ... of the reality."

R7412 Holmes, Richard. "Lord of the Exiled Asterisk." Times, (16 Sept.), p. 11. Maintains that Greene's deportment as biographer is "laboured" when compared to his novels. Though Greene does not manage to establish a convincing chronology of Rochester between 1672 and 1677, his feeling for the moral tensions beneath Rochester's "braggadocio" and the recreation of the "hot, doomed, aristocratic life" are extraordinarily sensitive.

R7413 Homer, Frank X. J. "Lord Rochester's Monkey." America, CXXXI:15 (16 Nov.), p. 297. Brief notice.

R7414 Lehmann, John. "Monkey Tricks." Spectator, CCXXXIII: 7631 (28 Sept.), pp. 403-04. Finds Lord Rochester's Monkey a "substantial piece of difficult research" that tends to establish Rochester's "powerful intelligence and the seriousness underlying all his frivolity" contrary to Pope's dictum that he is a "holiday" poet.

R7415 Lewis, Peter. "Now Those Were the Really Permissive Sixties." DaiM, (12 Sept.), p. 7. Even though the period comes richly to life, Rochester "remains an enigma in spite of Mr. Greene's sympathy with his melancholy and his remorse, both as a sinner and as a convert."

R7416 Lodge, David. "Grounds for Empathy." Tablet, CCXXVIII (23 Nov.), p. 1129. "... A judicious, lucid and engrossing account of Rochester and his times," which has "surprisingly little evidence" of the novelist in its "restrained almost scholarly" verbal style when compared to Greene's literary essays. Speculates on the possible grounds for empathy between subject and author.

R7417 McLellan, Joseph. "Pick of the Paperbacks: 1974." Book

World, (22 Dec.), p. 3. Brief notice of The Honorary Consul.

R7418 ______. "The Honorary Consul." Book World, (22 Sept.), p. 4. Brief notice of paperback edition.

R7419 Muller, C[harles] H. "Graham Greene's New Novel." UES, XII:1, pp. 67-69. Contends that The Honorary Consul is a "hybrid of his earlier 'Catholic' fiction and his later novels of 'absurd comedy,'" that its only action is centered in the "casual philosophical-theological discussions," and its force lies in the "vivid similes Greene uses to express the essence of character--Plarr as "l'homme absurde" and Father Rivas as "l'homme revolté, in revolt against the irrationality of the Church's teaching." Includes two photographs of Greene in South Africa in July 1973.

R7420 Newlove, Donald. "Lord Rochester's Monkey." VV, XIX (3 Oct.), p. 37. A general account of Rochester's life that pays little attention to Greene's treatment.

R7421 Nicol, Charles. "Lost Fathers." NR, XXVI (18 Jan.), p. 97. Describes The Honorary Consul as a "tragic entertainment" which offers a "profound collection of Argentine characters and characteristics," and whose minor characters are "sharply, even indelibly drawn."

R7422 Porter, Peter. "Out with It." NRev, I (Sept.), pp. 74-76. Notes Greene's "originality" in having written Lord Rochester's Monkey, a "valuable book, part biography and part critical assessment," as early as 1932 when Rochester's literary reputation was almost entirely negligible. Finds the book agreeable because it is "psychologically sound even if erroneous or improbable in fact" and especially because Greene emphasises Rochester as a poet.

R7423 Prescott, Peter S. "Rake's Progress." Newsweek, LXXXIV (23 Sept.), p. 92. Finds the "lavishly illustrated" Lord Rochester's Monkey "sympathetic and perceptive" in its treatment of what may well have been a hero from Greene's own fiction: "the restless victim, cynical, desperate and self-indulgent, alienated from, and yet attracted to, God...."

R7424 Pritchett, V. S. "Rogue Poet." NYRB, XXI (3 Oct.), pp. 17-18. Lord Rochester's Monkey is a "substantial" biography written with the "originality, thoroughness, and alertness to affairs of conscience" that one finds in Greene's fictional manhunts. Greene brings to life the Restoration scene. Though it is a "novelist's book it is not novelized" because Greene is a "firm but charitable examiner" of Rochester.

R7425 Raven, Simon. "Poetry and the Pox." Observer, (15 Sept.), p. 28. Though rather suspicious at first of the shelving of Lord Rochester's Monkey for some forty years, he finds the biography "excellent: chaste in style, sharp in narrative, balanced in judgment and shrewd in its (severely disciplined) speculations." Maintains that the volume, "prettified and naughtified" by its many illustrations, shows Greene rather sympathetic to Rochester's verdict on humanity.

R7426 Ricks, Christopher. "Enslaved by Liberty." SunT, (15 Sept.), p. 40. Rochester's life and times seem to be a perfect subject for Greene, just about tailor made for his preoccupations and obsessions. However, Greene treats his subject with great "economy and discipline" and, in spite of his "eye for the vulturish," has succeeded in writing a "succinct, deft and bracingly cool" biography.

R7427 Scannell, Vernon. "Love the Sinner." NSta, LXXXVIII (20 Sept.), pp. 388-89. Welcomes Lord Rochester's Monkey in the hope that this "very good" book will arouse a wider interest in Rochester's poetry. Finds the work "carefully researched, impartial, self-effacing yet stylish" with ample quotations and illustrations, and speculates on the causes of Greene's attraction to Rochester as a subject for biography.

R7428 Scott, Nathan, Jr. "Books: Critics' Choice for Christmas." Commonweal, CI:9 (6 Dec.), p. 242. Brief notice of The Honorary Consul.

R7429 Shea, John. "The Honorary Consul." Critic, XXXII (Jan.-Feb.), pp. 75-76. The novel is "vintage Greene" in style, landscape and characterization, and embodies Greene's enduring "Manichean temptation"; the argument about the "night side" of God is the "backdrop for the religious meaning" of the novel and the "subterranean flow of grace."

R7430 Sherr, Merrill F. "Lord Rochester's Monkey." LJ, XCIX (15 Sept.), p. 2146. A short review noting Greene's "delightfully written biography" in which he has succeeded in giving his subject a "three-dimensional quality."

R7431 Siggins, Clara M. "Lord Rochester's Monkey." Best Seller, XXXIV (1 Nov.), pp. 343-44. Maintains that Rochester emerges as a living character, "real and believable" and filled with contradictions on which Greene focusses his attention. Finds the biography engaging though rather "partisan."

R7432 Silverstein, Norman. "Graham Greene on Film." JML, III:3 (Feb.), pp. 515-17. One of three books reviewed on the cinema. Notices Greene's sharp film sense in the collection which stands as another example of "fine writing," as well as his talent in his ability to keep literature and film separated.

R7433 Steiner, George. "Burnt-Out Case." NY, L (28 Oct.), pp. 185-87. Describes Lord Rochester's Monkey as "quintessential Greene: spare, elegant, beautifully researched and wholly immersed in the topic of depravity." Greene gives a penetrating and fair-minded portrait of Rochester, and his treatment of the death bed conversion shows "a perfect tact and a psychological acuity."

R7434 Sullivan, Walter. "Old Age, Death, and Other Modern Landscapes: Good and Indifferent Fables for Our Times." SR, LXXXII, pp. 138-47. The Honorary Consul is the last of four novels reviewed on pp. 145-47. Notes that God is "lying low" in the novel and wonders whether Greene is less certain of his earlier beliefs. The characters are typical Greene--people desolated in spirit but interesting.

R7435 Sutherland, James. "Hedonism in Control." TLS, 3785 (20 Sept.), p. 992. Admits that Greene is "thoroughly well informed, often accurately perceptive" in Lord Rochester's Monkey. He has also succeeded in avoiding unacknowledged use of the imagination; he speculates critically and profitably but generally examines the life as closely as evidence will permit. The one serious reservation mentioned is connected with the reliability of some of the material on which the biography is based.

R7436 Theroux, Paul. "Monkeying Around." Book World, (13 Oct.), p. 3. Maintains that Lord Rochester's Monkey though "most lavishly" illustrated, is "rich in pleasure" well conceived and "beautifully written." Greene does not make too much of Rochester's death bed conversion but is "more understanding" of Rochester's flights and infidelities than earlier biographers.

R7437 Trotter, Stewart. "The Greene Within." Listener, XCII (24 Oct.), p. 549. Maintains that Greene in Lord Rochester's Monkey does not separate the poet's life from his work and sets out to trace "the embittered effect of drink and disease on Rochester's verse--and all but reduces it to a moral tale." Finds Greene's handling of religion "suspect" and the conclusion that Greene's Rochester owes "as much to self-projection as literary and historical research" difficult to resist.

R7438 Wade, Rosalind. "Quarterly Fiction Review." ContempR, CCXXIV:1296 (Jan.), pp. 45-46. The Honorary Consul is the second book reviewed. Though a deceptively simple tale exploring a situation of contemporary corruption and avarice, the novel conceals "formidable undercurrents" by giving "universal interest" to men and women "disintegrating" both spiritually and physically in the seedy provincial town. Also notes the lack of "novelty and bracing narrative movement" of earlier novels.

R7439 Wolfe, Peter. "The Honorary Consul." STC, 14 (Fall), pp. 117-20. Considers the novel to be "vintage Greene" in its discussion of the "twin theme ... of the lost father and the ambiguous national tie," in its suspense, in the deep religious questions it invites and in the mechanism of its well-built plot that "generates both wisdom and warmth."

R7440 ______. "Lord Rochester's Monkey." MFS, XX (Winter), pp. 597-601. Includes a review of the biography with two books on Greene by Gwenn R. Boardman and Gene D. Phillips. Maintains that the biography is "veiled autobiography"; Greene fails to "tune style to subject" and does not speak out on Rochester's eleventh-hour conversion or his passion for an actress. Moreover, Greene resists treating Rochester's life like a character in a novel; there are gaps in the written record.

R7441 Young, Vernon. "The Friends of Graham Greene." HudR, XXVII (Summer), pp. 245-51. A rather lengthy review of The Pleasure-Dome that finds the most impressive features of the collected film reviews to be Greene's "sense of reality" and the "unrivalled combination" of his "common touch and the uncommon style." Considers it one of Greene's major entertainments that is worth rereading.

R7442 Unsigned. "Paperbacks." Best Sellers, XXXIV (1 Oct.), p. 311. Brief notice of Pocket Book edition of The Honorary Consul and The Third Man.

R7443 ______. "Our Man in Havana." Best Sellers, XXXIV (15 Dec.), p. 428. Brief notice of Pocket Book edition.

R7444 ______. "Lord Rochester's Monkey." Booklist, LXXI (1 Sept.), p. 14. A short note describing Greene's approach to what turns out to be a "popular biography backed by considerable research."

R7445 ______. "Literary Lives." Book World, (8 Dec.), p. 5. Brief notice of Lord Rochester's Monkey.

R7446 ______. "The Honorary Consul and Collected Stories." Choice, X (Jan.), p. 1718. The short review notes that Greene has recovered the control exhibited in his middle period and the novel reveals him as a "brilliant entertainer and a serious moralist." Also describes the stories as being of "uneven technique and sureness of style."

R7447 ______. "Rakehell." Econ, CCLII (28 Sept.), pp. 104, 107. A short review of Lord Rochester's Monkey noting that the book is not aimed at scholars and that Greene's sympathetic treatment of his subject makes certain episodes in Rochester's life more understandable.

R7448 ______. "Lord Rochester's Monkey." Esquire, LXXXII (Oct.), p. 118. The short review describes the biography as "elegant, cool and compact" but it does not make particularly easy reading because of a "certain pedantry in the treatment" of this gay cavalier.

R7449 ______. "A Sort of Life." JML, III:3 (Feb.), p. 368. A brief annotation noting its limitation and value.

R7450 ______. "Lord Rochester's Monkey." Kirkus, XLII (1 Aug.), p. 849. Pre-publication notice of Greene's "only biographical venture" narrated with the "taut, restrained comparison which he always extends to fallen idols and angels."

R7451 ______. "The Honorary Consul." NYTBR, (8 Sept.), p. 34. Untitled brief review announcing publication as Pocket Book, and mentioning the "net of suspenses, unexpected combinations, unpredictable outcomes" on which the action rests, and whose characters "stand for something basic."

R7452 ______. "Lord Rochester's Monkey." NYTBR, (1 Dec.), p. 59. Notice of publication.

R7453 ______. "The Honorary Consul." PW, CCV (24 June), p. 61. Brief notice of paperback edition quoting from the earlier review. See R7367.

R7454 ______. "Lord Rochester's Monkey." PW, CCVI (5 Aug.), p. 54. Briefly noticed as a "graceful and perceptive study ... solid despite its brevity." Also notes that the "religious quality" of Rochester's atheism must have commended him to Greene.

R7455 ______. "Lord Rochester's Monkey." QQ, LXXXI:4 (Winter), pp. 652-53. Short notice describing the literary biography as "short on scholarship, long on good writing, very readable, and lavishly illustrated."

D741 Gaston, Georg M. A. Forms of Salvation in the Novels of Graham Greene. Auburn Univ. DAI, XXXV (Sept.), p. 1655A.

D742 Isaacs, Rita Maria. Three Levels of Allegory in Graham Greene's 'The End of the Affair.' M.A. Trinity Univ., San Antonio.

D743 Lattinville, Ronald Edward. Comic Characterization of the Fiction of Graham Greene. Univ. of Southern California. DAI, XXXV (Dec.), p. 3750A.

D744 Sinclair, Stephen Gerard. Moralists and Mystics: Religion in the Modern British Novel. Univ. of Michigan. DAI, XXXV (1975), p. 7328.

D745 Veitch, Douglas W. The Fictional Landscape of Mexico: Readings in D. H. Lawrence, Graham Greene and Malcolm Lowry. Univ. of Montreal. Published as Lawrence, Greene and Lowry: The Fictional Landscape of Mexico. Waterloo, Ont.: Wilfrid Laurier Univ. Press, 1978. See B782.

D746 Walker, Ronald Gary. Blood, Border, and Barranca: The Role of Mexico in the Modern English Novel. Univ. of Maryland. DAI, XXXVI, p. 913. Published as Infernal Paradise: Mexico and the Modern English Novel. Berkeley & London: Univ. of California Press, 1978. See B783.

1975

B751 Duran, Leopoldo. La Crisis del Sacerdote en Graham Greene. Madrid: Biblioteca de Autores Christianos. A perceptive and sympathetic study from a theological viewpoint of the role of the priest and the priesthood in Brighton Rock, The Power and the Glory, The Heart of the Matter, The End of the Affair, The Living Room, The Potting Shed and A Burnt-Out Case, followed by a survey of the changes that took place in religion over the previous thirty years. Maintains that the earliest "Catholic" novels are rather prophetic in pointing to the "crisis" or change in theology which took place later. Also shows how Greene strips the priesthood of everything which is unessential in order to reveal "its vital qualities."

B752 Gillie, Christopher. "The Critical Decade 1930-1940." Movements in English Literature, 1900-1940. London: Cambridge Univ. Press, pp. 122-50. Pages 137-42 attribute Greene's popularity to the vividness of his twentieth-century scenes and his then "unusual hypothesis--that God is not dead." Discusses the narrative line of The Power and the Glory, its structure which underlines the "irony of the difference between the real and supposed good and evil," notices the resemblance it bears to Conrad, but denies that the novel explores the "moral experience" of human beings.

B753 Kunkel, Francis L. "The Sexy Cross." Passion and the

Passion: Sex and Religion in Modern Literature. Philadelphia: The Westminster Press, pp. 157-69. In this last chapter of a serious study of the "symbiosis between sex and religion" in twentieth-century literature, Kunkel lumps together nine Catholic writers--Bloy, Claudel, Mauriac, Waugh, Greene, Péguy, Bernanos, O'Faolain and Chesterton--who share similar though not identical notions of the "subterranean trinity of blood, sex and anti-reason" which determine the view of Catholicism projected in their writings. The tendency to place perhaps undue emphasis on Greene's "bizarre erotic interest in cruelty and humiliation," the suffering and joylessness connected with sex and the "self-damnation" that is mistaken for "self-sacrifice" stems from regarding Greene as a Catholic novelist, not a novelist "who happens to be a Catholic."

B754 Lambert, Gavin. "The Double Agent." The Dangerous Edge. London: Barrie & Jenkins; New York: Grossman Publishers, 1976, pp. 132-70. A biographical investigation of Greene's intrigue-filled spy thrillers based on the assumption that "crime-artists" even while inhabiting the "brutal, menacing and conflicted world of melodrama" also give a "continuous secret autobiography" which reveals "impulses fiercely at war within the self." The investigation is replete with attempts to relate the views and attitudes of characters to Greene, and with generalizations based on speculation; e.g., "The Basement Room" tips off "the novelist as a detective of hell," or the events in Stamboul Train "are drawn from Greene's personal mythology."

B755 Nakano, Kii. "G. Greene to Gendaisei." [G. Greene and Modernism]. Kirisutokyo to Bungaku. [Christianity and Literature]. Ed. Tomoichi Sasabuchi. Tokyo: Kasama Shoin, pp. 155-72. In Japanese. Examines the shift from Freudianism to Communism and to Catholicism in Greene's works. Regards the three concepts, especially Catholicism, as determining factors of Greene's modernism. Bases his views on an interpretation of A Sort of Life.

B756 Raine, Kathleen. The Land Unknown. London: Hamish Hamilton; New York: George Braziller. This autobiography refers on pp. 178, 180-81, and 184 to the writer's acquaintance with Greene during the war years in London. Besides describing Greene as "invariably chivalrous; like a knight who does battle with every champion, but shows courtesy towards women," she admits that she has not "at all understood Graham either." She also reveals that Greene "was tormented by 'doubts'" in the forties and seems to have evinced to her an interest in "proof by physical evidence" in spite of his belief that "Catholicism is essentially a 'magical' religion."

B757 Takeuchi, Masao. "The Heart of the Matter no Kosei, Shuho oyobi Buntai ni tsuite." Gengo to Buntai: Higashida Chiaki Kyoju Kanzeki Kinen Ronbunshu. Ed. Chiaki Higashida. Osaka: Osaka Kyoiku Tosho, pp. 239-51. Unavailable for examination.

A751 Burgess, Anthony. "Graham Greene as Monsieur Vert." Tablet, CCXXIX (15 March), pp. 259-60. An interesting assessment of Greene's achievement by an expatriate English Catholic novelist. Maintains that Greene finds his conflicts within the faith, seems to have embraced Jansenism, and is rather intolerant of an achieved or settled society. The origins of his art is the popular "visualisable" story to which he has brought theology, wit and humor.

A752 Day-Lewis, Sean. "The Dominant Shades of Greene." DaiT, (15 Sept.), p. 7. Finds the Thames's Television adaptation of a selection of Greene's short stories unsatisfactory because producer Alan Cooke's "visual style" seems to emphasize their ephemeral quality. Notes Greene's lack of interest in writing directly for television in spite of the mass public he can then command.

A753 Dombrowski, Theo Q. "Graham Greene: Techniques of Intensity." Ariel, VI:4, pp. 29-38. Examines the technical devices Greene uses--emphasizing the significance of character, actions and objects, the juxtaposition of diverse elements, figurative language, and figures of speech "yoking abstracts and concretes"--to create intensity by the disturbing effect of "dislocation, disorientation, and enigma" which echo his intense vision of a life of "inherent brutality, transcendent significance and essential inscrutability."

A754 Duran, Leopoldo. "The Hint of an Explanation of Graham Greene." ContempR, CCXXVI, pp. 152-55. Asserts that the short story is a "metaphysical parable" that depicts the struggle between good and evil, between God and Satan.

A755 ________. "The Essential Priesthood as Portrayed by Graham Greene." CR, NS LX:2 (Feb.), pp. 103-16. Examines Greene's dramatic presentation of the "essential priesthood" and the theological concept of the priest's sacramental character as understood by the Catholic Church through a study of the Whiskey Priest, Father Brown and Father Callifer--priests in critical and extreme situations who illustrate the threefold crisis: the moral, pastoral and intellectual crisis which many priests are undergoing after the winds of change brought about by Vatican II.

A756 Greisch, Janet Rohler. "Patterns of Evil and How to Break Them." CT, XIX (20 June), pp. 13-14. Maintains that though Greene's characters expound the evidence of his "pattern-breaking," it is in his conception of God and the way he writes compellingly of God and His mercy that Greene invites particular interest.

A757 Harwood, Ronald. "Time and the Novelist. Graham Greene Interviewed." Listener, XCIV (4 Dec.), pp. 747 & 749. On Radio 4, "Kaleidoscope." Discusses his latest play The Return of A. J. Raffles, the influences that have acted on him as a novelist, especially Conrad, his irritation at being labelled a "Catholic" novelist and consequently with The Heart of the Matter, his "discovery" of comedy and his current favorite novel, The Honorary Consul.

A758 Heilpern, John. "On the Dangerous Edge." Observer, (7 Dec.), pp. 17-18, 21, 23, 25. An account of an interview with Greene in his Paris flat and over lunch. Greene speaks of his writing habits, dreams, experience of the "paranormal," boredom, and travel as one form of escape from it, childhood reading, the writer's instinct and belief in God.

A759 Isaacs, Rita. "Three Levels of Allegory in Graham Greene's The End of the Affair." LNL, I:1, pp. 29-52. Originally an MA thesis submitted in 1974 to Trinity Univ., San Antonio, Texas. Presents an allegorical interpretation of the novel through a study of its language, imagery, symbols and parallel structures. Maintains that the second level of allegory involves Greene's use of The Dark Night of the Soul by St. John of the Cross--a "matrix on which he [Greene] bases the structure of the novel."

A7510 Kahler, Klaus. "Der Syntax des Dialogs im modernen Englisch untersucht an Werken von Harold Pinter und Graham Greene." ZAA, XXIII, pp. 41-63. A linguistic analysis of "spoken prose" in selected excerpts from Pinter and Greene for the preparation of material for second language instruction purposes.

A7511 Koszty, Gabriella. "Biralatok kereszttuzeben: Graham Greene 'homalyos teologiaga.'" Vigilia, XL:7, 456-63. Unavailable for examination.

A7512 McCann, Janet. "Graham Greene: The Ambiguity of Death." ChrC, XXX (April), pp. 432-35. Maintains that Greene's fascination by the irony of possible damnation or salvation and his notion of life as a moral drama are reflected in his treatment of death and dying, a treatment that emphasizes the ambiguity of death. Such ambiguities and ironies in The Man Within, Brighton Rock, and The Power and the Glory emphasize Greene's theme of human love as a "destructive and redeeming force which clouds all moral issues and makes the world an even more dangerous place."

A7513 McDougal, Stuart Y. "Visual Tropes: An Analysis of The Fallen Idol." Style, IX:4 (Fall), pp. 502-13. A study of the techniques used in the film adaptation of "The Basement Room" to create a range of visual equivalents for the figurative language of the story.

A7514 McManus, June. "The Power and the Glory for Freshmen." PCCTT, 40, pp. 24-30. An instructor's justification for teaching the novel to freshmen at San Antonio College, Texas, and her experiences with the various literary topics researched for class presentations, as well as the sociological, philosophical undertones and the historical background.

A7515 Monge Rudin, Patricia E. "Elementos descriptivos evocadores de muerte en The Power and the Glory." RUCR, XLI, pp. 193-98. An analysis of Greene's masterly use of descriptive elements that speak of disintegration, desolation and violence to indicate the continued presence and reality of death, its "inminencia palpable," in the novel.

A7515a Nasrulaeva, F. "Tragicheskiy konflikt v romankh G. Grina i Dzh oldridzha." Sovetskii Dagestan (Makhachkala, USSR), I, pp. 68-71. Unavailable for examination.

A7516 Ogude, S. E. "In Search of Misery: A Study of Graham Greene's Travels in Africa." Odu, 11 (Jan.), pp. 45-60. The first of two articles that examine the Africa that emerges in Greene's works. (See A766). Argues that two different impressions of Africa emerge from his travel books, World Without Maps and In Search of a Character. One is a picture of Africa that suggests simplicity and innocence in the world as it was conceived, a picture of Africans as a child race that brings spontaneous joy to the mere act of living, and the other is of an Africa that Europe and the white man knows, the Africa of the late Victorian Empire builders.

A7517 Ower, John. "Dark Parable: History and Theology in Graham Greene's 'The Destructors.'" Cithara, XV:1, pp. 69-78. Considers the short story as a "symbolic theological parable" whose thematic richness is remarkable in its scope and whose significance lies in its "'enveloping action,' of the implicit connection" of the story with the spiritual crisis and the cultural disintegration of Europe.

A7518 Trifu, Sever. "Greene in Romania." Steaua, XXVI:5, pp. 53-55. In Romanian. Analyzes the reaction of the Romanian public and critics to Greene's literary achievement. Finds the critics in general agreement over Greene's growing realism, and the restlessness resulting from his vision of life as he attempts to reach a satisfactory solution to the problems of the 20th century.

R751 Avery, G. S. "Lord Rochester's Monkey." MLR, LXX (Oct.), pp. 857-58. Maintains that despite his "sharp, historical concern" with detail and thorough investigation of the Wilmot family connections, Greene fails to develop his promising view of Rochester's character, and his interpretation of major actions is "thin and often unconvincing." The "uneven quality" of the biography makes it more likely to "perplex" than to engage the general reader. Also has "reservations" about the reliability of some of Greene's comments.

R752 Hirsch, Foster. "Rake and Poet." Progressive, XXXIX (Feb.), pp. 58-59. Considers the research that went into Lord Rochester's Monkey to be "thorough" but the writing to be "sometimes choppy" with details that are not always pertinent or engaging. Tends to regard Rochester as one of Greene's "burnt-out cases" on whom Greene has grafted the "conflicts, denials and transformations" of his own religious history. Notes Greene's interest in Rochester as poet and wit and appreciation of his skill with words.

R753 Hurren, Kenneth. "Return of the Native." Spectator, CCXXXV:7694 (13 Dec.), pp. 770. A review of The Return of A. J. Raffles and the performance. Rather disappointed with Greene's "disrespectful spoof"; the plot is little more than a "series of unrelated diversions and decorations," devoid of Greene's gift of storytelling for which the fashionable introduction of nudity is no substitute.

R754 Mayne, Richard. "TLS Commentary: Second Innings." TLS, 3848 (12 Dec.), p. 1486. A review of The Return of A. J. Raffles and the performance at the Aldwych Theatre. Discusses the appeal of the "extravaganza" and questions the suitability of the sub-title.

A755 Mudrick, Marvin. "The Offending Member." HudR, XXVIII (Summer), pp. 271-78. A review of the Earl of Rochester's life and poetry occasioned by Greene's Lord Rochester's Monkey.

R756 Nightingale, Benedict. "Through the Slips." NSta, XC:2334 (12 Dec.), p. 764. A review of The Return of A. J. Raffles and its performance. Finds the play a "not-very-successful comedy-thriller, an anticlimactic end" to Greene's eleven year exile from the stage. Notes the effect of "sexual seediness and moral disintegration" in the play, the open, unashamed and pervasive homosexuality being Greene's "main contribution" to the Raffles myth.

R757 Wimsatt, Margaret. "Lord Rochester's Monkey." Commonweal, CI:16 (14 March), pp. 465-66. Describes the book as "sumptuously produced" and its "lavish style" reflecting the "affection and respect its author has earned in the years between."

R758 Unsigned. "Der Honorarkonsul." Booklist, LXXI (1 March), p. 672. Notice of the German translation of The Honorary Consul.

R759 ______. "Lord Rochester's Monkey." Choice, XI (Jan.), p. 1630. A short note describing the volume as the "most handsome study" of the poet whose portrait is drawn "with sympathy" and rescued from the "taint of his lechery."

R7510 ______. "The Honorary Consul." ChrC, XCII (14 May), p. 501. Brief notice of Pocket Books paperback edition.

R7511 ______. "The Honorary Consul." EJ, LXIV (Jan.), p. 112. Title appears on the "1973-74 Honor Listing" for the most popular books.

R7512 ______. "Lord Rochester's Monkey." Scriblerian, VII:2 (Spring), p. 117. Finds Greene's presentation of Rochester's "cavalier-puritan tension" rather simple today, and disappointed by the limited discussion presented of Rochester's poetry. This "rehabilitation" of Rochester in the eyes of the general reader whom Greene has in mind, would have been more welcome in the thirties than it is now.

R7513 ______. "Lord Rochester's Monkey." VQR, LI (Spring), p. xliv. A note on the "skillfully written" biography that provides "fresh and valuable insights." Finds it "persuasive" especially the explanation of Rochester's "religion of aestheticism." Mentions two faults: its lack of footnotes and cavalier dismissal of Vieth's edition of Rochester's poems.

D751 Baker, M. A. A Study of the Use of Environment in the Novel, with Particular Reference to Some of the Novels of Graham Greene. M. Phil. London Institute of Education.

D752 McCullagh, James Charles. Aesthetics and Religious Mind: Francois Mauriac, Graham Greene and Flannery O'Connor. Lehigh Univ. DAI, XXXV, 7316A.

D753 McDonald, Horace Thelton. Africa as a Fictive World: Seven Modern Responses from Joseph Conrad to Graham Greene. Univ. of Southwestern Louisiana. DAI, XXXVI (1976), 7440A-41A.

D754 Milbury-Steen, Sarah Louise. Contrasting and Reciprocal Views of Africans and Europeans by Selected European and West African Writers. Indiana Univ. DAI, XXXVI (1976), 7413A.

D755 Morrison, Patrick John. The Quest Motif in the Fiction of Graham Greene. Univ. of Toronto. DAI, XXXVIII (March 1978), 5464A.

D756 Nesaule, Valda. The Christ Figure and Idea of Sacrifice in Herman Melville's Billy Budd, in Graham Greene's The Potting Shed, and in Fedor Dostoevskij's "The Dream of a Ridiculous Man." Indiana Univ. DAI, XXXVI (1976), 5284A.

D757 Riesen, David Herman. Retreat into Wilderness: A Study of the Travel Books of Five Twentieth-Century British Novelists. Madison, Wisconsin. DAI, XXXVI, 1534A.

D758 Soliman, Soliman Yousef. Non-British Setting in Twentieth-Century British Fiction. Univ. of Indiana. DAI, XXXVI, 881A.

1976

B761 Burton, H[arry] M[cGuire]. Notes on Graham Greene's 'The Quiet American.' Study-Aid Series. London: Methuen Educational. The "Notes" are rather elementary and are meant as an aid for examination purposes. Tries to place The Quiet American in the perspective of the modern novel, gives some background material on it, summarizes chapters and gives character sketches. This is followed by explanatory notes on the text and both general and context questions.

B762 Faulkner, Peter. "Recent Religious Novelists: Waugh, Greene, Golding." Humanism in the English Novel. London: Elek Books Ltd.; New York: Barnes & Noble, pp. 156-78. Pages 165-69 of Ch. VI focus on Brighton Rock and Travels with My Aunt as being characteristic of Greene's "dogmatic Christian anti-humanism"; Brighton Rock for extolling the superior spiritual status of those aware of religious values--Pinkie--over those who are only aware of the moral values--Ida--and Travels with My Aunt for being unable to find meaning in ordinary human experience or raise it to a higher level. Defines humanism as an "ethical tradition" that regards happiness as a "central concern," is skeptical about the supernatural or the transcendental, ascribes value to human achievements, and recognizes the "achievement of a full humanity rather than a passing beyond the human" as the ideal or the challenge.

B763 Gregor, Ian and David Lodge. "Graham Greene." The English Novel. Questions in Literature. Ed. Cedric Watts. London: Sussex Books, pp. 153-71. A "critical dialogue" discussing Greene's vision of life or presentation of religious assumptions that invite a reader's "imaginative assent" and the inevitable "lopsidedness" or distortion attendant on the representation of such truths, his reputation, popularity and general position in the literary world, and thirdly, the "characteristic techniques and style of a Graham Greene novel." Focus on Brighton Rock, The Power and the Glory and The Heart of the Matter. No discussion of, or debate on, later novels.

B764 Lodge, David. "Graham Greene." Six Contemporary British Novelists. Ed. George Stade. New York: Columbia Univ. Press, pp. 1-56. Rpt. from Columbia Essays on Modern Writers, No. 17. See B664.

A761 Bergonzi, Bernard. "Graham Greene Supplied the Lyrics. A Footnote to the Thirties." Encounter, XLVII (Dec.), 67-71. Examines Greene's use of popular music in the thirties in Brighton Rock and earlier novels. Shows how his use of popular songs ranges from the purely decorative in Stamboul Train to the functional or "Flaubertian counterpoint" in The Confidential Agent or to the inventive, and extensive too, in Brighton Rock, in much the same way as he has used other conventions of the popular arts, like the cinema and the thriller, for literary creation.

A762 Deedy, John. "News & Views: Graham Greene." Commonweal, CIII (23 April), p. 260. Tidbits of information culled out from "TLS Commentary: 'Second Impressions.'" TLS, (26 March 1976), p. 346. See A7610.

A763 Domenichelli, Mario. "L'incredible messia: Il primo Greene fra Eliot e James Joyce." LdProv, XXV-XXVI, pp. 117-31. In Italian. Notes the absence of allusions or references in A Sort of Life to the two "grandi matrici" of the first part of the twentieth century--Joyce and Eliot--and examines England Made Me, A Gun for Sale and Brighton Rock to show Greene's indebtedness to The Waste Land and Ulysses for much of the "Greenean" imagery that figures prominently in the three novels.

A764 Duran, Leopoldo. "A Priest Reads The Honorary Consul." CR, NS LXI:9 (Sept.), pp. 343-49. Concentrates on Fr. Rivas, "the central figure" of the novel, because he incarnates the "theological, social and political dilemmas" confronting priests in Latin America. Admits that Fr. Rivas, "the highest personification of the 'borderline' priests depicted," creates a "problem" for modern theology. Also points out the affinites between him and the Whiskey Priest.

A765 Larsen, Eric. "The Quiet American." NRep, CLXXV (7-14 Aug.), pp. 40-42. A reconsideration of the novel as a "serious" book that also dismisses American heated reaction to the novel in the fifties and, in retrospect, recognizes it as the best novel that came out of the Vietnam war, as truly "prophetic" and whose caricature and satire of the fictionalized American are by and large true.

A766 Ogude, S. E. "Graham Greene's Africa." Odu, 14 (July), pp. 41-65. The second of two articles that examines the Africa that emerges in Greene's works. (See A7516). Examines the set of values and assumptions behind Greene's attitude to Africa as it is represented in his novels especially his portrayal of black characters in Ali, Deo Gratias and Wordsworth. Maintains that Greene's "odd African fixation" is "probably, very probably" an extension of his admiration of an imperial past that sees a cultural gap between white man and black man, and continues the former's condescending and patronizing attitude towards the loyal and grateful negro. Also examines Greene's "almost pathological" interest in black women and his caricature of the educated middle class of Sierra Leone.

A767 Vargo, Edward P., S. B. D. "Struggling with a Bugaboo: The Priest Character in Achebe and Greene and Keneally." FJS, IX, pp. 1-13. Rpt. in Awakened Conscience: Studies in Commonwealth Literature. Ed. C. D. Narasimhaiah. New Delhi: Sterling Publishers Pvt. Ltd., 1978, pp. 284-94. Compares the elements which the concept of the priest in Chinua Achebe's Arrow of Gold, Greene's The Honorary Consul and T. Keneally's Three Cheers for the Paraclete share in common, especially their dramatization of "transcendent realities" which the priest, as spiritual leader is constantly aware of, his role as intermediary between God and man and the failure of organized religion. Notes how Greene's Father Rivas feels himself "a criminal estranged from God," struggling with his transcendent reality, and rationalizing his own evil and that of the community into the essence of God himself. Maintains that Greene's treatment is "ironic and equivocal."

A768 Viola, André. "Graham Greene et 'Le Tombeau de l'homme blanc.'" EA, XXIX, pp. 167-78. An analysis of Greene's frequent allusions to West Africa in general and to Freetown in particular, and the place the latter occupies in his universe, in an attempt to assess the symbolic value with which it is invested in his works. Notes that critics have been generally preoccupied with the general significance of his African trips but have not brought out the fact that Freetown is "le point de passage obligatoire, l'étape nécessaire avant l'épisode central" as well as a sort of "décor priviligié pour ratés." Journey Without Maps, The Heart of the Matter, In Search of a Character and "Across the Border."

A769 Weselinski, Andrzej. "Irony and Melodrama in The Heart of the Matter." SAP, VIII, 167-73. Attempts to show that humor and the "existential irony pervading the whole novel" add a tragic dimension to what would have been "superfluous sentimentality and cheap pathos" in Scobie's drama. Notes Greene's reinsertion of an important scene insofar as Louise is concerned in The Collected Edition of the novel.

A7610 Unsigned. "TLS Commentary: 'Second Impressions.'" TLS, 3863 (26 March), p. 346. On the reissue of The Man Within and The Third Man/Loser Takes All in the Collected Edition. Notes the importance of the introductions as autobiography, the omissions and additions, as well as the circumstances of their writing.

R761 Breen, Jon L. "Raffles, Puzzles, and Bosworth Field." WLB, LI (Sept.), pp. 38-39. A brief review of The Return of A. J. Raffles as a "spirited comedy that reads well and should play better."

R762 Esslin, Martin. "The Return of A. J. Raffles." P&P, XXIII (Feb.), p. 30. A favorable review of the play and the performance by the RSC at the Aldwych Theatre, London. Notices the sophisticated character of Greene's Raffles in this "nostalgic pastiche," and Greene's indirect comment about his own time "by contrast as well as tragic irony."

R763 Peereboom, J. J. "Playing with Words: The London Drama Scene." DQR, VI:4, pp. 318-33. Includes a brief review of The Return A. J. Raffles on p. 331 as a comedy not "worth mentioning if it was by somebody else" and which, in spite of "some lively moments" in Act II is "too easy-going for its own good."

R764 Unsigned. "The Return of A. J. Raffles." Choice, XIII (Oct.), p. 980. Describes the play as "witty, clever, and amusing," with much of its humor coming from the "ironic conflict between 'normal' morality and 'homo' morality."

R765 ________. "The Return of A. J. Raffles." Booklist, LXXII (15 April), p. 1154. A brief review noting Greene's "sense of satire" as it is directed in this "smart" comedy against the decadent "British upper crust" at the turn of the century.

R766 ________. "Letter from London." NY, LI (26 Jan.), pp. 100-01. Rather critical of Greene for "modishly" updating Hornung's characters in The Return of A. J. Raffles. The play is a "curious concoction, with its laboured jokes and plot" and the now standard nude scene.

D761 Moore, Karen Rae. The Comic Technique of Graham Greene. Georgia State Univ.--School of Arts and Sciences. DAI, XXXVI, 5322A-23A.

D762 Navarro, Lenore Mary. From Fiction to Film: A Critical Analysis of Graham Greene's The Fallen Idol, The Third

Man, and Our Man in Havana, Directed by Carol Reed. Univ. of Southern California. DAI, XXXVII (March 1977), 5405A.

D763 Pearson, Sheryl Marie Sherman. The Anglo-American Novel of the Mexican Revolution, 1910-1940: D. H. Lawrence, B. Traven, Graham Greene. Univ. of Michigan. DAI, XXXVII, 1543A.

D764 Ragheb, G. A. A. M. The Vision of Life Presented in Graham Greene's Fiction and the Presentation of Some of His Novels to University Students in Egypt. London Institute of Education.

1977

B771 Koga, Hideo. Essays on Graham Greene and His Work. Hiroshima: Hiroshima Univ. Publishing Society. This is a collection of six separate unconnected "essays" strung together for publication in book form. "Greeneland and Greenelander" describes Greene's world and gives brief character sketches in novels from The Man Within up to and including The Heart of the Matter. "On A Burnt-Out Case" is a general examination of the novel that touches upon the various states of belief, half-belief and non-belief. "Graham Greene as Short Story Writer" examines description and style in several short stories. "Graham Greene as Literary Thriller Writer" examines the "hunted-versus-hunter pattern" in The Man Within, Brighton Rock, The Power and the Glory, The Heart of the Matter and two entertainments, A Gun for Sale and The Confidential Agent. "Graham Greene as Playwright" focusses on The Living Room as a play describing the dilemma of human beings when forced into an emotional impasse. The last essay, "Greenesque" is in two parts: The first deals with Greene's nostalgia for childhood and the second surveys briefly The Comedians and The Honorary Consul. Though the book quotes from, and refers to, critics extensively, it has no footnotes, no bibliography and no index.

B772 Kulshrestha, J. P. Graham Greene: The Novelist. New Delhi: Macmillan Co. of India. A study of the themes and the world Greene has imagined and of the characters who inhabit it. Contends that Greene's primary obsession with evil accounts for the recurrent themes and motifs in the novels, that they are inextricably linked with his religious consciousness, and that his characters, in their attitudes and sensibilities, reflect the attitudes and sensibilities of Greene himself.

Ch. 1 investigates Greene's "obsessional motifs" and the moulding of his sensibility in childhood. Ch. 2 discusses the characters in The Man Within, It's a Battlefield and England Made Me, and his dramatization of personal guilt, isolation and failure in a "corrosively malignant world" as a recreation of the experiences which haunt Greene most. Ch. 3 maintains the same approach in Brighton Rock, The Power and the Glory and The Heart of the Matter and maintains that despite the preponderance of the religious dimension, Greene's view remains basically unchanged. Ch. 4 asserts that Greene's belief in the presence of God modifies the "realism" of the relationships of characters in The End of the Affair and that Greene's religious stance undergoes a change in A Burnt-Out Case. Ch. 5 discusses The Quiet American, The Comedians and The Honorary Consul in which the relationship between man and God either "does not figure at all, or, if it does, figures only marginally." Human commitment in the face of social evil is also explored. The last chapter examines the "entertainments," and shows how Stamboul Train, A Gun for Sale, The Confidential Agent and The Ministry of Fear bring into sharp focus "Greene's obsessive awareness of crime and violence," and project a "disheartening" image of life. Each of the post-war entertainments, The Third Man, Loser Takes All, Our Man in Havana and Travels with My Aunt is unique, but they all express the "innate oneness" of Greene's material. The Conclusion sums up Greene's vision of life. Includes a select bibliography. Footnotes are well documented.

B773 Mahood, M. M. "The Possessed: Greene's The Comedians." The Colonial Encounter: A Reading of Six Novels. London: Rex Collings, pp. 115-41. The book attempts an "exegetical" study of six masterpieces selected from novels of the Third World and the English 20th-century novel, and which are concerned with the experience of colonial rule and its aftermath. Attempts to show that in this "novel of neo-colonialism," Greene attains the "lost objectivity" he had long sought since his Liberian trip, but it is marred somehow by "literary overkill." Greene's heavy emphasis on humanism makes it "one of the most engagés books of his time."

B774 Merry, Bruce. Anatomy of the Spy Thriller. London: Macmillan; Montréal: McGill-Queen's Univ. Press. The study attempts to describe "the ground rules of this literary genre and establish its recurrent patterns of characterization and structure" and to account for its success. Notes the unusual attributes of the professional killer in the spy thriller--Simon Raven with his tragic parents and harelip (pp. 80-81)--and examines Greene's parody of the professional agent's paranoia in Our Man in Havana (pp. 153-56) and the "moral ambiguity" surrounding "D" in The Confidential Agent (pp. 204-05). Makes no reference to The Ministry of Fear.

A771 Camano Rencoret, Marie Esther. "El triple asedio en Sarah Miles, heroina de El fin de la aventura de Graham Greene." Kanina, I:1, pp. 15-21. An analysis of the three major forces, "el triple asedio," that besiege and determine Sarah Miles' personality and action: the carnal or physiological pressures inherent in the flesh, the psychological pressures manifested by her obsessive ideas, remorse, and anxiety, and lastly Divine Grace.

A772 Dworkin, Martin S. "The Writing on the Screen." Trivium, XII (May), pp. 17-25. Discusses two opposed views on the screen-writer as a "kind of skilled illiterate" or as an "embattled litterateur." Examines briefly Greene's views on the motion picture medium and his mixed feelings about film version of his work--it is likely that Greene had more "to do with screen work, directly and indirectly, than any major literary figure, so far in the century."

A773 Fay, Teresita, and Michael G. Yetman. "Scobie the Just: A Reassessment of The Heart of the Matter." Renascence, XXIX (Spring), pp. 142-56. Investigates the nature of pity and its "correlatives, corruption and responsibility, as these qualities insinuate themselves into the psychology and moral choices" of Scobie. Contends that though pity may account for Scobie's corruption, it is simultaneously his glory too, for it is this same capacity for pity which, despite his "relentless deteriorating self-estimate," also reveals Scobie to be a man who in both thought and action is set apart from other characters and is to be admired "for his singular openness to the claims of others." Also maintains that his suicide, disturbing but defensible in its heroism, is also "courageous because it is selfless."

A774 Hanlon, Robert M., SJ. "The Ascent to Belief in Graham Greene's A Burnt-Out Case." C&L, XXVI:4 (Summer), pp. 20-26. Proves that Greene's "dramatic expression" of three "types of belief, half-belief, and non-belief" in the novel correspond, in substance, to Kierkegaard's three stages on life's way, the religious, the ethical and the aesthetic.

A775 Higdon, David Leon. "Graham Greene's Second Thoughts: The Text of The Heart of the Matter." SB, XXX, pp. 249-56. Argues that the extensively revised text of the Collected Edition (1971)--it contains 23 additions, one involving the restoration of a manuscript chapter, 131 deletions and 158 changes--offers the reader an "excellent opportunity to observe an author clarifying intention, satisfying his own sense of craftsmanship, and remaking his fictive reader." Examines the significance of each category of revisions. Uses the 1960 Viking Compass edition to determine the extent of the changes in the 1971 edition of the novel.

A776 Mewshaw, Michael. "Greene in Antibes." LM, XVII (June/July), pp. 35-45. An account of an interview with Greene in Antibes in which Greene speaks of his present working habits and describes The Honorary Consul as a novel that does not contradict what he had written earlier. Reminisces on his travels to Chile, Cuba and his meetings with Castro, Haiti, Vietnam, all of which show his "sense of timeliness, an instinct for stories which afterward seem prophetic," and reveal him as a writer who is "fiercely independent, politically engagé." Also narrates the circumstances of his surreptitious screen debut.

A777 Miller, R[obert] H. "Graham Greene: The Potting Shed, Act III." PBSA, LXXI (Jan.), pp. 105-07. Shows from an "Uncorrected Proof Copy" in the Graham Greene collection at the Univ. of Louisville, Louisville, Kentucky, that the same text for The Potting Shed was in press in both England and the U.S. in 1957 and that the decision to publish an English edition with a different third act was made later. (See also pp. 45-48 of his Graham Greene: A Descriptive Catalog. Lexington, Ky.: Univ. Press of Kentucky, 1979).

A778 _______. "Textual Alterations in Graham Greene's Stamboul Train." PBSA, LXXI (July), pp. 378-81. Examines the original readings of the novel before Greene altered them at his publisher's request following J. B. Priestley's claim that he was libelled. This copy of Stamboul Train, presumably a pre-publication copy distributed for review, is now in the possession of Mr. Eugene Higgins, New York. All editions of the novel carry the altered text. (See also pp. 14-16 of his Graham Greene: A Descriptive Catalog. Lexington, Ky.: Univ. Press of Kentucky, 1979).

A779 Morita, Akiharu. "Aspects of Pity: Brighton Rock." AnRS, XXVIII, pp. 188-200. Unavailable for examination.

A7710 Raphael, Frederic. "Sacred Cows: Dishing the Dirt." SunT, (15 May), p. 78. Takes a look at Greene's reputation as "a kind of fictional St. Augustine" whose later novels embarrass by their "laboured and threadbare contrivance" and their "moral complaisance." Questions why Greene has not written about the Holocaust and thinks him "uniquely equipped to write the great modern obituary on traditional notions of God and man."

A7711 Thale, Jerome, and Rose Marie Thale. "Greene's 'Literary Pilgrimage': Allusions in Travels with My Aunt." PLL, XIII, 207-12. Finds the novel a "compendium" of allusions and quotations--over one hundred items--sometimes obvious but at times their detailed implications are quite obscure and constitute Greene's "most elaborate and circuitous" jokes. Shows the similarities in character, theme and situation between Rob Roy and Travels with My Aunt and the elaborate allusions in it to The Viper of Milan, and maintains that Greene is playing on the relationship between literature and life in that the former will tell us nothing about life "unless we ourselves understand the ways in which literature is not life but only like life, and the ways in which it can be serious or playfull, or both at the same time."

A7712 Webb, Bernice Larson. "Whiskey and Women: Problems of the Priesthood in Graham Greene's The Power and the Glory and J. F. Powers' 'The Valiant Woman.'" NLauR, VII:2, pp. 62-71. Compares the conflicts of the two priests, the opponents against whom they contend, their choices to suffer or to make a break for freedom, their reliance on God, and how, in their separate ways, they let themselves be trapped in their respective environments.

A7713 Wobbe, R. A. "Graham Greene's Literary and Theater Reviews and Articles in The Spectator, 1932-1941." BB, XXXIV (Jan.), pp. 21-28. Some 220 items chronologically arranged in two sections: 192 under Literary Reviews and Articles, and 28 under Theater Reviews. An Introductory note remarks on the absence of such a list and explains the need for it to reveal Greene's "acute critical insight" and to provide us with a "writer's look at the writer's world of the thirties."

A7714 Unsigned. "1978 Jurors and Their Candidates for the Neustadt International Prize for Literature." WLT, LI (Autumn), p. 578. A biographical note on Greene listing his achievements as a candidate for the prize when he was nominated by R. K. Narayan.

D771 Adamson, Judith Emily. Greene on Film. Univ. of Montreal.

D772 Brannon, Lilian Borop. Iconology of the Child Figure in Graham Greene's Fiction. East Texas State Univ. DAI, XXXVIII (Jan. 1978), p. 4155A.

D773 Friedman, Lois M., O.S.F. The 'Dark Night of the Soul' in Selected Dramas by Three Modern Catholic Authors. Purdue Univ. DAI, XXXIX (1978), p. 872A.

1978

B781 Vargo, Edward P., SVD. "Struggling with a Bugaboo: The Priest-Character in Achebe and Greene and Keneally." Awakened Conscience: Studies in Commonwealth Literature. Ed. C. D. Narasimhaiah. New Delhi: Sterling Publishers Pvt. Ltd., pp. 284-94. Paper read at the Fourth Triennial Conference of Commonwealth Literature in January 1977 in Delhi. Originally published in FJS, IX (1976), pp. 1-13. See A767.

B782 Veitch, Douglas W. "Graham Greene: The Dark Is Light Enough." Lawrence, Greene and Lowry: The Fictional Landscape of Mexico. Pref. George Woodcock. Waterloo, Ont.: Wilfrid Laurier Univ. Press, pp. 58-111. Originally a doctoral diss. presented to Univ. of Montréal, 1974. Greene is the second author whose creative response to the Mexican landscape and the ambivalent role it plays--the landscape is at once "omnipresent background" and a rich source of image and symbols that reflect the human drama--is analyzed and discussed. Examines Greene's emotional and intellectual response to Mexico through an analysis of The Lawless Roads, "Across the Bridge," and The Power and the Glory to show how Greene's recreation of landscape functions as a "component of meaning" in the fiction. Focusses on the novel where Greene's artistic creation of landscape, even while respecting verisimilitude, contributes to the meaning when the various landscapes--port, town, village, cell and finca--are seen as "places of betrayal and capture, temptation and justification, exclusion and inclusion, compression and decompression," and also as contributing to the "structure" of the novel. Ch. 1, "Mexico and the Mythic Response," also discusses in general terms the three writers' apprehension of Mexico.

B783 Walker, Ronald G. Infernal Paradise: Mexico and the Modern English Novel. Berkeley & London: Univ. of California Press. Originally a diss. presented to Univ. of Maryland, 1974. An attempt to define the nature of the fascination that Mexico exercised over Lawrence, Huxley, Greene and Lowry, to suggest reasons for its emergence and to examine the aesthetic response of each novelist in one of his novels. Ch. 6 examines Greene's Mexican trip to show that Greene's fullest and most explicit expression of the Mexican "myth" is given in The Lawless Roads (Another Mexico) which provides him at once with opportunities for self-exploration and for the pursuit of his own obsessions; it is in Mexico that Greene found the centrality of his own religious faith. Emphasizes the merits of the book as a testament for self-exploration, independent of its relation to the novel to which it gave rise. Ch. 7 focusses on The Power and the Glory and traces the "border imagery" in it which expresses the ambience of pain, of isolation and of spiritual abandonment, of dissolution and of loss that permeates the novel; for Greene is not really interested in description of landscape for its own sake but only in the meaningful way landscape reflects or affects the life of characters. This he does by conveying an overwhelming sense of atmosphere with a minimum of straight description.

B784 Weber, Antonie. Die Erzahlstruktur von Graham Greenes katholischen Romanen. Swiss Studies in English, 95. Bern: Francke Verlag. A scholarly and erudite investigation of Greene's narrative technique and its relationship to his concept of reality; i.e., the "peculiar relationship between religious theme and novelistic form." Bases the analysis of the structural technique on the early "Russian formalists and their elaborations by the French structuralists." Considers Greene's stylistic features, and after a detailed analysis of the narrative structure of Brighton Rock and The End of the Affair, attempts to show that most of the Catholic novels have, more or less, the same underlying structure and, though "mimetic and topical," they are largely "metaphoric and expressive of an unchanging outlook," a preconceived view of fallen man.

A781 Adamson, Judy, and Philip Stratford. "Looking for The Third Man. On the Trail in Texas, New York, Hollywood." Encounter, L (June), pp. 39-46. Traces the "interminable transformations" in names, plot, deletions and characterization from story to film by examining the six manuscripts housed in the Research Centre, Univ. of Texas, the abridged form of the story in The American Magazine (March 1949), and David O. Selznick's cabled requests, to reveal a "classic case-history of what can happen when in the great arena of contemporary culture the armies of finance, art and politics clash by night."

A782 Alley, Kenneth D. "A Gun for Sale: Graham Greene's Reflection of Moral Chaos." ELWIU, V, pp. 175-85. Maintains that A Gun for Sale has not received the critical attention it deserves because critics' responses to the "entertainments" have been "conditioned" by Greene's original distinction between them and the novels. Argues that A Gun for Sale is a "multi-levelled novel" not only because it is a "full-scale attack" on the traditonal or detective story, but is also a "biting indictment of modern society" with all its horror and depravity, from its lowest levels in the world in which Raven moves and Mather works to its highest rungs where Sir Marcus rests.

A783 Allott, Miriam. "Graham Greene and the Way We Live Now." CritQ, XX:3 (Autumn), pp. 9-20. Draws attention to the "phenomenon" of the "prolonged existence" of popular interest with serious literary and scholarly attention that Greene has been getting, for like Dickens, he possesses a "capturing narrative verve," an entirely "individual tone of voice," and an "uncanny, sensitized-plate responsiveness" to the actualities of the world he inhabits so that his sense of time and place are informed by an "acute and active social, political and religious sense." Examines The Human Factor as a case in point.

A784 Brannon, Lil. "The Possibilities of Sainthood: A Study of the Moral Dilemma in Graham Greene's The Power and the Glory and T. S. Eliot's Murder in the Cathedral." PAPA, IV:3, pp. 66-71. Demonstrates the parallelism between Thomas Becket's sermon on martyrdom in T. S. Eliot's play and the Whiskey Priest's fate in The Power and the Glory, and shows that the inward search of the individual cannot escape the paradox of suffering in a divinely ordered universe.

A785 Dennys, Louise. "The Greene Factor." SunTel, (12 March), p. 14. An "unusual" but sympathetic profile of Greene by his niece who interviewed him on the occasion of the publication of The Human Factor. Touches upon his kindness, lack of pretension, instinctive "evasiveness," his interest in dreams and the workings of the unconscious, as well as his interest in the "religious sense" in fiction.

A786 Duran, Leopoldo. "El poder y la gloria de Graham Greene. Parabola metafisica." Arbor, CCCLXXXVII, pp. 101-08. A study of The Power and the Glory as a "metaphysical parable" expressing vital truths professed by the Catholic Church on the supernatural function of the priesthood, and to show the mysterious ways in which God works in the soul of man by using both the established means of the institutional church as well as "innumerable extraordinary ways."

A787 Emerson, Gloria. "Graham Greene: Our Man in Antibes." RolS, 260 (9 March), pp. 45-49. A lengthy account of an interview with Greene in the Spring of 1977 in which he reminisces on Vietnam, the creation of Pyle, his travels, his dreams and the novels in general.

A788 Hoskins, Robert. "Hale, Pinkie, and the Pentecost Theme in Brighton Rock." MBL, III:1 (Spring), pp. 56-66. Examines "carefully selected parallels" through which the character of Hale, especially his pride, foreshadows and defines Pinkie; the first section of the novel anticipates what is to come later, both Hale and Pinkie turn to a woman for preservation, are "betrayed" by them, and both carry the indelible mark of their Brighton origins. Argues that Greene's purpose in choosing the Whitsun holiday is twofold: to establish Ida's "wholly secular character ... and thereby, to emphasize the important contract between sacred and profane which informs the work" and to dramatize Pinkie's "resistance to salvation as a failure to receive the Holy Spirit," a theme which is worked out by three closely related elements--an ironic allusion to the use of tongues, attrition of Pinkie's hatred for Rose, and images of the dove, symbol of the Holy Spirit.

A789 Karnath, David. "Bernanos, Greene, and the Novel of

Convention." ConL, XIX:4 (Autumn), pp. 429-45. An analysis of Bernanos' Diary of a Country Priest and Greene's The Heart of the Matter--two well made novels and moving spiritual portraits both "Catholic in interest"--to reveal the extreme tensions between literary form and world view in an attempt to demonstrate what the novel cannot be and what it is, i.e., its ideological limits. Shows in both novels how the literary form overrides the world view which reshapes itself in the direction predictable from the artistic form employed. The novel "untracks" the world view; i.e., the Catholicism or philosophical structure of The Heart of the Matter is "radically individualistic," the sort "required by fiction in general and the novel in particular,"--a fundamental implicit assumption that the novel is necessarily about the individual and explores his privacy and is opposed to the "liturgical world view committing itself to the collective and breaking individual patterns."

A7810 Kelleher, Victor. "The Heart of the Matter: Graham Greene and the Humanist Dilemma." UES, XVI:1, pp. 32-34. Argues that the novel transcends purely religious questions and deals with basic human problems because the world it depicts is "protean" in character, shifting, relativist, where nothing is absolute or unchanging and in which God and traditional attitudes have ceased to be fixed or absolute. Scobie's pity reflects this relativist and uncertain quality and his unaided effort to create meaning out of the chaos of experience after "usurping" the role of God is in itself the humanist dilemma.

A7811 Lambert, J. W. "The Private World of Graham Greene." SunT, (5 March), p. 37. Rpt. as "A Guide to Greeneland." Critic, XXXVII (July 1978), pp. 1 & 8. An account of an interview with Greene in Paris two weeks before the publication of The Human Factor. Greene speaks of his attempt "to evoke sympathy for people outside the border of public sympathy," and chats about Panama, his readings, the need for "level passages" in a novel, his love for the theatre and interest in dreams. Also includes "A Guide to Greeneland"--a brief account of his career and achievements in the novel, theatre and the cinema.

A7812 ________. "A Guide to Greeneland." Critic, XXXVII (July), pp. 1 & 8. Rpt. from SunT, (5 March 1978), p. 37. See A7811.

A7813 McCartney, Jesse F. "Politics in Graham Greene's 'The Destructors.'" SHR, XII, pp. 31-41. Cautions against an "allegorical" reading of the story for a "symbolic" one, and argues in his analysis of the story that the Wormsley Gang of "The Destructors" epitomizes "democratic socialism" in conflict with privilege and conservatism, and that the story depicts the post-war world of "traditional values of beauty, grace, individualism, and class distinctions ... succumbing to the new values of materialism, efficiency, democracy and group activity." Also points out paradoxes "inherent in the spirit" of Greene and his "ambivalent" attitude toward worldly reformers.

A7814 McConnell, F. "Reconsideration: The End of the Affair." NRep, CLXXVIII (11 March), pp. 35-37. A sensitive appreciation raising the question central to the novel: "Why does Greene write such an unpromising, offensive, perhaps fanatic book, and, beyond that, why does it, against all odds, work?" Draws attention to Greene's narrative subtlety, especially the "novel's insistence on its own quality as a novel," and to his idea of sainthood which has more to do with the "bitter purity of Camus' humanism than with the piety of C. S. Lewis's antiquarian fancies."

A7815 Pritchett, V. S. "The Human Factor in Graham Greene." NYTMag, (26 Feb.), pp. 33-36, 38, 40-42, 44, 46. Rev. and amended for English readers, and rpt. as "Graham Greene into the Light." Times, (18 March 1978), pp. 6-7. Excerpted and rpt. as "A Man of Disappearances." AWPR, XXV (July 1978), pp. 27-29. A portrait of Greene at 73 as a "londoner through and through" in spite of his residence in France, as a "joker" with a "bleak and sad mind," determined to be "unrespectable," to be the "odd man out" and "to laugh," but also as a person who is "very gentle, serious, self-centered (as an artist) and a man of great charity." The meeting between the 40-year-old friends takes place in Antibes. Also considers his boredom, conversion to Catholicism, his own description of self as a "manic depressive" and a "Catholic atheist," his travels, interest in technical questions and handling of sexual scenes. Greene maintains in that "interview" that he will not write his reminiscences.

A7816 Rama Rao, V. V. B. "Graham Greene and the Burden of Childhood." LHY, XIX:2, pp. 50-62. Illustrates from novels up to The Heart of the Matter and from "The Basement Room" the consistency of Greene's treatment of childhood as an "inexorable influence" conditioning the growth of personality. Also attempts to show the "formative" influences on Greene's mind.

A7817 Savage, D. S. "Graham Greene and Belief." DR, LVIII:2 (Summer), pp. 205-29. Scrutinizes Greene's religious beliefs which play a prominent part in Brighton Rock, The Power and the Glory, The Heart of the Matter, The End of the Affair, The Quiet American, A Burnt-Out Case and The Comedians, and relates these beliefs to Greene's "psychopathology ... as revealed in his more confessional writings." Doubts the authenticity of Greene's religious insights and vision--his conversion is "only in name" and his religiosity is "otiose"--and questions his artistic honesty and integrity as a writer. Argues that Greene is a minor writer who gives "little imaginative substance to his readers"--he is a mere "confectioner of melodramas," with "puerile" lovers that "centre upon the same obsessional concern with the same inescapable issues" of a writer whose "psychological development has been shockingly arrested at a pre-adolescent age."

A7818 Stratford, Philip. "Second Thoughts on 'Graham Greene's Second Thoughts': The Five Texts of The Heart of the Matter." SB, XXXI, pp. 263-66. Takes Prof. Higdon to task (see A775) for measuring the extent of the revision of the novel by using two Viking Compass editions of 1960 and 1974. "The 1960 Compass is identical to the American first edition, but not the British," because the American first and the British first, though published within two months of the same year, are different. Moreover, Greene started revisions for the Uniform Edition in 1951, so that revisions ascribed to 1971 may well have been made twenty years earlier. Cites a few examples. Again, the 1974 edition is set from The Portable Graham Greene (1973) text which is "similar but not identical" to the Collected Edition.

A7819 Weselinski, Andrzej. "Similes in the Novels of Graham Greene." KN, XXV, pp. 454-62. Analyzes and classifies into four categories Greene's similes in Brighton Rock, The Quiet American and A Burnt-Out Case and considers the "camera-eye" technique which has become a hallmark of Greene's literary style, to show that Greene's extensive use of simile serves as an artistic means for "veiled commentary" to attenuate the effect of impersonality and detachment resulting from his reliance on the "camera-eye" narrative manner.

A7820 Yamagata, Kazuni. "Jiken no Kakushin no Kaitei o megutti: Scobie wa Jisatsu o sake eta ka." EigoS, CXXIII, pp. 590-92. Unavailable for examination.

A7821 Young, Eric, and Louise Dennys. "A Novel Sort of Life." LHWM, (25 March), pp. 9-11. One account of an interview with Greene in January 1978 in which he expresses reluctance to analyze his works, comments on his travels which stem from his interest in life, on his recent escapade in the film world, on dreams and the workings of the unconscious, on the religious sense, and his desire to achieve "an unnoticeable style." See account of the same interview published in SunTel, (12 March 1978), p. 14. A785.

R781 Allen, Walter. "Human Face of Treason." DaiT, (16

March), p. 14. As the "most accomplished," "most expert," "most elegant" and "most beguiling of storytellers," Greene has subordinated all elements to reveal the "human face of treason," and his rendering of the relation between Castle and his wife is "tender" and most moving. Greene also writes with "special brilliance" and "affection" too, of St. James, and his picture of the Secret Service is "beautifully done." Moreover, the novel is also "very funny, and the humour is original."

R782 A[rthur], B[udd]. "The Human Factor." Booklist, LXXIV (15 March), p. 1164. Brief note on its publication.

R783 Bedford, Sybille. "Re-reading Graham Greene." B&B, XXIII (May), pp. 10-11. A favorable review of The Human Factor as a "serious work about the nature of human experience and the condition of man" in the twentieth century, even though it often is "sardonic, funny, extravagantly funny." Notes the anxiety and suspense in the novel, the "compressed despair" of the two last chapters, Greene's virtuosity with locale, the absence of "explicit violence" except perhaps for the shooting of the dog, and the theme of "grey treason." Finds, however, that though one can believe in Castle's existence and the reality of his dilemma, one finds it difficult to "accept or even entirely understand his actions."

R784 Binyon, T. J. "In the Direction of Moscow: The Human Factor." TLS, (17 March), p. 301. Finds it "disconcerting" to read the novel against the memory of Our Man in Havana; the laughs are fewer and the similes are loaded with irony. The novel lacks the "firm sense of place, the rich narrative texture" of previous novels: "it is thinner, drier almost skeletally schematic" but it is also masterfully told.

R785 Bragg, Melvyn. "Greene & Sharpe." Punch, CCLXXIV (22 March), p. 505. Finds The Human Factor one of Greene's "most intriguing and puzzling novels," continually compelling but not his best. Notes Greene's determination to give the reader a "sympathetic portrait" of Castle so that it is almost difficult not to admire him even though one is left puzzled as to "the moral certainties" that his actions arouse in the novel.

R786 Brudnoy, David. "The Human Factor." SatEP, CCL (Dec.), p. 86. Focusses on the moral dilemma that Castle confronts in the novel and Greene's ability to trap the reader in it to get a deeper understanding of the central problem. Notes Greene's skepticism about commonly held values such as patriotism and honesty.

R787 Burgess, Anthony. "The Quiet Defector." Observer, (19

March), p. 37. This fictional study of a defector is as fine as anything Greene has ever written--"concise, ironic, acutely observant of contemporary life, funny, shocking, above all compassionate" with the kind of "jolting apothegm" and the "bizarre yoking of the banal and the profound" which gives moral significance to the commonplace. However, it is not a novel about spies and the Secret Service--Castle hardly fulfils the "traitor paradigm"--but it is a novel primarily about people and love and loyalty.

R788 Caute, David. "Picture Frame for Treason." Guardian, (16 March). p. 9. Rpt. in GuardianW, CXVIII (26 March), p. 22. In The Human Factor, Greene seems to share the British establishment's fascination--a "sneaking respect verging on affection"--for defectors. The world of the SIS is used by Greene, perhaps amateurishly, as a mere picture frame for his story about the overlap of political and personal feeling. His explorations in this area against the "surprisingly confined geographical parameters" of his setting are "beautifully done, a pleasure to read, a succession of deft, unobtrusive, yet masterly touches."

R789 Christman, Elizabeth. "Graham Greene: The Human Factor." Critic, XXXVII (July), pp. 2-3. Finds the novel "disappointing" and more of a "regression rather than a triumphant return" to the world of espionage for the "human factor" is sadly lacking: Castle as a lever for the plot is effective but "flat" as a character, "colorless and unemotional."

R7810 Clemons, Walter. "A Master's Homecoming." Newsweek, XCI (6 March), pp. 97-98. Describes The Human Factor as a "marvelous novel, crystalline and understated, that tenderly, cruelly, almost regretfully refuses to gratify" the readers' romantic expectations. Greene, with great suavity and grace, enlists sympathy for Castle, the "most human" of his unheroic hunted men.

R7811 Cuffe, E. D. "Tangled Webs, Words, Worlds." America, CXXXVIII (15 April), pp. 310-11. Considers The Human Factor a "fine" novel, "literate, assured, marvelously put together, merciless, harrowing"--a sad story with an autumnal and finally wintry atmosphere and many lonely people.

R7812 D., R. "The Human Factor." WCR, IV (May), pp. 29-30. A brief review noting how real the characters are drawn and the human factor which proves to be Castle's undoing in this "truly exciting entertainment."

R7813 Delbanco, Nicholas. "The Human Factor." NRep, CLXXVIII (11 March), pp. 32-33. Highlights the dilemma of the typical Greene hero whose loyalties are at odds as well as the "well-made" plot. Though the book is described as "first-rate ... an instruction as well as 'entertainment,' an artful spy story and publishing event," the reviewer, on impression, finds the novel "flattish and faded," with a "sense of weary manipulation throughout."

R7814 Donoghue, Denis. "A Novel of Thought, Action and Pity." NYTBR, (26 Feb.), pp. 1 & 43. Though the story in The Human Factor is a good one, it is told for the sake of the characters--"Greene's abiding concern"--who are revealed by their thoughts, attitudes and feelings which, in turn, point to the moral of the novel. By making it impossible for the reader to condemn Castle, Greene has drawn attention to the cardinal sin of not caring, and has shown that ethical judgment upon a person's actions--Castle may be a traitor, but his motives are selfless, his feelings pure--is inept, inadequate and incomplete "until it is brought to the point at which pity is lavished upon everyone." Speculates on the possibility that the novel is about Kim Philby.

R7815 Flower, Dean. "The Way We Live Now." HudR, XXXI (Summer), pp. 343-54. Pages 352-54 review The Human Factor. The title alone gives "the sine qua non of Greeneland" and the "scrupulous austerity and ... deadly ironic touches which Greene gives the story make it authentic and irresistibly human." Maintains that the novel has a "powerful sub-text, which argues that loneliness is preferable to love, and isolation superior to attachment."

R7816 Fuller, Edmund. "Entertaining Novels of Life's Cynical Dilemmas." WSJ, CXCI (10 April), p. 18. The Human Factor is the first of two novels reviewed. As a strong narrative of suspense, it carries "extra depths of characterization," and the ambiguities and the moral ambivalences inescapable in espionage stories dominate the novel as a result of Castle's bond to his wife and son.

R7817 Grosvenor, Peter. "Traitor's Fate...." DaiE, (16 March), p. 24. A rather cursory review noting the "nasty taste" left by The Human Factor, and Greene's sympathetic treatment of Castle.

R7818 Hanlon, Robert M. "The Pity of Treachery: Graham Greene's The Human Factor." America, CXXXVIII (17 June), pp. 486-88. Scrutinizes the pressing problem of the morality in "treachery toward a perfidious government." Notes Greene's interest in the individual and his conscience in this "superb" novel whose characters "give it matter," especially Castle--"a sad outcast," for whom Greene, to his enduring praise, can sympathize with as well as arouse the reader's sympathy for him.

R7819 Hynes, Samuel. "The Unquiet Englishman." Book World, (12 March), pp. E1 & E6. Sees the essential conflict in The Human Factor to be "System versus System--the communist world versus its opponents"; in this struggle life and love become problems not values. The novel creates an "oppressive sense" of the helplessness of individual characters and the ending is the most "open and unresolved" in Greene's novels.

R7820 James, Clive. "Birthmarks, Chess Games and Wise Policemen." NSta, XCV (17 March), pp. 359-60. An appreciative review of The Human Factor, a "spy story with an intricate plot" but "very serious" as it explores the realities of life and their moral overtones--one of Greene's "best" books even though it may lack "the fearful symmetry" of The Heart of the Matter. Notices the "neurotically accurate" topography of the novel as well as its "serious flaw": not only is Castle too complacent over Davis' destiny but as a central character he is "less interesting than his dilemma warrants."

R7821 Jones, D. A. N. "The Agnostic Spy." Listener, XCIX (16 March), pp. 336-37. A review of The Human Factor that examines the "neatness of Greene's pattern-making and the elegance of his prose" as he weaves into the novel an imaginative discussion of the ethics of defection and double-dealing.

R7822 Kennedy, Eileen. "The Human Factor." Best Sellers, XXXVIII (May), pp. 36-37. Describes the novel as Greene's "best" over the previous twenty-five years, and as an "entertainment raised to a philosophic dimension" by emphasizing the sanctity of human relationships. The novel's power lies not only in Castle's character but in the way Greene "has honed his style to fit his meaning." Notes Greene's technique of naming characters ironically.

R7823 Klausler, Alfred P. "No Honor Among Spies." ChrC, XCV (12 April), pp. 398-99. Maintains that The Human Factor with all the qualities that make it "absolutely tops as a thriller" exposes the amorality and immorality of intelligence apparatuses and raises disturbing questions in its exploration of good and evil and defection in a world that has long abandoned ethical behavior.

R7824 Latham, Aaron. "Love Fragments Patriotism." Esquire, LXXXIX (14 March), p. 93. Though a "fine" book, The Human Factor shows evidence of a "slight decline but no fall"; Greene can still make a defector a sympathetic character and show defection as an act of love.

R7825 Leonard, John. "Books of the Times." NYT, (27 Feb.), p. C17. As a novel, The Human Factor "doesn't work" in spite of its interesting plot and "promising ideas" for characters; the portrait of Sarah is "non-existent," so that when the occasion demands passion, there is only "emptiness." Moreover, crucial incidents are implausible, and the novel generally contains "some indifferent writing" and is full of "scraps, homilies, analogies, generalizations."

R7826 Lewis, Peter. "Missing Link with Philby...." DaiM, (16 March), p. 7. "... Fairly and tautly written," The Human Factor entices the reader to the "trapdoor" beneath the ostensible spy story--to the "murkier regions of moral doubt and moral deception," especially the "moral position" of the double agent. Though the characters of the Firm seem to be "decisively drawn," Castle never seems to attract or even convince us of his human reality.

R7827 McMahon, Sean. "Back to Base." IP, (23 March), p. 6. "Funny and very exciting" in spite of its "blankness," The Human Factor has realistic and gripping suspense elements and a "dry humour" that serves to heighten the unease of the reader as he moves into the strange "Philby country" of espionage. The novel, however, provides a "lasting joy" to readers and asks many of the unanswerable questions about love, loyalty, patriotism and treason.

R7828 O'Brien, Conor Cruise. "Greene's Castle." NYRB, (1 June), pp. 3-5. Considers The Human Factor as a novel that expresses Greene's spiritual preoccupation, that though it appears political, it is the "most Christian" of his novels since The Heart of the Matter. The religious theme is so closely interwoven with Castle's professional activities that "the two in a sense become one." The spiritual current is real and tormenting and belongs to a Christian tradition which is subversive of established order. Also notes instances where the plot, like Camus's L'Etranger, is incredible at key points.

R7829 Raphael, Frederic. "The Man Who Gave Hostages to Treason." SunT, (19 March), p. 41. Though not a masterpiece, The Human Factor is a "piece by a master" that is almost an "abstract recension of ever-Greene themes." In spite of the customary "clipped uneasy tone," the ruthlessness displayed in the novel seems "less devilish than puerile, love less carnal than naive."

R7830 Ratcliffe, Michael. "Back in England." Times, (16 March), p. 12. Notices the return to a contemporary London setting in The Human Factor, and the fact that it is not a novel "about" Philby--in fact, treason is hardly acknowledged nor is Castle even accused of treachery. For a Greene hero, Castle's self remains "curiously opaque and undefined" and Sarah is unreal. The novel is full of tenderness and a subdued note of elegy and desolation, and not without humor and comic ironies. The sense of immediacy created through Greene's power of observation and the "uncluttered and seductive prose" with "every word in its place and a place for every word" show a mastery beyond mellowing age and fashions.

R7831 Reedy, Gerard. "The Heart of the Factor." Commonweal, CV (28 April), pp. 279-80. Maintains that The Human Factor "exhibits ... a curious bifurcation of imaginative energy: of building up human happiness only to destroy it." However, within the scale of values set up by the novel, Castle remains right in doing what he has done; his love for Sarah and Sam provide the only meaning in his life and also its only vulnerability.

R7832 Scott, Chris. "The Human Factor." BC, VII:5 (May), pp. 41-42. A short review describing the novel as "compassionate and witty" and which surprises conventional wisdom by asserting that "love and a sense of obligation" make a spy.

R7833 Sheppard, R. Z. "A Separate Disloyalty." Time, LXI (6 March), pp. 64 & 66. Maintains that though the development of Castle's motivation may be "a little thin" at times, the workmanship in The Human Factor is "superb." A "spiritual malaise" pervades the world of spies and their games as Greene seems to advocate disloyalty to institutions threatening the ideals of individualism and humanism. Finds Greene's "bitterness and sense of inevitability about 'the intelligent and the corrupt'" to be the novel's strong point rather than compassion.

R7834 Steiner, George. "God's Spies." NY, LIV (8 May), pp. 149-54. Though not one of Greene's major achievements, The Human Factor is a "lean, finely governed piece of work" that brings the reader into the presence of Greene's "spare diminished ambience" of a society "wheezing its way toward some faintly nasty future." Its flaws lie in the "shorthand of motive and characterization" which the reader is asked to flesh out. Asserts that the motif of the novel is Greene's suggestion that both "Catholicism and espionage provide an instrument of truth and solace which neither Protestantism nor secular rationalism ... can match."

R7835 Stewart, Ian. "Recent Fiction." ILN, CCXXVI (April), p. 79. The Human Factor is one of the novels briefly reviewed. As a thriller, it gives a "probing and moving" study of human character, its location of scenes is cinematically clear and its conclusion "dismal" but "grippingly related."

R7836 Stone, Robert. "Gin and Nostalgia." Harpers, CCLVI (April), pp. 78, 80 & 83. A review of The Human Factor as a "fatuous fake moralizing" tale where "everything is reduced to "piety, snobbery, and cliches." The rather sweeping condemnation of Greene's "phony personal decency" motivated by a "distaste" that has "ripened unpleasantly into contempt" is rather hostile and perhaps unwarranted.

R7837 Sullivan, Walter. "Documents from the Ice Age: Recent British Novels." SR, LXXXVI (April), pp. 320-25. The Human Factor is one of six British novels reviewed. Expresses dissatisfaction with the novel because the characters are "lifeless and the action contrived" as a result of the narrowing of the scope of Greene's artistic vision and his inability to transcend the specific causes of history and politics.

R7838 Todisco, Paula J. "The Human Factor." SchLJ, XXV (Oct.), p. 162. Briefly noticed as an espionage novel that goes beyond generating suspense and as a "masterful exploration of the dangers of love and loyalty."

R7839 Veit, Henri C. "The Human Factor." LJ, CIII (1 March), p. 585. A short review that finds the novel puzzling and disappointing and not up to the "strato-spherical level" of his other entertainments, and whose sense of time and place is "vague in the extreme."

R7840 Waugh, Auberon. "The Old Spyin' Game." EvS, (21 March), p. 25. The Human Factor is a "sad sour little tale" which, despite its "moments of high comedy" has a very serious intention. Greene pitches his tale on an "improbable note in order to emphasize the world of make-believe" in which "quaint period pieces" like 'C.', Doctor Percival and Colonel Daintry live.

R7841 Webb, W. L. "New Year Readers Start Here." GuardianW, CXVIII (22 Jan.), p. 22. Reviews publisher's lists for 1978 and notices the forthcoming publication of The Human Factor by the "one British novelist-still-of unchalleng(e)-ably international, non-parochial reputation."

R7842 Wheatcroft, Geoffrey. "Spinning the Chamber." Spectator, CCXL:7811 (18 March), p. 18. Discusses The Human Factor as a "novel about spies, rather than a spy novel" or a political novel. Notes its "incidental weaknesses," its "faulty" London topography as well as its "unique flavour" especially the singularly "capricious fashion" in which the central characters behave and take their "vital decision as though it scarcely mattered." Finds Greene, on the whole, to be always entertaining but never comfortable.

R7843 White, Terence de Vere. "The Master's Cunning." IT, (18 March), p. 11. Though "superficially a thriller and certainly entertainment," The Human Factor is written with Greene's customary "elegance," and is "representative" in that it brings in everything we had come to expect from the master. "The book loses nothing from being confined to earthly combatants," nor does it show any weakening of Greene's formidable powers. The last section of the novel is written with an air of authenticity.

R7844 Woodcock, George. "Corruptions of Love." CF, LVIII:681 (May), pp. 31-32. Focusses on the opposition between private love and public loyalties and the relativity of our ideas of corruption which The Human Factor, a "morally motivated thriller," arouses in the reader's mind. Detects a "stiffening of the imagination" that tends to turn the novel into a tract because the characters are "strangely empty within and leave little impact on the memory."

R7845 Unsigned. "Current Fiction: The Human Factor." America, CXXXIX (11 Nov.), p. 338. Briefly noticed as "vintage Greene," "stunningly wrought" and its "quiet irony" as a "brilliant image of the human condition."

R7846 _______. "The Human Factor." Book World, (10 Dec.), p. E3. Briefly noticed as a "shadow play of moralities" in spite of its seeming espionage story.

R7847 _______. "The Human Factor." Kirkus, XLVI (1 Jan.), p. 15. Pre-publication notice of the novel pointing out Greene's cinematic building of suspense, his characters "with surprise pockets of vulnerability" and the paring down of moral patterns to the barest essentials.

R7848 _______. "A Sort of Life." Kliatt, XII (Fall), p. 28. A short review of the publication in paperback. Notes Greene's "forthrightness" and "honesty" in the "life."

R7849 _______. "The Human Factor." Observer, (23 July), p. 21. Brief notice.

R7850 _______. "The Human Factor." Observer, (17 Dec.), p. 36. Chosen by A. J. Ayer as first choice in Books of the Year.

R7851 _______. "The Human Factor." PW, CCXIII (16 Jan.), p. 92. Advance notice of publication describing the novel as Greene at "his most riveting" as he unravels the tale of the "complex and compassionate" Castle.

R7852 _______. "The Human Factor." WSJ, CXCII (8 Dec.), p. 18. Brief notice.

D781 Diephouse, Daniel Jon. Graham Greene and the Cinematic Imagination. Univ. of Michigan. DAI, XXXIX (Dec.), p. 3572A.

D782 Hardwick, Patricia Anne. The Emergence of Humanism: A Study of Characterization in the Fiction of Graham Greene. Univ. of Colorado at Boulder. DAI, XXXIX (Feb. 1979), p. 4937A.

D783 Rosenkranz, Joel Harris. Graham Greene's Travel Writings: Sources of His Fiction. New York Univ. DAI, XXXIX (Oct.), p. 2262A.

1979

B791 Miller, Robert H. Graham Greene: A Descriptive Catalog. Foreword by Harvey Curtis Webster. Lexington: Univ. of Kentucky Press. A descriptive catalogue of first editions of works by Greene, English and American, which are presently in the collection at the Univ. of Louisville. Also includes letters, radio scripts, pamphlets and "subsequent editions of importance and scarcity." Arranged chronologically by title.

B792 Wobbe, R. A. Graham Greene: A Bibliography and Guide to Research. New York and London: Garland Publishing, Inc. An excellent and up-to-date guide for the scholar and the casual reader. Brings new information about Greene, his life, his works, his career and his critics. "Section A contains descriptions of the first English and American editions of books and pamphlets written by Greene, works written in collaboration with others and works edited by him. Reprints are listed in a subsection following the first-edition descriptions, but because they are so numerous, translations have been omitted entirely. Section B lists the first printings of books and pamphlets containing contributions by Greene. Section C lists Greene's contributions to press and periodicals and supplies a separate list of film criticism. Section C lists manuscripts and typescripts in collections and those of Greene's screenplays which have been produced. Section E is a bibliography of works about Greene. Sections F and G list published and broadcast interviews with Greene and his involvement with radio and television." The cut-off date is December 1977 but a few items in 1978 have also been included. The index covers works by Greene and works reviewed by Greene.

A791 Fetrow, Fred M. "The Function of Geography in The Power and the Glory." Descant, XXIII:3, 40-48. Discusses

Greene's accomplishment and application of the integration or fusion of "geography and consciousness" in the novel in relation to symbolism, characterization, thematic concerns and allegorical implications. Maintains that Greene's presentation of the Tabascan landscape creates a "spiritual climate" that argues forcibly the reality of his views, and that the setting becomes so "functional as to defy distinction between nature and natural depravity, between fact, fiction and theme," even when he "adjusts" details of geography to allegory.

A792 French, Philip. "Man of Mystery: The Enigma of Graham Greene." Listener, CII:2631 (4 Oct.), pp. 441-43. A shortened version of "Graham Greene at 75" (BBC, Radio 3), a symposium in which Paul Theroux comments on Greene as an explorer novelist, his elusiveness and his attitude to America, Sir Hugh Greene on his Berkhamstead days and contribution to the English novel, Dilys Powell on his film criticism, V. S. Pritchett on the influence of the cinema on his style and of Catholicism generally on his writing, Anthony Burgess on the novels and Greene's "brand" of Catholicism and the inspiration he draws from the "Third World," John Le Carré on Greene as a man of the thirties, his ability to convert any experience into artistic material and his status as an international novelist, and Michael Meyer on Greene's manic depression. Greene also comments on the price of success, the way he feels "at home" wherever he goes, but rejects the notion that he is a man of the thirties.

A793 Gaston, G. M. "The Structure of Salvation in The Quiet American." Renascence, XXXI (Winter), pp. 93-106. Argues that though war and politics are prominent issues in the novel, they only serve "to poise the ultimate concern of personal salvation," an issue which is concentrated primarily in the character of Fowler and the way he tells his story. Maintains that Greene's implicit purpose in the novel is to suggest that there are other forms of salvation than the "explicit presence of Grace" in the Catholic novels, that the "form of faith" is beside the point and that what counts is whether a faith is "wed to a creative view of life."

A794 Gilliatt, Penelope. "Profiles: The Dangerous Edge." NY, (26 March), pp. 43-44, 47-50. The profile is based on an interview with Greene and A Sort of Life. Considers Greene's views on the cinema, his sense of humor, his love of reading and literature in general, his unmistakable Englishness in spite of his travels and his outrage at national hypocrisy.

A795 Higdon, David Leon. "'Betrayed Intentions': Graham Greene's The End of the Affair." Library, 6th Series,

I, pp. 70-77. Traces the history of The End of the Affair from 1948 to 1973 and shows that Greene embarked on a "process of refinement" through the Uniform Edition of 1955 but this process was "reversed sharply when a new perceived aspect of intention" led to extensive revision in the Collected Edition of 1974. Wonders whether Greene, in making such changes, was "pursuing an original intention" or was merely responding to criticism of the novel.

A796 _______. "The Texts of Graham Greene's A Burnt-Out Case." PBSA, LXXIII (July), pp. 357-64. Compares the American first edition of the novel with the English first edition and discovers thirty eight substantive variants in the former, half of which resulted from the extensive "house styling casually imposed" by the American publisher, and notes Greene's "minor but continued revisions" as the text progressed towards the Collected Edition.

A797 Hoskins, Robert. "Through a Glass Darkly: Mirrors in The End of the Affair." Notes on Contemporary Literature, IX:3, pp. 3-5. Examines Greene's use of the numerous images of mirrors in the novel as a major literary device to reveal not only Bendrix's "confused attitudes toward love" but also to contrast his "spiritual blindness ... with the more perfect vision of Sarah."

A798 Ward, J. A. "Henry James and Graham Greene." Henry James Review, I, 10-23. Considers the problems raised by Greene's appraisals of Henry James in the five essays devoted to him. Questions the "curious affinity" Greene finds between James and Conrad, his creation of a James "in his own image," and whether betrayal is James's dominant theme. Notes the similarity between them in associating evil with sexual passion, but finds Greene's sense of kinship with James "rather paradoxical." Also examines in some detail the resemblance between The Wings of the Dove and The Heart of the Matter.

R791 Godbout, Jacques. "Graham Greene: une fuite dans la plomberie." L'Actualité, IV:1 (Jan.), p. 50. A short review of the French translation of The Human Factor which admits that the novel seems at first sight like a carbon copy of a John Le Carré spy story, but notes how Greene's vision imbues the story with compassion.

R792 Mambrino, Jean. "Le Facteur humain." Etudes, CCCL (Jan.), p. 126. A short review appreciative of Greene's mastery in plumbing "les abimes de l'ame humaine à partir des petits faits de l'existence." Notes that though God is nowhere mentioned, one's thoughts and feelings are indirectly drawn to Him.

R793 Shorter, Eric. "Regions." Drama, 133 (Summer), pp. 60-66. Includes a reivew of the "modest revival" at the Churchill, Bromley, of The Complaisant Lover which is described as a "snug comedy."

R794 Unsigned. "The Human Factor." NYTBR, (4 Feb.), p. 41. Title included among "New and Noteworthy" paperbacks.

R795 ________. "The Human Factor." PW, CCXV (1 Jan.), p. 57. Advance notice of the Avon publication.

D791 Browne, Phiefer L. Men and Women, Africa and Civilization: A Study of the African Stories of Hemingway and the African Novels of Haggard, Greene and Bellow. Rutgers--The State University, New Jersey. DAI, XL, 246A.

INDEX OF CRITICS

INDEX OF SELECTED TOPICS AND THEMES